Here's Holland

"Simply the best all-in-one guide to travel and life in Holland."

Sheila Gazaleh-Weevers
with
Shirley Agudo
Connie Moser

Eburon Delft

2007

DEDICATION

This book is dedicated to Patricia Erickson and the
years we worked together on *Roaming 'round Holland*.

THE HISTORY OF THIS BOOK

Here's Holland is a derivative work of *Roaming 'round Holland*, which evolved from
Roaming 'round Rotterdam in the early 70s, when Rotterdam was not the modern
international city it now is, and when it was certainly more difficult for foreign residents
to adapt to life here.

Patricia Erickson and her husband, Eric, then US Consul General, were very much
involved in the well-being of the American community and the International School of that
city. In an effort to help families adjust to their new home-away-from-home, she brought
out a practical book, *Roaming 'round Holland*, which answered their many questions about
day-to-day life.

It was published by the City of Rotterdam, ever supportive of the needs of the School
and the foreign community. With the proceeds, Pat Erickson established the William K.
Gordon Scholarship Fund which continues to give financial assistance to deserving students of
all nationalities at the American International School.

From 1976 when the Ericksons left Holland, Sheila Gazaleh-Weevers continued to
update and gather information for the book, and together they were able to continue
publishing for twenty years, up until its seventh edition. To date, Sheila has continued with
two more editions, this being the 9th.

Under Sheila's stewardship, the book has helped some 60,000 families settle into and
enjoy life in the Netherlands, introducing them to all this amazing little country has to
offer.

ACKNOWLEDGEMENTS

A word of thanks to our head sponsors, ABN AMRO bank and ZaZare Diamonds, and our media partners, *The Amsterdam-Hague-Rotterdam Times, Amsterdam Weekly, Dutch News.nl, Expatica, TheHagueOnLine* and *XPat Media*, as well as all of our advertisers, for their confidence in us to reach their target markets – both tourists and international residents of Holland, the 'expats' – with this dual-purpose, all-in-one-guide to the Netherlands.

Special thanks go to the NBTC, Fryslân Marketing, and Marketing Groningen organisations for the extra assistance they provided, as well as the various VVV and Tourist Information Offices who helped with the update of this edition. Their cooperation, expert advice and the support of their staff have been invaluable. We also want to mention the cooperativeness of the various museums and sites in the Netherlands in answering our queries. We consider ourselves very fortunate to live in a country where people are so willing to assist with our massive updating process, not to mention how ready and capable the Dutch are to switch to English for those of us who use that as our modus operandi. The response has been phenomenal.

In addition, we especially want to express our gratitude to those who have shared this daunting task with determination and dedication: Lara Geijsen and Carol Conover, our Research Assistants; Anne van der Zwalmen of Textcetera for her professionalism, attention to detail, and patience; Dick Heuff, our Website Manager; Grant Jonathan, our Systems Control Manager; Albert Dolmans, for his relentless, all-round support; and, last but not least, Maarten Fraanje, our Publisher extraordinaire, who didn't realise what he was getting into with three head-strong, determined women at the helm, but who handled it all with the utmost tact, calm, and incomparable professionalism. Eburon Academic Publishers in Delft, you're the best! www.eburon.nl

From a personal point of view, I should like to commend two very talented ladies with whom I have had, not only the pleasure, but the privilege to work on this 9th edition.

Connie Moser for her know-how and knowledge of what goes on in Holland, her incredible attention to detail, her competence, energy and enthusiasm. She has also been selflessly dependable, stepping into the breach on tight occasions, for which we are most grateful.

Shirley Agudo has been a true inspiration. Like Connie, she has great enthusiasm for what she does – and does it well. Not only has she shouldered the mammoth job of editing the book in a most professional way, but she developed and coordinated an effective business plan. A more positive, capable, tirelessly-devoted lady, always ready to go that extra mile – without allowing her feathers to be ruffled – would be hard to find.

Sheila Gazaleh-Weevers

MESSAGE FROM HOLLAND PROMOTION'S MANAGING DIRECTOR

Holland is a relatively small country, but it is an interesting and especially varied destination for visitors from abroad, be they tourists or on business – a country where in one day you can visit the most varied museums and attractions – from Dutch design to Rembrandt, from rollercoasters to flat-bottom boat sailing in Friesland or strolling along Amsterdam's canals and terrasses.

Here's Holland will help you discover Holland's treasures. It will guide you to historic cities, through picturesque landscapes and to the beaches of our coast and islands.

...In fact *Here's Holland* is essential for getting to know the Netherlands.

I wish you a pleasant voyage of discovery through our unusual and beautiful country.

Hans van Driem
Managing Director
Holland Promotion

Table of Contents

Dedication   3
The History of this Book   3
Acknowledgements   5
Message from Holland Promotion's Managing Director   6
Preface   10
How To Use This Book   10

PART ONE: SIGHTSEEING, MUSEUMS AND AMUSEMENT CENTRES

1   Touring Holland   13

Tourist Aid Organisations – Tips for Travellers – Transportation –
Eating Out – Staying Over – Holland Resources

2   The Province of North Holland   29

Amsterdam, Aalsmeer, Haarlem, Zandvoort, Zaanse Schans,
Alkmaar, Den Helder, Julianadorp, Texel, Medemblik, Twisk,
Kolhorn, Enkhuizen, Hoorn, Edam, Purmerend, Volendam, Monnickendam,
Marken, Broek in Waterland, Naarden, Laren

3   The Province of South Holland   94

Rotterdam, Delfshaven, Schiedam, Vlaardingen, Delft, The Hague,
Scheveningen, Wassenaar, Leiden, Valkenburg, Alphen a/d Rijn, Lisse,
Gouda, Haastrecht, Oudewater, Schoonhoven, Kinderdijk, Dordrecht,
Heinenoord, Brielle

4   The Province of Utrecht   160

Utrecht, Nijenrode, Oud Amelisweerd Estates, De Haar Castle,
Sypestein Castle, Zuylen Castle, Nieuw Loosdrecht, Amersfoort,
Amerongen, Doorn, Wijk bij Duurstede, Zeist, Soesterberg

5   The Province of Gelderland   179

Barneveld, Harderwijk, Elburg, Apeldoorn, Zutphen, Groenlo,
's Heerenberg, Doesburg, Arnhem, Rozendael Castle,
Doornenburg Castle, Doorwerth Castle, De Hoge Veluwe National Park,
Oosterbeek, Nijmegen, Tiel, Buren, Zaltbommel, Ammerzoyen Castle,
Culemborg, Woudrichem

6   The Province of Flevoland   202

Almere, Zeewolde, Lelystad, Dronten, Noordoostpolder, Emmeloord, Urk

7   The Province of Brabant   211

Willemstad, Bergen op Zoom, Roosendaal, Wouw, Huijbergen,
Biesboch, Breda, Etten Leur, Baarle-Nassau, Tilburg, De Efteling,
Beekse Bergen Safari Park, 's Hertogenbosch, Vught, Rosmalen,
Eindhoven, Overloon, Nuenen, Helmond

8   The Province of Friesland   230

Afsluitdijk, Harlingen, Franeker, Aeolus, Leeuwarden, Marssum,
Veenwouden, Grouw, Wieuwerd, Sneek, Makkum, Piaam, Ferwoude,
Workum, Hindeloopen, Stavoren, Sloten, Joure, Heerenveen, Dokkum,
Moddergat, Wierum, The Waddenzee Islands

9   The Province of Groningen   255

Groningen, Paterswoldse Lake, Haren, Leek, Grijpskerk, Lauwersoog,
Leens, Pieterburen, Warffum, Uithuizen, Delfzijl, Appingedam, Nieuwolda,
Nieuweschans, Fraeylemaborg Castle, Bourtange, Ter Apel

10   The Province of Drenthe   273

Assen, Veenhuizen, Norg, Roden, Zuidlaren, Emmen, Coevorden,
Schoonoord, Barger Compascuum, Orvelte, Westerbork, Meppel

11   The Province of Overijssel   286

Zwolle, Staphorst, Rouveen, Slagharen, Ommen, Hattem, Kampen,
Giethoorn, Vollenhove, Kuinre, Oldemarkt, Steenwijk, Almelo,
Hellendoorn, Vriezenveen, Denekamp, Ootmarsum, Enschede, Oldenzaal,
Delden, Diepenheim, Deventer

12   The Province of Limburg   297

Venlo, Roermond, Maasplassen, Thorn, Heerlen, Hoensbroek,
Kerkrade, Rolduc Abbey, Valkenburg, Margraten, Maastricht

13   The Province of Zeeland   319

Brouwershaven, Serooskerke, Zierikzee, Ouwerkerk Caissons,
Delta Expo Oosterschelde, Veere, Middelburg, Westkapelle, Goes, Yerseke,
Vlissingen, Terneuzen, Zaamslag, Axel, Hulst, Biervliet, Oostburg, Breskens,
Cadzand, Aardenburg, Sluis

14 Beaches   340

Oostvoorne, Rockanje, Brielle, Hook Of Holland, Kijkduin,
Scheveningen, Noordwijk Aan Zee, Zandvoort, Ijmuiden,
Egmond Aan Zee, Schoorl, Julianadorp

15 How It's Made: Crafts and Industry   351

Baking, Basketry, Beer, Candles, Cheese, Crystal, Diamonds, Distilleries,
Eel Smoking, Furniture, Peat Digging, Pewter, Pottery, Silver, Textiles,
Wine, Wooden Shoes

PART TWO: LIVING IN HOLLAND

16 Living in Holland   361

Newspapers, Relocation Services, Money and Banking, Medical Care,
Places of Worship, Libraries, Social and Business Organisations,
Adult Education, Shopping, Pets, Who are the Dutch?

17 The Good Life: Out and About   388

Movies, TV, Casinos, The Performing Arts, Theatres and Auditoriums,
Eating Out, Dutch Taste Treats, Randstad Restaurants, Fine Dining

18 Sports   405

Spectator Sports: Biking, Boating, Motor and Horse Racing, Ice Skating,
Soccer, Swimming, Tennis. Active Sports: Badminton, Baseball, Basketball, Biking,
Bowling, Fencing, Fishing, Flying, Horse Riding, Ice Skating, Martial Arts, Rugby,
Sailing, Squash, Swimming, Tennis, Football, Walking, Windsurfing and more

19 The Younger Set   421

Child Care, Schools, Museum Orientation, University Education,
Libraries, Cultural, Educational and Work Exchange Programmes,
Summer Camps and Schools, Fun & Games, Entertainment and The Arts

20 Yearly Special Events   437

The Calendar – Yearly Dutch Events – Yearly Foreign Community Events

21 Quick Reference   461

Car Rentals, Casinos, Places of Worship, Clubs and Organisations, Telephone
Assistance, VVV offices, Recommended Reading, Radio

Index   477

PREFACE

Here's Holland is unique. It's 'simply the best all-in-one guide to travel and life in Holland' – all in one easy-to-use source.

This 9th edition is a tried and true book whose merit is already measured by its over 25-year existence on the market. Sheila Gazaleh-Weevers treasures her long-time residence in Holland and wants to share its glories with others. *Here's Holland* provides an intimate look at this magnificent country, from someone who is 'in the know.'

In her travels, Sheila has managed to continue finding the most interesting sites and out-of-the-way places, to share with the tourists and expatriates who come to enjoy the beauty, diversity and pizzazz found in this tiny pinhead of a country. As a result, Part I of this book is packed with enough sights and sounds to keep you busy, literally, for years. From historic and exciting cities with world-class museums and nightlife like no other, to state-of-the-art recreation and amusement parks, extensive beaches, and folkloric and picturesque villages, Holland is like a diamond in the rough. No other country packs so much into so little.

Useful, easy-to-follow directions help to guide you, and a calendar of 'Yearly Events' serves as your personal assistant in scheduling your time wisely, so that you don't miss the ongoing, very special events throughout the country.

If you're not already living here, you may very well end up wishing that you did. In the meantime, enjoy it to the fullest, with *Here's Holland* in hand. If you are one of the lucky expatriates that now live here, congratulations! Part II is especially geared to living with the Dutch, providing you immediate access to a wealth of resources.

Whether you're a tourist or an 'expat,' we hope that this book helps to make your time here very rewarding – and, above all, fun!

HOW TO USE THIS BOOK

The first part of this book, 'Sightseeing, Museums and Amusement Centres', is organised by provinces (12 of them), with some useful hotel and dining recommendations throughout, and as much detail, including directions, as possible. The 'Living in Holland' section (Part II) provides many details on living here. Use it as a handy 'expat' resource and, for tourists as well, as a way of learning more about your holiday destination.

While every effort has been made to be accurate, please realise that establishments do go out of business and/or change phone numbers, hours, and even addresses. To be safe, call to verify, especially if you have a limited amount of time or a special 'day out' planned. We want this book to serve you well.

Part I

Sightseeing, Museums and Amusement Centres

Chapter 1 | Touring Holland

Welcome to the Netherlands, a tiny country that only extends, at its broadest, 312 km (194 mi) north to south, and 264 km (164 mi) east to west – although the land area increases slightly each year as a result of continuous land reclamation and drainage. With a lot of heart and much to offer, 'Holland,' as it is commonly known to most of us abroad – a name stemming from its once most prominent provinces – has more going on per kilometer than most countries, and more English-speaking natives. You'll be impressed by its historic cities and charmed by its countryside and villages, full of contrasts.

From the exciting variety on offer, you could choose a romantic canal boat tour in Amsterdam, a Royal Tour by coach in The Hague, or a hydrofoil tour around the biggest harbour in the world – Rotterdam. In season you could visit the dazzling bulb fields, enjoy a full day on a boat, or take a bike tour through the pancake-flat countryside spiced with windmills. The possibilities are countless and the nationwide tourist office, the VVV, is on hand to give you information and make reservations. You'll have few language problems here, as the Dutch are true linguists and English is spoken almost universally.

Part II of this book, 'Living in Holland,' is of special interest to foreign residents; however, as it includes things like Dutch food specialities, entertainment, children's interests, sports, shopping, rules of the road for both cars and bikes, medical care and churches, it proves useful to visitors also. Similarly, the chapters on beaches, evening entertainment and where to see special or 'typically Dutch' things being made by hand will expand the range of your itinerary.

For further trip planning before you leave home, we suggest you contact The Netherlands Board of Tourism and Conventions (NBTC) in your country (see below). You might also check our 'Recommended Reading' list in chapter 21.

▸ **NBTC – Netherlands Board of Tourism and Conventions**
Head Office The Netherlands: Nederlands Bureau voor Toerisme, Vlietweg 15, 2260 MG Leidschendam, ☎ (070) 370 5705. Email: information@holland.com, www.holland.com, www.nbtc.nl, www.holland.co.uk
Canada: 14 Glenmount Court, Whitby, Ontario, L1N 5M8, Canada: ☎ (905) 666 5960; fax (905) 666 5391; Email: information@holland.com, www.goholland.com
United States: 355 Lexington Avenue, 19th floor, New York, NY 10017
☎ (212) 370 7360; fax (212) 370 9507; Email: information@goholland.com
Other NBTC overseas offices are listed in 'Quick Reference' (chap. 21)

On www.goholland.com you can download brochures about the Netherlands.

NRC – Netherlands Reservation Centre Advanced Reservations: www.hotelres.nl
Established by the Dutch hotelkeepers and the NBTC, this organisation is your
link with all categories of hotels in the Netherlands, from budget to five-star:
www.worldtravelguide.net/country/187/accommodation/Europe/Netherlands

▶ VVV – National Dutch Tourist Offices

In Holland, this organisation is truly invaluable as a source of information and assistance for travellers. Look for the blue and white sign in most towns showing 'VVV.' An
authority on what's going on within its area, as well as on things of interest countrywide, each office is independent with a helpful multilingual staff. Hours are usually
Mon.-Fri. 9am-5pm, Sat. 10am-noon. In-season hours may be extended.

They will give you details of special events and places of interest, public transport,
walking and cycling routes and just about everything related to tourism in Holland.
They have tickets to events, theatre, concerts, etc., and the Museum Year Card, as well
as a wide selection of books, brochures, maps and souvenirs for sale. Reservations can
be made through them for hotels or other accommodations and also for package tours.
See www.vvv.nl to find a VVV in all locations throughout the country. Here are a few of
the main ones:

- Amsterdam: VVV, Stationsplein 10 and 15, platform 2, and Leidseplein 1
  ☎ (0900) 400 4040, www.amsterdamtourist.nl
- The Hague: VVV, Wagenstraat 193, Hofweg 1, Scheveningen; Gevers Deynootweg
  1134, ☎ (0900) 340 3505, www.denhaag.com, www.scheveningen.nl,
  www.thehagueonline.nl
- Rotterdam: VVV, Coolsingel 5, ☎ (0900) 403 4065, www.vvv.rotterdam.nl

> 📖 For a more complete list of VVV offices throughout the Netherlands, refer to
> 'Quick Reference' (chap. 21)

Note: All (0900) numbers (accessible only in Holland) have per-minute charges.

▶ ANWB – The Royal Dutch Touring Club

ANWB is the touring club of Holland, geared to making life easier for all who travel, by
providing information, assistance (see 'Road Service') and a great deal more.

The ANWB works closely with sister clubs in almost every country in the world,
such as the AA in England and the AAA in the United States. Already being a member in the sister clubs can be an advantage, as it may entitle you to all the benefits the
ANWB offers its own members. You only have to show a membership card. Their 'Show
your card' benefits programme entitles you to discounts both here and abroad. Unfortunately, most ANWB literature is only available in Dutch, but representatives in the
ANWB travel stores speak English, making guidance and information readily available

in person or by phone. Travel articles and clothing are also for sale there, as well as on their 'webwinkel' online store. For complete addresses, see www.anwb.nl

Here are a few:

Amsterdam:	Museumplein 5	☎ (020) 673 0844
The Hague:	Wassenaarseweg 220	☎ (070) 314 7147
Rotterdam:	Coolsingel 67	☎ (010) 414 0000
Maastricht:	Wycker Brugstraat 24	☎ (043) 362 0666
Utrecht:	van Vollenhovenlaan 277-279	☎ (030) 291 0333

If you are a long-term visitor or permanent resident, it's in your interest to join the ANWB. For more information and addresses of the nearest ANWB store or ANWB/VVV branch, call freephone ☎ (0800)-0503.

Road service: ANWB's yellow 'Wegenwacht' patrol cars will help you with mishaps on the road, around the clock. On-the-spot repairs can be made, or they will tow you to the nearest service station. There are roadside emergency phones located along all Dutch highways …just press the button and you will be connected to the nearest Road Service Station (or freephone ☎ 0800-0888). For memberships, choose the coverage that best suits your needs: for local, at-home service (Woonplaats Service), country-wide assistance (Nederland Service) or throughout Europe (Europa Service).

▶ **Transportation to Holland**

From the US and Canada:

All flights come into Amsterdam's Schiphol Airport. KLM is the major air carrier to Holland from Canada. In the US, KLM operates flights through Northwest Airlines. Many other airlines fly in and out of Schiphol. (See list of discount flights at the end of this chapter.) www.schiphol.com

For a listing of all airports in Holland see: http://travel.away.com/Netherlands.

From the UK:

By air: There are several daily flights from London to Amsterdam and Rotterdam by KLM, British Midland, British Airways, Transavia and VLM. KLM also operates flights to Amsterdam from most British airports, as do British Midland, British Airways, Easy Jet, and Aer Lingus (Dublin). There are also flights to Maastricht and Eindhoven from London's airports.

Schiphol Taxi is a door-to-door airport taxi service, to and from the Amsterdam airport to your destination, at a very reasonable rate. You must hold a flight ticket and reserve at least 48 hours in advance (0900 8876 or www.schiphol.nl). Other passengers may be collected along the way, but this is not always the case.

By ferry: One of the most popular ferry connections is Stena's Harwich-Hook of Holland line. The day and evening crossings take approximately four hours. Another, Hull-Rotterdam (Europort) by P&O North Sea Ferries, is overnight and takes 14 hours.

You could also come from Newcastle to IJmuiden with Scandinavian Seaways or DFDS Seaways. Ferries also cross to and from Breskens, Belgium.
www.POferries.com, www.stenaline.com and www.dfdsseaways.nl

By train: Eurostar via the Channel Tunnel runs from London Waterloo to Brussels South (*Zuid*) in three hours 15 minutes, and connects with trains to the Netherlands. www.eurostar.com

Onward by train: Ongoing air travellers can change money at the 'GWK' office while waiting for their luggage in Schiphol Arrival Hall, and need only walk a short distance to buy train tickets, get directions to the platform (*spoor*), and catch their train. During normal hours, trains run to Amsterdam, The Hague and Rotterdam every 15-30 minutes, with regular connections to other cities throughout Holland. NOTE: Banks no longer cash travellers checks or handle foreign cash. Currency exchange must be done at the GWK offices at train stations.

▶ **Transportation in Holland**
By domestic air service: KLM operates flights from Amsterdam to Rotterdam, Eindhoven and Maastricht. www.klm.com

By train: In Holland, the '*Nederlandse Spoorwegen* (NS)' trains are a popular form of transportation – efficient and convenient. Most of the 379 stations are in the centre of town and offer good security and facilities such as restaurants, bookshops, chemists, flower shops, etc.

As from 2007, trains run every 15 minutes in the Randstad (major metropolitan areas in and around Amsterdam/The Hague/Rotterdam) and every 30 minutes in the rest of the country. New connections and seven new stations will be added along with new high-speed trains and better inter-European connections. Trains run from 6am (Sundays and public holidays, 7am) until midnight, but an hourly night service is maintained to major cities and Schiphol airport until 4am. Trains are comfortable and efficient, and English is spoken.

Major stations have an Information Desk for general inquiries, and an Information Office for special-priced NS organised excursions, ticket and seat reservations. International reservations can only be made at 'NS International' offices in major stations, open 8am-8pm. High-speed trains bring passengers almost anywhere in Europe in a matter of hours: Amsterdam to Paris, for example, in 4hrs/15minutes.

☞ Dutch Railway Information: ☎ (0900) 9292 (70 euro cents per minute) 7am-midnight, for door-to-door travel information on public transport within Holland; schedules, prices, etc. International train inquiries ☎ (0900) 9296.

Websites: www.ns.nl or www.nsinternational.nl. See also:
- www.internationaltrainline.com – for rail passes worldwide and
- www.raileurope.com – for your European travels.
- www.ov9292.nl – for public transportation

The following may also be helpful:

Buying tickets: Most train station ticket windows are open 6am-10pm. There is a 50-euro-cents-per-ticket surcharge for the personal service versus the ticket machines, so we encourage you to use the yellow machines labelled 'Treinkaartjes,' as they are fairly easy to operate:

1. Click on the English icon.
2. Find the first letter of the name of your destination and touch it on the keypad screen.
3. Choose the ticket you want: 1st or 2nd class (first class offers very little added value, other than being less crowded); discount (*met korting*) or regular rate (*zonder korting*); one-way (*enkele reis*) or round-trip (*retour*); a ticket for today (*vandaag*) or without a date (*zonder datum*).
4. The machine will tell you how much to pay – be ready with coins or bankcard and 'PIN code,' as paper money is not accepted. Credit cards are not accepted at NS stations.

Note: For a demonstration of how the ticket machine touch screen works see: http://webdemo.ns.nl

Tickets are not sold on the trains. If you do not have a valid ticket before boarding, when the conductor asks for one you will be fined. Smaller stations have restricted hours and facilities, but tickets may be available from their 'Wizzl' mini market shops.

Fares: A basic return ticket valid one day (*dagretour*) is cheaper than two single tickets. See information below regarding special weekend fares, excursions and other fares. You have a choice of 1st class or 2nd class, which is 50% cheaper. As mentioned, first class is usually much less crowded but, otherwise, not worth the extra cost. Second class is almost as comfortable.

Special tickets and excursion passes

- 'Dagkaart' (Day Pass): Allows holder unlimited 1st or 2nd class travel for one day.
- 'OV Dagkaart': In conjunction with a Day Pass allows unlimited travel on metro, trams and buses for one day.
- 'Zomertoer' ('Summer Tour' Pass): Three days unlimited travel for two in Holland during a period of ten days in July and August.
- 'Railrunner' (Children's discount ticket): Up to 3 children aged 4-11 pay €2.00 each when accompanied by an adult, 19 or older.
- 'Weekendretour' ('Weekend Return' Tickets): Valid from Friday 7pm to Monday 4am, for the price of a day return.

- '*Voordeel-Urenkaart*': For regular train travellers, a 40% discount on Mon.-Fri. travels after 9am and all day on weekends. (Up to four persons traveling together can receive a joint discount or '*samenreiskorting*' on one discount card). The card is valid for one year and costs €55.00. For those over 60, the pass also entitles you to seven free days of travel per year.
- '*Euro Domino*': Three, five or ten days unlimited travel within a month.
- '*Rail Pass*': Entitles foreign travellers to 3-5 days travel in Holland in one month. Discount up to 25% for under 25s and seniors; companion 50%. Passport needed.
- See www.nsinternational.nl for special arrangements and international travel.

Day trips by train: You might like to visit Amsterdam by Museumboat and see Rembrandt's paintings, take a trip to the Delta Works, or enjoy the tulips at '*Keukenhof*.' The ideal way to do this is to buy a combined ticket that includes rail-bus travel and admission. How much more comfortable travelling through the bulb fields this way than being stuck in a traffic jam and then having to wait in line for a ticket on arrival. Countless day trip suggestions are listed in the NS booklet '*Er op Uit*' (in Dutch) and on many websites listed in this book.

Hiking and biking trips: Many beautiful walking and cycling tours are listed in '*Er op Uit*.' Upon buying your ticket, you will be given the appropriate map. If you choose to cycle, you can travel with your own bike at specific times (with a bicycle ticket), or you can rent one at your destination station. Look for '*Fietsenstalling*.' For information: ☎ (0900) 9292.

Disabled travellers will find stations and trains reasonably accessible. For extra help, call NS one working day before travel, Mon.-Fri. 8am-4pm ☎ (030) 230 5566.

Public transportation in town: In town there is a choice of tram, bus or metro (the latter in Rotterdam and Amsterdam). Tickets, available from bus or tram drivers, entitle you to one hour of unlimited travel; if you plan to take more than one trip, choose the cheaper option, a '*strippenkaart*.' These cards have either 15 or 45 strips. They are not available from drivers, but from newsagents, train station bookstores, supermarkets, VVVs and post offices. The entire country is divided into zones. The number of zones you pass through determines how many strips must be stamped at the start of your journey.

Some trams have a conductor (in the rear or middle) who stamps the tickets; others have machines where you may stamp the ticket yourself. When in doubt, ask the driver to assist.

Commuter tickets: You can buy a week, month or year ticket from the authorised ticket office, or post office. When applying, a passport photo and a valid ID, such as a passport, are required. Zone maps are also available.

☞ To get on the Tram or Metro: press the '*deur open*' button at the front, middle or back of the car. You must press it for the door to open; it will close automatically.

By bus: Holland is admirably organised, and bus travel is coordinated with trains to provide complete access to all towns and villages. For information ☎ (0900) 9292, or check www.ov9292.nl for public transportation. The online 'OV Planner' is a good way to see all of the schedules and to plan your train, bus and tram connections. Always board the bus by the front door where you can purchase or show the driver your valid ticket. Websites: www.eurolines.com and www.connexxion.nl

Public transportation city information:

- Amsterdam: www.gvb.nl   Utrecht: www.gvu.nl
- The Hague: www.htm.nl   Groningen: www.ovbgd.nl
- Rotterdam: www.ret.nl   Eindhoven: www.oveindhoven.nl

For an explanation of the '*strippenkaarten*' system for public transportation by bus throughout the country and by tram and metro (underground) in large cities, along with current fares: www.vbn-bv.nl/ovinfo

By taxi: Taxis operate privately and are relatively inexpensive. You cannot hail one in the street, but must either call one (Yellow Pages under 'Taxi') or find a taxi stand, which are usually in convenient city locations. There is also a '*Trein-Taxi*' ticket available for some destinations, whereby you can hire a special taxi to and from the train station for a much-reduced rate (approx. €5.00). See the list on the www.ns.nl website. (See also 'Schiphol Taxi' under air travel for transportation to and from the airport.)

By car: Holland is a perfect country to tour by car. Roads are outstanding – even the smallest country roads (highly recommended for true scenic beauty). The rules of the road, however, are strict, with heavy fines. ANWB Wegenwacht (see page 15) is on hand to rescue drivers with problems.

- For detailed driving route instructions: www.routenet.nl
- For maps (street, route and satellite): www.map24.nl
- For familiarisation with Dutch and international traffic signs: www.3vo.nl

Where you see the black and white 'i' sign, information maps are posted. In some places, yellow machines with '*plattegrond met route*' (map with route) are available free of charge.

> ☞ *Important points for drivers to keep in mind:* At intersections without traffic lights, cars coming from the right have the right-of-way, except when there are a series of painted triangles (sharks' teeth) on the road in front of you. Be constantly aware of cyclists; they are always around and will often take the right-of-way, even when they are supposed to stop. Before making a turn, motorists must wait for cyclists continuing on, to clear the intersection. In this instance, the cyclist has the right of way. Another word of advice: Always check in mirrors for passing cyclists before opening doors.

By bicycle: There are 16 million bicycles in Holland, where the current population is 16,491,461 (July 2006) (just about everybody has one – or more!), and 1.3 million new bicycles are purchased every year. The country boasts 19,200 kilometers of bike paths!
- http://holland.cyclingaroundtheworld.nl
- www.enfb.nl – the NL bicyclists' union (*fietsersbond*) with many pages of links, routes and clubs

Pointers for cyclists: Right of way: Always give hand signals to indicate your intention. Do not cut off automobiles. If you are turning, the automobilist should stop for you, however, they don't always yield, so caution is advised. Cyclists coming from the right on equivalent roads have priority. Sharks' teeth (triangle points painted on the road) indicate the need to stop on priority roads, indicated by an orange diamond sign. Cyclists must also stop to allow pedestrians to cross the '*zebra pad*' (striped crosswalk). Watch out for buses; they don't always give way to cyclists. Trams *always* have the right of way at all times, so be aware!

Maps:
Bookshops, petrol stations, the ANWB and the VVV all sell maps. Online you can have a look at:
- www.embassyworld.com/maps/Maps_Of_Netherlands
- http://netherlands.map-vista.com
- www.mapquest.com

▶ **Tips for travellers**
Local currency/foreign exchange
The local currency is the Euro (€), and Euro bills come in denominations of 500, 200, 100, 50, 20, 10 and 5. The Euro is further divided into 100 cents, and coins are available in 2 euro and 1 euro and 50, 20, 10, and 5 cents. When paying cash, prices are rounded up.

You may change your foreign currency into Euros at GWK Travellex exchange offices (usually found at most train stations or near most VVV tourist bureaus). GWK offices are also open late in the evenings; at Schiphol Airport and Amsterdam's Central Station, they are open 24 hours. They can arrange cash withdrawals on credit cards, travellers' checks and insurance, and sell practical things like phone cards and maps. Their Tourist Service can book last-minute hotel accommodation, excursions, events and attractions. You may also order currency and travellers' checks online before you leave for your trip: www.travelex.com/nl. In general, it is not customary for merchants in the Netherlands to accept foreign currency.

ATMs have become increasingly popular in the Netherlands, making it easier for travellers to withdraw euros from their own bank accounts. Cards with the Cirrus logo are widely accepted. Those with the Plus logo and EDC, EC, and Maestro logos are accepted at some banks. If you must use a credit card, it is recommended that you use it to get a cash advance from an ATM. Cash can be taken out on American Express,

Diners Club, MasterCard, and Visa cards at GWK currency exchange outlets and Change Express Offices. There are a number of ATMs at the airport.

Travellers' checks are accepted in the Netherlands. There is a small charge to exchange checks in foreign currencies, but not if the checks are in euros. American Express, Diners Club, MasterCard, and Visa are all widely accepted, though not everywhere. In some cases, you will find that only the more expensive restaurants accept credit cards.

Telephones: Most public phones accept only prepaid phone cards, which can be bought at post offices, stations, GWK, or VVV offices. Phones at train stations work with a different card (Telford). Some phones accept credit cards for long-distance calls. If you can't find a street phone box, try the post office. However, depending on the type of mobile phone, many have GSM capabilities for worldwide use.

> ☞ *Calling from overseas:* Phone numbers listed in this book begin with a city code in parenthesis. That number always begins with a zero. The zero must be dialed for all calls from a phone within the Netherlands to a phone located in a city with a different code. If you call from overseas, the city code should be dialed without the zero. For example, to call an (070) Dutch number from the US, dial 00 31 (country code) 70 (city code) and then the number.

Warning: In Europe, international calls made from your hotel can be double the price of calls from a phone box. Always enquire about surcharges before calling. International calls generally cost less at weekends, depending on where you call from. The *Gouden Gids* (Yellow Pages) includes an English-language section with valuable keywords and information to save you time.

- Yellow pages online: www.goudengids.nl
- White pages online: www.detelefoongids.nl
- Partial listings in English: www.markt.nl/dyp/index-en.html

Directory Assistance for numbers within the Netherlands: 1888 (€1.30 p. min.), or 0900 8008 (€1.15 per call); and numbers outside the Netherlands: 0900 8418 (€1.15 per call). **Note:** 0800 service-provider numbers are free; 0900 numbers are charged a per-minute or per-call rate.

Helpful hints about telephoning

- **Emergency:** ☎ 112, police, fire, ambulance assistance countrywide
- **Information:** Within Netherlands ☎ 1888 (€ 1,30 p.m.); or for operator assistance ☎ (0900) 8008; for numbers outside Netherlands ☎ (0900) 8418
- **Credit card and operator-assisted calls:** Dial 0800 04 10 for a Dutch operator. Collect calls to numbers abroad ☎ (0800) 0101. For an AT&T operator ☎ (0800) 022 9111; MCI ☎ (0800) 022 9122; Sprint ☎ (0800) 022 9119.
- **International access code:** US & Canada ☎ 001, then area code and local number; UK ☎ 00 44, then local code and number.

- **Other country codes:** Australia 00 61; Belgium 00 32; France 00 33; Germany 00 49; Ireland 00 353, New Zealand 00 64; South Africa 00 27.
  Country codes are listed in the Dutch phone book: www.detelefoongids.nl
- **Repairs:** ☎ (0800) 0407
- **Customer service:** ☎ (0800) 0402
- **KPN Telecom (Dutch phone company):** ☎ (0900) 0244 (€0.10 p.m.) www.kpn.com

Mail: The TNT Post Office has a brochure giving current prices, weights, etc. Post office hours are 8:30am-5pm. Main post offices in major cities may have longer hours, particularly on Thursdays or Fridays, and some are open on Saturday mornings. Delivery service is good – a letter to the US usually takes roughly four days to arrive; one to two days within Europe. Post boxes are red or orange. Website: www.tntpost.nl

Hours for shops and banks: Shops are open Mon.-Fri. 9am-5:30/6pm, Sat. 9am-4/5pm (some open at 1pm on Mondays). In Amsterdam and major cities, some shops stay open seven days a week until 10pm. Many towns have late-night shopping (*koopavond*) on Thursday or Friday evenings, and, on occasion, one Sunday a month (*koopzondag*), although on most Sundays shops are closed (except in Amsterdam and at Schiphol airport, The Hague, Rotterdam, Zandvoort) where many shops are routinely open). See www.shoppenopzondag.nl for listings of all the places where you can shop on Sundays.

Banks are open Mon.-Fri. 9am-4/5pm, some Mon. 1-4pm.

Museumjaarkaart (Museum Year Card): A good buy for museum lovers, this pass gives free access to 400 museums throughout the country (special exhibits may have a surcharge). It is available from any VVV, many museums, or ☎ (0900) 404 0910, or you can order it online (see below). The cost is €30 for adults and €15 for those age 24 and under.
- www.museumjaarkaart.nl – for participating museums.
- See also www.museum.nl for a list of over 1000 museums in the Netherlands.

Tipping: Tipping is not obligatory, but is customary in taxis, restaurants and hotels. Bills normally already include a 10–15% service charge, to which clients may add.

Emergency/tourist assistance: TAS (Tourist Assistance Service) helps crime and accident victims:
- In The Hague ☎ (070) 310 3274
- In Amsterdam ☎ (020) 625 3246

Eating out

Holland has not generally been known for its gastronomy. Today, however, there is a great deal of choice – particularly with other ethnic foods such as those from Indonesia (a former Dutch colony). Children's plates are frequently available at a lower cost. If you don't see '*Kindermenu*' listed, ask if they have one. (Dutch foods are described in Chapter 17.)

A number of Dutch restaurants have received Michelin stars, a sign of excellence. A complete list of these restaurants can be obtained by writing to any Netherlands Board of Tourism office (see addresses on www.viamichelin.co.uk), or you can check the latest

Michelin guide that includes all of the Benelux countries (Holland, Belgium and Luxembourg). The Alliance Gastronomique Neerlandaise ☎ (040) 263 1153, www.alliance.nl, consists of 39 restaurants representing the cream of culinary art. Relais du Centre ☎ (0499) 55 0674, (0653) 62 2356, www.relaisducentre.nl, is a group of 35 restaurants aiming to offer high quality at a moderate price.

Our own list of favourites can be found in each chapter under the heading 'Eating Out,' and also in a list in Chapter 17.

Restaurant guides: Dutch restaurant websites where you can search by city, type of food or cost, read independent reviews, and also purchase guides:
- www.dinnersite.nl – restaurant site, occasionally with some discount offers
- www.iens.nl – Iens Independent Index, in English and Dutch
- www.specialbite.nl – Special Bite also publishes a food /restaurant magazine.

Staying over

Excellent hotel information and reservation services are provided upon arrival by the Netherlands Reservation Centre (NRC), as well as the VVV and ANWB. Another option is the GWK, *Grenswisselkantoren*, whose currency exchange offices are in most major train stations (room reservations, theatre and event tickets). It is a national financial institution where you can exchange any currency and also use credit cards and travellers' checks. www.travelex.com/nl

For hotel reservations before arriving in Holland, contact the NBTC/NRC:

The Netherlands Reservation Centre (NRC) (Netherlands Reserverings Centrum)

Plantsoengracht 2, 1441 DE Purmerend, The Netherlands

☎ (0299) 689 144. www.hotelres.nl

Hotel chains:

Hilton, Marriott, Ramada, Holiday Inn, Best Western, Novotel, and Campanile are all represented in the Netherlands. However, there are several recommended Dutch hotel chains that may not be as well known:

Golden Tulip Hotels have 56 hotels, generally in the luxury category, including health spas, pools and recreational facilities. For a brochure, write: Stationsplein 26, 3818 LE Amersfoort, P.O. Box 448, 3800 AK Amersfoort, The Netherlands. Reservations: ☎ (0031) 33 254 4800, or www.goldentulip.com

Bilderberg Group offers their guests a special experience in unrivalled settings. Their 22 luxury hotels (often with pool or sauna, tennis or putting facilities) ensure every comfort. For information and reservations call ☎ (031) 731 8319, or www.bilderberg.nl

Holland Hotels are often in quiet, scenic places, with generally moderate prices. You can reserve directly, or from one Holland Hotel to another for your next night's stop. ☎ (076) 520 2888, www.hollandhotels.nl

Postillion (Postillion Hotels) is also highly regarded. One of their special services is to organise bike tours, transporting your luggage from one hotel to the next as you bike across Holland. They have nine hotels in the Netherlands. For information: Postbus 720, 7400 AS Deventer, ☎ (0570) 69 4131.

Hotels:

- www.worldtravelguide.net/country/187/accommodation/Europe/Netherlands.html
- www.bookings.nl – no registration fees and ample selection of hotels throughout the country
- www.tripadvisor.com – for Holland hotels

Bed and breakfasts:

There are currently some 3,450 B&Bs (sometimes called 'pensions') in Holland, offering good value for money, as well as a way to meet Dutch families. Rates vary, and they may be booked through local tourist offices, or you can easily view these characteristic and charming accommodations online and make reservations yourself.

- Bed and Breakfast Service Nederland, ☎ (0497) 33 0300, www.bedandbreakfast.nl, Veilig Oord 60, 5531 XC Bladel
- Farm Holidays in Holland, ☎ (017) 258 6340, www.dutch-farmholidays.com, and www.hoevelogies.nl, Postbus 73, 2390AB Hazerwoude
- Erfgoed Logies Nederland: Historical heritage stays in very characteristic Dutch farmhouses, castles, manor houses and the like, including two old sailing ships where you can spend the night. ☎ (020) 679 7441, www.erfgoedlogies.nl, Apollolaan 133-135, 1077 AR Amsterdam.
- The Pronkkamer Characteristic Bed & Breakfasts: ☎ (0519) 34 9473, www.pronkkamer.nl, 9033 ZX Leeuwarden.
- Stichting Neerlands Goed, (Netherlands Land/Estates) ☎ (029) 965 5726, www.neerlandsgoed.nl, Lagedijk 9A, 1145 PL Katwoude,

Self-catering: Farmhouses and holiday chalets for groups can be booked months in advance via the local tourist offices. Bungalow parks, also known as 'holiday villages,' can be booked through The Netherlands Reserverings Centrum (NRC). Most bungalow resorts offer a full range of recreational facilities, including swimming pools, golf and tennis. Prices depend on size, amenities and time of year. Families especially enjoy the combination of day trip excursions and holiday resort afforded by many.

- www.centerparcs.nl
- www.landal.nl
- www.bungalow.net/nederland
- www.vakantie-bungalowparken.nl

Camping:

There are about 2,500 registered campsites in Holland! Only 500 offer advanced booking; the others operate on a first-come, first-served basis. Camping is not allowed outside official campsites, only on-site. You may be charged per day or per 24 hours, and proof of identity, such as a passport, will be needed.

- Stichting Vrije Recreatie (information on camping/caravanning), www.svr.nl
- www.campingo.com/netherlands-camping
- www.eurocampings.co.uk (See 'The Netherlands' for inspected campsites.)

Hostels:
There are around 30 hostels in various surroundings, from castles to modern buildings. People with a Hostelling International card receive a discount of €2.50 for an overnight stay including breakfast. Information is obtainable from Stayokay (the Dutch Youth Hostel Association/Stichting Nederlandse Jeugdherberg Centrale): ☎ (020) 551 3155, www.stayokay.com
For more information: http://hostelworld.com, www.europeanhostels.com
Travelling students might also try: www.homestayweb.com

Useful phrases in Dutch
http://dutch.about.com/od/dictionaries/
www.worldreferences.net
www.unforgetabledutch.com

Holland resources
www.hollandhandbook.nl
www.netherlands.info
www.expatica.com
www.thehagueonline.nl
www.amsterdamcitytourist.com
www.hollandportal.info
www.holland.com/us
www.holland.com/uk

Air travel
www.ryanair.com
www.virgin-atlantic.com
www.airberlin.com
www.flylowcostairlines.org
www.whichbudget.com
www.attitudetravel.com
www.cheapflights.co.uk
www.cheapseats.com
www.cheaptickets.com
www.traveladvisor.com
www.e-bookers.com
www.bargainholidays.com

www.onlinetravel.com
www.mixfly.com
www.bargain-airfares.org
www.expedia.co.uk
www.travelocity.com
www.dohop.com – multiple leg journeys
www.momondo.com – compare Europe
www.flylc.com – European discounts
www.easylow.com – over 10,000 routes

Netherlands (NL) ticket sites
www.cheaptickets.nl
www.skybreakers.nl
www.vliegtarieven.nl
www.worldticketcenter.nl
www.flightemotions.nl
www.vergelijk.nl – comparisons
www.skyteam.com – 10 airlines' network of 728 destinations in 150 countries
www.nl.lastminute.com – Dutch deals
www.fly2start.nl
www.aireka.nl (click 'vluchten' for airfares only)

Who are the Dutch?

by Jacob Vossestein, author of **Dealing with the Dutch**

When trying to describe the Dutch character, one needs to probe deeply to reveal the origins of their soul. In Holland, this takes us on a vastly diverse journey, through its amazing water defences against the ever-threatening sea and rivers, its liberal and infamous policies on drugs and sexual freedom, and its successes in art, fashion (witness Viktor & Rolf), and even business and sports. The Dutch are known for trade and are fond of travel – resulting in a strong global presence. Paradoxically, they combine a reputation of stern frugality with a striking involvement in world-wide charity and aid.

At the heart of all these phenomena, there is a 'no nonsense' kind of pragmatism stemming collectively from the struggle against water, a republican past, and Calvinist-cum-Protestant values.

The Dutch are programmed for a rational outlook on the world as a place where one 'has a job to do' rather than playing fancy games of power and glory. Whether involving work or leisure, something almost always needs to be accomplished; success is wonderful but, in their minds, should not lead to strong pride or even basic vanity. "Down to earth, please." A popular Dutch expression is: "*Doe maar gewoon; dan doe je gek genoeg*," which translates as, "Just act normal; that's strange enough as it is." Famous paintings from the Dutch Golden Age characteristically depict simple people and, although visitors will encounter monuments, these rarely honour outstanding heroes but rather concrete projects and solid achievers.

You will quickly discover that Dutch pragmatism also seems to reflect itself in a rather no-nonsense attitude towards customers in shops or restaurants: "We will happily serve you if you are clearly not pompous or pretentious." Anyone counting on servility or great respect from the Dutch just for the sake of being important – or because they have a wallet full of fancy credit cards – may be in for a surprise. People in the Netherlands believe in a very basic kind of equality. They may, indeed, have the requisite number of cars, but they also don't frown on going anywhere and everywhere by bicycle.

In such a densely populated country – 16.5 million people in only 36,000 square kilometers – physical and mental space are at a premium, and that leads to another type of Dutch pragmatism: "Do whatever you like as long as it doesn't interfere with my freedom to do likewise. So do it there, in your space, and not here in mine. Fine if you want to come home at three in the morning, but don't make too much noise please; we're sleeping." Boundaries. They're important in Holland. →

Even the notorious 'Red Light District' is both geographically and socially a highly defined area, as are the 'coffee shops' – soft drug havens – and the nudist beaches. These are clearly pragmatic niches, solutions for what exists 'whether one likes it or not.' The Dutch don't quite understand what all the international fuss is about such issues. "After all," they say, "it's plain logical, isn't it?"

If you have respect for the Dutch in their pragmatic look on life and present yourself in a casual, non-glossy way, you are sure to have many pleasant encounters in this land of seeming contrasts.

For more information: www.kit.nl

Chapter 2 | The province of North Holland

North Holland is rich in history, natural beauty, and panache. It offers visitors a wealth of uniquely Dutch impressions, including the vibrant patchwork of the spring bulb fields, colourful cheese markets, and traditional old fishing villages. Travellers enjoy its surprisingly good beaches, its cornucopia of lakes and its ancient and vast woodlands. Windmill-dotted canals still cut their way through the notoriously flat countryside, gently infiltrating Holland's idyllic towns and cities where fine historic buildings and world-class museums join hands. In this province you'll find the world's largest flower market, and a city like no other – Amsterdam.

North Holland encompasses the arm of land bordered by the North Sea on the west, the IJsselmeer on the east, as far north as the island of Texel, and south to Schiphol Airport. In its early history, the west coast of Holland was considerably smaller in territory than today. The main towns were Haarlem, Hoorn and Amsterdam...the rest being villages surrounded by marshlands with islands. Still mostly below sea level, the land has been greatly enlarged through extensive reclamation.

While Amsterdam is its foremost city and main tourist destination, there are many other fascinating towns to visit and sites to see in this province. Roads and public transportation are excellent.

Information:
www.noord-holland-tourist.nl, www.holland.com/uk, and www2.holland.com/us

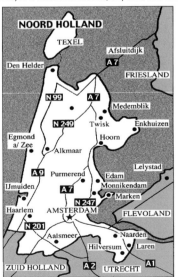

Amsterdam

Getting there: From The Hague or Rotterdam take Highway A4. Frequent train connections from Schiphol. (Tourist information booth at Schiphol Airport, Arrivals 2.)

Information: VVV, Stationsplein 10 (opposite Central Station); Platform 2 (*Spoor* 2) inside Central Station; Leidseplein 1, ☎ (0900) 400 4040 (€0.40 per min), www.amsterdamtourist.nl, www.vvvamsterdam.nl, www.visitamsterdam.nl

Amsterdam's history began before the 12th century, in what was a swampy area on the banks of the old Zuiderzee and the river Amstel. Count Floris V granted Amsterdam her city charter in 1275 and she became a member of the Hanseatic League in 1369. Her people were seafarers – tough and ambitious; they went as far as Portugal for salt and the Baltic for wood. Built on piles, the city took on its unique character when the city fathers decided to expand by building three principal semi-circular canals. There are now at least 100 canals crossed by 1,200 bridges. A town of immigrants, it reached its Golden Age in the 17th century with the influx of many talented artists, artisans and traders fleeing the rigours of Spanish rule in the south. Prosperity knew no bounds, as is reflected in the elegant patrician houses along Amsterdam's canals. The city was a storehouse of international goods, with a great merchant and banking class that supported the artistic and cultural life previously unsurpassed in Europe.

Amsterdam, like most of Holland, suffered under Spanish rule (16th century), French rule (Napoleonic period, 1795-1814), and the German occupation (WW II, 1940-45). It has an active stock exchange, and its busy port and air traffic centre make it an international commercial hub. In addition, it is a city of great tolerance, which is reflected in the number of young people who flock here from all over the world to 'breathe' the atmosphere. Ask a Dutchman how he would rate the three big cities of Holland and he would undoubtedly say: "Rotterdam is the city to work in; The Hague is the city to live in; but Amsterdam is the city to play in."

Unfortunately, the city's VVV tourist offices are often crowded, especially the two at the Central Station. To save time, gather as much information as you can before your trip. Special 1, 2 and 3 day 'I amsterdam' discount passes are available, as well as a wealth of information on: www.iamsterdam.nl. You can get a free map of all buses and tram routes in Amsterdam – available from tourist offices or the GVB ticket office in front of Central Station and next to the VVV. If you require public transport information, just call 0900 92 92, stating destination, times, etc. Calls cost € 0.50 per min. Service runs weekdays from 6am until midnight.

Walking is the best way to discover Amsterdam, but we do recommend a canal boat cruise to get oriented. It provides a perspective you can't get on land. Amsterdam is a wonderful city to discover – it can be shocking, amusing, beautiful, entertaining and educational, and certainly never dull. Its reputation for liberalness precedes it and, as such, you're likely to see almost anything here. If you don't believe us, just spend some time sitting at an outdoor café on Leidseplein!

Damrak

Location: Straight ahead of Central Station, walk down the Rokin. It runs to the 'Dam,' the main square.

As you leave Central Station, the street ahead of you is the **Damrak**, where you'll see several canal boat operators. At one time, this area was filled with boats, as the river Amstel originally flowed into the sea at this point. The Damrak is built right where the river once flowed.

Central Station is an architectural gem in itself. Designed by Dutch architect P.J.H. Cuypers, it was opened in 1889. Built in the area of what was once the mouth of the river Amstel, its construction was a great engineering feat. New islands had to be built, and thousands of piles were driven into the watery ground. The facade includes a wind direction gauge, a reminder of the days when wind-powered ships were the mainstay of the city's commerce.

Another architectural jewel is **Beurs Van Berlage**, Damrak 277, ☎ (020) 530 4141, www.beursvanberlage.nl, open Tues.-Sun. 10am-4pm. Its design was revolutionary in 1903 when H.P. Berlage built it as an exchange building. The building had a tremendous influence on future generations of Dutch architects. No longer an exchange, you can visit the building – now a concert/exhibition hall and community centre – and climb the tower to enjoy the view.

If walking down Damrak is your first look at Amsterdam, you'll soon discover that subjects considered 'taboo' elsewhere are treated quite casually here. For example, on this busy street you'll find the **Venus Temple Sex Museum**, Damrak 18, ☎ (020) 622 8376, www.sexmuseumamsterdam.nl, open daily 10am-11:30pm, which explores sex through the centuries.

Oude Zijde

Location: To your left after leaving Central Station.

This is the oldest part of Amsterdam. The first street running parallel to Damrak to the east, Warmoesstraat, is a major road on which people lived in the Middle Ages. The city's oldest church, which is also its oldest building, is located here. But the area is probably best known for its colourful participants in the world's oldest profession. This is the heart of Amsterdam's Red Light District.

▶ Oude Kerk

Location: Oudekerksplein 23, between Warmoesstraat and Oudezijds Voorburgwal
Information: ☎ (020) 625 8284; www.oudekerk.nl
Hours: Mon.-Sat. 11am-5pm, Sun. 1-5pm

In the 13th century the original church was built on this site. Proving too small for the growing city, work began in the early 14th century on what is now known as the **Oude Kerk**. By the 15th century it was again too small, but by then the city had closed in around it, leaving no room to expand.

Up until the late 16th century, the Oude Kerk was not only the religious centre for much of Amsterdam, but also its social centre. The church was open to people selling their goods, as well as to beggars who needed a place to stay. During the Reformation, it became a Protestant Church. Over the centuries, however, it fell into disrepair and, when the risk of its collapsing became too great, it was closed in 1951. It took 28 years to complete the restoration process. Inside, you can see 15th-16th-century ceiling paintings, stained-glass windows dating from 1555, and the grave of Rembrandt's wife, Saskia. Its Vater-Muller organ (1724) is renowned for its quality, and summer concerts are given regularly. You can climb the tower for one of the best views in the city.

▶ **Amstelkring Museum**
Location: Oudezijds Voorburgwal 40
Information: ☎ (020) 624 6604, www.museumamstelkring.nl
Hours: Mon.-Sat. 10am-5pm, Sun. 1-5pm

From the street, the **Amstelkring Museum** looks like just another 17th-century merchant's house along an Amsterdam canal. The elegant first floor living room is also what you would expect to see. A walk up the stairs to the attic, however, proves that this house is not at all what it appears to be. In fact, it served as a secret place of worship and has a large, hidden chapel in the attic. It became known as 'Ons' Lieve Heer op Solder,' or 'Our Lord In The Attic,' and is preserved in its entirety. After the Protestant Reformation, Amsterdam Catholics were not allowed to worship in public. Although Catholic services were not banned, the law insisted they be held in private, i.e. hidden from public view, so Catholics built clandestine churches. Most disappeared when the ban was repealed in the 19th century, but this one, built in 1661, was preserved and became a museum in 1888, with an altar, pews, an organ, and a confessional in the narrow space of the attic. The museum also has a collection of religious objects, as well as religious and secular art.

▶ **Red Light District**
Location: Houses on several streets, located in the area east of Warmoesstraat,
                west of Zeedijk, and north of Sint Jansstraat.
Information: www.red-light-district.nl

As strange as it may seem, one of the most popular tourist attractions in Amsterdam is its **Red Light District**, known as 'De Walletjes.' Visitors from all parts of the world wander through these streets to see what has to be one of the world's most unexpected tourist sights: scantily-clad 'women of the night' in shop windows, working their 'legal' trade.
    The Dutch view prostitution as something that cannot be stopped, but can be controlled. Prostitutes are licensed, medically checked, and restricted to 'red light' areas. They even have their own union. If you're interested in learning more, visit the

Prostitution Information Centre near the Oude Kerk. They also offer guided walking tours and have a gift shop, ☎ (020) 420 7328. www.pic-amsterdam.com

On the flip side, there is an organisation called the **Scarlet Cord** (Scharlaken Koord), located in the same area, which aims to help such women find alternative lifestyles, ☎ (020) 622 6897. www.bewareofloverboys.nl

The women in the Red Light District are accustomed to tourists, but do not try to take pictures; photography is frowned upon here. Also, although the area is generally safe, beware of pickpockets.

This area is the largest Red Light District in Amsterdam, but it is not the only one. They do exist in other Dutch cities as well, but this is the only one where tourists will not feel particularly out of place.

- **Also on the Oude Zijde:** In the spirit of this area's unique atmosphere, there's a sort of informal 'alternative' museum quarter on Oudezijds Achterburgwal. There's the **Erotisch Museum**, Oudezijds Achterburgwal 54, ☎ (020) 624 7303, open daily 11am-midnight; the **Tattoo Museum**, Oudezijds Achterburgwal 130, ☎ (020) 625 1565, open Tues.-Sun. noon-5pm, www.tattoomuseum.com; and the **Hash Marijuana Hemp Museum**, Oudezijds Achterburgwal 148, ☎ (020) 623 5961, www.hashmuseum.com, open daily 11am-10pm.

Besides being tolerant toward prostitution, the Dutch also have lenient policies on the use of marijuana, which is available at establishments throughout the city that call themselves 'koffieshops.' If you're actually interested in a real cup of coffee without the extra indulgences, you might want to go elsewhere. These so-called 'coffee shops' (as opposed to 'cafés') cater to those who want to smoke cannabis, or consume it in cookies or cakes. Although technically illegal in Holland, marijuana is tolerated as long as it is used discreetly indoors.

The **Waag**, a 15th-century structure – once a gate into the old city, later a weigh-house and now a restaurant – sits on the edge of this district, on Nieuwmarkt, where a Sunday antique market is held from May-Sept. If you follow St. Antoniesbreestraat from the Nieuwmarkt, you'll see the tall church tower of **Zuiderkerk**, Zuiderkerkhof 72, (020) 552 7987, www.zuiderkerk.amsterdam.nl, open Mon.-Fri. noon-5pm, Thurs. 8pm. It was built between 1603 and1614 by architect, Hendrik de Keyser, who is buried here. It was the first Protestant church built in the city. During the famine years of World War II, the church had to be used as a morgue. In 1944 an average of 50 corpses were brought here each day. It has become an information centre for the city's housing department. You can listen to its 35-bell carillon at noon on Thurs., and climb its 70-meter tower between June-Sept.

▶ **Dam Square**

Location: Due south of Central Station via Damrak

The **Dam** has always been the centre of the city, so-called since the 13th century when residents built a dam here to protect their homes from the floods. At one time, the Amstel flowed in the area where the monument now stands. Boats would dock here to unload their cargoes for the markets and weigh-houses on the square. The Dam has also been the site of political and military events, from grand parades of military might, to royal processions, and the protests in the 1960s and 70s.

The Amstel has been filled in, the markets moved to other locations, and the Weigh House torn down by Louis Bonaparte in 1808 because it blocked his view from the Palace. Two major buildings still stand on the square. It remains the centre of the city, filled daily with thousands of people going about their business, or just enjoying the charged atmosphere. For many years the National Monument, built in honour of Dutch victims of World War II, has been a popular spot for young people to congregate.

▶ **Nieuwe Kerk**

Location: The Dam
Information: ☎ (020) 638 6909, www.nieuwekerk.nl
Hours: Usually daily 10am-6pm, but depends on events.

This Gothic church, the second church to be built in the city of Amsterdam, dates from 1408. In January 1645 a fire destroyed its interior and, unfortunate as this was, the timing could not have been more opportune since this was the period of Holland's greatest artistic glory. Outstandingly-talented artists and artisans of the Dutch 'Golden Age' were available to restore and enhance the interior of the damaged church, making it the imposing structure it is.

There is no altar, but the monument-grave of one of Holland's heroes, Admiral de Ruyter, can be seen in its place. The organ, one of the most beautiful in Europe, is used for concerts and special musical services on Sundays. Its oak pulpit took 15 years to carve and was completed in 1664.

Queen Beatrix's investiture, like those of her predecessors since 1815, took place in the **Nieuwe Kerk**. At this ceremony the new monarch takes an oath, and all members of both chambers of Parliament swear allegiance to the throne. Originally a Roman Catholic church, it became part of the Dutch Reformed Church. It is now managed by a non-denominational Trust, whose aim is to make it a lively meeting place, as it was in the Middle Ages. Non-political meetings, discussions, exhibits, etc., take place here.

▶ **Royal Palace on the Dam**

Location: Dam Square
Information: ☎ (020) 620 4060, www.koninklijkhuis.nl
Hours: Irregular, as the palace is used for functions. Generally open
                    Tues.-Thurs., Sat.-Sun. 12:30-5pm. Call in advance to check.

When the Koninklijk Paleis, or **Royal Palace**, was built between 1648-55, some described it as the eighth wonder of the world. It is perhaps the grandest structure in Amsterdam, as its builders planned it to be, though it was not designed to be a palace. It was built as a city hall, at a time when Amsterdam was establishing itself as one the world's great cities. The city fathers wanted a building that would reflect Amsterdam's growing economic and political importance. It didn't become a Royal Palace until 1808, when Napoleon gave his brother Louis the title 'King of Holland.' Louis made this his home and, much to his brother's anger, protected Holland's interests against Napoleon's policies. Napoleon sent in troops and Louis fled in 1810. Today, the Dutch Royal family lives in The Hague, but still uses this building for some official functions.

It took over 13,000 wooden piles driven into the wet, sandy soil to support the building. Inside, much of the furniture is that left behind by Louis Bonaparte when he beat his hasty retreat. The most impressive room is the huge Burgerzaal with its marble floor, illustrated with maps of the world as it was known at that time, and its 95-foot-high ceiling. The building looks truly palatial throughout, with spacious rooms and numerous paintings and statues which were meant either to tell a story, or to impress the people of Amsterdam with some moral lesson, when they came there to conduct business with the city.

▶ **Madame Tussauds Amsterdam**

Location:	Dam 20
Information:	☎ (020) 523 0623, www.madametussauds.nl
Hours:	Daily 10am-5:30pm

World personalities, historical figures, Dutch painters, artists, sportsmen – all are represented in this exhibition in wax, including the likes of President Clinton, Winston Churchill, and the Dutch Royal Family. Here's your chance to be photographed with them or others, such as the Dalai Lama, Michael Jackson or Rembrandt. Scenes depicting 17th-century Holland, with beggars, rat catchers and merchants along an old canal, make this an easy museum to enjoy – not too big, colourful and fun.

● **Near Dam Square:** Behind the Palace and the Nieuwe Kerk on Nieuwezijds Voorburgwal, is a huge 19th-century Neo-Gothic building now called the **Magna Plaza**. It was built as the city's main post office in 1899, but has been converted into a shopping mall. www.magnaplaza.nl

South of Dam Square

Location: Boundaries are the Dam Square (north), Singel Canal and river Amstel (south), Oude Schans and Zwanenburgwal (east), Singel Canal (west).

This area has several sites of historical interest, with restaurants, hotels, most of the city's main shopping streets and canal boat rides on offer. Being almost at the centre of the city's main attractions, it is within walking distance of almost everything you may want to see in Amsterdam.

▶ **Begijnhof**

Location: Entrances on Spui and on Gedempte Begijnensloot
Information: ☎ (020) 622 1918; www.begijnhofamsterdam.nl
Open: Mon. 1pm -6:30pm, Tue.-Fri. 9am- 6:30pm, Sat. & Sun. 9am-6pm

The **Begijnhof**, a beautifully serene oasis, is centrally located in what has become the busiest shopping area on the Spui. The 164 small houses, formerly for lay sisters, open onto a picture-perfect courtyard bright with flowers, and is strangely peaceful in spite of the hubbub just outside its walls. In 1346, a group of lay women who lived and worked as nuns, but who had not taken their vows, came to Amsterdam from a nearby village to found a religious community. They built their own small houses instead of living in a monastery or cloister, but had to abide by strict rules: be sober of manner, live and dress simply, and not receive male company at night. They were to engage in charitable works and were not allowed to spend the night away from their Begijnhof home.

All was well until the Reformation. In 1578 their church was confiscated, and in 1607 it was turned over to the English Reformed (Presbyterian) Community. The Beguines as they were called, were allowed to remain, but since any public display of Catholicism was forbidden, they practiced their religion in secrecy. At first, Mass was held in different houses until 1655 when the parish priest bought two adjoining houses and converted them into a permanent, hidden place of worship. Still a Catholic Chapel, it is the unobtrusive structure opposite the English Church.

The **English Church** was originally dedicated in 1419. Having been seriously damaged by fires in 1421 and 1452, it was more elaborately reconstructed. The flags on display are the Union Jack and those of the Scottish Church, and the House of Orange. The American flag and the stained-glass window over the choir exit were presented by the Pilgrim Fathers Society. Church services in English are held every Sunday.

Across the way, on the corner, stands reputedly the oldest house in Amsterdam (number 34), dating from 1475. Its front and back gables are made of wood as is the Gothic inner framework, hence the name 'Houten Huis,' wooden house. After the Reformation, this house was used as a chapel for the Beguines and as a hospital ward.

Today, the Begijnhof houses are occupied primarily by self-supporting single women. Visit the Orientation Centre at #35 for more details.

▶ **Amsterdam Historical Museum**

Location: Nieuwezijds Voorburgwal 357 / Kalverstraat 92
Information: ☎ (020) 523 1822, www.ahm.nl
Open: Mon.-Fri. 10am-5pm, Sat.-Sun. 11am-5pm

The rich history of Amsterdam is told in a building that was once an orphanage. (Notice the carving of orphan boys over the entrance gate off Kalverstraat.) A generous number of paintings are used to portray the history of Amsterdam, including some by such well-

THE Hague Amsterdam Rotterdam TIMES

The Holland Times is the first newspaper to be published in the greater Amsterdam, The Hague and Rotterdam areas for international travellers and the large population of local expatriates who, for the very first time, can now read the Dutch news in an English paper.

Distribution points for The Holland Times:
- Embassies and consulates in The Hague and Amsterdam
- Fine bookstores such as Athenaeum, the American Book Center, Waterstone's and Scheltema
- Auction Houses such as Christie's, Glerum and Sotheby's
- Offices of the International Chamber of Commerce
- Restaurants and café's
- Several airlines, including Cathay Pacific, China Airlines and Iceland Air
- Virtually all of the three, four and five star hotels in Amsterdam, The Hague and Rotterdam
- Controlled Circulation: Canon, Shell, Cisco Systems, New Horizons, Adidas, KPMG, ABN-AMRO

argopress Delflandlaan 4 1062 EB Amsterdam 020-5849020

known artists as Rembrandt. There are also carillon bells that once hung in Amsterdam's Munt Tower, suits of armour, and maps of the world as it was known here in the years of exploration. An interesting display of paintings hangs on the walls in a glass-enclosed area: 14 group portraits of the Civic Guard. Walk through and admire.

- **Also south of Dam Square:** The **Allard Pierson Museum**, Oude Turfmarkt 127, ☎ (020) 525 2556, www.allardpiersonmuseum.nl, open Tues.-Fri. 10am-5pm, Sat.-Sun. 1-5pm, is a museum of Egyptian antiquities with mummies, model pyramids, and a computer that can print your name in hieroglyphics.

Western canals

Location: To the right as you leave Central Station. South of Brouwersgracht to Leidsegracht, and between Singel Canal and Prinsengracht. Canals crisscross the old city of Amsterdam. But there are four canals which almost form a complete ring around the old city: Singel, Herengracht, Keizersgracht and Prinsengracht.

The western side of the old city is a beautiful area for those who want to explore the canals. It is also home to one of the city's most popular tourist destinations: the Anne Frank House.

▶ **Anne Frank House**
Location: Prinsengracht 263/267
Information: ☎ (020) 556 7105; www.annefrank.nl
Hours: Mar.15- Sept.14, daily 9am-9pm; Sept.15-14-Mar., daily 9am-7pm; closed on Jewish holidays

_____

Anne Frank, her parents and sister, together with four other Jewish people, hid from the Germans in the upper floors of this house for two solid years, from 1942 until 1944. During this period Anne grew from a young girl to a teenager, and wrote her now famous diary – on display here – in which she described in detail her thoughts and feelings during that traumatic time during WW II. Eventually the Germans discovered the hiding place and its occupants who, together with young Anne, were dispatched to concentration camps. Ironically, she died only one month before the end of the war. Of the eight who hid in the annex, only Anne's father, Otto, survived. After the war he published his daughter's writings, little knowing that his 13-year-old's diary would become an international bestseller, with over 13 million copies sold in more than 50 languages.

Extensive restoration has helped preserve the building as it was when Anne and the others were arrested. A visitors' centre presents an excellent exhibition about her and the millions of others who died in concentration camps. Inside the house you can still see the collection of photographs of royalty and film star postcards that Anne had on the wall of the room where she slept, as well as the pencil marks her father made on the wall, recording the height of his two growing girls. A moveable bookcase, hinged like a door, separated the hiding place from the rest of the building, and is still in place.

This is one of the most popular tourist attractions in Amsterdam. Come early to avoid the longest queues.

The **Singel** is the first canal you reach when you come from the city centre, the oldest of the four inner canals that circle the city. When it was dug in the 15th century it formed Amsterdam's western boundary. At its northern end is the Stromarkt, with outdoor cafés where you can sit and watch the canal boats negotiate a difficult turn. Nearby is the former **Lutherse Kerk**, Kattengat 2. Its round shape was unusual for a church when it opened in 1671. Today it's a conference room for a neighbouring hotel.

One of the pleasures of walking in Amsterdam is to observe the canalside buildings and their different gables. Bell-shaped gables were popular on houses built between about 1660-1790. Some examples are at 96 (built in 1755), and 104-106 (1743). Numbers 140-142 (1602) were once the home of Frans Banning Cocq, who gained eternal fame by being the central figure in Rembrandt's painting 'The Night Watch'. Most canal houses are narrow (owing to less taxes in former days), but none more so than number 166 – not much wider than a door.

The bridge over the Singel at Oude Leliestraat is the **Torensluis**. It used to be graced with a tower, which explains why it is so wide. Today it provides spacious terraces for nearby cafés in summer. Notice the entrance to the old city dungeons at the base of the bridge. The next canal west is **Herengracht**. Before the bell gable was in style on its elegant houses, the step gable was most popular, reaching its peak between 1600-65. Some examples are Herengracht 77 (1632), 81 (1625), and 170-172 (1617) where two houses share a single step-gabled facade. Houses were embellished with gables in order to hide their slanted roofs which were not considered elegant at the time. The neck gable became popular between 1640-1775, the first example built in 1638 by architect Philips Vingboons. It can be seen on the building that now houses the **Theatermuseum**, Herengracht 168, ☎ (020) 551 3300, www.theaterinstituut.nl, open Tues.-Fri. 11am-5pm, Sat.-Sun. 1-5pm. The museum tells the history of Dutch theatre, with displays of old costumes and paintings. It also gives visitors a chance to see the inside of this old canal house, with its beautiful spiral staircase. The museum extends next door into the **Bartolotti House**, Herengracht 170-172 (1617), which curves to follow the bend in the canal.

Two other canal houses form the **Bijbels Museum**, Herengracht 366-368, ☎ (020) 624 2436, www.bijbelsmuseum.nl, open Mon.-Sat. 10am-5pm, Sun. 1-5pm. Vingboons designed these buildings in 1662. The property has a well-preserved kitchen, ceilings painted with mythological figures, and a large garden and pond. The museum displays include archeological finds, old Bibles, and models of ancient temples.

Keizersgracht is the next canal west. You'll notice many decorations on the facades of the old houses of Amsterdam, most of them near the top. You'll understand why the house at 123 (1622) is known as the **House with Heads**, when you look at the lower façade. Number 209 (1734) is graced with a female statue symbolizing hope.

One canal to the west is **Prinsengracht**. The step-gabled house at 175 (1661) has three animals on its facade. But what will impress you on this canal is the number of houseboats...2,500 at last count, and all lived in. If you are curious, climb aboard the **Woonbootmuseum** (Houseboat Museum), Prinsengracht, opposite 296, open Mar.-Oct. Tues.-Sun. 11am-5pm; Nov.-Feb. Fri.-Sun. 11am-5pm, ☎ (020) 427 0750, www.house-boatmuseum.nl. It's a 1914 riverboat converted into a cosy home.

● **Also along the western canals**: Almost next door to the Anne Frank House is the **Westerkerk**, Prinsengracht 281, ☎ (020) 624 7766, www.westerkerk.nl, open April-Sept., Mon.-Fri. 11am-3pm; July-Aug., also Sat. The church was built in 1631, and its 85-meter tower (275 feet) is the city's tallest. You can climb the tower when the church is open; a guide takes visitors up at the top of each hour. It's the best tower view of Amsterdam. The carillon chimes automatically every 15 minutes, but its 50 bells are played by hand every Thurs., noon-1pm. Rembrandt was buried in the church in 1669, but it is not known where.

At the northern end of all four canals is the **Brouwersgracht**, a canal that runs through an attractive tree-lined area with lots of old buildings and cafés. You will also see the **Homomonument** of three granite triangles, in remembrance of the gay men and women who lost their lives in WWII. www.homomonument.nl. In August the city hosts a world-famous Gay Pride parade on boats that sail through the canals.

Southern canals

Location: Boundaries are Singel and Binnen-Amstel (north), Singelgracht (south), Amstel River (east), Leidsegracht (west)

Amsterdam was growing rapidly at the end of the 16th century, so the city looked to the west to expand. Three new canals were dug, running parallel to the Singel. Having finished the northwest leg of the Herengracht, Keizersgracht, and Prinsengracht in 1660, work began on the southern loop of the project. The houses in this southern section were, therefore, more up-to-date, generally larger and more expensive than those to the west of the old city.

This part of the Singel once formed the southern boundary with a city wall. The **Munttoren**, or Mint Tower, is the only surviving reminder of this fortification. It was a city gate tower until 1672 when the French occupiers used it to mint coins. Almost next to the tower is the city's colourful **Bloemenmarkt**, also known as the floating flower market.

When the three canals beyond the Singel were dug, the Herengracht or Gentlemen's Canal, was closest to the city, and the most prestigious. This is evident in the houses built on what is known as the **Golden Curve**, the gentle curve followed by the canal between the Leidsegracht and the Reguliersgracht. The houses here are not typical canal houses, but more like canal mansions. Notice the size of the buildings, their windows and the stairways – the more windows and steps, the more prestigious. House number 510, as well as 543 across the canal, are good examples.

Number 518 is the **Geelvinck Hinlopen Huis**, ☎ (020) 639 0747, www.geelvinck.com, where tours for groups of up to 15 can be arranged. The **Willet-Holthuysen Museum**,

Herengracht 605, ☎ (020) 523 1822, www.willetholthuysen.nl, open Mon.-Fri. 10am-
5pm, Sat.-Sun. 11am-5pm, is a 17th-century patrician mansion with a lovely garden.
The museum's period rooms provide a view of life on the canal in the 18th and 19th
centuries.

The spot where the Herengracht crosses the Reguliersgracht is a favourite for canal
boat tours. From here there is an excellent view of seven bridges all at one time. (It's
difficult to see all seven from street level.) The arched bridges along Herengracht and
Keizersgracht are all made of brick, another sign of the prestige of these canals when
wooden bridges were the norm. Many arches are ringed with lights, making an attractive scene at night.

The **Museum Van Loon**, Keizersgracht 672, ☎ (020) 624 5255, www.museumvan-
loon.nl, open Wed.-Mon. 11am-5pm, is an elegant canalside mansion to visit. Built in
1671, it has 17th-18th-century furnishings, family portraits and a formal garden.

Prinsengracht, was the least prestigious of the three new canals when they were
built, as it had a mixture of homes and warehouses. You can spot a warehouse by the line
of large shuttered windows running down the centre of the building's facade. Today,
many of these have been converted into apartments or offices. Some good examples are
at numbers 534-36, and 771-73.

Note the hoist beams protruding from near the top of the buildings here and
throughout the old part of the city. These were necessary because of the very narrow
stairways inside most of the houses. The only way to move furniture in and out was, and
still is, to use a rope on a hoist beam to pull the object up, and then carefully through
a window. That also explains why some houses lean forward, enabling an object to be
lifted without hitting the front of the house. Although a slight lean forward may be normal for an Amsterdam house, lists to the side – which are also common – are due to the
soft ground on which a building is built, and were not planned.

The bridge over the Amstel between the Prinsengracht and Keizersgracht is known
as the **Magere Brug**, or Skinny Bridge, because of its delicate shape. It's a double drawbridge from 1840, and is still in use for foot and bike traffic.

Jewish quarter

Location: Boundaries are Oude Schans and Zwanenburgwal (northwest), Singelgracht (southeast), Rapenburg and Entrepotdok (northeast), river Amstel (southwest)

About 140,000 Jews lived in the Netherlands before World War II. Most were taken to
concentration camps, with only 22% surviving the war. Amsterdam was home to 80,000
of the country's pre-war Jewish community, and most lived in this section of town. It
was a colourful area – its centre the busy Waterlooplein Market, the shopping street
Jodenbreestraat, and the complex of synagogues that now make up the Jewish Historical Museum. It also contained areas of extreme poverty, such as the slums on Uilenburg.
The community disappeared at the hands of the Nazis, but there are several places to see
which act as reminders of those who lived here and of their rich culture.

▶ **Jewish Historical Museum**

Location:	Nieuwe Amstelstraat 3-5
Information:	☎ (020) 531 0310; www.jhm.nl
Hours:	Daily 11am-5pm; closed on Jewish holidays

Built between 1671-1752, the museum is housed in four synagogues. The displays cover the history, culture, and religion of the Dutch Jews, and relate the story of the Nazi attempt to eliminate the Jews, including quickly scribbled postcards and notes to loved ones tossed off trains en route to the death camps. There is also a section about the Jewish contribution to the city's economic life before the war.

Near the Jewish Historical Museum: A VVV booklet guides you to all the sites in the former Jewish quarter. One such site is opposite the museum, the **Portuguese Synagogue**, Mr. L.E. Visserplein 3, ☎ (020) 624 5351, www.esnoga.com, open April 1-Oct 31, Sun.-Fri. 10am-4pm; Nov.1-March 31, Sun.-Thurs. 10am-4pm, Fri. 10am-2pm.

When it was built in 1675 it was the largest synagogue in the world. It is still largely in its original state.

If you take Muiderstraat off Mr. L.E. Visserplein, it will take you to the **Hollandsche Schouwburg**, Plantage Middenlaan 24, ☎ (020) 531 0340, open daily 11am-4pm. www.hollandscheschouwburg.nl

One of the city's main theatres from 1892 to 1941, the Nazis converted it into an assembly point for Jews being shipped to concentration camps. Up to 80,000 Jews were brought here before being dispatched. Only the facade and two walls of the original building remain. A monument to the Dutch Jews murdered during the war lists 6,700 names of those killed.

On the way to the Schouwburg you pass **Hortus Botanicus**, Plantage Middenlaan 2a, ☎ (020) 625 9021, open Mon.-Fri. 9am-5pm, Sat.-Sun. 10am-5pm; until 4pm in Dec. & Jan. and until 9pm in the summer, www.hortus-botanicus.nl. A botanical garden founded in 1682, it now boasts over 6,000 plant species from around the world.

Amsterdam was the diamond capital of the world, and in 1894 the Dutch Diamond Workers Union became the country's first modern trade union. Its headquarters was designed by H.P. Berlage, and today it houses a museum on Dutch trade unions, the **Vakbondsmuseum**, Henri Polaklaan 9, ☎ (020) 624 1166, www.deburcht-vakbondsmuseum.nl, open Tues.-Fri. 11am-5pm, Sun. 1-5pm. The castle-like building is an architectural gem. Even if its theme doesn't interest you, do walk into the lobby to admire the interior.

▶ **Artis Zoo**

Location:	Plantage Kerklaan 38-40
Information:	☎ (020) 523 3400; www.artis.nl
Hours:	Daily 9am-5pm, in the summer until 6pm

This zoo from 1838 is the oldest in continental Europe, and with its large trees shading a series of winding paths, it still has a 19th-century atmosphere. There are over

700 species of animals in Artis, as well as a house for nocturnal animals, a beautiful hippo house and an authentic African savannah.

Admission to the zoo also gives you access to two museums on the grounds of the park. The **Geological Museum** has a wealth of fossils, minerals and geological models showing the development of the earth in a most interesting manner. The **Aquarium** is the largest in Holland. Both of these attractions have the same hours as the zoo. While you're in the park you also have the opportunity to stargaze from the **Artis Planetarium**. While you sit comfortably, the moon will go through its various phases as day changes to night. The large projector is a technical miracle made up of over 29,000 elements. An entry ticket for Artis also provides admission to the Planetarium, the Geological Museum, the Aquarium and the Zoological Museum. Dogs are not allowed in the zoo.

- **Near the Artis Zoo:** Down the street is the **Verzetsmuseum**, Plantage Kerklaan 61a, ☎ (020) 620 2535, open Tues.-Fri. 10am-5pm, Sat.-Sun. noon-5pm, www.verzets-museum.org, which tells the story of the resistance and life in Holland during WW II.

Follow Plantage Middenlaan, on the south side of the Artis Zoo, and you'll come across the **Muiderpoort** at Alexanderplein, the 1770 city gate through which Napoleon invaded Amsterdam in 1811.

Beyond the gate is the **Tropenmuseum**, Linnaeusstraat 2, ☎ (020) 568 8200, www.tropenmuseum.nl, open daily 10am-5pm. This is the largest anthropological museum in the country, focussing on the tropics. Its displays take you inside a Javanese courtyard, a Bombay slum, and a noisy Arab street. In its Kindermuseum (Children's Museum), adults are only allowed if accompanied by a child. Aimed at the 6-12 age group, it offers many activities to interest children, such as native dances and costumes. Various musical theatre performances are also hosted in their **Tropentheater.**

▶ **Rembrandt House**

Location: Jodenbreestraat 4
Information: ☎ (020) 520 0400; www.rembrandthuis.nl
Hours: Mon.-Sun. 10am-5pm, Fri. 10am-9pm

Rembrandt lived here for 20 years, during some of the most productive years of his life, and some of the most painful. Born in Leiden in 1609, Rembrandt was a well-known artist by the time he moved to Amsterdam in 1631. Three years later he married Saskia van Uylenburgh, and in 1639 they moved into this house. At the height of his fame, Rembrandt was receiving numerous commissions in the prosperous city of Amsterdam, and some of his most famous works were painted in this house – including 'The Night-watch,' now on display in Amsterdam's **Rijksmuseum**. Many of his students also came to the house, to study and work with him in a studio on the top floor.

While living here, Saskia gave birth to three children, none of whom survived. Finally their son Titus was born, but sadly, shortly after his birth in 1642, Saskia herself died. Rembrandt continued to live here until his lifestyle forced him into bankruptcy. In 1658 the house was sold, and he moved to a small apartment in the Jordaan district of the city. He died in 1669.

The house has been restored to look as it did when Rembrandt lived here. On show are some of the art and curios he amassed in his lifetime, as well as his studio and living quarters. An adjacent wing has 250 original etchings, almost the complete collection of those he created.

- **Near the Rembrandt house:** A few steps away is the **Holland Experience**, Waterlooplein 17, ☎ (020) 422 2233, open April-Sept., daily 9:30am-6:30pm; Oct.-March, 9:30am-5:30pm, ideal for those who would love to see 'all' of Holland, but don't have the time. This multimedia extravaganza takes you on a 25-minute tour of the sights, sounds, and even the smells of Holland. Guaranteed to whet your appetite to return to see the real thing. The **Waterlooplein Market**, open Mon.-Sat. 9am-5pm, is a giant flea market on the original site of the daily market in the city's Jewish quarter. You'll find just about everything in this popular, lively market.

    For additional markets in the city see: www.amsterdam.info/markets

    Overlooking this market is the **Mozes en Aaronkerk**, Waterlooplein 205, ☎ (020) 622 1305, www.mozeshuis.nl, a Catholic church built in 1841 on the site of a 17th-century secret church from the days when Catholics were not allowed to worship in public.

Eastern docks

Location: IJ river (north), Prins Hendrikkade and Nieuwevaart (south), Singelgracht (east), Central Station (west)

At one time, if you stood more or less where the Dam Square is now situated and looked north, you'd get a good view of Amsterdam's connection to the sea. This view was blocked when Amsterdam's Central Station was built. Nowadays, if you want to see the waterway that carried Amsterdam to international importance, the dock area just east of the station is a good spot. Ships used to come and dock here, dropping off their cargoes at the numerous warehouses. Today, most of those warehouses have been converted into apartment buildings or offices, but many of the attractions in this area do still relate to shipping. The impressive Scheepvaart, or Maritime Museum, is located close by in an over 300-year-old former naval storehouse.

▶ **Scheepsvaartmuseum – Netherlands Maritime Museum**

Location: Kattenburgerplein 1
Information: ☎ (020) 523 2222, www.scheepvaartmuseum.nl
Hours: Tues. Sun. 10am-5pm; mid June-mid Sept., daily 10am-5pm
Note: Closed through 2007-2008 for two years of renovations.

A major feature at the beautifully appointed **Scheepvaartmuseum** is docked outside – a replica of an 18th-century sailing ship, 'Amsterdam.' The original 'Dutch East Indiaman' sank off the coast of England on its maiden voyage. You can climb aboard this

47

giant three-master and watch the crew swab the decks and sing old shanties, or wander around and see where an 18th-century crew would have eaten and slept.

Inside the museum is a display of Dutch sailing from before its 17th-century golden era, to its continued importance today. Of particular interest are the Royal Barge, beautifully constructed pleasure craft of by-gone days, magnificent ship models and world maps which show the Americas as they were known in the 17th century. Take a close look at the cities which were important enough to be indicated at that time, and at California, which was thought to be an island! There's a multimedia theatre where you can experience the rough seas on a journey to the Indies, and a periscope for spying on those outside.

▶ **NEMO – New Metropolis Science and Technology Centre**
Location: Oosterdok 2; almost next to the Maritime Museum
Information: ☎ (0900) 919 1100 (€ 0.35 per min); www.e-nemo.nl
Hours: Tues.-Sun. 10am-5pm; July-August and school vacations open daily

There are two obvious things about the **NEMO**: it appeals to all age groups, and it's very 'hands-on.' Designed with the philosophy that the best way to learn is to 'do,' business, technology, energy, science, and human emotions are all dealt with in various interactive displays that are educational and fun. Everything is presented in English as well as in Dutch.

In one section of this centre, a pre-schooler is wearing a hard hat while building a house. In another, a pair of ten-year-olds are learning that it's not easy to dam up a small, raging river, while one floor below some pre-teens are navigating tanker ships and learning about the danger of oil spills. Meanwhile, a group of teenagers is putting on white coats as they enter a crime lab to help investigators solve a mystery. Downstairs a few adults are busy watching a news broadcast, then making quick decisions on whether it means they should buy, sell, or hold some of the stocks in their computer game portfolio.

The giant green building is hard to miss. Across the water from the Scheepvaart Museum and looking like a ship, it's situated right over the IJ tunnel. There's a restaurant on the top floor with great views of the city and surrounding water.

▶ **Stedelijk Museum**
Location: Temporarily at Oosterdokskade 5 (2nd & 3rd floor Post CS building) near the Central Station
Information: ☎ (020) 573 2911; www.stedelijk.nl
Hours: Apr.-Sept., daily 10am-6pm; Oct.-Mar., daily 11am-5pm
Note: Currently renovating the permanent location at Museumplein. Highlights on show at Oosterdokseiland location.

The **Stedelijk Museum** is one of the world's foremost museums of modern art. It has an important collection of international paintings and sculptures dating from 1850 to the present, though a great part of the collection consists of post-1945 art. There are constantly-changing exhibitions of contemporary international art, and samples of the permanent collection on view, including photography and video exhibits.

- **Also in the Eastern Docks area:** Near the Maritime Museum is the 18th-century **De Gooyer Windmill**, Funenkade 5, not open to the public, but it does make a nice photo. Clearly visible from Central Station is **St. Nicolaaskerk**, Prins Hendrikkade 73, ☎ (020) 624 8749, www.muziekindenicolaas.nl, open Tues.-Sat. 1:30-4pm. The Church of St. Nicholas (1887) with its rich interior and imposing exterior, was the most impressive of the churches built after the 200-year ban on Catholic worship was lifted.

A little further down the street is the **Schreierstoren**, or Criers' Tower, Prins Hendrikkade 94, ☎ (020) 428 8291, www.schreierstoren.nl, so named because it was part of an old city wall where sailors' wives came to wave goodbye to their husbands as they sailed for parts unknown. It now houses a café. Look for the bronze plaque commemorating this as the spot where Henry Hudson departed on the Half Moon, April 4, 1609, heading for Nieuw Amsterdam, today's New York.

Further east is the **Scheepvaarthuis** (1916), Prins Hendrikkade 108-114, which originally housed offices for shipping companies.

Jordaan

Location: Boundaries are Brouwersgracht (north), Leidsegracht (south), Singelgracht (east), Prinsengracht (west)

Of the three major canals dug west of the old city in the 17th century, Herengracht is closest to the centre. It was also home to the wealthiest and most important Amsterdam residents of the time. Prestige declined as you moved away from the centre. And then, there was the **Jordaan** ... where Amsterdam's working class lived. It was the most crowded part of the city, and by the start of the 20th century it was a rundown slum. A massive redevelopment plan was drawn up in the 1970s to tear it all down and build modern housing units. It almost happened. Instead, a decision was taken to restore the buildings that could be saved, and preserve the character of the neighbourhood. Today, the Jordaan is known for its abundance of small shops and cafés, and as a somewhat fashionable place to live. Visitors enjoy exploring the side streets.

Bruin (brown) cafés – which derive their name from their brown, tobacco-smoke-stained interiors – are typically Dutch, and you'll find some of the best examples of them in the Jordaan. Liquor, coffee and at least a snack are served. Two examples are **'t Smaaltje**, Egelantiersgracht 12, as tiny as the name implies, and **De Pieper**, Prinsengracht 424, a three-centuries-old brown café complete with beamed ceiling and sand on the floor.

Another characteristic of the Jordaan is its *hofjes*, or almshouses. In the 17th century, some wealthy Dutchmen would 'buy their way to heaven' by bequeathing money for a home for the needy. The resulting *hofjes* were usually small houses built around a courtyard garden – isolated, quiet and pretty. The **Claes Claesz Anslohofje** (1626), is on Eerste Egelantiersdwarsstraat; enter through the wooden door across the street from number 4. Three others are the; **Hofje Venetiae** (1670), Elandsstraat 102-142, and **Hofjes**

Pieter-Jansz Suyckerhoff (1667), Lindengracht 149-163, and **St. Andrieshofje** (1617), Egelantiersgracht 107-145, with a passageway lined with Delft tiles. You may visit the courtyards of most *hofjes*, as long as you respect the peace and quiet of the surroundings and the privacy of those living there.

As you walk through the Jordaan, look for gable stones on the front of some buildings, as there are quite a few in the neighbourhood. Some of these carved stones indicated the trade of the owners, such as a tobacconist at Prinsengracht 226, or a butcher at Tweede Goudsbloemdwarsstraat 26.

Museum quarter

Location: Boundaries are Singelgracht (north), Amstel Kanaal (south), Schinkel (east), Boerenwetering (west)

Some of the most important museums in Amsterdam, and in the Netherlands, are situated very close together in this part of town.

▶ ## Rijksmuseum – National Gallery

Location: Stadhouderskade 42
Information: ☎ (020) 673 2121, www.rijksmuseum.nl
Hours: Daily 9am-6pm, Fridays also 6pm-10pm
Note: Major renovations are currently underway until at least 2010. However, a special wing with the highlights of the museum has been dedicated and, in reality, is a perfect time/place to see the crème of their crop.

This world-famous museum – the largest one in the Netherlands – must not be missed, even if you have small children with you. The most complete collection of Dutch paintings from the 15th to 19th century is located here. The main collection is the 17th-century work of the Dutch masters of the 'Golden Age.'

Be sure to see Rembrandt's 'The Night Watch.' Besides this most famous work, Rembrandt's 'Syndics of the Drapers' Guild,' and 'The Jewish Bride' are here. Jan Vermeer, known for his attention to detail, and portrayal of space and light, is represented by several paintings, including 'The Kitchen Maid,' and 'View of Houses In Delft.' Haarlem artist Frans Hals is known for his lively portraits, and the 'Wedding Portrait of Isaac Abrahamsz Massa and Beatrix van der Laen' is a good example.

In addition, there are some elegant period rooms displaying old Dutch silver, porcelain and other objects. Its history section tells the story of the nation through paintings.

There is a self-guided audio tour available in English, a museum guidebook, and a brochure that points out some of the highlights of the Dutch Golden Age collection.

▶ **Van Gogh Museum**

Location:	Paulus Potterstraat 7
Information:	☎ (020) 570 5200, www.vangoghmuseum.nl
Hours:	Daily 10am-6pm, Friday evenings also 6pm-10pm (with music and drinks in the lounge)

The **Van Gogh Museum** contains the world's largest collection of works by Vincent Van Gogh (1853-90), born in Zundert in the Dutch province of Brabant. It houses about 200 of his paintings, 500 drawings, and 700 letters he wrote to his brother Theo. The core of the collection belonged to Theo who, although an art dealer, did not succeed in helping his brother to fame and fortune.

The works are from both the Dutch and French periods of Van Gogh's life, which was cut short by his suicide. The collection gives a broader understanding of this strange man's life and development, and should be especially appealing to children because of Van Gogh's strong colours and sometimes wild approach to his subjects. Most of his best-known works are on display.

The building itself was specially constructed to house this collection, with the nephew of Vincent Van Gogh acting as advisor. It is among the most popular of the many fine museums to be found in the Netherlands. The collection also includes works by many of Van Gogh's contemporaries.

A visit to Amsterdam would hardly be complete without thoughts of diamonds, as the city is well-known for its suppliers, and **ZaZare Diamonds** is the place to go if it's personal service you want. Located literally a stone's throw from the Rijksmuseum, ZaZare offers a complete tour, with a fascinating explanation of the various gems and why certain cuts are more valuable than others. With that knowledge in hand, you can intelligently select your personal stone, and a goldsmith will assist you in selecting the ideal setting. What better souvenir? Open 7 days a week, 10am-5:30pm, Weteringschans 89, ☎ (020) 626 2798, www.zazarediamonds.com. (See their display ad on page 4 for a discount offer and special tour package.)

Coster Diamonds, on the other side of the Rijksmuseum, has recently opened the **Amsterdam Diamant Museum**, Paulus Potterstraat 8, (020) 305 5300, www.diamantmuseumamsterdam.nl, featuring the history of diamonds and a beautiful collection of jewels and crowns. You can also visit their diamond factory for a demonstration of diamond cutting. www.costerdiamonds.com. Another company, **Gassan Diamonds** is located at Nieuwe Uilenburgerstraat 173, www.gassandiamonds.com.

Museum **The Hermitage Amsterdam** showcases some of the finest collections from the Hermitage museum in St. Petersburg, Russia. This museum is located on the Amstel river at Nieuwe Herengracht 14, ☎ (020) 530 8755, open daily from 10am-5pm. www.hermitage.nl

For the largest collection of handbags and purses in Europe – over a thousand pieces – head to the **Tassenmuseum Hendrikje (Bag or Purse Museum Hendrikje)**, Herengracht 573, ☎ (020) 647 8681, www.tassenmuseum.nl, Thurs.-Sun., 1pm-5pm; groups by appointment only, Tues.-Sat., where 500 years of the development of bags and purses is presented, with every woman's dream gift shop offering an unusual selection of the same. By request, an afternoon tea, British style, can be served on the beautiful, historic premises.

- **Near the museum quarter:** Follow the Singelgracht canal to the right after leaving the Rijksmuseum and you'll come upon the former brewery, now the **Heineken Experience**, Stadhouderskade 78, ☎ (020) 523 9666, www.heinekenexperience.com, tours Tues. thru Sun. 10am-6pm. Beer was brewed here for 120 years before a move to the suburbs in 1988. There are tours of the old facility, with a highlight for many being a free glass of the famous brew. Down the canal to the left is the attractive, wooded, **Vondel Park**, just across the canal from the Leidseplein. In summer it hosts free entertainment, and is a great place to 'people-watch.'
- **Outside the city centre:** To the south is the **Botanical Garden** of the Vrije Universiteit (Free University), Van der Boechorststraat 8, ☎ (020) 598 9390, www.vu.nl, open Mon.-Fri. 8am-4:30pm. Near it, is the **Electric Tram Museum**, Amstelveenseweg 264, ☎ (020) 673 7538, www.museumtram.nl, open Easter-Oct. 10:30am-5:40pm. It has around 70 historic trams, most built between 1910-50 and from cities like Amsterdam, The Hague, Rotterdam, Groningen, and even foreign cities like Kassel (Germany) and Vienna (Austria). You can take a ride on some of these historic, colourful tram cars, starting from behind Haarlemmermeer Station, or Amstelveen Station, en route to the Amsterdam woods. They have the original wooden seats and coloured destination boards.

Also south on the A2, is the **Amsterdam ArenA**, ☎ (020) 311 1333; www.amsterdam-arena.nl; tours daily 10am-6pm, except during events. This modern stadium with a retractable roof is open for one-hour guided tours and is best known to soccer fans as the home of the Ajax 'football' club. At the stadium is the **World of Ajax**, ☎ (020) 311 1444, www.ajax.nl, open daily 10am-6pm, a museum about the club's 100-year history. Another relic of sports history is the **Olympisch Stadium**, off Amstelveenseweg, the site of the 1928 Summer Olympics at which, despite objections by the Pope, women competed for the first time. www.olympisch-stadion.net

Other attractions to the south are at **Schiphol Airport** itself. Near Gate One of Arrivals is the **Schiphol Visitors Centre**, open Mon.-Fri. 10am-6pm, Sat.-Sun. 12am-5pm, which tells you all about Schiphol – past, present and future. Admission free; ☎ (020) 601 3652.

If you need more excitement while waiting for a flight, there's a **Holland Casino**, ☎ (023) 574 0574, open daily 6am-10pm, in the west terminal (for ticketed passengers only).

Shopping in Amsterdam

Amsterdam is a shopper's delight, with diamonds and Delftware topping the list. Here's a summary of the main shopping areas, places to find specific items, and a list of the city's many markets.

- **Main shopping areas:** Amsterdam has numerous neighbourhood shopping areas with their own personalities, but here are the major ones:

  Kalverstraat: This is one of Amsterdam's busiest shopping streets, and at weekends it can be very crowded. It has all kinds of shops, from department stores to small specialty shops. It runs south from Dam Square, where De Bijenkorf, a major department store, is located. To the north is Nieuwendijk, also a major shopping street. Rokin runs parallel to Kalverstraat, and also has a good mix of stores.

  Leidsestraat: Another main shopping artery. (Watch out for the trams that run down its centre.)

  Magna Plaza: A good place to shop on a rainy day because it's all under one roof. This attractive and upscale shopping mall – albeit small by American standards – is a converted post office located behind the Royal Palace. It is rumoured that it may close.

  P.C. Hooftstraat: This is the trendy boutique area, extending into van Baerlestraat and Beethovenstraat, where you'll find international fashions, brands, and respective prices. It's located in the Museum Quarter neighbourhood, just a stone's throw from the Van Gogh Museum, and Rijksmuseum.

  Jordaan: Small specialised shops and boutiques are in abundance in and around the Jordaan district.

- **Luxury items:** Amsterdam's diamond industry began in 1586, and flourished because of the cutting and polishing skills brought to the country by Jewish immigrants. The largest diamond in the world, the Cullinan, weighing over a pound, was cut here by Jacob Asscher, becoming the largest cut stone. It is now in the sceptre of the British Crown Jewels. (See also Chapter 15.) (See also Zazare Diamonds ad, page 4 for special offer.)

  Historically, antiques have always been sold near the important museums. The best area to explore here is Nieuwe Spiegelstraat, near the Rijksmuseum, where about 70 antique shops will tempt you.

- **Markets:** Amsterdam is rich in outdoor markets, with more than one operating every day of the week. A few words of advice: watch your wallet or purse, as markets are favourite hunting grounds for pickpockets. See also: www.amsterdam.info/markets

  - *Art Market de Looier*: Elandsgracht 109, Sat.-Thurs. 11am-5pm. A covered market selling antiques, art, collectibles and whatever.
  - *Antique Market*: Nieuwmarkt, May-Sept., Sun. 9am-5pm.
  - *Art, Antique and Flea Market*: Looiersgracht 38, Sat.-Thurs. 11am-5pm.
  - *Art Market*: Thorbeckeplein, March-Nov., Sun. 10:30am-6pm, Spui, April-Nov. Sunday 10:30-6pm.
  - *Bird Market*: Noordermarkt, Sat. 8am-11am.

- *Book Market:* Spui, Fri. 10am-6pm.
- *Flea Market:* Waterlooplein, Mon.-Sat. 9am-5pm. If flea markets are your thing, this famous market in the heart of Amsterdam's former Jewish quarter is for you – from cracked toilet bowls to small treasures.
- *Farmers' Market,* Nieuwmarkt, organic products, Sat. 9am-5pm.
- *Floating Flower Market:* along the Singel (not to be missed), Mon.-Sat. 8:30am-6pm.
- *General Goods Markets:* Albert Cuypmarkt, Mon.-Sat. 9:30am-5pm; Noordermarkt, Mon. 9am-6pm. This is the city's largest market, with food from around the world, as well as clothing, etc.
- *Organic Food Market:* Noordermarkt, Sat. summer 9am-4pm, winter 9am-3pm.
- *Stamp Market:* Nieuwezijds Voorburgwal (near #280), Wed. & Sat. 1-4pm.
- *Textile Markets:* Westerstraat and Noordermarkt, Mon. 9am-2pm.

Entertainment

There's always a lot happening in Amsterdam. Your best guide is *What's On In Amsterdam*, a monthly magazine sold by the VVV. It lists concerts, exhibitions, tips on shopping, nightlife and dining out. (There's a more complete discussion of theatres, the symphony, dance, etc., in Chapter 17.) You can also pick up a free copy of *Amsterdam Weekly*, for cultural information and articles, or read it online at: www.amsterdamweekly.nl. Check out www.amsterdamhotspots.com for nightlife suggestions.

- **Night life:** Saying that Amsterdam is alive at night is an understatement, especially on the Leidseplein, Rembrandtplein and Reguliersdwarsstraat. For jazz, a popular choice is the **Bimhuis**, Piet Heinkade 3, ☎ (020) 788 2188, www.bimhuis.nl, or the **Bourbon Street Jazz and Blues Club**, Leidsekruisstraat 6-8, ☎ (020) 623 3440. For the latest in music, there's **Paradiso**, Weteringschans 6-8, ☎ (020) 626 4521, www.paradiso.nl, or **De Melkweg**, Lijnbaansgracht 234, ☎ (020) 531 8181, www.melkweg.nl. For dancing, **Odeon**, Singel 460, ☎ (020) 521 8585, www.odeontheater.nl, has three floors – disco on the top floor, newest hits on the ground floor, and jazz in the basement. If you're looking to join Amsterdam's young and beautiful crowd, you can try to get into the exclusive **Roxy**, Singel 465, ☎ (020) 620 0354. For the outrageous, there's **iT**, Amstelstraat 24, ☎ (020) 625 0111, a gay club with a mixed crowd, where everyone makes a statement with their clothing ... or they don't get in the door. For comedy in English, **Boom Chicago**, Leidseplein 12, ☎ (020) 423 0101, is the place, (see display ad page 40). For something a bit on the edge, with fantastic 'lounge music,' reserve a night at the **Supperclub**, one of several such clubs around the world, where you can dine on mattresses (or normal tables, if so desired) placed around an all-white room, while a DJ mixes it up, and you dine to the beat of a 5-course, always delectable meal that's worth it in itself; reservations highly recommended, Jonge Roelensteeg 21 (discreetly hidden down a rather small alleyway near Dam Square), ☎ (020) 344 64 00, www.supperclub.nl.

- **Cafés:** Cafés are open day and night as a place for a drink, coffee or tea, a snack, or in some cases a meal. Popular with the young are 'white' or 'art deco' cafés. Some examples are **Café Americain**, Leidsekade 97, ☎ (020) 556 3010; www.diningcity.nl/cafeamericain/; **Dantzig Aan De Amstel**, Zwanenburgwal 15, ☎ (020) 620 9039; and **De Jaren**, Nieuwe Doelenstraat 20, ☎ (020) 625 5771. More typically Dutch are 'brown (bruin)' cafés, so-called because of their dark panelled walls, smoke-stained ceilings and their old and cosy atmosphere. Some examples are **Café Hoppe**, Spui 18-20, ☎ (020) 420 4420, with stained-glass windows and sand on the floor; **Papeneiland**, Prinsengracht 2, ☎ (020) 624 1989, which once had a tunnel through which the Catholics who frequented this 'Papists' Island' could quickly escape in the days of the Protestant Reformation; or **De Tuin**, Tweede Tuindwarsstraat 13, ☎ (020) 624 4559.
- **Casino:** Amsterdam's **Holland Casino**, Max Euweplein 62, ☎ (020) 521 1111, is open daily 1:30pm-2am. Minimum age is 18, passport ID necessary, and obligatory dress code. www.hollandcasino.com

Eating out

Amsterdam has an endless variety of restaurants, cafés and pubs of virtually every ethnicity, with Indonesian in full force. (Indonesia was a former Dutch colony.) For Dutch food in an old-world atmosphere, there's **Haesje Claes**, Spuistraat 273-275, ☎ (020) 624 9998, www.haesjeclaes.nl. **The Pancake Bakery**, Prinsengracht 191, ☎ (020) 625 1333, www.pancake.nl, serves a variety of huge Dutch-style pancakes, i.e. crepe-like with innumerable fillings/toppings, in an old canal-side warehouse. If you're looking for places with decided character, **De Silveren Spiegel**, Kattengat 4, ☎ (020) 624 6589, www.desilverenspiegel.com, is in a step-gabled building from 1614, next to the Lutheran Kerk, and **Café Kort**, Amstelveld 12, ☎ (020) 626 1199, offers meals inside a 17th-century wooden church or, in good weather, in a square overlooking the Prinsengracht. Indonesian food should be tried by anyone who loves a spicy meal. One possibility is **New Bali**, Leidsestraat 95, ☎ (020) 622 7878. For Chinese food, the **Sea Palace**, Oosterdokskade 8, ☎ (020) 626 4777, www.seapalace.nl, is a large floating restaurant east of Central Station. (For evening dining out, a number of restaurants are mentioned in Chapter 17.)

Tip: For great dining throughout the Netherlands, check out www.specialbite.com, and *Iens Independent Index* restaurant guides, www.iens.nl, where you can search by city, type of food and price, as well as read reviews written by patrons.

Yearly events

Some yearly events are: April 30, the Queen's Birthday (*Koninginnedag*) celebration includes huge flea markets in the city centre, Vondel Park being a prime place; May 4th and 5th, Memorial Day and Liberation Day ceremonies on Dam Square commemorate the war dead and the liberation; June, Holland Festival (international and national productions of performing arts); August, the Uitmarkt, a three-day cultural market, with classic to pop music, theatre, dance and opera – all free – also the Grachtenfestival when over 60 concerts are performed in canal houses, courtyards, from roof tops, and even on pontoon boats on the canals; September, flower parade (Aalsmeer-Amsterdam), Jordaan Festival (typical Amsterdam neighborhood event); November, International Cat Show, the Horse Show, Jumping Amsterdam, and the St. Nicolaas parade.

Check the Expatica website, www.expatica.com, for events, including Valentines and Halloween parties, speed-dating events, and their annual 'I Am Not a Tourist' expatriate fair in October.

- **Money-saving options:** Amsterdam has over 60 museums, so avid museum-goers should get a **Museumjaarkaart (Museum Year Card).** Purchase of this card entitles you to one year of free access to hundreds of museums across the country, including most major ones. It usually pays for itself after about five or six museum visits. If you're not going to stay around long enough to make that worthwhile, you might try an **Amsterdam Culture & Leisure Pass.** It provides free entry into some museums, discounts on others, and extras such as a free canal cruise, and restaurant and transportation discounts. Details are available from the VVV. www.museumjaarkaart.nl

- **Dutch news in English:**

  The XPat Journal

  An outstanding quarterly publication, The XPat Journal, has been keeping expats informed since 1998, covering issues related to working, housing, legal and financial, education, daily life, health care, art, culture, events, book reviews and more. The website www.xpat.nl is a great resource with links and addresses for many organisations of interest to foreigners, as well as cultural and business events and an online archive with the possibility to purchase back issues. With a circulation of 10,000 copies, it is without a doubt the best-read magazine for internationals in the know! Keep informed by ordering your own subscription from the expat-specialized publisher and premier source of information for Holland's international community.

  The Amsterdam-Hague-Rotterdam Times – www.thehollandtimes.nl – This full-colour, English-language newspaper with Dutch news and cultural events is distributed free in many locations and hotels throughout Amsterdam, the Hague and Rotterdam.

  Dutch News.nl – the www.dutchnews.nl website is updated every day at 4 o'clock with the latest news reports online. It's a free, 2-page daily round-up of the day's main Dutch news in English, keeping you up to date with stories that make the Netherlands buzz. (Sign up to receive the daily newletter by e-mail, via the website.) Free 'classifieds' and 'what's on' calender of cultural events.

  Expatica – offers extensive online news and resources for living and working in the Netherlands. They also have events, an annual Survival Guide, and an expatriate fair in October. www.expatica.com

  Amsterdam Weekly – Award-winning arts and culture newspaper, free every Wednesday at various places throughout Amsterdam. www.amsterdamweekly.nl

  TheHagueOnline – activities in The Hague, Social Club, articles and news for the region, www.thehagueonline.com

Tours

For the first-time visitor, a general tour can provide a good, basic orientation to Amsterdam. The VVV is your best source. They can tell you where to find any guided trip, from a peaceful cruise past windmills in the Dutch countryside, to a behind-the-scenes look at the Red Light District. Here are some choices:

● **Canal tours:** Everyone should take a canal tour. Generally, all operators offer similar trips that take about an hour. Commentary is given in several languages, including English. You can find tour boat operations at the Prins Hendrikkade, (to the right as you exit Central Station); on Damrak, (straight ahead as you come out of Central Station); from the Rokin, (just south of Dam Square); on the Singelgracht, (opposite the Heineken Experience); and near the Leidseplein on the Singelgracht.

For adults, some of the companies offer romantic evening tours in the summer. These candlelight tours last about three hours (reservations necessary). Some also have special brunch and dinner cruises. **Amsterdam Canal Cruises Nicolaas Witsenkade**, opposite the Heineken Brewery, De Pijp, ☎ (020) 626 5636; **Canal Bus**, Weteringschans 24-1, Leidseplein, ☎ (020) 623 9886, www.canal.nl; **Holland International**, Prins Hendrikkade, opposite Centraal Station, ☎ (020) 622 7788; **Meyers Rondvaarten**, Damrak 4, Dam, ☎ (020) 623 4208; **Museumboot Rederij Lovers**, Stationsplein 8, ☎ (020) 530 1090; **Rederij Lovers**, Prins Hendrikkade 26a, opposite Central Station, ☎ (020) 530 1090; **Rederij P. Kooij**, Rokin, near Spui, ☎ (020) 623 3810; **Rederij Noord/Zuid**, Stadhouderskade 25, opposite Parkhotel, Leidseplein, ☎ (020) 679 1370; **Rederij Plas**, Damrak, quays 1-3, Dam, ☎ (020) 624 5406.

For something more energetic, sightsee by **Canal Bike,** Weteringschans 24, ☎ (020) 626 5574, a stable, dry pedalboat that seats up to four. There are four possible starting points: Leidseplein; between Rijksmuseum and Heineken Brewery; Prinsengracht at the Westerkerk near the Anne Frank House; and on the Keizersgracht near Leidsestraat. You pick the bike up at one point, and leave it at another. Operates all year 10am-6:30pm, in the summer 10am-10pm. Deposit required. Another option is www.bootnodig.nl/rent_a_boat, where you can rent small boats as well as yachts.

For boat tours outside the city, the Historic Ferry that leaves from landing #8 behind Central Station, Sun. noon, 2pm & 4pm, gives a 2-hour ride on the IJ River. **Rederij Naco**, ☎ (020) 626 2466, has trips along the Vecht River to Muider Castle, on the Amstel River, and dinner or candlelight cruises. Departure point is landing #7 behind the station.

● **Bicycle tours:** There are numerous bike rental shops for those who want to see Amsterdam the Dutch way. **Mac Bike**, Mr. Visserplein 2, ☎ (020) 620 0985, Weteringsschans 2, ☎ (020) 620 0985, Marnixstraat 220, ☎ (020) 626 6964, Stationsplein 12, ☎ (020) 620 0985, www.macbike.nl, is one option. From April-Oct. **Yellow Bike**, Nieuwezijds Kolk 29, ☎ (020) 620 6940, www.yellowbike.nl, conducts a 3-hour city tour by bike (9:30am & 1pm). **Let's Go Amsterdam**, April-mid-Oct., will take you through the Dutch countryside on a 6-and-a half-hour castle or windmill tour, www.letsgo-amsterdam.com, ☎ (020) 600 1809. The VVV has information on bike rental and bike tours.

- **Walking tours:** For those who like to keep their feet on the ground, the VVV has walking tour booklets to guide you. For a city walk with a difference, join a Mystery Tour packed with discoveries and fun, **Let's Go,** ☎ (020) 600 1809, April-mid Oct., Tues.-Thurs. 5pm, Sat. 10:30am. Another option is to rent **Audio Tourist,** Oude Spiegelstraat 9, ☎ (020) 421 5580, www.angelfire.com/id/audiotourist/, with tapes, and maps that guide you along the canals and across the city.
- **Bus tours:** City sightseeing tours by bus are conducted by **Lindbergh,** Damrak 26, ☎ (020) 622 2766, daily 10am & 2:30pm; and **Tours and Travel Services,** TT Melissaweg 15, ☎ (020) 635 3110, www.tandts.nl. Their two-to three-hour tours visit some of the main city attractions. They also conduct tours outside the city, including the Alkmaar cheese market, Marken, Volendam, Delft, The Hague, and more.
- **Carriage:** A horse and carriage is a relaxing way to see the city. The carriages operate from April-Sept. from 11am-6pm. You can arrange the length and the route of the trip with the driver. Contact the VVV or Let's Go, www.letsgo-amsterdam.com.

Transportation

The best advice for anyone driving into Amsterdam is to park the car on the periphery and take public transportation into the centre, which is difficult to navigate because of its narrow streets and the over-abundance of bicycles, pedestrians and trams. Public transportation is convenient and easy to use. You can buy a special tram-bus-metro ticket for the day, either from the VVV or the tram or bus driver. Enter at the front and ask for a day ticket (*dagkaart*). With this ticket, you can travel all day. A regular tram/bus ticket allows you to travel for one hour.

For more information about the public transportation system in Amsterdam, pick up the '*Tourist Guide to Public Transport Amsterdam*' folder put out by GVB – Amsterdam Municipal Transport – at their office in front of Central Station. There are 30 bus, 17 tram and four Metro routes in the city. Parking can be a problem, and it's expensive. On www.parkeren.amsterdam.nl you will find everything you need to know about getting around the city, from Park & Ride locations to taxis, trams and bicycles.

For those who reside in Holland and frequently visit Amsterdam and other major cities, there is now a GSM parking service called Park-line, based on paying through your mobile phone, by inputting a number displayed on the 'P' (for parking) signs on designated streets. Payment of the standard parking rate is made by automatic bank debit or credit card, saving you the hassle of having the right change or, worse yet, your meter time running out. When you return to your car, you simply call the service again, and the payment stops. Subscriptions are only €10 (free with an American Express card), and €1.75 per month. www.park-line.nl

- **Circle-tram 20:** Tram number 20 leaves from Central Station and makes a loop around the city centre, stopping at 29 places on its circular route. All the stops are located near one or more of the city's main visitor attractions. You can get on and off the tram at any of them. Tickets can be bought for one full day, or up to nine days of unlimited use. Tickets are also good for all tram, bus and Metro lines. They can be bought from the VVV, or GVB office, or the driver. Tram 20 operates every 10 minutes from 9am-7pm.

- **Canal bus:** The **Canal Bus** ☎ (020) 623 9886, www.canal.nl, has three routes along the city's canals, with stops at the Central Station, Museum Quarter, the Anne Frank House and eight other popular areas. You can get on and off at any stop with a day-long ticket which is valid until noon on the next day. They also provide a commentary on the sights along the way.
- **Museum boat:** A museum boat tour is a pleasant way for you and your family to get indoctrinated to the city. This canal boat operates between the Anne Frank House, the Floating Flower Market, Rijksmuseum, Rembrandt House, Maritime Museum and the pier in front of the VVV Tourist Office at the Central Station, Prins Hendrikkade 25 – 27. Smoke-free and reasonably priced, it operates from 10am-6:30pm, ☎ (020) 530 1090, or www.lovers.nl for more details.

Staying over

For help in finding a place to stay, you have the following options: call the Amsterdam VVV, ☎ 0900 40 04 40 or, alternatively, try Bed and Breakfast Holland, ☎ (0497) 33 300, www.bedandbreakfast.nl, or the Stayokay Hostels, ☎ (020) 551 3155; www.stayokay.com, www.amsterdam-hotels-guide.com, www.hotels.nl.

- **Hotels:** If you're looking for the best, try the **Grand Westin Demeure Hotel**, Oudezijds Voorburgwaal 197, ☎ (020) 555 3111, www.thegrand.nl; or the **Amstel Hotel**, Prof. Tulpplein 1, ☎ (020) 622 6060, on the river Amstel. Two other choices at a somewhat lower price include the **Pulitzer**, Prinsengracht 315-331, ☎ (020) 523 5235, located in 24 old canal houses; and the **Amsterdam Renaissance**, Kattengat 1, ☎ (020) 621 2223. A moderate-priced choice along the canals is the **Tulip Inn**, Nassaukade 387-390, ☎ (020) 420 4545, www.tulipinnamsterdamcentre.com. The **Hotel de l'Europe**, Nieuwe Doelenstraat 2, ☎ (020) 531 1777, www.leurope.nl, has a central location near the Muntplein and overlooks the Amstel river. The **Doelen Hotel**, Nieuwe Doelenstraat 24, ☎ (020) 622 0722, is practically next door, but at a lower price. It's also where Rembrandt's 'Nightwatch' was first hung. For something different, the lower-priced **Amstel Botel**, Oosterdokskade 2-4, ☎ (020) 626 4247, is located on a large boat docked east of Central Station.
- **In the neighbourhood of Amsterdam: Amstelveen** is conveniently and pleasantly situated on the southern fringe of Amsterdam. Its 76,000 inhabitants enjoy not only the **Amsterdamse Bos** (woods) but also some first-class museums and an extremely modern town centre with good shopping. Together with Ouder-Amstel, Uithoorn and Diemen, it belongs to an area called Amstelland. The romantic villages of Ouderkerk and Uithoorn owe their existence to the Amstel river that linked Amsterdam to the rest of the Netherlands.

Amstelveen has two important museums, the **CoBrA Museum**, Sandbergplein 1, ☎ (020) 547 5050, www.cobra-museum.nl, open Tues.-Sun. 11am-5pm – an important museum of modern art. CoBrA was the name of a post-war movement of artists from Denmark (Copenhagen), Belgium (Brussels), and the Netherlands (Amsterdam). Most famous are Alechinsky, Karel Appel, and Corneille whose works are on display. The **Jan v.d. Togt Museum of Modern Art**, Dorpstraat 50, ☎ (020) 641 5754, open Thurs.-Sun. 1-5pm has a collection of sculpture, glass and paintings from the 20th century, including works of Zadkine. www.jvdtogt.nl

Aalsmeer
Largest flower auction in the world

Getting there: Aalsmeer is at the intersection of Highways A4 and N201, south of Schiphol Airport.

Information: VVV, Drie Kolommenplein 1, ☎ (0297) 32 5374; www.hollandsmidden.nl

In the 17th century, most people in Aalsmeer dug peat for a living. For their own use, they grew a few fruit trees and other plants. As Amsterdam grew just a few kilometers away, so did the market for their fruits, vegetables, flowers and other plants. Their success led to the first greenhouses being built in the late 1880s, enabling them to have longer growing seasons and to protect sensitive plants. By 1910, the growers were doing well, but the system of selling to a middleman was not working to their advantage. So they formed a cooperative in Aalsmeer in 1912 to establish an auction where they could sell their products directly to buyers. That cooperative still exists, with over 7,000 growers today, and their auction house is now the largest flower auction in the world. Along with the gardens of Keukenhof, the **Aalsmeer Flower Auction** is the best place for visitors to see the famous world of Dutch flowers.

Aalsmeer Flower Auction

Location: Legmeerdijk 313
Information: ☎ (0297) 397 000; www.vba-aalsmeer.com
Hours: Mon.-Fri. 7:30-11am

This flower auction building is as large as 120 football fields – an impressive sight. Every day, about 17 million flowers and two million plants are sold in it. It's the centre of the world's flower industry, with daily prices watched closely by flower buyers and sellers worldwide. There are other flower markets in the Netherlands, but this is the largest, with 55% of the country's annual flower sales.

A catwalk has been constructed over the auction floor so visitors can see every aspect of the sales process, which is explained in any of six languages of your choice. You'll see many of the auction's 1,800 employees wheeling flowers in for auction, and out again as soon as they have gone under the hammer – about to begin their rapid journey to their ultimate place of sale, which could be anywhere in the world.

Roses are the most-sold flower, followed by chrysanthemums, tulips and lilies. It's an incredibly colourful sight, especially on Mondays – the busiest day of the week –

during late spring and early summer. Most of the flowers and plants are destined for European florists, where they'll arrive later in the day. Germany is the biggest market, with France second, the United Kingdom third. The United States ranks 10th among countries receiving flowers sold here. This trip is for the early riser, as you should be in Aalsmeer before 9am to take full advantage of the flower auction; it closes when the day's supply of flowers runs out.

● **Yearly events:** The annual Flowerparade Aalsmeer, from Aalsmeer to Amsterdam and back, takes place the first Saturday of September with gorgeous floats, a Flower Queen, bands and drum majorettes. Floats can be seen the Friday before and the Sunday after the parade, in the auction hall. www.bloemencorsoaalsmeer.nl

For obvious reasons, flower parades are popular in Holland. In August there's the Flowerparade Rijnsburg, from Rijnsburg to Leiden, Katwijk, and Noordwijk; in late August, the Flowerparade Leersum in Utrecht province. In early September, the Dahlia Parade, the oldest flower parade in the country, is held in Brabant province; and the most famous, the Flowerparade Bollenstreek, goes from Noordwijk, to Sassenheim, Lisse, Hillegom, Bennebroek, Heemstede and Haarlem in late April. www.bloemencorso-bollenstreek.nl

Haarlem
Home of artist Frans Hals

Getting there: A5 from Amsterdam. A4 from The Hague and Rotterdam, to the Haarlem turnoff at N201 or A5 going west.

Information: VVV, Stationsplein 1, ☎ (0900) 616 16 00, www.vvvzk.nl and www.haarlemonline.nl, and the local guide: www.haarlemshuffle.com

Haarlem is over 900 years old and a veritable treasure house. Count William II granted the town its charter in 1245 and started building a hunting lodge there in 1250. This became the Town Hall in the 14th century. In front of the lodge on what is today the Market Square, jousting events were held. The Great Church (*Grote Kerk*) was built between 1390 and 1520; however, most historic buildings still standing date from the 17th century – Haarlem's greatest period of prosperity.

In 1572, Haarlem joined other nationalistic Dutch towns to oppose Spanish rule – an action they paid for – the town being besieged for seven months. After great suffering, Haarlem surrendered, on condition that its citizens would not be punished. The Spanish commander went back on his word, killing the Governor, all the Calvinist ministers and almost 2,000 townsfolk. Three years later, a fire destroyed most of Haarlem, and in 1577 the Dutch army returned unopposed. The war against Spain and the religious battles between Protestants and Catholics ruined the Town Hall and the monastery complex behind it, and brought hardship to its citizens. By the 17th century, all of Holland (including Haarlem) was enjoying the prosperity brought by an influx of skilled workmen and artists from Spanish-occupied territories to the south.

Today, Haarlem is the capital of North Holland province. It has some industry, but is best known as the Dutch bulb export centre, primarily tulips. A good-sized town, most of its historic sites are within a kilometer radius. Walking is the best way to get around, allowing the town's enchanting atmosphere to envelop and seduce you. The VVV has a tour map to help you explore. Visiting the characteristic almshouses, or *hofjes*, might be a good place to start. Haarlem has some 22 of these homes originally built for laypersons connected with the church; the homes are still lived in today, usually by single persons. Timing your visit during the April Flower Parade might be an added bonus.

▶ **Grote Kerk – St. Bavo Church**
Location: On Market Square, but entrance is on Oude Groenmarkt
Information: ☎ (023) 532 4399; www.bavo.nl
Hours: Mon.-Sat. 10am-4pm; Sunday church service at 10am

This late Gothic church is of particular interest to music lovers. It houses the Muller organ, one of Europe's most famous, which has three keyboards, 68 registers 5,000 pipes, and is nearly 30 meters (about 100 feet) high. Built in 1738, it was played by Mozart, when he was the ten-year-old musical sensation of Europe, and twice by Handel. Free organ concerts are held mid-May to mid-Oct., Tues. 8:15pm; July-Aug., also Thurs. 3pm. Built on the site of a former church (1300s), the oldest part of the structure dates from 1390. For centuries, it marked the centre of Haarlem, visible for miles, and was part of most early paintings of the city. The early 16th-century choir screen has wonderful animal carvings at its base, and the choir stalls date from 1512. This is also where famed artist Frans Hals is buried, his grave marked with a lantern. Three colourful sailing ships hang from the rafters, and not far from them another curious addition to a church – two scratch marks on a pillar indicating the heights of two unusual men of Haarlem, one 2.64m tall (8'8"); and the other only 84 cm (2'9"). Attached to the exterior of the church building is a series of little houses with interesting shops, just as in the Middle Ages.

● **Near the Grote Kerk:** The **Grote Markt** (Great Market Square) is one of the finest in Holland. At one end is the **Grote Kerk**. Next to it is the **Vleeshal** (former meat market or Butcher's Hall). It dates from 1602, built by architect Lieven de Key, and is sure to catch the eye with its highly ornamented step-gables. The **Archeologisch Museum**, Grote Markt 18, ☎ (023) 542 0888, open Wed.-Sun. 1-5pm, is in the basement of the Vleeshal. Next door is **De Hallen**, Grote Markt 16, ☎ (023) 511 5775, open Mon.-Sat. 11am-5pm, Sun. 1-5pm, with displays from the modern art collection of the Frans Hals Museum. Next door is the **Verweyhal**, a museum devoted to the Haarlem painter Kees Verwey. www.dehallen.com

At the far end of the square is the ornately gabled **Town Hall**. The oldest part of the building is what remains of Count William II's hunting lodge (mid-1200s) and part of a medieval Dominican monastery that stood behind the lodge. Shortly after the fire of 1351 levelled much of the city, Count William V built the Count's Hall. In the 15th century, several rooms were added along the Zijlstraat, as well as the public high court, where judgements were pronounced. The gallows were torn down in 1855. Religious battles during and after the Spanish period, along with another serious fire in the 16th century, destroyed much of the Town Hall and the buildings of the monastery. The property came into the hands of the city, and a Prince's Court was added where members of the House of Orange and other important guests could stay. Visitors are welcome during the week if rooms are not in use.

The **Hoofdwacht** (Guard House), one of Haarlem's oldest buildings, is located on the northeast corner of the Grote Markt and Smedestraat. Near it is a statue of Laurens Jansz Coster. Some claim he invented printing before Gutenburg, inspired by the imprint left in the sand by a carved wooden letter he dropped. On the same side of the church is the old **Vishal** (Fish Market), where free art exhibitions are held.

Around the square are narrow pedestrian shopping streets with attractive boutiques and cafés. As you cross the market square to the Town Hall, imagine the many jousting tournaments that were once held here.

To the west of the Grote Markt is **Hofje van Loo**, Barrevoetestraat 7. Dating from 1489, this almshouse lost its courtyard when the street was widened in 1885. Not far away is another, **Brouwershofje** (1586) with its distinctive red and white shutters. The secret gardens of Haarlem, or '*Haarlemse Hofjes*' can be found in various secluded courtyards dotted around the historic centre of town. For the complete list, visit www.haarlemshuffle.com/tourism. You can also get a *hofjes* map from the VVV.

▶ **Frans Hals Museum**
Location: Groot Heiligland 62
Information: ☎ (023) 511 5775; www.franshalsmuseum.nl
Hours: Tue.-Sat. 11am-5pm, Sun. noon-5pm

Frans Hals (1580-1666) was a native of Antwerp, but spent most of his life in Haarlem. He painted many large canvases depicting groups, such as the officers of the 'Corps of Archers of St. George,' a painting that brought him fame when he was only 36 years old. Also on display is his painting of the 'Governors and Governesses of The Oudemannenhuis' (old men's home), painted when he was over 80. At first, you might think that seeing one large canvas after another of stuffy citizens or self-important military officers would be pretty dull, but Hals painted differently from his colleagues. If subjects drank too much, he portrayed them that way. If he saw meanness or pettiness in their eyes, he would paint that too. This must have created quite a stir among his clients as, according to the custom of the day, each person depicted in a painting paid for the privilege with his percentage of the artist's fee for the whole painting.

In addition, the museum shows paintings by a number of old Dutch masters. Of special note is the collection of Haarlem silverware and 18th-century Delftware found in the reconstructed pharmacy. There's an 18th-century doll's house and a paper-doll tableaux showing cut-out scenes of old-fashioned homes behind glass and lighted to give a three-dimensional impression. The modern art collection consists of works by such well-known Dutch artists as Isaac Israels, Jan Sluyters and Karel Appel.

The museum building dates from 1608. During Frans Hals' time it was an almshouse for older men. It later became an orphanage, and around 1913 it was transformed into a museum.

- **Near the Frans Hals Museum:** The attractive street on which the museum stands has several 17th-century *Gasthuisjes* (literally 'guesthouses' but referring to hospitals), a series of buildings that made up the St. Elizabeth's Hospital. Also in this area is the **Historisch Museum Zuid-Kennemerland**, Groot Heiligland 47, ☎ (023) 542 2427, open Tues.-Sat. noon-5pm, Sun. 1-5pm. It has displays and a good video presentation in English on the history of Haarlem. www.historischmuseumhaarlem.nl

To the west, and across the canals is **St. Bavo Kathedraal**, Leidsevaart 143, ☎ (023) 553 2040, open April-Sept. and autumn break, Tues.-Fri. 10am-4pm, Sun. 1-4pm. This Catholic cathedral, built between 1895 and 1906, has beautiful stained-glass windows, sculptures, and an interesting treasury of ecclesiastical art. Visitors sometimes confuse it with the Grote Kerk, which was originally named St. Bavo Kerk, and sometimes still goes by that name. Like the Kerk, the Kathedrale has regular free organ concerts, mid-April to late Sept., Sat. 3pm. After the concerts you can take a close look at the organ. www.rkbavo.nl

▶ **Teylers Museum**

Location:	Spaarne 16, at the corner with Damstraat
Information:	☎ (023) 516 0960; www.teylersmuseum.nl
Hours:	Tues.-Sat. 10am-5pm; Sun. noon-5pm

Teylers is so unique, it's a museum piece in itself. Founded by scholars in 1778, it is Holland's oldest museum, created when having a museum was 'avant garde,' since they were only to be found in a few major cities like Paris and London. Part of the charm of visiting Teylers is seeing how museums used to be, because, with the exception of a few 'conveniences' like electricity and indoor plumbing, this museum has hardly changed over the years.

Its collection is as varied as you would expect from a museum from before the era of specialisation. The first rooms contain cases filled with an incredible variety of fossils. One, bought by the museum in 1802, was known as the 'Diluvian Man' and, like Noah, thought to be a human who survived the great flood. Later research showed it to be a 12-million-year-old giant salamander.

There's a collection of 18th and 19th-century scientific instruments, such as the almost six-foot wheel of an electrostatic generator that dazzled visitors in the late 1700s with the two-foot-long spark it produced.

Don't miss the tiny room with phosphorescent or 'glow-in-the-dark' minerals, or the collection of old coins, or the two galleries of Dutch art. In 1790, an important nucleus of the museum's international drawing and print collection was established when a group of 2,000 works, previously part of Queen Christina of Sweden's private collection, was acquired. In this group were works by Raphael and Michelangelo.

- **Near the Teylers Museum:** The Spaarne river runs in front of the museum, with its picturesque bridge, the Gravenstenenbrug. Centuries ago, this area was a centre of Haarlem's economy, as the **Waag**, or 'weigh house' (1598) on the corner near the museum indicates. This part of the river is also where Spanish soldiers drowned many Haarlem residents. After capturing the city in 1573, residents were tied together back-to-back, and tossed into the river. The only other remaining town gate, the **Amsterdamse Poort** built around 1400, is across the river via Spaarnwouderstraat.

Walking further along the Spaarne river (turn left outside the museum) you will see the **Adriaan Windmill**, which has been beautifully reconstructed to its original glory. If there is enough wind on Saturdays, the sails are set to working. Visitors can also enjoy a bite to eat there after touring inside. Open Wed.-Fri. 1pm-4pm, Sat.-Sun. 1-4pm; from 1 Nov. to 1 Mar. closed Wed. & Thur., Papentorenvest 1a, 023-545 0259. www.molenadriaan.nl

The oldest almshouse in the Netherlands dating from 1395, the **Hofje van Bakenes**, is just off the Bakenesser Gracht (Canal), not far from the Grote Kerk and Teylers Museum. Following the canal east of town, you might have to search for the entrance which is off one of the small back streets. This pretty courtyard garden, lined with two-story, whitewashed houses with dark green shutters and red-tiled roofs, is in its own hushed world of quiet dignity. The **Bakenesser Kerk** stands quietly by, now privately owned.

▶ **Corrie ten Boomhuis Museum – The Hiding Place**
Location: Barteljorisstraat 19, just north of the Grote Markt
Information: ☎ (023) 531 0823; www.corrietenboom.com
Hours: April 1-Oct.31, Tues.-Sat. 10am-3:30pm; Nov.1-March 31,
                      Tues.-Sat. 11am-2:30pm

This museum is devoted to the amazing story of a watch-making family with great courage and strong religious beliefs. Willem ten Boom founded a shop here in 1837, handing it down to his son Casper, and to Casper's daughter, Corrie, the first woman watchmaker in Holland. The narrow house (4m/13ft.) is still a shop, and the museum is the former living quarters upstairs. If it hadn't been for the Nazi persecutions of WW II, the Ten Boom family would have lived ordinary lives. Instead, Casper and his children undertook to hide people in danger – Jews and members of the Dutch resistance. The house was a refuge for many, hidden here until they could be smuggled to safer locations.

Known as 'The Hiding Place,' the house is shown by a guide who points out its secret places – a false step just outside Corrie's bedroom where ration cards were hidden; and a false wall with a trap door and air hole against the outside wall. The Gestapo often came to search the house and Corrie would sit on her bed and pretend nothing was amiss.

Several other bedrooms just large enough to hold a bed, and perhaps a dresser, were under the eaves towards the front of the house. A space was fitted in one of these for others to hide, high in the wall between it and the roof. The family was betrayed – arrested in early 1944 when the Gestapo raided the house. Corrie alone survived the concentration camp – released by mistake just days before all the women her age were killed. Before dying, her sister Betsie asked Corrie to devote her life to preaching that the Lord is always there, no matter how dire the situation. Remembering those words, Corrie gave lectures and preached in over 60 countries. She also wrote many books before her death in 1983 at age 91 – including one that you may want to read before your visit: The Hiding Place. A film by the same name, about the family, was made in 1975.

Though entrance is free, donations are welcomed. Check on the door for the times of English-language tours, and try to be early as groups are limited.

● **Near the Corrie ten Boom House:** The former **Janskerk**, originally a 14th-century monastic church, is on the corner of Janstraat and Begijnesteeg. The oldest church in Haarlem, the 14th-century **Waalse Kerk** is near Janskerk in the Begijnhof. The late 15th-century Bakenesserkerk with its elegant sandstone tower, is across the Bakenesser Gracht on Bakenesserstraat. Another attractive almshouse **Hofje van Staats** (1730) has an elevated central area. It is near the Central Station on Jansweg.

▶ **Het Dolhuys – The Madhouse**
'Psych' museum in former asylum

Location: Schotersingel 2, short distance to the north of Central Station
Information: ☎ (023) 541 0670; www.hetdolhuys.nl/engels/
Hours: Tues.-Fri., 10am-5pm; Sat. and Sun. 12-5pm

Experience the world of madness and explore the boundary between 'crazy' and 'normal' in **Het Dolhuys** (The Madhouse), an interactive museum in a former insane asylum where you can meet madmen and lunatics, or 'clients' as they are known today, and find out how the Netherlands has dealt with madness throughout the centuries.

Eating out

A number of attractive cafés and restaurants can be found on the southern side of the Grote Kerk on Spekstraat (literally 'Bacon Street'). Look for the historic **De Karmeliet**, Spekstraat 6, ☎ (023) 531 4426, www.karmeliet.nl, a coffee shop on the site of an old Carmelite Cloister (1249-1578). Good salad plate, hamburgers and soup. Forty-four kinds of pancakes can be had at **De Smikkel**, Kruisweg 57, ☎ (023) 532 0631; or various cuts of Argentinian meat at **Los Gauchos**, Kruisstraat 9, ☎ (023) 532 0358. The **Grand Café Brinkmann**, Brinkmannpassage 41, ☎ (023) 532 3111, www.grandcafebrinkmann. nl, on the market square, is also recommended, as are **Jill's** at #10, ☎ (023) 532 9494, and behind the church in the Spekstraat **Spektakel** at #4, (023) 532 3841.

Yearly events

The Houtfestival (theatre, music, folk dancing and art market) June, and a Barrel Organ Festival July (www.organfestival.nl). In August, there is a big jazz festival, Haarlem Jazz Stad, on the Grote Markt, www.haarlemjazzstad.nl, and food; and an antiquarian booksellers' market every Saturday, starting the second Saturday in April to second Saturday in October (dates subject to change), www.kollektorsitem.nl. See www.haarlemonline. nl, city directory for events, restaurants and shopping.

Tours

You can cruise the canals of Haarlem with **Woltheus Cruises**, ☎ (023) 535 7723, April-Oct., daily 10:30am, noon, 1:30pm, 3pm & 4:30pm. Trips depart from Spaarne 11a, which is on the river Spaarne at Damstraat, near the Teylers Museum. www.woltheus-haarlem.nl. The VVV also organises guided walking tours. The 2-hour '*hofjes*' walk is very popular.

In the neighbourhood of Haarlem

Zandvoort has plenty to offer in the way of recreation and natural beauty with miles of sandy beaches. Once a sleepy fishing village, it's now one of the country's major beach resorts. There's also a **Holland Casino**, Badhuisplein 7, ☎ (023) 574 0574, open daily 1:30pm-3am. The **Zandvoorts Museum**, Swaluëstraat 1, ☎ (023) 574 0280, open Mid April-Aug., Wed., Sat.-Sun. noon-4:30pm, covers the town's history, with traditional clothing and period rooms among its displays. Except for the beach, Zandvoort is probably best known for the **Circuit Park Zandvoort** racetrack, Burg. van Alphenstraat 108, ☎ (023) 574 0740, with regularly scheduled bike and motor races. It hosts a major race at Easter, and others throughout the summer. (More about Zandvoort's beach in Chapter 14.)

Further north is **IJmuiden**, an excellent choice if you're looking for seafood. It's also the best place in North Holland to see the ships going to and from Amsterdam. Situated at the mouth of the Noordzee Kanaal, it has a kilometer-long breakwater extending out into the sea. Inland are the mighty locks through which the ships must pass. There's an information centre to tell you all about the workings of the canal, **Noordzeekanaal In Zicht**, Noordersluisweg 20, ☎ (025) 551 9112, open May-Sept., Tues.-Sat. 11am-5pm, Sun. noon-4pm; Oct.-April, Tues.-Fri. noon-4pm.

Beverwijk is best known for its **Beverwijkse Bazaar**, Montageweg 35, ☎ (025) 126 2666, www.debazaar.nl, open Sat. 8am-4:30pm, Sun. 8am-5:30pm, and billed as Europe's largest indoor market. It has 3,000 stalls and shops, including many that sell Middle Eastern food and goods. There are over 55 eating places in the complex and lots of bargains!

The **Zuid-Kennemerland National Park**, between Haarlem and the coast is a beautiful natural scenic area with bird habitats, lakes, woods, beaches and dunes. The Visitor's Centre, Tetterodeweg 27, Overveen, ☎ (023) 541 1123, is open mid-April to mid-Sept., daily 9am-4:30pm; the rest of the year, Sat.-Sun. 9am-4:30pm.

South of Santpoort, are the 13th-century ruins of **Brederode Castle**, Velserenderlaan 2, ☎ (025) 221 1597, open March-Nov., Sun.-Fri. 10am-5pm.

South of Haarlem in Bennebroek, the **Linnaeushof Recreation Park**, Rijksstraatweg 4, ☎ (023) 584 7624, www.linnaeushof.nl, open April-Sept., 10am-6pm is a playground with 350 attractions, such as water bikes, motor carts and midget golf.

In Cruquius, just outside Heemstede, is the **Museum de Cruquius**, Cruquiusdijk 27, ☎ (023) 528 5704, www.museumdecruquius.nl, open March-Oct., Mon.-Fri. 10am-5pm, Sat.-Sun. 11am-5pm, and containing one of the three pump stations used to drain the Haarlemmer lake. This was the greatest 19th-century land reclamation project, resulting in new land stretching from Amsterdam to Leiden. In operation from 1849-1933, the original one-of-a-kind steam engine is on view. A scale model of Holland at storm tide shows how the low land was reclaimed from the sea and then kept permanently dry.

Halfway between Haarlem and Amsterdam is Halfweg (no, they weren't very creative), where you'll find the **Stoomgemaal Halfweg**, Haarlemmermeerstraat 4, ☎ (020) 497 4396, open April-Sept., Wed.-Thurs. 1-4pm, Sat. 10am-4pm – a steam pumping station built in 1852.

Spaarndam has a special meaning to readers of *Hans Brinker, or the Silver Skates*, the legendary boy who used his finger to stop a leak in the dike in order to save the area from floods. So many tourists asked about Hans that the local citizens put up a statue of him with a plaque that reads: 'Dedicated to our youth to honour the boy who symbolises Holland's perpetual struggle against water.' The story is considered a classic of children's literature, even though its American author, Mary Mapes Dodge (1830-1905), never visited Holland before writing the book. The village is charming with a sluice gate (from 1611) to control the water level. (Spaarndam is difficult to find, as the way is not well marked. It is northeast of Haarlem, along the Spaarne River.)

De Zaanse Schans
Old Dutch windmill village/living museum

Getting there: A4 from Rotterdam and The Hague, to A10 on the west side of Amsterdam. Then take A8 to A7, and get off at exit 2, 'Zaandijk.' Zaanse Schans is 3 km (2 mi) further on the right. The address is Schansend 7, Zaandam.

Information: ☎ (075) 616 8218; www.zaanseschans.nl

Hours: The Visitor Centre is open daily, April-Sept. 8:30am-5pm; Oct.-March 8:30am-6pm. The various attractions have their own opening times, but most are open daily from April-Nov. Some are closed in the winter.

De Zaanse Schans is a living museum of homes, buildings and windmills dating from the 17th-19th centuries. The houses are actually lived in by private citizens, the intention being to eliminate the ghost-town feeling that is often felt in open-air museums.

These characteristic wooden houses and mills were transported from the neighbouring area by boat, and reconstructed with loving care and attention to detail. There are a number of working windmills to visit, including one where you can buy excellent mustard that has been milled on the spot.

The Visitor Centre has a brochure listing all the attractions, along with a map, following this route:

1. The Zaans Museum, Schansend 7, ☎ (075) 616 2862, www.zaansmuseum.nl, open Tues.-Sat. 10am-5pm, Sun. noon-5pm, offers an overview of the history of the region.

2. The craft shop De Saense Lelie, Zeilenmakerspad 7, ☎ (075) 635 4622, www.saenselelie.nl, open March-Oct., daily 8am-6pm; Nov.-Feb., daily 9am-5pm, has demonstrations of glass-blowing, ceramic-making, and other Dutch crafts.

3. Cheesefarm Kaasmakerij Catharina Hoeve, Zeilenmakerspad 5, ☎ (075) 621 5820, is open March-Oct., daily 8am-6pm; Nov.-Feb., daily 8:30am-5pm. Edam and Gouda cheese are made here in traditional manner.

4. Bakkerij Museum Oude Stijl, Zeilenmakerspad 4, ☎ (075) 617 3522, open Tues.-Sun. 10am-5pm, is an old bakery and sweet shop.

5. The antique shop, Het Jagershuis, Zeilenmakerspad 2, ☎ (075) 616 8886, is in the oldest house in Zaanse Schans, built in 1623.

6. Mustard mill De Huisman, Kalverringdijk 23, ☎ (075) 616 8888, was built as a snuff mill in 1786. Though not open to the public, you can buy the delicious Zaanse mustard that is made here. The last Saturday in September is Zaanse Windmill Day, when all the mills will be in operation.

7. Landing stage

8. Sawmill De Poelenburg, Kalverringdijk 27. Only open the second Saturday of the month from April-Sept.

9. Paint mill De Kat, Kalverringdijk 29, ☎ (075) 621 0477, open April-Oct., daily 9am-5pm; Nov.-March, Sat.-Sun. 9am-5pm, is a 1782 windmill where visitors can see pigments being produced for use by artists.

10. Oil mill De Zoeker, Kalverringdijk 31, ☎ (075) 628 7942, open March-Sept., daily 9:30am-4:30pm, is a 1610 windmill where oil is made.

11. 17th-century mill De Bonte Hen, Kalverringdijk 39, ☎ (075) 621 5148, open Sat. 9am-5pm, has two large wind-powered rollers to crush oil seed.

12. Cruise on Rondvaartrederij De Schans, Jan van Goyenkade 15, ☎ (075) 617 2920, for a nice view of the village from the water.

13. Gallery Aan 't Glop, Kalverringdijk 21, ☎ (075) 617 6585, has wooden toys, etchings and watercolours for sale.

14. Museum Het Noorderhuis, Kalverringdijk 17, ☎ (075) 617 3237, open March-June & Sept.-Oct., Tues.-Sun. 10am-5pm; July-Aug., daily 10am-5pm; Nov.-Feb., Sat.-Sun. 10am-5pm, is equipped to show how a rich merchant lived in the beginning of the 19th century. The building is from 1670.

15. De Hoop Op d' Swarte Walvis, Kalverringdijk 13-15, ☎ (075) 616 5629, is a restaurant whose name means 'Hoping For The Black Whale.'

16. Garden

17. Museumwinkel Albert Heijn, Kalverringdijk 5, ☎ (075) 659 2808, open March-Oct., daily 10am-1pm & 2-5pm; Nov.-Feb., Sat.-Sun. 11am-1pm & 2-4pm, is the original Albert Heijn grocery store from 1887, and now an international leader in the supermarket trade.

18. Museum Van Het Nederlandse Uurwerk, Clock Museum, Kalverringdijk 3, ☎ (075) 617 9769, open March-Oct., daily 10am-5pm; Nov.-Feb., Sat.-Sun. noon-4:30pm, presents Dutch clocks from 1500-1850 in working order.

19. De Tinkoepel, Kalverringdijk 1, ☎ (075) 617 6204, www.tinkoepel.nl open Jan.-Feb. 11am-4pm; March-Dec. 10am-5pm, is a pewter shop with working craftsmen. The building is an 18th-century teahouse from Zaandam.

20. Old-fashioned shipyard De Sleephelling, De Kwakels 2, ☎ (075) 635 1689, is where you can see traditional Dutch boats being made.

21. Restaurant De Kraai, Kraaienpad 1, ☎ (075) 615 6403, specialises in 10 kinds of pancakes, cold snacks, and a 'Koffietafel' (coffee, cookies and sandwiches).

22. Giftshop De Bezem, Kraaienest 3, ☎ (075) 615 7680, www.souvenirsandgifts.nl, has all kinds of gifts from Holland and abroad.

23. Photostudio J. Engels, Kraaienest 1, ☎ (075) 617 9517, is a place to have a family picture taken in traditional costume.

24. Wooden shoe workshop and museum, Zaanse Schans Klompenmakerij, Kraaienest 4, ☎ (075) 617 7121, www.woodenshoeworkshop.nl, open March-Oct., daily 9am-6pm; Nov.-Feb., daily 9am-5pm, has 7,000 pairs of clogs (klompen) in stock and special demonstrations of how they're made.

In the neighbourhood of De Zaanse Schans

The Zaan district is the oldest industrial region in Europe. Of the 600 windmills that once dominated the skyline – grinding flour, and making mustard, paint and oil, as well as sawing wood, only 12 remain. A windmill museum is at Koog aan de Zaan, the **Molenmuseum**, Museumlaan 18, ☎ (075) 628 8968, www.zaansemolen.nl, open June-Sept., Tues.-Fri. 11am-5pm, Sat. 2-5pm, Sun. 1-5pm; Oct.-May, Tues.-Fri. 10am-noon & 1-5pm, Sat. 2-5pm, Sun. 1-5pm.

At Zaandijk, you can see Zaanse objects and 17th- and 18th-century clothing at the **Zaans Historisch Museum**, Lagedijk 80, ☎ (075) 621 7626, open Tues.-Fri. & Sun. 1-5pm.

Zaandam is where you'll find the **Czar Peterhuisje**, Krimp 23, ☎ (075) 616 0390, open Tues.-Sun. 1-5pm. Russia's Czar Peter the Great (1672-1725) lived here in 1697. At the time, some of the finest ships in the world were built in the Netherlands, and Zaandam was one of the shipbuilding centres. Using an alias, the Czar came to Zaandam to learn how the Dutch made their famous ships. John Bergamini, in his book, The Tragic Dynasty, reports: "Peter Michaelov was working in the shipyards... as a labourer, and boarding with an old carpenter he had known in Archangel...The Csar's disguise served him only about a week: his height, his twitch and a wart on his cheek gave him away, and it did him no good to turn his back on officials who called him 'Your Majesty' and on the crowds of the curious." He returned to Zaandam three more times, the last in 1717. The wooden house he stayed in was built in 1632 and now stands protected inside a stone building, commissioned by Nicolas II, the last of the Russian czars.

Alkmaar
Cheese galore

Getting there: A4 from The Hague to A9 northwest to Alkmaar. From Amsterdam go via Zaandam to A9 then north to Alkmaar.

Information: VVV, Waagplein 2, ☎ (072) 511 4284; www.alkmaar.nl

Alkmaar is an attractive, old Dutch town with canals, lift bridges, a beautiful town hall, magnificent patrician houses, boat tours, and picturesque shopping streets in its old centre. Most visitors come here in summer for one reason though, to see the traditional Friday morning cheese market.

Cheese has made Alkmaar what it is today. Land in this part of Holland is flat, soggy and unsuitable for most farm crops, but perfectly fine for grazing cows. As far back as 1365, farmers in the area were bringing cheese into Alkmaar to be weighed. The city was granted exclusive weighing rights for the region by the Count of Holland, and prospered from the taxes it charged on each cheese that was weighed.

The city's prosperity was brought to a violent halt in 1573 when Spanish soldiers laid siege to the town. Having held off the invasion, the city grew again, thanks largely to new export markets for cheese. In the late 16th century, a new cheese weigh-house was built, followed by other buildings in the prosperous 17th century. These buildings are still standing, and make it worthwhile to linger and explore Alkmaar after visiting the cheese market.

▶ **Cheese Market**

Location: Waagplein, follow signs to Waag, or Kaasmarkt

Information: VVV ☎ (072) 511 4284

Hours: Mid April-Mid Sept., Fri. 10am-1:30pm

The weekly **Kaasmarkt**, or **Cheese Market**, is popular and well worth the trip. Held every Friday morning during the tourist season, it is on the itinerary of every guided tour group, so expect a crowd and come early to get a good view.

At this traditional cheese market, you'll see business conducted as it has been on this square since 1693! Of the piles of various cheeses spread out on the ground, the most popular are big, wheel-like cheeses called Gouda; the smaller, ball-like ones, Edam. Though similar in taste, Gouda has a higher milk fat content, so its texture is somewhat creamier.

The cheeses are laid out for wholesalers and exporters to examine and taste before bidding. With a special scoop they bore out a long, round piece, smelling, tasting, and crumbling it between their fingers to determine the fat and moisture content. When eventually two people, the buyer and seller, start slapping one another's hands, they are negotiating prices in the traditional manner. A final slap clinches the deal.

That done, the cheese is carried to the scales by a team of six men – members of the 'Cheese Porters' Guild.' The guild has four companies, each with its own colour: green, blue, red or yellow. Each company has a team of six porters and a collector (or treasurer). It also has a foreman – his silver insignia hanging from his neck on a ribbon of the appropriate company colour. The porters are all dressed in spotless white, with lacquered straw hats. By means of leather shoulder slings, they carry their trays loaded with up to 80 cannon-ball-sized cheeses weighing around 160 kilos (330 pounds). In the process, the porters take on the distinctive bobbing gait necessary to carry such a heavy load. Traditionally, the oldest and youngest of each company work together – the elder one at the back.

At the Weigh House, the collector weighs the cheese, marking the weight of the total load. The 'weighmaster' calls out the weight, notes it on a blackboard, and the porters deliver it to the buyer.

Because of this market's popularity, you are advised to arrive early and come by train. Alternatively, follow the parking signs on the highway to a special parking area, which has a shuttle bus service.

● **Near the cheese market:** The **Waag** was built in 1341 as a chapel dedicated to the Holy Ghost. It was converted into a weighing house in 1582, the tower added around 1595. Those who love carillons should arrange to be on the square on Friday, 11am-noon (in season), or Thurs., 6:30-7:30pm and Sat., noon-1pm. The chimes sound every hour, accompanied by a mechanised show of trumpeters blowing their horns and horsemen 'charging out to do battle.' (Best seen from the bridge at the Mient – the canal next to the Waag.) www.alkmaar.nl/monument/monument/waag

Het Hollands Kaasmuseum, Waagplein 2, ☎ (072) 511 4284, www.kaasmuseum.nl, open April-Oct., Mon.-Thurs & Sat. 10am-4pm, Fri. 9am-4pm, has several videos in English about cheese. It also has numerous displays, such as a collection of cheese presses from the 1800s, when families made their own cheese. This was a common wedding gift at the time. Note the initials and wedding dates painted on them.

Just a block from the cheese market is **Biermuseum De Boom**, Houttil 1, ☎ (072) 511 3801, www.biermuseum.nl, open April-Oct., Tues.-Fri. 10am-4pm, Sat.-Sun. 1:30-4pm; Nov.-March, Tues.-Sun. 1-4pm. In this 17th-century brewery you can see how beer is made, and even choose a brew from among nearly 90 Dutch varieties.

● **Also in Alkmaar:** Some of the more interesting town sights include the **St. Laurens Church**, Koorstraat 2, ☎ (072) 514 0707, www.grotekerk-alkmaar.nl, open June-Sept., Tues.-Sun. 10am-5pm, and built between 1470 and 1516. The **Hof van Sonoy**, Gedempte Nieuwesloot, is a former convent, shelter for the homeless, and residence of the Governor Jonkheer Diedrick Sonoy. Also of interest are the **Huis van Achten** (House of Eight) (1656), Lombardsteeg 23, a home for eight old gentlemen; and the **Hofje van Splinter**, Ritsevoort 2, (1646) an almshouse for eight elderly ladies.

YOUR WEEKLY CULTURAL GUIDE.

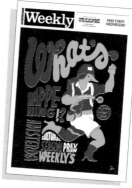

The **Town Hall** can be visited on weekdays when the reception rooms are not in use. Late Gothic in style, the oldest part dates from the beginning of the 16th century. The Mayoral Council Chambers, the hall (with its Schermer chest), the Polder Room, and the Nierop Room with its original wooden ceiling, are of special interest.

The Municipal Museum, or **Stedelijk Museum**, Canadaplein 1, ☎ (072) 548 9789, www.stedelijkmuseumalkmaar.nl, open Tues.-Fri. 10am-5pm, Sat.-Sun. 1-5pm, is northwest of the square. The collection of antique toys will interest young and 'old'; history buffs will be interested in the displays relating to the town's early days, especially the Spanish siege in 1573.

Tours

Alkmaar has two companies offering sightseeing trips on the city's canals, in season: Grachtenrondvaart Alkmaar, ☎ (072) 511 7750, leaves from the canal near the Waag; Rederij Woltheus, ☎ (072) 511 4840, also offers cruises to Zaanse Schans and Amsterdam.

In the neighbourhood of Alkmaar

The **Alkmaarse Hout** is a wooded area where you can take beautiful walks to nearby Heiloo. In Limmen, the **Hortus Bulborum**, Zuidkerkenlaan 23a, ☎ (025) 123 1286, www.hortus-bulborum.nl, open mid April-mid May, Mon.-Sat. 10am-5pm, Sun. noon-5pm, is a garden with over 1,400 varieties of tulips and 200 other flower varieties.

To reach the coast, drive about seven kilometers (4mi) west to Egmond aan Zee. Besides its popular beach, it has the **Museum Van Egmond**, Zuiderstraat 7, ☎ (072) 506 1678, open June-mid Sept., Sun.-Fri., 2-4pm; June-Aug. also open Tues.-Thurs. 7-9pm. Housed in a former church, it covers the rich history of the region, much of it centered around Egmond aan de Hoef where the powerful Egmond family made their home in the Middle Ages. Destroyed by the Spanish in 1573, the ruins of the family estate can still be seen. Egmond Binnen had one of the most influential abbeys in 16th-century Holland, when abbeys played a major role in society. Founded in 950, it is now the **Museum Abdij Van Egmond**, Abdijlaan 26, ☎ (072) 506 1415, open by appointment. www.egmondaanzee.info/nl

Further north is **Bergen aan Zee**, a charming artists' centre. Its **Zee Aquarium**, Van der Wijckplein 16, ☎ (072) 581 2928, www.zeeaquarium.nl, is open April-Sept., daily 10am-6pm; Oct.-March, daily 11am-5pm. For some beautiful scenery, continue north past Schoorl to Groet.

Broek op Langedijk, north of Alkmaar, has a unique museum, and the oldest vegetable market in Europe, where you can bid in a real auction. Established in 1887, sellers brought their vegetables in via a canal that ran through the auction hall itself. Buyers made their bids from seats on either side of the waterway as the boat floated by. Nowadays, visitors are shown how the system works and are invited to bid on various products. **Museum Broeker Veiling**, Museumweg 2, ☎ (022) 631 3807, www.broekerveiling.nl, open April-Oct., Mon.-Fri. 10am-5pm, Sat.-Sun. noon-5pm, also offers 30-minute boat trips through the town and countryside, with regular craft demonstrations in the summer.

Den Helder
Home of the Dutch Navy

Getting there: Den Helder is at the northern tip of North Holland. From Rotterdam and The Hague, take A4 north past Schiphol Airport; then west on A9 to Alkmaar, then N9 north. From Amsterdam, A5 to A9 and continue as above.

Information: VVV, Bernhardplein 18, ☎ (022) 362 5544; www.vvvkopvannoordholland.nl

---

The first records of **Den Helder** appear about 1500. Before then, only the village of Huisduinen was known. Still existing as a part of Den Helder, it has retained its village-like qualities. Den Helder was a fishing village until the French occupation in 1811, when Napoleon turned it into a fortress town – the 'Gibraltar of the North.' Today it is home to the Dutch Fleet. Another developing industry is tourism. Locals boast that Den Helder has more hours of sunshine per year and cleaner water than any other resort in the Netherlands. It is also an active fishing centre, as well as the ferry link with the island of Texel. In July, National Naval Days are organised with visits to ships, exhibits, demonstrations, brass bands, etc.

▶ **Marinemuseum**
Location: Hoofdgracht 3
Information: ☎ (022) 365 7534; www.marinemuseum.nl
Hours: Mon.-Fri. 10am-5pm, Sat.-Sun. noon-5pm. Nov-April closed on Mon.

The Dutch Navy's five centuries of history reached its peak in the 17th century, when it was probably the world's most powerful. Those years of glory are remembered in the **Marinemuseum**, the Dutch Naval history museum. A few less auspicious occasions are also remembered, the most unique being the capture of the Dutch fleet by the French cavalry – the ships having become icebound between Den Helder and Texel. There are two ships visitors can explore. You can squeeze your way through the cramped quarters of the submarine, the Tonijn, or visit the Abraham Crijnssen, a famous minesweeper whose heroic crew escaped through Japanese naval lines in the waters off the Dutch East-Indies in 1942, having ingeniously disguised the ship as a tropical island.

● **Also in Den Helder: Nationaal Reddingmuseum Dorus Rijkers,** Oude Rijkswerf Willemsoord / Cape Holland terrein, Willemsoord 60-G, 1781 AS Den Helder, ☎ (022) 361 8320, www.reddingmuseum.nl, open Mon.-Sat. 10am-5pm, Sun. 1-5pm, tells the tale of Dorus Rijkers, a local lifeboat skipper who helped rescue 487 people during his years on the sea. Den Helder is renowned for its efficient sea rescue teams, and this museum also shows how lives are saved today, with a simulation in which you feel you're on a lifeboat on the storm-tossed seas. The lighthouse **Vuurtoren De Lange Jaap** is over 60 meters (200 ft) tall. Fort Kijkduin, Admiraal Verhuellplein 1, ☎ (022) 361 2366, www.fortkijkduin.nl, has guided tours 10am-6pm. Napoleon had this fort built in 1811. It has a number of underground tunnels, including one that has been converted into a sea aquarium. **Kathe Kruse Poppenmuseum (Doll Museum)**, Binnenhaven 25, ☎ (022) 361 6704, www.kathekrusepoppenmuseum.nl, is open March-Dec., Thurs.-Sat. 2-5pm; also Tues. 2-5pm in July-August.

In the neighbourhood of Den Helder

In springtime, you will be enchanted by the brilliant colours of the many bulb fields in bloom around **Julianadorp**. This is also the place to stay if you want to enjoy a beach holiday in the area. There are a number of parks, and many hiking places around the dunes.

The **Afsluitdijk (Enclosing Dike)**, about 24 km (15 mi) east of Den Helder, will take you to the province of Friesland. Even if there's only time to drive to the observation point on this magnificent dike (about halfway), it's an impressive sight. www.afsluitdijk.org

Texel
'Sheep island' and bird preserve

Getting there:	Follow directions to Den Helder, then signs to Texel or the TESO ferry terminal. It's a 20-minute ferry crossing with departures every hour. Cars allowed. ☎ (022) 236 9691
Information:	VVV, Emmalaan 66, Den Burg, ☎ (022) 231 4741; www.texel.net

Still a world apart, **Texel** has traditionally been known as the 'sheep island.' Approximately 16,000 sheep contribute to its economic base, along with tourism, agriculture, bulb-growing and fishing.

Texel, 15 miles (24km) long and 5 miles (8km) wide, is the largest of the North Sea islands, and part of a dune area that extends to Jutland in Denmark. It is protected by its immense sand dunes on the west. Even today, it offers a relatively isolated area with some of the most beautiful sand beaches in the world. The most southerly of the Wadden islands which run along the northern coast of Holland, it is the easiest to reach. Tourism increases annually, and is important to the economy of the island. If you want to stay overnight, do make reservations. Beaches along the whole length of Texel are accessible by road with good parking facilities. The National Forestry Service, which is responsible for the protection of the dunes, offers guided walks in the nesting areas. In addition, there are many special walking paths marked for visitors to enjoy on their own. Originally planted to keep the sand dunes from blowing away, the woods between Den Hoorn and De Koog provide ideal spots for picnics.

Den Burg is Texel's main town. Its fine shopping centre has a Mon. morning market, and a folkloric market on Wed. in summer. The **Oudheidkamer**, Kogerstraat 1, ☎ (022) 231 3135, open April-Oct., Mon.-Fri. 10am-12:30pm & 1:30-3:30pm, is a museum with a collection of Texel art. The white tower of the church on De Binnenburg has been a landmark for seafarers since the 16th century.

- **Also on Texel: De Koog** is the main beach area on the island, and its most crowded. It's also where you'll find **Ecomare**, Ruijslaan 92, ☎ (022) 231 7741, www.ecomare.nl, open daily 9am-5pm, an environmental education centre set in 170 acres of dunes. It has a seal refuge where you can approach the seals, (they are fed at 11am and 3pm), a bird sanctuary and nature history museum dealing with the area. This is also where the annual 100km (62 mi) catamaran race around the island begins in early June.

  Oudeschild was once an important port for navigators. Ships docked here waiting for the right weather conditions to begin their journeys. As many as 3,000 ships a year came in the 17th-18th centuries, and the local people prospered by supplying provisions. All this local history is told in the **Maritiem en Jutters Museum**, Barentszstraat 21, ☎ (022) 231 4956, www.texelsmaritiem.nl, open Tues.-Sun. 10am-5pm; July-Aug., also Mon. 10am-5pm. It also has a collection of flotsam washed up on the shore from passing ships over the centuries. In the summer there are demonstrations of eel smoking, net mending, and other maritime skills, as well as a beachcomber storyteller, daily 11:30am & 1:30pm. If you call in advance, this 'old tar ' will tell his tales in English for groups. From April-Oct, Wed. 10am, the museum has a tour of **De Schans**, a fortress built in 1572 by William of Orange to protect the Dutch ships, and expanded by Napoleon in 1811, a kilometer south of Oudeschild.

  Den Hoorn has a church built between 1500-1700, and a cheese-making farm, **Zuivelboerderij St. Donatus**, Hoornderweg 46, ☎ (022) 231 9426, www.sintdonatus.nl, open Jan.-March, Tues. 2-6pm, Thurs. & Sat. 9am-6pm; April-Oct., Tue.-Sat. 9am-6pm. The 15th-century **Martinuskerk** in **Oosterend** is the oldest church in Texel. **De Waal** has an **Agrarisch en Wagenmuseum**, Hogereind 4-6, ☎ (022) 231 2951, open two weeks before Easter to autumn vacation, Mon. 1:30-5pm, Tues.-Sat. 10am-5pm, Sun. 2-4pm, a farm museum with wagons from the 1700s. www.wagenmuseum.nl

  De Cocksdorp has a museum of aviation in Texel, **Luchtvaart Museum Texel**, Postweg 120, ☎ (022) 231 1267, www.texelairport.nl, open May-Oct, daily 11am-6pm.

- **Biking and birding:** With 120km (74.5 mi) of trails, Texel is wonderful for biking. Bring your own, or rent one on the island. Any one of four 30km (19 mi) routes available from the VVV will give the visitor an idea of the island's diversity. We cannot leave Texel without mentioning its importance to serious and amateur students of ornithology. There are many species of birds breeding on the island and innumerable migrants stay on Texel in spring and autumn. Among the breeding birds are several rare and interesting species, the Hen Harrier, Little Tern, Sandwich (and Arctic) Tern, Bittern and Bluethroat.

Staying over

The old-fashioned and moderately-priced hotel on the market square of Den Burg, the **Lindeboom**, Groenplaats 14, ☎ (022) 231 2041, is a good place from which to observe local happenings. On Wednesdays in July-August, the place jumps with a market, sheep-shearing demonstrations and an arts-and-crafts fair. In **De Koog**, **Hotel Opduin**, Ruyslaan 22, ☎ (022) 231 7445, www.opduin.nl, is about 300 meters from the beach. Den Hoorn or De Koog might appeal to beach lovers with their miles of sandy beaches backed by high dunes and pine woods. Campers have a choice of numerous campsites. Other hotels, and bed and breakfasts, are also available. All-in holidays, including parachuting, catamaran sailing, sea kayaking, or Ecomare courses can be arranged with the VVV.

Medemblik, Twisk and Kolhorn
Three charming villages

Getting there: Medemblik is north of Hoorn. From points south, follow directions to Amsterdam, through the Coen Tunnel, west on A8 and then north on A7 to exit 11. Twisk and Kolhorn are in the vicinity of Medemblik.

Information: VVV Medemblik, Kaasmarkt 1, ☎ (022) 754 2852; www.vvvmedemblik.nl

Medemblik, **Twisk**, and **Kolhorn** are three very special stops north of Hoorn. Located on the IJsselmeer, Medemblik is one of the oldest and most important mercantile towns in West Friesland with a recorded history from the year 334. It comes alive during the summer when boats and their crews stop here. International sailing races are held regularly.

Radboud Castle, Oudevaartsgat 8, ☎ (022) 754 1960, open Easter to Nov. 1st, Mon.-Sat. 10am-5pm, and all year on Sun. noon-5pm, built by Floris V in 1288 to keep an eye on his newly-conquered subjects, was originally square, with four round defensive towers, one in each corner. The castle was restored in 1890 by architect P.J.H. Cuypers, and is only a quarter of its original size. It has a weapons and flag museum, as well as furniture, paintings and items dealing primarily with the history of Medemblik. www.castles.nl/rad

Some of the interesting buildings in town include the 15th-16th-century **Bonifacius Church**, the 17th-century weigh-house on the Kaasmarkt, the old widows' houses on Heeresteeg, and City Hall with its 17th-century brick step-gables. The orphanage, **Die Oudtheytkamer**, on Torenstraat, has an interesting collection of Dutch coins, ceramics, and silver from the 14th-17th centuries. It also has a 1785 gate, with figures of four orphan children carved in a niche at the top. You can visit the **Herder windmill**, Westerdijk 3, ☎ (022) 754 3198, open Sat. 10am-5pm, where various grains are ground. They sell flour that's good for making brown and white breads, cakes and pancakes. There is also an old bakery museum, **De Oude Bakkerij**, Nieuwstraat 8, ☎ (022) 754 5014, open April-Oct., daily noon-5pm; rest of year, Sat.-Sun. noon-5pm. It has old cake moulds and other baking utensils on display, as well as an old oven that is used during demonstrations of how scrumptious-smelling Dutch cookies and gingerbread are made. Special hands-on activities during school holidays.

The **Nederlands Stoommachinemuseum**, Oosterdijk 4, ☎ (022) 754 4732 open Tues.-Sun. 10am-5pm, is a museum of Dutch Steam Engines. It shows the exciting historic development of the steam engine from the mid-18th-19th centuries. There are many working models from ships and factories. www.stoommachinemuseum.nl

Staying over

A pleasant hotel stop is **Tulip Inn** Medemblik, Oosterhaven 1, ☎ (022) 754 3844. A hotel since 1897, it offers traditional hospitality and comfort. Some rooms overlook the old harbour.

In **Twisk**, just a few kilometers from Medemblik, is a small village worth a detour. The houses are charming and colourful. Literally built on either side of its one principal road, the houses are reached by private bridges. We recommend you leave the car at one end of this unique village and walk its length to fully enjoy it. **Kolhorn** is an example of what a typical dike village was like before the original draining of the Wieringer-waard land in 1844. From the top of the high mid-14th-century enclosure dike, there is a beautiful view of the village and surrounding polderland. In former times, Kolhorn was known for fishing and its peat storage sheds. Peat was brought in sailing ships from Friesland. Shell fishing near Texel was another source of income. Ships too large to dock at Amsterdam used to bring their exotic cargoes from the East Indies to towns like Kolhorn, where they transferred their goods to 'coasters,' smaller lighters, which could navigate the shallower waters. This way of life ceased, however, with the damming of the Zuiderzee. The area, now about 10 km (6 mi) from the water, was pumped dry to create farmland. It took some time and experimenting, however, to find a way to eliminate the remaining salt. Finally a root was discovered which made the land porous enough for the salt to escape.

Enkhuizen
Boats, boats, boats and a very special museum

Getting there:	From Rotterdam and The Hague, follow directions for Amsterdam, through the Coen Tunnel, west on A8 to the intersection with A7 north to exit 9, and then east on N302.
Information:	VVV, Tussen Twee Havens 1, ☎ (022) 831 3164; www.vvvweb.nl/enkhuizen

At one time, **Enkhuizen** was a prosperous town on the Zuiderzee with a population of 40,000. A major port, it rivalled Amsterdam in importance in the 16th century. Misfortunes struck over the centuries – silt blocked its harbour, and the plague struck its people. Amsterdam grew in economic importance, as Enkhuizen's fortunes waned. The final blow came in the 1920s with the damming of the Zuiderzee. Enkhuizen's fishermen found themselves without saltwater fish and, therefore, without work.

Enkhuizen today is a photographer's paradise. It has many beautiful historic buildings from its glorious days and gives an impression of life in the fishing towns of yesteryear. At every turn, there are facades, scenic drawbridges, ships of all classes and sizes at anchor. But most visitors come to Enkhuizen to see one of Holland's most exciting museums, the Zuiderzee Museum.

▶ **Zuiderzee Museum**

Location:	Indoor Museum: Wierdijk 12-2, in the Peperhuis. Open Air Museum: Look for signs to the Zuiderzeemuseum parking area, from where you will board a ferry to the Open Air Museum.
Information:	☎ (022) 835 1111; www.zuiderzeemuseum.nl

| Hours: | Open Air Museum, open April-Oct., daily 10am-5pm; Indoor Museum, open daily 10am-5pm throughout the year. |
| Note: | Admission tickets to the Open Air Museum can be bought at the car park before boarding the boat. You can return by boat to the car park, or walk to town to see the Indoor Museum and then take a boat back to the car park from the jetty near the station. |

Zuiderzee Museum takes you back in time. It consists of two parts: an open-air museum, and an indoor museum nearby. The **Open Air Museum**, or the **Buitenmuseum**, is the main attraction.

The Open Air Museum is a reconstructed, old Dutch village on the shores of the IJsselmeer (formerly the Zuiderzee). When it was enclosed by a dam in the 1930s, it was obvious that life for the fishing communities was going to change significantly. Before most of the threatened buildings were destroyed, plans were made to dismantle and rebuild them, creating a picture of life as it was when fishing was so important to the local economy.

Reassembled along streets and canals are 130 buildings, providing a glimpse of life from 1880-1932. Craftsmen from all trades demonstrate their work: a blacksmith, a butcher, a baker, even the organist playing hymns in church. Perhaps you'll take part in a short lesson on penmanship in the old schoolhouse. There's also a working steam laundry (1900), fish-smoking, sail-making and net-mending. Children can play with old-fashioned toys, and dress in traditional Dutch costumes, clogs included. Breathe in the atmosphere, look across the still waters of the IJsselmeer and enjoy a quick visit into the past.

The **Indoor Museum** is located in an historic building, the Peperhuis, once the headquarters of the Enkhuizen Chamber of the Dutch East India Company. In it are seven centuries of Zuiderzee history, including national costumes in authentic period interiors, painted furniture from the Hindeloopen and Zaan areas, ship models, and all sorts of nautical objects. There are old-style anchors, fishing nets, and farmhouse utensils, including cheese presses. Particularly unique is the fleet of Zuiderzee and inland ships moored at the quay, and the covered hall of ships where old vessels can be viewed from a walkway. A ticket to the Open Air Museum entitles you to a visit to the Indoor Museum at no extra cost; tickets for the Indoor Museum itself are available, be we recommend the combination.

- **Also in Enkhuizen:** There's more to be seen in Enkhuizen beyond the Zuiderzee Museum, including buildings like the **Drommedaris**, Paktuinen 1, ☎ (022) 831 2076, a 16th-century tower with vault paintings; the 16th-century **Weighhouse**, Kaasmarkt 8; the 17th-century **Town Hall**; the **Stadsgevangenis**, the old city prison behind the Town Hall on Swaanstraat; the **Koepoort** (1649), a city gate; the 15th-century **Westerkerk** with its wood carvings and choir screen; and the **Vestingwal** (1590), city walls with bulwarks and water gates. Enkhuizen also has the **Flessenscheepjesmuseum**, Zuiderspui 1, ☎ (022) 831 7762, open daily, 1pm-5pm, with over 600 ships in bottles on display.

Another attraction in the centre of Enkhuizen – and sure to delight the younger set – is **Sprookjeswonderland (Fairy-tale Land)**, Kooizandweg 9, ☎ (022) 831 7853, open daily winter Nov.-Mar. 11am-6:30pm and summer April thru Oct. 10am-5:30pm. There are dollhouses, a mini-train, small electric boats, fairy-tale characters, as well as a children's zoo. Another recreational centre is **Enkhuizer Zand**, Kooizandweg 12, ☎ (022) 832 3173. There you can enjoy a sandy beach, heated pool, playground, mini-golf course and water sports facilities for small craft. www.sprookjeswonderland.nl

Staying over

This part of Holland deserves an overnight stay. If you decide to enjoy the local, rural atmosphere, try the moderately priced **Die Port Van Cleve**, Dijk 74-78, ☎ (022) 831 2510, a hotel with old-world charm. **Hotel Driebanen**, Driebanen 59, ☎ (022) 831 6381, is slightly lower-priced, and also has apartments. There are a number of camping sites in the area. www.hoteldriebanen.com

Tours

Enkhuizen is probably the best starting point for anyone interested in a boat trip on the IJsselmeer. **Rederij Naco**, ☎ (020) 626 2466, offers trips to Medemblik and across the IJsselmeer to Stavoren in Friesland. **Rederij FRO**, ☎ (0527) 68 3407, also sails to Friesland, with trips to Urk in season. Departs hourly from 11am-5pm, April-Sept. from Westerstraat 164.

In the neighbourhood of Enkhuizen

A yearly event in Bovenkarspel of interest to plant and flower-lovers is the **Westfriese Flora**.

▶ **Westfriese Flora**

Location: After you turn off A7, follow signs to Enkhuizen then to Westfriese Flora. Cars must park just outside the village where a shuttle will take you to the entrance. There are bus services from major cities in North Holland, and special half-hourly train services. Ask for the combined train/entrance ticket. From the Flora stop (Bovenkarspel-Grootebroek) it is only a 3-minute walk to the exhibition entrance.

Information: ☎ (022) 851 1644; www.hollandflowersfestival.nl and www.westfrieseflora.nl

Hours: Open for 10 days, about mid-February. Those interested should call for precise opening and closing dates each year, or see the website.

The **Westfriese Flora** is a preview of what will be seen at later flower exhibitions such as the Keukenhof, but it's also a fascinating, hurly-burly, old-fashioned country fair with a real Dutch flair! For ten days in February, hundreds of thousands of plants and flowers are on display at the auction hall. With 14,000 m^2 of exhibition space, it is the world's largest exhibition of bulb flowers under one roof. All the latest developments in the field are featured, with plenty of advice on growing them. Plants are on sale and on auction.

Hoorn
A rich history of land and water

Getting there: Hoorn can be reached by land or by water; it attracts sailors of all kinds. From Amsterdam and other points south, take A7 north to exit 8.

Information: VVV-ANWB, Veemarkt 4, ☎ (072) 511 4284; www.vvvhoorn.nl

It's easy to see that **Hoorn** was once a rich international town. A former base of the Dutch East India trading company, it was known throughout the world of that time. It was from here that daring adventurers started out, braving the hazardous seas in search of merchant treasures. They brought back spices, gunpowder and all manner of exotic items from the Baltic, the Levant and the West Indies.

Hoorn was founded in the 14th century on the site of a natural harbour that was to bring its citizens wealth and power during the 17th century. In this 'Golden Age' it became the central administrative and commercial centre of all of Holland north of Amsterdam. It was the birthplace of Willem Schouten (1580-1625) who discovered 'Cape Horn' in 1616 and named it after his native town.

The character of Hoorn changed with the building of the Afsluitdijk in 1932, linking North Holland with Friesland and cutting it off from the Zuiderzee. It's an ideal town to explore, with interesting historical landmarks, an attractive harbour area, and many nice small shops to be discovered.

▶ Westfries Museum

Location: Rode Steen 1 (Town Square)
Information: ☎ (022) 928 0022, www.wfm.nl
Hours: Mon.-Fri. 11am-5pm, Sat.-Sun. 2-5pm

The **Westfries (West Frisian) Museum** is housed in the former State Council building, a beautiful baroque structure built in 1632. In the 17th century, Hoorn was an important and prosperous town. Delegates representing the major cities of the region met in this building to agree on policy before attending sessions of the States of Holland in The Hague. Voting in a block gave them a stronger voice than they would have had individually. The meeting room is the showpiece of this museum, its walls covered with large paintings of the civic guards who kept law and order and protected the city.

City coats of arms decorate the front of the building: from left to right, Medemblik, Edam, Alkmaar, Hoorn, Enkhuizen, Monnickendam and Purmerend. Prince Maurits, the major political figure of the period in North Holland graces each gable. The collection has something for everyone: period rooms, prison cells, coins, coats of arms, ship models, and archaeological finds. Much of the history of the East India Company can be discovered here.

● **Near the Westfries Museum:** The museum is on the town square, the most picturesque part of Hoorn. The square is known as the Rode Steen, referring to the 'red stone' on the ground just to the side of the statue – a spot where public executions took place. The statue is that of J. P. Coen, a native of Hoorn who headed the Dutch East India Company, which helped make the Netherlands one of the 17th century's greatest economic powers. Opposite the Westfries Museum is the **Waag**, or **Weigh House** (1609), now a restaurant. From the square, Kerkstraat leads to the **Grote Kerk**, a 19th-century structure, which was formerly a church. Facing it is **St. Jans Gasthuis**, one of the city's most attractive buildings, a former hospital built in 1563. Notice how the stone on the side of the front door has been worn down by the touch of thousands of hands. Doing so, it was believed, would protect you from the plague. The statue on the facade is that of St. John. It is now an art gallery.

Just up the street which becomes Nieuwstraat, is the **Statenpoort**, (1613) with twin step gables. Government officials from the seven main towns of the northern half of North Holland stayed here when they came to Hoorn on official business.

▶ **Binnenhaven**

The **Binnenhaven (Inner Harbour)** is primarily for leisure yachts. A pleasant place to stroll, the main attraction is its romantic **Hoofdtoren**, on Veermanskade. This defense tower has stood guard at the port entrance since 1532. There are attractive buildings and facades all along Veermanskade and across the bridge on Oude Doelenkade. Look at the old warehouses on Veermanskade 2, 3 & 6, and the buildings 17, 19, 21 on the Oude Doelenkade. Continue until you reach Slapershaven. At the corner of Grote Oost, are the **Bossuhuizen** with ornamental Frisian sculptures. From here, citizens witnessed the great naval battle of October 1573 when a Spanish fleet, under the command of Admiral Bossu was defeated by the Dutch.

The battle is commemorated in relief and verse on the side of the corner house. If you turn around, cross the bridge and continue down Kleine Oost, you'll come to the **Oosterpoort**. This **East Gate** (1578) is the only gate remaining of the original five.

● **Near the Binnenhaven: Oosterkerk**, with its 17th-century facade, on Grote Oost, used to be the seamen's family church. Notice the clock extending from its facade like a signboard.

Between the Binnenhaven and the main square is the **Museum Van De Twintigste Eeuw** (Museum of the 20th Century), Bierkade 4, ☎ (022) 921 4001, open Tues.-Fri 10am-5pm, Sat.-Sun. noon-5pm, with displays of household items showing how people lived in the 20th century. A scale model of Hoorn shows it as it was in 1650. www.museumhoorn.nl

Tours

What could be nicer than a train ride through the West Frisian countryside? **Museumstoomtram Hoorn-Medemblik**, Van Dedemstraat 8, ☎ (022) 921 4862, open Easter-autumn holiday, Tues.-Sun. 9:30am-5:30pm; July-Aug. also on Mon., offers old-fashioned steam locomotive rides between Hoorn and Medemblik. It also runs during the Christmas season, and has combined train/boat trips to Enkhuizen.

If a boat trip is what you want, there's a leisurely boat excursion from Medemblik and Enkhuizen; **Rederij Naco**, ☎ (020) 626 2466, for details. www.museumstoomtram.nl

In the neighbourhood of Hoorn

To the northwest, in Spanbroek is the **Frisia Museum**, Spanbroekerweg 162, ☎ (022) 635 1111, www.frisia-museum.nl, open daily Sun. 10am-5pm, with its collection of Dutch Magic Realist art. The core of the collection revolves around paintings by Carel Willink, one of Holland's most important artists of the 1930s.

To the southwest, **Schermerhorn** is a good place to see windmills (*molen*) in action. The **Museummolen**, Noordervaart 2, ☎ (072) 502 1519, www.museummolen.nl, open April-Oct., daily 10am-5pm; Nov.-March, Sun. 10:30am-4:30pm, is one of three examples in the vicinity. **De Rijp** was a prosperous 17th-century town, as we can see by its **Waag** (1690), and its **Stadhuis** (1630). The **Rijper Museum In 't Houtenhuis**, Jan Boonplein 2, ☎ (029) 967 1286, open Easter-June & Sept.-Oct., Sat.-Sun. 11am-5pm; July-Aug., Tues.-Sun. 11am-5pm, is an attractive 17th-century home and the local history museum.

Edam
The round, red cheese town

Getting there: Edam is north of Volendam. From the south, take A10 around Amsterdam to exit S116, then N247 to Edam.

Information: VVV, Damplein 1, ☎ (029) 931 5125; www.vvv-edam.nl

Edam is now known principally by those red, round, balls of cheese that bear its name. Originally, after receiving its city rights from Count Willem V in 1357, it was the shipbuilding of its 33 shipyards that made the city prosper, including the one which built the 'Halve Maan' (Half Moon) on which Henry Hudson sailed in 1609 to what is now New York. In those days Edam rivalled Amsterdam, Hoorn and Enkhuizen as a centre of commerce. Those prosperous days ended when the harbour silted up. Edam's many old buildings bear witness to the golden era of the 17th century, making it an interesting town for those who enjoy the picturesque. Between 1778 and 1922, Edam was the marketplace for local cheese-producing farmers. Their cheese had its own distinctive flavour, and because it was sold here, it became known as Edam cheese. Although the cheese market no longer exists, the old weigh-house still stands, and every summer there are demonstrations of how the cheese used to be marketed.

▶ **Edams Museum**

Location: Damplein 8

Information: ☎ (029) 937 2644, www.edamsmuseum.nl

Hours: 14 April-30 Oct. Tues.-Sat. 10am-4:30pm, Sun. 1pm-4:30pm

Edam's oldest brick building (1530), the home of a merchant family, became a museum in 1895, displaying the history of Edam. It continues to look much as it did nearly five centuries ago.

The most unique feature of the house is a cellar that floats on its own groundwater. In the 16th century, groundwater levels fluctuated. When cellars were built, they could be under severe pressure as groundwater levels rose. Such pressure could not only cause damage to the cellar, but also lead to cracked walls and dislocated floors above. The solution was a cellar without connections to the house, one that would rise freely as the water levels rose. You have to be small or flexible to climb into the cellar, but you can feel it bounce like a waterbed just by putting your foot on the ladder that leads down to it. Above the kitchen are the sleeping quarters, with cupboard beds built into the walls.

- **Also in Edam:** The Town Hall, **Raadhuis van Edam** on Damplein 1, is also the VVV office. It was built in 1737, and has a beautiful Council Chamber, magnificent wedding room, antique furniture, hand-painted wallpaper, and ... sand on the floor. It also sponsors temporary exhibits. Don't miss the **Captain's House** opposite the Town Hall with its paintings of regional folktale characters.

The **Weigh House** (1778), Kaaswaag, Jan Nieuwenhuizenplein 5, ☎ (029) 937 2842, open April-Sept., daily 10am-5pm, still sells cheese, and the re-enacted cheese market takes place here every summer for visitors. Close to the Kaaswaag is the 15th-century **St. Nicolas Church**, Grote Kerkstraat, open Easter-Sept. 2-4:30pm. Look for the fine choir screen and stained-glass windows, mostly from 1606-24. On the other side of the canal, the 16th-century **Proveniershuis** (1555) was formerly the home of the Beguines, a sisterhood of nurses. Near Breestraat and Achterhaven, the 16th-century **Houtenhuis** is the oldest wooden house here. Somehow it managed to escape fires and a law that made wooden houses illegal. The fact that it survived makes it a rare example of houses of the 1500s. (Not open to the public.) The **Speeltoren** of the former Onze Lieve Vrouwe Church, near Kleine Kerkstraat and Kapsteeg, also dates from the 15th-16th centuries. The carillon (1561) is played every 15 minutes. The tower was originally part of a church that stood here until 1882. It was braced and restored so as not to fall. www.edam-volendam.nl

Yearly events

Edam re-enacts its traditional cheese market at the Kaaswaag every Wednesday, 10:30am-12:30pm, in July and August.

Tours

Two-hour boat trips can be taken from Edam harbour on the IJsselmeer on Wed., in July-August, also on Saturdays. Check with the VVV.

In the neighbourhood of Edam

Purmerend has been a market town for 500 years, and is still known today for its Cattle Market, Tues. 7am-1pm. There is a general market on the same day, 8:30am-12:30pm. The **Purmerends Museum**, Kaasmarkt 20, ☎ (029) 947 2718, open May-Oct., Tues.-Fri. 10am-4pm, Sat.-Sun. 1-5pm; Nov-April, Wed., Sat.-Sun. 1-4pm, has a collection of Art

Nouveau pottery produced in Purmerend, as well as town history. www.purmerends-museum.nl

Volendam, Monnickendam and Marken
Old-world charm

These three villages, clustered together just north of Amsterdam, along with Zaandam, Broek in Waterland, Edam and Purmerend, are among the most charming in the Netherlands. Their old-world character has been noted by visitors for years, and their proximity to Amsterdam has made them popular. Try to visit just before or after the heaviest summer influx.

Volendam
A Roman Catholic fishing village

Getting there: North of Amsterdam, take exit S116 on the A10, then north on N247 past Monnickendam to Volendam. From The Hague and Rotterdam, A4 to A10 at Amsterdam, then as above. In summer, there are boat trips from the harbour to the island of Marken.

Information: VVV, Zeestraat 37, ☎ (029) 936 3747; www.vvv-volendam.nl

Originally a fishermen's village, **Volendam** is a Roman Catholic town as opposed to Marken, which is Protestant. Like Marken, since the draining of the Zuiderzee and the demise of the local fishing industry, the town turned to tourism. Volendam is larger than Marken, but both towns have retained some of their traditional feel, despite the tourists.

One of the attractions of Volendam is that you see traditional costumes. Old Dutch costumes varied from town to town, but those of Volendam no doubt match the picture most foreigners have in their minds. But don't expect a town full of men with baggy pants, fishermen's caps, and wooden shoes, and women with winged lace caps on their heads. A few older villagers still wear their traditional dress and you're most likely to see them on Sundays...for tourists!

This is a busy town where most of the crowd stays along the harbour, with its dozens of shops aimed at tourists. Included are fish stands and restaurants where you can try smoked eel – the local speciality. There are also wonderful views across the IJsselmeer as you walk along Haven, the main street.

These views were part of what lured many artists to the town in the 19th century. Often they spent time at the **Hotel-Restaurant Spaander**, Haven 15-19, ☎ (029) 936 3595 – a good stop for a cup of coffee, a meal, or just to see a collection of more than 100 old paintings from those artists. Should cigar bands fascinate you, there's a collection of 11 million of them at the **Volendams Museum**, Zeestraat 41, ☎ (029) 936 9258, www.volendams-museum.com, daily 10am-5pm. A 'local' collected them, and pasted them into collages of world-famous sites like St. Peter's, Rome, the Statue of Liberty, etc. The museum also has a collection of traditional costumes, and numerous old photographs and paintings of people wearing them. There are also four model interiors of Zuiderzee homes. There's a fish auction on the Haven on Mon.-Fri. mornings in May-June. You can visit the cheese farm **Alida Hoeve**, Zeddeweg 1, ☎ (029) 936 5830. Then, last but not least, head to one of the many photographers on the dike and have your picture taken in traditional Dutch costume! But before you leave, be sure to wander away from the harbour and walk along the narrow streets behind Haven. They are less crowded, with attractive small houses.

Monnickendam
Smoked eel and wooden shoes

Getting there: From Amsterdam, take A10 to exit S116, then go north on N247 to Monnickendam. From The Hague or Rotterdam, take A4 to Amsterdam, then as above.

Information: VVV, De Zarken 2, ☎ (029) 965 1998

This small town dates back to the 13th century when Frisian monks built a dam in the sea and a lake was formed. It was a leading port on the Zuiderzee, and one of the country's most prosperous cities. Before the Afsluitdijk was built and the Zuiderzee became the IJsselmeer, fishing was the lifeblood of **Monnickendam**. Today its harbour is popular with boaters, and visitors enjoy its narrow streets and buildings of yesteryear.

The 13th century **Grote Kerk**, De Zarken, open late May-early Sept., Tues.-Sat. 10am-4pm, Sun.-Mon. 1-4pm, is one of the important sites in town. The **Town Hall** (1746), Noordeinde 5, was originally a patrician mansion. Notice the town emblem on the façade – the figure of a monk.

The **Speeltoren**, Noordeinde 4, ☎ (029) 965 2203, open mid April-May, Sat. 10am-4pm, Sun. 1-4pm; June-mid Sept., Tues.-Sat. 10am-4pm, Sun.-Mon. 1-4pm, has a 16th-century carillon that chimes on the hour, while two knights perform a slow parade. The carillon is played by hand on Saturdays from 11am-noon. The local history museum is housed in the Speeltoren, with a collection that includes ceramics, old ship models, and archeological finds.

Nearby is the **Waag**, the 17th-century weigh-house, now a restaurant. Try the local speciality, smoked eel. See the traditional smoking process at Havenstraat 12, ☎ (029) 965 4256, open Tues.-Sat. in summer, only Wed. in winter. The **Weeshuis** (1638), Weezenland 16, is a former orphanage. The '*Speeldozencollectie*' at the **Stuttenburgh** restaurant, Haringburgwal 3-4, ☎ (029) 965 1869, open Tues.-Sun. noon-11pm, is all about music boxes.

Marken
'Island' village full of charm

Getting there: From Monnickendam, N518 east
Information: VVV, Monnickendam, ☎ (029) 965 1998; www.vvv-volendam.nl

For eight centuries, **Marken** was an island in the Zuiderzee. It was occupied by monks in the 13th century, who built a dam around it. From the 17th century it was a prosperous fishing community, until the decision to build the Afsluitdijk was taken early in the 20th century, cutting off the Zuiderzee from the North Sea. Since then, Marken has relied on tourists coming to see their old-fashioned fishing village with its green and white wooden houses built on piles.

The dike connection to the mainland was made in 1957. Approaching Marken by boat is far more picturesque, however. The **Marken Express**, operated by Rederij Veerman en Co., ☎ (029) 936 3331, April-Oct., leaves every 30-45 minutes to and from Volendam.

If you drive, leave your car at the town's car park. The walk from it will take you past some shops, including Marker Klompenmakerij, Kets 50, ☎ (029) 960 1630, a wooden shoe maker open all year 9am-6pm. After walking along the narrow streets lined by old fisher-men's houses, you will come to the **Havenbuurt**, a harbour lined with fishing boats, shops and places to eat. The **Kijkhuisje Sijtje Boes**, Havenbuurt 21, open March-Oct., Mon.-Sat. 9am-6pm, is an old Marken home where you can see how the old seamen and their wives looked and lived. The house is cosy and as compact as a ship's cabin.

Away from the harbour is the **Kerkbuurt** with, in its centre, the **Dutch Reformed Church**, open mid April-Oct., Sat. 10am-5pm. Look up to see the six sailing ships constructed by local craftsmen and hanging from the ceiling...one is a herring boat. The **Marker Museum**, Kerkbuurt 44-47, ☎ (029) 960 1904, open Easter-Oct., Mon.-Sat. 10am-5pm, Sun. noon-4pm, is in four former fishermen's homes, their interiors as they were, showing Marken life and history. www.markermuseum.nl

Yearly events

Don't forget your camera on the Queen's Birthday (April 30) when the citizens of Marken – as well as everywhere else in Holland – dress in orange-coloured clothing. In July, fish-ing boats compete in colourful sailing competitions.

Broek in Waterland
Marsh in water land

Getting there: A4 to Amsterdam, to the A10 west ring, to exit S118, and north on N247. Immediately after turning left off the highway, you will cross a bike path; turn right and follow the parking signs. Just 10 km (6 mi) from Amsterdam.

Information: VVV Monnickendam, ☎ (029) 965 1998; www.noord-holland-tourist.nl

You will agree the name is apt as you approach this village with its small lake, and then walk along its many canals. This attractive old village is full of surprises and has something to offer everyone.

The only way to see it is on foot (everything is so close by). Notice the lovely restored homes, many with the upper stories jutting forward, a feature unique to this area. Some say that it protected them from the harsh storms, others that upper stories being storage areas, access was made easier by this construction. No matter the reason, these attractive green and white houses and their unusual architecture give the village a special charm.

The **Hervormde Kerk** (Reformed Church), Leeteinde 11, open May-Sept., Mon.-Sat. 10am-5pm, should be your first stop – lest you be diverted by the clog-maker or antique shops. Off-season, ask the Rector for permission to visit; he lives next door. Built before 1400, the church was consecrated to Santa Claus...which should intrigue the younger set. It was destroyed by the Spanish in 1573, and rebuilt by 1628. Many of the objects you see in the church were given by townspeople. An interesting feature is the hourglass at the pulpit – for everyone to time the sermon! The arrangement of chairs and benches dates from the Hedge-sermons, whereby armed men manned the benches which were placed in a protective ring around the women and children.

Eating out

De Witte Swaen, Dorpstraat 11-13, ☎ (020) 403 1525, www.dewitteswaen.nl, is rustic and informal with 'specials' at moderate prices. For something more stylish, try the Neeltje Pater, Dorpsstraat 4, ☎ (020) 403 3311, with a lakeside view. On Sunday afternoons you can enjoy an English tea with homemade scones, and a variety of delicious cakes. Reservations recommended.

In the neighbourhood of Broek in Waterland

To the west in Oostzaan is the recreation area 't Twiske, Noorderlaaik 1 ... wonderful for biking. And a small museum at Landsmeer, the Museum Grietje Tump, Zuideinde 69, ☎ (020) 631 3455, open Sun. 2-5pm, has a large collection of antiques in an old farm-house.

Naarden
A fortified town

Getting there:	A1 east from Amsterdam. From The Hague and Rotterdam, A20 northeast to A12 east, past Utrecht to A27 north, A1 northwest. For a scenic route, A12 east to A2 north to turnoff for Maarssen. Then follow the Vecht River past the castles at Nijenrode, Oudaen and Gunterstein, and past Breukelen (Brooklyn, NY was named after it.), Loenen, Hilversum, Bussum.
Information:	VVV, Adriaan Dortsmanplein 1B, ☎ (035) 694 2836; www.vvvnaarden.nl

Naarden is like a large open-air museum and one of Holland's best examples of a fortified town. It has a double ring of walls in the shape of a star. This fort was built in the late 17th century, when Dutch forts were made of stone with earth ramparts. Naarden's old inner city is also well preserved, with many old buildings and attractive streets to explore.

Naarden's history is hazy, since most town records were destroyed during years of regional fighting, but the name Naarden appears as early as 968. In 1280, Count Floris conquered Naarden. He was later murdered at Muiderberg, not far away. One of Naarden's most traumatic episodes occurred in 1572 when the Spaniards burned the town to the ground and killed most of its inhabitants as an example to other Dutch rebels. This, combined with a later invasion by the French army, explains why the building of strong-walled fortifications around the city was necessary.

▶ **Vesting Museum (Fortress Museum)**
Location: Westwalstraat 6
Information: ☎ (035) 694 5459 www.vestingmuseum.nl
Hours: Mar.16-Nov.1 Tues.-Fri. 10:30am-5pm, Sat.-Sun. noon-5pm; Nov.1-Mar.16
                Sun.noon-5pm, group visits possible on Mondays.

Naarden's distinctive monument, this 17th-century fortress, is still largely intact. It is built with six bastions, arrow-shaped projections from the main wall designed to give defenders a better firing angle. The **Fortress Museum** is located in one of those bastions, the Turfpoort. Part open-air and part underground, it relates the history of Naarden. Youngsters will enjoy the ramparts and the ancient cannons on top of the high wall.

Inside this 17th-century building are scale models of the Turfpoort that explain the ingenious defence system, model figures ready to fire a cannon, a gunpowder room with old engravings of the town and, for gun enthusiasts, an arms collection showing gun development from flintlock and percussion, to breech loading and repeating rifle. There's a long underground tunnel known as 'the listening gallery.' The holes in its ceiling were actually used in time of war to listen for the enemy's possible sneak approach above.

There are boat rides on the moat around the fort, and walks in the surrounding woods. In May-Sept., every third Sun. 2-4pm, men dressed as cannoneers demonstrate the loading and firing of a twelve-pound cannon.

● **Also in Naarden**: It is easy to believe yourself in the 17th or 18th century here as you drive through small streets lined with interesting houses and historic monuments. **St. Vituskerk**, Marktstraat 13,☎ (035) 694 9873, open June-mid Sept., was built between 1380-1440. Its tower has a great view of the town and surroundings, July-Aug., Tues.-Sun. 1pm, 2pm, 3pm & 4pm, ☎ (035) 694 2836. Across the street is the fine Renaissance town hall (1601), **Stadhuis**, Marktstraat 22, ☎ (035) 695 7811, open April-Sept., Mon.-Sat. 1:30-4:30pm. A former town hall, Turfpoortstraat 27 is known as the **Spaanse Huys**, or Spanish House (1615). Its name comes from the stone tablet on its facade commemorating the slaughter of its people by Spanish troops in 1572. The **Arsenal** (1688) was the storeroom of the town's weapons. Renovated after a fire in 1954, it was converted to a pleasant centre with shops, cafes, etc. As you approach Naarden, you can already see the fortress' layout. Cross the moat and enter through the lovely **Utrecht Gate** (1877), one of several. Nearby is a large statue of Jan Amos Comenius (1592-1670), the scholar-educator. The **Comenius Museum**, Kloosterstraat 33, ☎ (035) 694 3045, open April-Oct., Tues.-Sat. 10am-5pm, Sun. noon-5pm; Nov.-March, Tues.-Sun. 1-4pm, tells the story of his life and work.

Eating out

Choose a picnic-type day to visit Naarden, and enjoy eating on the ramparts or in the lovely countryside. There are also many local restaurants to choose from, including famed restaurateur Paul Fagel's **Restaurant Het Arsenaal**, where you'll find 'haute cuisine' from Provence, Kooltjesbuurt 1, Naarden Vesting, ☎ (035) 694 9148, www.paulFagel.nl, adjacent to Het Arsenaal complex of high-end shops.

In the neighbourhood of Naarden

For a castle that really looks like a castle, try the one in **Muiden**. The **Muiderslot**, Herengracht 1, ☎ (029) 426 1325, www.muiderslot.nl, open April-Oct., Mon.-Fri. 10am-5pm, Sat.-Sun. 1-5pm; Nov.-March, Sat.-Sun. 1-4pm, is at the mouth of the Vecht river 7 km (4 mi) northwest of Naarden and 12 km (7.5 mi) southeast of Amsterdam. It is a massive red brick structure topped with pointed towers and step-gables, set within and protected by its moat. The castle dates from 1280 and Count Floris V. Its history recounts the damage it has suffered through the ages. It was at its zenith in the 17th century when Dutch historian P. C. Hooft restored it, living there until his death in 1647. It lost its splendour thereafter, especially during the French occupation. It was saved from demolition by King William 1, and restored between 1895 and 1909, as it was again in the last century. Guided tours available (English possible); last tour an hour before closing. The Tavern provides snacks, and it's quite pleasant to picnic at the tables in the castle grounds. The nearby fortress island of **Pampus** may be visited by boat, and offers special lunch and sailing arrangements, ☎ (029) 426 2326. www.pampus.nl

Hilversum
'The Media Town'

Getting there: A1 east from Amsterdam; A27 north from Utrecht.
Information: VVV, Noordse Bosje 1, ☎ (035) 623 7460; www.vvvhilversum.nl

The area to the east of Amsterdam is known as **Het Gooi**, or the 'Garden of Amsterdam.' As early as the 17th century, the wooded land along the river Vecht was attracting Amsterdam's wealthy. As you drive along it you will see an endless string of imposing residences built by rich merchants in the 17th-18th centuries. Most of these large houses are now used as offices and conference centres, but today's residents could also be either descendants of the old families, or new families – with larger than average incomes – that commute to work in Amsterdam or Utrecht.

Hilversum, the main town in this green region, is the country's major media centre where most Dutch television and radio shows are produced. Appropriately, the broadcasting institute, **Nederlands Instituut voor Beeld en Geluid** (Sound and Vision) is housed in a spectacular new glass building, opened in Dec. 2006, ☎ (035) 677 3434, http://portal. beeldengeluid.nl, Media Park, Sumatralaan 45, Mon.-Fri. 9am-noon and 1:30 -5pm. Archives of around 700,000 hours of television, radio, music and film make Sound and Vision one of the largest audio-visual archives in Europe, with old broadcast control rooms, a TV film set, and opportunities to see and hear Dutch broadcasts from the past.

Being relatively new, Hilversum has few buildings of historical interest. **St. Vituskerk**, Emmastraat 7, ☎ (035) 624 7415, open July-Aug., Wed. & Sat. 2-4pm, with its 98 meter tower, was designed by P.J.H. Cuypers. Hilversum is better known for its modern architecture. The **Raadhuis**, Dudokpark 1, the town hall built by architect W.M. Dudok (late 1920s), is considered one of the best examples of modern architecture in the country. Dudok was heavily influenced by the work of American architect Frank Lloyd Wright. It now serves as the **Goois Museum**, Kerkbrink 6, ☎ (035) 629 2826, open Tues.-Sun. 1-5pm, with a collection of objects on the history of the Gooi region.

In the neighbourhood of Hilversum

A very pleasant town, **Laren** has always attracted artists and writers. A mix of old estates and typical farmhouses, plus a small, tree-lined lake right in the heart, make this a popular place to visit – not to mention the fine (but high-scale) shopping for which people travel far and wide. William H. Singer, Jr. (1868-1943), a wealthy American steel magnate from Pittsburgh, PA, cum art collector and painter, chose to live here with his wife, Anna. Some of his romantic canvases and other pieces from their vast collection are in the **Singer Museum**, Oude Drift 1, ☎ (035) 539 3939, open Tues.-Sun., 11am-5pm, part of their former home. Housed here is also an excellent collection of Dutch and international 19th- and 20th-century painters, many of whom lived in the area. The museum has fine temporary exhibits and a sculpture garden, including works by Rodin. www.singerlaren.nl

Nearby **Huizen** is popular with beach and water lovers. Its **Huizer Museum Het Schoutenhuis**, Achterbaan 82, ☎ (035) 525 0223, www.huizermuseum.nl, open Tues.-Sat. 1:30-5pm, shows how people lived in this region in former days. The **Huizer Klederdrachtmuseum**, Havenstraat 81, ☎(035) 526 9080, open May-Oct., Tues.-Sat. 2-5pm; Nov.-Feb, Wed. and Sat. 1:30-4:30pm, shows how they dressed. And the **Bakkerij-museum**, Schippersstraat 5, ☎ (035) 525 0223, open May-Sept., Wed., Thurs. and Sat. 2-5pm, shows how their bakers and bakeries worked.

Chapter 3 | The province of South Holland

South Holland has long been one of the most influential provinces in the Netherlands – due in no small part to its location. Europe's most important commercial river is the Rhine, which in Holland becomes the Maas. It flows past Rotterdam into the North Sea, and contributes to making that city the world's foremost port. Historically, this vital transportation link has also fostered the development and prosperity of other towns along its banks – including Schiedam and Dordrecht, as well as Maassluis and Vlaardingen on its 'New Waterway' section to the coast.

In South Holland, Leiden, Delft and Gouda were among the most prosperous cities in the Dutch Golden Age of the 17th century. They are still among the most interesting and beautiful for visitors to see. The bulb fields near Leiden and the gardens of Keukenhof attract thousands of visitors every year. Delft, Gouda and Dordrecht are popular destinations for their historic canals, old streets and atmosphere, as well as their world-famous ceramics and cheese. The country's best display of windmills is here in South Holland at Kinderdijk. Its North Sea beaches, such as Scheveningen and Noordwijk, are among the country's best. In a league by itself is The Hague, the seat of Dutch government (although Amsterdam is officially the capital) and home of the Royal Family.

South Holland is the centre of the most heavily populated part of the country: an area including Amsterdam, The Hague, Rotterdam, and Utrecht, known as the 'Randstad,' where almost forty percent of the nation's population live, on approximately ten percent of the country's land.

Rotterdam
A dynamic modern city

Getting there: Major highways are A4 (Amsterdam), A13 (The Hague); A12, A20 (Utrecht); A16 (Breda).

Information: VVV, Coolsingel 67 ☎ (0900) 403 4065; www.rotterdam.info and www.rotterdam.nl

In the 18th century, **Rotterdam** had charm and elegance. It was a typical Dutch town with 17th-century gabled buildings along its tree-lined canals, and colourful street markets specialising in butter, cheese and fish. Majestic old windmills stood in the town centre and numerous bridges crossed its waterways. Few vestiges remain today, due to the bombing in 1940. As a result Rotterdam developed a character of its own, becoming a dynamic, exciting city fitting perfectly into today's modern world. It has wide streets with elegant modern architecture and large, covered pedestrian shopping areas, excellent concert and convention facilities and a wide choice of hotels and restaurants. If its fine museums, the Architecture Institute, KunstHal and outstanding zoo are not enough, then being the busiest port in the world surely must be. The humanist Erasmus, a native son, would have been proud of the dogged determination of its people to make the city what it is today.

Rotterdam faced its greatest test during that infamous May bombing of WW II. The port and city centre were obliterated and enveloped in thick black smoke for three days. Some of the hundreds of fires burned until August. There being no resources for such an overwhelming task, rebuilding seemed impossible. Nevertheless community leaders lost no time in making plans for reconstruction. With the war over, the city fathers gave priority to rebuilding the port in order to reactivate the economy. They gradually re-housed the population and then turned to more exciting modern architecture. If you want a taste of modern Europe, come to Rotterdam.

Located at the mouth of two of Europe's greatest rivers, the Rhine from Germany and the Meuse or 'Maas,' as the Dutch call it, from France, Rotterdam has excellent access to the North Sea and oceans beyond. Today, it is the largest port in the world, with much to offer on the cultural and entertainment scene.

As the whole city centre was rebuilt, architecture buffs can indulge themselves here with everything from pre-war and reconstruction, to state-of-the-art modern buildings (special VVV tours). The thoroughly modern city centre is like no other in the country. Its buzzing shopping centre developed from the country's – possibly even Europe's – first shopping mall. Visitors can enjoy its impressive structures, world-class museums, and well-preserved old harbours like Oude Haven and Delfshaven, dotted with outdoor cafés and restaurants. Take a harbour boat tour and enjoy its maritime flavour, or ride to the top of the Euromast to survey it all. Kop van Zuid, with its impressive buildings and pleasant waterside living space, is developing south of the river near Erasmus Bridge, offering us even more to explore. Information centre: Stieltjesstraat 21.

▶ **Boijmans-Van Beuningen Museum**
Location: Museumpark 18-20
Information: ☎ (010) 441 9400; www.boijmans.rotterdam.nl
Hours: Tues.-Sat. 10am-5pm, Sun. 11am-5pm

One reason the **Boijmans-Van Beuningen Museum** is considered to be one of the best in the country, is its rich collection of paintings by Old Masters. There are works by Peter Breughel: *Tower of Babel*; Hieronymus Bosch: *Prodigal Son*; Rembrandt: the portrait of his son, Titus; Rubens: the *Achilles* series; as well as those by Frans Hals, Van Eyck, Jan Steen, Teniers, and Van Goyen, among many others. One of the museum's earliest pieces, *Norfolk Triptych*, dates from about 1415.

This museum's important modern and contemporary collection has works by Impressionists including Monet, Van Gogh, and Degas; Surrealists Dali and Delvaux; and more contemporary artists like Ernst, Kandinsky and Appel. This is the only museum in the Netherlands which spans six centuries with its own collection.

Known as the Mecca for modern ceramics, the Boijmans also has an impressive collection of old Delftware, clocks, glass, silver, furniture and prints. It is also known for its Industrial Design section. To top it all off, you can restore yourself in its light and airy restaurant, looking out over an elegant sculpture garden.

• **Near the Boijmans-van Beuningen museum:** The **Chabot Museum**, Museumpark 11, ☎ (010) 436 3713, open Tues-Fri 11am-4:30pm, Sat 11am-5pm, Sun. noon-5pm, is devoted to the war paintings of Henry Chabot, a Rotterdam artist born in 1894; www.chabotmuseum.nl. Nearby is the **Nederlands Architectuur Instituut**, Museumpark 25, ☎ (010) 440 1200, www.nai.nl, with one of the world's largest architectural collections on display. **Natuurmuseum**, Westzeedijk 345, ☎ (010) 436 4222, www.nmr.nl, Tues.-Sat. 10am-5pm, Sun. 11am-5pm, has a collection of birds and mammals of Holland, as well as changing exhibitions of regional nature. **KunstHAL**, Westzeedijk 341, ☎ (010) 440 0300, www.kunsthal.nl, is a large art centre with some 25 changing exhibits each year.

▶ **Euromast**
A tower like no other
Location: Parkhaven 20
Information: ☎ (010) 436 4811; www.euromast.nl
Hours: Open daily all year round. April- September, 9:30am to 11pm;
              Oct-March, 10am-11pm; last ride 9:45pm; brasserie restaurant open
              until 11pm. Wheelchair accessible.

On a clear day, the **Euromast** offers a magnificent view in all directions. From it you can fully appreciate the tremendous scope and vitality of the active port, the city, and the park gardens below. The ride to the top is not to be missed, as you climb 605 feet (185 meters) in the space cabin and enjoy a real bird's eye view. If heights give you a thrill, you'll enjoy the **Space Adventure**, a super-fast elevator ride simulating a rocket take-off. For refreshments or a meal while taking in the scenery, try the Panorama Restaurant, a mere 300 feet (90 meters). Extensions are planned for trips to even dizzier heights in the future. For the extremely adventurous, try rappelling off the side or being suspended diagonally and aerially with ropes! www.abseilen.nl

- **Near the Euromast:** The area around the Euromast (Parkkade and Parkhaven) is pleasant for a stroll along the river or through the park. (For restaurants, see 'Eating Out'). You can also take The **Flying Dutchman** hydrofoil or the **Pancake Boat** (opposite the Euromast), touring the harbour or going through the busy river traffic and waterways to Dordrecht.

▶ **St. Laurenskerk**
Location: Grotekerkplein 3
Information: ☎ (010) 413 1494 or (010) 413 1989
Hours: Tues.-Sat. 10am-4pm; 11 April thru October. On Saturday 12:30 to 2pm and Sundays 1pm to 4pm, you can climb the tower, www.laurenskerkrotterdam.nl

St. Laurenskerk, the oldest building in Rotterdam, was built between 1449 and 1525. Destroyed by fire during the war, restoration began in 1952 and was only completed at the end of 1968. The church is very simple in its construction – its wooden roof typical of Dutch church buildings. (Stone vaulting would be too heavy for the soft soil.)

St. Laurenskerk's three organs are internationally famous for their unrivalled tone. The principal one is situated in the nave. In summers there are Thursday lunch concerts, while Friday evening concerts are held all year. (See the website for a complete schedule.)

Look for the marble tombs of the Dutch naval heroes who fought against the English from 1650-88, and for the wooden model of a 17th-century vessel located in one of the chapels. At the back of the church, you will find a cone-shaped canopy that is part of a monument to the victims of the Rotterdam bombardment. There are also video and photo exhibits of the devastation and reconstruction of the city.

- **Near St. Laurenskerk:** In front of the church stands the nation's oldest statue: the **Erasmus Statue** honouring Desiderius Erasmus (1469-1536), one of the most influential scholars and writers of his time, and a native of Rotterdam. His humanist philosophy urged basic rights for the common man at a time when this was considered heresy. It remains a controversial statue. An earlier version was thrown into a canal by invading Spaniards. Placed on the main square in 1622, this new statue became the subject of fierce debate. Despite the angry objection of the Calvinists to Erasmus' Catholic beliefs, the city kept the monument to its most famous native son. It survived the war – secretly buried in the North Holland dunes.

▶ **Oude Haven**

The **Oude Haven**, or Old Harbour, was Rotterdam's main shipping port as long ago as the 13th century. Today, the old waterways are still there, but the focus has changed as dozens of outdoor cafés and restaurants do business in this picturesque and lively setting. (Open air pop and jazz concerts in summer.)

Moored just a few feet away are historic vessels waiting for technical assistance or being restored, thanks to a foundation that operates out of the **Koningspoort** slipway. The foundation was established by lovers of old ships to keep the vessels from disappearing simply because their owners lacked funds for repairs. In so doing, the area developed as an open-air museum. The **Openlucht Binnenvaartmuseum**, Koningsdam 1, ☎ (010) 411 8867, provides berths for these inland sailing vessels. Enjoy a walk along the docks and take a look. www.buitenmuseum.nl. Rising nearly 150 feet, (45 meters), over the Oude Haven is the **Witte Huis** (White House). Constructed in 1898, it was the tallest building on mainland Europe until 1922. Remarkably, this 19th-century skyscraper withstood the bombing of 1940 when little else in the harbour did. Next door, the **Mariniersmuseum Der Koninklijke Marine**, Wijnhaven 7-9, ☎ (010) 412 9600, open Tues.-Sat. 10am-5pm, Sun. 11am-5pm, has displays on the Royal Navy, and a ship to visit. Continue along Wijnhaven to another floating museum: **Museum Schepen Uit Verre Landen**, Wijnhaven 20a, ☎ (010) 413 8351, open Tues.-Fri. 10am-4pm, Sat.-Sun. noon-5pm, a collection of 'ships from faraway lands,' including a whaler from the Azores, a gondola, and an actual craft used by Chinese and Vietnamese 'boat-people' to escape to freedom. If this has whet your appetite, keep walking. The **Maritiem Museum Prins Hendrik** is one of two more shipping museums just a short walk away. On the weekend, stop and enjoy **Kunst aan de Kade** at Wijnhaven 20, featuring modern art in a floating boat. www.kunst-aan-de-kade.nl

● **Near the Oude Haven:** Because this area was so devastated in the war, it became a challenging workplace for modern architects once the war ended. One striking example of their experimental styles is the **Kijk-Kubus**, Overblaak 70, ☎ (010) 414 2285, open daily 11am-5pm, Jan.-Feb., only Fri.-Sun. Designed by Piet Blom in 1984, these cube-shaped houses are perched on one corner, with windows angled downward to the street or upwards to the sky. If you are curious about this avant-garde architecture, one of the houses is open for visits. www.kubuswoning.nl. There are other examples of Rotterdam's post-war architecture nearby. **Blaak Station** (1995) dominates the large open square on which it sits looking as much like a flying saucer as it does a Metro station. Vying for attention on that same square is the **Bibliotheek** (Public Library), an equally impressive work of modern architecture. The city market is held close by, Tuesdays and Saturdays.

The **National Museum of Schools**, Nieuwe Markt 1a, ☎ (010) 404 5425, open Tues.-Sat. 10am-5pm, Sun. 1-5pm, has furnished classrooms from the time of Charlemagne to the present; videos and dioramas show how education has evolved. (Children's party arrangements possible.) Nearby is **De Ontdekhoek**, or Discovery Corner, Pannekoek-straat 55, ☎ (010) 414 3103, open Tues.-Sat. 10am-5pm, where children aged 4-14 can discover the technicalities of different trades, such as building dikes, laying bricks, frying chips, etc. Hands-on fun. www.ontdekhoek.nl.

To the east of the Oude Haven, along the Maas, is **Tropicana**, Maas Boulevard 100, ☎ (010) 402 0700, open Mon.-Fri. 10am-10pm, Sat.-Sun. 10am-8pm, a subtropical swimming and leisure paradise (29° C/84 °F all seasons). Built alongside the river, this glass structure encloses a decor of exotic tropical vegetation, pools and water chutes. You can swim, be swept along by turbulent rapids, or enjoy a tingling massage in hot whirlpools. There's a sauna, solarium, paddling pool for the little ones, cafés and terraces. www.tropicana.nl. The **Openbaar Vervoer Museum**, Oostplein 165, ☎ (010) 433 0762, open Sat.-Sun. 11am-5pm, has models, uniforms and displays on public transportation.

▶ **Maritime Museum Prins Hendrik**

Location:	Leuvehaven 1
Information:	☎ (010) 413 2680; www.mmph.nl
Hours:	Tues.-Sat. 10am-5pm, Sun. 11am-5pm (in July and august on Monday, 10am-5pm)

The **Maritime Museum** is located at the end of the Coolsingel where the city centre meets the Maas River, once the site of Rotterdam's first man-made harbour and historically, one of the city's busiest. The museum consists of displays dealing with ships, waterways, navigation and harbour activities past and present. There's an extensive collection of ship models – including one that is 13 feet (4 meters) long. If the little ones need more to keep them entertained, they can visit Professor Splash – a children's activity centre for 4-12 year olds, complete with chutes and conveyor belts for them to use in loading cargo, and a periscope they can look through to see the harbour basin close up.

Berthed outside is the restored turret ship 'Buffel,' an integral part of the museum. Built in 1868 in Scotland, this Dutch Royal Navy warship houses models, machines and other material to do with steam power and iron ship construction. It has been outfitted to explain Dutch naval history and to show how sailors lived in the second half of the 19th century.

● **Near the Maritime Museum:** Most visitors to the Maritime Museum and the 'Buffel' continue along the harbour toward a collection of historic sailing barges, tug boats, harbour cranes, etc. All part of the **Maritiem Buitenmuseum Leuvehaven**, Leuvehaven 50, ☎ (010) 404 8072, open Mon.-Fri. 10am-4pm, Sat.-Sun. noon-4pm. It is free of charge, and visitors can climb on board some ships. www.buitenmuseum.nl

On Churchillplein, look for Rotterdam's most dramatic statue: Russian sculptor Ossip Zadkine's **Monument for a Devastated City** (1953). A stark piece, its powerful message serves to remind us of the cruelty of war.

▶ **Rotterdam Zoo Blijdorp**
Location: Abraham van Stolkweg
Information: ☎ (010) 443 1495; www.rotterdamzoo.nl
Hours: Daily summer 9am-6pm, winter 9am-5pm

The Rotterdam zoo is one of the best. It houses approximately 2,234 animals and 532 species in environments as close as possible to their natural habitat. Thanks to the clever use of glass barriers rather than walls, you can get very close to observe the animals. The little ones will love the many baby animals, the Gorilla Island, and the latest project, Oceanium.

There's a good guidebook and map available, and an audio guide (the Zoophone) that will take you from one continent to another – in English. Feeding times are posted at the entrance to the zoo. Remember, a drowsy lion isn't nearly as exciting as one who is roaring eagerly for his imminent meal.

▶ **Het Schielandshuis – Historical Museum**
Location: Korte Hoogstraat 31, close to the Maritime Museum.
Information: ☎ (010) 217 6767; www.hmr.rotterdam.nl
Hours: Tues.-Fri. 10am-5pm, Sat.-Sun. 11am-5pm

The **Schielandshuis** is the only 17th-century building in the centre of Rotterdam that was spared in the bombing of May 1940. Completely restored, it is now a museum that gives a varied picture of Rotterdam's history, including its rich art period of the 17th and 18th centuries. The city's development and the daily life of its inhabitants are well-documented in an inviting, progressive way.

The top floor deals with clothing, textiles and toys from the 18th-20th centuries. The first floor covers city history in period paintings, models, glass artifacts, carvings and coins. A film shows the bombing of Rotterdam. There are style rooms with original furniture and decor of the 17th-19th centuries, and displays of porcelain, silver and curiosa. The ground floor has statues, tiles and fragments of buildings. The building also houses the Atlas Van Stolk collection of prints and drawings showing the history of the Netherlands. There is a museum shop and a charming restaurant with garden views.

• **Near Het Schielandshuis:** Two major buildings that survived the 1940 bombing are Coolsingel 40 and 42, the **Stadhuis** (City Hall) and the Post Office. The Stadhuis, built in 1920, has tours by reservation, ☎ (010) 417 2459. The Post Office, next to it, was built in 1923.

▶ **Wereldmuseum – World Arts Museum**

Location: Willemskade 25
Information: ☎ (010) 270 7172; www.wereldmuseum.nl
Hours: Tues.-Sun. 10am-5pm

This renovated museum, formerly the Museum of Ethnology, is beautifully located on the Maas – a visit can easily be combined with watching the ships, or a stroll along the quay. The exhibits represent, primarily, the folk art of primitive peoples and ancient cultures. In addition to contemporary art exhibits from the non-western world, there are photo exhibits and a permanent collection, including the instruments of an entire Indonesian orchestra. Children of all ages are fascinated by the masks and primitive carvings, etc., so even the young ones can find something of interest. In addition, film and live shows showing the cultures of other countries are held regularly. Visit their Wereldcafe where the food follows the themes of the exhibitions.

● **Near the WereldMuseum:** Completed in 1996, the **Erasmus Bridge** is one of modern Rotterdam's most famous landmarks. This elegant 800-meter (2600-foot) bridge crosses the Maas River in impressive fashion. Because of the angle of its 139-meter (455-foot) tower, it has been nicknamed the 'Swan.' Connected to that tower is a series of steel cables, spread apart fan-like as they extend gracefully to the ramps of the bridge. Just to the east is the smaller, complementary **Willems Bridge** (1981).

The **Belasting & Douane Museum**, Parklaan 14, ☎ (010) 440 0200, www.belasting-douanemus.nl, open Tues.-Sun. 11am-5pm, a museum about taxes, certainly falls into the category of 'unusual subjects' for museums. It has some attention-getting displays on smuggling, fraud and tax revolts. All are told with the help of paintings and artifacts, such as a 3,000-year-old statuette of a tax official found in the tomb of an Egyptian pharaoh – probably placed there to ensure the pharaoh's financial security in the afterlife.

▶ **Port of Rotterdam**

The **Port of Rotterdam** is a fascinating place to visit. About 30,000 ocean-going ships a year come and go from it, as well as over 130,000 inland vessels. There are 26 miles (42km) of loading, storage and industrial facilities along the docks, mainly involving containers. Oil, coal, chemicals, farm products and much more are carried here by ships from around the world. Rotterdam is Europe's most important port, and the busiest in the world.

There are two ways to see this huge shipping complex. One is by car. If you follow A15 west as it becomes N15, the road will continue past numerous oil refineries and other facilities along the banks of the port's channel, the Nieuwe Waterweg. The route ends at the North Sea, where you will see ships sailing into the port, and out to sea. You can obtain the ANWB map with English text from the VVV, and follow the Harbour Route with its distinctive road markers, or take a closer look from a tour boat in the centre of Rotterdam. If you want to know more about the port, it has its own website: www.portofrotterdam.com

▶ Also in Rotterdam

To the east of town in **Kralingen**, one of Rotterdam's more elegant residential areas, is the **Toy-Toy Museum**, Groene Wetering 41, ☎ (010) 452 5941, open Sat.-Tues. 11am-4pm, closed June-Aug., with such treasures as dolls created by famous French and German doll makers. Among many there is a life-size Jumeau doll and a number of character dolls, i.e., dolls with faces modelled on those of real children. There are all sorts of mechanical toys: planes, antique cars and doll houses depicting the lifestyles of many countries in the 1800s and 1900s.

Kralingen has pleasant woods for walks and rides (bike or horse), and a sizeable lake for water sports. There are animal reserves (deer, goats and feathered friends to feed), windmills (De Ster and De Lelie, both on Plaszoom), pancake houses, and plenty of play space for the tots. **Arboretum Trompenburg**, Honingerdijk 86, ☎ (010) 233 0166, open Mon.-Fri. 9am-5pm, Sat. 10am-4pm; Nov. thru March noon to 5pm, also open Sun. 10am-4pm, is a unique botanical garden laid out in 1820, noted for its oaks, beeches, and rhododendrons. www.trompenburg.nl

To the northwest is an old flourmill from 1712: **De Speelman**, Overschiese Kleiweg 775, ☎ (010) 467 7299, open Tues.-Sat. 10am-4pm, for visits and flour. To the north, **Plaswijk Park**, Ringdijk 20, ☎ (010) 418 1836, is open daily 9am-5pm. Set in a lovely lakeside location, this recreation park has animals, a traffic circuit for children, and boat trips. Special arrangements can be made for birthday parties, complete with ice cream and snacks.

To the south of the river is the **Oorlogsverzetsmuseum Rotterdam**, Veerlaan 82, ☎ (010) 484 8931, open Tues.-Fri. 10am-6pm, Sun. noon-4pm, a museum which tells the complete story of wartime Rotterdam – the bombing of the city, its resistance movement, and the Nazi collaborators. www.ovmrotterdam.nl

Football fans will want to visit the **Home of History**, Van Zandvlietplein 1, ☎ (010) 492 9444, open Wed.-Thurs. 1-5pm, Sat. 9am-5pm, for a look at the history of the Feyenoord football club. The 75-minute tours include the stadium, visits to the VIP stands, dressing rooms, players' tunnel and more.

Near Central Station is **Holland Casino Rotterdam**, Weena 624, ☎ (010) 206 8206, open daily 1:30pm-3am, dress code enforced. www.hollandcasino.nl. You must be at least 18 years of age to gamble, and you must conform with the dress code... no training/jogging suits and no white trainers/sneakers.

Markets

A change of pace from museum-viewing is a browse through Rotterdam's open-air market, Tues. & Sat., 9am-5pm, on the Binnenrotte near St. Laurens Church. Interesting items can often be found in the flea market section, May-Dec., also Sun. noon-5pm. Flea market on Schiedamsedijk on Sun.; stamp market on Grotekerkplein, Tues. & Sat. 10am-4pm.

Rotterdam's main shopping area is around the **Lijnbaan**; built on the ruins of WW II, it became Europe's first pedestrian shopping area in 1953. It's still popular, partly due to the numerous stores on the adjacent streets, and because, unlike most other towns, the shops are open until 9pm on Fri. and from noon-5pm on Sundays.

Eating out

The **Parkheuvel**, Heuvellaan 2, ☎ (010) 436 0766, is often cited as one of Holland's top restaurants. Also in the park are **Chalet Suisse**, Kievitslaan 31, ☎ (010) 436 5062, and the less expensive **Parkzicht**, Kievitslaan 25, ☎ (010) 436 8888, both with large summer terraces. You might enjoy the Chinese floating restaurant, **Ocean Paradise**, Parkhaven 21, ☎ (010) 436 1702, berthed across the street from the Euromast. More central, and for 100 years a unique favourite, **De Pijp**, Gaffelstraat 90, ☎ (010) 436 6896, is highly informal. In the Old Harbour, **De Tijdgeest**, Oost Wijnstraat 14, ☎ (010) 433 0619, serves good food in a young atmosphere. The new Kop van Zuid area is full of restaurants; among our favourites are **Zilt** (for fish), Cargadoorskade 107, ☎ (010) 290 9091; and **Pasta e Basta**, Vijf Werelddelen 1, ☎ (010) 290 8080. For the best pizza in Rotterdam, you must visit **Angelo Betti**, Schiekade 6a, Rotterdam Noord, ☎ (010) 465 8174, the 4th generation of Italian immigrants who started it in the 1920s as a gelataria; worth the wait, no reservations. **Brasserie Boompjes**, Boompjes 701, ☎ (010) 413 6070, has a fine view on the river. For Indonesian, an ethnic specialty in Holland, try **Raden Mas**, Kruiskade 72, ☎ (010) 411 7244; **Anak Mas**, Meent 72, ☎ (010) 414 8487, or **Dewi Sri**, Westerkade 20, ☎ (010) 436 0263. Many Chinese-Indonesian restaurants are less expensive, but pancake restaurants are even more informal. Try **Boshut de Big**, Kralingseweg 20, ☎ (010) 452 6874, in the woods, or take a cruise on the **Pannenkoekenboot**, Parkhaven, across from the Euromast, ☎ (010) 436 7295, with an all-you-can-eat pancake buffet on board. In Kralingen, **In den Rustwat**, Honingerdijk 96, ☎ (010) 413 4110, serves good food in the elegant atmosphere of an old inn.

Staying over

Most pleasant of Rotterdam's central hotels are perhaps its most recent, the imposing **Westin**, on Weena 686, (010) 430 2000; the **Hilton**, Weena 10, ☎ (010) 710 8000; and the **Bilderberg Park Hotel**, Westersingel 7, ☎ (010) 436 3611, with its pleasant garden and restaurant. Moderately-priced choices include the **Tulip Inn Rotterdam**, Willemsplein 1, ☎ (010) 413 4790; **Hotel Wilgenhof**, Heemraadssingel 92, ☎ (010) 425 4892; and revamped **Hotel New York**, on the river at Koninginnehoofd 1, ☎ (010) 439 0500, originally (1901) headquarters of the Holland America Shipping Line. Rotterdam has a fine youth hostel, **City Hostel Rotterdam**, Rochussenstraat 107, ☎ (010) 436 5763.

Yearly events

Rotterdam's yearly events start in January with the **International Film Festival**; Feb.-March the **ABN-AMRO World Tennis Tournament** at the Ahoy Hall; mid-April the

Generale Bank Marathon; in June poetry lovers from around the world converge for Poetry International; in July the Zomercarnaval Straatparade is a lively event with colourful floats and carnival parades through the city; and in Sept. the World Harbour Festival opens up the harbour with visits on-board ships, fireworks and more. The world famous North Sea Jazz Festival, formerly in The Hague, now takes place in Rotterdam. www.northseajazz.nl

Tours

The best way to see the Port of Rotterdam is on a tour boat. Spido Harbourtrips, Leuvehoofd 5, ☎ (010) 275 9988, offers daily trips year-round. (From June-Sept. every 45 minutes from 9:30am-5pm; other trips in July-Aug., including a trip to Dordrecht which passes the windmills of Kinderdijk, and a day trip to the Delta Works in Zeeland.) www.spido.nl, www.kinderdijk.nl and www.deltawerken.com. If you like a little more zip in your trip, the Flying Dutchman, Parkhaven opposite the Euromast, ☎ (010) 426 1222, takes you through the port or as far as Dordrecht on a high-speed hydrofoil. It operates from April-Oct.; call for schedule. Other tours on boats include De Croosboot, Crooswijksestraat 126, ☎ (010) 414 9751, which offers rides to Delfshaven as well as to the Rottemeren recreational lake area; and Waterbus, Leuvehaven, ☎ (010) 404 8072, which includes the Oude Haven and the city's inland waterways.

You can also see the city on a walking tour with Gilde Rotterdam, Westersingel 23, ☎ (010) 436 2844, conducted by city natives who still remember the early post-war days. There are also Architectural Excursions and Industrial Tourism visits organised for groups by the VVV, ☎ (010) 402 3234.

▶ Delfshaven

Delfshaven is a must for any visitor to Rotterdam. Formerly independent, but a part of Rotterdam since 1886, it has a fine historic church, warehouse museum, the Zakkendragershuis (formerly headquarters for the longshoremen's union), antique and craft shops and galleries, all in a picturesque setting. It is located west from the Euromast on the Westzeedijk.

Delfshaven was originally the port of the city of Delft. At that time (1340) Delft was an important city while Rotterdam was just a village. Rotterdam was looking for ways to expand, however, and planned to dig a canal from the Maas to Delft, to share in Delft's prosperity. Understandably, the merchants of Delft were not keen to let this happen. But Rotterdam obtained permission to construct its own canal, the Delfshavense Schie, which was completed in 1404.

A town grew up at the point where this new canal ran into the Maas and it became Delfshaven. Thwarted by misfortune, it has been destroyed in several wars, damaged in a fire in 1536, and much maligned by Delft, jealous that it might take away precious trade. In fact, it finally did pass laws ensuring Delfshaven would not prosper at the expense of the parent city. Despite these obstacles Delfshaven grew as a home port for herring boats, whaling fleets, and later for distilleries. In the 16th century, the East India Company also established its dock and warehouses here.

By 1792, however, Delfshaven had slumped into a deep decline. The herring industry and distilleries were in severe recession, and a sandbar in the harbour forced some shippers to abandon the port in favour of Rotterdam. Its fate was sealed with the arrival of Napoleon's armies, which closed down the East India Company and many of the distilleries. All of Holland suffered from the French occupation, but Delfshaven never recovered.

Although it had gained independence from Delft in 1811, economic problems led Delfshaven to request incorporation into Rotterdam in 1841. The city refused, but as Delfshaven became more of an eyesore and health hazard on the edge of their prosperous city, Rotterdam authorities agreed to annex it in 1886.

Delfshaven has a particular significance to Americans as this was the port from which the Pilgrims sailed for the New World in July 1620.

▶ **Historical Museum De Dubbelde Palmboom**
Location: Voorhaven 12
Information: ☎ (010) 476 1533; www.dedubbeldepalmboom.nl
Hours: Tues.-Fri. 10-5pm, Sat.-Sun. 11am-5pm

This beautifully renovated 19th-century warehouse deals mainly with the development of Rotterdam as a world port and with the history of Delfshaven. There are archeological finds that illustrate how this area relied on the trading of goods as far back as 2500 BC; plus displays on Piet Heyn, one of the greatest Dutch naval heroes. There are reconstructed stores and living quarters that show what life was like in the Netherlands in the early 20th century.

▶ **Zakkendragershuisje – Porters' Guild House**
Location: Voorstraat 13-15
Information: ☎ (010) 477 2664
Hours: Tues.-Sat. 10am-5pm, Sun. 1pm-5pm

The **Zakkendragershuisje** was built in 1653. It belonged to the Sack Carriers' Guild (similar to dockers or longshoremen of today). They would gather in front of this guild house when the bells above it were rung, indicating a ship needed to be loaded or unloaded. Inside the house, an old tin pot holding dice was kept in a niche at the bottom left-hand side of the stairs. A throw of the dice decided who would work.

A pewterer works here daily, casting pewter items from original 18th-century moulds belonging to the Rotterdam Historical Museum. Demonstrations are held on Sunday afternoons throughout the year at 2, 3 and 4pm, or by request. The items are exceptionally accurate copies and may be purchased as gifts or as a souvenir of your visit.

▶ **Also in Delfshaven**

At the end of the Voorhaven towards the Maas is a windmill that once processed grain for some of the 34 distilleries around Rotterdam in the Golden Era. **De Distilleerketel**, Voorhaven 210, ☎ (010) 477 9181, open Sat. 10am-4pm, was built in 1727. It has had a dramatic past, having burned and been restored three times. During WW II, the Dutch Marines set fire to it, suspecting it to be a hideout for collaborators. You can see grain being ground there, and buy freshly ground flour in their shop. The former Delfshaven Town Hall was restored and is now converted into the **Stadsbrouwerij de Pelgrim**, Aelbrechtskolk 12, ☎ (010) 477 1189, a small brewery using traditional methods. Meals are served and the beer can be sampled. The bricks and ceiling beams were part of the original building.

According to legend, the night before their journey began the Pilgrims who sailed to America in 1620 stayed in a barn next to the **Pilgrim Fathers' Church**, Aelbrechtskolk 20, ☎ (010) 477 4156, open Sat. 1-4pm. They were known as Separatists – persecuted in England for their religious beliefs that were not those of the official church. They fled to Holland in 1608, settled in Amsterdam, and moved to Leiden a year later. After eleven years, they decided to move on again before becoming completely absorbed into the Dutch way of life. They came to Delfshaven to board the Speedwell, the ship they hoped would take them to the New World. After worshiping in the church, they departed for England to join up with fellow Separatists on a second ship. Shortly after setting sail for America, the Speedwell proved not to be seaworthy enough to cross the ocean. It returned to England, where the entire group crowded onto the Mayflower for the 65-day journey. The church has been restored and is most beautiful during candlelit evening services.

Behind the Old Church on Piet Heyn Plein is a statue of Piet Heyn. Born in Delfshaven in 1577, he became the world-famous Lord Admiral of the Dutch Fleet. Another famous native son was the artist Kees van Dongen.

Eating out

Over the bridge, the old **Henkes Gin Distillery**, Voorhaven 17, ☎ (010) 425 5596, has been converted into a brasserie, its terrace looking over the old sailing boats. You can also dine in a renovated warehouse, **Miller's**, Voorhaven 3, ☎ (010) 477 5181. At the Kop van Delfshaven are some interesting bruin (brown) cafés, the most authentic being **De Oude Sluis**, Havenstraat 7, ☎ (010) 477 3068, and the **Ooievaar** (Stork) next door.

the only website in English for expats and the international community in The Hague!

local, national and community news
arts & entertainment features five days a week, plus...

weekly e-newsletters keep you informed
THOL Social Club keeps you connected

TheHagueOnLine.com

Schiedam
A 'spirited town'

Getting there:	From The Hague and Amsterdam, A4 south to the edge of Rotterdam, then west on A20, exit Schiedam. www.waterweg-westland.nl, www.ontdekschiedam.nl
Information:	VVV, Buitenhavenweg 9, ☎ (010) 473 3000; www.vvvschiedam.nl

The historic old town of **Schiedam** lies just to the west of Rotterdam. It received its municipal rights in 1275 and owes its origins to a dam built on this spot in 1260. A town developed, with the 'Schie' at the centre of its activities until 1850, when it flooded, bursting the old ramparts and moats.

About three centuries ago the city developed into a *jenever*-making centre. *Jenever* (Dutch gin) has always been the nation's most popular 'tipple.' It is made by distilling malt-wine with juniper berries and other herbs and flavouring spices. The drink's popularity spread beyond the Netherlands, and by 1880 it brought prosperity to the 400 or so distilleries in Schiedam.

Over the years, the industry has declined as other alcoholic drinks have become popular. Today, there are only a few distilleries left, but the elements of the industry remain Schiedam's main attraction for visitors: the Dutch Distilleries Museum, and five remaining windmills which ground the grain used for the drink. From its days of prosperity there are also attractive 18th-19th-century buildings in the Baroque inner town.

▶ **Dutch Distilleries Museum – De Gekroonde Brandersketel**

Location:	Lange Haven 74-76
Information:	☎ (010) 426 1291; www.hetgedistilleerdmuseum.nl
Hours:	Tues.-Sat. 12am-5pm, Sun. 1-6pm

You can learn all about Dutch *jenever* and try a free sample of the national drink at the **Dutch Distilleries Museum**. In the museum's small working distillery you will be shown how the liquid is processed, and stored in underground vats. The museum's exclusive *jenever* is made in the traditional way – by distilling malt wine and 40% alcohol. (Most of today's *jenever* is 35% proof.) You can also see the museum's collection of 12,000 miniature bottles of alcohol from around the world, and smell some of the essences that are added to liqueurs and *jenevers*.

● **Near the Dutch Distilleries museum:** A few doors down is the **Nationaal Cooperatie Museum**, Lange Haven 84, ☎ (010) 427 0920, open Thurs. 1:30-5pm & 7-9pm, Fri. 1:30-5pm, Sat. 11am-5pm. It's a typical 1920s corner grocery, as well as being a grocery store museum. Next-door is the **Appelmarktbrug** (Apple Market Bridge), one of three picturesque cast-iron bridges in Schiedam, which is still raised manually by the bridge-masters.

Close by is the **Stedelijk Museum** (Town Museum), Hoogstraat 112, ☎ (010) 246 3666, open Tues.-Sat. 11am-5pm, Sun. 12:30-5pm. The building was constructed in the 18th century as a home for the elderly; it later became a hospital with a church separating the men and women's wards. Contents of the museum include town antiquities, archaeological discoveries and modern art.

The harbour has been restored and a stroll along the **Maasesplanade** waterway gives you a good view of the activity on the river Maas.

▶ **Netherlands Working Flourmill Museum – De Nieuwe Palmboom**
Location: Noordvest 34
Information: ☎ (010) 426 7675; www.schiedamsemolens.nl
Hours: Tues.-Sat. 11am-5pm, Sun. 12:30-5pm

Of its original 24 gigantic mills, Schiedam now has five: De Noord (The North), 1803; De Drie Koornbloemen (The Three Cornflowers), 1770; De Walvisch (The Whale), 1794; De Vrijheid (The Liberty), 1785; and **De Nieuwe Palmboom** (The New Palmtree), 1791 – the world's tallest. Only the Nieuwe Palmboom and De Noordmolen are open to visitors.

De Nieuwe Palmboom, the latest to be restored, is also the **Netherlands Working Flourmill Museum.** If you want to see inside a windmill, this is a good example. Eight stories high, a tour to the top will take you through a number of displays explaining how windmills have been used over the years. They still grind grain here, which is used in a local distillery to make *jenever*, and by local bakers. Call in advance to see if they're working on the day you plan to visit. Even if they're not, the sails of the windmill may be turning and you can get a close-up view of them from the outdoor platform on the 5th floor. It also offers a good view of the town's other windmills. (Note that since the steps to the upper floors are very steep, you should come down backwards.)

• Near the Nieuwe Palmboom: **De Noordmolen**, Noordvest 38, ☎ (010) 426 3104, is the only other windmill open to the public... but you have to eat there. It's been a bar and restaurant since 1973, and is open for lunch and dinner during the week; dinner only on Saturdays.

The **Korenbeurs** (Corn Exchange) is where the grain for distilleries was formerly traded. Look for the **Zakkendragershuisje** (Porters' Guild House) of 1275. The porters were warehousemen who carried bags of grain from the ships to the warehouse for the munificent sum of € 4.50 (approx. $6) per week. As soon as a ship arrived, the tower bell was rung and all the porters who lived in the distillers' quarter congregated at their guildhall for work.

▶ **Also in Schiedam**
The **Grote Kerk** (also known as St. John's Church), Lange Kerkstraat 37, ☎ (010) 426 6241, has a unique baptistry screen from 1642, magnificent windows, and Venetian glass chandeliers; and its walls are covered with gold-tooled leather.

The **Town Hall**, on Grote Markt, is not open to the public. It was originally made of wood but was partly destroyed by fire in 1604. The facade is typical Dutch Renaissance style from about 1782. The courtyard of the 18th-century **Almshouse** on Proveniersplein is open to the public. Originally a leper-house, this building with a white rococo facade later became a home for the elderly.

Eating out

Highly recommended is **Bistro Hosman Frères**, Korte Dam 8, ☎ (010) 426 4096, with its half block of red awnings, and fine French cuisine and wines! Also recommended: **La Duchesse**, Maasboulevard 7, ☎ (010) 426 4625; **Le Pecheur**, Nieuwe Haven 97, ☎ (010) 473 3341; **De Mouterij**, Noordvest 61, ☎ (010) 473 0962; or **Noordmolen** above.

Vlaardingen
From herring port to containers

Getting there: A20 from Rotterdam towards Hook of Holland. From The Hague, A13 south then A20 west. From Amsterdam, A4 south towards Rotterdam and A20 west. There are many charming back roads.

Information: VVV, Westhavenkade 39, ☎ (0900) 192 192; www.vvv-vlaardingen.nl

Vlaardingen received its city charter from Count Floris V in 1273, but people have lived here much longer. Excavations unearthed pottery and other finds which indicate this was the site of a settlement about 2500 BC, where residents sought their livelihood primarily by fishing and hunting. Eventually, like so many other Dutch towns along the Maas, Vlaardingen became a centre for trade and fishing – in fact the biggest Dutch port for herring fishing in the 18th century. Digging the New Waterway led to the creation of new harbours and docks, which transformed Vlaardingen into a commercial port. Today, over 2,500 ocean-going ships and more than 20,000 inland navigation ships call at this harbour every year. Vlaardingen is third among Dutch ports, surpassed only by Rotterdam and Amsterdam. Take a river trip along the New Waterway to see for yourself.

This town is truly a mixture of the old and the new. It's surprising when you finally happen upon the old town centre, hidden behind winding streets and the modern facades of 'new' Vlaardingen. Suddenly, you could be in the 17th century. Don't miss the historic old port of Vlaardingen, the **Ton Stolk Music Museum**, Westhavenkade 45, ☎ (010) 434 7240, and the **Jan Anderson Regional Museum**, Kethelweg 50, ☎ (010) 434 3843.

▶ **Visserijmuseum (Fishing Museum) Vlaardingen**
Location: Westhavenkade 53-54
Information: ☎ (010) 434 8722; www.visserij-museum.nl
Hours: Tues.-Fri. 10am-5pm, Sat.-Sun. noon-5pm

The small pool of fish at the entry of this **Fishing Museum** is so fascinating it is tempting to spend the whole time trying to locate a big eel, crayfish, or whatever is hiding in the sand or under the rocks. But don't stop there. The unique videos and dioramas are well done and give a clear idea of the many techniques used in commercial fishing. You'll see that the method of catching shellfish is quite different from that used for eel, cod, halibut or sole. In the 'ships' hall,' the development of Dutch fishing boats from earliest times to the complicated electronic navigational and fishing equipment of today can be seen. The exhibit also includes costumes and jewellery from fishermen's families throughout the ages. It has 18th-century model rooms, and a small studio upstairs where films about fishing are shown.

▸ **Also in Vlaardingen**

The **Grote Kerk** (1582) is a restored church originally of late Romanesque style. Its tower (1745) houses the well-known Oranje Chime. It has a copper lectern (1778), guild plates, stained-glass windows, and a famous organ (1763). There are free lunch concerts in summer, Thurs. 12:45-1:15pm. Many old buildings line the small street around the marketplace, giving you a glimpse of Vlaardingen's historical past. Across the street from the marketplace is the **Town Hall** (1650), a blend of traditional and modern architectural styles that exemplify the history of this old town.

Eating out

'**t Scheele Hoeke**, Markt 21, ☎ (010) 434 8570, is recommended for French cuisine. **Delta Hotel**, Maasboulevard 15, ☎ (010) 434 5477, sitting practically in the Maas – part of it built on piles – has a restaurant with a splendid view of passing river traffic. If wine interests you, visit **Holland Natuurwijnen**, Zuidbuurt 40, ☎ (010) 460 3120, for tasting delicious fruit wines, dining, and even enjoying the occasional musical evening.

Delft
The town of blue and white porcelain

Getting there: From Rotterdam, A13 northwest. Charming small roads lead to Delft, especially the Rotterdamserweg along the canal. From The Hague, A13 south; from Amsterdam, A4.

Information: Tourist Information Point, Hippolytusbuurt 4, ☎ (015) 215 4051; www.delft.com

To those outside the Netherlands, **Delft** is known as the home of blue and white glazed pottery called 'Delftware.' To the Dutch, it is also known as the city of their royalty. Both are reasons why this is one of the nation's top tourist destinations, but even without these claims to fame, Delft would remain a popular town, simply because it is very picturesque.

Founded in 1075, Delft is more much more intimate than Amsterdam. Its splendid Gothic and Renaissance houses lining tree-shaded canals easily transport one to another period in time. A number of famous native sons include the painter Vermeer (celebrated by a brand-new Vermeer Centre), www.vermeerdelft.nl, and the famous lawyer and scholar, Hugo de Groot. It is also the last resting place of William of Orange, also known as William the Silent. He made Delft his home in his fight against Spanish rule, and it was here he was assassinated and buried. Over 40 of his descendents of the Royal House of Orange-Nassau are also buried here.

The best ways to see Delft are to take a horse-drawn tram, a canal tour or to walk away from the hubbub of the busy Market Square into the narrow, primarily residential streets with elegant historic buildings along the canals. The VVV's guided walking tour pamphlet will help you spot places of note, but don't let too many facts interrupt the pleasure of personal discovery.

▶ Delftware

As early as the 1300s, Delft was a prosperous town, thanks in part to its breweries – nearly 200 of them – that used water from its many canals to make their beer. As the town grew, however, the beer industry declined – not only because of growing competition, but also because the canal water was becoming increasingly dirty. In the 17th century, while the breweries were having to close, the Dutch East India Company traders were beginning to import blue and white porcelain from China. Demand for it grew quickly – so quickly in fact that Delft craftsmen began making it themselves, imitating the designs. They took over the vacant brewery buildings, until some 30 factories were producing what is still internationally known and admired as Delftware.

Today, there are many original Dutch motifs to choose from, in black, multi-coloured, or traditional blue and white. Plates can be ordered for special gifts such as weddings or births, with dates of the event, etc. Three potteries are open to visitors, still creating Delftware the original hand-painted way:

De Porceleyne Fles (The Royal Delftware Factory), Rotterdamseweg 196, ☎ (015) 251 2030, www.royaldelft.com, open 27 March-31 Oct., Mon.-Sun. 9am-5pm, 1 Nov.-26 March, Mon.-Sat. 9am-5pm, was established in 1653 and is the best-known maker of Delftware both for quality and price. Entrance includes demonstrations of pottery-turning on the wheel, hand-decorating, the factory and ovens, a video show, and a small museum of Delftware – and, of course, a shop full of porcelain! Located at the southern end of town.

De Delftse Pauw, Delftweg 133, ☎ (015) 212 4920, www.delftsepauw.com, 1 April-31-Oct., daily 9am-4:30pm; 1 Nov.-31 March, Mon.-Fri. 9am-4:30pm, Sat.-Sun. 11am-1pm. Artists at work; guided tours free of charge; shop prices moderate.

Atelier de Candelaer, Kerkstraat 14, ☎ (015) 213 1848, open mid-March-mid-Oct., daily 9am-6pm; Nov.-March, Mon.-Sat. 9am-5pm, is a small, family shop just off the main market square, with artists at work and moderate prices.

▶ **Nieuwe Kerk**
Location:	Markt 80
Information:	☎ (015) 212 3025; www.nieuwekerk-delft.nl
Hours:	April-Oct., Mon.-Sat. 9am-6pm; Nov.-Mar., Mon.-Fri. 11am-4pm, Sat. 11am-5pm

The main attraction in the **New Church**, the black and white marble sarcophagus of William the Silent surrounded by allegorical statues representing Fame, Valour, Religion, Justice and Liberty, is most impressive. His little dog that died, having refused to eat after his master's death, adds a poignant note. William, who led the fight against Spanish rule in the 16th century, is one of the most revered figures in Dutch history. It was he who established the House of Orange-Nassau as the governing family, and now, more than 400 years later, they still occupy the royal throne. More than 40 of its members are buried in the vaults beneath the church. (Not accessible to the public.) There are exhibits relating to the House of Orange and to the history of the church, the oldest part of which dates from 1300. Be sure to climb the tower. The view of Delft from 110 meters (360 feet) is marvellous. On good days you can also see The Hague and Rotterdam,

● **Near the Nieuwe Kerk:** One of the main attractions in Delft is its picturesque **Markt** (Market Square). In summer on non-market days, the cafés and restaurants extend their seating into the square – a perfect place to listen to the carillon of the Nieuwe Kerk. In the centre is a statue of Hugo Grotius (1583-1645), a native of Delft who was a scholar and political leader. Other places of note include the early 17th-century **Town Hall**, Markt 87. Its tower was built in the 13th century as part of a prison that stood on this site. The **Waag** (Weigh House), Markt 11, is behind the Town Hall and is now used as a small theatre. The **Boterhuis** (Butterhouse) is adjacent to the back of the Town Hall and dates from 1765. The **Vleeshal**, Voldersgracht 1, former meat market, is on the same small street. It is now a student society. Opposite is the **Fish Market**, plying its trade as it has, on the same spot for centuries.

▶ **Het Prinsenhof**
Location:	Sint Agathaplein 1
Information:	☎ (015) 260 2358; 'Combi-tickets' are available for Prinsenhof, Nusantra and Lambert van Meerten museums. www.prinsenhof-delft.nl
Hours:	Tues.-Sat. 10am-5pm, Sun. 1-5pm

The Prinsenhof is the site of the most famous assassination in Dutch history. It was originally a convent, built in the late 14th century. But from 1572 until 1584 this beautiful building was the residence of William the Silent, who led the Dutch revolt against Spanish rule. On July 10, 1584, William left the dining hall to climb the staircase leading to his study when he was shot three times and killed. The assassin was a devout Catholic who saw the revolt as a threat to his religion. Today you can still see the evidence of his assassination – two bullet holes near the foot of the staircase where he fell. They now appear oversized, because generations of tourists couldn't resist the temptation to poke them. As a result, they are now covered by a small plate of glass.

Beside the historic importance of the building, the museum also exhibits objects dealing with the history of Delft and the Eighty Years' War: paintings, tapestries, beautiful antique silver and Delftware. Included in the 'Prince's Court' is the Orange-Nassau Museum, with portraits of the Royal Family from William the Silent to the present day. The grounds retain some of the tranquility of days gone by when this was a convent.

- **Near Het Prinsenhof:** The small ethnographic museum **Nusantara**, Sint Agathaplein 4, ☎ (015) 260 2358, open Tues.-Sat. 10am-5pm, Sun. 1-5pm, is just across the square from Het Prinsenhof. There is a fine display of Indonesian culture, arts and crafts, textiles, musical instruments, masks, etc. www.gemeentemusea-delft.nl

▶ **Oude Kerk**

Location:	Heilige Geestkerkhof 25
Information:	☎ (015) 212 3015; www.oudekerk-delft.nl

You know a town is old when its Nieuwe Kerk (New Church) was built in the late 1300s. By the time the Nieuwe Kerk was built, there had been a church on the site of the **Oude Kerk** (Old Church) for about three centuries. The present structure dates from 1246. One of the first things you may notice is that its tower leans about six feet. Experts say the problem may be due to the church being built on a filled-in waterway.

The pulpit is considered one of the most beautiful in the country. Carved in 1548, it was about the only religious object in the church to escape the vandalism of 1566 when the iconoclasts tried to destroy every symbol of the Catholic faith. Surprisingly, the stained-glass windows are modern, made by a master in this field, Joep Nicolas, between 1955 and 1972. Before they were installed, the church had been without stained-glass windows since 1654, when a gunpowder explosion blew them out.

Several famous people are buried here and the church is known for some of the elaborate mausoleums which mark their places of rest, the most impressive of which honour Dutch admirals and naval heroes Piet Heyn (1577-1629) and Maarten Tromp (1598-1653). By contrast, there is only a plaque to honour one of the great Dutch artists, Jan Vermeer (1632-75). He died in poverty, and although he is presumed to be buried here, no one knows precisely where. Scientist Anthony van Leeuwenhoek (1632-1725), known for his pioneering work with microscopes, also rests here.

- **Near the Oude Kerk:** Across the street is **Delfland Gemeenlandhuis**, Oude Delft 167. It has a magnificently decorated facade with sculptures and coats of arms. It was built as a mansion in the 16th century, but now houses the offices of the agency responsible for the dikes in the Delft region.

▶ **The Vermeer Centre**
Location: Voldersgracht 21
Information: ☎ (015) 213 8588; www.vermeerdelft.nl
Hours: Mon.-Sat. 10am-6pm (Nov.-March 5pm), Sun. 10am-5pm

The 'Master of light', Johannes Vermeer, native son of Delft, is paid due homage in the brand-new Vermeer Centre that takes you on a voyage through his life and work. The Centre is housed in the former St. Lucas Guild where Vermeer was Dean of the Painters for many years. His home was situated opposite.

▶ **Museum Lambert van Meerten**
Location: Oude Delft 199
Information: ☎ (015) 260 2358; www.lambertvanmeerten-delft.nl
Hours: Tues.-Sat. 10am-5pm., Sun. 1-5pm

In addition to being a showcase for an extensive display of tiles and other Delftware, this building (1893) provides an enchanting mixture of the neo-Renaissance style and older architectural fragments, among which are splendidly carved windows from 1537. Once the home of a wealthy Delft industrialist, after whom the museum is named, its spacious rooms serve as a backdrop for the many art treasures on display. Especially noteworthy are early tiles from Delft, Italy and Spain. If you're particularly fond of Delftware, this is a good place to visit.

▶ **Leger Museum – Army Museum**
Location: Korte Geer 1
Information: ☎ (015) 215 0500; www.legermuseum.nl
Hours: Mon.-Fri. 10am-5pm, Sat.-Sun. noon-5pm

There's probably no better place for an army museum than a former arsenal. The **Royal Netherlands Army and Arms Museum** is located in a 17th-century arsenal built by the Dutch during the 80 Years War against Spain. There is plenty of space to display tanks, cannons, a large variety of guns, suits of armour, swords, shields, pikes and other weapons from past centuries.

Those who aren't particularly interested in weaponry might enjoy seeing the changing face of military fashion. There are hundreds of life-size models wearing what soldiers wore over the years, from 17th-century suits of armour and the ornate uniforms of the 19th century, to today's simple khaki. Displays also explain changes in the tactics of warfare, especially the revolutionary methods developed by the Dutch Prince Maurits that helped win the war against Spain. There are a number of paintings of military men and battles, plus medals, flags, and an assortment of other material used in warfare.

- **Near the Leger Museum:** Near the station is **Reptielenzoo Serpo**, Stationsplein 8, ☎ (015) 212 2184, www.serpo.nl, open daily 10am-6pm, a reptile zoo brimming with snakes, lizards and their reptilian cousins.

Opposite the Leger Museum entrance is a street called **Koornmarkt**, ideal for photographing some typical canal houses. Note the attractive step-gabled houses at Koornmarkt 81 and 36, and the 19th-century **Synagogue** at Koornmarkt 12.

Museum Paul Tetar van Elven, Koornmarkt 67, ☎ (015) 212 4206, open mid April-late Oct., Tue.-Sat. 1-5pm, is in an 18th-century canal mansion. It was named after its owner, a teacher of art who was an accomplished copier of master paintings. You'll see many familiar paintings as well as some of his original works. The house is kept as it was at his death in 1896, giving visitors an idea of how perhaps the only wealthy Dutch artist of that era lived.

▶ Also in Delft

The picturesque **Oostpoort** (East Gate), on Oosteinde, is the only remaining gate of the eight built around the city in 1400. Three almshouses remain: **Klaeuw's Hofje** (1605), Oranje Plantage 58-77, with its regency room and 17th-century paintings; **Hofje van Pauw** (1707), Paardenmarkt 54-62, which housed needy married couples; and **Hofje van Gratie** (1575), Van der Mastenstraat 26-38, for 'god-fearing spinsters.'

Markets

The General Market on the Markt Square and the Flower Market along the canal by Hippolytusbuurt take place every Thursday. Fruit, vegetable and flower markets at Brabantse Turfmarkt and Burgwal are held on Sat., and an art/flea market on the Heilige Geestkerkhof, Sat., mid April-mid Sept.

Eating out

Delft has a wide choice of places to eat along the canals, on the square, or near its museums. **Stads-Koffyhuis**, Oude Delft 133, ☎ (015) 212 4625, a bakery since 1881, serves 12-inch-wide pancakes with a wide selection of fillings. Try homemade Dutch apple pie with coffee at **Kobus Kuch**, Beestenmarkt l. **Cafe de Vlaanderen**, in the Beestenmarkt area, has a garden and serves quality food, also Sunday brunch buffets. **De Kurk** on Kroonsrraat also offers a good value menu.

For a different night out, there's a medieval inn where dinner is served by wenches in costume. Entertainment and food is in the style of the times, i.e. you can eat your chicken with your fingers, **Stadsherberg de Mol**, Molslaan 104, ☎ (015) 212 1343 ... three hours of eating and carousing. Closed Mondays.

Tours

From Apr.-Oct., **Rondvaart Delft**, ☎ (015) 212 6385, has canal cruises that depart from Koornmarkt (corner Wijnhaven), daily 9:30am-6pm, every 45 minutes. www.rondvaart-delft.nl. They also rent out canal bikes. To see the inner city, you can rent a canoe from **Kano Delft**, ☎ (015) 257 1504. Delft is not only a great town to cycle round, but also a departure point for scenic bike tours. ANWB Delfland and Westland Routes are marked, and maps are available from the VVV. During the summer, **Horse-drawn Carriage Tours** depart from the Market Square, ☎ (015) 256 1828 ...no set times, but a schedule is posted at the departure point.

In the neighbourhood of Delft

't Woudt, 3 km (2 mi) west of Delft, is a charming village whose church, pastoral build-ings, farms and labourers' cottages are just as they were centuries ago. **Maasland** is an historic town divided in two by a canal, its centre and 15th-century church are restored. Visit the **Schilpen Museum**, a grain chandlers' shop with period rooms. **De Lier** and **Schi-pluiden**, villages close by are also worth a detour. Cycle through this **Midden Delfland** area with its rural villages, waterways, typical farms, liftbridges and windmills. **Delftse Hout**, lying east of Delft, is an extensive recreation area for watersports, fishing and cycling. There is a deer park, arboretum, botanical and herb garden, children's farm, water play-ground, and go-cart track. In **Naaldwijk**, the **Holland Flower Auction**, Middel Broekweg 29, ☎ (0174) 63 3333, open Mon.-Fri. 8-10am, but closed Thurs., offers a different way to see Holland's pride and joy. Visitors are welcome each morning to witness the entire pro-cess of the international flower trade. You watch the action on the trading floor and see the flowers wheeled off for destinations around the world. Millions of flowers a year pass through this virtual landscape of glass houses, which is larger than 150 football fields.

The Hague (Den Haag)
The Seat of Parliament

Getting there: Rotterdam is 20 minutes southeast via A13; Amsterdam, about 40 minutes northeast via A4.

Information: VVV, Koningin Julianaplein 30 (in front of Central Station); VVV Schevenin-gen, Gevers Deynootweg 1134 (Palace Promenade,)
☎ (0900) 340 3505; www.denhaag.com, www.the-hague.info, and www.thehagueonline.com

---

There's a saying among the Dutch that Rotterdam is where money is made, Amsterdam is where it's spent, and **The Hague** is where they talk about it and tax it. While Amsterdam is the official capital of the Netherlands, The Hague has been the seat of government and diplomacy since the 13th century. This is where the Dutch Parliament and cabinet offices are located, where the Queen lives and works, and where your country's Embassy will be located. All this contributes to the exclusive atmosphere of the city.

In the 13th century the Count of Holland built a hunting lodge here called 's Gravenhage, or the Count's Hedge. This remained an official name until recently, although the Dutch call the city 'Den Haag'. When Count William was crowned King of the Holy Roman Empire in 1248, he established his royal court here, commencing its history as the seat of government.

The town did not grow rapidly, however. While Amsterdam became a major city of commerce in the 17th century, The Hague remained relatively small. It wasn't until the 19th century that its population exceeded 100,000. Today, it is the country's third largest city, with nearly 450,000 residents.

Gracious and subdued compared to Amsterdam or Rotterdam, The Hague's centre is relatively quiet in the evenings. However, there is much cultural activity with theatre, concerts and dance, and a wide variety of restaurants. The Hague's tree-lined avenues, lovely shopping streets and stylish traditional architecture give it a grace and serenity that sets it apart. It also has excellent museums, seaside resorts and 26 parks.

Among its other attractions are the numerous stately government buildings, and international organisations, such as the International Court of Justice, with their headquarters here. The Hague has become a truly vital international city.

▶ **Binnenhof**

Location: Between Hofweg & Korte Vijverberg, in the centre
Information: ☎ (070) 364 6144; http://historie.denhaag.org/binnenhof.htm
Hours: Mon.-Sat. 10am-3:45pm. Conducted tours take 45 minutes. Groups are limited. If you arrive late for the ongoing tour, obtain your tickets for the next tour to be sure you get in.

Approximately 775 years ago the history of The Hague began on this spot. It remains the heart of the city and the seat of Dutch government. The **Binnenhof** is an historic complex of buildings housing government offices and the Dutch Parliament. It was here in the 13th century that Count Floris IV built a hunting lodge on a small lake, and here that his son William II built a palace when he became king of the Holy Roman Empire. He completed the project by building the **Ridderzaal**, Hall of Knights, the most important building in the medieval courtyard.

The Ridderzaal was a meeting place for knights of the Golden Fleece in the 15th century, a residence for royalty, a hospital, and even stables. Today, it is primarily used for ceremonial functions, the most important being the Queen's Opening of Parliament on Prinsjesdag, on the third Tuesday of September when she can be seen in full regalia, riding through the city in a horse-drawn golden coach, to deliver a speech outlining the policies of her government for the coming year.

Inside the building is the royal throne, the flags of the 12 provinces of the Netherlands, and stained-glass windows bearing the coats of arms of major Dutch cities. A tour of the Binnenhof includes some of the current governmental buildings and the Second Chamber of the legislature.

Outside the Ridderzaal in the attractive courtyard is a fountain from 1885, topped with wrought iron and gargoyles. Equally picturesque is the **Hofvijver**, the small lake which used to be part of the moat surrounding the castle.

- **Near the Binnenhof:** Contrasting with the old town is the startling ultra-modern architecture of what's called **The Hague's New Centre**, located east of the Binnenhof. This massive redevelopment of the area between the city's main shopping district and Central Station began in the late 1980s. The result of this lengthy project is a distinctive new look for The Hague, designed by some of the world's top architects. Among the first buildings completed was the **Town Hall**, Spui 70, designed by American architect Richard Meier, whose buildings are renowned for their 'whiteness.' Inside this 11-storey white structure is a giant atrium, ringed by interior windows and walkways, and topped by a glass ceiling. The building is open 7am-7pm. If you want to view the atrium from the highest walkway, an elevator will take you to the 11th floor. The **Xpat Desk** of The Hague Hospitality Center is the first point of contact for new residents of The Hague, providing information and resources; located on the ground floor, open Mon.-Fri. 9am-5pm, ☎ (070) 353 5043. See also www.denhaag.com under 'Living in The Hague.'

Connected to the Town Hall is the **Central Library**, Spui 68, a part of the Town Hall complex. Next door is the **Anton Philips Concert Hall**, Spuiplein 150, where the Hague Philharmonic perform, and the **Lucent Dance Theatre**, Spuiplein 152, home of the Nederlands Dans Theatre. They all form a complex with a hotel, restaurants and coffee shops. The only old building of note in the area is the **Nieuwe Kerk** (1656), Spui 175, ☎ (070) 363 4917, open Wed. 1:30-3pm. The philosopher Spinoza and both of the De Witt brothers, prominent politicians, are buried here.

▶ **Mauritshuis Museum**

Location: Korte Vijverberg 8, just outside the Binnenhof
Information: ☎ (070) 302 3456; www.mauritshuis.nl
Hours: Tues.-Sat. 10am-5pm, Sun. 11am-5pm

Originally a nine-room palace, the **Mauritshuis** was built for Count Johan Maurits van Nassau-Siegen, nephew of the ruling Prince Maurits. Completed in 1645, it is architecturally noteworthy for its perfect proportions and is one of the most beautiful examples of Dutch classical architecture. Destroyed by fire in 1704, and later rebuilt, the State of Holland leased it to high-ranking officials. From 1807-19 it was used as the Royal Library, but in 1819 the State bought it for 35,000 florins and designated it a museum.

The basic collection includes outstanding paintings donated by the Orange-Nassau families, Stadhouders, and the Princes William IV and V. It includes 17th-century works by Rembrandt *(The Anatomy Lesson of Dr. Nicholas Tulp)*, Jan Steen *(The Way You Hear It Is The Way You Sing It)*, Vermeer *(View Of Delft, and Girl With A Pearl Earring)*, Frans Hals, Van Goyen, Ruisdael, Hobbema, Dou, Metsu, and others. There are important 15th-16th century Flemish masters represented, such as Rubens, Van Dyck and Jordaens.

This museum is highly recommended as an introduction to the early masters. It is one of the richest small museums in the world.

- Near the Mauritshuis: **The Hague Historical Museum**, Korte Vijverberg 7, ☎ (070) 364 6940, open Tues.-Fri. 10am-5pm, Sat.-Sun. noon-5pm, is devoted to the history of The Hague. The collection includes paintings of the city and prominent citizens, models, commemorative medals and The Hague silverware. There is also a dollhouse from 1910, which shows in amazing detail what a Dutch home of standing looked like at the time. www.the-hague.info/museums/historical_museum

The **Bredius Museum**, Lange Vijverberg 14, ☎ (070) 362 0729, open Tues.-Sun. noon-5pm, is in an elegant 18th-century house. It contains a unique collection of 17th-century paintings and drawings that were owned by a former director of the Mauritshuis, Dr. Abraham Bredius, who died in 1946 at the age of 92. Among his treasures are works by Rembrandt, Cuyp, Steen, and van der Neer, as well as The Hague School and some lesser masters. www.museumbredius.nl

Across the street on the side of the Historical Museum is a tree-lined avenue ahead to the right. The **Lange Voorhout** is one of the most attractive promenades of The Hague. The **United States Embassy**, Lange Voorhout 102, is on the right. A few doors away is the 18th-century **Palace Lange Voorhout**, Lange Voorhout 74, ☎ (070) 362 4061, open Tues.-Sun. 11am-5pm, once home to members of the royal family, but a museum since 1992. A unique collection of the work of M.C. Escher, one of the most famous Dutch graphic artists, can be viewed here in **Escher in het Paleis**, ☎ (070) 427 7730, www.escherinhetpaleis.nl. Nearby, the **Hotel des Indes**, Lange Voorhout 54, has taken care of many prominent visitors to The Hague since opening in 1881. It is a nice stop for afternoon tea. Lange Voorhout continues to the left, where it passes the **Embassy of the United Kingdom**, Lange Voorhout 10. The **Pages' House**, Lange Voorhout 6, built in 1618, is one of the few remaining step-gabled houses in The Hague. Pages from the Royal Court once lived here. The **Kloosterkerk**, Lange Voorhout 2, ☎ (070) 346 1576, open Apr.-Oct., Mon.-Fri. noon-2pm, has served as a hospital, arsenal and stables, as well as a place of worship since its construction in 1403.

To the north of the Lange Voorhout is the **National Book Museum, Meermanno-Westreenianum**, Prinsessegracht 30, ☎ (070) 346 2700, open Tue.-Fri. 11-5pm, Sat.-Sun. noon-5pm. Based on the collections of two 19th-century gentlemen, it contains over 340 handwritten and rare books, including many elaborately designed medieval manuscripts. On the last Sunday of each month from 2-5pm, the museum has a unique activity for the entire family. Visitors from age nine can dress in monk's robes and take a lesson on how to write with quill pens and ink on parchment. www.kb.nl

▶ **Museum Gevangenpoort – Prison Museum**

Location: Buitenhof 33. Near the Binnenhof in the town centre.
Information: ☎ (070) 346 0861; www.gevangenpoort.nl
Hours: Tues.-Fri. 10am-5pm, Sat.-Sun. noon-5pm. Hourly guided tours.
 Last tour at 4pm

This is a medieval prison with the requisite heavy wooden doors, narrow stairs and passages. Visit the cells where as many as 15 men were jailed in one tiny room. In another part of the building, where debtors and war prisoners were held, you can see the names they carved into the wooden walls centuries ago. Look for the elaborate ship carved by an English prisoner-of-war. There is a 'well-equipped' torture chamber, and a variety of unpleasant methods of imprisonment described or demonstrated. You can also visit the section where the rich and noble were imprisoned, including Cornelis de Witt, a 17th-century mayor of Dordrecht and brother to Johan. Cornelis was tortured here by political opponents. The building is small, but the half-hour tour is likely to leave a vivid impression. (Printed sheet in English available.)

- **Near the Gevangenpoort:** Next to the Gevangenpoort is a statue of Johan de Witt (1625-72). He led the Dutch government from 1653-72, during some of the country's most glorious years, but was despised by those who preferred a monarchy. Johan and his brother Cornelis were blamed by political opponents for a French invasion of the country, abducted and murdered by an angry mob. Their mutilated corpses were hung from a stake near this spot that is now a pleasant square filled with outdoor cafés.

If you cross the square you reach **Noordeinde**, one of several pedestrian streets in the shopping core. Noordeinde also has the distinction of being the street where Queen Beatrix works. **Noordeinde Palace** was built in the 16th century, and today serves as the Queen's office. It is not open to the public. **Noordeinde 66**, next door, is the home of Prince Willem-Alexander (born in 1967) – the current Prince of Orange and heir to the throne – and his wife, Princess Maxima, and their children. When the Prince is in residence, an orange flag flies from a flagstaff on the roof. Opposite the palace on Noordeinde is a **statue of William the Silent** (1533-84) the royal ancestor who led the Dutch revolt against Spain. Behind it is a **statue of Queen Wilhelmina** (1880-1962), grandmother of the present Queen, who won the hearts of her countrymen with her inspirational radio broadcasts from exile in London during the German occupation of Holland. On www.koninklijkhuis.nl/English you can view all six royal palaces.

Nearby is the **Schuilkerk**, Molenstraat 38, ☎ (070) 346 3912, open Wed. 2-4pm, a secret Catholic church from the years when these parishioners were not allowed to worship openly.

▶ **Galerij Prins Willem V**

Location: Buitenhof 35; next to the Gevangenpoort
Information: ☎ (070) 302 3435; www.codart.nl
Hours: Tues.-Sun. 11am-4pm

This collection of 17th-18th century Dutch paintings has an interesting history – collected by Prince William V (1748-1806), who in 1774 took the unprecedented step of opening his gallery to the public a few days a week. This is therefore the oldest museum in the Netherlands. When Napoleon invaded, the Prince fled the country... without his collection. Napoleon sequestered it and for 20 years the paintings hung in the Louvre in Paris, before being returned. Today most of them are displayed as they used to be in the days of William, covering the entire wall from eye level to ceiling. There are some 200 paintings in the collection, including works by Steen, Potter, Rembrandt and Jacob Jordaens.

- **Near the Galerij Prins Willem:** To the right, and around the corner from the gallery is the **Buitenhof**, a square with several outdoor cafés and restaurants. On the corner is the **Vijverhof**, Buitenhof 37 (1643), which was once a nobleman's home. Further down on your right is the **Passage**, Buitenhof 4, the country's only remaining late 19th-century shopping arcade. Built in 1883, it still contains many popular shops. Across the street is **Maison de Bonneterie**, Gravenstraat 2, a beautiful, early 20th-century department store built in 1913 and still thriving. Step inside to look at its stained-glass dome.

▶ **Grote Kerk**

Location:	Rond de Grote Kerk 12
Information:	☎ (070) 302 8630; www.grotekerkdenhaag.nl
Hours:	Mon.-Sat. 11am-5pm, see website for special events and concerts

The best view of The Hague is from the tower of the **Grote Kerk**, also known as St. Jacob's Church. There has been a church on this site since the 13th century, but the present building is from 1420-92. The oak pulpit has some of the most beautiful Renaissance wood carvings in the Netherlands. Dating from 1550, the carvings depict Moses, John the Baptist, and the four evangelists. Along the left wall is a row of seats for city leaders with carvings from 1647. The large monument near the back of the church is to Admiral Jacob van Wassenaar Obdam, who died in battle in 1665. Behind it is the burial site of statesman and poet Constantijn Huygens (1596-1687) and his son Christiaan Huygens (1629-95), inventor of the pendulum clock and discoverer of Saturn's rings. Be sure to notice the beautiful 19th-20th century wooden ceiling. The hexagon-shaped watchtower was built by the city. (Guided tour to the top.)

- **Near the Grote Kerk:** As the Binnenhof has always been the political centre of the Netherlands, so the area around the Grote Kerk was for centuries the political, religious and economic centre of the village of The Hague. The **Old Town Hall**, built in 1565, is behind the church.

If you turn left as you leave the church and walk five to ten minutes down the street, you will reach a canal and the **Dunne Bierkade**, an old section of The Hague that is gradually being restored to its 17th-century glory. Famous men from the city's past lived and worked here, such as artists Jan van Goyen (1596-56) who built the house at Paviljoensgracht 72 in 1646, and Jan Steen (1626-79) who married van Goyen's daughter, rented the house and lived in it. Later, the philosopher Spinoza lived and died there. A **statue of Spinoza** stands outside the house in the middle of Paviljoensgracht. A private home, it is not open to the public. Well-known artist Paulus Potter (1625-54) also lived in the area, as did Pieter Post (1598-1665), the most renowned Dutch architect of the time.

He designed Dunne Bierkade 17, another charming building and garden. Opposite the Spinoza House is a Red Light District – perhaps a bit unsettling if you are not expecting it.

This side of town has several almshouses or *hofjes*. Found hidden away in many Dutch towns, they are all unique, restful oases 'far from the madding crowd.' Some were built to house needy religious laypersons (there is often a chapel within the walls), and in the 19th century when housing was scarce, they often housed widows and single people who had fallen on hard times. Those eligible had to be of good character, churchgoing, and able to pay a nominal rent. The largest and most beautiful almshouse in The Hague is the **Hofje van Nieuwkoop**, Warmoezierstraat 36-52 and 92-202, open Mon.-Fri. 10am-5pm. Pieter Post designed it in 1665. The building faces Prinsengracht, but the entrance is opposite the hospital on Warmoezierstraat. Press the button to the left of the door to unlock it, and enter to discover a box-hedged, flower-bedded courtyard surrounded by well-kept little houses. http://homepage.residentie.net

▶ **Panorama Mesdag**

Location:	Zeestraat 65
Information:	☎ (070) 3644 544; www.panorama-mesdag.com
Hours:	Mon.-Sat. 10am-5pm, Sun. noon-5pm

In the late 19th century panoramas were a popular form of entertainment in parts of Europe. The **Panorama Mesdag** is one of the last remaining examples of this art form, and one of the best.

Through a gallery of paintings by artist H.W. Mesdag and his wife Sina, and via a spiral staircase, one suddenly emerges into the world of Scheveningen (the beach area of The Hague) in 1880. The immense panorama (circumference 394 ft., height 46 ft.) surrounds you, and has a three-dimensional feel. The town is on one side, the beach on the other, with fishing boats drawn up and cavalry exercising, just as if one were standing in the dunes over a century ago.

The work was the idea of Mesdag, a prominent 19th-century artist who specialised in paintings depicting the North Sea coast. Assisted by his wife and three other painters, it was completed in just four months. The building was specifically built for it.

The panorama is all the more relevant as it captures a pivotal moment in Scheveningen history. You see exactly how the village looked just before it was transformed from an old fishing village into a modern seaside resort. It is also an important example of The Hague School of painting.

● **Near Panorama Mesdag:** Close by is the **Museum voor Communicatie** (formerly the PTT post office museum) Zeestraat 82, ☎ (070) 330 7500, open Tue.-Fri. 10am-5pm, Sat.-Sun. noon-5pm. Its collection covers all aspects of communication, from the boots worn by early horseback messengers, to modern telephone systems, with many working and hands-on models. For example, there are displays that let you type out your name in

Morse code, surf on the Internet, and see who is on the other end of the phone. There's also a collection of thousands of Dutch and foreign stamps.

▶ **National Museum H. W. Mesdag**
Location: Laan van Meerdervoort 7F
Information: ☎ (070) 362 1434; www.museummesdag.nl
Hours: Tues.-Sun. noon-5pm

This museum, established by the Dutch painter, H. W. Mesdag (1831-1915) in an annex to his own home, contains a collection of The Hague Romantic School (Maris, Mauve, Israels, as well as Mesdag himself) and the largest collection of 19th-century paintings of the Barbizon School outside of France (Delacroix, Corot, Courbet, Millet, etc.). There is also a collection of Oriental ceramics, as well as those by Dutch artist Theodoor Colenbrander. Enjoy the views of the Peace Palace from the museum windows.

▶ **Vredespaleis – The Peace Palace**
Location: Carnegieplein 2
Information: ☎ (070) 302 4137; www.the-hague.info/court/
Hours: Tours Mon.-Fri. 10 & 11am, 2 & 3pm, but **no tours when court is in session.** Call in advance to check.

The permanent home of the International Court of Justice, the Permanent Court of Arbitration, and the International Law Library was donated by the American, Andrew Carnegie. Notice the many interesting and valuable gifts from different nations such as Ming vases from China, stained-glass windows from Holland, etc. All tours are guided – each guide assembling a party of one language – and they enjoy relating amusing anecdotes about Court happenings to suit the nationalities in their party. The Palace gardens are open in season.

▶ **Madurodam**
Location: George Maduroplein 1, about midway on a line drawn from the Binnenhof to the Scheveningen Pier.
Information: ☎ (070) 416 2400; www.madurodam.nl
Hours: Daily, 1 Sept. – 14 March 9am-6pm hrs.; 15 March – 30 June 9am-8pm hrs; 1 July – 31 August 9am-11pm; 1 Sept. – 31 December 9am-6pm

Madurodam is a tribute from loving parents of George Maduro to commemorate his life. (Look for the memorial plaque on the left of the entrance gate.) Maduro served with honour during the May 1940 invasion by the Germans. Later interned, he died at the Dachau concentration camp.

Even if you have seen model towns before, this is well worth a visit. It is advisable to have a supply of small change, because it will be needed in various slots to make a band or an organ grinder play, a parade march past, etc., while supporting worthy charities.

Different Dutch towns can be recognised by their well-known buildings. Much is mechanised: ships launch, cable cars climb, railways and motorways buzz with activity – only the planes don't fly. If possible go at dusk and see the lights turn on over this enchanting mini-Holland.

- **Near Madurodam:** Some 20,000 roses are on display from early July-Oct. in **Westbroek-park**. The park is a short walk along the canal which runs past Madurodam. It can also be entered from the Cremerweg, Nieuwe Parklaan, Nieuwe Duinweg, or Kapelweg. Apart from its roses, there are family attractions such as midget golf and a playground. Open 9am-sunset.

▶ **Gemeentemuseum Den Haag – Municipal Museum The Hague**
Location: Stadhouderslaan 41
Information: ☎ (070) 338 1111; www.gemeentemuseum.nl
Hours: Tues.-Sun. 11am-5pm

Opened in 1935, the **Municipal Museum** was the last building built by innovative Amsterdam architect H.P. Berlage. Extensive, it includes a special Music Section with traditional instruments as well as modern electronic music. The European instrument collection is world-famous and includes a tiny dancing-master's fiddle (which had to fit in the pocket of a tailcoat). Other curious instruments include a flute carved into a walking stick to help while away the miles. The non-European instruments include huge African drums and a Javanese Gamelan (orchestra consisting of gongs, drums and other instruments).

The Modern Art Section has the world's largest collection of paintings by Piet Mondriaan, including *Victory Boogie Woogie*, which he was working on at the time of his death in 1944. It came to the museum in 1998 at a cost of $40 million. There are also works by Picasso, Monet and other 19th-20th century painters. The Applied Arts Section has Italian, Islamic and Chinese ceramics, Venetian glass, Delft pottery, Dutch silver, period rooms, and Indonesian art.

The important Fashion Section has displays and accessories dealing with such subjects as emancipation, sport, social status, fashion photography and jewellery, and changing exhibits on costume through the ages.

- **Near the Gemeentemuseum:** Two other interesting sites are next to the Gemeentemuseum. **Museon**, Stadhouderslaan 37, ☎ (070) 338 1338, www.museon.nl, open Tues.-Sun. 11am-5pm, is a hands-on museum of science. There are videos, computer terminals and other interactive devices to entertain and educate. Displays explain Indian culture, an Egyptian section has a real mummy, and a vibrantly-coloured doll display shows native dress from around the world. Serious scientific and ecological subjects are treated in an easy-to-understand fashion. Be sure to see the tropical rainforest exhibit. There are five sections in the museum: history, geology, biology, physics and ethnology.

Next to it is **Omniversum**, President Kennedylaan 5, ☎ (0900) 666 4837 (€ 0.35 p.m.) for reservations and information; shows are hourly, Mon. 11am-3pm, and 8pm to 10pm, Tues.-Wed. 11am-5pm, Thur. & Sun. 11am-9pm, and Fri. & Sat. 11am-10pm. Reservations recommended. A 300-seat amphitheatre with an 840-sq.-meter screen. Films feature space, oceanography, geology, meteorology, biology, the cultures of exotic countries, mysteries of the Nile, the magic of flight, and wild forces of nature. A planetarium programme shows the stars as they were over a million years ago. Be sure to rent the sound track in your language...plugs are behind your seat.

▶ **Also in The Hague**

On the far south end of The Hague is the community of **Loosduinen**. Independent for over 100 years, it became a part of The Hague in 1923. The **Museum De Korenschuur**, Marg. v. Hennenbergweg 2a, ☎ (070) 397 3342, open July- Aug., Sat.-Sun. 1-5pm, focuses on the history of farming on the sandy soil between the dunes and the polder lands. **Abdijkerk** (Abbey Church), Willem III-straat 40, ☎ (070) 397 4182, open July-Aug., Sun. 3-4:30pm, is the oldest church in The Hague (ca. 1240). To the west of Loosduinen is the resort of **Kijkduin**. (More details in Chapter 14.)

The **Haagse Bos** is a wooded area not far from Central Station. Several walking and biking trails run through it. At one end is the **Malieveld**, a large open area where concerts, fairs, circuses and other major events are held, and at the north end is **Huis Ten Bosch**, the 17th-century home of Queen Beatrix and her family. (Not open to the public.) The castle was built in 1645 by the architect Pieter Post and is considered an important building of the period. Back toward the station is the **Letterkundig Museum**, Prins Willem Alexanderhof 5, ☎ (070) 333 9666, open Tues.-Fri. 9am-5pm, Sat.-Sun. noon-5pm. The museum features displays of 250 years of Dutch literature, including a look at children's literature. www.letterkundigmuseum.nl

Another of The Hague's many parks is just west of Haagse Bos. **Clingendael Park** (133 acres) boasts a lovely formal Japanese garden dating from 1896 with teahouse, lanterns, bridges, and typical and rare Japanese plants with an especially lovely show of azaleas. This part of the park is only open from mid-May to mid-June, 9am-8pm. The main garden is open all year and has an exciting display of rhododendrons in spring. It can be entered from Van Alkemadelaan, not far from the main ANWB office on Wassenaarseweg.

To the south is the spacious **Zuider Park**, open Mon.-Fri., 8am-4pm and most weekends. Its many attractions include a recreation park, bird park, small animal centre, swimming pool, mini-golf, children's farm, open-air theatre, walking and biking paths, a miniature steam train with child-sized carriages, an herb garden with free picking privileges, and a restaurant. The park is open all year, but not all the facilities. Miniature Railway information: ☎ (070) 380 2660. Operates daily April-Oct, including Sat. and Sun., 11:30am-4:30pm and during school holidays. For a look at multicultural neighbourhoods, Transvaal, Schilderswijk and De Stationsbuurt make up **City Mondial.** VVV offers walking tours for a colourful day, ☎ (070) 402 3336. www.citymondial.nl

An excellent way to find out what's going on in The Hague is via **The Hague Online:** www.thehagueonline.com. (More on this on pages 130-131.)

▸ Scheveningen

Scheveningen is the primary Dutch resort town on the North Sea. For centuries a sleepy fishing village, it began its transformation into a beachfront resort in the 19th century. Today there are few reminders of its village days. The beach is the main reason to visit Scheveningen. Even if you don't like to swim or lie in the sun, there's a boulevard and a pier for you to explore, miles of bike trails through the dunes, restaurants, shopping, theatres and a casino. Since Scheveningen is a part of The Hague, we will mention here some of its visitor attractions. In addition, see Chapter 14 for information on Scheveningen as a seaside resort. www.scheveningen.nl

▸ Scheveningen National Sea Life Centre

Location:	Strandweg 13, on the sea front next to the Kurhaus
Information:	☎ (070) 354 2100; www.sealifeeurope.com/holland
Hours:	Daily 10am-7pm; Aug., daily 10am-8pm

In one part of the **Sea Life Centre** you are literally underwater, with fish swimming above you and at your side. Made possible by a long, glass underwater tunnel, and a walkway running through it, this particular aquarium is one of several in the Sea Life Centre that gives visitors a close-up look. The aquariums are built at 'child's eye level,' enabling even the smallest child to look the fish in the eye. Several show North Sea fish, including stingrays, crabs and an octopus or two. Another section is devoted to the colourful and unusual fish of the tropical reefs.

The Centre is very child-friendly, with games designed to keep children interested as they tour the displays. There's also a play area for the youngsters who need more than fish to entertain them.

● **Near the Sea Life centre:** The first time you visit Scheveningen your eyes will probably be drawn to the sea, and to the **Steigenberger Kurhaus Hotel.** This large structure is the focal point of the pedestrian Boulevard that runs along the beach. In its early days of the 18th century it was an elegant establishment for those wanting to 'take the cure.' Today, the Kurhaus remains a fine hotel with restaurants, convention facilities, and a concert hall, overlooking the North Sea. Go inside and climb the stairs to see the beautiful ceiling of the elegant main hall, where you can sit and enjoy the surroundings with a meal or a cup of coffee. The five-star hotel may not be within everyone's budget, but if you are interested in some luxury by the sea, you can call ☎ (070) 416 2636. www.kurhaus.nl

A short walk away is **Beelden Aan Zee**, or Sculptures by the Sea, on the Boulevard at Harteveltstraat, ☎ (070) 358 5857, www.beeldenaanzee.nl, open Tues.-Sun. 11am-5pm.

It's a collection of 20th-century sculpture, displayed both in and outdoors. The museum is constructed around a beach pavilion built in 1826 by King William I, and has good dune and sea views.

Each summer the beachfront is lined with temporary buildings that house restaurants, bars and sunbathing facilities. They offer a wide variety of comfort, food and refreshments for visitors. To get a better view of the sea, and still shop, you might venture out onto the **Scheveningen Pier.**

The **Muzee Scheveningen** is a fusion of Museum Scheveningen and the Zeemuseum, Neptunusstraat 90-92, ☎ (070) 350 0830, open Tues.-Sat. 10am-5pm – about the only place where you can still get a feel for the Scheveningen of old. It deals with the history of the village and the fishing families who lived here. Displays include Scheveningen's distinctive costume jewellery and ship models. On Wed. and Sat. you can climb up the lighthouse tower!

Holland Casino, Kurhaus 1, ☎ (070) 306 7777, open daily 1:30pm-2am, closed May 4 and Dec. 31, is just across the street from the Kurhaus. To enter you must be appropriately dressed and at least 18 years of age. www.hollandcasino.nl/scheveningen

▸ **Zee Museum – Marine Biological Museum**
Location: Dr. Lelykade 39
Information: ☎ (070) 350 2528
Hours: Tues.-Sat. 10am-5pm, Sun. 1-5pm

A huge green turtle, a giant clam, and one of the world's largest snails are all on display in the **Zee Museum**. Despite the presence of these mighty creatures from the deep, this is a small museum. Some of its most fascinating attractions are the tiny seahorses, crabs and other seldom-seen sea creatures, which are kept in several small aquariums. The museum covers everything connected with the sea, telling the story of lobsters and oysters, as well as of mermaids and sea monsters. There are hundreds of seashells, and a display of gorgeous mother-of-pearl shells and jewellery made with them. Collectors will find countless varieties of shells for sale in the gift shop.

● **Near the Zee museum:** The Zee Museum is located in the Scheveningen Harbour area, which is a short distance from the beach. There are numerous restaurants, as well as possibilities for boat trips. It also has the **Mercuur Ship Museum**, 2e Binnenhaven, ☎ (070) 354 0315, open Tues.-Sun. 10am-5pm. The Mercuur was originally an American ship, but became part of the Dutch Navy in 1954. When it was retired in 1987, it was the Dutch Navy's last wooden ship. Now a museum, it's open for visitors.

Markets

The **General Market** is held on Herman Costerstraat, Mon., Wed. & Fri. 8am-6pm; Sat. 8am-5pm. The indoor **Markthof** at Gedempte Gracht/Spui, Mon., 11am-6pm; Tues., Wed. & Fri., 9am-6pm; Thurs. 9am-9pm; and Sat., 9am-5pm. **Antique, Curio Market:**

Lange Voorhout, May-Sept., Thurs. 10am-7pm; Sun., 10am-6pm; on the Plein, Oct.-May, Thurs. 10am-6pm.

Eating out

In the small shopping streets in the centre of town, various places offer snacks, but the Denneweg offers all sorts of possibilities should you want something more substantial. If you want to watch the world go by, 't Goude Hooft, Groenmarkt 13, ☎ (070) 346 9713, has typical Dutch fare and a pleasant terrace for outside eating. For a more historic stop, go to **De Boterwaag** (Butter Weighing House) (1681) at Grote Markt 8, ☎ (070) 365 9686. It's great fun to get weighed on the original butter scales and receive a certificate telling 'all.' For Indonesian food a good choice is **Bogor**, which has two locations in town, or **Bogor Dua**, Noordeinde 163, ☎ (070) 360 2983, open Tues.-Sun. 6-10pm. The **Pannekoekhuis Maliehuys**, Maliestraat 10, ☎ (070) 346 2474, will delight youngsters with their pancakes. Try bacon, apple, raisins and syrup! In Scheveningen, there's **van der Toorn**, Tweilerdwarsweg 2, ☎ (070) 354 5783, and **Simonis**, Visafslagweg 20, for a simple but good seafood meal, and **Ducdalf**, Dr. Lelykade 5, ☎ (070) 355 7692, open daily noon-10pm, a smarter restaurant on the Dr. Lelykade. (More ideas in Chapter 17.)

Yearly events

Some special events include the **CPC Half-Marathon** of The Hague in March, and the **Queen's birthday celebration** on April 30; **Sand Sculpture Festival** in Scheveningen in May; **Flag Day** (Vlaggetjes Dag) and the **Fishing Festival**, beginning of June; **Hague Horse Days**, **National Kite Festival** and **Parkpop** in June; the **International Rose Show** in Westbroek Park, **Passion for Jazz Festival** (www.apassion4jazz.net) in Scheveningen in July; the **International Fireworks Festival** from Scheveningen Pier in August. (There are fireworks every Fri. at 11pm in July.) September brings **Haagse Kermis**, the largest fun-fair (like an American carnival) in Holland (Malieveld), and, on the 3rd Tues. the **Opening of Parliament**.

TheHagueOnLine

An excellent way to keep on top of everything that's going on in The Hague and surrounding area is www.TheHagueOnLine.com, a daily English-language website that informs the international community in and around The Hague about national and local news, upcoming social and cultural events, clubs, associations, business initiatives, goods and services, charity events, and more.

TheHagueOnLine also runs a Social Club, offering at least four events every month, providing many wonderful opportunities to meet other people while having fun or learning something new. The two weekly newsletters, 'Arts &Entertainment' and 'Weekly News', give information on leisure, dining, sports and much more.

In September, TheHagueOnLine co-organises (with ACCESS) the annual 'Feel at Home in The Hague, The International Community Fair,' a one-day event introducing expats to a variety of local organisations, services, goods and activities.

TheHagueOnLine is the gateway to the growing expatriate and international community currently estimated at 50,000 in The Hague region alone. www.TheHagueOnLine.com (see ad on page 108.)

Tours

The Royal Tour (by bus) operates May-Aug., Tues.-Sat., also on Sun. in July and Aug. Departs from the Central Station at 1pm and from the VVV Scheveningen at 1:15pm. The 2-hour tour takes you past the Queen's residence and other points of interest in The Hague. They also offer an Architectural Tour on Saturdays at 10:30am from Central Station. It highlights the old and new architecture of the city, ☎ (0900) 340 3505 for reservations.

HTM Specials operates bus tours, Spui 256, ☎ (070) 384 2725 (brochures available at the VVV) lasting 3 hours and taking you to many highlighted spots in and around The Hague and Delft, including the pottery factory. Groups may book throughout the year for day tours to Avifauna, Delfshaven, etc., or for a candlelight trip to Leidschendam.

Lovers of boats may enjoy a tour or fishing expedition from Scheveningen. **Trip Sportviscentrum**, Dr. Lelykade 3, ☎ (070) 354 1122, www.rederijtrip.nl; June-Sept., daily 4pm, takes you through the fishing port of Scheveningen and out to sea. Sport fishing starts with breakfast at 6am, returning about 3pm. You can catch mackerel in summer and cod or sprat in winter. Fishing rods, reels and bait can be rented. There are other companies offering boat trips from the Dr. Lelykade area. **Rederij Groen/ Rederij Fortuna**, ☎ (070) 355 3588, www.rederijgroen.nl, **Rederij Vrolijk**, ☎ (070) 351 4021, www.rederijvrolijk.nl All sail daily at 4pm for an hour-and-a-half tour of the North Sea, from June-Sept.

▶ Biking

To rent bikes, check the phone directory under 'Fietsverhuur,' then follow the VVV bike routes. A particularly nice ride is through the dunes along the coast. Trails from Scheveningen or Kijkduin take you south to Hoek van Holland and beyond, or to Wassenaar and points north.

In the neighbourhood of The Hague

Rijswijk is home to **Drievliet Recreation Park**, Jan Thijssenweg 16, ☎ (070) 399 9305, open April weekends, from April 22–Sept. 3, daily 10am-6pm; Sept.-Oct. only weekends. Practically in town, this huge park includes a monorail, bumper cars and all the fun-fair attractions imaginable, plus a children's farm. Admission includes them all. There's also a large restaurant. www.drievliet.nl/english Close by is **Museum Rijswijk 'Het Tol-**

lenshuis,' Herenstraat 67, ☎ (070) 390 3617, open Tues.-Fri. 2-5pm, Sat. 11am-5pm, Sun. 2-5pm, which deals with Rijswijk town history and holds occasional art exhibits.

Voorburg is a pleasant and historic town southeast of The Hague. It has Roman origins, a 13th-century church, a 17th-century mill, **de Vlieger**, and an octagonal watermill that has kept its water at the right level for centuries. The **Huygens Museum Hofwijck**, Westeinde 2, ☎ (070) 387 2311, www.hofwijck.nl, open Tue., Wed., Thur., Sat. & Sun. 1-5pm, is in a charming building from 1641. This former country manor owned by poet and statesman Constantijn Huygens, was designed by Jacob van Campen and Pieter Post. It contains memorabilia of Constantijn and his son, Christiaan Huygens, physicist, astronomer and inventor of the pendulum clock. **Museum Swaensteijn**, Herenstraat 101, ☎ (070) 386 1673, open Wed.-Sun. 1-5pm, contains Roman archeology, town history, and the works of local artists. www.swaensteyn.nl

About 10 km (6 mi) north in **Voorschoten** is **Duivenvoorde Castle**, Laan van Duivenvoorde 4, ☎ (071) 561 3752, with tours May-Sept., Tues.-Sat. 2pm and 3:30pm. Restored to its original state as an 18th-century country manor, its brass chandeliers, handpainted rafters, and oriental rugs are well worth seeing. It also has a fine collection of antique furniture and porcelain.

Wassenaar is an elegant residential and recreational area to the north of The Hague. The horse racetrack **Renbaan Duindigt**, Waalsdorperlaan 29, ☎ (070) 324 4427, open Mar.-Nov., Sun. 1pm & Wed. 2:30pm, is located here. Wassenaar is also known for its natural beach and Duinrell Recreation Park.

▶ **Duinrell Recreation Park**

Getting there: Duinrell 1, Wassenaar. From Rotterdam, take A13 towards The Hague, then north on N44. From Amsterdam, take A4, then A44 south to the sign for Duinrell.

Information: ☎ (070) 515 5155; www.duinrell.nl

Hours: Park open mid April-Oct. 10am-5pm or 6pm. Tiki Pool and Sauna open daily; hours vary, but generally open 'til 10pm.

Duinrell is one of the largest recreation facilities in the Netherlands. It has an amusement park, an indoor wave pool, a complex of saunas, campgrounds and bungalows. For the brave of heart, there are many breathtaking experiences, both in the amusement park and the wave pool. The amusement park includes roller coasters, a giant 500-meter-long white-water slide, and a lightning-fast toboggan ride from the 'highest point' in Holland.

The Tiki Pool, or wave pool, contains some massive water slides as well as waves and whirlpools. If you're not up to that much excitement, the Tiki Pool has more leisurely options, such as a ride called 'The Lazy River,' with underwater music. Tiki Sauna is an independent facility with a separate admission fee. It has Finnish saunas, Turkish steam baths, and an ice-cold immersion bath.

For the smaller ones, there's a huge playground, a sea of balls to play in, puppet shows, and a Fairy Tale Wonderland. There's also a 3-D cinema, bike rental, and the Wassenaar beach only 4km (2.5 mi) away. Duinrell is located in an area of dunes and woods. You can rent bungalows, but camping is also possible, at 'all comfort' sites (including a cable TV hookup) ... or the roughing-it kind.

In winter the amusement park closes but the Tiki Pool and Sauna remain open. The park is also open weekends throughout winter, when the permanent playgarden, trampolines and midget golf are still available. Something else goes on at Duinrell in wintertime, however – skiing on brush slopes! The ski school has qualified instructors, approximately 100-meter slopes, with a special slope for children – all floodlit for evening classes.

Leiden
Home of Holland's oldest university and the Pilgrim Fathers

Getting there:	The A4 and A44 encircle Leiden, but many country routes are possible. Canals and narrow one-way streets make driving difficult. Look for 'P' signs and leave the car.
Information:	VVV, Stationsweg 2D, ☎ (0900) 222 2333; www.hollandrijnland.nl/leiden

Leiden is a city with a rich history, the nation's oldest university, picturesque canals, and an assortment of museums. But to understand the city you must go back to 1574, when the Spanish army had Leiden surrounded and tried to starve its people into submission. For months they refused to surrender, even though over a third of them had already died from hunger and disease. William the Silent came to the rescue, his militia breaking down dike after dike to reach the city, sending the Spaniards running from the rushing floodwaters.

The heroism of the people won William's praise, and he granted Leiden the right to establish the nation's first university. The **University of Leiden** became, and is still today, a major centre of medical, legal and scientific study in Europe. Two of its scientists have been awarded Nobel prizes for physics in the 20th century, and one for physiology.

The city prospered after the end of the Spanish siege, thanks in part to the university, but even more to the textile industry. Refugees from what is now Belgium led a huge influx of newcomers to Leiden in the late 16th century. They came for work that was available in cloth-making. By 1664, Leiden was home to 70,000 people and was the second largest city in the Netherlands. More than half of its people worked in the textile industry.

Besides being an intellectual and economic centre, the city was known for its tolerance of religious minorities. In 1609 a group of Separatists from the Church of England settled here to escape persecution in their homeland. Today, they are known to us as the Pilgrims. For eleven years they lived and worked in Leiden before sailing from Delfshaven via England to North America (1620) where they established the colony of Plymouth. During this golden era of Leiden's history, some of the greatest Dutch artists were born here, including Rembrandt van Rijn (1606), Jan Steen (1625), Jan van Goyen (1596), Gerrit Dou (1613) and Gabriel Metsu (1629). The textile industry-gradually declined, eventually disappearing completely in 1982, unable to compete with low-cost foreign cloth. Today, this city of about 117,000 people is just slightly larger than it was during the golden era of the 17th century. But Leiden is still a lively university town, with numerous museums and other attractions along its many canals. It also benefits from being only 33 minutes from Schiphol airport by train, 12 minutes from The Hague, and right next door to the bulb fields and North Sea beaches.

▶ **Pieterskerk**

Location: Pieterskerkhof 1a
Information: ☎ (071) 512 4319; www.pieterskerk.com
Hours: Daily 1:30-4pm, and during special events.

Like many of the old churches in the Netherlands, **Pieterskerk** is no longer a church. But at one time this massive building was a major place of worship in Leiden; some of the Pilgrims worshiped here, and John Robinson, one of their leaders, is buried here. There's a plaque on the side of the church commemorating Robinson and the Pilgrims. Artist Jan Steen is also buried here. Today the building is used as a community centre, and even events such as flea markets take place on the century-old stones that mark the graves.

● **Near Pieterskerk:** At Heerensteeg 17A, William Brewster ran the **Pilgrim Press**, which published leaflets criticising the Church of England, until King James applied enough pressure to have it shut down. A plaque marks the spot. At Kloksteeg 21, another plaque indicates the location of 'The Green Gate,' where Pilgrim pastor John Robinson lived and where services were held. Twenty-one small houses were built around the garden for members of the congregation. Some years after Robinson's death (1625) and the Pilgrims departure in 1620, the **Jean Pesijnshofje** almshouse was built on this site. Across the square from the almshouse is the **Gravensteen,** which was a residence for the Counts of Holland, a prison, and is now part of the University.

▶ **Leiden American Pilgrim Museum**

Location: Beschuitsteeg 9
Information: ☎ (071) 512 2413; www.pilgrimhall.org/LeidenMuseum
Hours: Wed.-Sat. 1-5pm

This is a tiny museum, located in a building which existed in the early 17th century, when the Pilgrims lived in Leiden. Inside you will get an idea of how they lived during the eleven years that Leiden was their home, before they sailed to America. The museum's curator has studied and written about the Pilgrims, and has a wealth of information to share with the visitor. For a Pilgrim walking tour of Leiden, see the route description on: www.pilgrimhall.org/leidenwalkinglong

● **Near the American Pilgrim Museum:** The **Burcht** is an 11th-century fortification built on an artificial hill, to overlook the Oude and Nieuwe Rijn. The ornate gate at the bottom of the hill was built in 1658. You can climb to the top for a view of the city, but if the trees are in leaf you'll only get a limited view. The Burcht does provide a very good view of the **Hooglandse Kerk**, a massive church built between the 14th and 16th centuries.

Not far from the museum is the **Koornbeursbrug**, a partially-roofed, 15th-century bridge where the grain market used to be held. On the other side of the bridge, on Breestraat, is the old Town Hall or **Stadhuis**. Its facade dates from 1595-97. In 1929 it came very close to being destroyed. On a bitterly cold February night someone decided to keep the stoves burning all night. By 4am, the building was in flames. Its contents were lost, including many valuable works of art. The facade, one of Leiden's architectural gems, was saved.

▶ **Rijksmuseum Van Oudheden – National Museum of Antiquities**
Location: Rapenburg 28
Information: ☎ (071) 516 3163; www.rmo.nl
Hours: Tues.-Fri. 10am-5pm; Sat.-Sun. noon-5pm

As strange as it may seem, this museum of archeology appeals to young children, perhaps because of its large collection of mummies! Founded in 1818, there are over 80,000 objects in its fascinating collections. One of its main exhibits is the Temple of Taffeh, which was presented by Egypt in 1979 in appreciation of Dutch assistance in a project to save its ancient temples from submersion after the construction of the Aswan Dam. Besides examining the ancient Roman and Greek cultures, the museum also has an extensive display on Dutch archeology.

▶ **Molenmuseum De Valk – Windmill Museum**
Location: 2e Binnenvestgracht 1
Information: ☎ (071) 516 5353; http://home.wanadoo.nl/molenmuseum
Hours: Tues.-Sat. 10am-5pm; Sun. 1-5pm

The windmill was not invented in Holland, but it has been used here more than anywhere else in the world. Of the 10,000 windmills that once existed, **De Valk** is one of about 950 that remain in the country. This brick windmill, dating from 1743, was used for grinding grain. On the ground floor, you can see how a miller lived around 1900, including his working tools and smithy. Upstairs, displays explain how windmills work, and their history. There are seven floors to explore, including a platform which gets you as close as you want to be to the powerful spinning blades. The ladder-like stairs inside may be difficult for some to climb. Come down as if you're climbing down a ladder, not walking down stairs.

▶ **Rijksmuseum Voor Volkenkunde – National Museum of Ethnology**
Location: Steenstraat 1
Information: ☎ (071) 516 8800; www.rmv.nl
Hours: Tues.- Sun. 10am-5pm

This museum is entitled to call itself the first scientific ethnological museum of Europe. King William I (1772-1843) was deeply interested in spreading education throughout his kingdom, and he personally acquired important collections that were the basis for the national museums. The museum has an informal atmosphere in which children are quite at home. The collection is too extensive to describe in detail but you will find displays on prehistoric art, the Islamic culture of the Middle East, Buddhism and its art, and the cultures of people from all parts of the world, including the people of the polar regions of Asia and America. The American Indian display is of particular interest to American children.

▶ **Stedelijk Museum de Lakenhal**
Location: Oude Singel 28-32
Information: ☎ (071) 516 5360; www.lakenhal.nl
Hours: Tues.- Sun. 10am-5pm

For 160 years this building was the centre of Leiden's prosperous cloth trade. From its construction in 1640, all the cloth woven in town was brought here to be inspected and given the official seal of approval. Displays tell the story of those days when the textile industry employed over half the city's population. There is also a collection of paintings showing Leiden's contribution to art, with works by Lucas Van Leyden, Rembrandt, Jan Steen, and Van Goyen, as well as a large collection of furniture and silver. The section on Leiden's history takes visitors on a tour of the city's historic neighbourhoods.

▶ **Museum Boerhaave – Museum for the History of Science**
Location: Lange St. Agnietenstraat 10
Information: ☎ (071) 521 4224; www.museumboerhaave.nl
Hours: Tues.-Sat. 10am-5pm; Sun. noon-5pm

Herman Boerhaave (1668-1738) was one of the world's first surgeons. His lectures on surgery attracted scientists from around the world to this building. In the 15th century the building was a convent, and in the 16th century a home for lunatics and plague victims. Today it is the foremost museum of surgery, medicine, and dentistry in the Netherlands. It contains exhibits on five centuries of medical science, as well as a reconstruction of Leiden's anatomy theatre as it was in 1610. In those days, people used to flock here to watch public dissections of corpses. Also on display is the oldest pendulum clock in existence (1657), designed by Dutch scientist Christiaan Huygens, as well as microscopes built by Dutch inventor Antoni van Leeuwenhoek.

▶ **Hortus Botanicus – Botanical Gardens of Leiden University**
Location: Rapenburg 73
Information: ☎ (071) 527 7249; www.hortus.leidenuniv.nl
Hours: Apr.- Oct. 3, Mon. – Sun. 10am-6pm, Nov. 1-Mar. 31, Mon.–Fri. &, Sun.
10am-6pm.(Nov. thru Mar. closed Saturday).

Work began in 1587 on creating a botanical garden behind the University of Leiden. The garden still exists, and continues to be used for research. It's a popular spot for anyone looking for a peaceful place to enjoy nature. Footpaths wind through the garden, taking you past roses, ferns and one of the biggest collections of passion flowers in Europe. There are also greenhouses that keep a collection of Asian plants comfortable during the Dutch winters.

● **Near Hortus Botanicus:** The **University History Museum** near the garden entrance is open Wed.-Fri. 1-5pm, and tells the story of the university. The gardens face the **Rapenburg**, a canal that is considered to be one of the most beautiful in the Netherlands. It is lined with many 17th-century patrician houses whose original owners kept food on the table of artists such as van Goyen and Steen by buying many of their works.

▶ **Naturalis – National Museum of Natural History**
Location: Darwinweg 2
Information: ☎ (071) 568 7600; www.naturalis.nl
Hours: Tues.-Fri. 10am-5pm; Sat. & Sun. 10am-6pm, school holidays, daily
10am-6pm

Leiden's newest museum is devoted to nature – from the rocks and minerals that make up the earth's surface, to the plants and animals that inhabit it. On display are fossils and dinosaur bones, an impressive collection of stuffed animals from around the world, and numerous stones and minerals from the museum's geology collection. There are also exhibits which explain how the elements of nature interact with each other. All of the displays in this modern, well-designed museum are explained in English as well as in Dutch. There are also interactive displays, especially designed to catch the interest of children.

Tours

If you enjoy walking, you'll find Leiden an interesting city to explore. To help you see the sights on foot, the VVV has put together four walking tours. The tour booklets are in English. They include a tour of most of Leiden's 35 almshouses, a walk through areas associated with the Pilgrims, a tour of locations related to 17th-century artists Jan van Goyen and Jan Steen, and a walk in the footsteps of young Rembrandt.

Canal boat trips are available from **Rembrandt Rederij**, ☎ (071) 513 4938, www.rederij-rembrandt.nl, Apr.-Sept. 11am-4pm. Boats leave from the Beestenmarkt. **Rederij Slingerland**, ☎ (071) 541 3183, has sightseeing tours across the nearby lakes, with boats leaving from the harbour. Rowboats and canoes can be rented near the Rembrandt bridge from Rent-A-Boat, ☎ (071) 514 9790.

Markets

On Wed. and Sat., colourful markets are held in the shopping centre of town (Nieuwe Rijn and Botermarkt areas).

Eating out

Like all university towns, there are many inexpensive places to eat such as **'t Pannekoekenhuisje**, Steenstraat 51, ☎ (071) 513 3144, (annex of one of the best restaurants in town, the **Rotisserie Oudt Leyden**) which specialises in wagon-wheel-sized pancakes served on Delft-blue plates. **Annie's Verjaardag**, Hoogstraat 1A, ☎ (071) 512 5737, has a nice location in a cellar that looks out onto the Oude Rijn, with seating by the river. The menu includes sandwiches, and such Dutch favourites as *uitsmijters*, open-faced sandwiches with ham or roast beef, cheese and lightly fried eggs on top. The café-restaurant **Koetshuis**, located at the foot of the Burcht, Burgsteeg 13, ☎ (071) 512 1688, is also a delightful spot. It was built in 1692 as a carriage house for a large private home, the Herenlogement opposite, now a library.

Yearly events

Several special events occur annually in Leiden. The first takes place the third week in January, the **Leyden Jazz Week**. On Maundy Thursday and Good Friday the famous **Matthew's Passion** is performed by the Bach Choir in Sint Pieterskerk. The beginning of July is time for the big summer festival celebrating Rembrandt's birthday and **Leiden's Cloth Festival**. Another major festival on October 3rd commemorates **Leiden's Ontzet**, the town's liberation from the Spanish who tried to starve them into submission. Legend has it that the Spaniards fled in haste from the floods initiated by William the Silent's men. When the hungry people of Leiden entered a newly-deserted Spanish campsite, they found a pot of white beans, carrots and onions (*hutspot*) still cooking. The same day, the waterbeggars (pirates) sailed into Leiden bringing with them raw herring and loaves of bread. These have become the three traditional foods of the day. Festivities begin at 7am with 'reveille'; at 7:30, herring and white bread are distributed as the 'pirates' make their entry into town. There are fireworks and all the fun of a fair.

Another historic event of note is celebrated in Pieterskerk on **America's Thanksgiving Day,** the last Thursday in November. It commemorates the first harvest of the Pilgrims in the new world. The US President's Thanksgiving Day Proclamation is read by the American Ambassador, and there is usually a guest speaker, a choir and a coffee hour after the well-attended ecumenical service.

In the neighbourhood of Leiden

One of the area's nicest beaches is close by in **Noordwijk**. In fact, Noordwijk also has a wide selection of hotels for overnight stays. (See Chapter 14 for details on what to see there.)

Valkenburg, a village west of Leiden, is where a horse market has taken place for over 1,150 years. The town developed on a mound along the banks of the old Rhine in the first three centuries A.D., producing flax and linen. Market days are Wednesday and Thursday, but the main event is on the second Wednesday in September, **Luilakmarkt**. People waken to the sound of bicycle bells ringing and tin cans being dragged along the streets. The bright lights of the fair await, not to mention many attractions, and market stalls to tempt one's purse.

Valkenburg is home to the **National Narrow Gauge Railroad Museum**, J. Pellenbarg-weg 1, open Easter to end of Sept., Sat.-Sun. 10:30am-5pm, ☎ (071) 572 4275. There are displays of small trains that are used primarily for industrial purposes. The main attraction, especially for children, is a 45-minute lakeside train ride. It runs hourly from 11am to 4pm.

▶ Avifauna

Location:	Hoorn 65, Alphen a/d Rijn
Getting there:	From The Hague or Amsterdam, A4 toward Leiden and follow signs; from Rotterdam, a scenic route is the back road from Hillegersberg to Bleiswijk, Kruisweg Hazerswoude-Rijndijk, and then along the Oude Rijn. Or, take a boat trip from The Hague, Leiden or Amsterdam.
Information:	☎ (0172) 48 7575; www.avifauna.nl
Hours:	Daily 9am-6pm

The unique aspect of **Avifauna** is its collection of more than 450 types of exotic birds housed in areas matching their natural habitat in an attractive park. Avifauna is a wonderful day's excursion for the entire family. There's even a motel with a good restaurant, ☎ (0172) 48 7502, reachable by boat from The Hague, Leiden, or Amsterdam from April-Nov. The children will naturally make a beeline for the recreation park with its mini-cars and countless other attractions, but there's also swimming, fishing, pony rides at the children's farm, and a covered amusement hall...should the weather change! At night, Avifauna is illuminated to add a romantic touch.

Lisse
Springtime riot of colours

Getting there:	The multi-coloured bulb fields are north of Leiden between Sassenheim and Lisse. Take 'Nieuw Venne' turnoff from A4 or N208 from A44 and follow signs.
Information:	VVV, Grachtweg 53, ☎ (0900) 222 2333 (€ 0.50 p.m.); www.hollandrijnland.nl/lisse

One reason that tourists come to the Netherlands is to see flowers. Though grown in other parts of the country, the largest growing area is here, between Sassenheim and Haarlem, in the **Bollenstreek** (bulb region). The season is at its peak from late March to mid May when the area is filled with glorious colours and scents, as well as tour buses and automobiles. Most visitors are on their way to **Keukenhof**, a huge and very popular outdoor exhibition park of flowers that first opened in 1949.

Tulips originated in Turkey and didn't appear in the Netherlands until the late 16th century. Austrian-born botanist Carolus Clusius (1526-1609) planted the first bulbs in this sandy soil. The Dutch immediately fell in love with the flower, and a huge demand developed. The bulbs were so rare that only the rich could afford them. Prices, particularly for exotic varieties, were astronomical, and many 'investors' lost fortunes when the market collapsed in 1636.

Although bulbs have fortunately come down in price since those years, the flower industry is still big business in this region. You will see thousands of acres of land devoted to flowers and bulbs. Besides viewing them from a bus or car, the VVV has information on bike routes you can follow through the bulb fields.

▶ **Keukenhof**
A festival of spring flowers

Location:	In season, Keukenhof is marked on road signs. There is a special train from Amsterdam and Leiden; or regular trains to Leiden or Haarlem, then bus 54 from Leiden, or 50 or 51 from Haarlem to Lisse, and then bus 54 from Lisse. At the station, ask for a reduced-rate ticket that includes train, bus and entrance.
Information:	☎ (0252) 46 5555; www.keukenhof.com
Hours:	Late March to mid-May, daily 8am-7:30pm; also open for Zomerfest from mid-August to mid-September, 9am-6pm

Keukenhof is said to be one of the three most photographed places in the world. When you arrive you will see why. Over six million flower bulbs are planted in this 69-acre park – a dazzling display of colours and fragrances. Every year the plantings are different, and the show is always new. Early in the season, you see crocuses, hyacinths, narcissi and azaleas; later, trees in blossom, and then the tulips, in all their glory.

Don't be discouraged if the weather isn't perfect – you can see the complete range of flowers in large pavilions, protected from rain and wind. Some have weekly-changing flower shows, elaborate cut flower arrangements, over 600 varieties of tulips, daffodils and other spring plants, garden layouts, etc.

Although Keukenhof should not be missed during the bulb blooming season, it sometimes seems the whole of Europe is visiting on the day you have chosen. The park receives almost 900,000 visitors in the few weeks it is open every year. Your best chance of avoiding the crowds is to go early.

Many growers are represented at Keukenhof, all eager to take your orders for delivery abroad. Sculpture is exhibited throughout the park, and there are model gardens, self-service restaurants, flower shops, and a working windmill open for visits. (Push-chairs and wheelchairs are available.)

Originally, the park closed in May when bulbs were dug up and the ground prepared for the next year. But from its 50th-anniversary year of 1999, Keukenhof organised its first **Zomerhof**, from mid-August to mid-September, now a permanent feature. It covers about 17 acres and includes bulb and tuberous plants such as lilies and begonias, as well as roses and perennials.

- **Near Keukenhof:** To complement the visual experience of the bulb fields, Lisse has the **Museum de Zwarte Tulp** (Museum of the Black Tulip), entrances on Grachtweg 2A and Heereweg 219, ☎ (0252) 41 7900, open Tues.-Sun. 1-5pm, A small but interesting museum, it gives the history of tulip-growing in the region. Upstairs they show a video of how tulips were planted in the old days, and a collection of implements used in the planting process. There is a free English-language visitor guide. www.museumdezwartetulp.nl

Yearly events

A yearly flower parade takes place on the main road between Noordwijk and Haarlem, via Sassenheim, Lisse and Hillegom, usually the last Saturday in April. Cars and floats, decorated with flowers follow a 40-km (about 25-mile) route. Well worth watching, the floats are usually on display the day before in Noordwijk and the day after the parade in Haarlem, also known as flower city or 'Bloemenstad.' For information about exact dates, locations and the parade route, check with the VVV.

In the neighbourhood of Lisse

Another place to enjoy fields of flowers is in the near-by North Holland town of **Vogelenzang** at **Holland Tulip Park Showgarden** (former Tulip Show Frans Roozen), Vogelenzangseweg 49, ☎ (023) 584 7245, www.hollandtulippark.com, open late March-late May, daily 8am-6pm, with thousands of flowers on display. If the weather doesn't cooperate, **Panorama Tulip Land**, Jacoba van Beierenweg 79 in **Voorhout**, ☎ (0252) 21 2472, open late March-late May, daily 10am-5:30pm, is a good place to come out of the rain. A large panorama painting of a field of flowers and a village encircles visitors. www.tulipland.nl/panorama

When gangsters Bonnie and Clyde robbed American banks in the 1930s, they wrote to carmaker Henry Ford complimenting him on his new V-8 automobile, which they would 'always choose to steal.' The **Den Hartogh Ford Museum**, Haarlemmerstraat 36, Hillegom, ☎ (0252) 51 8118, www.fordmuseum.nl, open Wed.-Sun. 10am-5pm, has more than a few V-8s. In fact, this is the largest collection of Fords in the world, including also trucks, motorcycles, racing cars, etc., all made between 1906 and 1948.

Gouda
Cheese, and a special Christmas festival

Getting there: From Amsterdam, take A2 south to A12 west; from The Hague, Highway A12. From Rotterdam, take A20 northeast.

Information: VVV, Markt 27, ☎ (0900) 4683 2888; www.vvvgouda.nl and www.gouda-online.nl

Known internationally for the cheese that bears its name (characterised by its large wheel shape), the **Gouda** area produces about 60 percent of all Dutch cheese. Every Thursday from mid-June through August from 10am-12:30pm, the old-fashioned cheese market is re-enacted for the benefit of tourists.

But cheese is only one of the interesting things going on here. It's a great place to get the true flavour of Holland in a short time and without too much driving. Most impressive is probably the marvellous collection of seventy 16th-century stained-glass windows in **St. Janskerk**. Best seen on a sunny day.

Situated on the banks of the Gouwe, Gouda began to develop when the river was connected to the Oude Rhine. That made it an important regional trading centre on the Amsterdam and Rotterdam shipping route. Its importance is reflected in the size of the town square, the largest in the country.

Besides the cheese, you should sample the *stroopwafels*. These caramel-filled wafers are sold throughout Holland, but Gouda *stroopwafels* are considered the best. The city was also known for pottery in the early 20th century, and for centuries before that for the typical long, white pipes that were crafted here. (You might like to know that 'Gouda' is pronounced 'Howda,' not with a strong 'G' and long 'u' as most tourists say.)

▶ **St. Janskerk**

Location: On Achter de Kerk, east of the Market Place on a small winding back street. Use the church tower as a guide.

Information: ☎ (0182) 51 2684; www.vrtour.nl/stjanskerkgouda

Hours: Nov.-Feb., Mon.-Sat. 10am-4pm; Mar.-Oct., Mon.-Sat. 9-5pm

St. Janskerk is one of the most impressive churches in the Netherlands, not only because it is the longest in the country, (123 meters/400 feet), but because of its incredible stained-glass windows – 70 of them in all, some of which are 20 meters in height. These windows tell about Dutch history as well as depicting events in the Bible, and are definitely worth a visit. One of the windows depicts Philip II, King of Spain; another Mary Tudor, Queen of England.

The 42 oldest windows were crafted between 1555 and 1571 in what was then a Catholic church. Ten were made by Dirck Crabeth (1505-74) and four by his brother Wouter (1520-89). The fact that the windows survived this long is somewhat miraculous. In 1573, when iconoclasts in Holland were destroying anything associated with the Catholic Church,

St. Janskerk turned Protestant. The windows survived the destruction that hit many churches in those years, and during the early Protestant years another 22 were added. In the last war, the windows faced another threat and were removed piece by piece, to be stored in a shelter under the dunes of North Holland until the hostilities ended.

We advise you to purchase the descriptive pamphlet at the entrance. (Summer carillon concerts on Thursdays 11-11:30am.)

▶ **The Catharina Gasthuis Museum**

Location:	Oosthaven 9 or Achter de Kerk 14 (behind the church)
Information:	☎ (0182) 58 8440; www.museumgouda.nl
Hours:	Tues.-Sat., 11am-5pm

There are two entrances to the **Catharina-Gasthuis**, but the most attractive is via the small street that runs along the south side of St. Janskerk. Then cross a little bridge, go through a lovely ornamental gate which used to be that of the town's leper hospital, to a charmingly planted garden and the entrance.

The present building, dating from 1542, is actually two buildings, the older rear section which was the hospital proper, and the front part which was the Governor's Building. Originally a *gasthuis* was an old-peoples' home and not necessarily a hospital. The *gasthuis* of Gouda existed as early as 1310, becoming a hospital sometime later and remaining so until 1910.

The dispensary houses all sorts of equipment and supplies from mortar and pestle to herbs used for the treatment of various diseases. Note the gruesome 'tools' that were used for pulling teeth, and how much better things are today! Another grisly scene is the painting located in the Surgeon's Guild Room called the 'Anatomy Lesson.' To make it more realistic, there is a case containing surgical instruments and a cupboard for storing the skeleton.

The museum has several period rooms. The Gasthuis kitchen is extremely well-equipped. There is also a collection of dolls and antique toys from the 18th and 19th centuries. Those more inclined toward the gruesome will much prefer the 'torture' room where you can see a body-stretching rack and all sorts of terrible instruments of pain and torture.

▶ **Town Hall and Market Square**

Location:	Markt 1
Information:	☎ (0182) 58 85 78
Hours:	Mon.-Fri. 10am-noon & 2-4pm; Sat. 11am-3pm

Gouda has the largest **market square** in the Netherlands, and sitting in the middle of it is the oldest freestanding Gothic **Town Hall** in the country, dating from 1450. The Trouwzaal (Marriage Room) on the first floor is worth a visit. The tapestries covering its walls are great works of art, and the Council Chamber, just under the roof beams, has true atmosphere.

Gouda received its town charter in 1272 from Count Floris V. The story is enacted every half hour when the clock on the east side of the Town Hall strikes. On the wall by the clock you can see colourful parading figures as the castle door opens – there are two groups of spectators and two standard-bearers on either side. Five seconds after the first chime of the bells, the spectators turn their faces towards the door and the standard-bearers swing round to form a guard of honour. Then the castle door opens and Count Floris emerges, accompanied by a representative of the townsfolk, to whom he hands the charter.

- **Near the Town Hall:** Another building of note on the square is the **Kaas Waag**, or Weigh House, built in 1668 by renowned Dutch architect Pieter Post. Like the Town Hall, it is a fine subject for photographers. This was the centre of Gouda's cheese industry. In its prime, all six entrances were busy, receiving cheese from thousands of farmers who brought their product here to be weighed, graded and sold. Today, the cheese and craft markets are primarily held for the benefit of tourists, but they're interesting to watch. They are held at the Weigh House, mid-June-Aug., Thurs. 10am-12:30pm. In the Weigh House, you can see the huge cheese-weighing scales and sample the cheese, which comes from about 1,500 farms in the vicinity. Upstairs in the Weigh House is the **Cheese Museum**, ☎ (0182) 52 9996, open Apr.-Oct., Tue.-Sun. 1-5pm; Thurs. 10am-5pm. It tells the story of cheese, as well as its importance in the history of Gouda.

A few blocks from the square is **Zuid Hollands Verzetsmuseum**, Turfmarkt 30, ☎ (0182) 52 0385, open Apr.-Sept., Tues.-Fri. 10am-5pm, Sat.-Sun. noon-5pm; Oct.-Mar., Tues.-Fri. 1-5pm, Sat.-Sun. noon-5pm. It deals with the resistance movement in South Holland during the last war.

▶ **De Moriaan – National Pharmaceutical Museum**

Location:	Westhaven 29, opposite the front entrance of the Catharina-Gasthuis
Information:	☎ (0182) 33 1000
Hours:	Mon.-Fri. 10am-5pm, Sat. 10am-12:30pm & 1:30-5pm, Sun. noon-5pm
Note:	April 2007 new pharmacy museum opens, pipes (see below) move to Catharina Gasthuis.

Although cheese is Gouda's claim to fame, the city was once one of Europe's premier makers of pottery and clay pipes, both of which can be seen here. Gouda's pottery trade reached its peak early in the 20th century – its art nouveau and art deco creations still valued by collectors today. This was a natural progression, for Gouda had been home to some of the world's most talented pipe makers for generations. In the mid-18th century, there were as many as 350-pipe making firms in the city. Some characteristic Gouda pipes are on display, with their long stems and elaborately designed oval bowls. One has a stem almost three feet long. The pipe industry vanished in the late 19th century as cigars and cigarettes became popular.

The building has historical significance and has been beautifully restored. Note the facade from 1617. Originally a sugar refinery, spices, coffee, tea and tobacco were later sold here. Upon entering the building, you see an antique tobacco shop fitted with wall cupboards containing tobacco jars and tin boxes, and an antique wooden counter. There are also tiles of many styles and designs throughout the museum – a good many dealing with pipes. www.museumgouda.nl

- **Near the Museum de Moriaan:** Windmill enthusiasts will want to see the restored flour-mill **De Roode Leeuw** (The Red Lion), Vest 65, ☎ (0182) 52 2041, open Thur. 9am-2pm, Sat. 9am-4pm. Built in 1727, it's a working grain mill. Besides taking a tour you can buy some of the products ground there. Nearby is the **Binnenhavenmuseum**, or Inner Harbour Museum, Schielands Hogezeedijk 1, ☎ (0182) 58 4230, an open-air museum located on a canal. On display are early 20th-century boats that sailed the Dutch waterways. www.museumhavengouda.nl

▶ **Also in Gouda**

Adrie Moerings, Peperstraat 76, ☎ (0182) 51 2842, is the only traditional pipe maker (those long white ones) left in Holland. Visitors who want to see how the pipes are made can do so and, there are pipes for sale. At **De Vergulde Kaars**, Hoge Gouwe 45a, ☎ (0182) 51 0825, you can see how candles are made. They'll even let you pour the wax and add colours for your own candle. www.deverguldekaars.nl. Another delectable Gouda speciality is the Gouda *stroopwaffel* (a delicious treacle cookie). At **Tearoom van der Berg**, Lange Groenendaal 32, ☎ (0182) 52 9975, you're welcome to come in early as they make their daily batch. Note, they usually wrap up their work by noon.

Yearly events

From mid-June through August the traditional **Cheese and Crafts Market** takes place Thurs. 10am-12:30pm; **Goveka**, Gouda's cattle and cheese market is held on a Wed. early in Aug. 9am-2pm; and **Gouda Pottery Festival**, with potters from all over Holland, is held on Ascension Day.

Gouda has a special **pre-Christmas event** that takes place in mid-December. It has become so popular that the main square is jammed with people, but it is such a lovely experience that we highly recommend it. It's not hard to imagine you're in the 16th century as the lights are extinguished – none are allowed in the buildings facing the square – and they, along with City Hall, are illuminated by literally thousands of candles. The Mayor will throw the switch illuminating a huge Christmas tree, a gift from Gouda's sister-city in Norway. After a few short speeches, everyone joins in singing Christmas carols. After the carols you can attend St. Janskerk where a special free concert is given. (A word of warning, **dress warmly**. Also, note that the centre of town is closed to traffic then. Public transportation is recommended; parking is limited.)

Tours

Rederij 't Groene Hart, Elckerlijkstraat 6, ☎ (0182) 51 9297, offers boat trips to the nearby Reeuwijk Lakes, where you can relax in the typical polder landscape. The VVV has a self-guided walking tour booklet for a few euros, which takes you past all of Gouda's major attractions.

Eating out

For those huge Dutch pancakes (*pannekoeken*), which everyone loves, try the charming old restaurant close to St. Janskerk, **Het Goudse Winkeltje**, Achter de Kerk 9a. On Oosthaven, **Mallemolen** is a small tavern with white frilly curtains and an old Dutch atmosphere. There are other restaurants on the Market Square...or if you go during Market Day, you can always buy *frites* (fries) or a sausage at one of the stands.

In the neighbourhood of Gouda

To visit a **cheese farm**, call the Gouda VVV for up-to-date addresses. However, there is one at **Kamerik**, a village near Woerden (off the A12 toward Utrecht) where visitors can make cheese; reservations at least 24 hrs. in advance. **Wilhelminahoeve**, ☎ (0348) 40 1200, open daily except Sun. 8am-6pm. Group visits by appointment. Other possibilities are the **Kaasboerderij Jongenhoeve**, Benedenberg 90, Bergambacht, ☎ (0182) 35 1229, open Mon.-Sat. 9am-5pm; and **Kaasboerderij P. Hoogerwaard**, Lageweg 45, Ouderkerk a/d Ijssel, ☎ (0180) 68 1530, open Mon.-Fri. **Boskoop** has the largest expanse of tree, plant and rose nurseries in Holland – a gardener's paradise. Call the VVV in Boskoop ☎ (0172) 21 4644.

Haastrecht
Mrs. Bisdom van Vliet's beautiful 19th-century home

Getting there: Take A12 following the signs for Gouda. At Gouda, take the bridge crossing the IJssel River. Immediately after crossing, you will come to a large intersection. Haastrecht is on the road heading east ... look for the signpost.

Information: VVV, Hoogstraat 31, ☎ (0182) 50 313; www.vvvhaastrecht.nl

This area encompassing Gouda, Oudewater, **Haastrecht**, and the IJssel and Vlist rivers, is exceptionally scenic... a lovely day's drive. Another nice way to see it is by canoe and/or bike. **Kanocentrum Haastrecht**, east of town, ☎ (0182) 50 2245, open May-Sept., offers a canoe trip down the river to Schoonhoven (11 km/7 mi; 3 hours). You can combine it with a bike trip back to Haastrecht, or vice versa.

▶ **Museum Bisdom van Vliet**

Location:	Hoogstraat 166. A large private residence on your left coming from Gouda. If parking is difficult, pass the museum, turn right, and park in their parking area.
Information:	☎ (0182) 50 1354; www.bisdomvanvliet.nl
Hours:	Mid April-mid Oct, Tues.-Thurs. 10am-4pm, Sat. & Sun. 2-5pm

You might call this a sort of 'non-museum' if there were such a word! Everything is just as it was when the lady of the house, Mrs. van Vliet, was alive. Built between 1874 and 1877, the house was the official residence of the Mayor of Haastrecht, Bisdom van Vliet. It's filled with treasures, the most impressive of which is the extraordinary collection of Chinese blue porcelain. The van Vliet family has a long and interesting history but, since they had no children, this lovely house and its treasures became a museum. Since Mrs. Van Vliet stipulated that all must be maintained just as it was, the visitor does feel as if he or she were walking into someone's home.

Oudewater
Site of the witches weighing scale!

Getting there:	In the province of Utrecht, but just a few miles east of Gouda along the IJssel River.
Information:	VVV, Kapellestraat 2, ☎ (0348) 56 4636; www.vvvoudewater.nl

Once a moated and fortified town, **Oudewater** received its town charter in 1265. Its rich history is evident in its beautifully restored 17th-century houses with fancy gables and many charming bridges. It's a pleasant town for walking, and the VVV has a brochure guide in English. The polder area surrounding town is also nice for hiking and bicycling. The VVV has maps and suggested routes for those interested. The main attraction in Oudewater is its association with witchcraft, and its **Heksen Waag**, or Witches Weighing House.

▶ **De Heksen Waag – The Witches Weighing House**

Location:	Leeuweringerstraat 2, on the main street in Oudewater
Information:	☎ (0348) 56 3400; www.heksenwaag.nl
Hours:	April 1-Nov. 1, Tues.-Sat. 11am-5pm, Sun. 11-5pm

Oudewater was a rope-making town known for the uprightness of its merchants. During the witch-hunting mania in the 16th century, it began to lose business because its people were over enthusiastic in the persecution of witches. To solve the problem, they hit on the idea of weighing anyone accused of witchcraft. The accused would be put on the scales and the weighmaster would indicate whether or not they were too heavy to be able to fly on a broom! It is to the credit of the governors of those days that they always weighed honestly, despite believing in the existence of the evil influence of witches. With their

'Certificate of Proof of Innocence of Witchcraft' in hand, the victims would return home, relieved to be able to keep their lives and property. This museum deals with the history of witch-hunting. The best part of the visit, for the children at least, is the weighing ceremony and the 'Certificate of Proof of Innocence of Witchcraft' that they will receive to take home.

- **Near the Heksen Waag:** The historic **Town Hall** was destroyed by the Spaniards in 1575 and rebuilt in 1588. You may see the beautiful hall, council-chamber and Mayor's room by appointment. For 300 years the huge nest on the roof was occupied by storks. Some still stop to rest there, but none have made it their home since around 1990. Dominating the skyline is the unique Frisian-style tower of **St. Michael's Church**, Noorder Kerkstraat 27, with saddle-back roof. When it was restored in 1960, remains of a Roman church dating from 1100 were discovered. **Touwmuseum De Banenschuur**, Reijersteeg 4, shows the history of rope-making in this quaint museum, ☎ (0348) 56 7832. www.touwmuseum.nl

Schoonhoven
The 'silver city'

Getting there: From Amsterdam, south on A2 towards the Lek River, turning off the main highway just before crossing the Lek. The drive along the river is slow but very scenic. From The Hague, A12 to the Gouda turnoff. From Gouda, you might stop at Haastrecht enroute, then south along the Vlist River to Schoonhoven. From Rotterdam, you can approach Schoonhoven along the Lek River, past Kinderdijk, and across the Lek by car ferry; or via Gouda and down the small country road bordering the Vlist River (slightly longer but lovely scenery).

Information: VVV, Stadhuisstraat 1, ☎ (0182) 38 5009; www.vvvschoonhoven.nl

For over six centuries, some of the most talented Dutch silversmiths have worked in **Schoonhoven**. Around 1375 the ruler of the area decided his town needed a silversmith, and by 1638 there were enough in Schoonhoven to form a guild. By the end of the 1800s nearly a third of the population worked in the silver and gold industry. Although much smaller today, it still plays an important role in the town. There are numerous silversmiths at work, and Schoonhoven is the home of the State School of Silver and Goldsmiths, with over 850 students. Obviously, most of the tourist attractions are connected with silver.

Schoonhoven is also noted for its architecture. Inhabited as early as 1280, much of the old town grew up around the central canal, where you'll still find many of its attractive old buildings. Once a walled town with an inner and outer moat, these walls, some of which still exist, protected it from frequent attacks during the Eighty Years War in the 16th century.

Although its central area is attractive, the main reason to visit Schoonhoven is its silver. There are many shops selling a wide range of items crafted from the metal. The VVV has a brochure indicating where they are located.

▶ **The Gold, Silver and Clock Museum**
Location: Kazerneplein 4
Information: ☎ (0182) 38 5612; www.ngzkm.nl
Hours: Tues.-Sun., noon-5pm

This interesting collection is housed in a former barracks, built in 1861. On the first floor, clocks from the Dark Ages to the present outline the development of this craft. Half the fun is listening to the hundreds of clocks ticking, the occasional chime, and even a cuckoo. There's also a lot happening visually. Pendulums swinging back and forth from clocks over 200 years old, mechanical figures moving on the faces of others – such as one of a woman milking a cow, or another of a soldier marching at his post. The 18th century was the Golden Age of clock-making in Europe. There are some fine examples of the Frisian stool-clock, the Amsterdam longcase clock, and the English bracket clock. Spanning five centuries, there's the oldest turret clock (Gothic) in the Netherlands, and today's state-of-the-art wristwatches.

The splendid gold and silver departments are on the second floor, with special attention given to the 19th century, and to a beautiful collection of Dutch silver dating from 1650. The gold collection is small, but the extensive silver collection includes miniatures as well as monumental pieces made for royalty and the wealthy. If you call to make arrangements in advance, the museum will have a silversmith or engraver present to give a demonstration.

▶ **Edelambachtshuis – Museum of Antique Silverware**
Location: Haven 13
Information: ☎ (0182) 38 2614
Hours: Tues.-Sat. 10:30am-4:30pm

A former synagogue along the town canal was restored in 1983 to become a museum with the largest collection of antique Schoonhoven silver from its 'Golden Era' to 1948. On the first floor there is an enormous and unique collection of old Dutch silver objects. Of note in the collection are several small, silver 'knot boxes.' They were used primarily in Friesland by young men proposing marriage. The man would put a small bag of coins in the box and tie the bag loosely. If the knot was subsequently untied by the woman of interest, it meant the answer was no. But if she tied the knot...so would they.

There is also an extensive collection of present-day gold, silver and jewellery on display, and a workshop where a silversmith demonstrates how silver is crafted. There's a small fee to enter the museum, but you can watch the silversmith at no charge. The museum is part of the Rikkoert silver shop, so be prepared to be tempted by the many objects for sale.

► **Also in Schoonhoven**

If your approach to Schoonhoven is via the Lek River, you will enter the town through the 17th-century **Veerpoort**, a narrow gateway through which kings, merchants, bishops and pilgrims have passed for centuries. If you come from Gouda, you will pass through typical polderland, farms, and meadows and your first view of the town will be **St. Bartholomew's Church** with its tower that leans 4 feet. It was built in 1354 as a cruciform church, rebuilt in 1653 in Doric style and, after restorations in 1927 and 1935, acquired its present look. In the choir is the tomb of Olivier van Noort, the first Dutchman to sail around the world. Summer visits on Wed. and Sat. afternoons.

As you thread your way along the narrow main street bordering the town canal, you will find the **Town Hall** and a most unusual town square. The canal being directly in front of the Town Hall, a particularly wide bridge was built to form a sort of square providing the necessary space for official ceremonies and wedding parties. A less happy occasion was when Marrigje Ariens, condemned as a witch, was burned at the stake here – a circle of white and grey cobblestones on the bridge marks the spot. The Town Hall, with its easily identifiable hexagonal cupola tower and white facade, was built in 1452 and renovated in 1775 and 1927. The VVV is located in an old peat cellar of the Town Hall. Ask for their walking route which takes you past the places of special interest.

Next door, the **Nederlands Museum van Knipkunst**, Stadhuisstraat 7, ☎ (0182) 38 7000, Tues.-Sat. noon-5pm, is a unique collection of intricate cut-out art – paper items cut in various designs and images with nothing more than a pair of scissors. Some items on display are over 100 years old.

The **Weigh House** on the Dam is now a restaurant. Facilities for weighing products were offered here by Jan Van Blois in 1356, and the first weigh-house was built between 1616 and 1617, the stone pillars added in 1756. The weighing rights were given to citizens for a few florins per year. Local agricultural products, including hemp, were the primary items weighed here.

A commercial silver shop, **Rikkoert**, Haven 1-13, the largest silver shop in town, has a wide selection of gift items for sale, as well as a superior collection of antique silver. Another option, if you're in the market for silver, is the gallery **Zilver In Beweging**, Bij de Watertoren 25. Located in the city's old water tower, it features contemporary work by Schoonhoven silversmiths.

Eating out

A nice stop for lunch, dinner or a cup of coffee is the **Belvedere Restaurant** on the dike overlooking the Lek River. Other recommended restaurants in town are **De Hooyberch**, **De Stadsherberg**, and the **Lekzicht**. There are also many pleasant coffeeshops for a quick bite.

In the neighbourhood of Schoonhoven

If you have a good map, you will note that there are many green markings indicating scenic roadways along the Hollandse IJssel, the Vlist and the Lek rivers – all within easy exploring distance. Gouda, Oudewater, and Schoonhoven are centrally situated in this flat polderland, a land of water and meadows, edged with willow trees, small lanes following winding creeks, narrow roads running on tops of dikes, and various villages. You might follow the winding road along the Lek towards **Vreeswijk** where you can enjoy a picnic and visit the **Princess Beatrix Locks**, one of the large lock gates in Europe. It is here that the Amsterdam Rhine Canal joins the Lek. It is interesting to watch the boats and the lock gates at close quarters. The drive to the locks along the northern dike of the Lek from Schoonhoven is very beautiful.

Another interesting stop is in **Groot Ammers** and the **Stork Village Het Liesveld**, Wilgenweg (follow the signs to Ooievaarsdorp), ☎ (0184) 60 2616, open Apr.-mid Sept. 10am-5pm. About 250 storks make this their summer home. The Society for Bird Protection opened this facility in 1969 when storks were becoming extinct in the Netherlands. The visitor centre has a film and displays, but the birds are the real attraction. You can watch them take off and land as well as soar in the sky above. There are a number of impressive stork nests. The Village is open only in season. The storks migrate to Africa for winter.

▶ **Kinderdijk**
Nineteen working windmills
Getting there: Take A16 south from Rotterdam, exit at Ridderkerk, then A15 to
Alblasserdam, and follow signs.
Information: VVV Zuid-Holland, ☎ (078) 613 2800; www.zuid-hollandinfo.nl
Hours: The mills work July-Aug., 1:30-5:30pm; April-Oct., a windmill is open
daily 9:30am-5:30pm. www.kinderdijk.org

A visit to **Kinderdijk** is included on almost all the tours. The reason for its fame is that 19 windmills stand here. Nowhere else will you see more than two or three in the same vicinity.

There is a legend about its rather odd name. It appears that following the very destructive flood of 1421, a crying baby and a meowing cat in a cradle were saved from drowning by being washed ashore at this point. From then on, the area was known as 'Kinderdijk' – *kinder* meaning 'child's' in Dutch. The second story (unlike the legend, and probably true) is that the dike along the river was built by the children who lived in the village of Giessen. Plan your visit, if at all possible, for a Saturday during July or August between 1:30pm and 5:30pm. The mills are turning then, and one is open for visits. Of course, it is possible to pass this scenic area by car along the Lek (on top of the dike) and see the windmills any day of the year, or take a stroll down the long path that runs alongside the canals and windmills. This is particularly pleasant in early September, when for one week the mills are illuminated at night. In the summer you can also take a boat tour among the mills (departs every half hour). For a group visit to a mill in operation call the VVV in Dordrecht. www.zuid-hollandinfo.nl

Dordrecht
Where three rivers meet

Getting there:	Dordrecht is reached by A16 (via Brienenoord Bridge) from the north, A15 from the east, A16 from the south.
Information:	VVV, Stationsweg 1, ☎ (078) 32 2440 www.vvvdordrecht.nl

If you climb the tower of Dordrecht's Great Church you can see why this was once one of the most important towns in the country. **Dordrecht** is surrounded by water. The Oude Maas (known as the Meuse at its source in France), Merwede and Noord (both branches of the Rhine, which flows through Germany from its source in the Alps) meet here before emptying into the North Sea. These rivers played an important role in the development of the Netherlands and its neighbours, and Dordrecht has benefited from being at the world's busiest river junction.

Dordrecht's earliest beginnings go back to 837 A.D., but it wasn't until a castle was built here in 1010 that a town began. The town prospered because it controlled the river traffic and could levy tolls on passing ships. Upon receiving its town rights in 1220, 'Dordt' (as it is familiarly known) became the first town of Holland. In 1572, an assembly of the twelve towns comprising the first Free States Assembly was held here under authority of William the Silent. This marked the Netherlands' independence. During this time, Dordrecht was the country's most important and powerful town.

Until the late 17th century, Dordrecht was known as the 'Wine City.' Because of its position on the rivers, all wine shipped to Holland from France and Germany had first to be unloaded here and taxes levied on it. Its location has also had its disadvantages. It suffered badly from flooding in the 15th century, and German troops parachuted into the area to capture control of the waterways in the 1940s. The city is no longer a wealthy town of commerce, but many buildings remain from its days of glory which, together with its canals and attractive waterfront, make it a pleasant city to visit.

▶ **Grote Kerk**

Information:	☎ Langekelderskade 2, (078) 614 4660; (078) 631 0113 (tower); www.grotekerk-dordrecht.nl
Hours:	Apr.-Oct., Tues.-Sat. 10:30am-4:30pm, Sun. 10am-4pm; Nov.-Mar. 1pm-4pm Tower climb: Apr.-Oct., Tues.-Sat. 10:30am-4:30pm, Sun. noon-4pm; Nov.-Mar., Sat.-Sun. 1-4pm

With its square, slightly leaning, grey tower, Dordrecht's 15th-century **Great Church** can be seen for miles. The interior is kept light and cheerful with its white marble pulpit

(1756) and gleaming bronze screen. Look for the Renaissance choir stalls built between 1539-42, predating the time the Church became Protestant, and the stained-glass window showing the disaster of the great flood of 1421. There are wonderful views from the tower.

• **Near the Grote Kerk:** An interesting story is told about the house at Engelenburgerkade 18, known as **Huis Bever-Schaep** (Beaver-Sheep House). Three brothers made a wager to see who could build the most beautiful house with the most controversial decorations. The first brother's house was decorated with a mermaid. The second brother built his house at Wijnstraat 125, displaying a statue of a naked young boy on the facade...the residence became known as **De Onbeschaamde** (The Shameless). The third brother won the wager, however. He decorated his house on Grotekerksplein with something so scandalous that it has not survived, and no one can say what it was.

Notice the sayings on various gables, such as, 'Inde weelde siet toe' (When you prosper, beware), on the **Groenmarkt** between numbers 103 and 117. These houses were built in 1540. Don't miss **De Sleutel**, the gate and buildings of a former brewery, on the Varkensmarkt. Number 105 on the Groenmarkt is now a library. Across from it is the **De Witt statue** honouring Dordrecht natives Cornelius and Johan de Witt, two of the most powerful men in the country in the late 16th century. Cornelius was mayor of Dordrecht, and Johan, as the nation's Grand Pensionary, controlled the nation's political fortunes for nearly a decade. His rival, William III, blamed him for a French invasion and did nothing to stop a mob lynching both brothers in The Hague.

▶ **Simon van Gijn Museum**
Location: Nieuwe Haven 30
Information: ☎ (078) 639 8200; http://cms.dordrecht.nl/gijn
Hours: Tues.-Sun. 11am-5pm

This museum is located on a harbour in an attractive, old part of Dordrecht. It dates from 1729 and was a gift to the town from Mr. Van Gijn, a prominent banker. The house has beautifully-furnished period rooms in various styles – a Louis XIV drawing room, a neo-Renaissance dining room, a study and kitchen of around 1800, and Mr. van Gijn's personal library and bathroom.

Children would be most interested in the superb collection of antique toys, model ships, arms, coins and medals. In addition, there are tapestries, costumes, guild silver, antique furniture, glass, clocks, pottery and china. Other exhibits include a selection of local antiques, while a unique collection of 24,000 prints and drawings is available for inspection upon request.

• **Near the Simon van Gijn museum:** In May 1940, many people in Dordrecht gave little thought to the German warplanes flying overhead. It wasn't the first time they flew over the town, and besides, news reports said Germany had no intention of invading the Netherlands. The **Museum '40-'45**, Nieuwe Haven 28, ☎ (078) 613 0172, open Tues.-

Wed. & Fri.-Sat. 10am-5pm, Sun. 1-3pm, tells the story of how wrong they were. There are collections of items here from the war years when the Netherlands was occupied by the Germans – from the guns and uniforms worn, to the food canisters dropped by the Allies to the starving people of Dordrecht in the final days of the war. Interestingly, it is staffed by people who not only lived those years, but were a part of the Dutch underground resistance. If you're fortunate, one of them may be available to show you around and tell you what life was like under Nazi occupation during the war years.

▶ **Het Hof**

Location: Hof 12
Information: ☎ (078) 613 4626; www.het-hof.nl
Hours: Tues.-Sat. 1-5pm

If any one place can lay claim to being the birthplace of the Netherlands, **Het Hof** could make a strong case. In 1572, representatives from 12 city-states met to form an alliance against the Spanish occupation. They met here in a room known as the Statenzaal, or Hall of States, and chose William the Silent to lead their revolt. You can visit the room, and see the coats-of-arms of those cities.

The Hof used to be a monastery, and has a medieval feel to it; the Statenzaal was the refectory. Across from it is the **Augustijnenkerk**. Built in 1293, it was the church where the monks worshipped. Inside are hundreds of graves, including that of artist Albert Cuyp (1620-91).

- **Near Het Hof:** Down the street is the **Munt**, Voorstraat 188, where between 1367-1806 Dutch coins were struck. A gate built in 1555 stands at what was once its entrance. Further down the street, attractive buildings are at 170 and 178. When you reach a 19th-century bridge over the canal with a cast iron rail, look to your right. You'll see the narrowest street in town (4 feet wide) called **Zakkendrageresstraat**, (Porter Street). If you're not claustrophobic, walk through it, look up and you'll notice it's even narrower at the top. Centuries of sinking have caused the buildings to lean this way.

▶ **Groothoofdspoort**

Location: The end of Wijnstraat and Kuipershaven

Groothoofdspoort, the city's most attractive old gate, is in an historic spot where the rivers of Dordrecht meet. Said to be the busiest river junction in the world, 1,500 ships pass this point every day. It was the busiest spot in Dordrecht, as many European travellers used to join or leave their ships here in the days when this was the principal means of travel.

One of the most impressive city gates still standing in the Netherlands, it was built in 1440, rebuilt in 1617, and a dome was added in 1692. On the land side is the city coat of arms, and on the water side an image of the Virgin of Dordrecht, the city's patron saint, and the coats of arms of other Dutch cities.

- **Near the Groothoofdspoort:** Anyone interested in Dutch architecture, ancient gables and historic carvings should wander around the inland harbour to see the many beautiful houses and warehouses built in the 17th and 18th centuries. Walk down the two streets leading to the Groothoofdspoort. **Wijnstraat** has some interesting houses, the oldest in town built in 1495 at number 113, then 127, and De Onbeschaamde (see page 155) at 125.

If you take the water side of Groothoofdspoort you'll be on **Kuipershaven**, where you'll see a unique drawbridge known as **Damiatebrug**. Before you cross it, take a look at the building at Kuipershaven 17-18, a picturesque warehouse from 1658. On the other side are a number of nice old buildings along Wolwevershaven harbour, with its colourful pleasure craft and tug boats.

▶ **Dordrecht Museum**

Location: Museumstraat 40
Information: ☎ (078) 648 2148; http://cms.dordrecht.nl
Hours: Tues.-Sun. 11am-5pm

An interesting museum whose collection includes mainly Dutch paintings (many from the Dordrecht School) dating from the 17th century to the present. There are paintings by Albert Cuyp (1620-91), who lived his entire life in Dordrecht. Jan van Goyen's *View of Dordrecht* is on display along with works by Nicolas Maes, Ferdinand Bol and Arent de Gelder, all pupils of Rembrandt.

- **Near the Dordrecht Museum:** The **Arend Maartenszhof**, Museumstraat 56, are almshouses built for war widows around 1600 by a wealthy man of that name. It has an attractive entrance gate which opens onto a tree-shaded courtyard with a well in the centre. Look to your right as you enter and push the little button on the wall. It will light up a room, allowing you to see the meeting hall where the almshouse governors held their meetings with residents. The portraits on the wall are those of the former governors. You can easily imagine yourself in the 17th century.

Eating out

On the waterfront there is an excellent restaurant with a river view at the **Bellevue Hotel**, Boomstraat 37, ☎ (078) 613 7900.

Tours

For a boat tour of Dordrecht, contact **Waterrondje Dordt**, ☎ (078) 613 3250 or 613 0094. Canal tours last an hour and leave from Wijnbrug, near Augustijnenkerk and Het Hof. This is also a great city to walk in. The VVV has an English walking-guide booklet.

Heinenoord
Location of an 18th-century farm residence and estate

Getting there: On A29 south from Rotterdam, take the first exit (exit 21) after passing through the Heinenoord Tunnel, and then follow the signs northwest to Heinenoord.

Information: VVV Oud-Beijerland ☎ (0186) 61 6000; www.vvvhoekschewaard.nl

This quiet area resembles Zeeland with its open fields, never-ending skies and healthy atmosphere. The island of the Hoeksche Waard is primarily agricultural, but also benefits from the recreational facilities which have developed around its neighbouring island, Voorne-Putten. Close by there's a nature reserve and bird sanctuary, and just a few kilometers south the watersports recreational area, Mijnsheerenland.

▶ Streek Museum Hoeksche Waard

Location: Hofweg 13. In Heinenoord, watch out for the left turn sign, 'Streek Museum.'

Information: ☎ (0186) 60 1535; www.streekmuseumhw.nl

Hours: The house is open Wed. 10am-5pm. Thur.-Fri. 2-5pm. and Sat. 10am - 5pm. Farm is temporarily closed.

The museum consists of two buildings, **'t Hof van Assendelft** being the main one. Built in 1768 as a private residence and meeting place for area rent collectors and polder officials, some rooms have been restored to reflect the style of that period. The first room you visit is the Polder Kamer, where government officials met to deal with matters of importance to the District. On the walls are large panels depicting the Greek-Turkish War of 1820; this type of wall decoration was not unusual in wealthy farmers' homes. This room houses a collection of antique toys. The kitchen is interesting and complete – even to a wine cellar. Just off it, the former stable is now a display room for old sleds and farm implements. Look for the small window in the second room you visit, which looks into the kitchen. In former days the wall or 'closet' bed (*bedstee*) was in that corner of the room, and the window in the closet door permitted the lady of the house to supervise the housemaid in the kitchen from her bed!

Upstairs are several rooms with life-size models in various types of dress, a collection of old tobacco pouches, pipes, lace caps, and so on. One interesting item is a 'clacker' (1800), which was used at night throughout town to signal the time. The attic is also interesting, fitted out to resemble a town square.

The second building of the museum, **Hofstede Oost Leeuwenstein**, is a lovely old farmhouse and barn. Only the barn is open to visitors. An old shop, built in 1911 and in operation until 1970 in Oud-Beijerland, has been incorporated into it. Opposite is a small bakery.

In the neighbourhood of Heinenoord

Not far away at **Mijnsheerenland**, a few kilometers south of Heinenoord, there is a café-restaurant worth mentioning: **Vrouwe Huisjesweg**, ☎ (0186) 60 1629, an attractive and reasonable place with good food.

Brielle (Den Briel)
First town liberated from Spanish occupation (1572)

Getting there: Brielle is on N218. From the north, take A13 to Maas Tunnel then left towards Rozenburg (signs 'Pernis') and Brielle. From the east, A15; from the south, A29 to Barendrecht, then A15 west, or N57 north.

Information: VVV, Markt 1, ☎ (0181) 47 5475; www.brielle.nl and www.zuid-hollandse-eilanden.nl

This small town received its town rights in 1330. Today, it is a veritable open-air museum, with countless monuments, charming narrow streets, squares, and cared-for houses that have witnessed history through the ages. A most significant event took place on April 1, 1572, when the Geuzen ('water beggars' or pirates), encouraged by Dutch nobles and burgers, successfully routed the Spanish who occupied the town. This was the first such victory in a campaign that ended in the formation of the Kingdom of the Netherlands. Vestiges of the original city walls, the **Wallen**, still exist – including the foundation of the gate which the water beggars broke down to enter the city. Don't miss **Den Briel Historical Museum**, Markt 1, ☎ (0181) 47 5475, open Apr.-Oct., Tues.-Fri. 10am-5pm, Sat. 10am-4pm, Sun. noon-4pm; Nov.-Mar., Tues.-Sat.. 10am-4pm, Sun. closed. www.historischmuseumdenbriel.nl

The museum presents the history of the town, including its native son Maarten Tromp (1598-1653). One of the greatest admirals of his time, he led the fleet that defeated the second Spanish Armada. Children might enjoy walking into the city's old jail cell, which dates from 1623 and still has writing on its walls from its occupants of centuries ago. You can visit **St. Catharijnekerk** (15th century) where William the Silent married his third wife, Carlotte de Bourbon. It's open mid May-June and Sept. 1:30-4pm; July-Aug. 10am-4pm. Take a deep breath and climb the 318 steps of its tower, as Mary Stuart did in 1688. The future Queen of England knew it was the best vantage point to watch her husband Prince William III and his army sail off to claim the British throne. On a clear day it's still a great place to see the surrounding polders, the North Sea, and the port of Rotterdam.

Locals and summer visitors enjoy the area because of its proximity to the great family beaches of Rockanje, Oostvoorne, and Briellse Meer (see Chapter 14). Golfers might like to try the public course, **Kleiburg**, Krabbeweg 9, ☎ (0181) 41 3330 for reservations.

Yearly events

On April 1, Brielle takes on a medieval feel as it celebrates its 1572 victory over Spain. Many stalls display old crafts (carving of wooden shoes, weaving of chair seats, etc.), while the aroma of roasting meat wafts from a barbecue in the centre of town. In the afternoon, actors dressed in the medieval costume re-enact the battle with the Spaniards.

Chapter 4 | The province of Utrecht

Centrally located, **Utrecht** is the smallest of the 12 provinces. It has had a long and influential history, particularly in its role during the long Eighty Years War against the Spaniards. The provinces of Holland tried to offer combined resistance, but disputes developed between the Catholic south and the Protestant north. The northern provinces refused to deal with the occupiers, while the southern group wanted reconciliation with the Spanish Duke of Parma, then Governor of the Netherlands. The northern provinces signed the Union of Utrecht on January 23, 1579. There followed a long war, the Spaniards being finally ousted in 1648, after which the Union of Utrecht served as the foundation for the Netherlands State.

The history of the area can be found in the province's ancient towns such as Utrecht (same name as the province itself) and Amersfoort. Its countryside offers many corners of relaxation: the southeast with fruit orchards whose blossom draws many visitors, and castles to titillate the imagination; the southwest, its peaceful polderlands hiding behind the dikes along the picturesque rivers IJssel and Lek; the northwest with the Loosdrecht lakes where all kinds of water sports are available; and the northeast with its old forestlands, former hunting grounds of Dutch royalty, its grand country hotels and restaurants. Indeed, Utrecht is a small province with a great variety of natural beauty and appealing places to explore.

Information: VVV, Utrecht ☎ (0900) 128 8732 (€ 0.50 p. min.)

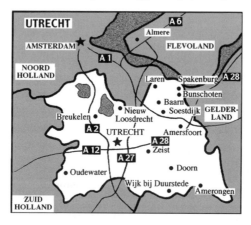

Utrecht
A city with a medieval past and active present

Getting there: From Amsterdam, A2 south until you see signs for Utrecht Centrum;
From The Hague and Rotterdam A12

Information: VVV, Vinkenburgstraat 19, ☎ (0900) 128 8732 (€ 0.50 p.m.)

The fourth largest town in the Netherlands, **Utrecht** has a history that dates back to 48 A.D. when the Romans built a fort on the spot now called Domplein. From the time its first bishop was appointed in 696, through the Middle Ages, Utrecht was the most important religious centre north of the Rhine. The bishops had tremendous power over all aspects of life. Many of Utrecht's tourist sites are connected with that period. Its major church, the Domkerk, attracts many visitors and the Domtoren is the tallest church tower in the country. On a clear day, visitors can see most of Holland from its viewing platform.

In the old city centre is the 'Museumkwartier' (Museum Quarter), a cultural paradise with medieval churches and historic buildings ringed by canals. It is where six of Utrecht's principal museums can be found, including the country's foremost one on religion, and its most entertaining, the Musical Clock to Street Organ Museum.

Thanks to its central position, Utrecht is a transportation centre – headquarters of the Dutch railway system. Its train station is connected to the largest indoor shopping mall in the country.

Stroll along the many canal-front streets lined with old, gabled buildings, or take a boat tour through the unique canal system. In an old city like Utrecht with its narrow streets you won't miss the car. It's much more interesting to discover on foot. (We recommend the VVV walking tour.)

Utrecht is also home to Holland's largest university, Utrecht University, and the atmosphere is decidedly student-based.

▶ **Domtoren – Cathedral Tower**

Location: Domplein, in old part of town. The tall tower is visible from most parts of town.

Information: ☎ (030) 233 3036

Hours: Tower tours summer 10am-5pm, winter 12am-5pm, Sat. 10-5. Otherwise irregular, call to check; www.domtoren.nl

---

Completed in 1382, it took 62 years to build the **Domtoren**, the tallest church tower in the country – 367 ft. (112 m) – the only remnant of a huge cathedral destroyed by a storm in the late 17th century (see Domkerk). Inside the tower are two chapels, and 13 bells that weigh from 880 to 18,000 lbs and are named after saints. They were cast in 1505, raised into the tower and positioned entirely by hand. It takes 25 people to ring them. More than 50 carillon bells are at the next level. Listen for them during your visit.

There are conducted tours (last one at 4pm) almost to the top of the tower, but only the fit should consider climbing the 465 steps. On clear days you can see the steeples of

Amersfoort, Rhenen and other neighbouring cities, and the distant skylines of Amsterdam, Rotterdam and The Hague. The narrow staircase was designed to wind in the direction that allowed defenders of the tower to fight with their right hand, while forcing invaders to fight with swords in their left hands.

Tickets for the tower (and other tours, including a canal trip) are available at Ron-Dom, an information centre located on the square near the tower, at Domplein 9. The tour, lasting just under an hour, makes several stops along the way, giving everyone a chance to catch their breath.

- **Near the Domtoren: Flora's Hof**, next to the Domtoren, is the court of the former Episcopal Palace and now a restful and attractive flower garden. The gate dates from 1634. North of the tower is the **Museum Voor Het Kruideniersbedrijf** (Grocery Shop Museum), Hoogt 6, ☎ (030) 231 6628, which sells a few 19th-century candies (*snoepjes*), tea (*thee*) and spices (*kruiden*). Upstairs is a display of grocery items from olden days. Open Tues.-Sat., 12:30-4:30pm; free entrance.

  A little further north is **Margaretenhof**, Jansvelt 4-20, with almshouses built in the 16th century. Nine of the original 20 almshouses remain. It is located close to Janskerk, a church founded in 1040, with a nave and transept from that period.

▶ **Domkerk – Cathedral**

Location: On Domplein, just behind the Domtoren
Information: ☎ (030) 231 0403
Hours: Open May-Sept., weekdays 10am-5pm, Sat. 10am-3;30pm, Sun. 2-4pm;
               Oct.-April, weekdays 11am-4pm, Sat. 10am-3:30pm, Sun. 2-4pm. Guided
               tours; free concert every Sat. at 3:30pm

A Roman fort was built on this site in 47 A.D. Just over 600 years later, two churches were built within its crumbling walls. The church we see today was built in stages between 1254 and 1517 and has had a chequered past. In 1674, it fell victim to a mighty storm, recorded as a freak tornado that destroyed a whole section between the tower and the present church. Due to the lack of funds it was never rebuilt, which is why the church and tower are not connected.

Inside the **Domkerk** is a sepulchral monument to Admiral Baron Van Gendt, who was killed in a naval battle against a British-French fleet in 1672. The French occupied Utrecht at that time and made Domkerk a Catholic church again. However, when the Dutch Protestants eventually won it back, they defiantly placed the admiral's tomb exactly where the Catholic altar had stood. Look in the choir gallery for the Holy Sepulchre including the black marble tomb of Bishop Guy van Avesnes. Like other religious images in the Domkerk, it bears scars inflicted by the iconoclasts who attacked the church in 1580.

- **Near the Domkerk:** This area is the oldest and most attractive part of Utrecht. In front of the church is the **Domplein**, or Dom Square. The nave of the Domkerk stood here until the storm destroyed it in 1674. Grey bricks on the pavement outline the contours of the nave of the church as it once was. The plan of the two small churches which were built on the site in the 7th century is indicated by heavy basalt rocks. There is also a plaque to show where a Roman fort stood in the first century.

Next to the church is the **Pandhof** or **Kloostergang**. This peaceful garden, a 15th-century cloister, has a formal herb garden with medicinal plants, and is encircled by a wall on which the life story of St. Martin, patron saint of Utrecht is depicted in carved stone tablets. They are original. Notice the stone seats along the wall facing the Domplein, close to the church; one has long scratch marks made by Napoleon's soldiers, who occupied the city from 1797-1813 and sharpened their bayonets there.

Next to the Pandhof is the Academy Building of **Utrecht University** (the largest university in Holland), Domplein 29, built in 1896. Behind the Academy Building is the **Kapittelzaal**, on Achter de Dom. Now a university auditorium, it was here in 1579 that the Union of Utrecht was signed. That agreement sparked the birth of the Netherlands as a nation, uniting seven provinces against Spanish rule.

The streets in front of the Domtoren are busy, modern shopping streets, but those behind the Domkerk have a quiet medieval feel. Look for the **Paushuize**, (Pope's House), a large building on Pausdam. It was built in 1520 by Adrian Florensz of Utrecht, who became Pope Hadrian VI in 1522. He was the only Dutchman to serve as Pope and was the last non-Italian Pope until John Paul II of Poland in 1978. Pope Hadrian died in 1523 and never lived in what is reputed to be the most beautiful house in Utrecht. Near the Paushuize is the **Nieuwe Gracht**, a picturesque canal built in the late 14th century.

Pieterskerk (1048) is also behind Domkerk, built on the remains of a Roman civilian settlement. Inside is a crypt with the remains of Bishop Bernold, who was responsible for the church's construction. He also had five others built in close proximity, positioning them to form a giant cross with the Domkerk at the centre. Pieterskerk forms the eastern arm of that cross, but apart from the Domkerk, the only other remaining church of the five is **Janskerk**, to the north of the city centre.

▶ **Oudegracht**

There are many canals in the Netherlands, but none like the **Oudegracht**, which runs through Utrecht's old town centre. It was dug in stages, the earliest around the year 1000. It was dug deep and lined with high walls to protect the city from flooding. These high walls made it impossible to load or unload canal boats at street level, so the canal was lined with wharves. The buildings above had cellars giving onto these brick wharves, which opened out onto the canal. This construction is not only unique in the Netherlands, but also in Europe. Some of the wharves are still used for loading and unloading goods, but many have been converted to terraces for the numerous restaurants and nightspots that have taken over the cellars. It's a popular and pleasant spot for a summertime drink or meal.

- **Near the Oudegracht:** The early residents of the Oudegracht were wealthy merchants and landowners who built large fortified houses. The best example is Oudegracht 99. This medieval mansion was known as the Castle Oudaen when it was built around 1300, but today it is the **Oudaen Brewery** with a restaurant. In the cellar is an authentic steam brewery where beer is made in the traditional way. Brewery tours are available for groups of 15 or more, ☎ (030) 231 1864.

  To the west of the canal is **Hoog Catharijne**, the largest indoor shopping mall in the country. It has over 200 shops and is connected to the main train and bus stations of Utrecht.

▶ **Museum Catharijneconvent**
Location: Nieuwegracht 63 (at corner of Lange Nieuwstraat)
Information: ☎ (030) 231 3835; www.catharijneconvent.nl
Hours: Tues.-Fri. 10am-5pm, Sat.-Sun. 11am-5pm

This museum's collection of medieval art is the most significant of its kind in the country, and includes works by Rembrandt and Frans Hals. This building was a convent, then a hospital and later a way-station for military troops. A particularly significant painting in the museum is a portrait of a Pope, which if reversed becomes a picture of the devil. This is a typical example of the religious hatred during the years of the Protestant Reformation. It is one of many paintings, woodcarvings and other displays here that recount the history of religion in the Netherlands. (Cross the first-story walkway for a splendid view of the cloister gardens.)

- **Near the Catharijneconvent:** There are two almshouses (*hofjes*) nearby. The remains of 14 original houses built in 1579 are at **Kameren van Jan van Campen**, Schalkwijkstraat 6-14. **Brutenhof**, near the Lepelenburg, was built in the 17th century on the least expensive piece of land overlooking the city wall. It also has a garden. Across the Oudegracht in the opposite direction from the museum is yet another almshouse, **Mieropskameren**, built in 1583.

▶ **Nationaal Museum van Speelklok tot Pierement**
(Musical Clock to Street Organ Museum)
Location: Steenweg 6
Information: ☎ (030) 231 2789; www.museumspeelklok.nl
Hours: Tues.-Sun. 10am-5pm, Thurs. till 9pm
Note: Guided demonstration tours in English every hour (highly recommended); last tour at 4pm; special activities for children

The **National Museum from Musical Clock to Street Organ** contains an amazingly varied and fascinating collection of automatic musical instruments from the 16th-20th centuries. The tour of this musical wonderland is full of surprises, with demonstrations of many of the exhibits ranging from simple but unique musical boxes to garish, resounding barrel organs that take up an entire room. Holland pioneered this form of musical entertainment. Well-known composers like Beethoven, Mozart, and Handel even wrote music especially for them – with musical boxes often in the form of clocks, and snuff and jewellery boxes.

The tour gives visitors a chance for hands-on fun or a sing-along, as the guide grinds out tunes on a portable barrel organ. You might consider taking a group to the museum on off hours – say, for a birthday party with a difference; call the museum for possibilities.

The museum building was a 10th-century church, the Buurkerk. In 1457 Sister Bertken, ashamed at being the illegitimate child of the parish priest, came and lived here as a hermit until her death 60 years later. The main street in this part of town once ran through the centre of the church. Livestock and wagons regularly passed through the building, except during church services when a detour was ordered. On the facade of the church, to the left, there are two cannon balls embedded in the wall. They were fired from Spanish cannons when the city was under siege in the 16th century.

▶ ## Nederlands Spoorwegmuseum – Dutch Railways Museum

Location: Maliebaanstation, Johan van Oldenbarneveltlaan 6
              (easy walk from city centre)
Information: ☎ (030) 230 6206; www.spoorwegmuseum.nl
Hours: Mon.-Sun. 10am-5pm

Utrecht is the headquarters of the Netherlands Railways and it has the country's best railway museum. The **Spoorwegmuseum** is well worth a visit, with a fascinating collection of old locomotives and train accessories of the past, present and future, including moving models, paintings, films and memorabilia.

It is located in a decommissioned 19th-century station with over 60 locomotives, carriages and wagons on its tracks. You can climb onboard some, including the cab of one old locomotive. There are miniature train rides, a restaurant and picnic area. The huge exhibit is divided into three 'Worlds' (*Werelden*), one taking you on an audio tour through an English coalmine, another with a theatre production journey onboard the Orient Express, and the third virtually taking you in, under and toward steam locomotives in an exciting recreation of the Golden Age.

Indoors you will see model trains zipping along a track, with modern signals and barriers working as they make their way over recognisable bridges and landmarks. There is even a simulated train ride where you drive the train from the cab of a modern express train. And outside is the 'Jumbo Express,' an adventure ride just for kids. Youngsters love this place.... parents will too.

▶ **Centraal Museum**
Location: Nicolaaskerkhof 10
Information: ☎ (030) 236 2362; www.centraalmuseum.nl
Hours: Tues.-Sun. 12am-5pm; Fri. till 9pm

The outline of the Agnieten Convent can be seen in the centre of this museum which is known for its collection of paintings from the 15th-16th century Utrecht School, as well as its Gerrit Rietveld Wing that recognizes this well-respected architect and furniture designer, of which there is a large collection here. (You can even book tours through the museum to two of the houses he designed.) Children may be more interested in the scale model 'doll house' of 1680. As was common in those days, this was not built as a toy, but as a scale model of a rich merchant's home. The Decorative Arts Section and Period Room give a perspective of life in early Utrecht. Art buffs will also find much to interest them in the Antiquities Collection, such as 15th-century sandstone statues. There is also fashion and contemporary design, including the 'A-Bomb coat' from the 'hot' Dutch design duo, Viktor & Rolf. In a separate building is a children's museum about Holland's famous children's book author Dick Bruna.

● **Near the Central Museum:** You can gaze at the stars through a telescope, or just watch them in a slide show, at the **Sterrenwacht Sonnenborgh**, Zonnenburg 2, open Tues.-Fri. and Sun., 11am-5pm (closed Saturdays!), ☎ (030) 230 2818. It's the second oldest observatory in the Netherlands (the oldest is in Leiden), the bastion of which was established in 1551. www.sonnenborgh.nl

The **Universiteitsmuseum**, Lange Nieuwstraat 106, ☎ (030) 253 8008, open Tues.-Sun. 11am-5pm, www.museum.uu.nl, contains the world's largest collection of dentists' instruments through the ages. It also has a collection of scientific equipment, rocks used by students of geology, and skeletons used by anatomy students. Behind the museum is an 18th-century botanical garden.

There are two almshouses nearby. **Beyerskameren**, Lange Nieuwstraat 108-132, or Agnietenstraat 4-6, built in 1597. Residents used to receive a yearly supply of wheat, cheese and peat. **Pallaeskameren**, Agnietenstraat 8-30 and Nieuwegracht 205, was built in 1651. Above the gate is written: 'Maria van Pallaes, Driven by God's Love, Being a Widow of Mr. Schroyestein, Has Founded These Almshouses – Not Heeding the Favour of the World – But a Place in Heaven's Square.'

De Doelen, Doelenstraat 12, dates from 1337, and was originally a convent for lay sisters. It was later a prison, a headquarters for the local militia, and then a workhouse for vagrants and prostitutes.

▶ **Also in Utrecht**
One of the largest brick tower windmills in the country is north of the city centre: **Rijn en Zon**, Adelaarstraat 30, open Saturday 10-11am, ☎ (030) 271 7352. West of the centre is a windmill restored in 1998, **De Ster**, Molenpark. There are also windmills in the sur-

rounding towns of Breukelen, Kockengen, Loenen, Lopik, Maarssen, Montfoort, and Tienhoven. For information about these windmills call Stichting de Utrechtse Molen, ☎ (030) 220 5555. www.utrechtslandschap.nl

Geld Museum (Money Museum), Leidseweg 90, open Mon.-Fri. 10am-4pm, ☎ (030) 291 0492, has a collection of Dutch coins and military medals from the 7th century to the present. It is the only official mint of royal coins. www.geldmuseum.nl

Julianapark, Amsterdamsestraatweg, is a pleasant city park with playing fields, ponds with flamingos, and aviaries with tropical birds.

East of the city centre are the **University Botanical Gardens**, Fort Hoofddijk, Budapestlaan 17, ☎ (030) 253 1826. These gardens have a splendid show of flowers and shrubs in summer. Open daily 10am-4pm; May-Sept., 10am-5pm; closed Dec.1-March 1. www.botanischetuinen.uu.nl

The **Rietveld-Schröderhuis**, Prins Hendriklaan 50, ☎ (030) 236 2310, open Wed.-Sat. 11am-5pm (by appointment only), is a part of the Centraal Museum. Designed in 1924 by the architect and furniture designer Gerrit Rietveld, this house is the best example of 'De Stijl' architecture popular in the early 20th century. It appears on the world list of protected buildings. www.centraalmuseum.nl

Markets

General Markets: Vredenburg, Wed. 10am-5pm; Fri. 10am-5 pm; Sat. 8am-5pm
Flower Markets: Janskerkhof, Sat. 8am-5pm; Oudegracht between Zakkendragerssteeg and Bakkerstraat, Sat. 8am-5pm;
Drapery and Ragbag Market: Breedstraat, Sat. 8am-1pm
Animal Market: Veemarkthallen, Sartreweg, horses, Mon. 8am-1pm; cows, Wed. 7:30am-1pm; sheep, Thurs. 7:30am-1pm

Eating out

You might like to try some food specialities of the area such as *Domtorentjes* (chocolate cup with whipped cream, mocha and chocolate topping), *Utrechtse sprits* (a brittle kind of shortbread) and *Utrechtse theekantjes* (a local cookie).

Utrecht has many good restaurants. Try **Stads Kasteel Oudaen**, Oudegracht 99, ☎ (030) 231 1864, www.oudaen.nl, a beautifully restored medieval castle. Or try **Chez Jacqueline**, close by at Korte Koestraat 4, ☎ (030) 231 1089 (closed Sun. and Mon.). The local parks have pleasant restaurants: **Het Oude Tolhuys**, Weg naar Rhijnauwen 13-15, ☎ (030) 251 1215, www.hetoudetolhuys.nl, and **De Zakkendrager**, Zakkendragerssteeg 26, ☎ (030) 231 7578, www.zakkendrager.nl. At Utrecht Station, in the popular shopping centre, the **Hoog Catharijne**, you'll find a great choice of convenient cafeterias, snack bars, cafés and restaurants. (Vroom & Dreesman's 'La Place' – a department store chain – is one of our favourites for a quick but excellent quality meal, cafeteria-style, with one of the few salad bars in Holland.)

Yearly events

In late Aug.-early Sept., Utrecht holds its Festival of Early Music with Baroque and Renaissance music. On Christmas Eve, *Kerstklokkenluiden*, there's a carillon concert at the Domtoren, complete with choirs and carols. Every Saturday from mid-May to end Sept., there's a VVV-guided walking tour of the city.

Tours

Rederij Schuttevaer, at the Viebrug (Vie Bridge), all year, 11am-5pm, ☎ (030) 272 0111, www.schuttevaer.com, has a daily one-hour tour of the city canals. They also offer a day boat trip on the Vecht River to Breukelen from June to late September, boat trips to the ancient village of Maarsen; through the nature area along the Kromme Rhine between Utrecht and Bunnik, as well as trips to a cheese farm. **Rederij Lovers**, Nieuwekade opposite no. 269, ☎ (030) 231 6468, www.loversutrecht.nl, does canal trips and organises dinner boat trips (min. 12 people), in summer. If you prefer to row your own boat, **De Rijnstroom**, Weg naar Rijnauwen 2, March-Oct., ☎ (030) 252 1311, www.rijnstroom. nl, gives you the opportunity with boat rental. In Loosdrecht, **De Rederij in Jachthaven Wolfrat**, ☎ (035) 582 3309, organises one to three-hour boat trips around the lakes.

In the neighbourhood of Utrecht

Utrecht's past can be discovered by visiting the castles in its vicinity, though it might take some time – there are 63 of them! The VVV sells a special castle booklet. The most interesting and beautiful castles are **De Haar, Zuylen** and **Sypesteyn Castles** – descriptions follow.

Nijenrode, along the left bank of the Vecht, is historically interesting but cannot be visited. It is worth driving past, because of its true castle-like setting within a moat, and its wooden drawbridge. It is now a prestigious Dutch business school.

It might be useful to note that **Oudewater**, with its Witches Scales, is only 20 kilometers (12 mi) southwest of Utrecht. Its rich history is covered in Chapter 2, together with its proximity to Gouda, Haastrecht and Schoonhoven.

The **Oud Amelisweerd Estates**, Koningslaan 11-A, ☎ (030) 656 3427, outside of town on the road to Bunnik, is a country estate built in 1770. Louis Napoleon bought it in 1808 during the period when he ruled the Netherlands, but stayed here no more than eight days. It has 116 acres of nature trails and bridle paths, (Appointments with the park ranger once a month, Sunday mornings, for garden tours only, with a theme; activities for children on Wed. afternoons. Also an organic garden and café – all homemade goods, 12-5pm weekdays, 11am-5:30pm weekends). www.veldkeuken.nl

Rhijnauwen Estate, Laan van Rhijnauwen, Bunnik, has 32 acres of woodlands and footpaths for lovely walks. Rederij Schuttevaer's 'Kromme Rhine (Rhine River)' tour, mentioned earlier, operates in June only. It stops at the summerhouse, and there's a charming pancake restaurant on the property.

The **Loosdrechtse Lakes** are located about 8 km (5 mi) north of Utrecht, and 8 km west of Hilversum. It's a family water sports paradise for swimmers, water-skiers and boaters. For the less active, summer days are filled with sailing meets and lots to watch. Encircled by woods and moorland, there are wonderful walking and cycling tours – or you can rent a rowboat to enjoy the Vuntusplas as well as the nearby nature reserve.

▶ **Kasteel De Haar – De Haar Castle**

Location: Kasteellaan 1, Haarzuilens, 8km (5 mi) west of Utrecht off A2. Direction Maarssen to Haarzuilens and follow signs for Kasteel de Haar.

Information: Kasteel de Haar, ☎ (030) 677 8515; www.kasteeldehaar.nl

Hours: All year, 10am-5pm; one-hour guided tours on the hour; last tour starts at 4pm (Note: 10-min. walk from parking lot to castle); no children under 5 years of age on tours.

The original castle on this site was built in the 12th century, but it was demolished and rebuilt several times before being destroyed by French soldiers serving under King Louis XIV. In the 1890s, the castle was rebuilt by Baron Etienne Van Zuylen van Nijevelt, a descendant of the family which has owned the castle since 1434.

The castle is unique, with its beautiful grounds, moat and spiky turrets reaching skyward. Among the curiosities is a small carriage in which King Louis XIV, the Sun King, rode as a child. There are huge tapestries, Persian carpets, paintings, antique furniture, and Chinese and Japanese porcelain.

The gardens are beautiful with an abundance of colourful flowers, and the spacious lawn is a popular place for family picnics. The charge for the castle tour is separate from the park entrance.

The red and white colours of De Haar Castle are repeated in the town of Haarzuilens, showing the influence of the castle on the town that is still the Baron's property. Along with the antique pump in the town square, you'll find cafés and restaurants for refreshments.

▶ **Slot Zuylen – Zuylen Castle**

Location: Tournooiveld 1, Oud-Zuilen, Maarssen. From Utrecht, take any small road going north towards Maarssen. The castle, obscured by trees is hard to find. Look for a tree-lined road followed by a serpentine brick wall. The castle is behind it.

Information: ☎ (030) 244 0255; www.slotzuylen.com

Hours: Mid-May to mid-Sept., Tues.-Thur. guided tours hourly 11am-4pm, Sat. 2-4pm, Sun. 1-4pm. Mid-March to mid-May & mid-Sept. to mid-Nov.; Sat. tours hourly 2-4pm, Sun. 1-4pm

Zuylen Castle gives an overview of life during five centuries. The present structure dates from about 1300, the gate from the 1600s. In the 18th century the fortress was altered into a stately country house with a magnificent garden. The main feature of the garden is the famous serpentine wall, ideally suited for growing citrus trees. The garden is open to the public during regular hours.

The collection includes paintings, furniture and tapestries. There are books and writings by the feminist, Belle van Zuylen (1740-1805) who spoke out against the hypocrisy of the social mores of her day. She maintained an active correspondence with such prominent men of letters as Voltaire and James Boswell. It was the latter who told her to hold her tongue which was too quick to criticise normal conventions. She married, but found her husband dull and had an eight-year 'intensive friendship' with Benjamin Constant. She wrote under the pseudonym 'Abbe de la Tour.'

▶ **Kasteel Sypesteyn – Sypesteyn Castle**
Location: Nieuw Loosdrechtsedijk 150 (south of Hilversum)
Information: ☎ (035) 582 3208; www.sypesteyn.nl
Hours: Apr.-Oct., Sat./Sun. noon-5pm; May-Sept. also Tues.-Thurs. 10am-5pm.
                   Guided tours noon-4pm. Foreign language groups, call in advance.

This castle is famous for its beautiful garden laid out in 16th-century style with a maze. It should be visited during the rose season if possible. Built on what were thought to be the remains of a 13th-century castle, it was the home of Sir Catharinus van Sypesteyn until 1937. There are twelve rooms with furnishings from the 16th, 17th and 18th centuries. It has an incomparable collection of Chinese, Loosdrechts and other Dutch porcelain, a large collection of 16th- to 18th-century paintings, valuable furniture, clocks, glassware and weaponry.

Amersfoort
A step back into the Middle Ages
Getting there: From Amsterdam, take A1 southeast. From The Hague or Rotterdam go
                     east on A12 to Utrecht, then A28 Zwolle.
Information: VVV, Stationsplein 9-11, ☎ (0900) 112 2364

Amersfoort is a growing town almost exactly in the centre of the country. Its narrow streets, canals, and over 350 buildings which are considered monuments, make Amersfoort an enjoyable place for a day of walking. Wall houses, archways, canals, and bending alleyways combine to give a beautiful picture of a medieval town. Most of Amersfoort's main attractions are quite close together.

For the perfect companion to your visit here, look for a colourful, pocket-sized book by Carol Conover – an American resident of Holland with ancestry from this town: *Amersfoort: Fragments of Time*, available through the local VVV and bookshops.

▶ **Muurhuizen – Wall Houses**

In the 14th century Amersfoort was growing quickly. To make room for the growing population, they tore down the town walls and built a new ring of walls a little further out. Being practical and resourceful, they built the houses on the foundations of the old walls. They varied in size and design, but almost all were attached to one another and built on the exact lines of the walls which circled the old city. These *muurhuizen*, or wall houses, still exist and form the core of the town.

Muurhuizen can be found on a street of the same name. Together with a section of Breestraat, it almost forms a complete circle around the old city. You can also take a look at the houses from the other side, by walking the ring of streets that border the old moat that surrounded the walls – streets named 't Zand, Weversingel, Zuidsingel, and Westsingel. The **Tinnenburg**, #25, is the oldest wall house dating from before 1414. The **Flehite Museum**, Westsingel 50, ☎ (033) 461 9987, open Tues.-Fri. 11am-5pm; Sat.-Sun. 1-5pm, is within three wall houses – two of which have been restored – and illustrates Amersfoort's history from early times to the present. www.museumflehite.nl One item on display is the cane used for support by Johan van Oldenbarnevelt (1547-1619), as he walked to be beheaded. An Amersfoort native, he became the highest official in the nation but, in one of Holland's less proud moments, he was caught in a political and religious dispute and executed by his adversaries.

Across from the museum is the **Mannenzaal**, Westsingel 47, ☎ (033) 472 0669, open July/Aug. Tues.-Fri. 11am-1pm and 2-5pm, Sat.-Sun. 1-5pm; May-Sept. daily 1-5pm. In the 16th century this building – financed by prominent citizens – contained hospital wards and a chapel for the poor and elderly. The women's ward was demolished in the early 20th century, but the men's ward and the chapel remain, looking as they did when the hospital itself closed in 1907. The main room is lined with 22 wooden compartments built into the wall, each containing a patient's bed, curtained off for privacy. www.museumflehite.nl

Close by is the most picturesque of the town's three remaining gates, the **Koppelport**, connecting Grote Spui and Kleine Spui. It is a water and land gate built over the river around 1400, and designed so that a wooden door could be lowered into the river to close the town off from menacing marauders. Nearby at **De Drie Ringen**, Kleine Spui 18, ☎ (033) 465 6575, open Thurs.-Sat. 1-7pm, you can take a free guided tour to see how beer is made...and, of course, sample the brew.

▶ **Also in Amersfoort**

The tallest structure in town is the **Onze Lieve Vrouwetoren (Tower of Our Lady)**, Lieve Vrouwekerkhof, all that remains of a church built in the mid-15th century that was destroyed by an explosion in 1787. You can see the outline of the old church marked in coloured stones in the pavement and hear the carillon bells ringing every 15 minutes. (There is a world-famous carillon school here in Amersfoort, De **Nederlandse Beiaardschool**, Grote Spui 11.) The 330 ft. (100m) tower may be climbed only in July and August.

Group visits to the tower also Apr.-Oct. can be arranged by calling the VVV at ☎ (0900) 112 2364 (€ 0.50 p. min.).

Amersfoorters are often teased about their unique boulder, **De Kei**, located on the corner of Arnhemsestraat and Stadsring...and referred to as 'boulder haulers.' The story goes that in the 17th century a man bet his friends he could get the gullible people of Amersfoort to drag a 9-ton boulder across town to his new house. We are told he succeeded, but not how. From the boulder, a path leads to the **Waterpoort Monnikendam**, Plantsoen-Ouest 2, a town gate, now a restaurant. Nearby is the **Marienhof**, built in 1480, a former convent with a beautiful garden, www.marienhof.nl, home to the **Culinary Museum**, Kleine Haag 2, (033) 463 1025, for appointments – a fascinating museum about the riddles of Dutch food through the ages, with table settings, utensils, etiquette, etc.

Amersfoort is the birthplace of cubist/Neo-Plasticist artist Piet Mondriaan (1872-1944). The **Mondriaanhuis**, a museum for geometric/abstract art, Kortegracht 11, ☎ (033) 462 0180, open Tues.-Fri. 10am-5pm, Sat.-Sun. 1-5pm, is the house where Mondriaan spent the first eight years of his life. The museum tells the story of his life and career and has a full-size model of his Paris studio. When you enter, it feels as if you're walking into one of his paintings. A room is devoted to his last work, *Victory Boogie Woogie*, which was left unfinished when he died. It is now in The Hague Gemeente Museum, along with other works by him (see Chapter 3). www.mondriaanhuis.nl

In the centre of town, **St. Joriskerk** (1442-1534; base of church, 1243), Hof 1, is worth looking at. The other old gate, the **Kamperbinnenpoort**, Langestraat and Kamp, is the only one of the three gates in the original town wall.

The **Dieren Park Amersfoort (Amersfoort Zoo)**, Barchman Wuytierslaan 224, ☎ (033) 422 7100, open April-Oct. 9am-6pm, is located in the Birkhoven woods on the western edge of town. It has 700 animals of over 90 species. Get the free trail sheet at the zoo entrance so you don't miss anything: www.amersfoortzoo.nl. Near the zoo is the **Museum Nederlandse Cavalerie**, Barchman Wuytierslaan 198, ☎ (033) 460 6996, open Tues.-Fri. 10am-4pm, a collection showing the history of the Dutch cavalry from 1813 to the armoured squadrons of today.

In the neighbourhood of Amersfoort

The Eemland area is extremely scenic with beautiful farms, extensive polders, and impressive lakes such as the Eemmeer, the Gooimeer and the Veluwemeer. There are some small towns to the east and north worth investigation.

Baarn was the home of many kings and queens. **Soestdijk Palace** was presented to King William II in 1816 in recognition of his bravery at the Battle of Waterloo. More recently it has been the home of Princess Juliana, the Queen mother. The Palace is on the road between Baarn and Soest. Tickets are available at the door, and for the park, tickets are available on-line: www.paleissoestdijk.nl. Also in Baarn – and a beautiful place to walk around – is **Kasteel Groeneveld**, Groeneveld 2, ☎ (035) 542 0446, open

Tues.-Sun. 11am-5pm, built about 1703, with displays about the Dutch landscape. Contact the VVV in Baarn for more Information: (035) 541 3226.

Spakenburg is a former fishing village that celebrates Spakenburg Days on the last two Weds. of July and the first two of August. A bonanza for shutterbugs, the whole village turns out in traditional dress, the only costume in the Netherlands in which parts of the medieval dress are preserved. In addition to its historic restored buildings along narrow streets, there is a folkloric market, fun fair, and displays of arts and crafts. For specifics, contact the Amersfoort VVV.

An exhibition of traditional costumes from the villages of Bunschoten and Spakenburg, and artifacts from the fishing industry can be seen at the **Klederdracht en Visserijmuseum (Traditional Costume and Fishing Museum)**, Kerkstraat 20 (behind the Noorderkerk), ☎ (033) 298 4634, open 14 Apr.-8 Sept., Mon.-Sat. 10am-5pm. www.kenvmuseum.nl

Spakenburg Museum 't Vuurhuus, Oude Schans 47, ☎ (033) 298 3319, open Thurs./Sat. 11:30am-2:30pm, is worth a stop to see a completely furnished farm, a fisherman's family living room of about 1915, an old shop, and a smokehouse where you can see how herring was smoked. www.vuurhuus.nl

Amerongen
Castle town and tobacco museum

Getting there: Take A12 to Maarsbergen (exit 22), south on N226 to N225, then 8 km (5 mi) east to Amerongen.

Information: VVV, Drostestraat 20, ☎ (0343) 45 2020 (closed Nov./Dec.)

Amerongen is an historic village with old arcades, and a moated feudal castle (little evidence of the original structure) dating from 1166. Historically, tobacco has been the traditional crop for the region. The **Amerongen Historical Museum** or **Tabaks Museum** (Tobacco Museum), Burg. Jhr. H. v.d. Boschstraat 46, ☎ (0343) 45 6500, open April-Oct., Tues.-Sun. 1-5pm, is located in a former tobacco shed. The museum gives the history of tobacco-growing in southeast Utrecht from 1640 to 1965, with drying shed, tools and carpenter's workshop. In summer, there is a demonstration in the tobacco field.

Between Amerongen and Utrecht, there are roughly 17 castles...a challenge to anyone wanting to cover them all. This area is called the **Langbroeker Wetering**. Aristocracy settled here because hunting was good and there was sufficient land to lease out for farms. The Duke of Gelder and the Bishop of Utrecht were constantly battling over territory, which explains the number of local 'fortifications.' Most cannot be visited, but Amerongen Castle and Doorn House are open to the public.

▶ **Kasteel Amerongen – Amerongen Castle**

Location: Drostestraat 20

Information: ☎ (0343) 45 4212; www.kasteel-amerongen.nl

Hours: By appointment only (in restoration until 2010, but still able to visit); please call or e-mail: info@kasteel-amerongen.nl

Amerongen Castle belonged to the powerful Bishop of Utrecht and later to the Counts of Holland. In 1672, Louis XIV even slept here. Not long afterwards, the castle was destroyed by the French, then rebuilt in 1676 to the plan of Maurits Post. Over the moat there is an interesting double bridge. The upper entrance led to the reception rooms while the lower entrance was for the use of servants.

The original castle had two towers. Unfortunately, today it lacks any outer decoration. Kaiser Wilhelm II of Germany stayed here from late 1918 to the summer of 1920. It was here he signed papers abdicating and bringing the monarchy to an end in Germany. The interior with its silk wall coverings is filled with priceless objects, including Delft and Japanese Imari porcelain. In 1879, Count van Aldenburg-Bentinck inherited the castle, and it is now owned by a foundation called the Stichting Kasteel Amerongen. Gardens are open to the public from April through October, weekdays (except Mondays) 11am-4:30pm; weekends 12:30-4:30pm.

In the neighbourhood of Amerongen

About 10km (6 mi) east is **Rhenen**, a town with a long history and a huge church tower. The tower of **St. Cunerakerk** was built around 1500. Legend has it that St. Cunera – an English princess who is reputed to have traveled to Cologne, Germany, with 11,000 virgins – escaped being killed by pagans while on a pilgrimage to Rome in the 5th century. Rescued by the king of Rhenen, she returned here with him but died at the hands of the king's jealous wife. A number of miracles were attributed to her and, as her legend grew, so did the number of pilgrims who came to Rhenen. It was they who made it possible for this relatively small village to build such a large church tower. **Gemeentemuseum Het Rondeel**, Kerkstraat 1, ☎ (0317) 61 20 77, open Tues.-Fri. noon-5pm, Sat. 1-5pm, Sun (only in July-Aug.) 1-5pm, tells the story of St. Cunera and of the town. www.rhenen.nl

Doorn
Home of Kaiser Wilhelm

Getting there: East/West on A12 take Doorn exit. North/south, take A2 past Utrecht, then A12 east to exit 21 (Maarn).

Information: VVV, Dorpsstraat 4, ☎ (0343) 41 2015

Doorn, just a few kilometers from Amerongen, has a famous manor house, **Huis Doorn**. On the third Sunday in August the annual **Horse and Carriage Castle Tour** in the area starts here – and quite a sight it is. (Viewing only; no rides) Located in a wooded area influenced

by two rivers, the Rhine and the Lek, it's a wonderful area for hiking and biking. Tree lovers will enjoy the **Van Gimborn Arboretum**, Velparegh 13, ☎ (034) 341 2144, open March-April, Mon.-Fri. 8am-4pm, Sat./Sun. 10am-4pm; May-Oct., weekends only, 10am-4pm, appreciated for its rhododendrons, heather-garden and immense collection of conifers. There are concerts in the **St. Maartenskerk.**

▶ **Huis Doorn**

Location:	Langbroekerweg 10
Information:	☎ (0343) 42 1020; www.huisdoorn.nl
Hours:	Check website for sporadic hours; closed on Mondays; last entrance 4pm.

In 1918 Germany was clearly losing WW I, and the man who led the country into war knew he had to leave. Kaiser Wilhelm II fled to the Netherlands, which was neutral and close by. He was granted asylum. The Dutch refused Allied requests to have him extradited for trial as a war criminal. So from 1920 until his death in 1941, he lived in exile at **Huis Doorn.**

It was a very comfortable life. The house he purchased was originally a 14th-century castle, used as a summer residence by the dean of the Utrecht Cathedral. It became a manor house in 1536 and underwent radical changes in 1780.

Never inhabited after the Kaiser's death, Huis Doorn is furnished and arranged as it was when he lived there. There are mementos relating to his stay, as well as antique furniture, porcelain and a famous collection of snuffboxes that belonged to Frederick the Great. There are portraits of the Kaiser, his family and other royalty. You can visit the bedroom where he died, aged 82; the dining room where he entertained guests in royal style; and the cellar with the collection of silver he brought from Germany.

World War II began before the Kaiser died, and German troops occupied the Netherlands. Despite having had no admiration for each other, Hitler was prepared to repatriate the Kaiser's body for burial in Germany. The Kaiser, however, had stipulated in his will that it could only be returned if the monarchy was restored to Germany. He remains buried on the estate here.

In the neighbourhood of Doorn

In **Driebergen**, the **Museum of Military Traditions**, 't Schilderhuis, van Rijckevorselsraat 2, ☎ (0343) 51 7588, open Wed. 2-5pm, Sat.-Sun. noon-5pm, has a collection of uniforms, equipment, videos and a model of part of the battle of Waterloo. www.schilderhuis.nl

Wijk bij Duurstede, with its unique alleys, arches and restored buildings, lies on the Rhine south of Doorn. If you visit by car, look for the only windmill we know you can drive 'through.' It is built over the old town gate. You can visit the dungeon and tower of **Duurstede Castle**, Langs de Wal 7, ☎ (0343) 57 13 03, every first Sunday of the month, 1:30-5pm by appointment; terrace open May-September. www.kasteelduurstede.nl.

The **Museum Dorestad**, Volderstraat 15, ☎ (0343) 57 1448, open Tues.-Sun. 1:30-5pm, has exhibits on the rise and decline of Dorestad, an early medieval settlement and precursor of Wijk bij Duurstede.

On the other side of the Rhine in Gelderland is the moated town of **Culemborg**. Together with Buren and Zaltbommel, it is well worth a visit.

Zeist

Old woods, private mansions, and Air Force Headquarters

Getting there: Take A12 east to exit 20, then north to Zeist.
Information: VVV, Het Rond 1, ☎ (0900) 109 1013

Zeist is between Utrecht and Amersfoort in a lovely wooded area. There are many large homes once owned by rich Dutch planters from Indonesia. In 1746, it was the refuge of the Evangelical Brotherhood who fled Moravia. In 1950, the City Council took over these houses on the square flanking Zeist Palace.

▶ Zeist Palace

Location: Zinzendorflaan 1, on the western outskirts of Zeist.
Information: ☎ (030) 692 1704; www.slotzeist.nl
Hours: Open all year, but by reservation only, with guided tours. The palace is often closed for weddings, so call in advance.

This superb palace is worth a detour (and an advance booking) both on its own merits and to learn something of its unusual history involving the Community of the Moravian Brethren who used to occupy part of the buildings. The front and back facades of the structure carry the date 1686. In 1676, William Adriaan of Nassau (the son of Prince Maurits) received virtually infinite powers over his territory. **Zeist Palace** became his headquarters where he made laws, levied taxes, coined his own money, etc. The palace is superbly furnished and has restored period rooms which are a delight to the eye. In addition, temporary exhibitions are held here.

In the neighbourhood of Zeist

Camp Zeist is a base for the Dutch Royal Air Force. Its **Military Air Museum**, Militaire Luchtvaart Museum, is north of Zeist (Huis ter Heide turnoff), then east to Camp Zeist, Kampweg 2, Soesterberg, ☎ (0346) 35 6000, open Tues.-Fri. 10am-4:30pm, Sun. noon-4:30pm. The museum has documents, photos, paintings and uniforms depicting the history of military aviation since 1913, as well as about 30 airplanes. www.militaireluchtvaartmuseum.nl

Chapter 5 | The province of Gelderland

Gelderland is the largest province in the Netherlands, with fingers of land going as far west as Gorinchem, north to Flevoland, east to the German border and south to the Waal River.

The beginnings of Gelderland are complicated, not least because it was made up of four areas: Zutphen, Arnhem, Nijmegen and Roermond. For centuries it was under the control of German counts that constantly battled for power. In 1579, Zutphen, Arnhem and Nijmegen signed the Union of Utrecht and became part of the United Provinces (of the Netherlands). Roermond remained loyal to Spain, and in 1713 became a part of Austria. With the end of the Napoleonic era it returned to the fold as part of the Province of Limburg.

A most popular area in Gelderland is the Veluwe, which extends south to Arnhem and north toward Zwolle. Its forests, hills, and natural beauty make it a favourite for those who are looking for a change of pace from the flat polderlands of North and South Holland. Gelderland's numerous castles also draw visitors, as do the sites which saw some of the heaviest fighting in the Netherlands during WW II. Arnhem is a good choice as a base for exploring the region, with Nijmegen an attractive alternative.

Information: VVV Gelderland ☎ (026) 751 7030

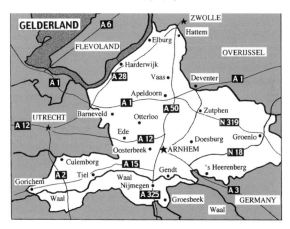

Barneveld
The old Veluwse Market

Getting there: Barneveld is east of Amersfoort. From Amsterdam, A1 to N30 south. From The Hague and Rotterdam, A12 to N30 north.

Information: VVV, Langstraat 85A, ☎ (0342) 42 0555; www.vvvbarneveld.nl

Most Thursdays in July, and on two in August, everything seems to happen in **Barneveld**, an old market town in the Veluwe. The yearly programme may change slightly, so if the following appeals to you, call the VVV for this year's events.

There is a market with over 100 stalls where antiques and just about everything else can be bought, locals in national costume can be photographed, and old-fashioned crafts observed, such as clog or basket-making, horse-shoeing and 'cake-beating' – the latter of which must be seen to be believed. There are costumed processions, demonstrations of folk dancing, puppet shows for the children, horse-drawn tram tours and, if you have the energy to climb to the top of the tower, the view of the Veluwe is most rewarding.

Don't miss the antique sale behind the Café Het Schaap in Nieuwstraat (see 'Eating Out'). Viewing is in the morning and the auction takes place at 2pm (not every Thursday, so do check). A traditional animal market is held every Wednesday morning.

There are two museums. Items dealing with Barneveld's history are at **Veluws Museum Nairac**, Langstraat 13, ☎ (0342) 41 5666, www.nairac.nl, open Tues.-Fri. 10am-5pm, Sat. 1-5pm. It also has an archeological collection. Barneveld has a college of agriculture, and is a leading poultry-producing town. The **Dutch Poultry Museum** (Nederlands Pluimveemuseum), Hessenweg 2a, ☎ (0342) 40 0073, www.pluimveemuseum.nl, open April-Oct., Tues.-Sat. 10am-5pm, is indeed all about chickens and eggs, though it doesn't explain which came first.

Eating out

To counteract those hunger pangs, consider a Dutch-style pancake at **Café Het Schaap**, Nieuwstraat 48, ☎ (0342) 41 2003.

Harderwijk
Home of the largest dolphinarium in Europe

Getting there: From Amsterdam A1 east, A28 north to Harderwijk; from The Hague and Rotterdam A12 east, A27 north, A28 northeast.

Information: VVV, Bleek 102, ☎ (0341) 42 6666; www.vvvharderwijk.nl

Harderwijk is an old Hanseatic port town which dates from 1231. It was prosperous enough to have its own university, where famed botanist Linnaeus studied. Its Town Hall, Grote Kerk, and two town gates are reminders of its historic past. The small **Veluws Museum**, Donkerstraat 4, ☎ (0341) 41 4468, www.stadsmuseum-harderwijk.nl, open Mon.-Fri. 10am-5pm, Sat. 1-4pm, covers the history of Harderwijk.

▶ **Dolfinarium Harderwijk**

Location:	Strandboulevard Oost 1
Information:	☎ (0341) 46 7467; www.dolfinarium.nl
Hours:	mid-Feb.- Oct., 10am-5pm, July-Aug. 10am-6pm

This is the largest marine mammal zoo in Europe, and there are several shows per day. Among the offerings are a dolphin show in the large covered pool area and other amusing shows with sea lions and walruses. You can watch seals feeding in their natural surroundings, pet and feed the rays, or stare eye to eye at killer whales through large glass windows. This is also a rescue centre for ailing dolphins. There is usually a film or two to be seen, a play beach and several places to get a snack.

Elburg
A town with historic architecture and charming streets

Getting there:	From Amsterdam, A1 east to A6, N309 through Dronten to Elburg. From Rotterdam and The Hague, east to Amersfoort, A28 north to 't Harde, follow signs to Elburg.
Information:	VVV, Ledige Stede 31, ☎ (0525) 68 1520; www.vvvelburg.nl

Once an important town in the Hanseatic League, **Elburg** is now a quiet village hidden from the surrounding fields and moors by its moat and old city walls. To be there in the early evening and see its main street lit with tiny clustered lights in its espaliered trees and the old Fish Gate is a delightful start to a romantic adventure. It's a treasure-trove of historic architecture with structures from the 14th-18th centuries. The facades of the 17th-18th-century houses are worth the trip alone. The Town Hall dates from about 1200, and there are widows' almshouses from 1650. The best way to visit is to put on your most comfortable shoes and walk the narrow streets. The old defense system is worth exploring, with the city walls, moat and gates all still largely in place.

St. Agnes Cloister (1418) houses the **Gemeentemuseum Elburg**, Jufferenstraat 6, ☎ (0525) 68 1341, open Tues.-Fri. 10am-5pm, a collection of local history. The **Fish Gate** (1392-94) and **Casements** are an annex to the museum, open July-Aug., Tues.-Fri. 10am-noon & 1-4:30pm. **St. Nicolas Church** and tower, open June-Aug, Mon.-Fri. 1:30-4:30pm, Tues. also 10am-noon, were first built in 1396.

Elburg has two popular herb gardens that are open to visitors: **A. Vogel Tuinen**, Landgoed Zwaluwenburg between 't Harde and Elburg, ☎ (0525) 68 7373, www.avogel.nl, open daily, year round from sun up to sun down; and **Kruidentuin De Groene Kruidhof**, Ellestraat 52, ☎ (0525) 68 1711, open May-Oct., daily 10am-8pm.

▶ **Anton Pieck Museum and Voerman Museum**
Location: Achterstraat 48, Hattem
Information: ☎ (038) 444 2192
Hours: May-Oct., Tues.-Sat. 10am-5pm, Mon. 1-5pm; Nov.-April, Tues.-Sat.
                   10am-5pm; July-Aug. also open Sun. & Mon. 1-5pm

Hattem is a picturesque town with ancient walls and buildings from Holland's Golden Age. It has more to offer...two museums under one roof – one originally the regional archeological museum, expanded with a collection of pre-war scenes of Hattem and the area by well-known Dutch illustrators of the 1900s, Jan Voerman and his son; the other, the **Anton Pieck Museum**, with 150 illustrations that this artist bequeathed to it in 1987. Pieck's work delights his admirers with nostalgia, as does the picturesque well in the courtyard and the Dickensian-type figure in the wrought iron sign above the entrance. The barn walls are covered with Pieck's charming works, capturing the period of tow barges, post coaches and the horse-drawn sleigh.

Staying over

Elburg has few 'fancy' facilities; but how many chances are there to stay overnight in a moated and walled town? The **Elburg Hotel**, Smedestraat 5, ☎ (0525) 68 38 77, is modest and inexpensive, but it has a room fit for a princess, with a four-poster bed!

Walibi World, an amusement park, is just across the bridge in the province of Flevoland (see Chapter 6), www.walibi-world.nl.

Apeldoorn
Playground of royalty
Getting there: Apeldoorn is easily accessible via a series of highways. North/south
                     highway A50 bypasses the town on the east and east/west, the A1
                     bypasses it to the south.
Information: VVV, Deventerstraat 18, ☎ (055) 526 0200; www.vvvapeldoorn.nl

Apeldoorn is in a wooded area embracing 50,000 acres of nature. Its beginnings as a town date from the 700s. From the 17th to 20th centuries, paper-making was the major industry. As it declined, commercial laundries (70 of them) sprang up in its place. Today it is a holiday and convention centre with charming inner-city streets, outdoor cafés, old facades, and many shops. In the summer, the Market Square is active almost daily with sales and special events (you can park underneath). Its claim to fame and chief tourist attraction is the palace which has housed generations of the Dutch Royal Family.

▶ **Het Loo Palace Museum**

Location:	Turnoff A1 heading north to Nieuw-Millingen, then right on the Amers-foortseweg until you see signs for Het Loo Paleis. Plenty of parking. Bus 102 or 104 from the train station.
Information:	☎ (055) 577 24 00, www.paleishetloo.nl
Hours:	Tues.-Sun. 10am-5pm
Note:	The Palace tour is self-conducted. A brochure in English is for sale, and is very helpful. Groups can call for conducted tours.

In the 1680s the sparsely populated land around Apeldoorn was one of the best hunting areas in Europe – and William III of Orange loved to hunt. He had a palatial lodge built, which also served as his country residence. When William and his wife Mary Stuart were crowned King and Queen of England in 1689, the palace was enlarged. It was also used by William's successors until 1806-10, when the French occupied the Netherlands. Louis Napoleon, King of Holland and brother of Napoleon, then used it as his home.

Queen Wilhelmina (1880-1962) spent her childhood here and retired to Het Loo when she abdicated in 1948. Princess Margriet, sister of Queen Beatrix, and her family lived here until 1975. After a seven-year renovation, the palace reopened in 1984 as a national museum commemorating the House of Orange-Nassau. All the earlier 19th-20th-century 'improvements' were removed, and each room of the palace decorated in a different style to depict the various periods over the 300 years that royalty lived here. The children may enjoy Wilhelmina's playroom.

The French Gardens were restored to their 17th-century glory, and there are excellent views of them from the back of the palace. There is an upper garden, a sunken lower garden, and two side gardens. Look for both the Queen's garden and the King's Garden. With luck, the King's Fountain will be working; it spurts almost 14 meters into the air. For those with unlimited energy, the grounds comprise some 1,606 acres. There are concerts in the Palace the last Friday of the month; reservations necessary.

▶ **Also at Palace het Loo**

The **Royal Stables** are what you will first see on arrival, built from 1906-10. On display are carriages and cars used to transport the royal family, as well as toy vehicles they played with as children. In the west wing of the palace is the Museum of the Chancery of the Netherlands Orders of Knighthood, with displays of royal medals and insignia, as well as uniforms. There is also a video explaining the Palace's restoration process.

▶ **Also in Apeldoorn**

Apenheul, Berg en Bos, J.C. Wilslaan 31, ☎ (055) 357 5757, www.apenheul.nl, open Apr.-June. & Sept.-Oct. 9:30am-5pm; July-Aug. 9:30am-6pm, is famous for its 400 monkeys which move freely among the visitors; especially fun for children. An island is reserved for gorilla families.

Koningin Juliana Toren, Amersfoortseweg 35, ☎ (055) 355 3265, recreation park has motorboats, caves, www.julianatoren.nl; Apeldoorn also has a children's farm, **Malkenschoten**, Arnhemseweg 355, ☎ (055) 533 2803, www.malkenschoten.nl. Steam train, boat and covered wagon rides to the village of **Dieren** are popular, ☎ (0900) 168 1636 (VVV). Gliding, parachuting and plane rides can be arranged at **Teuge Airfield**, De Zanden 55, ☎ (055) 323 8585.

CODA Museum, Vosselmanstraat 299, (055) 526 8400, open Tues.-Sat. 10am-5pm, Sun. 1-5pm, gives the history of the city, including displays of the paper-making industry and laundries that thrived here. The **Nederlands Politie Museum**, Arnhemseweg 346, ☎ (055) 543 0691, open Tues.-Sun. 1-5pm, is fun for youngsters, with its displays of uniforms, weapons and other items that tell the story of 200 years of police work in the country. They can climb into police cars and helicopters, try on a bullet-proof vest, and even have their fingerprints taken. In addition to the national forests nearby, Apeldoorn's oldest park, the **Oranjepark** is a lovely relaxing place, and certainly worth the trip in autumn when the trees take on their brilliant colours.

▶ ## De Cannenburgh Castle

Location:	Maarten van Rossumplein 4 in Vaassen, about 6-8 km (4-5 mi) north of Apeldoorn.
Information:	☎ (0578) 57 1292
Hours:	April-June & Sept.-Oct. Mon.-Thurs. 10am-5pm, Sat.-Sun. 1-5pm. July-Aug., Tues.-Sun. 10am-5pm

Built in 1365, this angular building with square towers was rebuilt in the mid-16th century from its medieval remains. The natural stone tower was the original main entrance, but in 1751 a Louis XIV-style entrance was added. There are portraits of the owners' ancestors in the 18th-century hall. The museum collection also includes antique furniture, paintings and porcelain. **Het Koetshuis**, the coach house restaurant, is a good place for lunch, a cup of tea, or even dinner. Open all year.

Zutphen
Ancient city of towers

Getting there:	A1 From Amsterdam around Apeldoorn to N345 south (exit 21), follow signs to Zutphen; from The Hague and Rotterdam, east on A12 to A348 north, then N348 to Zutphen.
Information:	VVV, Stationsplein 39, ☎ (0900) 269 2888; www.vvvzutphen.nl

A town of many battles and rulers, **Zutphen** was a prominent city in the 12th century due to its position on the river IJssel – a major trade route at the time. It declined in importance as the river silted up, but still had 7,500 inhabitants when in 1572 the Spanish stormed it to put down a revolt. They massacred over 100 Zutphen citizens, hoping to discourage rebellion to the Spanish rule in other cities. Instead of leading to surrender, the massacre resulted in stronger resistance in many cities. Zutphen declined under 19 years of Spanish occupation, and never regained its former prominence. There were more wars: the French occupied Zutphen twice, and it suffered a great deal of damage during WW II.

The English poet Sir Philip Sidney died in Zutphen. He is revered as a great writer of English verse, and as the ideal Renaissance gentleman. He died in battle as English troops assisted the Dutch against Spain in 1586.

▶ **St. Walburgiskerk and Library**
Medieval library with chained books
Location: From the Groenmarkt, take the Lange Hofstraat to 's Gravenhof, the church and the City Hall.
Information: ☎ (0575) 51 4178

This 13th-century Protestant church was transformed into its present Roman-Gothic style in the 15th century. It has suffered war damage and fires – the north Door of the Virgin being replaced between 1890 and 1925. Notice its impressive ceiling and wall fresco, and fine wrought iron work. It has an important library (1561), with the building and furniture preserved in their original medieval state; home to 750 books, many printed before 1500 (the oldest in 1469), with their beautiful stamped covers, brass bindings and clasps. There are also ancient manuscripts which, like many of the books, have been bequeathed to the library. This was a public library from the outset – built by a churchwarden to enable regular citizens, tempted by reform, to read about Catholicism – where books could only be studied in situ. Note the original locks and chains of the more than 300 books chained to the rows and adjoining monastic benches. This really is a fascinating place for lovers of books and history. (Must be toured with a guide; check times.)

▶ **Also in Zutphen**
In spite of so much damage, Zutphen retains some gates and towers of historic interest. The **Wijnhuistoren** (Wine House Tower), originally part of a 14th-century inn, became part of the fortifications in the 17th century. The **Berkel Gate**, although in ruins, still sits prettily over a canal. The **Bourgonje Tower** (1457), a rampart **Drogenaps Tower** (1444), the **Spanish Gate**, and **Gunpowder Tower** can all be visited.

Just walking the streets is a treat, especially for those interested in architecture. On the 's Gravenhof, you will see the 15th-century **Town Hall** and a complex of buildings with fine Gothic and Renaissance facades. An unusual feature in such a small town is its three large market squares: the **Groenmarkt** (vegetable market), the **Houtmarkt** (wood market), and the **Zaadmarkt** (seed market).

The **Stedelijk Museum**, Rozengracht 3, ☎ (0575) 51 6878, open at the end of 2007 after renovation, Tues.-Sun. 11am-5pm, is housed in the cloisters of a 13th-century Dominican monastery. It contains archeological and historical artifacts from the region.

The **Museum Henriette Polak**, Zaadmarkt 88, same phone number and hours as the Stedelijk Museum, has a collection of modern Dutch figurative art. Next to St. Walburgskerk is the **Grafisch Museum**, Kerkhof 16, ☎ (0575) 54 2329, open Weds.-Fri. 1-4:30pm, Sat. 11am-3pm, devoted to printing, with demonstrations on how it was done in the early 20th century.

's Heerenberg
Home of the Catholic Counts

Getting there: 's Heerenberg is a few kilometers southeast of Arnhem on the German border off the main east-west highway A12. Take the Emmerich turnoff heading north (N316).

Information: VVV, Stadsplein 73, ☎ (0314) 63 2822

Bergh Castle is the important stop here, but take a look around the town itself. The **Town Hall** steeple is Roman. There are a few houses from the late Middle Ages and a small castle, **Boetselaarsburgh**. The northwest wing and tower of this patrician house are probably 16th century; the remainder mostly 18th century.

▶ **Kasteel Huis Bergh – Bergh Castle**

Location: Hof van Bergh 2, southwest part of town.

Information: ☎ (0314) 66 1281

Hours: Visits by tour only. Call for hours.

Bergh Castle was built in 1200 for the Counts van den Bergh who held important positions in church and state and possessed many large properties. Set in hilly woodlands, the castle is one of the largest in the Netherlands. It has been damaged by fire several times, most recently in 1939, when its contents were fortunately saved by the local people.

Inherited by a noble German family, though hardly used by them, the castle was let (or rented out) between 1799 and 1912 for various purposes. A Dutch industrialist, Dr. J. H. van Heek, bought the estate in 1912, gradually restoring and refurbishing it to its former glory. It has a valuable collection of medieval furniture, art and porcelain, coins, maps, weapons, heraldry and books.

Do not miss the Bergh Mint where you can mint your own coins (by appointment); the 18th-century plantation, with its ancient oak trees; one of the oldest flour mills in Europe; and the Counts' tennis court. There's a lovely 20-minute walk along the medieval town walls.

For refreshments or a meal visit the historic tearoom restaurant next to the castle – or the **Montferland Hotel** restaurant in the middle of the woods. This was a small hunting lodge built to commemorate the last Count Van den Bergh.

In the neighbourhood of 's Heerenberg

The part of Holland east of 's Heerenberg to the German border is so beautiful; a drive or picnic on a warm day is really worthwhile. **Groenlo**, almost on the border, is one place to stop. It has medieval city walls and ramparts, a Spanish cannon from 1627, and Callixtus Church, which dates from 1234 (wall paintings, stained-glass windows, carillon). The **Stadsmuseum**, Mattelierstraat 33, ☎ (0544) 46 1247, open May-Oct. Mon.-Fri. 9:30am-5pm, Sat. 9:30am-4pm, Nov.-April Mon.-Fri. 10am-12:30pm & 1:30-5pm, Sat. 10am-1pm, is worth a special visit. Grolsch beer items, pottery, weapons, cannon balls, a fire engine, loom and paintings of the region form the collection.

Doesburg
15th-century trading town in the Achterhoek

Getting there: Doesburg is 11 kilometers (7 mi) northeast of Arnhem. Follow directions to Arnhem, bypassing to the north on A12. At Velp, turn off north on A348 to Doesburg.

Information: VVV, Kerkstraat 6, ☎ (0313) 47 9088; www.vvvdoesburg.nl

This attractive 15th-century trading town on the river IJssel has an arts and crafts centre, picturesque shops, and one of the last mustard factories in Holland. The **Doesburg Mustard and Vinegar Museum**, Boekholtstraat 22, ☎ (0313) 47 2230, open Mon.-Fri. 10am-5pm, Sat. 11am-4pm, demonstrates how mustard used to be made. Nearby is the former **Guildhall** with small shops selling handmade jewellery, wooden shoes, and varieties of vinegar and perfumes. The restaurant **De Mosterdhoeve**, Meipoortstraat 43, ☎ (0313) 47 3691, specialises in 'mustard dishes,' also pancakes, salads, etc.

Other places of interest are the imposing Gothic **Martini Church** and **Gasthuis Chapel** (15th century); a 16th-century **Town Hall**, with a renaissance entrance; a 16th-century **Weigh House**; ruins of a former fortress and ramparts from 1607; and some interesting buildings along the Koepoortstraat. The **Museum De Roode Tooren**, Roggestraat 9-13, ☎ (0313) 47 4265, open Tues.-Fri. 10am-noon & 1:30-4:30pm, Sat.-Sun. 1:30-4:30pm, deals with the town history.

In the neighbourhood of Doesburg

Didam is the archery capital of the Netherlands, with an archery festival in July, ☎ (0900) 202 4075 (VVV Arnhem). There's also an **Archery Museum**, Gelders Schuttersmuseum, Raadhuisstraat 9, ☎ (0316) 22 7520, open Tues.-Thurs. & Sun. 2-4pm. In **Zevenaar**, you can see bricks being made in an old-fashioned kiln at **De Panoven**, Panovenweg 18, ☎ (0316) 52 3520, open April-Aug. daily 10am-5pm, rest of year Tues.-Sun. In **Aerdt**, **'n Aerdts Paradijs**, Heuvelakkeresestraat 7, ☎ (0316) 24 7319, open June-Aug., Wed. & Sun., is a rose garden with 5,000 square meters of flowers and plants.

Arnhem
Capital of Gelderland and great national forests to the north

Getting there: From Amsterdam, south on A2 then east on A12. From The Hague or Rotterdam, east on A12.

Information: Tourist Information Office, Velperbuitensingel 25, ☎ (0900) 112 2344 or (026) 372 0792; www.vvvarnhem.nl

Arnhem, capital of Gelderland, is on the slopes of the Zuid-Veluwe hills and the Rhine River, one of the most wooded and scenic areas in the country. Once it was a flourishing Roman settlement and, according to the first century historian, Tacitus, the region was called 'Arenacum.' Its location has blessed it with great scenic beauty, but also cursed it through the ages as a strategic military prize. During WW II it was almost totally destroyed during the Battle of Arnhem. Arnhem's main attractions include the Burgers' Zoo, Open Air Museum, Hoge Veluwe National Park and Kröller-Müller Museum, and WW II sites.

▸ **Openluchtmuseum – Netherlands Open Air Museum**
Location: Schelmseweg 89
Information: ☎ (026) 357 6111; www.openluchtmuseum.nl
Hours: April-Oct., 10am-5pm

This museum is a fascinating collection of authentic buildings from all over Holland, brought together to show what life for the rural population used to be like, particularly their traditional culture and their homes. Farms, windmills, watermills, a church, etc., are represented. The buildings are all original, furnished as far as possible in a traditional manner, so one can even smell the 'fragrances' that come with living among the animals, as was common in the early days.

Here you can see paper being made in a mill, a farmer milking a cow, and a boat being built in a shipyard. There are opportunities for children to join in the fun, from learning to read in the old schoolhouse, to riding an antique bicycle. And the whole family can take a ride on a historic tram.

There's much more to see: an herb garden, a collection of farm vehicles, a laundry from 1900 (run by real horse power), a cheese and butter factory, a dairy farm, and some traditional Dutch quilts. Throughout the months when the park is open, special events are held, e.g. concerts in a Zeeland chapel, the reenactment of a farmer's wedding, or an old-fashioned Dutch fair.

In this park of about 100 acres, be prepared to walk. If you bring babies or toddlers, have a stroller for them and comfortable shoes for yourself. There are places for rest and refreshments. The charming Museum Restaurant serves warm and cold meals, and by the herb garden there's a pancake restaurant, **De Hanekamp**. However, fresh bread and biscuits are baked daily in the park!

▶ **Burgers' Zoo**
Getting There: Take A12 to Arnhem and follow the signs for Burgers' Zoo along the roads. Bus 3 from Arnhem station.
Information: ☎ (026) 442 4534; www.burgerszoo.nl
Hours: Summer hours: 9am-7pm; winter season: 9am-5pm

A zoo with over 3,000 animals, hundreds of which roam freely, is bound to be popular with almost everyone. **Burgers' Zoo** is one of the most popular in the Netherlands. The zookeepers try to give animals the space they need to roam freely, in a setting that's as close as possible to their natural habitat. To see the giraffes, zebras, rhinos and other animals roaming about in the Burgers' Safari Park, visitors progress along a wooden bridge overlooking the area. Lions and cheetahs are in a separate area, as is the chimp colony which can be studied from special observation posts. There are also woods with wolves, and a large attractive bird collection.

Burgers' Bush is the largest covered tropical forest in the world. Visitors can explore plants and animal habitats from Asia, Africa and South America...swamps, waterfalls, trees, flowers and palms intermixed with big and small game. A tunnel connects it to Burgers' Desert where bobcats and other desert creatures roam freely. There's also Burgers' Ocean, with fish and other marine life found in tropical seas. There are four restaurants in the park, a tropical restaurant in the Bush, and a Mexican restaurant in the desert.

● **Near Burgers' Zoo:** The zoo is adjacent to the Open Air Museum. A short distance south is **De Watermolen**, Zypendaalseweg 24, ☎ (026) 445 0660, open Tues-Fri 10am-5pm, Sat-Sun 11am-5pm, a 15th-century watermill still in operation during the week. Close by is **Kasteel Zypendaal**, Zypendaalseweg 44, ☎ (026) 355 2555, open mid-April-Oct., Tues-Fri and Sun 1-5pm, an 18th-century castle in an attractive landscaped park. To the west is **Arnhems Oorlogsmuseum** 40-45, Kemperbergerweg 780, ☎ (026) 442 0958, open Tues-Sun 10am-5pm, which tells the story of Arnhem during the 1940-45 German occupation, resistance efforts, local battles and the liberation.

▶ **Also in Arnhem**
Most of Arnhem's sites of interest are close to the Market Square. During the battle of Arnhem in 1944, the 15th-century **Eusebius Church**, Kerkplein 1, ☎ (026) 443 5068, open April-Oct. Tues.-Sat. 10am-5pm, Sun. noon-5pm, Nov.-March Tues.-Sat. 11am-4pm, Sun. noon-4pm, caught fire and its tower came crashing down. It took 50 years to rebuild. One advantage is that you don't have to climb a narrow staircase to enjoy the views from the 93-meter-high tower now. A glass elevator takes you to the top.

To one side of the church is the 18th-century **Waag**, or Weigh House. Behind it is city hall, the oldest part of which is known as **Duivelshuis**, or Devil's House. The name has nothing to do with the administrators who use the building these days, but with the figures of devils on its facade. This 16th-century house was built for Maarten van Rossum, a Dutch military commander, whose statue can be seen on the roof.

Since Arnhem's old town centre was demolished in the battle of Sept. 1944, one can imagine how close-by that battle was. Southeast of the centre is the **John Frostbrug**, popularised as 'A Bridge Too Far,' where Nijmeegseweg crosses the Rhine. The bridge is named after British Colonel John Frost, whose troops took the north end and held it for four days against intense German attacks. A plaque commemorates their heroism.

There are two art museums. The **Historisch Museum Het Burgerweeshuis**, Bovenbeekstraat 21, ☎ (026) 442 6900, www.hmarnhem.nl, open Tues.-Fri. 10am-5pm, Sat.-Sun. 11am-5pm, has pre-20th century paintings, glass, silver, and ceramic art. Housed in an old orphanage, it also has a section on Arnhem's history. The **Museum Voor Moderne Kunst**, Utrechtseweg 87, ☎ (026) 351 2431, www.mmkarnhem.nl, open Tues.-Sun. 10am-5pm, is a museum of modern art, famous for its collection of 'Magic Realistic' paintings by Carel Willink, Pyke Koch and Wim Schuymacher. It also has contemporary, industrial and applied art, Delft and Chinese pottery, and original Gelderland silver. There is a sculpture garden and outstanding views of the Rhine.

Slightly north and east of the city centre are two more museums. **Museum Bronbeek**, Velperweg 147, ☎ (026) 376 3535, open Tues.-Sun. 10am-5pm, shows the history of the Dutch Army in its former Indonesian colonies. The **Nederlands Wijnmuseum**, Velperweg 23, ☎ (026) 442 4042, www.wijnmuseum.nl, open Tues.-Fri. 2-5pm, Sat. 11am-5pm, is all about wine – from the soil in which vines grow to the cork that tops the finished product. It's located in an old wine cellar that was used by a Dutch wine merchant.

Eating out

For something different, the **Boerderij**, Parkweg 2, ☎ (026) 442 4396, is a 19th-century farm restaurant in Sonsbeek Park. **Rijzenburg**, Koningsweg 17, ☎ (026) 443 6733, situated at the entrance to the Hoge Veluwe Park amid trees and meadows, is known for its cuisine. You can dine here in style or choose something light from their luncheon menu.

Staying over

For a quiet rest overlooking the Rhine, try the **NH Rijnhotel**, Onderlangs 10, ☎ (026) 443 4642. **Papendal-National Sports Centre**, Papendallaan 3, ☎ (026) 483 7911, is a hotel with basic accommodations, camping, restaurants and every possible sports facility, for groups.

Tours

For boat trips, **Rederij Eureka**, ☎ (0570) 61 5914, has different day trips on the Rhine from Arnhem.

In the neighbourhood of Arnhem

Four castles are nearby. **Kasteel Rosendael**, Rosendael 1, ☎ (026) 364 4645, open mid-April-Oct, Tues.-Sun. 11am-5pm, is northwest at Rozendaal. This 14th-century castle has the largest brick dungeon in Holland. Try imagining yourselves in its small, low-ceiling prison chamber, chained to the wall – it's enough to make your skin crawl. Built in 1314, it was rebuilt in 1615. The massive round stone tower surrounded by water dates from 1350. The model castles on display from other countries are also worth a look. The very popular 1,200-acre park, open 11am-5pm, has a French-style, manicured garden, a grotto with rare inlaid shells, and waterfalls.

Kasteel Doornenburg, Kerkstraat 27, ☎ (0481) 42 1456, with tours generally April-June & Sept.-Oct. Sun. 1:30, 2:30, 3:30; July-Aug. Fri.-Sun. 1:30, 2:30, 3:30, Tues.-Thurs. 11:00, 1:30, 2:30, 3:30, is about 20km (12 mi) south near the village of Gendt. This is not just a castle but a moated complex of buildings with courtyard and apparently the country's longest and most beautiful stables. Built in the 14th and 15th centuries, this impressive castle gives an excellent impression of how feudal lords were able to defend themselves from attack.

Kasteel Doorwerth, Fonteinallee 2, ☎ (026) 333 7406, open Tues.-Fri. 10am-5pm, Sat. 1-5pm, Sun. 11am-5pm, is west of Oosterbeek, east of Heelsum on the Rhine. The 13th-century castle was largely destroyed in WWII, with restoration beginning in 1947. The Knights Hall, bedroom, small dining room, main kitchen with its centuries-old wall steps in the north and east wings are all furnished and complete. The 300-year-old acacia tree in the courtyard is the oldest in Europe. There is also a Nature, Wildlife and Hunting Museum.

Kasteel Middachten, Landgoed Middachten 3, ☎ (026) 495 2186, is a 17th-century castle completely furnished in authentic style. It's only open in July, Sun.-Tues. 1-4pm, and in early Dec., Tues.-Sun. 11am-4pm. Its walled gardens, double moat, and rose and herb gardens are open July, Sun.-Tues. 9:30am-4:00pm.

National Park Veluwezoom has 10,000 acres of forest, dunes and hills for walking and cycling. There's a visitor's centre in Rheden, Heuvenseweg 5a, ☎ (026) 497 9100, open Tues.-Sun. 10am-5pm. Close to it is a sheepfold you can visit. The shepherd is there around 4:30pm to tend to his flock of 150 sheep.

In Dieren the **TV Toys Museum**, Wilhelminaweg 21, ☎ (0313) 49 0888, open daily 10am-5pm, Sept.-Easter closed Mon.-Tues., has a collection of 45,000 toys and props that were made for use in various Dutch TV programmes and movies.

De Hoge Veluwe National Park

Getting there: North of Arnhem, between Otterloo, Hoenderloo and Schaarsbergen. By train to Apeldoorn and then bus 110. In season, by train to Arnhem and then bus 12.

Information: ☎ (0553) 378 8166, www.hogeveluwe.nl

Hours: Daily, 8am 'til sunset, 9am-6pm in the winter

This nature reserve has over 13,000 acres of woods, heath, dunes and fens, with hundreds of red and roe deer, wild boar and pheasant to see...if you're lucky. It once belonged to Anton Kröller, a successful industrialist, and his wife. Before they died they created a foundation to operate their land as a national park, and built a museum on it to house their extensive art collection.

Spring or autumn are good times to watch the deer being fed. This is done from an enclosure raised six feet or so from the ground. If you are quiet and still, the animals may come into the clearing from the woods some distance in front of you. In the spring, they are especially wary, and you will see the buck leading the pack. Once he is satisfied there is no danger, they start to eat.

A good way to see the park is to take advantage of the 500 'white bicycles' provided free of charge to visitors. Just pick one up at one of the three locations, including De Koperen Kop restaurant. There are trails set out for 10, 18 and 26 km (6, 11 and 16 mi) rides. Camping is possible from April-October.

▶ **Kröller-Müller Museum**

Location: Houtkampweg 6, located inside the park.

Information: ☎ (0318) 59 1241. www.kmm.nl

Hours: Tues.-Sun. 10am-5pm

It may be a little surprising to discover that within the scenic wooded parkland of the Hoge Veluwe, a major collection of paintings by famous 19th and 20th-century artists is hanging. This museum is an art lover's dream. The main collection has 275 works by Vincent Van Gogh. There are also works by Picasso, Seurat, Redon, Braque, Juan Gris and Mondriaan, among even more.

Sculptures are displayed indoors against a background of greenery seen through large picture windows, while the outdoor Sculpture Garden is the largest in Europe. Children can play on the grass or enjoy watching the ducks while parents ponder the meaning of some modern sculptor's creation. There are many works, including some by Marta Pan, Hepworth, Rodin, Lipchitz, and Henry Moore.

▶ **Also in de Hoge Veluwe**

Entrance to the park includes a visit to **Museonder**, ☎ (0553) 78 8175, open daily 9:30am-5pm, April-Nov. 9:30am-6pm, the world's first underground museum. True to its name, the museum explores the world beneath our feet, including the creatures that inhabit it.

The **Jachthuis St. Hubertus** (St. Hubert Hunting Lodge) was designed for Helene Kröller-Müller by Dutch architect H.P. Berlage in 1920. Hubert is the patron saint of hunters who, according to legend, saw a deer with glowing antlers beneath a shining cross. Berlage designed the building with its two wings representing the deer's antlers, and its tower, the cross. The rooms follow in a sequence from dark to light, representing Hubert's spiritual development from agnostic to saint.

Eating out

De Koperen Kop, ☎ (0318) 59 1289, a rustic restaurant in the park, is convenient for a snack, or try the nearby **Schaarsbergen Pancake House**, Kemperbergerweg 673, ☎ (026) 443 1434.

In the neighbourhood of De Hoge Veluwe

In Otterlo, the **Nederlands Tegelmuseum**, Eikenzoom 12, ☎ (0318) 59 1519, open Tues.-Fri. 10am-5pm, Sat.-Sun. 1-5pm, www.nederlandstegelmuseum.nl, is worth a visit if you have time. It shows the development of tiles in the Netherlands from 1550 to 1850.

Oosterbeek
Site of the largest airborne battle of WW II

Getting there:	Southwest of Arnhem along the Rhine River, between A50 and A52.
Information:	VVV, Raadhuisplein 1, ☎ (026) 333 3172; www.vvvoosterbeek.nl

Located in the middle of a forest near Arnhem, this is one of the major sites in Operation Market Garden – the largest airborne operation of World War II. During the battle, British Major-General R.E. Urquhart made his headquarters in the Hartenstein Hotel – now a museum and Oosterbeek's main attraction. For more war sites, check out the **National War and Resistance Museum** at Overloon (in Brabant), and the **Museum of the 1944 Liberation** at Groesbeek.

▸ **Operation Market Garden**

Operation 'Market Garden' was a daring military operation in Sept.-Oct. 1944, and the brainchild of British Field Marshal Montgomery at a time when Germany seemed to be near defeat. His plan was to end the war quickly. To do so, he developed a massive airborne operation. Thousands of paratroopers were dropped behind enemy lines from the Belgian border to Eindhoven, Nijmegen and Arnhem. They were to capture key bridges and clear the way for the main British force to advance quickly. The Brits would then be able to get around the main German defenses, sweep into the heartland of Germany – depriving the German Army of its sources of supply – and quickly move on to Berlin.

American paratroopers were dropped to the south near Nijmegen. They were able to capture key canals and bridges, but a stronger-than-expected German resistance slowed them down. The main British force was able to advance, but three days behind schedule. British troops dropped near Arnhem were even less fortunate. Their goal was to take the bridges over the Rhine and they expected few German troops. When the Dutch Resistance warned them of a much larger German presence, their warnings were not believed. The Dutch had it right. By chance, the Germans had positioned two battle-tested tank divisions in the area in order to give them a rest period after fighting in Normandy.

Despite Polish paratrooper reinforcements, only one battalion got through to the bridge in Arnhem, and they could only take the northern end of it. The original plan was that the main British force would reinforce them within two days. Four days later, despite intense German fire, this small group of British soldiers was, amazingly, still holding the position on its own.

The paratroopers who couldn't reach the bridge took up positions near headquarters in Oosterbeek and waited for the main British force while facing heavy German fire. It was soon obvious; both the battalion on the bridge and the soldiers around the Hartens-tein had to move back to safety. Of the 10,000 or so men parachuted in to fight near Arnhem, only 2,293 were left to retreat. The Allies did make important gains during Operation Market Garden, but because crack SS troops held their position in Arnhem, the war continued another seven months. Many more lives were lost, and the Russians were the first to enter Berlin. Arnhem wasn't liberated until April 1945.

▶ **World War II Cemeteries**
There are many war cemeteries in the area, including one in Oosterbeek with the graves of over 1,700 young men, most of whom died in Operation Market Garden and in the battle to take the Arnhem bridge. Many of the Americans who died are interred in the **U.S. Military Cemetery** in Margraten, Limburg.

Military Cemeteries in the Arnhem Region

Oosterbeek	British Airborn Cemetery	1,746 graves
Nijmegen	Jonkersbos British Cemetery	1,636 graves
Groesbeek	Canadian Cemetery	2,595 graves
Mook	British Cemetery	322 graves
Milsbeek	British Cemetery	210 graves
Uden	British Cemetery	703 graves
Overloon	British Cemetery	280 graves
Ysselstein	German Cemetery	31,576 graves
Venray	British Cemetery	692 graves
Mierlo	British Cemetery	665 graves
Eindhoven	British Cemetery	686 graves
Nederweert	British Cemetery	363 graves
Valkenswaard	British Cemetery	222 graves
Lommel	German Cemetery	39,158 graves

▶ **Hartenstein Airborne Museum**

Location:	Utrechtseweg 232, Oosterbeek.
Information:	☎ (026) 333 7710, www.airbornemuseum.com
Hours:	April-Nov. Mon.-Sat. 10am-5pm, Nov.-April 11am-5pm, year round Sun. noon-5pm

The **Airborne Museum** was founded in 1949 as a tribute to the British and Polish troops who fought in the Battle of Arnhem in 1944. It is housed in the former Hartenstein Hotel, which was the Allied headquarters. Much fighting went on around the hotel, and today there are still anti-tank guns and a Sherman tank standing where they were left after the battle.

The course of the battle is explained with a number of visual aids: films taken during the battle, military and civilian photos, weapons, uniforms, etc. Don't miss the door on which instructions from an Allied commander to his troops, as well as his words of encouragement to them, are written.

In the cellar are several dioramas depicting various aspects of the campaign. One, for example, recreates a scene in that very same cellar where wounded soldiers were brought in for treatment during the fighting.

Yearly events

In early September there's a walking tour of the battlefields; in mid-September, special commemorative ceremonies are held.

Eating out

Located on a hill overlooking the Rhine, **De Westerbouwing**, Westerbouwing 1, ☎ (026) 333 2019, open Sundays only, 11am-4pm, can add a highlight to the day's outing. www.dewesterbouwing.nl

Nijmegen
A Roman town called 'Noviomagus'

Getting there:	From The Hague A13 east through Rotterdam, A15 to Nijmegen; from Amsterdam A2 south, A15 east.
Information:	Tourist Information Office, Keizer Karelplein 32H, ☎ (024) 322 8344 or (0900) 112 2344; www.vvvnijmegen.nl

Nijmegen is an old Roman town that was a hilltop command post in a revolt against Rome in 69-70 A.D. The rebels were defeated and 'Noviomagus' was established as a frontier town and stronghold in 105 A.D. That makes Nijmegen one of the oldest towns in the Netherlands. Although famous personages from history books, like Charlemagne and Barbarossa lived here, its ancient history has been superseded in the minds of many by its 20th-century tragedy. When Allied troops failed to take Arnhem in 1944, Nijmegen became the front line of the war for the next seven months. Much of the town was destroyed, but a few historic structures are left. Today it is a bustling, lively university town where culture has an important place, with festivals, concerts and art galleries.

▶ **Waalkade Riverfront**

Many attractions are along the Waal River, on or near the **Waalkade** promenade. It's also a good place to watch the busy river traffic and enjoy a meal or drink at one of the many cafés there.

For an overview of the surroundings, start at the **Valkhof**, the top of the hill where that battle of 69-70 A.D. took place. Charlemagne built his palace here in 777. It was rebuilt by Frederick I Barbarossa in 1155. All that's left is a chapel wall, and a small chapel built in 1045 modelled after the Aachen Cathedral. The gardens are a pleasure and the view of the river well worthwhile. There's another good view if you take the path from here to the **Belvedere**, a 16th-century watchtower that's now a restaurant. It's located in **Hunnerpark**, where heavy fighting took place in WW II.

Nearby is Nijmegen's newest museum, **Museum Het Valkhof**, Kelfkenbos 59, ☎ (024) 360 8805, open Tues.-Fri. 10am-5pm, Sat.-Sun. 11am-5pm. It deals with the area's art, archeology, culture and history. The archeology goes back to prehistoric times, but the emphasis is on Nijmegen's Roman period.

Go underground to examine medieval Nijmegen at the **Museum De Stratemaker-storen**, Waalkade 83, ☎ (024) 323 8690, open Tues.-Fri. 12am-5pm, Sat.-Sun. 1-5pm. A 14th-century tower was built here, manned by members of the road workers' guild (*stratemakers*) whenever the city was attacked. The subterranean corridors of the tower still exist. There are slides and videos in the underground passageways, including one giving the feel of approaching the medieval city gates at night.

What's more appropriate in the Netherlands than a museum devoted to the bicycle? The **Nationaal Fietsmuseum Velorama**, Waalkade 107, ☎ (024) 322 5851, open Mon.-Sat. 10am-5pm, Sun. 11am-5pm, has about 250 bicycles on display. There's the pedal-less Pedestrian Carriage which graced the streets of London in the 1820s, the Boneshaker which was popular in America in the 1860s despite the accuracy of its name, and the five-foot-tall High Wheel bike of the 1880s. How did they climb on and off that thing?

Rolling the dice was a popular pastime for Roman soldiers, and today people can still do that on the banks of the Waal – as well as playing roulette, blackjack, and other games of chance – at the **Holland Casino**, Waalkade 68, ☎ (024) 360 0000, open 1:30pm-2am, with bars and a restaurant.

South of Hunnerpark is the **Natuurmuseum Nijmegen**, Gerard Noodtstraat 121, ☎ (024) 329 7070, www.universal.nl/users/museum, open Mon.-Fri. 10am-5pm, Sun. 1-5pm, with its collection of over 50,000 specimens of the flora, fauna and geology of the Nijmegen region.

▶ **Market Square**

The **Market Square** (Grote Markt) area is where most of the old buildings that survived the war are located, and the place for shopping. **St. Stevenskerk**, ☎ (024) 360 4710, open Tues., Wed., Fri. 10am-2pm, was founded in 1254, but rebuilt and renovated many times. Its tower and facade were badly damaged in WWII. You may climb the tower, by appointment, ☎ (024) 323 0156, for a view of the square and the Waal River (minimum five people necessary). Behind the church is the impressive-looking **Latin School** built in 1545, with statues of the 12 apostles on its facade.

Next to the Latin School is the **Kerkboog**, a vaulted gateway built at about the same time. On the other side is the **Markt**, with the old **Weigh House** (Waag) from 1612 and the **Cloth Hall** (Lakenhal). A short distance from the Markt down Burchtstraat is the **Town Hall** (Stadhuis). Built in 1554, it had to be rebuilt after the war. It contains Gobelin tapestries, paintings, porcelain and antique furniture. Tours by appointment, ☎ (024) 329 2403.

Next on tap are beer-flavoured mustard, vinegar and liquor, as well as plain beer, all made at the **Museumbrouwerij De Hemel**, Franse Plaats 1, ☎ (024) 360 6167, open Tues.-Sun.11am-6pm. It's located in the **Commanderie van St. Jan**, which has also been a hospital, school and church since it was built in 1196. You can watch the beer-making process, and yes, sample the products they make.

▶ **Also in Nijmegen**

Kronenburger Park, west of the town centre, contains ruins of 15th-16th-century fortifications. One is the **Kruittoren** (powder magazine) at Parkweg 99, home to **Grootmoeders Keukenmuseum**, ☎ 06 5341 0107 by appointment. A peep into an old-fashioned kitchen, it contains kitchen utensils from about 1900 – grandma's collection, or probably great-great grandma's collection, of tins, egg cups, grocery shop articles, etc. **Het Rondeel**, Parkweg 65, is another fortress tower. If you walk west from Kronenburger Park along Lange Hezelstraat, you will come to the **Waalhaven harbour**. The site of the original Roman town, **Noviomagus**, is along the river at the western end.

Worthwhile playgrounds in Nijmegen are **De Leemkuil**, Luciaweg, ☎ (024) 360 5198, April-Oct. and **'t Brakkefort**, Kan. Mijlinckstraat, ☎ (024) 355 7283.

Markets

There are several markets in town. The flea market on Monday mornings is the most interesting.

Yearly events

From May to mid-Sept. many interesting events take place, including the **Four Day Marches** (3rd Tues. in July) when Nijmegen is inundated with physical fitness enthusiasts from all over the world. Originally made up mainly of military participants, civilians joined in greater numbers after 1916. Nijmegen hosted its first march in 1917, and has been its permanent host since 1925. Over 1,000 took part in 1928; today more than 30,000 participate. The walks were never competitive. The only objective is to complete the route, for which you receive a medal. Anyone over 12-years-old is welcome, and, depending on age and sex, must complete 30, 40, or 50 km (19, 25, or 31 mi) per day. If interested, reserve a room in advance with the VVV – unless you don't mind sleeping in the fields! During the march there are many festivities with performances by well-known artists, and the biggest fireworks display in the country.

There's also a **Four Day Cycling** event in August, covering distances of 25, 40, 60 and 80 km (15.5, 25, 37, and 50 mi). August is also the month for **Waalkade a la Carte**, when you can sample specialities of top restaurants and enjoy music and dancing along the riverfront. Early October is the time for **Kermis**, the city's big fair.

In August, the village of **Deest** holds its well-known market. There are arts and crafts of yesterday and today, antiques, clowns, puppet shows, and more.

Tours

In July-Aug., **Stoomboot Brandaris – Rederij Tonissen**, ☎ (024) 323 3285, offers steamboat cruises up the Rhine and Waal rivers. The one to two-and-a-half-hour trips leave from the Waalkade, opposite the Holland Casino. They also offer day trips to Rotterdam and Emmerich.

In the neighbourhood of Nijmegen

Three very different museums outside Nijmegen are worth exploring. The **Museum of the 1944 Liberation** (Bevrijdingsmuseum 1944), Wylerbaan 4, ☎ (024) 397 4404, open Mon.-Sat. 10am-5pm, Sun. noon-5pm, is in **Groesbeek**. It was founded in honour of the men who participated in the massive Allied operations in this area. Americans were the first to arrive. Many of them moved on to fight the Battle of the Bulge (mid-November 1944) leaving behind 1,800 dead. British, Canadian, some Polish and Dutch troops came next, also suffering heavy casualties. There are scale models and videos explaining the battles and the German occupation of 1940-44. Operation Market Garden was considered a failure because it did not achieve its aim of ending the war early, but the museum clearly emphasises the campaign's many successes.

Biblical Open Air Museum, ☎ (024) 382 3110, open 20 March-Oct. 10am-5pm, Nov.-March 11am-4pm, is 3 km (2 mi) east of Nijmegen. Follow the signs to 'Heilig Land-stichting.' The Holy Land Foundation is an outdoor park with Biblical scenes...just as they were in Christ's time. Regardless of religious preferences, this museum is very worthwhile. The walk through the woods is also lovely. There are two restaurants for the hungry and a museum train for the weary.

About 4 km (2.5 mi) east of Nijmegen in **Berg en Dal** is a museum devoted to African art and culture. Inside the **Afrika Museum**, Postweg 6, ☎ (024) 684 7272, www.afrika-museum.nl, open Mon.-Fri. 10am-5pm, Sat.-Sun. 11am-5pm, Nov.-March closed Mon., is a collection of brightly displayed artifacts, African masks, pots, warrior shields, etc.

Outside, five different African compounds have been rebuilt on 12.5 acres of land surrounding the museum. They are designed to give visitors an idea of what traditional
African homes are like, and include a life-size replica of a Pygmy settlement, and dwellings typical of Lesotho.

In June there's a home and garden **Castle Fair** in **Wijchen**, in the gardens of **Kasteel
Wijchen**, Kasteellaan 9, ☎ (024) 642 4744, open Fri. 11am-5pm, Sat.-Sun. 1-5pm. The
castle contains a museum covering Wijchen's Roman and Middle Age periods, and its
scenic setting between the Maas and Waal rivers.

Tiel
The heart of the Betuwe and castles galore

Getting there:	A13 from The Hague & Rotterdam, to A 20, to A16, then A15 east. From Amsterdam A2 south to A15 east.
Information:	☎ 0900 636 3888; www.rivierenland.nl

Tiel is said to have existed by the mid-5th century. Strategically situated on the Waal River,
it has suffered often from war – most recently in WW II. Almost daily from Oct. 1944 – May
1945, Tiel was heavily shelled by Allied forces while the Germans plundered and set fire to
the town. One of few surviving historic buildings is the **Ambtmanshuis** (1525), Ambtman-
straat 17, formerly the residence of the peace officer. **St. Martin's Church** (1400), Achterweg
11, was rebuilt in 1965. Its tower contains a beautiful carillon with 47 bells. **Church of St.
Cecilia**, Kerkstraat 34, was destroyed but has also been rebuilt. **Streek Museum de Groote
Societeit**, Plein 48, ☎ (0344) 61 44 16, open Tues.-Fri. 1:30-5pm, Sat.-Sun. 1:30-4:30pm, has
antiquities of local interest, and a watergate that can be visited during museum hours.

Yearly events

In spring, mid-April to mid-May, a drive in this area is a real treat when the orchards of
plum, cherry, pear and apple trees are in bloom. Early in September, the fruit garden of
the Netherlands presents its **Harvest and Fruit Show**, which includes a parade through
Tiel on the second Saturday in September.

In the neighbourhood of Tiel

Culemborg is a moated and fortified town northwest of Tiel on the lovely river Lek. You
can still see the moat and part of the ramparts; the **Binnenpoort** (the only remaining
town gate); the beautiful step-gabled **Town Hall** designed in the 1530s; the **Grote or St.
Barbarakerk** (14th and 15th centuries), and the **fish-auction house** at the Havendijk, both
of which have been restored. Another restored building is the 16th-century orphanage,
now the **Museum Elisabeth Weeshuis**, Herenstraat 29, ☎ (0345) 51 3912, open Tues.-
Sat. 1-5pm, Sun. 2-5pm. It deals with the history of Culemborg. The orphanage has a
pleasant garden.

There are a number of small towns and many castles in the close vicinity of Tiel. **Ophemert**, southwest of Tiel, has an ancient castle. **Waardenburg**, a few km further west, has two. The largest inland locks in Europe are just east of Tiel where the Amsterdam-Rhine canal runs into the Waal River – a most impressive civil engineering project.

Buren
'Orange Town'
Getting there: From Amsterdam, take A2 south, N320 east, look for the Buren turnoff. From The Hague & Rotterdam, A12 east to A2 south and follow directions above. West of Tiel.

Information: ☎ (0344) 57 1922; www.rivierenland.nl

The first wife of William the Silent, Prince of Orange was from the ruling family of medieval Buren. They were married in 1551 in **St. Lambertus** Church, open May-Oct., Tues.-Sat. 10:30am-noon & 2-4pm, built in 1395. Their first child, Maria van Oranje (1553-54) is buried in the crypt. Because of these royal ties Buren is nicknamed 'Orange Town.' **Museum Buren en Oranje**, Markt 1, ☎ (0344) 57 1389, open April-Oct., Mon.-Sat. 10am-4:30pm, Nov.-March, Mon., Tues. Wed. Sat. 11am-3pm, explains the connection of the royal family with Buren. **Museum Der Koninklijke Marechaussee**, Weeshuiswal 9, ☎ (0344) 57 1256, open May-Sept., Tues.-Fri. 10am-4:30pm, Sat.-Sun. 1:30-5pm, is in an orphanage founded in 1612 by another Dutch Royal, Maria van Nassau. It's a museum of the Royal Military Police with paintings, uniforms, arms and other items detailing their history.

Almost the entire town of Buren has been restored. Interesting buildings include the **Weigh House**, and the **Prins van Oranje Mill**, circa 1716, (call VVV for a Saturday visit), and the **Muurhuizen** (houses built into the town walls).

Zaltbommel
Old fortress town
Getting there: A2 south from Amsterdam. A13 south from The Hague & Rotterdam, A15 east to A2, south to Zaltbommel.

Information: ☎ (0900) 636 3888; www.rivierenland.nl

Zaltbommel is an interesting town with much to see and do. A small settlement in 850 A.D., it gained its town rights in 1231. Its ramparts date from that time. A former stronghold, it has many historical, gabled buildings and a pleasant atmosphere as you stroll through it.

Its distinguished visitors include Karl Marx, who worked on 'Das Kapital' while here in 1863. In 1842 the composer Franz Liszt, perhaps not only charmed by the musical chimes, took the carillonneur's daughter to Paris where she was introduced to Edouard Manet, the painter. Manet married her here in **St. Maartenskerk**. This 13th-15th-century church, ☎ (0418) 51 3125, open March-April & Oct.-Dec., Sat.-Sun. 1:30-4:30pm; May-Sept., Tues.-Sun. 1:30-4:30 pm, has beautiful frescoes, the oldest choir stalls in Holland (14th century) and a Louis XVI organ. Other worthwhile sites are the **Town Hall** (1762) with sundial and clock; the **Fish Market** (1776); **Weigh House** (1797); and the **town pump** (1800).

Another early building is the **Maarten van Rossum Museum**, Nonnenstraat 5, ☎ (0418) 51 2617, open Tues.-Fri. 10am-12:30pm and 1:30-4:30pm, Sat.-Sun. 2-4:30pm; closed Sat. Oct.-April. Built in 1535, it houses a fine collection of prints, furniture, artifacts and ornaments, as well as items from prehistoric and Roman excavations.

In the neighbourhood of Zaltbommel

Seven km (4 mi) south in **Ammerzoden** is **Ammersoyen Castle**, Kasteellaan 7, ☎ (073) 594 9582, open April- Oct., Tues.-Fri. 10am-5pm, Sat.-Sun. 1-5pm, Nov.-March Wed. 1-5pm (last tour at 4pm). It's an original 12-14th-century stronghold with four round towers and a medieval facade. Once a monastery, it is now the **Town Hall** and a museum of antiquities. The restored town of **Heusden** across the river is worth a visit.

Woudrichem
Site of Loevestein Castle

Getting there: Woudrichem is about 40 km (25 mi) southeast of Rotterdam and 35 km (22 mi) southwest of Utrecht. The castle is across the river from town, where the Maas and Waal rivers meet. In the summer, there's a special ferry from Gorinchem and Woudrichem.

Information: ☎ (0183) 44 7171

Hours: May-Sept., Tues.-Fri. 10am-5pm, Sat.-Mon. 1-5pm, Oct.-April Sat., Sun., Wed. 1-5pm, Nov.-March, Sat., Sun, Wed. 1-4pm

One of the pleasures of visiting **Loevestein Castle** is getting there. You can reach it by land, but it's easier to take a passenger ferry from Woudrichem or Gorinchem. It's not only fun for the kids to ride on the boat but also to ring the bell on the castle side of the water to call it back to pick you up. What makes Loevestein difficult to reach is its location at the junction of the Maas and Waal rivers.

The castle is worth the trip, with its thick walls and moat. It also has an interesting history. Built in 1357-66, it was a manor house before becoming a prison. Badly damaged about 1400, the present walls were constructed about 1576. As a 17th-century prison, it housed some of the great names of the Netherlands. The most prominent was Hugo Grotius, leading Dutch intellectual and prominent statesmen of his time. He was imprisoned for being opposed to the religious convictions of those in power and his legend grew when he escaped from the prison – hidden inside a wooden chest – in 1621.

Chapter 6 | The province of Flevoland

Originally a unique experiment, **Flevoland** is now a symbol of modern Dutch ingenuity and engineering skill. It is an entirely man-made province, for until the 20th century most of what is now Flevoland was under the sea – the Zuiderzee.

For centuries, areas bordering the Zuiderzee lost their uneven battle with nature. Farmland, homes and towns were swallowed up time and again by violent storms. In an effort to protect the central Netherlands from the floods, Dr. Cornelius Lely devised a plan to dam the entrance to the Zuiderzee. Work began on the Afsluitdijk in 1920, and when the great dike was completed in 1932, the Zuiderzee lost its connection to the North Sea and became a fresh water lake, the IJsselmeer.

Then came the task of creating land from the seabed, a project partly motivated to create more agricultural farmland, but also by the need to provide more housing for this densely populated country, especially for the ever-expanding Amsterdam area. Flevoland was officially proclaimed The Netherlands' twelfth province by Queen Beatrix in 1986. Its attractions include the former island, and old fishing community of Urk; the modern architecture of its new towns; its Land Art; major museums in Lelystad and Schokland; Walibi World themepark; water recreation and nature reserves; forests, colourful bulb fields and brilliant carpets of rapeseed. Flevoland is now the Netherlands largest bulb-growing area. It is also a province in evolution, with many more parcels of land still being reclaimed from the sea bed.

Information: VVV Flevoland, ☎ (0527) 61 2000, www.vvvnoordoostpolder.nl

Almere
The gateway to Flevoland

Getting there: A1 east from Amsterdam, and cross the Hollandsebrug. From The Hague and Rotterdam, A4 to A1.

Information: VVV, Stadhuisplein 1, (036) 548 5041

Almere is one of the more ambitious towns in the Netherlands. In existence only since 1975, it is aiming to become the fourth largest city in the country. With over 125,000 inhabitants already, it would seem to be getting there. Almere owes its reputation as 'the fastest growing city in the country' to relatively inexpensive housing, and its proximity to Amsterdam – 20 minutes by train. Its harbour on the Gooimeer is also a magnet to boaters, water and nature lovers. The **Muiderzand** and **Zilverstrand** beaches, and the harbour beach, are crowded with bathers on sunny days.

Almere is also something of a leader in modern and contemporary Dutch architecture and art. There are about 50 sculptures throughout the city, and two experimental housing neighbourhoods. **Fantasy** consists of nine houses on the Weerwater in the southern part of Almere-Stad, and **Reality**, of 17 homes on the Noorderplassen on the north side. These very unusual houses were chosen from designs submitted by 250 architects in the 1980s. Almere's museum of contemporary art, **ACHK-De Paviljoens**, Odeonstraat 5, ☎ (036) 545 0400, www.achkdepaviljoens.nl, open Wed., Sat.-Sun. noon-5pm, Thurs. – Fri. noon-9pm, has a growing permanent collection, as well as its temporary exhibitions.

In the neighbourhood of Almere

Flevoland's wide-open spaces make it a perfect setting for land art. Two examples are close by. Marinus Boezem's **Groene Kathedral**, Tureluurweg, east of town, was designed to represent the Notre Dame Cathedral of Reims. It is built using different grasses, stones, shrubs and trees, with Italian poplars as its columns. Daniel Libeskind's **Polderland Garden of Love and Fire**, Pampushavenweg, west of town, consists of five wide lines in nature, three of which are canals crossed by two paths. One canal points to Almere, another to Berlin (the artist's home), and the third to Salamanca, birthplace of Spanish mystic Juan de la Cruz, who inspired the work. It is advisable to have the VVV folder explaining this original art form and where to find it.

Among the nature reserves around Almere is the **Oostvaardersplassen**, which stretches along the western edge of the landmass from Almere to Lelystad. As many as 250 species of birds have been spotted here, including the marsh harrier hawk, a bird which is the symbol of Flevoland. There are two bird observation posts, and a walking/ bicycling path through the reserve.

Zeewolde

Water sports and colourful fields

Getting there: Exit 11 on A28, and then west. West of Ermelo, southwest of Harderwijk.

Information: VVV, Raadhuisstraat 1, ☎ (036) 522 1405

Inaugurated in 1984, **Zeewolde** is Flevoland's newest town. On the southeast side of the province, its situation on the Veluwemeer makes it a centre for water sports – swimming, sailing, windsurfing and fishing. Bordering the town is the largest single deciduous forest in Europe, 9,884 acres of trees. There are many sites for camping in the woods and along the water.

In May, fields around Zeewolde are brilliant with the intense yellow of rapeseed in bloom. Harvesting the seed for its oil starts the first half of July when it is cut and arranged in windrows. About a week after the cutting, the IJsselmeerpolders Development Authority's 40 combine harvesters, 40 tractors and 130 trucks roll into action. Quite a sight.

This area is also known for its land art. The VVV has a 7 km (4 mi) Art Route if you want to see it all. Included in it is **Sea Level**, Landschapspark De Wetering in Zeewolde. It consists of two cement walls showing the water level in Zeewolde if the protective dikes did not exist. Northwest of town is **Aardzee**, Vogelweg, one of the largest examples of land art in the country, where the land has been made to look like the waves of the sea that once covered it.

Lelystad

Flevoland's museum centre

Getting there: After crossing the Hollandsebrug, continue on A6 past Almere to turnoff for town centre.

Information: Tourist Information Centre, Stadhuisplein 2, ☎ (0320) 27 8222

The first residents settled in Flevoland's capital in 1967. Today, with over 60,000 people, **Lelystad** has also become a centre for visitors. Several museums have been created, including two major ones located side by side just north of the harbour: the **Nieuw Land Erfgoedcentrum**, and the **Batavia-Werf**, both well worth a visit. Lelystad also has four yacht harbours, and is next to wooded areas which offer camping, biking and walking paths. A special drive takes you from Lelystad to Enkhuizen via the Markerwaarddijk (N302)...it's like 'walking' on water.

▶ **Nieuw Land Poldermuseum**

Location: Oostvaardersdijk 01-13

Information: ☎ (0320) 26 0799; www.nieuwlanderfgoedcentrum.nl

Hours: Tues.-Fri. 10am-5pm, Sat.-Sun. 11:30am-5pm

If you were always curious about how polderland is created and how water can be turned to mud and then mud turned to land, you will want to visit this interesting museum. The immensity of the project must be seen to be understood. Since 1920, over 407,724 acres of new land have been created several meters below sea level. The museum shows how this tremendous undertaking came about, using films, slides, models, photographs and displays of objects that have been discovered. They show how the polders were created, but also why and how they are being developed. Booklets and headsets are available in English to guide you through the museum.

▶ **Aviodrome – Air Museum**

Location:	Nationaal Luchtvaart-Themapark Aviodrome, Pelikaanweg 50 Lelystad Airport
Information:	☎ (900) 284 6376 (€ 0.25 p.m.), www.aviodrome.nl
Hours:	Apr.-Sept. daily 10am-5pm; Oct.-Mar., Tues.-Fri., 10am-5pm; Sat. Sun., noon-5pm

This interesting museum shows the development of air travel. Over two dozen planes are on display, as well as hands-on exhibits, such as a computer flight simulator for the would-be pilot. You can also book sightseeing flights in a vintage plane, a helicopter and a hot air balloon!

▶ **Batavia-Werf**

Location:	Oostvaardersdijk 01-09
Information:	☎ (0320) 26 1409; www.bataviawerf.nl
Hours:	Daily 10am-5pm; July-Aug., daily 10am-8pm

Batavia-Werf is a shipyard where replicas of 17th-century Dutch ships are constructed. On display is its first creation, a replica of the Batavia – a Dutch East India Company ship that sank off the Australian coast in 1629. The replica was built over a period of ten years by young Dutch volunteers, who under the supervision of a master shipbuilder are learning new skills. The result is a beautiful ship, as true to the original in every detail as possible. You're free to explore on board. There's also a second ship, **De Zeven Provincien.** Work began on it in 1995.

At the same location is the **Centre for Maritime History**, which displays finds from shipwrecks. When the Zuiderzee was drained, more than 300 shipwrecks from the last 700 years were discovered. These have provided archaeologists not only with considerable information about the history of shipbuilding, but also an insight into ancient cultures. Artifacts, such as household goods, have been discovered, some dating as early as the 13th century. The wreck of a 16th-century merchant ship is also on display.

In the neighbourhood of Lelystad

Natuurpark Lelystad, Meerkoetenweg 1a, ☎ (0320) 28 6130, www.flevolandschap.nl, open daily, sunrise to sunset, is full of wild animals. Beavers, badgers, otters and birds mingle with herds of European bison, elk and the Przewalski horse. There's a visitor's centre (noon-5pm daily) to show you what you might encounter as you walk through the park. It's located south of Lelystad on the road to Harderwijk, near the A6.

Also in the park is **Prehistorische Nederzetting,** a farm from the Bronze Age (1750-750 B.C.) modelled on a 1966 archeological find in nearby Swifterbant. Every year on Easter day they demonstrate Bronze Age skills, such as stoneworking and pottery. Group arrangements can be made for short Bronze Age holidays. Check with the VVV.

Between Lelystad and Swifterbant is another of Flevoland's land art creations. **Observatorium,** Swifterringweg, was created by American artist Robert Morris in 1977. Made of stone and earth, this work of art should be seen at sunrise in each of the four seasons. You can watch the sun come up through peepholes – quite a different impression with each season.

Staying over

Hotel Mercure, Agoraweg 11, ☎ (0320) 24 2444, is a 4-star possibility; or the budget **Hotel Herberg Oostvaarder,** Oostvaardersdijk 29, ☎ (0320) 26 00 72; or **B&B Doors Logies,** Bronsweg 18, ☎ (0320) 23 3801.

Dronten
A place with Stone-Age roots

Getting there: Dronten is northeast of Lelystad. From points south, take A6 to Lelystad, then N309 following signs for Dronten.

Information: VVV/ANWB, De Rede 80-82, ☎ (0321) 31 3802

In a lengthy throwback – long before Flevoland was raised from the sea – people lived here as early as the Stone Age, before the land disappeared to be replaced by swamps and lakes. Today it is a modern town with a large 'congress centre' that includes a cinema, market, café-restaurant, theatre and exhibit halls. There are a number of sign-posted touristic routes that you can follow through bulb areas by taking the small local road north to Ketel Lake.

▶ **Walibi World amusement park**

Location: Spijkweg 30, Biddinghuizen. Take A6 to Lelystad, or A28 to Harderwijk, and then follow signs for Walibi World.

Information: ☎ (0321) 32 9999; www.walibiworld.nl; VVV Harderwijk, ☎ (0341) 42 6666

Hours: April – Nov., from 10am. Closing hours vary seasonally.

Close to Dronten you'll find 'Hollywood' in the little village of **Biddinghuizen.** This huge new theme park is part of the world's largest group of 35 similar parks in the US, Europe and Latin America. Cutting-edge technology has made for even bigger, faster and more exciting roller coasters, river raft adventure rides and aerodynamic experiences. Of a total of 50 attractions, twenty or more thrill rides are all here for the taking. Some of them extend for a whole kilometer, climbing 100 ft (30 meters), before taking their first breath-stopping plunge and swinging round their curves at 80 km (50 mi) an hour.

For the less hardy, there are more relaxing attractions involving the Looney Tunes characters in live shows and theme presentations. The Looney Tooter train, the mini teacups and frog hopper will surely be more the little ones' cup of tea. Batman and Superman are also in attendance, ensuring as ever that good triumphs over evil, in action-packed shows full of special effects.

Apart from all the excitement, the area itself is delightful and well-laid-out with every facility. A bungalow park (141 units), and camping sites for mobile campers and tents are also conveniently close by. They will undoubtedly tempt visitors to spend more time in the area, making Walibi World one of the major highlights of your holiday or stopover.

Emmeloord
In the heart of flower country

Getting there: Take A6 crossing from the southern part of Flevoland. From Friesland, A32 south to A6.

Information: VVV, de Deel 21a, ☎ (0527) 61 2000

The northeast polder was drained between 1937-42, making it the first of the new lands created by the Zuiderzee project. At the centre of the additional 123,553 acres of land is **Emmeloord**, the largest town as well as geographic and commercial centre for the area. Concerts are held in summer at the foot of the 65-meter **Polder Tower**, which you čan also climb. If you want to enjoy the springtime flowers, the area around Emmeloord is an option. It's not as crowded as the traditional flower regions of Holland. In fact, Flevoland is now the largest bulb growing area in the country. The VVV recommends a route through the area of Espel, Creil, Ens and Rutten. There's also an Orchid farm northeast of town, **De Orchideenhoeve**, Oosterringweg 34, Luttelgeest, ☎ (0527) 20 2875, open Mon.-Fri. 9am-6pm, Sat. 9am-6pm, Sun. noon-5pm, with over 30,000 square meters of exotic flowers. To the south is the important **Schokland Museum**.

▶ **Museum Schokland, Archeological Museum**

Location: Middelbuurt 3, Ens. Exit 13 off of A6, then east on N352....due east of Urk and south of Emmeloord.

Information: ☎ (0527) 25 1396

Hours: April-June. & Sept.-Oct., Tues.-Sun., 11am-5pm; July-Aug., daily 11am-5pm; Nov.-March, Fri.-Sun. 11am-5pm.

Once upon a time **Schokland** was an island. When the Zuiderzee, specifically the northeast polder was drained, Schokland was attached to the mainland. The treasures found after the waters were drained make up this museum collection. The little village is raised from the surrounding polderland and consists of a series of colourful red-roofed houses constructed in the Zuiderzee style of 1859. The museum is in the ancient chapel of **Middelbuurt**.

The collection includes ship-rudders, figureheads, pieces of Roman galleys and Norman dragonships, as well as bones of prehistoric mammoths, woolly-haired rhinoceros, giant deer and wild horses. There are stone tools and weapons, Neolithic hunting gear, and pre-Christian cooking pots.

Urk
After 700 years, an island no more
Getting there: A6 to exit 13, then east on N352
Information: VVV, Wijk 2/2, ☎ (0527) 68 4040

Urk has a longer history than the polder it is a part of. For at least 700 years it was an island, home to a fishing community, and isolated from the rest of the country. But in 1941 the land around it was reclaimed. It has retained its traditional seaport atmosphere, however, and is one of Flevoland's most pleasant towns.

Urk's charm lies in its old town with its fishermen's cottages. Walk through the small streets and notice the picturesque compact homes with their green facades and red and white shutters, and their neat front gardens behind painted picket fences. Take a walk along the harbour to see the fishing boats. The **lighthouse** at Wijk 3-80, ☎ (0527) 68 1582, can be climbed in the summer months. The huge anchor just in front of its entrance came from one of Admiral de Ruyter's ships in the 17th century.

On Sundays, you can still see a few older residents wearing their traditional dress to church – the men with their colourful outfits, baggy pants and wooden shoes. And on Monday some women still observe the traditional washday, and can be seen hanging clothes on lines between houses. But by and large, the old customs of this once isolated village are lost. To see some of the old culture, visit the **Museum Het Oude Raadhuis**, Wijk 2/2, ☎ (0527) 68 3262, open April-Sept., Mon.-Sat. 10am-5pm, with its collection of costumes, an interior dating from 1900 and displays explaining the life of old Urk. You can see the whole town dressed up in traditional costume on **Urkerdag**, usually held in late May.

Tours

From late June-early Sept., **Rederij Duurstede**, ☎ (0527) 68 3407, takes passengers and bicycles from Urk to Enkhuizen. The boat leaves Urk at 9:30am, 1:15pm & 5pm; and Enkhuizen at 11:30am, 3:15pm & 6:40pm... but not on Sundays. The trip takes about an hour and a half.

Eating out

Although it's not open to the public, Urk still has a fish market every Mon. & Fri. Eel is one of the specialities. The best places to eat fish are at **Restaurant 't Achterhuis Visafslag**, Burg. Schipperskade 2, ☎ (0527) 68 2796; **De Kaap**, Wijk 1-56, ☎ (0527) 65 2092; and **De Zeebodem**, Wijk 1-5b, ☎ (0527) 68 3292.

Chapter 7 | The province of Brabant

Brabant is one of the largest of the Dutch provinces, with its southern boundary falling just short of running the entire length of the Dutch-Belgian border. All major highways north/ south pass through some part of Brabant. It has a varied landscape, offering a wide choice of outdoor activities. It also has its fair share of castles, a fine selection of recreation parks (De Efteling, Land van Ooit, Beekse Bergen Safari Park and Autotron), not to mention WW II sites, and attractive towns. 's Hertogenbosch, popularly known as Den Bosch, is the provincial capital, and along with Breda probably the most interesting of the towns to visit.

The province has special celebrations and folkloric events throughout the year. Traditionally Catholic, it has a reputation for being more relaxed than the Protestant provinces to the north, and its pre-Lenten Carnival celebrations are popular and lively.

Brabant was under Spanish control during much of the Dutch war of independence, but joined the northern provinces in 1648. After years of differences with those provinces, South Brabant became part of the newly formed country of Belgium in 1839, while North Brabant remained in the Netherlands.

Information: Call local VVVs listed throughout chapter.

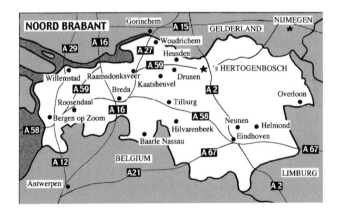

Willemstad
Fortress town and boating centre

Getting there: From Amsterdam and The Hague A13 south via Rotterdam, then A29 over to Willemstad.

Information: VVV, Hofstraat 1, ☎ (0168) 47 6055

Most Dutch boaters know about **Willemstad**, but it's not as well known to foreigners. This charming fortress town was named after William the Silent who in 1583 had it enclosed with a moat 125 feet wide, and ramparts laid out in the shape of a seven-pointed star. Two openings were left in the fortress: a land gate and a water gate, both now replaced.

Willemstad can vie with Naarden (in North Holland) for the title of 'best-kept fortress town.' It is a quieter place, becoming more animated at weekends and during holiday periods when boats arrive in droves to sail the **Biesbosch**, an area of innumerable inlets and outlets perfect for fishing or other watersports. Surfboards, boats, etc. can also be rented.

Next to the harbour in the centre of town is the **Arsenal** (1794) and jutting out in front of it the former **Town Hall**, now the VVV, graced with an elegant mermaid weathervane.

Stroll down the charming streets with their 17-19th-century houses to the square of the **Domed Church**, completed in octagonal design in 1607, and the first Protestant church building in the country. Then take the Hofstraat to the **Mauritshuis**, built as the hunting castle of Prince Maurits in 1587. On the ramparts near the water is the **Oranje Mill** (1734), Bovenkade 11. The VVV has walking tours for groups, which visit the church, climb the tower for a spectacular view of this precisely laid-out town, and follow the ramparts.

Bergen op Zoom
Asparagus, strawberries and anchovies!

Getting there: About halfway between Rotterdam and Antwerp. From Rotterdam, The Hague and Amsterdam, take A29 to N259.

Information: Tourist Information Centre, Grote Markt 1, (0164) 27 7482

Founded in the 12th century, **Bergen op Zoom** is a stately old town that was often under attack. During its heyday, this fortress town was besieged 14 times. Victorious against the Spaniards in 1588 and 1622, it was known as the 'virgin' city until 1747, when the French took it and bombarded it heavily. It was an important trading town in the Middle Ages, particularly with England and Belgium. There is little to be seen today of its distinguished past as a result of these military manoeuvres. There are, however, plenty of appealing and unexpected things to catch your interest. Today Bergen op Zoom is known for its asparagus, oysters, strawberries and anchovies...so May and June are the ideal months to visit.

▶ **Markiezenhof City Museum**

Location:	Steenbergsestraat 8
Information:	☎ (0164) 27 7077
Hours:	Tue.-Sun. 11am-5pm

The late Gothic palace of the Marquises of Bergen, with its interesting grillwork on the ground floor windows, was built between 1485-1525. Inside, look for the Christoffer Chimney with Renaissance stone motifs designed by Rambout Keldermans. Its 12-room museum contains local archeological finds, fishing displays, old toys, 16th-century carpets, paintings, sculptures and furniture from the 15th-18th centuries, all displayed in rooms in the style of those periods.

▶ **Also in Bergen op Zoom**

The beautiful facade of the **Stadhuis** (Town Hall), Market Square, open May-Sept., Tues.-Sat. 1-4:30pm, dates from 1611. The inscription on the front reads, 'I have overcome thousands of dangers.' While on the Market Place, notice the **St. Gertrudis Church** with its remarkable domed tower (the pepper box).

Look for the house called **De Olifant** (The Elephant) built over St. Anna Street, which runs from the Town Hall through a late Gothic gateway. On **O.L. Vrouwestraat**, you will see a Flemish-shaped building with the town's most beautiful baroque facade. The **O.L. Vrouwepoort**, Gate of the Blessed Lady, is particularly impressive with its lower walls seven feet thick – all that remains of the former ramparts. In July-Aug., Mon. 7:30pm and Wed. 2pm, there are guided walks through old town.

In the neighbourhood of Bergen op Zoom

Roosendaal was a 13th-century peat-cutting village, but today industry is its mainstay along with plenty of shopping. Its **Museum Tongerlohuys**, Molenstraat 2, ☎ (0165) 53 6916, open Tues.-Sun. 2-5pm, is in St. Jan's Church (1762). The collection includes silver, glass, crests, pewter, toys, tools, porcelain, earthenware, a little shop and a print cabinet.

Wouw, west of Roosendaal, is called the 'Geranium Village' because they bloom profusely here in summer. You can't miss the splendid silhouette of **St. Lambertuskerk** (15th century). Inside are 17th-century choir stalls and lovely stained-glass windows. There is a **Graphics Museum**, Roosendaalsestraat 43, ☎ (0165) 30 2290, open Sun. 1-5pm and a flour mill, **De Arend**, Akkerstraat 13, ☎ (0165) 30 1273, open if the mill is working, Sun. 2-6pm. Located in a wooded area, this is a place to enjoy the outdoors. **Wouwse Plantage** has nature trails and campsites.

Huijbergen, southeast of Bergen op Zoom, was inhabited by monks for centuries. There is a 17th-century gate as a reminder of times gone by, and a small museum, **Wilhelmietenmuseum**, Staartsestraat 2, ☎ (0164) 64 2568, open April-Sept., 2nd and 4th weekends 2-5pm, with items of the village heritage.

The Biesbosch
Largest valuable nature reserve in Holland

Getting there: Encircled by both major and minor highways; A16 to the west, A27 to the north, A15 to the east and A59 to the south. The closest towns are Dordrecht and Breda.

Information: Information Centre 'Drimmelen,' Biesboschweg 4, Drimmelen, ☎ (0162) 68 2233 open Tues.-Sun. 10am-5pm.
Information Centre 'De Hollandse Biesbosch,' Baanhoekweg 53, Dordrecht, ☎ (078) 630 5353

When the Haringvliet Dam was completed in 1970, what had been a freshwater tidal area was replaced by a man-made, controlled, non-tidal, alluvial landscape. There were vast changes with losses of certain plant and animal species, and gains when they were replaced by others...and changes continue to take place.

The **Biesbosch** as a wetland (an area rich in water; important as a waterfowl habitat), dates from 1421 when the polder became an inland sea after a severe flood, and tides entered the area freely. At the same time, sludge and sand were deposited from the Maas and Waal rivers. With the buildup of the sludge, rush, reed and willows grew, and by 1850 over two-thirds of the former inland sea was being used for agriculture.

The flora includes reed beds, stinging nettles, willow-herb, marsh marigold, and yellow iris. Birds have always come here to roost, feed and breed, especially migrating birds. You will find ducks, cormorants, swans, herons, meadow birds, wild geese, and even a rare kingfisher and night heron. Among the mammals are bats, roe deer, polecats and beavers.

The area is managed by the National Forest Service. Start your visit at one of the information centres: 'Drimmelen,' on the south shore of the Maas; or 'De Hollandse Biesbosch,' just outside Dordrecht. They will advise you about recreational facilities and organised day-trips. You may experience the joys of the Biesbosch on bikes, by canoe, boat, swimming or walking. Yachting is subject to navigation regulations.

In **Werkendam**, the **Biesbosch Museum**, Hilweg 2, ☎ (0183) 50 4009, open April-Oct., Tues.-Sat. 10am-5pm, Sun. noon-5pm, deals with the history of the area before 1970. It tells the story of creatures that used to live here, such as the 9-foot-long sturgeon, which is extinct due to pollution and overfishing. Fishing, basket and thatch-making are explained. Fascinating slide show.

Tours

There are numerous boat rental facilities (motor, sail, canoe, kayak, rowing) as well as boat tours, many leaving from Drimmelen. Check with the information centres for specifics. **Rondvaartbedrijf Avontuur,** ☎ (0165) 34 8104, has tours from Willemstad.

Breda

In the neighbourhood of the Biesbosch

The **National Automobile Museum** at **Raamsdonksveer** makes for a total change of pace!

▸ **The National Automobile Museum**

Location: Steurweg 8, Raamdonksveer (north of Breda on A27)
Information: ☎ (0162) 58 5400
Hours: April-Oct., Tues.-Sat. 10am-5pm, Sun 11am-5pm

This 12,000-square-meter national museum has a fascinating international collection of antique cars from as far back as 1894. There are over 200 cars, 40 motorbikes, carriages, fire engines, an airplane and even bicycles...not to be missed. Films about unusual forms of transport, inventions, and racing car history are usually shown every hour.

Breda
Home of the Counts of Burgundy

Getting there: A2 south from Amsterdam, then A27 south; A13 from The Hague and Rotterdam, A20 east, A16 south.
Information: VVV, Willemstraat 17-19, ☎ (0900) 522 2444

Breda is known for its historic town centre, its church with magnificent gravestones of the ancestors of the Dutch royal family, its castles, parks and the ancient woods that surround it. It has a rich past, receiving its town rights in 1252. In 1350, it passed as a Brabant fiefdom to the Lords of Polanen. One of the women of that family, Johanna van Polanen, married Engelbrecht I (1370-1442) of the House of Nassau. Four generations later came William the Silent, Prince of Orange – the leader of the Dutch revolt against Spain, and from whom the current royal family (House of Orange-Nassau) is descended.

During the 80 Years War, Breda changed hands many times as battles raged around the castle belonging to the family of William the Silent. Once, Breda was retaken in a legendary ruse reminiscent of the Trojan Horse. According to local lore, in 1590, 70 soldiers under the command of Prince Maurits (the son of William the Silent) entered the city hidden in a peat barge. This surprise attack led to their victory over the Spaniards.

Charles II of England lived here in exile before being restored to the throne in 1660. And in 1667 a treaty was signed in Breda which transferred the American colonies of New York and New Jersey from Dutch to British control.

▶ **Grote Kerk (Great Church) or Onze Lieve Vrouwe Kerk**

Location: Market Square. Getting here can be tricky because of the canals that surround the town. Follow signs for 'Centrum.'

Information: ☎ (076) 521 8267

Hours: Mon.-Sat. 10am-5pm, Sun. 1-5pm

The **Grote Kerk** took 150 years to build. The result was one of the most beautiful towers of the Netherlands and one of its tallest (97 meters). If possible, come here on a Tuesday or Friday morning when the 45 bells of the carillon in the church tower ring out over the heads of the market shoppers in the square.

Originating from about 1400, this is a fine example of Brabant Gothic style. There are interesting gravestones from the Polanen and Nassau families. A huge mural of St. Christopher (1500) covers one wall, while a restored mural of the Annunciation of Mary is on another. There is a simple wooden seating area called the 'Princes Pew' (1663), which has always been reserved for members of the royal family. Look for the satirical wooden sculptures on choir seats in the choir of the church, some from the 16th century and some as recent as the 20th century.

In the neighbourhood of the Grote Kerk

The **Town Hall** (1768, enlarged in 1924) is across from the church on the Grote Markt. Inside is a copy of a famous painting by Velasquez, *De Overgave van Breda* (The Surrender of Breda) and portraits of members of the House of Nassau.

Further south is **Breda's Museum**, Parade 12, ☎ (076) 529 9300, open Tues.-Sun. 10am-5pm. It deals with the history of the Barony of Breda, and contains a collection of art from the region.

▶ **Breda Castle**

Location: North of the town centre at Kasteelplein 10.

Information: VVV, ☎ (0900) 522 2444

Hours: Visits only with VVV guide. Walking tours in the summer.

The Renaissance castle was built from 1536 under Henry III of Nassau, uncle to William the Silent. Henry married Claudia of Chalon and Orange, thus uniting the Dutch and French houses of Nassau and Orange. William the Silent lived here, and it has been the scene of many important struggles in Dutch history. In the quiet inner court there are interesting tunnel vaults which still evoke memories of its warlike history. The castle is home to the Dutch Royal Military Academy. It is only open to visitors accompanied by a VVV guide.

● **Near Breda Castle:** The **Stadhouderspoort** is the main entrance to the castle. Just outside that gate is **Kasteelplein** (Castle Square) where many battles took place in the days when this was the castle's only entrance. Kasteelplein is also where Protestants were burned at the stake during the Inquisition.

The **Spanjaardsgat** (Spaniard's Gate) is next to the castle at the end of Cingelstraat. It is a water gate flanked with two big gun towers. It is said this is the gate through which the peat barge with its cargo of soldiers under command of Prince Maurits sailed into the city to do battle with the Spaniards.

On the other side of the castle is a fine public park with rare plants and flowers. **Valkenberg** (Falcon's Mount) was part of the castle grounds where falcons were trained for hunting. In the 17th century it was the castle's ornamental garden, containing 17 large statues – four remain, including that of Hercules. At one end of the park is the **Nassau-Baronie Monument**, dedicated by Queen Wilhelmina in 1905 to mark 500 years of the House of Nassau.

On the edge of Valkenberg is the **Beguinage**, its entrance on Catharinastraat, next to the ancient Walonian Church. It is a peaceful little quadrangle surrounded by medieval dwellings. The original occupants were Beguines, religious women dedicated to the church. Elderly women now live here, protected from the hustle and bustle of the outside world. In the middle of the quadrangle is a small 18th-century church and an herb garden.

Not far away is the **De Beyerd Art Centre**, Boschstraat 22, ☎ (076) 522 5025, under renovation but generally open Tues.-Fri. 10am-5pm, Sat.-Sun. 1-5pm. Exhibits of contemporary art, photography, architecture and ceramics.

▶ **Also in Breda**

The manor house **Bouvigne**, Bouvignelaan 5, was built in the early 16th century. This estate was called 'The Boeverie' which means 'landed property' in old French. A number of noblemen have resided here, including William the Silent, and later his son Maurits. It is a lovely spot to admire the elegant lines and onion dome of this graceful brick castle.

In addition to things cultural, Breda offers sports activities such as riding schools, swimming pools, bowling alleys and several parks and gardens. A relaxing way to explore is to rent a canoe at **Akkermans Outdoor Centre**, Kraanstraat 7, ☎ (076) 522 4813, near the Spaniard's Gate...reasonable rates. For adult evening entertainment there's the **Holland Casino Breda**, Kloosterplein 20, ☎ (076) 525 1100.

Markets

Weekly markets are held Tues. & Fri. 9am-1pm on the Grote Markt; Sat. 9am-5pm Ginnekenmarkt (a flea market); Sat. 1-5pm on the Nieuwe Haagdijk/Haagweg; Thurs. 9am-12:30pm in the Winkelcentrum Moerwijk; and Sat. 9am-1pm on the Vijverstraat.

Eating out

A wide selection of international foods includes Portuguese, Italian, Cantonese, Mexican and over 25 Chinese-Indonesian restaurants! **Kloostertaverne**, Kloosterplein 5,

☎ (076) 521 9871, is a pancake restaurant. **De Boschwachter Mastbos**, Huisdreef 4, ☎ (076) 565 2880, and **De Boschwachter Liesbosch**, Nieuwe Dreef 4, ☎ (076) 521 2736, are farm restaurants in the woods. For gourmet meals: **De Stadstuin**, Ginnekenweg 138, ☎ (076) 530 9636. Look for restaurants near the Grote Kerk at the Grote Markt (in front of the church) and Havermarkt (behind the church).

Yearly events

Carnaval draws lively crowds just before Lent; **St. Matthew's Passion** is presented before Easter. **Netherlands Art and Antique Fair**, ten days before and including Easter weekend. **Jazz Festival** in May (four-day Ascension weekend) with street and pubs alive with music. Several horse events – one at Whitsun, and the Derby, 1st weekend in Aug. Also in Aug., **Breda Balloon Fiesta** at Rietdijk, with over 30 colourful hot air balloons; and the equally colourful **Breda National Taptoe**, end of Aug.-beginning of Sept., at Trip van Zoutland Kazerne.

In the neighbourhood of Breda

Oosterhout, north of Breda, has a toy museum: **Op Stelten**, St. Vincentiusstraat 86, ☎ (0162) 45 2815, open Wed.-Sun. 1-5pm. The **Bakkerij Museum**, Klappeijstraat 47, ☎ (0162) 42 9700, open by appointment only, has exhibits of traditional Dutch baked goods, and an old fashioned bakery store. Groups can make arrangements to bake their own bread or cookies. The **Brabant Museum**, Bredaseweg 129, ☎ (0162) 42 6815, open April-Oct., Tues.-Fri., 10am-5pm, Sat.-Sun. 11am-5pm, Nov.-March, Tues.-Thurs. 11am-4pm, Sun. noon-5pm, has exhibits relating to the Dutch way of living and working around 1900. There's also a full-scale recreation area, **De Warande**, Bredaseweg 127, ☎ (0162) 45 3800, with swimming pools (including impressive waterslide), lake, playground, midget golf, and restaurant with terrace.

Etten Leur, 5 km (3 mi) west of Breda, has the **Drukkerijmuseum**, Leeuwerik 8, ☎ (076) 503 4826, open Wed. & Thurs. 1-4:30pm, 1st Sun. of the month and the Sat. before it, 1-5pm. This printing museum shows early book-printing techniques, including binding, engraving and setting; 19th-century tools and machines are still in use. **Recreation Park Bosbad Hoeven**, Oude Antwerpsepostbaan 81a, Hoeven, ☎ (0165) 50 2570, open July-early Sept., Mon.-Fri. 10am-7:30pm; late April-June, daily 10am-6:30pm, has pools for every age: paddling, racing, diving and a 60-meter super waterslide, a playground with over 50 attractions, electric motorboats, sightseeing train, horses and a campground.

In the beautiful wooded area of **Dorst** there's a recreation park **Surae**, Suraeweg 61, ☎ (0161) 41 1559, with swimming and rowing, midget golf, trampolines, etc., and a restaurant with a lovely terrace.

Baarle-Nassau and **Baarle-Hertog** are southeast of Breda. Since South Brabant broke away from Holland and joined Belgium, these twin towns, one Dutch and one Belgian, have represented a unique political and economic phenomenon. This situation has created many unusual predicaments. For instance, some residents of Baarle-Hertog must pass through Holland in order to go from their Belgian home to their office in Belgium. Everything is duplicated: two electrical systems, two post offices, two police departments, two mayors with two City Halls. **Kathedrale Kaarsenmuseum**, Kerkplein 2, ☎ (013) 507 9921 (VVV), open Easter-Sept., Tues.-Thurs. 11am-4pm, Sat.-Sun. noon-4pm, has elaborately designed candles on display, most with finely carved and painted religious figures.

Tilburg
Home of antique and modern textiles

Getting there: A 13 from The Hague and Rotterdam, to A16 south, and A58 east.
                  From Amsterdam, A2 to A27 to A58.
Information: VVV, Stadhuisplein 128, ☎ (0800) 023 4004

Tilburg is an education centre, with a textile school, well-known University of Economics, the Brabant Academy of Music and an excellent ballet school. Its location made it a wine trading centre. Ships and carts that transported textiles across Europe brought back various products, including wine. Its heyday came with the development of modern factories in the 18-19th centuries. Workers and their families settled in Tilburg close to its many textile factories. Under Louis Napoleon (Bonaparte's brother), it received its town charter.

The factory owners had excellent relations with King William II who lived in Tilburg during much of his reign. He gave his palace to the town which serves today as part of the Town Hall and VVV Tourist Office.

The wool trade has been replaced with a variety of service industries and companies specialising in modern technology. Industrial giants are often good supporters of the arts, and Tilburg has a number of museums, art galleries, theatres, and venues for enthusiasts of modern jazz. In addition, there are sidewalk cafes, good shopping and a wide choice of restaurants.

▶ **Textile Museum**
Location: Goirkestraat 96
Information: ☎ (013) 536 7475
Hours: Tues.-Fri. 10am-5pm, Sat.-Sun. noon-5pm

When you walk into the exhibition area of the **Textile Museum**, your first thought might be that you've made a wrong turn – it looks like a factory. But don't hesitate to walk right up to the people running the spinning, rattling and chugging machines to watch what they're doing. The Textile Museum is a lively place with machines at work making cloth – weaving, knitting, and spinning textiles; and the workers are there to explain it all to you.

The museum is located in a former textile mill. On the first two floors, 19th and 20th-century machines are exhibited. On the two upper floors are examples of textile art, such as rugs, clothing, etc. There's also a gift shop, where you can buy items made in the museum.

The **DePont Foundation for Contemporary Art**, Wilhelminapark 1, ☎ (013) 543 8300, open Tues.-Sun. 11am-5pm, has modern paintings and sculptures, and is housed in a large, old, wool spinning mill, making it possible to display works which have unusual space requirements.

▶ **Also in Tilburg**

Museum Scryption, Spoorlaan 434 ☎ (013) 580 0821 open Tues.-Fri. 10am-5pm, Sat.-Sun. 1-5pm, is a museum of writing instruments. Over 500 typewriters, ink pots, pens, and letter openers are part of the display; also interesting material on calligraphic art, ancient writing materials, and old writing styles. Next door is **Noordbrabants Natuur-museum** ☎ (013) 535 3935, same address and hours. Its collection includes plants, animals, rocks, prehistoric fish, petrified wood. If you want to see live animals, **Dierenpark Reptielenhuis De Oliemuelen**, Reitse Hoevenstraat 30 ☎ (013) 463 0026, open daily 10am-6pm, has snakes, crocodiles, frogs and more.

Maison Du Vin Wijnmuseum, Geminiweg 9, ☎ (013) 584 1202, open Tues.-Fri. 9am-6pm, Sat. 10am-5pm, is a little bit of France in the middle of Brabant. This wine museum is something for the adults that the kids will also enjoy. Enter through the Orangerie, then visit the 'Cinema du Vin' (movie on wine), then follow the 'Route du Vin' past a barrel or cask-maker, art gallery, a glass store, wine library and a Grand Cru shop. For the thirsty or hungry, there's a French-style café and an open market with wine tasting.

Poppenmuseum Tilburg, Telefoonstraat 13, ☎ (013) 543 6305, open Wed., Thurs., Fri. & Sun. 1-4pm, has a collection of over 3,000 modern and antique dolls, along with the clothing and other accessories that accompany them.

Yearly events

In June the **Festival Mundial** is held with hundreds of musicians from all over the world. **Tilburgse Kermis**, the biggest fair in the Benelux region (3 km/2 mi long), is in July. End of Sept., **Tilburg Wijnstad/Culinair** celebrates good food, and particularly good wine. Every Saturday near the Town Hall the **Kruikenmarkt** has antiques, curiosities and secondhand goods.

In the neighbourhood of Tilburg

At **Waalwijk** there's a **Leather and Shoe Museum**, Elzenweg 25, ☎ (0416) 33 2738, open Tues.-Fri. 10am-5pm, Sat.-Sun. noon-4pm, in a former shoe factory. Shoes from around the world and from all periods. Boot and shoe-making tools and machines dating from 1870 are still functioning and are used for demonstrations.

▶ **De Efteling**
Amusement/fairyland park
Location: Near Kaatsheuvel, 8 km (5 mi) north of Tilburg on A261
Information: ☎ (0900) 0161; www.efteling.nl
Hours: Apr.-Oct., daily 10am-6pm; mid-July- Aug., open to 9pm

De Efteling was designed in the 1950s by Anton Pieck, a well-known Dutch artist and great lover of children. His aim was to bring his drawings and characters from fairy tales of Holland and those from around the world to super-life-size. It took 10 years to complete what you see today. Each year there are more changes and additions to the park, so you can always count on a surprise. Efteling is outstanding and has won many international awards.

Set in a beautiful woodland area, the Enchanted Forest is full of recognisable characters such as Sleeping Beauty, Little Red Riding Hood, Hansel and Gretel, and Snow White. There's also an amusement park for the little ones, with the usual fare, plus a play area for the tots with a paddling pool and an elephant spouting water high in the air. There's a boating lake, a monorail around the whole complex, an original steam carousel, and puppet, slide and video shows.

Another attraction is the haunted castle where an audience of 500 can watch a 25-minute spook show. It's the biggest in Europe and compares to the one in Disneyland, USA. If the spinning rooms of Villa Volta don't shake you up, you might enjoy a not-so-restful ride on turbulent waters in round, rubber-bottomed boats, passing waterfalls and other hazards. There are three rollercoasters, a bobsled ride, and plenty to keep fans of exciting amusement park rides lining up again and again at Efteling. Afterwards, you can always relax in a gondoletta!

There's enough to warrant spending more than a day, perhaps even over-nighting in their own on-site **Efteling Hotel**, ☎ (0900) 0161, with its special theme rooms.

▶ **Het Land van Ooit – 'Once Upon a Time Land'**
Location: Parklaan 40, Drunen. On A59 take the Drunen exit.
Information: ☎ (0416) 37 7775; www.ooit.nl
Hours: 10am-5pm. Late Apr.-mid Sept., daily. Mid Sept.-mid Oct., weekends only. Late Oct.-end of Oct. (autumn holiday) daily.

Het Land van Ooit, which we have translated as 'Once Upon a Time Land,' is a theme park with a difference. Why? Because it is based on the unique concept that children are in charge! There are countless imaginative attractions, water and play activities in which boys (Knights) and girls (Lady Knights), can take part...twelve theatres where tales of yore are enacted with elaborate costumes of yesteryear, fiery horses, adventure and song – an unforgettable day for the whole family. Adults are welcome too, and will appreciate the tranquil beauty of this old country estate.

▶ Beekse Bergen Safari Park

Location: 3 km (2 mi) SE of Tilburg at Hilvarenbeek off N26
Information: ☎ (0900) 233 5732 0200
Hours: Daily: Jan.-Dec. 10am-4pm; Feb. & Nov. 10am-4:30pm; March-June & Sept.-Oct. 10am-5pm; July-Aug. 10am-6pm

Lions, leopards, and cheetahs run loose and tigers prowl freely...but no need to worry. Although those imposing creatures are allowed a lot of freedom at **Beekse Bergen Safari Park**, the park is safe for humans, as well as for the relatively peaceful zebras, elephants, rhinos, giraffes, ostriches and many monkeys.

Beekse Bergen is a controlled Safari Park. It keeps incompatible animals apart from one another, and humans a safe barrier away. But you can still get a good view of the bison, warthogs and bears. A ticket into the park offers you three different ways to view the animals: by motorised vehicle, either your own car or a bus; by boat, which floats along the park's waterways; on foot, via a path that winds its way to all sides of the park, or, if you like a bit of each.

The park is designed with children in mind. If the camels, flamingos or kangaroos don't hold their interest for long, there are playgrounds scattered throughout, and demonstrations designed to interest all members of the family.

If you drive, do not open car doors or windows, even when sorely tempted by the cute baby animals, or those mischievous apes will be tearing off your side mirror – or worse. The monkeys are the greatest fun because they are so active and full of naughty tricks. They will jump on your car for a ride, peer in through the windows showing their teeth, look at themselves in the side mirrors, and handle anything loose or interesting – do keep an eye on your car antenna.

- **Near Beekse Bergen Safari Park:** The Safari Park is part of a recreation complex at Beekse Bergen. There is also a bungalow park and campsite with a beach, and a lake for boating. **Speelland**, ☎ (0900) 233 5732 0200 open mid-April-June, daily 10am-5pm; July-early Sept., daily 10am-6pm, has ponies, mini-cars, trampolines, water bikes, miniature golf, etc.

Eating out & staying over

Special arrangements can be made through the VVV for two or three-day stays in typical three-star farm hotel//restaurants near to these attractions. One example is the 18th-century **Joremeinshoeve**, Lange Zandschel 1, Kaatsheuvel, ☎ (0416) 27 4527. Pancakes, etc. available from **d' Ouwe Brouwerij**, Baarschotsestraat 48, Baarschot (near Hilvarenbeek), ☎ (013) 504 2079.

's Hertogenbosch
Medieval town with magnificent Gothic cathedral

Getting there: A2 South from Amsterdam; A13 from Rotterdam and The Hague, then A16 south to A15 east, then A2 south.

Information: VVV, Markt 77, ☎ (0900) 112 2334

This medieval town was once the wooded hunting preserve of the Duke of Brabant – which is how it got its name. 's Hertogenbosch means 'The Duke's Woods.' Today, it is most often referred to as 'Den Bosch' (The Woods).

A village grew on the Maas River along the Duke's estate, and in 1185 it received its municipal charter. Its city walls and ramparts kept enemies out, which helped preserve some of the old buildings that still grace the canals and narrow streets of its old town section. Den Bosch is the political and cultural capital of Brabant. Its splendid cathedral – one of the most beautiful in the country – is one of its main attractions. Also worth seeing is its triangular-shaped town square – a busy place on most Saturdays.

▶ **St. John's Cathedral (St. Janskathedraal)**

Location: Choorstraat, in the centre of the old city

Information: ☎ (073) 614 4170

Hours: Daily 9am-5pm except when services are in progress (Sun.); carillon concerts Weds. 11:30am-12:30pm

St. John's Cathedral is considered by many to be the most beautiful cathedral in Holland. It was constructed between 1330 and 1530 on the foundations of a previous church which was destroyed by fire in 1240. It suffered heavy damage during many wars, requiring it to be restored in 1860 and 1955.

The spacious interior boasts 150 pillars! There are numerous superb features to see: the highly decorated stalls of the choir; a Renaissance-style chair; a copper baptismal font (1492); fine statues; and two paintings, the *Virgin with Child* and *St. John*, attributed to the School of Bosch. The chapel of Zoete Lieve Vrouwe (Sweet Dear Lady) contains a 13th-century statue that was credited with playing a role in hundreds of miracles in the Middle Ages. It has drawn thousands of pilgrims to the church over the centuries.

Do take a look at the strange grotesque creatures scampering over the flying buttresses, reminiscent of the characters in Hieronymus Bosch's paintings. If you have binoculars, look at them in detail. A local tale is that each time someone drinks a pint of beer, these little characters change their position. You can test that theory...and get a good view of the church...from the **Parade**, an area with numerous cafés and restaurants adjacent to the church.

● Near St. John's Cathedral: **Museum Slager**, Choorstraat 16, ☎ (073) 613 3216, open Tues.-Fri. & Sun. 2-5pm, is just behind the cathedral. It deals with the works of three generations of the Slager family of artists – over a century of work. The **Zwanenbroedershuis**,

Hinthamerstraat 94, ☎ (073) 613 7383, open Tues. & Thurs. 1:30-4:30pm, houses a collection of rare books of music and medieval carvings belonging to a religious, charitable order that has existed since 1318.

▶ **North Brabant Museum**
Location: Verwersstraat 41
Information: ☎ (073) 687 7877; www.noordbrabantsmuseum.nl
Hours: Tues.-Fri. 10am-5pm, Sat.-Sun. noon-5pm

North Brabant Museum is in the 18th-century Government House built for the Military Governor after Den Bosch was liberated from Spanish rule. The main building houses the collection of ancient art, including an archeological collection about Brabant, which is very enlightening. One wing covers the history of Den Bosch and Brabant, while the other holds changing contemporary exhibits. There is also an attractive sculpture park.

● **Near the North Brabant Museum:** If you enjoy walking, stroll through the **Uilenburg Quarter** (near Molenstraat), west of the museum. There are a number of attractive-looking buildings, as well as bridges that gracefully arch over the canals and reflect in their waters. There are also numerous outdoor cafes along the canals in this area.

The **Refugiehuis**, at Spinhuiswal and St. Jorisstraat, now an arts and crafts centre, was originally a safe haven for those persecuted for their religious beliefs.

▶ **Also in 's Hertogenbosch**
The town centre is full of atmosphere with many buildings worthy of note. On the **Market Square** is a statue of Hieronymus Bosch (1450-1516) the famous painter and native son. From the tower of the 16th-century **Town Hall,** carillons chime every half hour while a group of mechanical horsemen ride into view; there's a one-hour concert on Wed. 10-11am. The oldest house in town is **De Moriaan House** (13th century), now the VVV offices. It was built as a hunting lodge for the Duke so he could escape the pressures of 'business' in Brussels.

North of the city centre is the **Stedelijk Museum**, Magistratenlaan 100, (073) 627 3680, open Tues. & Thurs. 1-9pm and Wed., Fri., Sat., Sun. 1-5pm, a museum of modern art specialising in ceramics. Nearby is the **Citadel**, a renovated section of ancient fortifications with moat and high ramparts. At the **Oranje** southern bastion is a huge cannon, **De Boze Griet** (The Devil's Woman), cast in 1511 in Cologne. The German inscription reads 'Brute force I am called, Den Bosch I watch over.'

Markets

On Wed. morning, there's a cattle market in the **Brabant Halls** on the Veemarktkade and on Thursdays horses are 'on the block.' The general market is held on the **Market Square**, Wed. 8:30am-2pm, Sat. 8:30am-5pm.

Eating out

Informal, often rustic eateries are found in the cellars of town halls. Though not as common in Holland as in Germany – fewer cellars perhaps – there is one in Den Bosch. The **Raadskelder,** Markt 1a, ☎ (073) 613 6919, dates from 1520. Try it for old-world character.

Yearly events

Den Bosch and Maastricht have a reputation for the most colourful **Carnivals** in the country...just before Lent. When in full swing, it's quite an experience. So dress the kids up, put on a crazy mask and join in the fun! In May, Den Bosch has its **Jazz In Duketown** music festival.

In the neighbourhood of 's Hertogenbosch

Archeological data shows **Heusden,** 5 km (3 mi) north of Drunen, was a Roman settlement by 50 B.C. It offers much charm, with little side streets and squares, and well-preserved facades with house names. It is unique for its two windmills on the town wall at the harbour. The **Great St. Catherine's Church** dates from the 13th century.

As for castles, they abound. **Maurick Castle,** south of the village of **Vught** on the road between Den Bosch and Eindhoven, ☎ (073) 657 9108, may not be visited, but the garden is open during the week. In 1601 the castle was a military base under Prince Maurits of Orange (an ancestor of Queen Beatrix) and used by his brother Frederik Hendrik in 1629. **Kasteel Heeswijk,** Kasteel 4, ☎ (0413) 29 2024, open by appointment, is an 11th-century medieval castle, southeast at **Heeswijk-Dinther,** where you can also visit a local farm museum, the **Meierijsch Museumboerderij,** Meerstraat 28, ☎ (0413) 29 1546, open May-Sept., Wed., Sat.-Sun. 2-5pm. **Wildhorst Forest,** Meerstraat 30, has midget golf, a children's playground, heated open-air swimming pool, etc. It's also possible to rent a bungalow, pitch your own tent, or rent a covered wagon here, ☎ (0413) 29 1466.

Overloon
Site of fierce tank battle in WW II

Getting there: A73 from Nijmegen, exit seven, and then west.

It was here in the autumn of 1944 that one of the fiercest tank battles of WW II took place. An American Armoured Division and the British Infantry met the stubborn resistance of the Germans and fought for 20 days – 2,400 men were killed. Over 300 tanks were destroyed and the city was devastated. After the soldiers moved on, the people of **Overloon** were left to rebuild their homes and lives. They used the tanks and weaponry left behind, to create a museum in honour of those who died and to remind the living of the futility of war.

▶ **Nationaal Oorlogs en Verzetsmuseum, Liberty Park –
National War and Resistance Museum**
Location: Museumpark 1
Information: ☎ (0478) 64 1250; www.oorlogsmuseum-overloon.nl
Hours: Sept.-June 10am-5pm, July-Aug. 10am-6pm

This museum consists of a 35-acre park, the actual location of the battle. You can see tanks, planes, guns, antitank devices and many other remnants of the fighting. An English-language guidebook, available at the gate, tells the story of each item you pass on the route, including an American tank whose crew was killed after receiving two direct hits from German antitank guns.

Housed in three buildings: the largest, the main museum consists of 17 rooms outlining the history of the war as it affected the Netherlands and the Dutch resistance; another is a hall with military equipment, uniforms and other materials of war; the third is devoted to the history of the Nazi concentration camps.

Best
Wooden shoes and wings of liberation
Getting there: Follow direction to 's Hertogenbosch and then south on A2. Just north of Eindhoven.
Information: VVV, Oranjestraat 12, ☎ (0499) 37 4177

If there are more wooden shoemakers in **Best** than in any other town in the Netherlands, it's because of the woods. Fast-growing poplar trees abound here, providing excellent material for the ideal wooden shoe. This area was also in the centre of military action during WW II, a part of Operation Market Garden.

▶ **Museum Bevrijdende Vleugels – Wings of Liberation Museum**
Location: Sonseweg 39
Information: ☎ (0499) 32 9722; www.wingsofliberation.nl
Hours: Daily 10am-5pm

The town of Best suffered heavy casualties during Operation Market Garden in WW II. The **Wings of Liberation Museum** is in an area where many American paratroopers landed to take part in the largest airborne battle in history.

In the museum you feel as if you are walking the streets in 1940. A panorama of 340 square meters depicts the German occupation of the city, and its liberation by the Americans. There is a slide show and a document centre with an astonishing collection describing the rise of the Nazi movement, the work of the resistance, and the history of the Jewish people in Holland. There are scale models of planes, uniforms and a large firearms collection.

There were many heroes in the fighting near Best. One was American PFC Joe Mann who saved his buddies by throwing himself on a grenade. He is honoured by a memorial east of town, by the road to Son en Breugel.

▶ **Klompenmuseum De Platijn – Wooden Shoe Museum**
Location: Broekdijk 12
Information: ☎ (0499) 37 1247
Hours: Apr.-Oct., Tues.-Fri., 1-5pm, Sat., Sun. noon-6pm, July-Aug., daily noon-6pm

The **Klompenmuseum De Platijn** shows wooden shoes made for all purposes, and in many styles: for gardening, ice skating, even dancing. Wooden shoes have been worn by people in many lands – examples from 30 countries are on display – but they became popular in Holland because of the wet ground. Wooden shoes keep the wetness out and the feet warm, better than any other material. Although wooden shoes are, for the most part, only worn by some farmers and workers in the field and at old-fashioned cultural events, they are highly popular with tourists. Here you can see how they're made – both the old and the modern way.

Eindhoven
City of light, science and commerce
Getting there: A2 from Amsterdam. From The Hague and Rotterdam, take A13, A16 south to Breda, then east on A58.
Information: VVV, Stationsplein 1, ☎ (0900) 112 2363; www.vvveindhoven.iaehv.nl/index.html

It's hard to believe this bustling industrial metropolis had barely 5,000 inhabitants in 1900. **Eindhoven's** rise as a city of great importance (5th largest in the Netherlands), with worldwide influence on electronic and commercial development, has occurred since 1891. That was the year Gerard Philips opened a small factory to make light bulbs that soon made Eindhoven the 'Lighting Capital' of the world. Today, Philips is a leader in electronics, and the company is at the heart of the city's economy.

▶ **Van Abbe Museum**
Location: Bilderdijklaan 10
Information: ☎ (040) 238 1000; www.vanabbemuseum.nl
Hours: Tues.-Sun. 11am-5pm. Thurs. till 9pm

In 1936, industrialist H. J. van Abbe presented a gallery to the city of Eindhoven. The collection started with a few Dutch paintings, then a Chagall, and in recent decades the collection has grown to include painters representative of expressionism, cubism, neoplasticism, the COBRA school, and surrealism. The once meagre **Van Abbe Museum** is now one of the most vibrant galleries of modern paintings to be found anywhere. See Picasso's *Seated Woman*, Braque's *La Roche-Guyon*, Leger's *Accordion*, Kokoschka's *The Power of Music*, as well as action paintings and chromatic abstractions by Morris Louis, Robert Indiana and Frank Stella.

▶ **Historisch Openluchtmuseum – Historic Open Air Museum**
Location: Boutenslaan 161b
Information: ☎ (040) 252 2281
Hours: Daily April-Oct., 10am-5pm Nov.-March, Sun. 10am-5pm

The **Historic Open Air Museum** takes you back in time – way back. It represents a village from 750-50 B.C. The structures are based on archeological finds in the Brabant town of Oss-Ussen. They are built with natural materials like loam, as in the Iron Age.

The best time to visit is from April-Oct. when people dressed as they were in pre-historic days are doing prehistoric work, such as hewing a boat out of a log, or baking bread in an outdoor oven. At the weekend there are special events – the reenactment of a Viking invasion, prehistoric music festivals, etc. During **Historic Days** held on the first weekend in October, a large range of handicrafts are demonstrated. For a small fee you can join in and learn to forge iron, spin wool, or just live the prehistoric life for a day. There are special weekends for children, giving them the opportunity to bake bread, play games, or learn to play music and dance – prehistoric style. Arrangements can also be made for overnight stays. Groups sleep in the huts, feed the hogs, or just sit by the riverbank and think how much easier life is in the 21st century...or is it?

▶ **Also in Eindhoven**
The most significant industrial site in Eindhoven is only open for visits on the last Saturday of each month. The **Philips Incandescent Lamp Factory of 1891**, Emmasingel 31, ☎ (040) 297 9115 (VVV), open for tours only Tues.-Sun. 2pm and Sun. 1pm, is the building where Gerard Philips first began producing lightbulbs. Retired Philips employees conduct the tours, during which they show how these incandescent lamps were made over a century ago.

Another Eindhoven success story is told at the **DAF Museum**, Tongelresestraat 27, ☎ (040) 244 4364, open Tues.-Sun. 10am-5pm. The van Doorne brothers opened a forge on this site in 1928. It grew to become DAF, an international manufacturer of trucks and trailers. From 1958-75, DAF made an innovative small car. The museum has a large display of DAF cars, trucks, buses and other vehicles, as well as the original smithy that sparked this successful company.

Other museums include the **Museum Kempenland**, St. Antoniusstraat 5, ☎ (040) 252 9093, www.dse.nl/kempenland, open Tues.-Sun. 1-5pm. Housed in a former church, it covers the history and culture of the region. The **Milieu Educatie**

Centrum, Genneperweg 145, ☎ (040) 259 4700, open Tues.-Fri., 9am-5pm, Sat.-Mon. 1-5pm, is a natural history museum.

Churches worth a visit include **St. Catharinakerk**, Kerkstraat 1, ☎ (040) 244 8897, open May, Tues.-Fri. 9:30am-4:45pm, a neo-Gothic basilica built in 1867 by P.J.H. Cuypers. Nearby is the **Augustine Monastery**, Augustijnendreef, a 17th-century church and monastery. It can be spotted by its tall steeple topped by a five-meter (16 ft) statue of Christ with outstretched arms.

There are also two mills. **De Collse Watermill**, Collseweg 1, ☎ (040) 281 7818, open Sat. mornings, is a grain mill, and the **Genneper Watermill**, Genneperweg 143, ☎ (040) 257 1772, open Mon.-Fri. 9am-5pm, closed Wed., was built in 1249.

The family could take a break from sightseeing at **Tongelreep Recreation Centre**, Antoon Coolenlaan 1, ☎ (040) 238 1112, complete with several pools (in and outdoor), a subtropical wave pool with slides, a jacuzzi and tanning area, a billiard room and a bowling centre. There's also a restaurant on the premises. It's a great place for a bad-weather day. Eindhoven has a luxurious ice skating complex, **Kunstijsbaan Eindhoven**, Antoon Coolenlaan 3, ☎ (040) 238 1201, with indoor and outdoor rinks; skates can be rented.

Yearly events

In late June, Eindhoven moves with a Latin beat for the popular **Fiesta del Sol Music Festival**. In Oct. there's the **South-Dutch Fair**, and in mid-Sept. the **Floral Parade** in neighbouring **Valkenswaard**.

In the neighbourhood of Eindhoven

Son en Breugel is thought to be the birthplace of Breugel senior, of the famous family of painters.

Nuenen, northeast off A270, is where Vincent Van Gogh lived from 1883-85. His painting studio has been preserved and his home is still intact. The park has a memorial. The **Van Gogh Documentation Centre**, Papenvoort 15, ☎ (040) 236 9615, open Tues.-Sun., 11am-4pm, has a collection of photos, reproductions and items connected with his stay here.

The castle in **Helmond**, east via A270, is from 1402, and now a cultural centre and museum with changing exhibits: **Gemeentemuseum Helmond**, Kasteelplein 1, ☎ (0492) 58 7716, open Tues-Fri. 10am-5pm, Sat-Sun. 1-5pm.

Heeze Castle, Kapelstraat 25, in **Heeze**, ☎ (040) 226 4435, open Mar-Nov., tours Wed. 2pm, Sun. 2pm & 3pm; July-Aug, Wed. tours also at 3pm, has 17th and 18th-century furniture, paintings and tapestries.

Asten, east on A67, is home to the largest collection of clocks and bells in Europe. The **National Carillon Museum** (Beiaard Museum), ☎ (0493) 69 1865, www.carillonmuseum.nl, open Sat.-Mon. 1-5pm, Tues.-Fri. 9:30am-5pm, tells the story of bells, and also houses the local natural history collection.

Try not to miss some of the many picturesque old villages such as **Eersel**, **Duizel**, **Steensel**, **Oirschot**, **Hulsel**, **Knegsel**, **Netersel**, **Reusel** and **Wintersel**.

Chapter 8 | The province of Friesland

Friesland is a province of proud, resourceful and independent people. Over half of them have retained their original Frisian language (*Fryske*), with many English-sounding words due to its west-Germanic origin. In fact, you'll see city and street names sometimes given in both Dutch and Frisian.

This is one of the oldest inhabited areas of the Netherlands. Over 2,000 years ago, Frisians built mounds upon which they established villages to escape the floodwaters. The marshy land was difficult for outsiders to conquer. The Romans were never able to control Friesland, but carried on trade with its residents. The Counts of Holland, determined to obtain this fertile land, fought many battles over it, until King Charles V of Spain incorporated it into his empire. In 1579, Friesland joined with five other provinces to form the Union of Utrecht, but maintained the right to choose their own 'Stadhouder' (Governor) – a privilege they maintained until 1747.

Though spring and summer are the best times to visit, winter has its own attraction with the famous ice-skating race 'Elfstedentocht.' Bird watchers and beach lovers should not miss the northern islands. There are ferry services, and for the adventurous it is sometimes possible to walk to an island ... in the mud (*wadlopen*). A drive along the 30 km (19 mi) dike to Harlingen is also a unique experience.

Friesland is a summer sports paradise. It's ideal for biking, with miles of trails winding along canals, and past fields full of black and white Frisian cows. There are also many folkloric events to enjoy that are unique to Friesland.

Information: ☎ (058) 2330 740; www.visitfryslan.com

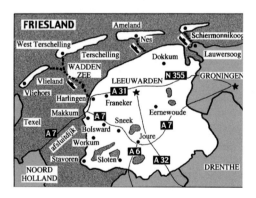

230

Harlingen
A national historic site

Getting there: From the Afsluitdijk, take the immediate left turnoff A31. Harlingen is about 8 km (5 mi) north.

Information: ☎ (0566) 84 0840; www.visitfryslan.com

The seaport town of **Harlingen** is so rich in historic buildings that the old centre has been declared a national historic site that will be preserved without change as an inheritance for future generations. Along with its interesting architecture, which includes over 500 gabled houses, there is an attractive **Town Hall**, Noorderhaven 86, ☎ (0517) 49 2222, dating from 1730.

Centuries ago, much of the city's prosperity came from shipping and whaling. It still has a harbour with access to the North Sea, and remains a busy shipping centre. From here you can catch a ferry boat to two of the islands off the Frisian coast: Vlieland and Terschelling.

Harlingen was once a major manufacturer of tiles. **Harlinger Aardewerk en Tegelfabriek**, Voorstraat 84, ☎ (0517) 41 5362, open Mon.-Sat. 8am-4pm, still practices the old craft, making tiles and hand-painted earthenware. Also interesting is the **Harlinger Aardewerk Museum**, where pieces of tiles from Harlingen, Makkum and Bolsward (period of 1600-1925) can be found, Zoutsloot 43, ☎ (0517) 41 3341. www.harlinger-aardewerk-museum.nl

You can learn more about the city's past at the **Gemeentemuseum Het Hannemahuis**, Voorstraat 56, ☎ (0517) 41 3658, open April-June, Mon.-Fri. 1:30-5pm; July-mid Sept., Tues.-Sat. 10am-5pm, Sun. 1:30-5pm, with an excellent collection of silver, porcelain, ship models, and a unique tile collection.

Franeker
Photogenic town hall and special planetarium

Getting there: Six km (4 mi) east of Harlingen on A31

Information: VVV, Dijkstraat 26, ☎ (0900) 540 0001

In 1811, Napoleon left his mark in **Franeker**. He closed a university that had existed since 1585 and been one of the top universities in the country. Included among its students was Peter Stuyvesant (1610-72), the last governor of the Dutch colony of New Amsterdam. The university was never reestablished, but today's heritage are several professors' homes on the main street, the Voorstraat. Two of them are now the **Museum Martena**, Voorstraat 35, ☎ (0517) 39 2192, www.coopmanshuis.nl, open Tues.-Sat. 10am-5pm; April-Sept., also open Sun. 1-5pm. This museum exhibits history of the university and Frisian folk art, including a special collection of 17th-century cutout work by Anna Marie van Schuurman. The **Martenahuis** was built in 1498 as a fortified house, and has a garden that was restored according to the original plans of the French landscape architect Lenotre. It includes a maze and an Orangerie.

Town Hall, Raadhuisplein 1, ☎ (0517) 38 0480, was built in 1591 in the elaborate Dutch Renaissance style. The elegant octagonal tower is worth a photo, as is the entire facade. The Council Chamber walls are lined in tooled leather – in the typical Dutch green – and a fine crystal chandelier hangs from the beamed ceiling. A painting of Queen Beatrix graces the wall.

Just a little further east on Eise Eisingastraat along the small canal, look for the **Korendragershuisje**, the guild house for the corn porters, which dates from 1634.

Every summer, Franeker hosts a 'Kaatsen' competition, a 500-year old Frisian game, similar to handball. The **Kaatsmuseum**, Voorstraat 2, ☎ (0517) 39 3910, open May-Sept., Tues.-Sat. 1-5pm, tells the story of the sport.

▶ **Eise Eisinga Planetarium**
Location: Eise Eisingastraat 3, across from the Town Hall
Information: ☎ (0517) 39 3070; www.planetarium-friesland.nl
Hours: Mid Sept.-mid April, Tues.-Sat. 10am-5pm; mid April-mid Sept., also
                          open Sun.-Mon. 1-5pm

Eise Eisinga, a wool comber by trade, was a self-taught astronomer. In 1774, an article about an unusual alignment of the planets led some to believe that the end of the world was near. Eisinga knew better, and for the next seven years he worked on a project to show his neighbours how the solar system worked.

He lowered the ceiling in the living room of his house, and installed a system of complicated cogs and wheels. He built the central clockworks over the cupboard bed, with the eight weights necessary for the operation hanging in the presses on either side of the bed. He must indeed have had a most understanding wife! His finished product was a planetarium that is still in working condition. On the ceiling of his living room you will see the planetary system, showing the orbits of the planets Mercury, Venus, Mars, Earth and the moon. A fascinating place for the entire family.

Leeuwarden
Getting there: From the Afsluitdijk, take A31; from Groningen, N355 is the main road; from the south A32.
Information: VVV, Sophialaan 4, ☎ (0900) 202 4060; www.vvvleeuwarden.nl

---

Leeuwarden is the capital as well as the administrative, economic and cultural centre of Friesland. Its earliest-known inhabitants built three separate settlements on artificial hills, known as 'terps,' to protect them from the marshy waters. In 1435 these settlements merged and became the city of Leeuwarden. It grew quickly, thanks to its location in the centre of a rich agricultural region. It also gained political prominence from 1582 until 1747 as the residence of Friesian Stadholders, the Counts of Nassau (ancestors of Queen Beatrix).

Leeuwarden has several buildings of interest, and two excellent museums. It's also known as the birthplace of the infamous World War I spy Mata Hari. A fact less well-known, is that in 1782 the people of Leeuwarden were the first to vote for Holland's recognition of the newly-formed United States of America, accompanied by a very substantial loan of funds to the fledgling nation.

▶ **Fries Museum**
Location: Turfmarkt 11
Information: ☎ (058) 255 5500; www.friesmuseum.nl
Hours: Tue.- Sun. 11am-5pm

The **Fries Museum** is the largest provincial museum in the Netherlands. A visit is recommended for those interested in understanding the political, economic and cultural history of Friesland. Its collection of antiquities is justly famous. An example is a 1397 drinking-horn of the St. Anthony Guild of Stavoren, part of one of the most valuable collections of silver in the country. Leeuwarden is famous for its 16th-18th-century silver, and many fine examples are on display here.

There are several other period rooms in the museum, which give an insight into how people lived in the past, including rooms reflecting home life in the Frisian village of **Hindeloopen** in the late 19th century, with brightly-painted Hindeloopen furniture and walls. There are displays of old, Frisian costumes, and paintings from the 16th-17th centuries. A hall of 19th-century paintings is displayed in 19th-century style, i.e. almost covering the walls of the large hall. Modern art is also represented, and a print room displays some of the museum's collection of 40,000 pieces. In addition, an archeology section has a significant collection of Roman coins that were found in Frisian mounds. There's also a section on Friesland's resistance to German occupation, and a room devoted to the story of Mata Hari, Leeuwarden's infamous, native spy.

Near the Fries Museum: One of the loveliest buildings in town is the **Kanselarij**, now part of the Fries Museum. It was built in 1566-71 as a Chancellery, the seat of the Frisian Court.

Just down the street to the south is an attractive little building from the 1930s: **De Utrecht**, Tweebaksmarkt 48, close to the **Provinciehuis**, Tweebaksmarkt 52; its facade of 1784 was built over a 1570 abbot's house. A bronze plaque on the building notes that in 1782, Leeuwarden was the first Dutch community to recognise the independence of the United States from British rule.

If you return west on Korfmakersstraat you will find the canal. Follow it west to the Waagplein, where you can relax and have a bite outdoors in front of the **Weigh House**, on Nieuwestad.

Walking along the canal, away from the front of the Waag, you'll come upon a small statue of a dancer-cum-spy at the Korfmakerspijp bridge. The **Mata Hari Statue** is in front of Kelders 33, where she was born and lived the first seven years of her life. Her real name was Margaretha Geertruida Zelle (1876-1917). She had a happy childhood as the pampered daughter of a well-to-do merchant. But when she was 13, his business failed and he abandoned his family; eight months later her mother died. After a disastrous marriage in 1895 to a man 20 years her senior, she became an international sex symbol. In 1905, she made her stage debut in Paris, with the exotic sounding name 'Mata Hari,' and a dance routine that started with veils and ended without them. During WW I she was accused of spying for the Germans, but even today the story is not clear. A French military court found her guilty, however, and she was executed by a firing squad in 1917.

To the north, the church with the tall steeple is **St. Bonifatiuskerk**, Voorstreek, open July-Aug. Wed. & Sat. 2-4pm. Built in 1882-84, it's a good example of Dutch neo-Gothic architecture, designed by P.J.H. Cuypers.

▶ **Museum Het Princessehof**
Location: Grote Kerkstraat 11
Information: ☎ (058) 294 8958; www.princessehof.nl
Hours: Mon.-Sat. 10am-5pm, Sun. 2-5pm

The **Princessehof Museum** houses a rich collection of ceramics in a former royal mansion. Princess Marie Louise van Hessen-Kassel, widow of Johan Willem Friso lived here between 1731 and 1765. Her husband was the Governor of Friesland, and heir to House of Orange-Nassau, until he drowned in 1711 at the age of 24. His son, later to become William IV the Stadhouder of all the United Provinces, was born six weeks after his death. The family portraits on the walls are identified, so you can tell who's who.

Three buildings make up the museum: a 15th-century east wing (formerly a convent), 17th-century central block, and an 18th-century west wing. The Princess joined the three together and furnished them in the style of the day. The central block is the only part of the museum where original interiors remain from when the Princess resided here.

The Princessehof's principal collection of Asian ceramics can be subdivided into a number of groups: Japanese, Chinese, Vietnamese and Siamese porcelain and stoneware. Look for the earthenware jars from Vietnam and Thailand, dating from 3600-250 B.C. – the most sophisticated prehistoric examples in the world. Also, the Japanese kilns such as Mino (Shino and Oribi ware), Kutani and Arita are well represented. The 18th-century white marble Buddha from Burma is a lovely piece. Another interesting group is the 7th – 11th-century stoneware jars. Found in the ground in Central Java, they were called Hindu-Javanese 'martabans' by collectors. Leak-proof and pest-proof, they were used on ships, in temples, shops and villages to keep drink pure and grain safe. The largest examples weigh about 43 pounds (20 kilos).

The tile collection forms one of the principal sections of the museum. There are Spanish, Portuguese and Islamic tiles on display, and the collection of Dutch majolica tiles is one of the largest in Europe. Tiles became popular in the 17th century for use as an interior finish to damp walls. The wealthy used oak and leather to panel the walls; the middle-class used tiles. Early tiles were profuse in their artwork, using geometric designs or exotic fruits and flowers. After 1625 the fashion became more sober, and most tiles were painted only blue on white. In the 18th century, walls were tiled in white with ornamental tiles as borders, or sparingly decorated with tiles depicting children's games, occupations, etc.

Near Het Princessehof: Down the street is the 40-meter (131-foot) tall **Oldehove Tower**. If you think it is leaning, you are right. It's leaning six feet out of line. You're also correct if you think it looks unfinished. It was built between 1529-32, but when it began to lean they abandoned plans for the cathedral that was to stand there. You can climb the tower May-Sept., daily 2-5pm. Across from the tower is **Noorder Plantage** and **Prinsentuin Park**, the former gardens of the Nassau family. The **Pier Pander Museum**, ☎ (058) 294 8958, open Tues.-Sat. 2-5pm, is in the park, with sculptures by Frisian artist Pier Pander (1864-1919).

Across the water from the park is a statue of a large cow sitting in the middle of a traffic roundabout on the opposite bank. It's **Us Mem**, or 'Our Mother,' a symbol of Friesland's economic reliance on cows. In the dreams of the cattle association that donated it, it's a cow with ideal measurements.

▶ **Also in Leeuwarden**

The area south of Prinsetuin Park is the old city centre, and the location of the **Natuurmuseum Fryslaân**, Schoenmakersperk 2, ☎ (058) 23 3224; www.natuurmuseumfryslân.nl, open Tues.-Sun. 11am-5pm. Hundreds of stuffed birds and small creatures from Friesland are on display. The largest exhibit is the skeleton of a 50-foot whale. In 1994 it took a fatal left instead of a right turn when approaching Scotland from the north. That took him into the North Sea...too shallow for whales. The poor whale ended beached on the Frisian coast and his skeleton in a museum. In the basement is an interesting Under Water display.

Nearby is the 15th-century **Jacobijner Kerk**, ☎ (058) 212 8313, open June-Aug., Tues.-Fri. 2-4pm, which contains the burial vault of the Nassau family. Over the south entranceway is a small orange tree, symbolic of the house of Orange. The square next to the church is **Jacobijnerkerkhof**, with a monument to the Jews who lived in this neighbourhood before the war. A double-arched entrance to **Boshuizen Gasthuis**, a 17th-century almshouse, is also in this courtyard.

Further south on Grote Kerkstraat 212, is the now private house where Mata Hari lived from about the age of seven to thirteen, when her father was a prosperous and well-connected local merchant of hats and capes. For genealogy enthusiasts, there is **TRESOAR**, the **Friesland Historical and Literary Centre**, Boterhoek 1, ☎ (058) 789 0789. www.tresoar.nl

The **Stadhuis** (Town Hall), built in 1715, is to the south on Raadhuisplein. It has a dome-shaped belfry with a carillon from 1668. Nearby is a statue of Count Willem Lodewijk, the first Frisian Governor. Across from it is the **Stadhouderlijk Hof**, a white stucco building which has served as the Governor's house and official residence of the

Queen's Commissioner. Today it is a fine hotel that is highly recommended (see 'Staying Over.')

To the east of town is **Aqua Zoo**, De Groene Ster 2, ☎ (0511) 43 1214, open April-Oct. 9:30am-5:30pm, www.frieslandzoo.nl, Nov.-March 10:30am-4:30pm, with otters, beavers, storks, etc.

Markets

The open-air market takes place on the Wilhelminaplein, Fri. 7:30am-3pm & Mon. 1-4pm. Leeuwarden formerly boasted the largest covered cattle hall in Europe. Located on Heliconweg, the **Frieslandhall**, also known as the Frisian Expo Centre, hosts numerous events. Friesland's dairy cooperatives are famous. It leads the country in cheese, milk and butter production, and in the export of cattle.

Eating out

The family will enjoy a pancake or snack on a 100-year-old, two-masted clipper ship called **'t Pannekoekschip**, moored at Willemskade 69, ☎ (058) 212 0903. **De Koperen Tuin**, Prinsentuin 1, ☎ (058) 213 1100, www.dekoperentuin.nl, enjoys the peaceful setting of Prinsentuin Park. Another option is **De Nieuwe Mulderij**, Baljeestraat 19, ☎ (058) 213 4802, www.denieuwemulder.nl.

Staying over

There's good selection on the high end with: **Hotel Paleis Het Stadhouderlijkhof**, Hofplein 29, ☎ (058) 216 2180, once a palace, now a hotel; **Eden Oranje Hotel**, Stationsweg 4, ☎ (058) 212 6241, www.edenoranjehotel.com; and the **Eurohotel**, Europaplein 20, ☎ (058) 213 1113, a little less expensive. Also slightly lower in price is the **Hotel Princenhof**, P. Miedemaweg 15, at Eernewoude ☎ (0511) 53 9206, about 15 minutes south of Leeuwarden. This tried and true hotel has a great location on lake Oude Venen.

Tours

Boat tours are possible in season on the Frisian Queen, ☎ (0566) 650 030; Salonboot Wetternocht, Spanjaardslaan 33, ☎ (058) 212 4522; or with Rondvaartbedrijf Middelsee, Rintsumasyl 13, ☎ (058) 254 1456. Get a copy of the VVV walking tour, in English, if you have the time for a leisurely exploration. There are many historical buildings, charming canals, shopping areas, and attractive cafés to visit.

In the neighbourhood of Leeuwarden

In **Marssum**, the Heringa-State, better known as the **Popta Slot**, Slotlaan 1, ☎ (0566) 650 030, is open April-May & Sept.-Oct., Mon.-Fri. for a 2:30pm tour; June, Mon.-Fri. at 11am, 2pm, 3pm; July-Aug., Mon.-Sat. every hour from 11am-4pm. This impressive, restored 18th-century manor house is filled with typical 16-18th-century furnishings. The park surrounding the manor house is well-tended with formal gardens, large trees, flower beds, and water lilies floating in the moat.

Dr. Popta, a bachelor, took pity on aged women and in 1711 founded the **Popta Gast-huis**, next door. Ladies could live there as long as they polished his furniture once a year. As you enter the Gasthuis through the elaborately-carved portal, notice the handsome pump. Neat brick houses face a green square...a lawn bordered by roses and a picket fence.

Veenwouden, about 15 km (9 mi) northeast, N355 to N356, is a small village. Its 12th-century square, fortified tower, **Schierstins**, is the last remaining watchtower for floods in Friesland.

Grou, about 15 km (9 mi) south of Leeuwarden on N32, is a popular water sports centre on the Pikmeer lake. The small village has a rather old-fashioned hotel, the **Oostergoo**, Nieuwekade 1, ☎ (0566) 62 1309; and a modern live-in sports centre, **Oer 't Hout**, Raadhuisstraat 18, ☎ (0566) 62 1528, with modest rooms accommodating several singles or families. Meals are included and are eaten family-style in two large dining rooms. Cheerful, busy, but very much for the young! Around February 21, Grou celebrates the feast of St. Pieter. It's a folk tradition honouring the town's patron saint – their own version of St. Nicholas.

Wiuwerd is worth a stop to see the four mummies in the crypt of the sepulchral vault of the church, Terp 31, ☎ (058) 250 1498, open April-Oct., Mon.-Sat. 9-11:30am & 1-4:30pm. Dating from 1609, no artificial means have been used to preserve the bodies that have not decayed in nearly 400 years. There is conjecture that cross-ventilation in the crypt (or a gas from the earth) is responsible for this interesting phenomenon. Even dead birds hung in the crypt do not decompose. A short visit is recommended!

▶ **Elfstedentocht – Eleven Cities (ice skating) Tour**

The **Elfstedentocht** took place only 15 times in the entire 20th century – limited to when it's cold enough – yet it is one of the most popular sporting events in the Netherlands. A speed-skating race bar none, part of its appeal stems from the legendary difficulty of completing the event. The course traverses 200 kms (125 miles) of Friesland's frozen canals. The race starts in the dark at 5:30am, with temperatures well below freezing, and often with a harsh Dutch winter wind blowing into the skaters' faces. (See photo on page 415.)

Despite the demanding conditions, a limit has to be placed on the number of partici-pants – only 16,000 in 1997, the last race to date. The number of spectators is also huge. If you want to watch the race in person (it is televised), take a train or bus, as highways are jammed. Hotel rooms are almost impossible to find. Estimates from 1997 put the crowd of spectators as high as 300,000.

The race begins and ends at Leeuwarden. As its name indicates, this 'Eleven City Tour' goes through the old eleven towns of Friesland (Sneek, IJlst, Sloten, Stavoren, Hindeloopen, Workum, Bolsward, Harlingen, Franeker, Dokkum, and Leeuwarden). It's a very colourful, typically Dutch event, with farmers on their tractors lighting the way as skaters glide through the dark Frisian countryside.

Record time is six hours 47 minutes, set in 1985. But long after the serious competitors are done, those whose goal is 'to just finish' are still crossing the finish line around midnight. More than half of the starters do not finish. Injuries are common, and there have even been some fatalities.

Although the race would seem to be a very old, Dutch tradition, it only came into existence when a sports journalist got the idea as he skated the route in 1890, and the first race was held in 1909. The goal is to have a race every year, but the ice has only frozen solid 15 times in the 20th century. In winter, if the temperatures drop well below zero, the country catches a severe case of 'Elfstedentocht fever,' as almost everyone watches the weather report to see if the cold spell will continue for the race to be held.

Sneek
Town with a sailing history dating back to the Vikings
Getting there: A7 goes through town east-west, and N354, north-south. Located about 21 km (13 mi) south of Leeuwarden.
Information: ANWB/VVV, Marktstraat 18, ☎ (0515) 41 4096; www.vvv.sneek.nl

Before the creation of the IJsselmeer resulted in the silting up of the harbour, **Sneek** (pronounced like 'snake') was an important seaport on the North Sea. It has been a sailing town since the time of the Vikings. Today, it is best known as a water sports centre. Three-quarters of the surrounding area offers lakes for sailing, fishing, swimming, wind surfing, water-skiing, etc..

Much of the old city centre is interesting with its picturesque buildings and streets. It used to be a walled city, but the walls of the town were demolished in 1720, and the **Watergate** by the Lemster bridge over the Geeuw is all that has survived of the early fortifications. The two-towered gate was built in 1613, and makes for a picturesque sight straddling the waterway.

The 15th-century **Martinikerk**, ☎ (0515) 41 2773, open mid June-mid Sept., Mon.-Sat. 2:30-5pm; Jul-Aug. also open 7:30-9pm, once had two towers which collapsed in 1681. The roof has a bell cupola with a carillon and a restored bell cage. The grave of a famous local warrior, Greate Pier, is inside. He fought against the Saxons and Burgundians from 1515-20 'on land and on sea.' His helmet is displayed in the guard room of the 18th-century **Town Hall**, the **Schutterskamer**, Marktstraat 15.

There are beautiful gables along the city streets. Behind the so-called captains' facade on the Oosterdijk promenade, look for the old, Frisian refreshment room with painted and tiled Hindeloopen interior.

The **Fries Scheepvaartmuseum**, or Frisian Maritime Museum, Kleinzand 14, ☎ (0515) 41 4057, open Mon.-Sat. 10am-5pm, Sun. noon-5pm, has a good collection of ships models, navigation instruments, ships' porcelain, paintings and an especially fine display of Frisian silver. www.friesscheepvaartmuseum.nl

Eating out

A speciality in town is dribbled cookies (*drabbelkoeken*), made at and available from the **Drabbelkoekenbakkerij**, 1ste Oosterkade 17, ☎ (0515) 41 2295. If you're in the mood for a drink, you'll enjoy relaxing in the **Weduwe Joustra**, Kleinzand 32, a distillery for the typical Frisian drink, Beerenburg, and also a café, in an authentic 19th-century interior, ☎ (0515) 41 2912. www.weduwejoustra.nl

In the neighbourhood of Sneek

In **Ysbrechtum** is the lovely **Epema-State** manor house/castle. Epemawei 8, ☎ (0515) 41 2475, www.epemastate.nl, open Mon.-Sat. by appointment only. This 19th-century castle is the family home of Baroness van Eisinga and the rooms have been kept as they were when the family was in residence. Its 1625 gatehouse is guarded by ferocious lions.

Bolsward
A starting point for the 'Aldfaers Erf Route'

Getting there: Located on A7, about 20 km (12 mi) from Harlingen (south then east) or 9 km (6 mi) from Sneek (west).

Information: VVV, Marktplein 1, ☎ (0515) 57 7701

One of Friesland's oldest towns and once a member of the Hanseatic League, **Bolsward** was settled even before 715. It was built on a mound as protection from regular flooding. It was a busy port before the Zuider Zee was closed off, reaching the peak of its prosperity in the 17th century. Bolsward was also the home of many well-known men of letters, artists, engravers and silversmiths.

Its attractions include **St. Martinikerk**, Grote Kerkhof, ☎ (0515) 57 2274, open Mon.-Fri. 10am-noon & 2-4pm; July-Aug., also open Sat. 2-4pm. This impressive Gothic church, built between 1446-66 has an organ, carved pulpit, choir stalls, and tombstones of note.

To see a fine example of Dutch Renaissance architecture, visit the **Town Hall**, Jongemastraat 2, ☎ (0515) 57 8735, open April-June & Sept.-Nov., Mon. 2-4pm, Tues.-Fri. 9am-noon & 2-4pm; July-Aug., Mon.-Sat. 10am-5pm. Built between 1614-17, it has a richly-decorated facade and beautiful Council Hall.

Bolsward can be a starting point for the **Aldfaers Erf Route**, a well-signposted excursion that takes you through several carefully preserved villages that recapture the rustic way of life found at the end of the 19th century. Check with the VVV.

In the neighbourhood of Bolsward

To the west is the dike that altered millions of Dutch lives in the 20th century. The **Afsluitdijk** shut off what had been the Zuiderzee from its connection to the North Sea. Since its completion in 1932, it has kept this part of the country free from disastrous floods, but it also put an end to much of the region's fishing and shipping industry. Highway A7 runs along the top of the 30-kilometer- (19-mi) long, 90-meter-wide dike. The complete flatness of view across the IJsselmeer and the long stretch of highway before and behind are quite awesome. Stop at the visitors' rest stop for a cup of coffee and the view, if the weather is clear. (In 2007 they will celebrate the 75 years existence of the dike. Check with the VVV.)

Before crossing the bridge, those interested in WW II history might want to stop in **Kornwerderzand** to see several bunkers built by the Germans in 1940. The **Kazematten-museum**, Afsluitdijk 5, ☎ (0515) 54 0550, www.kazematkwz.nl, open May-Sept., Wed. & Sat. 10am-5pm; July-Aug. also open Sun. 1-5pm, explains the war role of bunkers.

▶ **Aldfaers Erf Route – Heritage Route**

The **Aldfaers Erf Route** (Our Forefathers Heritage Route) extends within a triangle framed by Bolsward, Makkum and Workum. The primary villages within the triangle are: Exmorra, Allingawier, Piaam and Ferwoude. The drive should be taken leisurely to allow the atmosphere to soak in. Absorb the lovely meadows, crossed by streams, polderland, narrow twisting roads through tiny villages with their tiled roofs, red brick walls, and lace-curtained windows. Stop and explore the special sights each village has to offer. All attractions on the route are open April-Oct., daily 10am-5pm.

Exmorra has an old-fashioned grocery shop, licensed spirits provisioner, and a 19th-century village school.

Allingawier has several stops, starting with a farm museum, **De Izeren Kou** (The Iron Cow), an 18th-century farmer's house in its original state. The living quarters are interesting with an outstanding milk cellar; a slide show presentation describes life on the land at that time. There is also the **Meermin**, a pastry shop and coffeehouse where *drabbelkoeken* (dribbled cookies) are the speciality. Once your sugar level has risen, you can visit the crafts hall to see old-fashioned crafts; and **Woord en Beeld Kerkje**, which uses three screens, six projectors, and 500 slides for a presentation on the story of Creation. Nearby in Allingawier you can visit **Allingastate**, the house where Yde Schakel, the founder of the Aldfaers Erf Route, was living. Also take a look in the garden. Tours from Apr.-Oct., daily at 11am-1pm, and 3 pm.

Piaam has the charming farm restaurant **Nynke Pleats**, Buren 25, ☎ (0515) 23 1707, with formal dining in one section, and a relaxed luncheon fare in the main brick floor room, with Frisian roof decorations under the huge beamed ceiling – a folksy and fun atmosphere where you can choose a hearty Dutch dish such as an *uitsmijter* (a slice of bread topped with cheese, ham and two or more fried eggs), soup, etc. Also, see **It Fugelhus**, a bird museum in a former church, Buren 6, ☎ (0515) 23 2161.

In **Ferwoude**, the farmhouse-carpenter's workshop with tools and leather stacked high, is worth a quick stop.

Makkum
Town of tiles

Getting there: Almost on the IJsselmeer, a couple of km south of the entry point to Friesland from the Afsluitdijk.

Information: ☎ (0566) 84 0840

This small town on the IJsselmeer has been synonymous with outstanding pottery for a couple of centuries. A study of the archives revealed that **Makkum** was a place of great ceramic activity in the 16th century and that on the site of the present Tichelaar Factory, a ceramics workshop existed. Besides seeing, feeling, learning about, and buying pottery, there are canals, bridges, churches and beautifully-restored houses and gables. If time permits, try to see the Netherlands Reformed Church, the **Hervormde Kerk** (1660) that sits in the middle of an old *terp* (mound) in Kerkeburen. Makkum is also known for its shipyard, harbour, and as a water sports centre – a real surfer's paradise.

▶ **Tichelaar's Royal Ceramics and Tile Manufacturer**
Location: Turfmarkt 65
Information: ☎ (0515) 23 1341
Hours: Tours Mon.-Thurs. 10am-noon & 1-4pm, Fri. 10am-noon & 1-2:30pm; salesroom Mon.-Fri. 9am-5:30pm, Sat. 10am-5pm

Tichelaar's was founded in 1641, a few years before De Porceleyne Fles in Delft, and has been under the same family management for over 300 years. In 1960, Tichelaar's was allowed to add 'Royal' to its full title as a result of Queen Juliana's patronage. Its tiles and ceramics have a unique, luminescent quality that is a result of this company's use of what they call a 'mysterious white tin glaze.' In fact, they are the only remaining tin glazing factory in the Netherlands.

Manufactured Makkum pottery started as a rough, soft-baked product...usually cooking pots or tiles to cover the damp floors or walls of people's homes. At first, decoration consisted mostly of sculpting the clay. With the introduction of tin-glazing to the Netherlands from Spain and Italy, elaborate decoration became possible. Tin-glazing started in the Orient, was brought to Spain by the Moors in the 11th century, then went to Italy via Majorca, (hence the name 'Majolica' ware), and then found its way north. Another explanation for the quality of Makkum pottery is the care with which it is worked using mostly hand methods in traditional fashion, the continued use of the ancient tin-glaze recipes, and the special quality of the Frisian clay.

You can take a tour to see how ceramics are made, or visit the Tichelaar's salesroom, which is like a modern museum display.

Eating out

Possibilities include **De Waag**, Markt 13, ☎ (0515) 23 1447, or at the beach, **De Vigilante**, De Holle Poarte 10, ☎ (0515) 23 1772. The dining room has complete menus, including fresh fish, but also a snack counter.

Staying over

Recreatie Vigilante, De Holle Poarte 10, ☎ (0515) 23 8222, located right on the beach, offers perfect relaxation at moderate prices, with a choice of rooms or apartments (2-4 persons) by the day, weekend or week. In addition to the restaurant mentioned above, there are beach activities (swimming, wind surfing, boating), billiards, bowling and other games available.

Workum
Lovely main street, and pottery production

Getting there: Take one of the small country roads form Bolsward (N359 going south); or N359 north from Lemmer.

Information: ☎ (0566) 84 0840

This small town was once a centre of the weaving industry and of eel export to London. Today, **Workum** is a regional administrative centre and produces centuries-old Workumer pottery in several factories. Also of interest is the old shipbuilders yard, **De Hoop**, on Seburch, ☎ (0515) 54 2176.

On either side of the main street there are scores of houses with stepped or necked gables. Adjoining the **Town Hall** (15th and 16th century) on the market square is a charming Frisian house (1620). The **Weigh House** (1650) houses the local history museum, **Museum Warkums Erfskip**, Merk 4, ☎ (0515) 54 3155, www.warkumserfskip.tk, open April-Oct., Tues.-Sun. 1-5pm. The 16th-century **St. Gertrudis Church**, on Merk, open May-Sept., Mon.-Sat. 11am-5pm; Apr. and Oct., Tues./Thurs./Sat. 1-5pm, March and Nov., Sat. 1-5pm, has a beautiful choir-screen, carved pulpit, mourning-signs with nine, painted guild biers for boatmen, farmers, apothecaries, surgeons, gold and silversmiths, carpenters and their children. (Note the detached tower.) **St. Werenfridus Church**, on Noard, has ancient woodcarvings, and was a 17th-century clandestine church within a farmhouse. **Museum Kerkelijke Kunst**, Noard 173, ☎ (0515) 54 3159, open mid-May to mid-Sept., Mon.-Sat. 11am-5pm, has a collection of religious art.

A local painter and flea-market trader, Jopie Huisman painted objects we would normally discard, and was very talented. The **Jopie Huisman Museum**, Noard 6, ☎ (0515) 54 3131, www.jopiehuismanmuseum.nl, open April-Oct., Mon.-Sat. 10am-5pm, Sun. 1-5pm, has his works on display. If pottery is your thing, you can visit **Pottenbakkerij Kunst**, Begine 9, ☎ (0515) 54 1926.

Hindeloopen

Colourful Frisian furniture and cloth

Getting there: On the IJsselmeer south of Bolsward off N359
Information: ☎ (0566) 84 0840

Hindeloopen received its city charter in 1225 and joined the Hanseatic League in 1368. It carried on a flourishing trade with Scandinavia, being most prosperous as a seaport in the 17th century. In the 18th century, trade with the Balkans developed, and soon Hindeloopen sailors were bringing home brightly-coloured materials and decorative items from the Orient.

Like all seamen around the world, many of them spent the winter repairing sails and nets, or whittling useful items for the house. In Hindeloopen, the whittling led to making furniture, and that led to painting it the highly admired colours and designs of the East. In those days, small towns were quite isolated and it was possible for Hindeloopen to develop an independent and unique style of dress and decoration. Even the language used here was different from any other in Friesland, surprisingly incorporating words of Asiatic origin. Soon, the popularity of the Frisian designs extended beyond this village and others began ordering furniture and yardage with their unique hues. You can visit a factory that produces copies of the traditional painted and carved furniture of Hindeloopen, and perhaps be tempted to add a small piece to your own collection of treasures. You will be welcomed graciously at **Roosje**, Nieuwstad 19 and 44, ☎ (0514) 52 1251, www.roosjehindeloopen.com.

This small town is a maze of narrow streets and lanes, interspersed with small canals winding past traditional style homes painted in the local green and white, with detailed roof decorations. Boats of all kinds are moored at small private docks at the end of green lawns and flowering gardens. You may well feel that you've stepped back in time to another, more relaxed era.

As you walk around town, notice the summer cottages by the waterside, the **Commanders'** and **Captains' Houses**. The **Liar's Bench**, from 1785, got its name because it was a place where seamen gathered and swapped tales. Rest a moment on the **Ringmuorre**, the wall near the harbour that used to protect the town from encroaching waters. Then admire the **Westertoren**... doesn't it lean just a bit? During the summer, the historical buildings are illuminated in the evening, adding a further touch of romance. The local singing and dancing society, **Aald Hielpen**, makes its appearance at the Valdelingenplein, from time-to-time. Stay a bit longer for a real vacation...the area is known as a centre for aquatics, especially attractive for sailors and windsurfers. **Reddingsloods KNRM**, 't Ooste, in the blue rescue shed at the harbour, is an exhibition about the lifeboat service; open mostly afternoons in season.

The local history museum, **Hidde Nijland Stichting**, Dijkweg 1, ☎ (0514) 52 1420, open Apr.-Oct., Mon.-Fri. 11am-5pm, Sat./Sun. 1:30-5pm, is housed in the former Town Hall, www.museumhindeloopen.nl. Notice the statue of Justice over the side entrance and in front of the steps – a freestone pillory. The original interiors show the lifestyle, furniture and dress of the local people...especially interesting are the highly decorated tiled walls, the women's costumes in colourful Indian chintz and checked cloth that matched the colours of the furniture. There's a reconstructed 18th-century captain's house showing a bride trying on her bridal veil. About 1740, Hindeloopen was at the height of its prosperity with two-and-a-half times as many inhabitants as today. By 1880, women had stopped wearing their traditional dress.

Het Eerste Friese Schaatsmuseum, Kleine Weide 1-3, ☎ (0514) 52 1683, open Mon.-Sat. 10am-6pm, Sun. 1-5pm, is a skating museum with the largest collection of skates in the world, and the story of the Elfstedentocht skating race through the canals of 11 towns (see page 237), including a once-frozen, amputated toe on display. www.schaatsmuseum.nl

In the neighbourhood of Hindeloopen

To the south on IJsselmeer is **Stavoren**, famous today as a water sports centre. In its heyday it was known for its shipping and trade. The haughty Lady of Stavoren is legend here; her statue in bronze stands on the harbour wall. She overlooks a harbour crammed with pleasure-sailing craft instead of commercial vessels. From Apr.-Oct. there's a ferry service from Stavoren to Enkhuizen.

Warns and nearby **Rode Klif** are of interest because of the Battle of Warns in 1345. The Frisian villagers defended themselves ferociously with hayforks and clubs against the Counts of Holland, who were determined to obtain the rich, fertile land of Friesland. A monument commemorates the unsuccessful Dutch invasion. The Frisian inscription says: 'Better to be dead than a slave.' There are beautiful views from Rode Klif (Red Cliff). Warns is built on a sand ridge, 7 meters above sea level.

Sloten
One of 'the Eleven Frisian Towns'

Getting there: North of Lemmer, about midway on the road connecting N359 and N354, on the Slotermeer Lake.

Information: ☎ (0566) 84 0840

Smallest of 'the Eleven Frisian Towns' on the famous ice-skating circuit, **Sloten** is incredibly picturesque. In the former **Town Hall** you can visit **Museum Stedhus Sleat**, Heerenwal 48, ☎ (0514) 53 1541, open April-Oct., Tues.-Fri. 11am-noon & 2-5pm, Sat.-Sun. 1-5pm, and consisting of historical town artifacts, fans, costumes, jewellery, clocks, magic lanterns and their forerunners, antique cameras, etc. Next door is the **Dutch Reformed Church** (1647) and parsonage with a Renaissance double-stepped gable. The town's ancient protective walls and two water gates are still standing. There are many restored buildings with beautiful gables along the Diep.

Boaters might consider a special route: Lemmer-Sloten-Woudsend. Lemmer is the entrance to the polder canals, the Buma pumping station and many sluices. Woudsend's imposing homes remind one of the town's importance as a shipbuilding centre in the 18th century. Enjoy its waterside café terraces, its restaurant in a former clandestine church, and more.

Joure
Clocks through the ages
Getting there: Between Sneek and Heerenveen, just off A7 (at intersection with A50).
Information: VVV, D.E. Plein 6, ☎ (0513) 41 6030; www.joure.nl

Joure is synonymous with clocks. The ancient Frisian clocks – the best of their kind – came from Joure and are worth a small fortune today. However, the modern shopper can obtain good reproductions at reasonable prices. Three clockmakers in town are: **Jacob ten Hoeve**, Midstraat 37, ☎ (0513) 41 3339; **Jouster Klokkenmakerij**, D.E. Plein 8, ☎ (0513) 41 4104; and **Van der Meulen**, Roazenbosk 13, in Scharsterbrug, ☎ (0513) 41 2751.

If you want to see antique clocks, **Museum Joure**, Geelgietersstraat 1, ☎ (0513) 41 2283, www.museumjoure.nl, open Tues.-Fri. 10am-5pm, Sat./Sun./Mon. 2-5pm, has Frisian clocks galore. The museum also has a nice collection of pipes, and a coffee and tea cabinet on the ground floor where clocks are also on display.

In the neighbourhood of Joure

Heerenveen is the venue for Holland's world skating championships. They're held at **Kunstijsbaan Thialf**, Pim Mulderlaan 1, ☎ (0513) 63 7700, open from Oct.-March, www.thialf.nl, in case you want to get in shape for the Elfstedentocht. Also in town, the manor house **Crackstate**, Crackstraat 2, ☎ (0513) 61 2712 (by appointment), was built by Hypolitus Crack in 1608. The building has a classic facade surmounted by a clock tower. House and garden are surrounded by a moat with an arched bridge dating from 1776. **Museum Willem van Haren**, Minckelerstraat 11, ☎ (0513) 62 3408, open Tues.-Fri. 11am-5pm, Sat-Sun. 1-5pm, located in a 17th-century patrician house, focuses on regional history, especially the peat-cutting that gave life to Heerenveen around 1550. www.willemvanharen.nl

Dokkum
The demise of St. Boniface
Getting there: N355 east of Leeuwarden, then north on N356.
Information: VVV Lauwersland, Op de Fetze 13, ☎ (0519) 29 3800; www.vvvlauwersland.nl

Dokkum has had a long and eventful history as a port town. Built on a *terp* (mound), it has retained its hexagonal fortress shape with bulwarks, moats and bastions still intact. In fact, the Frisian Crusade fleet sailed from here in 1217 heading for Damietta in Egypt. It also has the dubious honour of being where the apostle of the Germanic tribes (later Saint Boniface) and his group (all 52 of them) were murdered by Frisians in 754. The Frisians resented his attempt to convert them to Christianity. This determination to retain their independence in matters of religion, State, language and culture is well documented and the special Frisian character continues to be fostered today.

On the ramparts, there are two windmills, one from 1847, the other dated 1862. **Town Hall**, Suupmarkt 2, ☎ (0519) 29 88 88, open weekdays 9am-noon & 2-4pm, dates from 1608. The ornately-decorated Louis XIV Council Room is worth a visit.

Streekmuseum Het Admiraliteitshuis, Diepwal 27, www.museumdokkum.nl, ☎ (0519) 29 3134, open Tues.-Sat. 1-5pm, is housed in a former naval affairs building from 1618. Its collection includes archeological finds, folk art, pottery, silver, local costumes, items dealing with fishing and maritime events of the area. There are also shows depicting scenes from around 1900, and an exhibition on St. Boniface.

Natuurmuseum Dokkum, Kleine Oosterstraat 12, ☎ (0519) 29 7318, open Mon. 1-5pm; Tues.-Fri. 10am-noon & 1-5pm; June-Sept., Sat. 2-4:30pm, specialises in the flora and fauna from the northeast corner of Friesland. www.natuurmuseumdokkum.nl

Staying over

You can combine an overnight stay in Dokkum with a visit to the Waddenzee island of **Schiermonnikoog**. A good option is **Hotel de Posthoorn**, Diepswal 21, ☎ (0519) 29 3500; or **De Abdij van Dockum**, Markt 30a, ☎ (0519) 22 0422, a bit more luxurious.

In the neighbourhood of Dokkum

Moddergat is 10 km (6 mi) north of Dokkum on the shores of the Waddenzee. **Museum 't Fiskershuske**, Fiskerspaad 4-8a, ☎ (0519) 58 9454, open March-Nov., Mon.-Sat. 10am-5pm, is a museum housed in four fisherman's cottages, showing the life of the fishing community around 1850. In **Moddergat**, they are also working on a replica of a fishing boat near the **Garnalenfabriek** (Shrimp Factory), It Grenaatfabryk 2-4, ☎ (0519) 58 9880, open Tues.-Fri. 9am-4pm, Sat./Sun. 1-5pm.

Wierum, close to Moddergat, is one of the departure points for organised *wadlopen* hikes through the muddy tidal marshes to Engelsmanplaat, from **Holwerd** to **Ameland**, or other destinations. Mud-flat walking season is from early May to early Oct. For safety reasons, try this *only* with a guided walk. They are usually organised on Fridays and Saturdays. For information, contact the **Wadloopcentrum Friesland**, ☎ (0519) 24 2100, or (0519) 56 1656. www.wadlopen.net (See photo on page 243.)

To the west, **Hogebeintum** is built on the tallest artificial mound in the country, almost 30 feet above sea level. Its church was built in the 12th century. Nearby, **Jannum** was also built on a mound. Its church was built in the 13th century, and is now the **Kerkmuseum**, Kerkstraat 6, ☎ (0519) 33 9342, open May-Oct., Tues.-Sun. 1-5pm, with exhibits of religious art and history.

The Waddenzee islands

Location: Wadden Sea, North of Noord Holland, Friesland and Groningen.
Information: VVV Vlieland, Havenweg 10, ☎ (0562) 45 1111; www.vlieland.net
VVV Terschelling, Willem Barentszkade 19a, ☎ (0562) 44 3000;
www.vvv-terschelling.nl
VVV Ameland, R. v. Doniastraat Bureweg 2, Nes, ☎ (0519) 54 6546;
www.vvvameland.nl
VVV Schiermonnikoog, Reeweg 5, ☎ (0519) 53 1233;
www.vvvschiermonnikoog.nl
Website for all the islands: www.vvv-wadden.nl

There are five major, and several smaller uninhabited islands located between the **Waddenzee** and the North Sea. The largest and most developed is Texel in North Holland, with access by ferry from Den Helder. (Chapter 3 gives full details about Texel.) The other four islands are a part of Friesland.

Each of the islands has its special charm. The are all very similar, with dunes, woods, bird sanctuaries, interesting architecture, sandy beaches, bracing air, sunshine (at times, of course) and a closeness to nature.

There are hundreds of bungalows that can be rented – nestled in the dunes or close to the villages. Some are simple and will sleep two people, and others are very elaborate with accommodations for eight, including a hot tub and other special features. The VVVs are prepared to help you make hotel, bungalow, campsite and ferry reservations. Ameland has the largest selection of hotels, followed by Terschelling, Schiermonnikoog and Vlieland.

The VVV can also help with arrangements for the numerous outdoor activities available on the islands, such as renting a horse to ride on the beach, para-sailing, biking, walking to the islands through the mud flats (*wadlopen*) during low tide (see photo on page 243), boat rentals, sailing lessons, hiking, bird-watching, and exploring nature.

One warning: the islands can get very crowded in the summer. Make reservations for overnight stays, and for the ferryboat if you plan on taking your car. Most of the islands are small and well-served by public transportation, and all have miles of bike trails, as well as numerous bike rental shops. Some people like to go off-season because it's a wonderful time to get away from the turmoil of everyday life with good accommodations available, even in the winter months. If you're looking for isolation, don't come in the summer.

Vlieland
The car-free island

If you want to get away from it all, try **Vlieland**. There is no pollution from auto or motor-cycle exhaust, as such vehicles are prohibited on the island, except to the 1,100 or so local residents. Bikes are the best way to get around...bring your own or rent one.

The only town on Vlieland is **Oost-Vlieland**. It is conveniently located next to 6,000 acres of dunes and pine forest, offering easy accessibility on foot or bike to beaches, dunes and woodlands. The island has two special attractions: the longest nudist beach in Europe and seals.

The island of Vlieland is also famous for its unique flora and fauna...96 species of birds have been observed, including the eider ducks that come during the breeding season. At that time, excursions are made to the breeding grounds, the woods and dunes with guides from the National Forest Service. You can also explore the 'wadden' (mud-flats or tidal marshes) at low tide. And if you come in winter after a snowfall, you can cross-country ski your way around.

The western end of the island is known as **Vliehors**. The town of West-Vlieland used to be there until it was literally washed away by an 18th-century storm. Now the area is used as a military training area, and is closed during the week, but accessible on weekends. It's a desert-like area with the dunes constantly being reshaped by the winds. One way to see it is on the **Vliehors Express**, a rebuilt Army truck that drives you over the dunes and through shallows. Ask about it at the bike rental shop, Dorpstraat 8.

In addition to swimming or sunbathing on the 12-km-long (7.5 mi) beach, there are walking tours, tennis, windsurfing, horseback riding, midget-golf, bowling, fishing, biking, and a lighthouse to climb. Culture-bugs will find two museums:

De Noordwester, Dorpsstraat 150, ☎ (0562) 45 1700, open Oct.-March, Wed., Sat.-Sun. 2-5pm; April-May & Sept., Mon.-Sat. 2-5pm; June-Aug., Mon.-Sat. 10am-noon & 2-5pm, is the Vlieland information and education centre. It deals with the island's history (including shipwrecks), but principally with the plants, animals and nature of the island. www.denoordwester.nl

Trompshuys Museum, Dorpsstraat 99, ☎ (0562) 45 1600, open Nov.-March, Wed. & Sat. 2-5pm; April & Oct., Tues.-Sun. 2-5pm; May-Sept., Tues.-Sun. 11am-5pm, is a 17th-century former Admiralty Building. Its collection includes paintings and interesting displays of porcelain, tile, copper, glass, tin and furniture.

Access is by boat ferry from Harlingen, with three departures a day in season; takes 90 minutes. Boats from Harlingen also go to Terschelling. If you want to go to Vlieland, be sure to board the 'Oost-Vlieland.'

Hotels include the **Golden Tulip Strandhotel Seeduyn**, Badweg 3, ☎ (0562) 45 1560, www.westcordhotels.nl; **Badhotel Bruin**, Dorpsstraat 88, ☎ (0562) 45 1301.

Terschelling
A 'National Park'

After Texel, **Terschelling** is the largest of the Waddenzee islands, and ranks with Texel as the most popular. Because of its beauty, this island was designated by the Dutch government as a 'National Park.'

People have been living here for 15 centuries – farming, fishing and seafaring. The villages reflect this rich past in their charming homes and gardens. **West Terschelling**, the largest town and capital of the island, offers some interesting sights. It would be pretty difficult to miss the 190-foot-tall **Brandaris lighthouse**, constructed in 1594. There is also a nautical school and a natural history museum, **Centrum Voor Natuur en Landschap**, Burg. Reedekkerstraat 11, ☎ (0562) 44 2390, open April-Oct., Mon.-Fri. 9am-5pm. Sat.-Sun. 2-5pm, www.natuurmuseumterschelling.nl

Het Behouden Huys, Commandeurstraat 30-31, ☎ (0562) 44 2389, open April-Oct., Mon.-Fri. 10am-5pm; July-Aug., also open Sun. 1-5pm; mid June-Sept., also open Sat. 1-5pm, is the local history museum. Before entering, notice the beautifully sculpted pavement. The interior contains furniture, costumes and practical items used by local people. In the attic there is a marine collection that includes items used in former whaling days. www.behouden-huys.nl

There are about a dozen other villages on the island, which has a population of about 4,600. Since most of the crowd stays in West Terschelling, taking a bus or a bike ride to the other villages can keep you 'away from it all.'

Terschelling has 64 km (40 mi) of duneland, woods and sandy shores. There are unique bird sanctuaries all over the island, the most important being **De Boschplaat**, with enough space and tranquility to encourage a collection of wild plants and dozens of species of birds numbering in the thousands. Cars are not allowed in the preserve, so explore on foot or by bike. Visits can also be made in a *huifkartocht* (covered wagon), ☎ (0562) 44 8837. www.behouden-huys.nl

A ferry goes from Harlingen two or three times a day. The crossing takes about 90 minutes. Reservations are a must if you have a car: **Rederij Doeksen**, Willem Barentsz-kade 21, ☎ (0900) 363 5736, www.rederijdoeksen.nl. There is also a hovercraft service; 45-minute crossing.

An interesting local crop is cranberries, also used in making cranberry wine. If you want to see how they are grown and processed, you can visit **Skylge**, Formerum 51a, Formerum, ☎ (0562) 44 8800, open May-Oct., Mon.-Fri. 2-3:30pm. www.terschellingcranberry.nl

Staying over

Golden Tulip Resort Hotel Schylge, Burg van Heusdenweg 37, Terschelling West, ☎ (0562) 44 2111, www.westcordhotels.nl, has the most rooms and the highest prices on the island. **Europa**, Europalaan 35, Terschelling West, ☎ (0562) 44 2241, is a little less expensive. www.hotelbornholm.nl

Ameland
A true Wadden diamond

The island of **Ameland** deserves an entire chapter. It is rich in natural beauty, with woods, dunes, sea, beaches and bird sanctuaries. Its four villages have been designated National Park areas, encouraging restoration and preserving the atmosphere of its early days when navigation and whaling were the principal means of livelihood. Look for the

17th-18th-century Commanders' dwellings, and notice if the sign is out indicating the captain is looking for cargo. The houses themselves can be identified by an extra row of bricks forming a ledge on the gable, and chiselled work on the front. Today, tourism and black and white Frisian cows support the economy. This is the only place where milk is transported by underwater pipeline to the mainland for processing!

There are 80-90 km (50-56 mi) of bike paths along the shallows and through the dunes; 27 km (17 mi) of beach with foaming surf (north side); tennis courts, bowling alleys, and horseback riding with special routes through the dunes and woods. In addition, you can arrange lessons for skydiving and windsurfing. In **Nes**, there's a subtropical swimming 'paradise' with sauna and fitness centre: **Aqua Plaza**, Molenweg 18, ☎ (0519) 54 2900, open April-Oct..

If you're interested in commercial tours and VVV-sponsored excursions, there are plenty to choose from: tours around the nature reserve the **Oerd** or in the **Briksduinen**, walks on the Wadden shallows, tractor trips to **de Hon**, and boat excursions to see the seals along the shore.

Hollum is home to an unusual local activity. Eight to ten times a year there is a practice for the lifeboat crew...and their horses. The lifeboat is drawn by 10 horses from the boathouse in Hollum to the beach, then launched by eight of them. In 1979 the horses drowned and were buried beside the dune crossing of the lifeboat track. If you're not fortunate to be here for a practice, you can learn more about the 160-year history of the lifesaving team on the island at **Reddingsmuseum Abraham Fock**, Orangeweg 18, ☎ (0519) 55 4243, open Nov.-March, Mon.-Fri. 1:30-5pm; April-June & Sept.-Oct., Mon.-Fri. 10am-noon & 1:30-5pm, Sat.-Sun. 1:30-5pm; July-Aug., Mon.-Fri. 10am-5pm, Sat.-Sun. 1:30-5pm.

Hollum, the most westerly village on the island, has a lovely town centre with a number of fine Commanders' houses. One of them is home to the **Sorgdrager Museum**, Herenweg 1, ☎ (0519) 55 4477, www.amelandermusea.nl/cultuurhistorisch/, open Nov.-March, Wed.-Sat. 1:30-5pm; April-June & Sept.-Oct., Mon.-Fri. 10-noon & 1-5pm, Sat.-Sun. 1:30-5pm; July-Aug., daily 10am-5pm, also open Thurs. 7-9pm. The collection in this Commander's house from 1751 includes objects of former whalers with their contributions to folk art, along with information on whaling.

One outstanding landmark in Hollum, the **Amelander Lighthouse**, built in 1880, is 193 feet high and stands 233 feet above sea level. One of the most penetrating lights, it measures 4 million candlepower and can be seen as far as 101 km (63 mi) under favourable weather conditions. The tower can be visited daily in season, 10am-4:30pm; out of season Wed., Sat-Sun. 11am-4pm.

The other landmark difficult to miss is the span roof tower (late 15th century) of the **Nederlands Hervormde Church** (1678) that used to serve as a beacon for sailors. The remains of three earlier churches were discovered on the site, the oldest dating from the 11th century.

Ballum is small, but has a rich history. The rulers of Ameland had their palace here. They sold the island to the van Oranje family, which makes Queen Beatrix the hereditary Baroness of Ameland. The castle was demolished in 1829, and its chapel destroyed three years later. All that remains of the chapel is its burial vault in the present cemetery. The huge stone that shuts it off was made in 1552/56 by a sculptor from Franeker. The present **Dutch Reformed Church** was built in 1832; its pulpit is among the oldest in the Netherlands (date of origin uncertain), and was brought to Ameland in 1771 from Harlingen.

The airfield north of Ballum is the island's lifeline when the ferry service is cancelled due to ice drifts on the shallows. It is also used to carry the mail and the sick or injured. In summer, sightseeing flights by small planes keep things humming, ☎ (0519) 55 4644.

Nes with its active VVV office will be the centre of planning for your time on Ameland. This charming old whaling village has numerous Commanders' houses, shops, restaurants, and an old-fashioned post office. Its 17th-century **Dutch Reformed Church** is on a picturesque square. The church tower, as in Ballum, stands approximately 100 meters away from the chapel, because in olden times these towers were built as beacons for sailors. The windmill **De Phoenix** on Mullensduin dates from 1880. The flour milled here is conveyed by the millers to local bakers who produce the Ameland Millbread.

The Natural History Museum, **Natuurcentrum Ameland**, Strandweg 38, ☎ (0519) 54 2737, is small but gives a good impression of this most important aspect of island life. The abundance of nature in and around the island is explained in videos, models and displays, as well as films. There is a small sea aquarium to interest the little ones. www.amelandermuseum.nl/natuurcentrum.html

Nes' **Mennonite Chapel** is the oldest church on the island (13th century, but rebuilt in 1843), and its **Roman Catholic Church** (1878) was designed by the architect P.J.H. Cuypers.

Buren has a little square with a bronze statue representing **Rixt the Witch** from Het Oerd. Legend has it that she purposely stranded ships by making fires on shore, and that she lived off their wreckage. Buren's neighbour, the nature reserve **Het Oerd**, well-known for its great variety of flora and fauna, is of great importance to the island. During the nesting season, the area is sealed off from the casual tourist, in order to protect the birds. Some sections are closed between April and August. There is a short biking path through some of the area with over 50 species of birds and at least 500 different plants to see or photograph.

Boat service from Holwerd to Nes takes about 45 minutes, with departures almost hourly from 6:30am-7:30pm (in season). Make a reservation if you want to take your car, ☎ (0519) 54 6111. Bus service on the island is very good.

Staying over

d'Amelander Kap, Oosterhiemweg 1, Hollum, ☎ (0519) 55 4646, has an indoor pool, charming lounge with fireplace, excellently-appointed dining room, and airy and spacious rooms. Bungalow accommodations are also available. More traditional is the **Hotel Nobel**, Gerrit Kosterweg 16, Ballum, ☎ (0519) 55 4157, in an old-world setting, and moderately-priced.

Schiermonnikoog
Bird Island – a National Park Island

The most northern and the smallest of the islands, **Schiermonnikoog** is only 16km (10 mi) long and 4km (2.5 mi) wide with around 1,000 residents. It is one big nature reserve and a paradise for bird lovers. Comprised of woods, dunes, salt meadows and shallows, it has an exceptional, fine sand beach on its north coast – reputedly the widest in Europe. Despite its many visitors in season, it retains its characteristic tranquility and, even at that time, the birds outnumber humans. We recommend the walking, bridal and biking trails especially, which bring you even closer to nature and to the almost tame animal and birdlife that abound.

This island's 'virtually-impossible-to-pronounce' name (unless you're Dutch) comes from its earliest inhabitants, Cistercian monks who wore grey habits or *schier*, meaning 'grey,' *monnik* for 'monk,' and *oog* for 'island.' Through the years it has changed owners several times, belonging for a period to the German Count Bernstorff. It has since been declared a National Park and its only village (with the same name), a National Monument. Built from 1720, this charming village replaced its predecessor, Westerburen, which lay further west and was washed into the sea by violent storms.

Wander through the old brick streets and lanes and admire the many characteristic island houses, particularly along de Langestreek, Middenstreek (look for one called **Marten** dated 1721), and the Voorstreek. The village has interesting shops and pleasant, terraced cafes and restaurants to relax in. Do not miss its very interesting visitors centre, **Bezoekerscentrum Schiermonnikoog**, Torenstreek 20, ☎ (0519) 53 1641, open Mon.-Sat. 10am-noon & 1:30-5:30pm; in season, also open Sun. 1:30-5:30pm, which has exhibits to acquaint you with all the natural wonders of the island.

You can reach Schiermonnikoog by ferry from **Lauwersoog**. As cars are not allowed on the island, you leave them behind in a designated parking area at the dock. Your luggage can be taken care of, but it is wise to travel lightly. Should you travel by train, buses can bring you to Lauwersoog from Groningen or Leeuwarden. The ferry crossing takes 45 minutes, and there are up to six a day, depending on the season. You will be welcomed on the island by taxis, buses and bikes. For ferry information, call **Wagenborg Passagiersdiensten B.V.**, Reeweg 4, ☎ (0519) 546 111.

Staying over

There is ample choice in all types of accommodation, from camping to luxury hotel apartments. The VVV will supply a comprehensive listing and make reservations. We can recommend the **Strandhotel**, Badweg 32, ☎ (0519) 53 1111, for its location in the dunes, impressive sea view and tranquility, or **Hotel Graaf Bernstorff**, Reeweg 1, ☎ (0519) 53 2000, in the village, www.bernstorff.nl.

Chapter 9 | The province of Groningen

Groningen, the most northern province, rich in history, culture and nature, has something for everyone. In 911, Groningen (then 'East Frisia') demanded its independence. In 1040, Emperor Henry III gave the city of Groningen and its surrounding area to the Bishops of Utrecht. The rest of the province remained under the control of major landowners, known as 'Jonkers;' these areas were called the 'Ommelanden,' separate from Groningen city and area. The Jonkers were rich and powerful and built themselves lovely manor houses and castles, a number of which still stand.

By 1440 Groningen was independent, but in 1536 Charles V united the area into greater Holland. The establishment of a university in 1614 brought learned men from around the world, making Groningen a major intellectual centre, even today.

The province is the chief peat region of the country, with fertile, well-drained land, much of it devoted to agriculture. Driving along, one is impressed by the huge Groningen farm buildings, unique in style to this area. There is much to do for nature lovers – lakes for sailing and water sports, and miles of watery polderlands for canoeing past ancient villages, historic manor houses and windmills. Needless to say, this flat, panoramic countryside is also a biker's paradise. Regular ferries from Lauwersoog (northwest) will take you to the smallest and quietest of the Waddenzee islands, Schiermonnikoog (see Chapter 8), where you can come even closer to nature.

Information: ☎ (050) 313 5713; www.groningen.nl/tourism

Groningen
Bustling hub of the north

Getting there: From the north take N355; from west and east A7; from south, A28.
Information: VVV, Grote Markt 25, ☎ (050) 313 5713 ; www.groningen.nl/tourism

The city of **Groningen**, capital of the province of the same name, has an atmosphere all its own. Even if one weren't aware that the second oldest university in the Netherlands (1614) is located here (Groningen University), it wouldn't take long to figure it out – especially on Saturday nights when everyone's out on the Grote Markt where the principal student association happens to have its Club House. Hundreds of bikes are gathered all around the square, their owners enjoying a pizza or simply sitting at a café with a 'Pils' (beer). College students number about 20,000 and, while they probably aren't all on the square at the same time, it might seem so. Don't be surprised if you see a bike perched precariously on a street sign or lamppost – it's a traditional joke played on student friends.

Groningen's importance and wealth date from very early times. In fact, Groningen provided ships and material for the Crusades. It was a fortress town in the 12th century and became an important commercial centre in 1251 when a contract between it and the surrounding towns established Groningen as the central market town for the area. After joining the Hanseatic League in 1594, Groningen became an even more important trading post.

Today, Groningen ranks fourth in commercial importance in the Netherlands. Being connected to the sea by three long canals has effectively made it an active seaport where commercial vessels come to do business. Agriculture and fishing have long been traditional activities; however, the discovery of large natural gas reserves in 1946 added to the province's importance and has turned a number of formerly sleepy townships into busy commercial centres.

The well-known and highly-reputed **Groningen University** continues to bring international educators and scholars to the city, greatly enhancing it culturally and intellectually. The city has a rich assortment of old almshouses to visit, and its Groninger Museum building is one exceptional example of the high-quality modern architecture found here.

▶ **Groninger Museum**
Location: Museumeiland 1
Information: ☎ (050) 366 6555
Hours: Tues.-Sun., 10am-5pm; www.groningermuseum.nl

It's been described as 'the most startling museum in the Netherlands.' No doubt about it...the **Groninger Museum** is an attention-grabbing sight. Italian Alessandro Mendini led the team of architects that designed the building. Completed in 1994, it is an assortment of colours, shapes and materials that is every bit as interesting and stimulating as the collection it holds. It sits both alongside and 'in' a canal opposite the station. In architecture, the term 'deconstructivism' is used to describe part of the building's style. This means that all architectural traditions have been rejected, e.g. a glass window becomes a floor, and a wall becomes a ceiling. It has to be seen.

The Decorative Arts section houses an impressive collection of Oriental ceramics, with explanations in English on their popularity in 17th-century Holland, and on how the Dutch eventually created their own version: Delftware. The collection is especially fine and highly valuable – a must for any Far East 'specialists.' The ceramics are displayed in a unique glass case that runs the circumference of the round room. French architect Philippe Starck has soft, white curtains gracefully dividing the room, creating a very peaceful atmosphere for the visitor. There's also an exhibit of 18th-century Chinese porcelain recovered in 1986 from a ship that sank in the South China Sea over 400 years ago. A few pieces are displayed showing how they spent most of the last five centuries – a pool of water covered with glass has been built into the floor.

Near the Groninger Museum: The street in front of the museum is lined with the homes of the city's late 19th-century elite. This tree-lined area has two small squares: **Emmaplein** to the west, and **Herenplein** to the east.

East of Herenplein is **St. Anthony Gasthuis**, Rademarkt 27. Built in 1517, it was a hospital for plague victims, but from 1644 and for 200 years, it was an institution for the mentally ill.

If you want to see Groningen's oldest and largest almshouse, going north on Rademarkt, take a left turn on Gedempte Zuiderdiep and a right to Pelsterstraat 43. The **Heilige Geest Gasthuis** (or Pelstergasthuis) dates from 1267. It once was a hospital for the poor, and an overnight stop for medieval travellers, but from 1600 until today it has been a home for the elderly. Over the years it has gradually expanded, and now it ranks among the largest almshouses in the Netherlands. There are three inner courtyards, separated by quaint old gates and corridors. A fourth courtyard has been added and is enclosed on all four sides by small modern houses. The back exit, with its Tuscan pilaster gate, renovated in 1724, gives access to Nieuwstad. There's a small church with a Schnitger organ.

You'll also find a small gem of an almshouse further north. The **Pepergasthuis**, or Geertruidsgasthuis, Peperstraat 22, has a 1640 gate which is a masterpiece. The sculptured sandstone pediment over the entrance door dates from 1743. There are two courtyards: the first has a water pump dating from 1829; the second presents a very charming sight with its 18th-century facades and the 1651 gate. The bars you see on some of the windows are remnants of the days when part of the building was a mental home.

Nearby is the **Holland Casino**, Kattendiep 150, ☎ (050) 317 2317, which offers blackjack, American and French roulette, and one-armed bandits.

▶ **Noordelijk Scheepvaartmuseum en Niemeyer Tabaksmuseum**
Northern Shipping and Tobacco Museum
Location: Brugstraat 24 (Gotische Huis), just west of Vismarkt
Information: ☎ (050) 312 2202; www.noordelijkscheepvaartmuseum.nl
Hours: Tues.-Sat. 10am-5pm, Sun. 1-5pm

The two buildings in which the **Noordelijk Scheepvaartmuseum en Niemeyer Tabaks-museum** is located are wonderfully restored 13th-14th-century structures with heavily beamed ceilings, and bright, well-ordered display space.

Fifteen centuries of history are represented in the superb Northern Shipping Museum. Stories are told of ships and their captains, the voyages they made, the far shores they visited, the cargoes they carried, the way they lived, and what they brought back to trade or to adorn their homes. There's a skipper's model room, ship models, machinery, and a collection of art dealing with maritime subjects.

The Tobacco Museum collection is quite famous with its fine quality objects, engravings and paintings depicting the history of tobacco in Western Europe from 1500-1930, its healing properties, its use as a luxury item and even present-day antismoking campaigns.

Near the Shipping & Tobacco Museum: The **Korenbeurs**, or Grain Exchange, facing the **Vismarkt**, was once a major exchange for domestic grains. Dating from 1865, the three Gods protecting this building were: Mercury, God of Commerce over the entrance; Neptune, God of the Seas; and Ceres, Goddess of Agriculture, on either side of the entrance.

Nearby stands the **A-Kerk**, A-Kerkhof 2, ☎ (050) 318 1433, a 15th-century Gothic church with a delicate Renaissance cupola. Apparently it has fallen off twice. In 1247 the original church that stood here was dedicated to Maria and St. Nicholas.

The **Natuurmuseum**, Praediniussingel 59, ☎ (050) 367 6170, open Tues.-Sun. 1-5pm, www.natuurmuseumgroningen.nl, has a collection of stones fossils and minerals, stuffed animals and insects – a very educational centre created for children and young adults.

▶ **Het Nederlands Stripmuseum – Dutch Comic Strip Museum**
Location: Westerhaven 71
Information: ☎ (050) 317 8470; www.stripmuseumgroningen.nl
Hours: Tues.-Sat. 10am-5pm, Sun. 12-5pm

See how comic strips are made at the **Dutch Comic Strip Museum**, the newest museum in Groningen, and the only one in the Netherlands that highlights comic strips. The museum is divided into special halls for children, adults and connoisseurs. In addition to an extensive collection of old and new comic strips, there are regularly-changing exhibitions. Sometimes you can watch a comic strip cartoonist at work.

▶ **Martinitoren and Martinikerk – Martini Tower and Martini Church**
Location: Martinikerkhof 1
Information: Tower, ☎ (050) 313 5713; church, ☎ (050) 311 1277
Hours: Vary with the season. Call for information.

Completed in 1482, the 315-ft-tall **Martini Tower** in the centre of old Groningen dominates the scene. Gothic in style, it is affectionately known as 'the Old Gray One.' Its bells are known internationally and its bell ringers' guild, established in 1982, now has about 50 members. You can climb the 251 steps to the second floor, which is about 185 feet.

Martini Church is Romano-Gothic in origin, as can only be seen from the exterior. It dates back to 1230 AD and has been preserved in its present form since the 15th century. The vaults have numerous 15th-century murals, and the walls of the choir are decorated with a series of exquisite frescoes. Various stained-glass windows show the coats of arms of the captains of the citizen soldiery (1770). The organ dates from 1480.

Near Martinitoren and Martinikerk: Nearby is the only 17th-century house that survived the destruction of the war. The **Goud** or Gold Office, Waagplein 1, built in 1635 as the tax house, has a Latin inscription over the entrance: 'Render unto Caesar that which is Caesar's.'

Beautiful buildings like this can be seen throughout town. The **Provinciehuis**, Martinikerkhof 12, home of the provincial government, dates from the 15th century. The caretaker's house (to the left) has an early Renaissance gable which was part of another house until 1893. The richly-sculptured facade with medallions representing Alexander the Great, King David and Charlemagne is why it is sometimes called 'the house with the Three Kings.'

The **Prinsenhof**, Martinikerkhof 23, originally housed a 15th-century order of friars who translated and transcribed books. It was converted in 1594 to accommodate the court of the Frisian Governors. Under Louis Bonaparte of France it served as a military hospital. The Pleinpoort (plaza gate) dates from 1642 and the annex, the Gardepoort (guard's gate), was built in 1639. It now houses the local TV and radio broadcasting offices.

Behind the Prinsenhof are its gardens, the **Prinsenhoftuin**, Turfsingel, ☎ (050) 318 3688, open April to mid-Oct. It's worth seeking out...especially in the rose season. The 1731 sundial in the gate of this 17th-century rose and herb garden has a Latin inscription: 'The past is nothing, the future is uncertain, the present is unstable; beware that you do not lose the latter which is yours.'

▶ **Also in Groningen:**
The northwest part of the old town is the University area. The **Academiegebouw**, Broerplein 4, (1909) is the main building – a large neo-Renaissance structure with the allegorical figures of Scientia, Minerva, Historia, Prudentia and Mathematica on its facade. Nearby is the **University Museum**, Oudekijk in 't Jatstraat 7-a, ☎ (050) 363 5562, open Tues.-Sun. 1-5pm.

There are some interesting buildings along the **Oude Boteringestraat**. Number 44, built in 1791, was the former residence of the Queen's Commissioner; number 36, the Court of Justice; number 23, the house with the Thirteen Pinnacles, with its ornate facade, but alas no longer 13 pinnacles; and number 24 on the corner of Braerstraat, a stone house built in the Middle Ages.

The University Museum, (Universiteitsmuseum) Oude Kijk in 't Jatstraat 7-a, ☎ (050) 363 5083, www.rug.nl/museum, open Tues.-Sun. 1-5pm, features diverse collections from anatomy, via ethnology, to zoology, with regular exhibitions on recent scientific developments, as well as the history of the university and student life.

South of the city centre is the **Grafisch Museum**, Rabenhauptstraat 65, ☎ (050) 525 6497, www.grafischmuseum.nl, open Tues.-Sun. 1-5pm, with an overview of printing through the centuries, and displays devoted to local artists and illustrators involved in printing and books.

On the southwest edge of the city, the **Stadspark** city park is a wonderful place to relax or let the children spread their wings. Besides a camping facility at Campinglaan 6, ☎ (050) 525 1624, there's plenty to do, with canoes for rent, horseback riding, midget golf, ice skating and a children's playground.

Markets

Markets are held Tues., Fri. and Sat. on the Grote Markt and the Vismarkt (fish and produce market).

Eating out

The VVV has a comprehensive list. For something a little different, that the children will also love, try the moderate-priced pancake ship, **'t Pannekoekschip**, Schuitendiep, ☎ (050) 312 0045. For a totally different atmosphere – lakeside – try the dining room of **Golden Tulip Paterswolde-Groningen** hotel, at Paterswolde Lake, Groningerweg 19 (see below), about 12 km (7.5 mi) south of town. For great Mexican fare – including small but potent Margaritas – head to **Four Roses**, Oosterstraat 71, ☎ (050) 314 3887, www.4roses.nl. The burritos are 'to-die-for.'

Staying over

For convenience, try the historic **Doelen Hotel**, Grote Markt 36, ☎ (050) 312 7041. For families or couples who want a bit of outdoors action, elegance, and time to relax, the **Golden Tulip Paterswolde-Groningen** hotel, ☎ (050) 309 5400, is an excellent choice. The hotel has an indoor pool, sauna, extremely comfortable rooms and a tearoom pavilion by the lake (short walk) where you can also sail and windsurf. Nearby are walks in the woods, biking, horseback riding, golf, and para-jumping. More expensive, but worth it.

Yearly events

Groningen's **Martiniplaza** (near the Stadspark) is booked solid Jan.-March with concerts, sports events, animal shows, antique exhibitions, and textile and other commercial markets. The yearly flower market is held on Good Friday; the City Fair in May. Between June and September there are organ concerts in the Martini Church, and in August the town jumps with 'Noorderzon,' a blast of special summer programmes. In December there's an Antiques Fair. Check with the VVV.

Tours

Canal boat tours are possible throughout the year, on the canal across from the Groninger Museum: **Rederij Kool**, Stationsweg 1012, ☎ (050) 312 8379.

In the neighbourhood of Groningen city

Paterswoldse Lake (6 km/4 mi) south of town) and **Zuidlaarder Lake** (15 km/9 mi) southeast) offer the complete spectrum of activities to enjoy these beautiful lakes and the surrounding wooded countryside. In neighboring **Drenthe**, two megalithic tombs can be explored, and the attractions of the pretty village of **Zuidlaren** enjoyed, including a popular horse and pony market at the beginning of October (see Chapter 10).

Haren (southeast 6 km/4 mi)) is home to **Hortus Haren**, Kerklaan 34, ☎ (050) 537 0053, www.hortusharen.nl, open daily 9:30am-5pm. This botanical garden has a greenhouse divided into three sections: desert, savannah and monsoon. The Hortus also has a Celtic garden. Its Hidden Empire of Ming is a Chinese garden complete with buildings and a Chinese teahouse in the style of the Ming dynasty period (1368-1644).

Noorderhoogebrug (northeast edge of town) boasts the biggest windmill in the province, **De Wilhelmina**, ☎ (050) 301 4899; check to find out when it operates and if demonstrations might be given.

A little further north in **Bedum** is the 800-year old **Walfriduskerk**, ☎ (050) 301 2780, open Jan.-May, Sat. 2-4pm; June-Sept., Tues. 10:30-11:30am, Weds. & Sat. 2-4pm. The tower of the church leans, and is known in the region as the 'Pisa of the Hogeland.'

To the west, in **Aduard**, there was once a 12th-century abbey of Cistercian monks. All that remains of this complex of 20-30 buildings is their infirmary, in use for centuries, but now a Protestant church, ☎ (050) 403 1724, open Mon.-Fri. 9am-noon & 2-5pm. You can learn about the abbey, which was a centre of religious thinking in medieval Europe, at the **Museum St. Bernardushof**, Hofstraat 45, ☎ (050) 403 2109, open April-Oct., Tue.-Sat. 10am-5pm; Nov.-Mar., Sun. 1-5pm.

West of Aduard in **Noordhorn** is a museum of dress and costumes from the 18th to early 20th centuries. At the **Kostuummuseum De Gouden Leeuw**, Langestraat 48, ☎ (0594) 50 3804, open all year (except Feb.) Wed.-Sat. 11-5pm, the focus is on Dutch clothing of that period.

An absolute 'must-do' for anyone visiting the Groningen area is to visit Dutch still-life artist Henk Helmantel's private studio, gallery and idyllic home, **De Weem**, Abt Emopad

2, in Westeremden, about a 20-minute drive from the city of Groningen, ☎ (0596) 55 1415, www.helmantel.nl, open May-Sept. Thurs.-Sat. 1-5pm, or by appointment. (See ad on page 277.)

Leek
A carriage museum, manor house and park

Getting there: From the west, off A7 about 20 km (12 mi) before Groningen. From Groningen, about 14 km (9mi) west.

Information: VVV, Tolberterstraat 39-1, ☎ (0594) 51 2280; www.nienoord.nl

Leek is a special treat whose origins stem from the historic manor house **Nienoord**, now called **Castle Nienoord**, which was founded about 1525. This castle comes complete with moat and two drawbridges. The 20-acre estate belongs to the municipality of Leek and the park is open to the public all year. A section has been converted to a museum (and restaurant) and is filled with antique furnishings. Don't miss the **National Carriage Museum**.

In town there's an interesting Protestant Church, the **Midwolde Church**, containing a 17th-century mausoleum with exceptionally fine marble sculptures.

The attraction park **Familypark Nienoord**, Nienoord 10, ☎ (0594) 51 2230, open April-Oct., daily 9:30am-5:30pm, offers many activities for the whole family. Take the miniature railway (1 to 8 scale) at the station and enjoy the ride. There are also around three dozen HO scale model railway trains covering 100 square meters. Model railway fans should visit around Ascension Day week when the big international collectors bring their trains to be admired.

▶ **Nienoord Castle – National Carriage Museum**

Location: Nienoord 1. Traffic is restricted so be prepared to walk around this green, wooded area.

Information: ☎ (0594) 51 2260; www.carriagemuseums.eu

Hours: April-Oct., Tues.-Fri. 10am-5pm, Sat.-Sun. 1-5pm

This 16th-century castle was greatly damaged by fire in 1850, necessitating its reconstruction. As home to the **National Carriage Museum**, it can be visited during museum hours. This is the only place in the world where you will find a complete national carriage collection! Well-known internationally, the museum works together with the Dutch Royal Mews, the Imperial Collection in Vienna, and the Royal Museum in Lisbon.

The small goat carriages and sleds belonging to former 'royal' children can put stars in many youngsters' eyes, while the sleds from the 17th and 18th century may hit a romantic, responsive chord with some adults. There are several coaches on display in the carriage house which belonged to the last German Kaiser. Also interesting is a 'Prince Albert' coach from 1900.

In addition, there's a summer pavilion of the 1700s, the interior completely decorated with shells and known as the 'Shell Cave.' There's a legend that explains the origins; be sure to ask about it.

Staying over

Camp (Apr.-Sept.) at **Westerheerdt**, Midwolderweg 19, ☎ (0594) 51 2059. www.campingwesterheerdt.nl

Yearly events

The major nationally-known events include a historic motorbike race, the **Horse Power Run**, the last Sunday in April (Leek-Assen-Leek); and an international 4-day show of steam train models, **Familypark Nienoord Stoomdagen**, Ascension Day through the weekend.

In the neighbourhood of Leek

Grijpskerk, about 16 km (10 mi) north of Leek on country roads, has unusual activities during the year, especially the national pole-vaulting events in mid-June and the local pole-vaulting championships that take place at the end of August.

Southwest of Grijpskerk is **Lutjegast**, the birthplace of Abel Tasman (1603-59), the first European to discover New Zealand and to circle Australia. In the **Abel Tasman Kabinet**, Kompasstraat 1, ☎ (0594) 61 3576 / 61 2521, open Thurs.-Sat. 1:30-4:30pm, is an exhibit about the navigator and his explorations.

Leens
To the manor born
Getting there: From Groningen, take N361 north to Leens
Information: VVV Winsum, ☎ (0595) 44 3388

Leens is the home of Verhildersum Castle, now a folklore museum with period rooms. It also has an historic church, **Petruskerk**, ☎ (0595) 57 1677, its organ made by Hinsz in 1733. The church is a fine tuffstone building from about 1000 AD, with a 13th-century saddle roof. **Leensterweek** is a festival at the beginning of September with street music, handicraft displays, special markets, etc.

▶ **Verhildersum Castle**
Location: Wierde 40, Leens, on the east side of town.
Information: ☎ (0595) 57 1430; restaurant, ☎ (0595) 57 2204
Hours: Mid April-Oct., Tues.-Sun., 10:30am-5pm; restaurant open 5-11pm, but closed on Mon.-Tues. in low season.

Verhildersum Castle is a wonderland to explore. Not only is it beautifully maintained and furnished, but its history dates back to the 14th century. What you see today, however, is more representative of the 19th century in style and decorations, as opposed to nearby Menkemaborg Castle which represents the 17th and 18th centuries. The story goes that there used to be a couple of witches in the house – one in the linen cupboard at her spinning wheel – but apparently they have moved on.

The original castle was restored in 1514. Its silhouette was greatly changed about 1786, as can be seen in an old painting of 1670 showing it as it was. A former owner, his wife and their ten children are in the foreground with the castle and town behind them.

The rooms are richly furnished and filled with objects of considerable value such as a splendid collection of 'Familie Rose' porcelain. In the same room is a rocking horse which would have made any four-year-old boy happy in 1885. The dining room, chairs and table were salvaged from a demolished manor house in Pieterburen. Notice the 19th-century highchair with its built-in chamber pot and a little foot-warmer. A charming contrast to the formal rooms is the high-ceilinged kitchen, the vaulted cellar, which dates to the 14th century, and the scullery with its peat funnel. It was through here that lumps of peat were dropped from the attic where they were kept dry, to fuel the fires below.

The top floor is furnished and has a variety of objects including photos relating to the history of the castle and its land. At the back are some Groninger costumes in what is like an old clothes attic.

There are often special exhibits in the coach-house, and you can visit the farmhouse museum, Welgelegen, with its agricultural implements. The gardens vary depending on the time of year, but are always a lovely place to relax. The storehouse is now a farm-style restaurant...where it is pleasant to sit outside and enjoy a drink while admiring the castle across its moat.

In the neighbourhood of Leens

To the north is **Lauwersoog**, on the Waddenzee and the **Lauwermeer**, a lake that connects with the sea. Naturally, this is a good spot for water recreation, ideal for learning to sail or windsurf...cycle, swim or fish. You can ply the canals by canoe or 'hooded boats,' spending the nights in log cabins. There are well-equipped campsites and comfortable bungalows.

Museum Wierdenland Ezinge, Torenstraat 12, ☎ (0594) 62 1524, open Apr.-Sept., Tues.-Fri. 10:30am-5pm, Sat.-Sun. 1-5pm, has exhibits that explain the *terp* villages, of which Ezinge is one. In Groningen, these artificial mounds that were built to protect inhabitants of the region from the sea are called '*wierden*.' In **Houwerzijl** there is an interesting **Tea Factory Museum**, Hoofdstraat 15, ☎ (0595) 57 2053, open April-Oct., Tues.-Sun. 10am-5pm., Nov.-March weekends only, 10am-5pm. A fascinating place to have tea.

Pieterburen

Seals, mustard and mudflats

Getting there: West of Warffum off N363 by the Waddenzee.
Information: VVV, Hoofdstraat 83, ☎ (0595) 52 8522

Here's a chance for lovers of seals to visit the **De Zeehondencreche** Lenie 't Hart, Hoofdstraat 94a, ☎ (0595) 52 6526, www.zeehondencreche.nl; open daily 9am-6pm, a research establishment where seals are studied with a view to preserving the remaining species, and discovering the causes of their rapidly depleting numbers. The organisation welcomes visitors – open daily as well as contributions to help with their work.

Pieterburen is one of the gathering points for that popular Dutch pastime, *wadlopen*, or mud-flat walking. Twice each day the tides leave little but mud between the Groningen shoreline and the Waddenzee island of **Schiermonnikoog**. So, dressed in swimsuits or shorts, a jacket or sweater and sturdy shoes, hundreds make the strenuous walk through the deep mud. For this taxing fun – an experience like no other – it's essential to go with a group led by an experienced guide. Three options in Pieterburen are: **St. Wadloopcentrum**, ☎ (0595) 52 8300 from May-Sept.; **Dijkstra's Wadlooptochten**, ☎ (0595) 52 8345, www.wadloop-dijkstra.nl, from mid March-Oct.; and **Dick Wiebenga**, ☎ (0595) 52 8207. It's best to book a place in advance. Most treks leave in the early morning. There are also *wadlopen* tours to Schiermonnikoog organised out of Ezinge, Uithuizen and Loppersum. Call the VVV for details: www.wadloop.nl (See photo on page 243.)

In the neighbourhood of Pieterburen

In **Eenrum**, the mustard museum **Abraham's Mosterdmakerij**, Molenstraat 5, ☎ (0595) 49 1600, open April-Oct., daily Thurs.-Sun., noon-9pm; Nov.-March, Thurs.-Fri. 5:30-8pm; restaurant open daily noon-9pm, but closed Mon.-Tues. from Oct.-March, offers a tour, coffee, slide show and a pot of Abraham's mustard. If you haven't the time for it all, you are welcome to watch a demonstration of mustard-making and have lunch. Eenrum is also home to the world's smallest hotel. **Grand Hotel de Kromme Raake**, Hoofdstraat 12, ☎ (0595) 49 1600, has only one room! It's a very comfortable one though – complete with a cosy, old-style Dutch cupboard bed (*bedstee*), literally a bed enclosed in a large cupboard (can be very romantic if you're not claustrophobic!) – and one of the most expensive in the province. Need we say, a reservation is highly recommended.

Warffum

An important agricultural area, 'Het Hoogeland'

Getting there: North of Groningen on N363, about halfway between Verhildersum and Menkemaborg Castles.
Information: VVV, Schoolstraat 4, ☎ (0595) 42 5245

Warffum has a **Protestant Church**, ☎ (0595) 42 2976, with a tower dating from 1638 and two clocks, one from 1686 and the other from 1701. Its organ is considered to be one of the most beautiful in the northern Netherlands. This area is a prosperous clay area in the important agricultural district 'Het Hoogeland.' There are fine farmhouses to be seen in this unusually picturesque region, such as the 'Groot Zeewijk' and 'Klein Zeewijk.'

▶ **Openluchtmuseum Het Hoogeland – Open-air museum**
Location: Schoolstraat 2
Information: ☎ (0595) 42 2233
Hours: April-Oct., Tues.-Sat. 10am-5pm, Sun. 1-5pm

To preserve the style of living of the local rural population, the **Hoogeland Open-Air Museum** has restored and furnished some really interesting buildings from the 1850s on. There's a kosher butcher's shop, a grocery and a pub, an almshouse (brought from Groningen), and houses furnished in the style of different periods, including a labourer's cottage and barn. Coffee, tea, soup and pancakes are served at a cosy 19th-century pub, 'bie Koboa.'

Staying over

A recommended campsite in the area is **De Breede**, De Breede 5, ☎ (0595) 42 4642, with swimming, midget golf and tennis courts.

Yearly events

In late June, there's an international folkloric dance festival called **Op Roakeldais** (in Frisian dialect), which means something like 'Hoping for the Best,' or 'For Good Luck.' An art and antique market is also part of the festivities.

Uithuizen
A lovely manor house
Getting there: North of Groningen on N363.
Information: VVV, Mennonietenkerkstraat 13, ☎ (0595) 43 4051;
                     www.toerisme-waddenkust.nl

The 'pièce de resistance' here is **Menkemaborg Castle**, but also look for the 13th-century church 'with a 12th century tower.' It has some unique pieces of furniture: a pulpit dating from 1711, a gentleman's bench and an organ from 1701. The **Lace Museum** (Kantmuseum), Oude Dijk 7, ☎ (0595) 43 2368, open April-mid-Dec., Wed.-Fri., 1-5pm has fine bobbin and needle lace from as early as the 16th century, from all parts of Europe.

Uithuizen | Delfzijl

▶ **Menkemaborg Castle**

Location:	Menkemaweg 2, Uithuizen. The castle is on the southeast side of town. There are small signs indicating the way.
Information:	☎ (0595) 43 1970; www.menkemaborg.nl
Hours:	March-Sept., Tues.-Sun., 10am-5pm; Oct.-Dec., Tues.-Sun., 10am-4pm

Menkemaborg Castle is considered to be one of the finest restored castles of the province. The original structure was a simple, square shape dating from the 14th century. The first owners were not remembered in history. It was only when the house was enlarged in 1700 that it took on its present shape and became an elegant fortified manor house. An English-language information sheet will help guide you around.

The castle is filled with authentic furniture, paintings, porcelain, glass and silver, and has carved oak fireplace mantels, a picturesque old kitchen and more, from the 17th and 18th centuries. There's a huge 18th-century four-poster bed in which King William III of the Netherlands slept. Note the comfortable toilet cupboards – a vast improvement on the 'out-house' – if not yet up to modern standards. The two round towers in the front garden forming a corner with the moat were also 'toilet facilities.'

The old kitchen is still cosy and inviting. The thick walls and heavily beamed, low ceiling are an indication this is part of the original house. Note the two pumps. One is for clean drinking water from the cistern; the other for water from the moat.

The garden has been planted according to an 18th-century plan found in the house. If you're here during the rose season, you will enjoy the famous rose bowers as well as the garden maze.

Eating out

The tearoom of the castle, **Schathoes**, ☎ (0595) 43 1858, is architecturally interesting. It was the former farm. On nice days, light lunches and drinks are served outdoors next to the moat where one can 'relax' to the honking of geese and ducks. Moderately priced, with pancakes a speciality.

Delfzijl
Largest port in the north

Getting there:	On the Eems estuary. From Groningen, take N360 northeast to Delfzijl.
Information:	VVV, J. v.d. Kornputplein 1a, ☎ (0596) 61 8104

Heavily fortified in the 16th century, **Delfzijl** now looks like the modern town it has become as the largest port in the north, with a harbour that has been expanded six times. The estuary is 19km (12 mi) long and 8km (5 mi) wide, allowing for the passage of large ships for the important shipbuilding and shipping trade. A walk along the seawall on clear days provides a fine view of the German coast and of the shipping activities on the Eems.

Salt and soda production is now surpassed by chemical production, agricultural products, aluminum, and other industrial goods. The shipbuilding and shipping trade also continue to bring increased prosperity to its citizens.

But life in Delfzijl isn't all work. There is an extensive recreation park along the seawall, with a swimming pool, midget golf, a traffic park for children, exhibition hall, youth hostel, campsite and open-air theatre. There is also a fine yachting harbour as well as an ocean terminal for big ships.

Georges Simenon, the well-known French author of mystery books (Maigret series), spent some time here in his youth, and his statue by Pieter d'Hont is at the port to greet all comers.

Staying over

The **Eemshotel**, Zeebadweg 2, ☎ (0596) 61 2636, sits on piles, with the sound of water to lull you to sleep. www.eemshotel.nl

Yearly events

Around the Whitsun holiday, in May or June, Delfzijl hosts **Pinksterfeesten** a five-day event which includes a fair, markets, and international deep-sea sailing races; in October it holds an Autumn Fair.

Appingedam
Picturesque 'kitchens' hanging over the canal

Getting there: From Groningen, N360 going east; from Delfzijl, N360 going west.
Information: VVV, Dijkstraat 26, ☎ (0596) 62 0300

Appingedam is worth a stop. Situated on the **Damsterdiep Canal**, it is known for its picturesque houses with little kitchens overhanging the canal. Located between Groningen and the Eems River, it was the most important sea harbour in this area until 1317 when the sluice gates were built in Delfzijl.

This medieval seaport town has been greatly restored in the past years. Look for the imposing **Nicolai Church**, (1225) ☎ (0596) 62 3313, open Mid June-mid Sept., Tues.-Sun. 2-5pm, with a Hinsz organ (1500), a vault painted with frescoes, a beautifully carved pulpit and pews, old gravestones and sarcophagi; and the **Town Hall** with a fine antique period facade dating from 1630 on what was originally the house of the Marksmen's Guild. **Blakenstein**, Blankenstein 2, ☎ (0596) 62 4488, is a clever combination of a 15th- and 19th-century building that houses changing exhibits of modern art. **Museum Stad Appingedam**, Wijkstraat 25, ☎ (0596) 68 0168, open Tues.-Fri. 11am-5pm, Sat.-Sun. 1-5pm, is the local history museum.

Appingedam will be a pleasant stop for the children, giving them a break from adult-oriented sightseeing. **Ekenstein Park**, Alberdaweg 70, ☎ (0596) 62 8528, is a fine recreational centre with a children's farm, playground, fishing ponds, deer park, aviaries, and an excellent hotel on the grounds.

Staying over

Hotel Ekenstein, Alberdaweg 70, ☎ (0596) 62 8528, offers something special for the whole family. There is rest and luxury in its peaceful surroundings and elegantly appointed lounge, with a roaring fire on cool evenings. There are special weekend arrangements and excursions such as sailing charters, or a week on the Wadden Sea aboard an historic Frisian barge.

Yearly events

Appingedam hosts numerous events, including festivals and markets: late June is **De Nacht van Appingdam** (Night of Appingedam), with music, food and celebrations from 6pm-6am. Mid-Sept. there's the **Damsterdag**, a parade with papier-mâché figures and, in Oct., a folk craft market.

Tours

Boat trips can be arranged with **Chez Bateau**, Wijkstraat 22, ☎ (0596) 62 6039.

In the neighbourhood of Appingedam

At **Nieuwolda**, south of Delfzijl and Appingedam on N362, there's a **Baby Carriage (Pram) Museum** (Kinderwagen Museum), Hoofdweg West 25, ☎ (0596) 54 1941, open April-Oct., Wed. & Sat.-Sun. 1-6pm. Located in an 18th-century farmhouse, this is a private collection of approximately 260 antique and old baby carriages from the 19th and 20th centuries. They have been beautifully restored.

Nieuweschans, on country roads to the German border is an old fortress town. The fortress is no longer, but the Voorstraat in the town centre has a parade-ground and fortress museum to visit: **Vestingmuseum**, 1ste Kanonniersstraat 2, ☎ (0597) 52 2020, open April-Oct., Mon.-Fri. 9:30am-noon & 1-5pm; Nov.-March, Mon.-Fri. 1-4pm. 'Taking the waters' is old hat in more southerly countries of Europe, but health spa centre, **Fontana Nieuweschans**, Weg naar de Bron 3, ☎ (0597) 52 7777, was the first of its kind in the Netherlands. The water pumped from the earth's depths has healing minerals such as iodine and iron, which together with its high salinity is said to benefit both mind and body. The outdoor pool is kept at a temperature of 36°C (96.8° F). There are massages and beauty treatments as well as a Thalassotherapy Centre.

At **Heiligerlee**, the **Klokkengieterij Museum** (Bell Casting Museum), Provincialeweg 46, ☎ (0597) 41 8199, open April-Sept., Tues.-Sat. 10am-5pm, Sun. 1-5pm; Oct., Tues.-Fri. & Sun. 1-5pm, is in the old Van Bergen Foundry. It was famous for its traditional method of casting bells and for its excellent workmanship. It closed in 1980, but today, demonstrations show the casting of small bells, and carillon concerts are held in the garden for visitors to appreciate the sound. There are changing exhibitions dealing with local industrial or regional history, modern production techniques, and contemporary local art. The **Museum Slag Bij Heiligerlee**, Provincialeweg 55, ☎ (0597) 41 8199, open April-Sept., Tues.-Sat. 10am-5pm, Sun. 1-5pm; Oct., Tues.-Fri. & Sun. 1-5pm, commemorates the Battle of Heiligerlee of 1568. It was the Dutch rebels' first victory over Spanish rule, and the first battle in what became known as the Eighty Years War.

Slochteren
Source of natural gas and a stunning castle

Getting there:	From Groningen, A7 east to Hoogezand intersection, then north toward Slochteren.
Information:	VVV, Noorderweg 1, ☎ (0598) 42 2970

Since the 1959 discovery of one of the largest deposits of natural gas in the world, **Slochteren** has been of great importance as the source of much of Holland's power requirements. The town has three mills, a 13th-century church, and a farm museum: **Boerderij Museum Duurswold**, Hoofdweg 271, ☎ (0598) 42 1573, open mid-March to Oct., Wed. 1-5pm, Sat. 10am-5pm. But the main attraction is the 16th-century Fraeylemaborg Castle.

▸ **Fraeylemaborg Castle**

Getting there:	Hoofdweg 30. After the village take direction Schildwolde. The castle is near the intersection to Noordbroek.
Information:	The castle, ☎ (0598) 42 1568, the restaurant, 'De Boerderij,' ☎ (0598) 42 1280; www.fraeylemaborg.nl
Hours:	Open March-Dec., Tues.-Fri. 10am-5pm, Sat./Sun. 1-5pm

At first sight, **Fraeylemaborg** is more an elegant country manor than a 'castle,' but the origins date back to the 13th century. The wings date from the second half of the 17th century, and it was restored in 1781. Johan de Witt held a conference here in the 17th century, with Jan Oesebrant Rengers. At the end of the 17th century, William III was the guest of Hendrik Piccardt, head of operations for the Ommelanden States. The large portraits of Willem and his wife Mary II Stuart were gifts of this royal couple.

There are other mementoes of the Netherlands Royal Family, and a precious collection of china. Exhibitions can be seen in the 'Schathuis,' the former farm of the estate. In the 'Koethuis' (the former coachhouse) you will find an art gallery. If time permits, take a walk through the part of about 25 acres, a unique sample of English landscape style.

Bourtange
A 400-year-old fortified town

Getting there:	From Groningen, A7 to Winschoten, then south on N368 and east on N976.
Information:	VVV, Willem Lodewijkstraat 33, ☎ (0599) 35 4600; www.bourtange.nl

Nearly 400 years ago, this small town in southeast Groningen was one of the most important fortified towns in the northern part of the Netherlands. The original fortification, in the shape of a five-pointed star, was built during the Eighty Years War by the Frisian landholder, Count Lodewijk of Nassau. In 1672, the bishop of Münster, a Spaniard named Verdugo, attempted to capture **Bourtange** but was unsuccessful. In fact, the fort was never captured, due mainly to its position on a sandy ridge in the middle of the greater Bourtanger marsh. Because these marshes slowly dried up and by 1851 the development of new methods of warfare had been developed, Bourtange was dismantled.

Now completely restored to its original star shape, **Vesting Bourtange**, Willem Lodewijkstraat 33, ☎ (0599) 35 4600, open April-Oct., Mon.-Fri. 10am-5pm, Sat.-Sun. 11am-5pm, gives visitors a chance to discover a unique fort.

You will arrive at Bourtange via the Frisian or Münster gates, both of which lead you to the picturesque marketplace with its fourteen ancient lime trees. Notice two partially restored, 17th-century officers' homes there. From this market square, ten little streets radiate out to the walls and bastions. Linked to each other, they form a perfect radial street pattern.

Among the reconstructed buildings are a number of barracks; a horse-powered mill; a synagogue built in 1842, which is one of the few this close to Germany to survive World War II; and **'s Landhuis**, a beautiful building which has now become a picturesque restaurant. There are also wooden drawbridges, wells, guard houses and many old cannons.

Shutterbugs might like to find out the precise dates for Bourtange's 'Feestweek,' a special celebration week, usually the end of July or early August, wherein local people dress in costume and special events are held. Bourtange may be a long drive, but it is interesting and can easily be incorporated into a general visit of Groningen. There are a number of hotels in Groningen city, Assen and Emmen. Check with the VVV and see Chapter 10.

Ter Apel
Site of a medieval cloister

Getting there: Ter Apel is on the German border, 18 km (11 mi) NE of Emmen. From Groningen, there is a very scenic route south of Winschoten through the small towns of Wedde, Vlagtwedde, Jipsinghuizen, Sellingen, etc.

Information: VVV, Molenplein 1, ☎ (0599) 58 1277

Ter Apel is the site of the medieval Crosier monastery, now known as **Klooster Ter Apel**, Boslaan 3, ☎ (0599) 58 1370, www.kloosterterapel.nl, open Tues.-Sat. 10am-5pm, Sun. 1-5pm; during summer holidays Mon.-Sat. 10am-6pm, Sun. 1-6pm.

First established and named Domus Novae Lucis or 'The House of The New Light' in 1465, it was a monastery of the Order of the Holy Cross until 1602. The existing structure dates from the mid-15th century. Reconstruction took place in the 1930s, and great care was taken to clean the original bricks by hand and replace them as before. The new west wing, designed by Prof. Johannes Exner, was completed in 2001.

The characteristic meeting rooms of the monastery are the Gothic church with the unique limestone rood-gallery, the refectory, the room of the prior and the chapter room.

On this site, designated by UNESCO as one of the 'Top 100 Monuments in the Nether-lands' you will find The Museum of Monastery and Church History & Religious Art, Gal-lery I & II of Modern Art, and The Cloister Café. The monastery garden is well-tended and attractive, with over 120 varieties of herbs. (Klooster Ter Apel has possibilities for business meetings, congresses and weddings.)

Ter Apel can make a convenient day-tour including Emmen, Barger-Compascuum, the *hunebedden* (dolmens), etc. Or, you can start from Groningen and make the swing clockwise, taking the most scenic provincial roads south of Winschoten and through Wedde, Ellersing-huizen.

In the neighbourhood of Ter Apel

To the north lies **Veendam**, once a major peat-producing settlement. The existing canals in the area are remnants of the waterways used by industry to transport the fuel it cut from the earth. **Veenkoloniaal Museum**, Museumplein 5, ☎ (0598) 36 4224, open Tues.-Thurs. 11am-5pm, Fri.-Sun. 1-5pm, tells the story of the local peat villages.

Chapter 10 | The province of Drenthe

Drenthe is a more rural province than Friesland and Groningen, its northern neighbours that were settled by the same tribal group around 3000 B.C. For years the region was an object of barter by the Romans, followed by the Frankish kings and German emperors. For five centuries the Bishops of Utrecht controlled this territory. Even at the time of Confederation, Drenthe had no representation, until it became a province in 1815. The discovery of oil in the 20th century has had a positive effect on the economy but, happily, it hasn't changed the peaceful, rural character of the province.

This is a region of archeological interest. In the Netherlands, 54 megalithic tombs have been found – 52 of which are in Drenthe. Called *hunebedden*, they consist of large boulders used by inhabitants 5000 years ago as tombstones. There have also been many bodies and artifacts recovered from the marshy peat bogs of Drenthe, providing archeologists with valuable clues about the ancient people who lived on the ridges and peat bogs of this area.

Drenthe has many recreation centres in the lake regions of Paterswolde, Zuidlaren, Midwolde and Noordlaren. The landscape is varied with clumps of dense forestland interspersed through an endless horizon of fields, heaths and grazing land.

Perhaps because Drenthe has not been a centre of international trade, the old traditions have remained closer to the surface. As a result, folklore and folkloric events can be found in many parts of Drenthe, especially in the summer.

Information: ☎ (0900) 202 2393

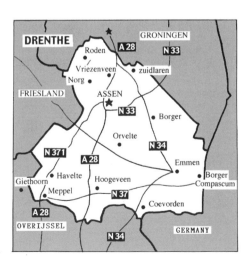

Assen

Provincial capital, and home to the bodies from the bog

Getting there: From Amsterdam, A1 east to Amersfoort, north on A28. From the south, A50 to Arnhem and then north.

Information: VVV, Marktstraat 8, ☎ (0900) 202 2393 or (0592) 314 324

Assen's earliest history has been estimated as beginning about 3000 B.C., according to data obtained from the ancient burial chambers. The Saxons overran the land in the 5th and 6th centuries. By 1024, the area had come under the jurisdiction of the Bishops of the See of Utrecht and was ruled by a governor from the House of Coevorden. It is interesting to note that nuns were the only inhabitants of Assen for 300 years. Their Cistercian convent, Maria in Campis, has played a large part in the history of the town. Assen was known as the 'Town of Palaces' in the 1700s, but is now famous as the home of Rizla & Dutch TT-Circuit Assen with its annual championship motorcycle races that take place at the end of June (www.tt-assen.com). For archeologists, it's known for the mummified bodies found in local bogs.

▶ **Drents Museum – Provincial Museum of Drenthe**
Location: Brink 1
Information: ☎ (0592) 37 7773; www.vvvdrentheplus.nl
Hours: Tues.-Sun. 11am-5pm

In 1897, while digging in a bog, two Drenthe farmers found a blackened body with bright red hair. The farmers dropped their shovels and ran. They were sure they had come face to face with the devil. Science has since confirmed that it was not the devil, but the remains of a 16-year-old girl who was apparently hanged about 2,000 years ago, possibly as a human sacrifice. Today that body is one of several on display in the **Drents Museum**. The 'bog girl' is known as the 'Girl from Yde,' named after the town where she was found. Science has also been able to determine what she looked like before her death, and a wax model of her face is on display. (We have to admit that the blond hair and blue eyes do give a more pleasant face to the mummified body nearby.)

The remains of prehistoric people preserved in the peat bogs for hundreds of years are just a part of the archeological finds on display. There's also the oldest canoe in the world, used in Drenthe some 8,000 years ago. It is a pine log hollowed out with a simple flint axe. The museum has an extensive collection of Dutch art from around 1900, including furniture, glassware and textiles, and beautiful gold jewellery from 400 A.D. There's a high-tech multimedia show about how Drenthe came to be – from the big bang onwards.

The museum building itself is fascinating with its highly ornamented walls, ceilings and fine mosaic work. Part of it is known as the **Ontvangershuis**, an 18th-century residence that is beautifully maintained and furnished. The oldest part dates from the Middle Ages, but a fire in 1676 caused considerable damage and much of the house was rebuilt. There are period rooms with fine furniture, china, needlework and, among other precious items, a collection of early toys.

▶ Also in Assen

The main square in town is the **Brink**, which in old Dutch is 'an open area used as a meeting place' – the same name given to such town squares throughout the country. The **Provinciehuis** (Provincial Hall), originally the chapel and part of the choir of the 13th-century Cistercian Convent, was used as the Town Hall until it was relocated to House Tetrode, a historic building on the Brink. Behind the Town Hall, there's a statue of Bartje – a little boy who is the hero in one of Anne De Vries' novels.

Verkeerspark Assen, de Haar 9, ☎ (0592) 35 0005, www.verkeersparkassen.nl, open April-Oct., daily Apr. 6-11, Apr. 28- Sept. 2, Oct. 12-28; but Apr. 12-27, and Sept. 3-Oct. 12, Wed./Sat./Sun. only, is the largest and most modern 'Traffic Park' in Europe. The midget-sized electrified vehicles (racing cars, autos, motorcycles) are set up so kids can learn the traffic rules on a special circuit. (Many of the instructors speak English.) There are also pedal cars available for driving over the 80,000 square meters of the park. Adults may also drive. It's also possible to tour the park by boat or by train, or operate radio-controlled boats on a pond.

The local woods, the **Asserbos**, has 250 acres of sports facilities and walks. It has deer, a children's farm with lots of animals to pet, and a swimming pool. In summer you can windsurf on Assen's lake.

Eating out

The **Hotel de Jonge** (see below) has a pleasant terrace that is glassed-in for cooler or inclement weather. Next door on the corner is **Café de Passage**, Gedempte Singel 1 (closed Sundays), where all manner of typical Dutch meals are to be had, with a hearty winter pea soup (*erwtensoep*) and delicious mustard soup (*mosterdsoep*). There are several pleasant sidewalk cafés and various places to grab a bite with the family in the Asserbos as well. If you're in the mood for the best ribs this side of Texas – not to mention some of the best steaks in Holland – hightail it out to pard'ner Jim's rural **Ribhouse Texas**, only 11km (7 mi) from Assen, at Hoofdweg 42, Zeegse, (0592) 54 13 60, www.ribhousetexas.nl. With servers in chaps, line dancing performance and peanut shells all over the floor, you'll think that you are in the good 'ol USA. Fred Flintstone rib eye weighs in at 26.5 ounces, but some will prefer the 'Lady's Steak,' a tender filet. Corn on the cob, jacket potatoes, and lobster as well. What are you waiting for? Very pretty drive through the back roads.

Staying over

The **Van der Valk Motel**, Balkenweg 1, ☎ (0592) 85 1515, and **Hotel De Jonge**, Brinkstraat 85, ☎ (0592) 31 2023, are the choices in town. **Witterzomer** camping facilities at Witterzomer 7, ☎ (0592) 39 3535, have been recommended ... 185 acres of space with playground and pool. And for the crème de la crème stay at a stunning Drenthe-style,

1860 farmhouse B&B, head just a bit out of town (10km/6 mi northwest) to the village of **Westervelde** where owner Dirkje Heida will coddle you at **Logement 't Olde Hof**, Olde Hofweg 5-7, with luxurious and well-stocked rooms in the main farmhouse, or in your private cottage, the 'Achterhuis,' a dream haven for up to six people, complete with private sauna; or the thatched-roof honeymoon gazebo, the 'Venhuis,' i.e. along the beautiful fen, with fireplace and outdoor hot tub (note: bathroom 'within walking distance' on this last option). Tennis court, pool, pond, boating, fishing, bicycles, free parking and babysitting make this an unforgettable experience. Book far in advance: ☎ (0592) 61 2733, www.oldehof.nl. (No credit cards, but definitely worth a trip to the bank.)

In the neighbourhood of Assen

At **Balloerkuil**, not far from town near the idyllic village of **Balloo**, provincial meetings were once held in the open air. Legal cases were tried and judgements made here until 1602.

Veenhuizen, west of Assen, has a museum dealing with the prison system: **Gevangenismuseum Veenhuizen**, Hoofdweg 8, ☎ (0592) 38 8264, open April-Sept. 11am-5pm., Oct.-March 1-5pm.

Norg (northwest of town), **Vries** (off N372 north) and **Anloo** (northeast off N34) are all charming and authentic Drents villages with village greens, medieval churches, and typical Saxon farmhouses. Norg also has two windmills and holds horse markets several times a year; Vries has a small bell foundry museum in the cellar of the 12th-century Roman church, the **Klokkengieterij-museum**, Brink 3, ☎ (0592) 54 2770, open by appointment; and Anloo has the oldest church in Drenthe, the **Magnuskerk** – Romanesque, with an 11th-century nave, 13th-century choir and Gothic chapel, ☎ (0592) 34 5044.

There are *hunebedden* (dolmens) in the neighbourhood at **Loon** (northeast city's edge) and at **Balloo** (east), and **Rolde**, (east of Balloo). Also in Rolde is **Collectie Harms Rolde**, Hoofdstraat 38 and Grolloërstraat 8, ☎(0592) 24 2521, www.collectieharms-rolde.nl, an art gallery that features, among others, the works of famed, Dutch still-life artist Henk Helmantel (See ad on page 277).

Roden has a museum of interest to all children. The collection of **Speelgoedmuseum Kinderwereld** (Child's World Museum), Brink 31, ☎ (050) 501 8851, open Tues.-Fri. 10am-5pm, Sat.-Sun. 1-5pm, includes antique children's games, dolls, tin soldiers, trains, books and so on. Let the children experience the toys of olden days in the outdoor play areas...hoops and stilts, a real 'penny-farthing', etc. You might combine this with a visit to **Nienoord Castle**, the carriage museum, at Leek, only 7-8 km (4-5 mi) away (details in Chapter 9).

There's more for the kids near **Beilen** at the **Speelstad Oranje (Orange Playtown)**, Oranje 8, ☎ (0592) 45 8080, open all year daily 10am-6pm, an enormous indoor-outdoor attraction park suitable for kids from 2 to 80! All the fun of the fair with everything from Ferris wheel, bumper cars, giant slides and roller coasters, to innumerable creative activities and sports. Perfect for a rainy day too, as much of it is inside.

HENK HELMANTEL

40 YEARS AS AN ARTIST

Exposition of 70 still lifes and church interiors

Roman glass and chinese skirt on table   22 × 171 cm - Oil on panel - 2001

MUSEUM DE WEEM

Helmantel's private gallery, studio and home
Westeremden, north of Groningen

May through September
Open Thursday, Friday and Saturday afternoons, 1pm - 5pm

Abt Emopad 2 - 9922 PJ Westeremden
Groups by appointment - +31(0)596 55 1415

New art book on Henk Helmantel available May 2007
www.helmantel.nl

Borger
Centre of the 'hunebedden' region
Getting there: On N34 between Emmen and Zuidlaren
Information: VVV, Grote Brink 2a, ☎ (0599) 23 4855

Centuries before the Romans built their great cities, the Greeks their temples, and the Egyptians their pyramids, the people living in this region built relatively simple grave markings that still exist – some 5,000 years later. In Dutch, they are called *hunebedden*. They are giant stones of granite that were somehow lifted, and then propped on top of other, equally large boulders. Mysteriously, almost all the tombs lie in a southwest direction and are entered from the south.

The word *Hondsrug* refers to a ridge of hills between Groningen and Emmen where many of these prehistoric graves have been found. The best route to reach these *hunebedden* is N34, from Emmen on the south and Zuidlaren on the north. Besides being almost at midpoint on the route, **Borger** has the largest concentration of *hunebedden*, and is also where you'll find a fascinating information centre that explains all about them.

▶ Hunebedcentrum – Hunebed Centre
Location: Bronnegerstraat 12
Information: ☎ (0599) 23 6374; www.hunebedcentrum.nl
Hours: Mon.-Fri. 10am-5pm, Sat.-Sun. 11-5pm

The largest of the *hunebedden* in the Netherlands is located here. It has 47 stones and is 20 yards long, with the heaviest stones weighing some 20 tons. Next to it is the **Hunebedcentrum**, which has scale models of various *hunebedden*. Displays explain how the formations may have been built, why they were built, and about the people who may have built them. There is also a collection of pots and other artifacts found in the graves. Children can dress up as Stone Age characters, build their own mini-Hunebed, and crawl inside a scale model thatched-roof house of that era.

In the neighbourhood of Borger

N34 is the route for the *hunebedden* hunter to follow. There are many to be found north of Zuidlaren, and south of Emmen. Finding them though, may not always be easy. Some are well marked and easy to find by following the signs '*hunebedden*,' while others can only be reached by trudging through the woods. Get a map from the Hunebedcentrum.

To the north, two *hunebedden* near **Drouwen**, as well as two near **Eext** and **Gieten** have produced many pots, axes, and other ancient finds. One can be found in a peaceful woodland setting 2 km (1 mi) south of Anloo. **Midlaren** too, has a picturesque example under an oak tree near a small farmhouse. To the south, there are *hunebedden* to be found near **Odoorn** and **Valthe**, while at **Exloo,** as well as *hunebedden*, you'll see lots of sheep with a sheep fold to visit on Hoofdstraat. There's also the museum farm **Bebinghehoes**,

Zuiderhoofdstraat 6-8, ☎ (0591) 54 9242, open May-Sept., Tues.-Sat. 10am-5pm, July-Aug., Mon.-Sat., 10am-5pm, Sun. 1-5pm, April & Oct.-Dec., Wed.-Sat., 10am-4pm.

Zuidlaren is at the northern end. Besides having *hunebedden* in the vicinity, it has the **Laarwoud Estate**, Laarweg 6, ☎ (050) 409 6868, a 17th-century moated house which now serves as the Town Hall; a 13th-century **Dutch Reformed Church** on Kerkbrink; and **De Sprookjeshof**, Groningerstraat 10, ☎ (050) 409 1212, open April-Oct., daily 10am-6pm, a recreation park that the small visitor will enjoy. It has a children's farm, and offers boat tours on the nearby lake, **Zuidlaardermeer**. Zuidlaren also has the largest horse fair in Western Europe on the third Tuesday in October. www.zuidlaardermarkt

Those in the mood for shopping for Delftware – the blue and white pottery for which Holland is famous – should head to a small, local factory/museum, **Royal Goudewaagen**, Glaslaan 29a, **Nieuwe Buinen** (bit difficult to find but worth the effort; use a map or GPS), (0599) 61 6090, weekdays 10am-4pm, where you can buy either first- or second-quality pieces in their shop. The seconds are about half price, and barely a sign of error, but do check. Surprisingly, this factory has produced pottery for Colonial Williamsburg in Virginia, USA, for years – and still does – and you can view some of the sample pieces. Shipping available. www.goudewaagen.nl

Staying over

The area has many campsites and holiday cottages. **De Bloemert**, de Bloemert 1, Midlaren, ☎ (050) 409 1555, is a lakeside camp.

Emmen
Peatfields, grave mounds and woods

Getting there: From Assen take N34 south about 27km (17 mi); from the south, take N34 north from Coevorden.

Information: VVV, Hoofdstraat 22, ☎ (0900) 202 2393

With a population of over 105,000, **Emmen** is the largest city in Drenthe. It is surrounded by huge peatfields, prehistoric *hunebedden* graves, and lovely wooded areas. It is a fascinating, folkloric area to discover, and its major visitor attraction is its popular zoo.

▶ **Dierenpark Emmen – Emmen Zoo**
Location: Hoofdstraat 18
Information: ☎ (0591) 85 0850; www. dierenpark-emmen.nl
Hours: Open daily: March-May & Oct. 10am-5pm; June-Aug. 10am-6pm; Sept. 9am-5:30pm; Nov.-Feb. 10am-4:30pm

The **Dierenpark Emmen** is one of the most attractive and modern zoos in Europe. Visitors mingle with the animals in what are, as near as possible, their natural habitats, with a minimum of railings and cages. You can imagine yourself in the African savannah surrounded by antelopes, zebras, giraffes, rhinos and ostriches, not to mention hippos, Kodiak bears, and Siberian tigers. It has the largest herd of Asian elephants in Europe, with many young. In fact this zoo holds records for the number of offspring reared each year. There are exotic birds, a butterfly house with over a thousand of the creatures fluttering freely about, sea lions in an immense pool, a natural history museum, and the 'Biochron,' where one can take a trip back in time, with fossils showing the evolution of animals. The little ones will enjoy the *kinderboerderij* where they can touch the small animals.

In the neighbourhood of Emmen

If you're fascinated by prehistoric matters, there are at least half a dozen *hunebedden* in the area. The **Emmen Scheermes** is called a 'Long Grave' because of its shape. It is the only one of its kind in the country. Look for the **Valtherbos** (woods), near the Westenesserbosje, if you've not yet seen enough *hunebedden*.

Ter Apel in Groningen, just a little further north, is worth a detour to see the magnificent Dutch Cloister (Chapter 9 has details). There is a fine restaurant opposite the church. To eat under the huge old trees while admiring the impressive architecture of the Middle Ages is also very relaxing.

To the west, **Zweeloo** is an attractive village with large, thatched-roof farmhouses and a pretty 13th-century church. Its side streets are a good place for a peaceful walk through a rural Drenthe community.

Coevorden, about 12 km (7.5 mi) south of Emmen, is one of the oldest towns in Drenthe. Primarily industrial, it retains some of its fortress-like qualities in the few remaining city walls and bastions. **Stedelijk Museum Drenthe's Veste**, Haven 4-6, ☎ (0524) 51 6225, open Tues.-Fri. 10am-5pm, Sat. 10am-3pm, is the local museum.

On the way to Orvelte, take the national road north toward **Schoonoord**, and stop on the way to see a rather special *hunebed*. Professor Cornelis Van Giffen of Groningen restored this ancient burial site in the early 1900s, to show what *hunebedden* really looked like when they were built some 5,000 years ago.

Schoonoord's open-air museum, **Drents Openluchtmuseum Ellert en Brammert**, Tramstraat 73, ☎ (0591) 38 2746, open April-Oct., daily 9am-6pm, tells the story of life in southeast Drenthe a century ago. There's an old country inn, a toll house, peatery, miniature lime kiln, turf huts with sheds, sheep pen with sheep, Saxon farm, old schoolhouse and carpentry shop from 1900, among other interesting things. The legend of two 'giants' is explained in the cave of Ellert and Brammert. Demonstrations of crafts are held during the week starting at 10am. There's also an old **Drenthe Inn** where you can have lunch.

Harmoniummuseum Drenthe
Site of the recreated Veenpark museum village

Getting there:	East of Emmen, close to the German border. From Zwolle, A28 east to N37, then north on N379.
Information:	Berkenrode 4, ☎ (0591) 32 4444; www.veenpark.nl
Hours:	Easter- Oct., daily 11am-4:30pm; July-Aug. 11am-5pm., Sun. 2-4:30pm.

This little excursion off the beaten path is highly recommended. It adds another piece to the puzzle of the history of the region. This reconstructed village shows how the peat dwellers of this area lived and worked. Demonstrations include the actual digging of peat; the baking of tasty bread filled with raisins, some plain and some sweetened with cinnamon and sugar; and the making of wooden shoes. Seeing the many loaves of different shaped breads being put into the outdoor oven paddle-by-paddleful will whet your appetite, making it impossible to resist buying one or more of the warm, fresh loaves.

Start your tour by visiting the Information Centre. If you have squirmy little ones, there is a playground to the right of the entrance. The displays describe the manner of digging peat and how the farmers and their families lived and worked. There are photographs explaining local customs, and a display of tools for collecting the peat. Look for the unusual shoes made especially to cope with the soggy, wet ground – there are even special hoof-pads for the horses so they won't get bogged down in the mushy earth. You'll feel the resilience of the ground when you walk where the demonstration of peat-cutting is being given.

Follow the paths to visit the tiniest, most simple one-room house for family and animals, made out of peat blocks with a steep thatched roof almost touching the ground, and then to a prosperous-looking brick house with several rooms. On entering even the simplest structure, one is surprised how light and pleasant it is.

Animals were even kept in part of the house. The poorest houses only had a little area reserved for them; more prosperous homes had well-defined separate areas, one for the family and one for the animals. Older farms – and there are some beauties in Drenthe – still have this unusual feature. It was a way of conserving heat in winter.

You'll see a large brick house that may have been the local pub; the former store, 'De Boete;' and a flourmill, the 'Korenmolen,' dating from 1870. Don't miss the schoolmaster's two-room house. His 15 or so pupils were probably quite cold in the school next door.

Orvelte
Museum village

Getting there:	On A28 take exit 31; go east on N381; north on N374. Follow signs to Orvelte, which is 25 km (15.5 mi) west of Emmen
Information:	Stichting Orvelte, Dorpsstraat 1a, ☎ (0593) 32 2335; www.orvelte.net
Hours:	May-Oct., 11am-5pm; May, June, Sept., Oct. closed Mon.
Note:	Parking outside the village; only residents may drive in. Your ticket is a small contribution (a 'toll' just as in olden days) which helps maintain the village, and is your entrance ticket.

The beautifully restored Saxon village of **Orvelte**, with its thatched-roof farmhouses and barns, isn't simply an open-air museum. People also live and work here. Before it deteriorated to the point of no return, a foundation was established to preserve the village. In 1974, Orvelte received international attention as a fine example of rural architecture. A surveyor's map from about 1830 was used as a guide in the reconstruction. The folder in Dutch includes a map and describes each building along your route; there's a flyer in English with corresponding numbers, so you shouldn't miss a thing.

Demonstrations usually include rope-making, lace-making, beekeeping, the old method of threshing wheat, and other ancient farming ways. During the holidays, special courses are offered in spinning, candle-making, caning chairs, dough doll-making, etc.

Some children-oriented pleasures include pony rides, a trip on a *huifkar* (a covered wagon used formerly on farms), and a visit to the old Fire Brigade building with its antique fire-extinguishing equipment. There are also lovely organised walks with explanations by a guide who might speak some English.

Eating out

De Schapendrift restaurant offers everything from a cup of coffee to a three-course meal. How about trying the herb drink, *kruiden borrel*? There's also a special berry gin or brandy with raisins!

Staying over

Camping is available in the area and there are several hotels and pensions in town, as well as in the neighboring village of **Westerbork**.

In the neighbourhood of Orvelte

In **Hooghalen** is a former Nazi transition camp from WW II: **Kamp Westerbork Remembrance Centre**, Oosthalen 8, ☎ (0593) 59 2600, www.kampwesterbork.nl, open Mon.-Fri. 10am-5pm, Sat.-Sun. 1-5pm; July-Aug. longer hours on Sat.-Sun. 11am-5pm. Over 100,000 Dutch people, primarily Jews, were brought here from their homes to be packed onto trains bound for Auschwitz or other Nazi death camps. This was the largest transit camp in the Netherlands. Among those imprisoned here was famous teen diarist Anne Frank, who was sent to her death on one of the last trains to leave Westerbork before it was liberated by Allied troops in September 1944. The camp was destroyed after the liberation, but a remembrance centre has been built on the site – a very worthwhile visit. A twisted rail track, serving as a symbolic and grim reminder of the transports, has been placed at the exact spot where the rail line into the camp ended.

Meppel
Gateway to Drenthe

Getting there: On the border of Drenthe and Overijssel. From the Randstad, take A28 to Meppel; from Assen, A28 south.

Information: VVV, Kromme Elleboog 2, ☎ (0522) 25 2888

Meppel is the largest town in the southwest corner of Drenthe, situated close by an extensive group of lakes in the neighbouring province of Overijssel: the **Bovenwijde** where Giethoorn is located, the **Beulakerwijde** and the **Belterwijde**, to name the largest. In addition there are six streams that converge at Meppel, providing extensive opportunities for water sports. The surrounding countryside has a special quality which comes when the sky and the land seem to blend, tied together by shimmering lakes and marshlands – enough to tempt you to leave the car in favour of a bicycle or canoe to explore the beauty of the countryside.

Those six waterways have also contributed to Meppel's reputation as the 'Rotterdam of Drenthe.' This crossroads of waterways has made the town a centre of inland navigation over the years; today it is a prosperous and busy industrial, shipbuilding and shipping, as well as agricultural, centre.

The **Reformed Church** steeple dates from the 15th century. The **Drukkerijmuseum**, Kleine Oever 11, ☎ (0522) 24 2565, open Tues.-Sat. 1- 5pm, focuses on the history of printing and bookbinding.

Staying over

Just off A28, east of Meppel in **De Wijk**, you have the chance to stay at a real castle-hotel, **Chateauhotel de Havixhorst**, Schiphorsterweg 34-36, ☎ (0522) 44 1487, where you will be 'pampered like a prince and princess.' For two centuries, the building was the home of the noble family De Vos van Steenwijk, and has now been renovated into an attractive hotel, complete with fairy-tale moat, www.dehavixhorst.nl. Children will enjoy the local stork sanctuary, **De Lokkerij**, just a five-minute walk through the forest. In Meppel, **Hotel de Poort van Drenthe**, Parallelweg 25, ☎ (0522) 25 1080, is pleasant and moderately priced.

In the neighbourhood of Meppel

Giethoorn, about 8 km (5 mi) west on the Beulakerweide (lake) in the neighboring province of Overijssel is a not-to-be-missed experience. (See Chapter 11 for details.)

Havelte, about 8 km (5 mi) north on N371 has many beautiful, traditional farmhouses as well as some interesting burial mounds. One, the second largest *hunebed* in the Netherlands, was ordered to be taken apart in 1945 for a German airfield to be built. The Dutch who did so, astutely kept the stones and put it back together after the war.

Just south of Meppel are the villages of **Staphorst** and **Rouveen**, known for their somewhat rigid traditional ways – more details in Chapter 11. **Hoogeveen**, to the east, is another straight-laced Protestant town, which still continues an old tradition of calling people to church with the beating of a drum. Nearby is the **Museum de 5000 Morgen** (Museum of 5000 Mornings), Hoofdstraat 9, ☎ (0528) 23 1530, open Tues.-Sun. 1-5pm. Located in a 17th-century mansion, it has rooms that show how a prosperous 19th-century Hoogeveen family lived, including antique tiles and a collection of old peat-digging tools. In the centre of Hoogeveen's main shopping street, Hoofdstraat, is a 250-meter winding and flowing structure known as the **Cascade**. This combination of art and water creates a unique attraction in the centre of town. On a side street, **De Zwaluw**, Van Echtenstraat 47, ☎ (0528) 27 7221, open Fri. 10am-5:30pm, Thurs. 9am-noon, Sat. 9am-3pm, is still in use as a flour-making mill, and has its products available for sale.

The first officially designated National Park in the country lies in the middle of Beilen, Hoogeveen and Dwingeloo. **Dwingelderveld** covers 8,000 acres of fens, ponds, heathland and woods. There are also many animals and rare plants, including juniper bushes for Dutch gin.

Chapter 11 | The province of Overijssel

Overijssel lies between the German border and the IJsselmeer. Its towns along the river IJssel – Deventer, Kampen, and its capital Zwolle – were the economic heart of northwest Europe in the Middle Ages. There are still many reminders of the days when they were major trading communities.

In the northwest (West Overijssel), Staphorst and Rouveen are intriguing villages steeped in rigid religious practices – its inhabitants still living in ways of the past. It also has lake areas with ancient 'peat-villages' like Giethoorn, a 'must-see' on your itinerary.

The 'Salland' is the centre section of Overijssel, a lesser-known region. Unspoilt and peaceful, it has comfortable hotels, campsites and bungalows for those who want to spend time fishing, canoeing, or just visiting its old villages. Deventer is the biggest town in the Salland area.

Lovely woods, ancient towns and interesting castles and manor houses are found in the eastern Twente area, which extends to the German border. It was mostly marshland until 200 years ago and much more accessible from the east, which explains the German influence on the language and architecture. Around the large towns of Enschede, Hengelo and Almelo, there are numerous country hamlets. Some, like Ootmarsum and Denekamp, continue centuries-old Easter traditions such as the lighting of bonfires for religious processions, as well as a colourful Advent tradition of midwinter horn-blowing.

Overijssel's network of waterways – its canals, lakes and rivers – is especially suitable for sports like canoeing. In winter, the sometimes snow-clad scenery is lovely, and the ice skating (although less frequent these days due to warmer winters) is outstanding.

Information: Tourist Office ☎ (0570) 68 0700

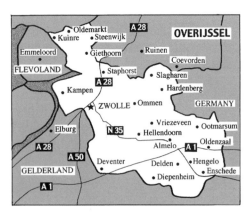

Zwolle
770-year-old market town
Getting there: Highway A28 or A50 direct
Information: VVV, Grote Kerkplein 14, ☎ (0900) 112 2375; www.vvvzwolle.nl

Zwolle, the capital of Overijssel province, has a history going back 770 years. Located on the river IJssel, it was a major trading centre in the Middle Ages. Spared of major wars and natural disasters due in part to its strong fortifications, it has retained its rich architectural heritage. Duke Charles of Gelderland attempted an invasion in 1524, but his army got trapped in the double-gated Sassenpoort. In 1621, Spanish General Spinola too was foiled in his attempt to take the city. Some of the old gates and part of the wall still stand. Throughout the compact city centre ringed by canals are many buildings from Zwolle's prosperous 15th century. Before exploring, ask the VVV for their recommended walking tour.

The five-spired **Sassenpoort**, Sassenstraat 53, ☎ (038) 421 6626, open Fri. 2-5pm, Sat.-Sun. 12-5pm, is one of the old city gates. Built in 1409, it has slit-like openings through which the city's defenders poured boiling oil on attackers. Inside are exhibits on its history. Two other gates are along a canal north of old town, as well as a part of the 15th-century town walls; the **Wijndragerstoren** was occupied by the town's wineporters; and the **Pelsertoren** was where furriers washed skins and furs in the canal and hung them along the wall to dry.

Next to the wall is **Broerenkerk**, Broerenkerkplein, part of a Dominican monastery founded in 1465. It's only open for special exhibits. **Onze Lieve Vrouwekerk**, Ossenmarkt, open Nov.-April, Mon.-Sat. 1:30-3:30pm; May-Oct., Mon. 1:30-4:30pm, Tues.-Sat. 11am-4:30pm, dates from 1395. You can climb its tower, the **Peperbus**. On Grote Kerkplein in the centre of town is the **Grote Kerk**, also known as St. Michael's Church, only open for visits May-October. They commenced this triangular Gothic church in 1406, completing it 40 years later. A 125-meter tower was added in 1548, but destroyed by fire in 1669. Notice the finely carved pulpit from 1620 and the world-famous Schnitger organ (1721) which has 4,000 pipes and four manuals.

Near the Grote Kerk is the **Town Hall**, actually two buildings: the old Town Hall, the 'Weehme' (formerly the 16th-century vicarage of the Grote Kerk), and the new Town Hall. Be sure to see the splendid **Schepenzaal**, Grote Kerkplein 15, ☎ (038) 422 2299, open by appointment only, dating from 1448, where the Council members met and where weddings now take place. The new Town Hall has a beautiful civic hall and council chamber. On the other side of the church is the picturesque **Hoofdwacht** (1614), the old guardhouse for the town's militia. Today it serves as police headquarters. Nearby is the **Karel V house**, Sassenstraat 33. Work started on it before 1555, but by its completion date in 1571, Karel V the German Emperor, had died.

Ecodrome, Willemsvaart 19, ☎ (038) 421 5050, open Oct.-March, Wed., Sat., Sun. 10am-5pm; April-Sept., daily 10am-5pm, is an environmental theme park with a maze, butterfly garden and dinosaur skeleton. The **Stedelijk Museum**, Melkmarkt 41, ☎ (038) 421 4650, open Tue.-Sat. 10am-5pm, Sun. 1-5pm, has period rooms from Gothic times to Art Nouveau.

The **Museum de Fundatie**, Blijmarkt 18, ☎ (0572) 38 8188, open Tue.-Sun. 11am-5pm, is devoted to art not associated with any specific school or movement.

Markets

From the Middle Ages, markets have been a major part of the town's economy. The cattle market on Rieteweg, Fridays 6am-noon, is the largest in Holland. The General Market is on the Grote Kerkplein, Fridays 8:30am-1pm; on the Melkmarkt and Grote Markt, Sat. 8am-5pm.

Staying over

Bilderberg Grand Hotel Wientjes, Stationsweg 7, ☎ (038) 425 4254, is first class, but expensive. Other options: **Mercure Hotel**, Hertsenbergweg 1, ☎ (038) 421 6031; **Hotel Campanile**, Schuttevaerkade 40, ☎ (038) 455 0444; **City Hotel**, Rode Torenplein 10, ☎ (038) 421 8182; or take an apartment for two outside the centre in an old canal house, **Thorbeckesuite**, Thorbeckegaat 34, ☎ (038) 423 1798; or in Blokzijl, another special stop is the hotel **Kaatje bij de Sluis**, Zuiderstraat 1, ☎ (0527) 29 1833.

Eating out

If you want to splurge on one of Holland's best and duly awarded restaurants, venture to **De Librije** (The Library), Broerenkerkplein 13 (very central), ☎ (038) 421 2083, housed in the beamed former library of a 15th-century monastery where owner/chef Jonnie Boer, known for his 'Cuisine Pure' based on fresh, locally produced ingredients, serves it up in style. Reservations essential; closed Sun. and Monday. www.delibrije.nl

In the neighbourhood of Zwolle

At **Staphorst** and **Rouveen** one can see the traditional dress and customs of people from this strict religious community. In contrast to towns such as Marken and Volendam in North Holland province, the people here do not readily welcome 'outsiders,' and taking pictures can be a difficult – even risky – affair. These stern people are highly religious, and do not even approve of riding bicycles on Sundays. They will tolerate visitors on weekdays, but do not point a camera at them! Get a rare glimpse into their culture at the **Gemeentelijke Museumboerderij**, Gemeenteweg 67, ☎ (0522) 46 2526, open April-Oct, Mon-Sat 10am-5pm. In **Slagharen**, the **Attractiepark Slagharen**, Zwartedijk 39, ☎ (0523) 68 3000, open March-Oct. 10am-5:30pm, has all the fun of the fair and is the ideal venue if your kids love horses.

Ommen is in the middle of woods and on the banks of the Vecht. It has four majestic windmills. Two are open regularly: **Den Oordt**, Den Oordt 6, built in 1824, is part of the Streekmuseum Ommen (see below); **De Lelie**, Molenpad 7, open Tues.-Sat. 9am-5pm, Mon. 1:30-5:30pm, was built in 1846. The regional museum, **Streekmuseum Ommen**, Den Oordt 7, ☎ (0529) 45 3487, is open Tues.-Fri. 10am-5pm; Sat. 1-4:30pm, www.museum-ommen.nl. The **Nationaal Tinnen Figuren Museum**, Markt 1 ☎ (0529) 45 4500, is open Mon.-Sat. 11am-5pm, Sun. 1-5pm, and has over 150,000 tin figures set up in dioramas.

288

Kampen
Important 15th-century seaport

Getting there: Take A50 or A28 to N50 north to Kampen
Information: VVV, Oudestraat 151, ☎ (0900) 112 2375

From 1240 until the late 1500s, **Kampen** was a major city. Located on the river IJssel, Kampen prospered as a member of the Hanseatic League, carrying on trade with England, Germany and the Baltic states. Emperor Maximilian bestowed the title 'Imperial Free Town' on Kampen, an indication of its wealth in the late Middle Ages. By 1400 it was the largest city in what is now the Netherlands, with a population four times that of Amsterdam at the time. It reached the height of its prosperity in the 15th century before its harbour silted up and the Spaniards occupied the city. Kampen is now a small town with an attractive old skyline. Its glorious past can be seen in its three city gates, and in some 500 historic buildings that line its streets.

▶ **Oude Raadhuis – Old Town Hall**

Location: Oudestraat 133
Information: ☎ (038) 331 7361
Hours: **Currently closed**; will house the Stedelijk Museum eventually

The city's most impressive building is probably the **Oude Raadhuis**, or old Town Hall. It dates from the first half of the 14th century, and was largely devastated in 1543 but immediately rebuilt. Notice the statues on the facade: Charlemagne, Alexander the Great, Moderation, Fidelity, Justice and Love.

Although you unfortunately cannot view it at the moment, the Aldermen's Room, the Schepenzaal, has hardly been altered in 460 years. Its ornate, stone chimneypiece was made in the 1540s by an out-of-town craftsman, while the adjacent wooden magistrates bench was made by a local cabinetmaker. The local man showed his anger at not being asked to make the larger chimneypiece by carving a satyr on the magistrates' bench...it looks at the stone chimneypiece and laughs cynically at what it sees.

● Near the Oude Raadhuis: The 17th-century New Tower, Oudestraat 146, ☎ (038) 331 7361, generally open summer Sat. 11am-5pm, is worth a look...even with the climb. The **Stedelijk Museum**, Oudestraat 158, ☎ (038) 331 7361, open Tues.-Sat. 11am-5pm, with local history, is in a merchant's home built in Kampen's glory years.

▶ **Also in Kampen**

Kampen has some of the country's loveliest gabled facades and three photogenic town gates. The **Broederpoort** and **Cellebroeders-poort**, both on Ebbingstraat, were built around 1617. The **Koornmarktspoort**, IJsselkade 1, ☎ (038) 331 7361, open during exhibitions or by appointment, has two 14th-century towers. **St. Nicholas' Church**, Koornmarkt, open May-mid-Sept., Mon.-Tues. 1-4pm, Wed-Fri., 10am-4pm, was built around 1400. The **Tobacco Museum**, Botermarkt 3, ☎ (038) 332 5353, is open April-Dec, Thurs.-Sat. 11am-12:30pm & 1:30-5pm.

You can stay at **Hotel van Dijk**, IJsselkade 30, ☎ (038) 331 4925; or **Party Hotel 't Haasje**, Flevoweg 90, ☎ (038) 331 3826.

Giethoorn
The 'Green Venice of the North'

Getting there: North of Zwolle about 25km (15.5 mi) via N331 to N334 continue north; from Meppel, N375 southwest, then N334 north.

Information: VVV, Beulakerweg 114a, ☎ (0900) 567 4637

Known as the Green Venice of the North, utterly picturesque **Giethoorn** is located in a lake area, and is one of the most popular tourist sites in Holland. It is set along a series of canals – the primary means of transportation here, as in Venice – with many of its thatched roof houses surrounded by water. Chances are you'll see the baker, milkman, a wedding party, or even cows going by – all in traditional punts. As you can't drive a car into town (you park just outside in designated areas), you either walk along the canals...or, do as the locals and take a boat.

Giethoorn's history started about 1280 when a group of flagellants, so named as they scourged themselves to atone for their sins, settled here. They were from the Mediterranean region, and believed the day of judgement was near. Few areas accepted their ideas, and they were forced to wander Europe. But the Lord of a nearby castle was sympathetic, and allowed them to remain here.

It seems the settlers found masses of ancient goat horns on the land, so they called their village 'Geytenhorn' (Goat's Horn), which eventually became Giethoorn. In order to pay taxes to the Count, the villagers dug peat and sold it. They worked in a very disorganised way, digging how and where they pleased, with the result that lakes and ditches formed. Canals also had to be excavated to transport the peat, creating little islands on which the houses stood, reachable only by boat or bridge. These canals and bridges give Giethoorn its present storybook appearance.

It isn't easy to find Giethoorn but don't get discouraged. Once there, we recommend you walk or choose from the numerous one-hour boat tours near the parking area. There are also small, low-powered electric motor boats for rent, easy to operate by most landlubbers.

Note: Giethoorn is a photographer's heaven, but gets very crowded in summer.

▶ **Also in Giethoorn**

Even this small village has a choice of museums. **De Oude Aarde**, Binnenpad 43, ☎ (0521) 36 1313, open, March-Oct., daily 10am-6pm; Nov.-Feb., Wed.-Sun. 10am-5pm, has a most interesting collection of semi-precious stones – also in the shape of pins, earrings, tie clips, etc. – from all over the world. **Museum De Speelman**, Binnenpad 123, ☎ (0521) 36 1776, open April-Oct., daily 11am-5pm, has a collection of street musicians' instruments from 1800 to 1925. **Gloria Maris Schelpengalerie**, Binnenpad 115, ☎ (0521)

36 1582, open April-Oct., daily 10am-6pm, has shells and corals. The **Museumboerderij 't Olde Maat Uus**, Binnenpad 52, ☎ (0521) 36 2244, open April-Oct., Mon.-Sat. 11am-5pm, Sun. noon-5pm; Nov.-March, Sun. noon-5pm, is a restored farm showing 150 years of farm life. **Automuseum Histo-Mobil**, Cornelisgracht 42, ☎ (0521) 36 1498, open April-Oct., daily 10am-6pm, displays over 300 model vehicles, with old cars and other transport. There are interesting shops and galleries on the Binnenpad and Zuiderpad.

Staying over

Giethoorn can be a one-day trip even from Amsterdam, but with small children an overnight is recommended. Two possibilities: **Hotel de Pergola**, Ds. T.O. Hylkemaweg 7, ☎ (0521) 36 1321; or **Hotel Grand Café Centrum**, Dominee Hylkemaweg 39, ☎ (0521) 36 1225. For other addresses, including B&B's and camping, for which Giethoorn is an ideal spot, contact the VVV.

Yearly events

Several days in late Aug. is **Gondelvaart**, a special parade with decorated and illuminated gondolas. The village is also enchantingly lit up during this time.

In the neighbourhood of Giethoorn

This is a region of water, woods and small towns not to be missed. **Vollenhove** was built around a bishop's hunting lodge. There are fine historic buildings and splendid facades as well as the ruins of an old castle, **De Toutenburgh**. The town flourished from the Middle Ages as can be seen by its old patrician houses and the area's many large farms. It has a busy harbour where traditional ships, fishing boats and yachts abound.

Blokzijl, once a prosperous Zuiderzee town, has 17th-century homes, the requisite canals, and a popular summer boating harbour, with a cannon from 1813 that was used to fire a warning when the tides rose dangerously high.

Kuinre, another border town off N351, has a **Town Hall** (1776) – formerly an old butter weigh-house – and a number of 17th-century houses.

The water areas surrounding **Oldemarkt** abound in waterfowl, the purple heron, bittern, marsh harriers, and more. Take time to visit the nature reserve, **De Weerribben**, and look out for the old peat-cutters' houses. If you take a boat trip you'll see countless windmills pumping water that irrigates the area.

Steenwijk was once a fortified town. The 90-meter **St. Clemenstoren** (1467), Kerkstraat 22, ☎ (0900) 567 4637 (VVV), can be climbed July-Aug., Tue.-Fri. 11am-4pm, Sat. 10am-3pm. The countryside abounds in natural beauty. You can make boat trips, windsurf and fish. **De Ramswoerthe**, Gasthuislaan, is a deer park. The **Kermis en Circusmuseum**, Onnastraat 3, ☎ (0521) 51 8687, open March-Oct., Tue.-Fri. 10am-4:30pm; July-Aug., Mon. 1-4:30pm, Tue.-Sat. 11am-4:30pm, is a fairground and circus museum with a play area and fair rides. **Stadsmuseum (Oudheidkamer) Steenwijk**, Markt 64,

☎ (0521) 51 1704, open Tue.-Fri. 10am-noon & 1-5pm; July-Aug., Mon. 1-5pm, Tue.-Fri. 10am-5pm, Sat. 11am-5pm, is a local history museum.

South of Giethoorn is **Zwartsluis**, a peaceful aquatic paradise.

Almelo
City with many different faces

Getting there: Almelo is southeast of Zwolle and northwest of Enschede; it is served by highways A1-A35, N36, N35, N349.

Information: VVV, Rosa Luxembergstraat 8, ☎ (0546) 82 8080

Almelo is in Twente, one of the most scenic green areas of Overijssel. It has a modern shopping centre with covered arcades, promenades and squares, yet within minutes is the **Gravenallee** with **Almelo Castle** (no visits) set in the Count's Forest with its lovely walks. (An ideal spot to bike and picnic.)

If you are interested in local history, visit the **Stadsmuseum Almelo**, Korte Prinsenstraat 2, ☎ (0546) 81 6071, open Tues.-Sat. 12:30-5pm; the **Wevershuisje**, Kerkengang 5, ☎ (0546) 85 2701, open Tues.-Sat. 10:30am-5pm, a restored 'town farm' showing different trades in times gone by. An interesting stop for coffee is **Bolletje Winkel en Koffieschenkerij**, Grotestraat Zuid 182, ☎ (0546) 81 5911, open Mon. 1-5:30pm, Tues., Wed., Fri. noon-5:30pm, Thurs. & Sat. 10am-5:30pm, a restored old bakery-cum-café with its own museum, **De Meelzolder** (grain attic).

The bucolic surroundings give you ample opportunity to 'get away from it all' on foot, bike, canoe or even horse – this is horse country. Check with the VVV for castles, ancient churches, gardens and nature reserves, wind and water mills and even astronomical observatories to visit.

In the neighbourhood of Almelo

Hellendoorn is the place for kids at **Adventure Park Hellendoorn**, Luttenbergerweg 22, ☎ (0548) 65 5555, www.avonturenpark-hellendoorn.nl, open April-Oct., 10am-5, 6, or 7pm. There's a monorail, log and white river rafting, sea-lion shows and rollercoaster. **Hengelo** provides yet another stop for the children, at **Recreatiepark De Waarbeek**, Twekkelerweg 327, ☎ (074) 250 4040, open weekends in April and October, 10am-5pm, and daily May through Sept., 10am-5pm, with a variety of rides.

Vriezenveen is an old fen colony. **Veenmuseum Het Vriezenveense Veld**, Paterswal 11, ☎ (0546) 65 8175, open by appointment and for groups, Mon.-Thur. 9am-3pm, Fri. 9am-noon, Sun. 1-4pm, tells about the peat industry. **Museum Oud Vriezenveen**, Westeinde 54, ☎ (0546) 56 3476, open Mon.-Fri. 10am-5pm, tells about the town's history and its textile trade with Russia that lasted 150 years. Look for traditional farmhouses and the nature reserve **De Kooyplas**.

Denekamp
Ancient town set in lovely scenery

Getting there: Northeast of Enschede and Oldenzaal on N342.

Information: VVV, Kerkplein 2, ☎ (0541) 35 5752

The attraction here is **Singraven Castle** (Huis Singraven), Molendijk 39, ☎ (0541) 35 1906, open April -Nov., tours Tues. & Wed. 11am, 2 and 3pm. Purchase your ticket at the watermill restaurant, **De Watermolen** (pancakes and other fare). The castle (1381) contains 17th and 18th-century paintings, Gobelin tapestries and antique furniture. The three-wheel watermill is from the 15th century.

Museum Huize Keizer, Kerkplein 2, ☎ (0541) 35 1003, open Mon.-Fri. 10am-noon & 2-5pm, is a 1900s-style shop and residence. **Museum Natura Docet**, Oldenzaalsestraat 39, ☎ (0541) 35 1325, open Mon.-Fri. 10am-5pm, Sat. & Sun. 11am-5pm, shows natural history. Note the 13th-century **St. Nicolaas** church.

Yearly events

Midwinterhoornblazen, the sounding of the mid-winter horns, is a colourful tradition. No one is sure if it was devised to drive away evil spirits at Christmas or to warn churchgoers of the Inquisition in the 15th century. The two-meter-long horns have five notes that carry far and wide, and are blown between the first Sunday in Advent and Epiphany.

Denekamp also has a special Easter celebration, wherein the townsfolk are led by 'Judas Iscariot' from St. Nicholas church to Singraven. From here an Easter pine tree is dragged to the 'Easter meadow,' its branches cut off and burnt with the trunk in the evening Easter fires.

In the neighbourhood of Denekamp

Ootmarsum is an extremely old town and a magnet for tourists because of its 18th-century-style timbered houses. There's an old town square with a 12th-century church, and three watermills. **Openluchtmuseum**, Smithuisstraat 2, ☎ (0541) 29 3099, open daily 10am-5pm, Dec. & Jan. weekends only, is a 1666 farmstead museum complete with tools and utensils, a wagon-makers shop, blacksmith, apiary and children's farm.

Ootmarsum is the only Dutch town to continue several Easter traditions; the **Pasenoptocht**, wherein children walk through the town carrying palms on Palm Sunday; and **Vlöggelen** on Easter Sunday and Monday, wherein groups of young men parade around the church singing Easter hymns. Their numbers gradually swell and by late afternoon, joined by others, their singing continues through the streets of town. Ootmarsum is also one of a few towns in Overijssel to have a festive **Paasvuur**, an enormous bonfire. Some say these Easter traditions go back as far as the 13th century.

Enschede
Former Saxon town, now the largest in Overijssel

Getting there: A12 from The Hague and Rotterdam, to A50, A1 to A35. From Amsterdam, A1 all the way to A35.

Information: VVV, Oude Markt 31, ☎ (053) 432 3200; www.vvvenschede.nl

Like most towns of significance on the German border, this old Saxon town lost almost all its ancient buildings to wars. A major fire, however, was responsible for destroying most of Enschede in 1862. But thanks to the success of its textile industry in the early 20th century, it is now the largest city in Overijssel.

▶ **Rijksmuseum Twenthe**

Location: Lasondersingel 129

Information: ☎ (053) 435 8675; www.rijksmuseumtwenthe.nl

Hours: Tues.-Sun. 11am-5pm

This museum has a collection of fine and applied arts from the 13th-19th century, as well as modern and contemporary art. Paintings – particularly Dutch paintings – are the core of its important collection. Holbein the Younger, Cranach, Brueghel the Younger and Van Goyen are represented. The religious art collection is of special interest because of its Primitives. Impressionists include Monet and Sisley, and it has Mauve, Israels, and Breitner from the Schools of The Hague and Amsterdam, and Appel, among others, in its Experimental and Cobra collection. There are also sections on Delftware, tapestries, glassware and silver.

▶ **Also in Enschede**

Museum Twentsewelle, a new museum opening at the end of 2007, will feature nature, textiles, fossils, minerals, and more, including innovation. www.twentsewelle.nl

The 15th-century **Grote Kerk** on the market square has 9th-century foundations. It was significantly rebuilt after a fire in 1862 and is open for visits April-Aug, Sat. 1:30-3:30pm, and mid-July-Aug. also Tues. 1:30-3:30pm.

There are 30 parks to choose from here. Little ones may enjoy the children's farm in **Wooldrikspark,** Boulevard/Gronausestraat, ☎ (053) 432 2932, or the **Hoge Boekel,** Hoge Boekelerweg 410, ☎ (053) 461 1378, a playground with midget golf. Adults may prefer the market, Tues. & Sat. 8am-5pm, Wed. & Thurs. 8am-1pm.

Eating out

The **Hoge Boekel,** Hogeboekelerweg 410, ☎ (053) 461 2777, is an option, or if money is no object, go for atmosphere in the old coach house **Koetshuis Schuttersveld,** Hengelosestraat 111, ☎ (053) 432 2866.

Staying over

The **Eden Dish Hotel**, Boulevard 1945 no. 2, ☎ (053) 850 6600, has all the amenities, but the VVV can give you less expensive options.

In the neighbourhood of Enschede

In **Oldenzaal** is the impressive **St. Plechelmusbasiliek**, St. Plechelmusplein, ☎ (0541) 51 4023, open daily 1-4:30pm, mid March-May, Mon.-Sat. 1-4:30pm, June-Aug., Tues.-Sat. 10am-4:30pm, Mon. 1-4:30pm, Sept. & Oct., Mon.-Sat. 1-4:30pm. The 12th-century basilica, made of Bentheim sandstone, has the largest bell-tower in Europe. St. Plechelm, who was Irish, converted the district. He died here in 730. **Museum Het Palthehuis**, Marktstraat 13, ☎ (0541) 51 3482, open Tue.-Fri. 10am-5pm, Sat.-Sun. 2-5pm, is a museum of antiquities.

The Counts of Twickel were very influential in the **Delden** area, and **Twickel Castle**, Twickelerlaan, ☎ (074) 376 1020, open Tues.-Sat. 11am-5pm, is an impressive monument to their wealth and power. The interior cannot be visited; but a walk through its grounds to admire the moats, towers and garden is recommended. Delden's **Grote Kerk**, Market Square, ☎ (074) 376 6363 (VVV), open mid June-mid Sept., Mon.-Fri. 10:30am-12:30pm & 2-4pm, Sat. 2-4pm, was built in 1464. Notice the pulpit, the pew of the Counts of Twickel, and ancient wall paintings. Salt was discovered underground here in the 18th century, hence the **Salt Museum**, Langestraat 30, ☎ (074) 376 4546, open Tues.-Fri., Sun. 2-5pm. Its interesting exhibits include a large collection of salt shakers.

Diepenheim, southwest of Delden, is a lovely town surrounded by five handsome castles. Only one, **Warmelo Castle** and gardens, can be visited, Het Stedeke 11, ☎ (0547) 35 12 80, open May-Aug., call for opening times; Sept., 1st Sun. of the month, 11am-4:30pm. The oldest watermill in Twente, **Den Haller** (13th century), is between Diepenheim and Markvelde, open daily 2-4pm, summer months Tues.-Sun. 11am-4pm.

In **Haaksbergen** the **Museum Buurt Spoorweg**, Stationsstraat 3, ☎ (053) 572 1516, has displays of old trains, and a steam train ride that you can take to Boekelo.

Deventer
Important Hanseatic League town

Getting there: On the A1, take exit 23 north; on the A50, exit 26 east leads to Deventer.

Information: VVV, Keizerstraat 22, ☎ (0900) 353 5355

Deventer was already an important town in the 6th and 7th centuries. Thanks to its location on the river IJssel, it was an early trading centre and important member of the Hanseatic League. By 1400 it was one of the most important market towns in Europe, the main place to obtain such staples as cloth, rye and salt. By 1500 it was also the leading Dutch town in the printing trade. There are still a number of places to visit in Deventer that have historic connections to those prosperous medieval years. The best place to start is the old town square.

▶ Brink – Town Square

The **Brink** is Deventer's town square – as it is in most Dutch towns. Although the markets held here are no longer as important as they were years ago, they still attract a good crowd of buyers and sellers every Fri. 8am-1pm and Sat. 9am-5pm.

The Square's most eye-catching building is the **Waag**, or Weigh House, built in 1528. There's a large pan hanging on its outside wall. When an official of the mint was caught counterfeiting, he was supposedly put in that pan and boiled alive in hot oil. Fastened to the wall, the pan was a warning to others. The holes in it were made by French soldiers who used it for target practice. They occupied Deventer in the early 19th century.

Inside **Historisch Museum Deventer**, Brink 56, ☎ (0570) 69 3780, open Tues.-Sat. 10am-5pm, Sun. 1-5pm, are various exhibits regarding the city's history. One covers theologian Geert Groote (1340-84) a native son, who founded a monastic order to which Erasmus, Descartes and Thomas a Kempis belonged.

Down the street, in two restored 15th-century houses, is the **Speelgoed Museum** (Toy Museum), Brink 47, ☎ (0570) 69 3786, open Tues.-Sat. 10am-5pm, Sun. 1-5pm. It has a collection of Dutch toys, tin soldiers, and mechanical toys primarily from around 1900, as well as model trains chugging down their tracks, dolls and doll houses, and kaleidoscopes and stereoscopes to peer through.

▶ Also in Deventer

The 15th-century **Grote Kerk**, or Lebuinus Church, Grote Kerkhof, ☎ (0570) 61 3744, open Mon.-Sat. 11am-5pm, was built on the foundations of an 11th-century Roman basilica, a crypt of which is still intact. Afternoons in July and August the tower can be climbed. The **Stadhuis** (Town Hall) is opposite the church. It consists of several buildings, the most remarkable of which is the **Landshuis**, built in 1632. Open 9am-5pm, you may enter the hall to see a painting of the town council by native artist and town counsellor, Gerard Terborch (1617-81).

Parts of the twin-towered **Bergkerk**, Bergkerkplein 1, ☎ (0570) 61 85 18, open Tues.-Sun. 11am-5pm, were built in the late 12th century. It's now an exhibition hall for modern art. The area around the church, the **Bergkwartier**, was extensively renovated in the 1960s and 70s. The streets, lined with stately patrician houses, form an interesting medieval pattern.

Staying over

There's a **Mercure Hotel Deventer**, Deventerweg 121, ☎ (0570) 62 4022, just outside of town, and another choice, **Hotel Royal**, Brink 94, ☎ (0570) 61 1880, in the centre of town.

Eating out

In the Middle Ages, Deventer's bakers invented a bread using rye flour, honey and ginger. It was called '*Deventer koek*' and was particularly popular because it didn't spoil during long journeys. You can still buy it today. Try some with a cup of coffee or tea at **Bussink**, Brink 84, a little café on the Square, or take it along on your continued journey.

Chapter 12 | The province of Limburg

Limburg is the most southerly province of the Netherlands, hugging the borders of Germany and Belgium. A scenic area, it changes from farmland and woods in the north, to flat, river and lake-dominated terrain in the centre, and to hilly, undulating countryside in the south.

People lived in Limburg as early as 750 BC. Roman warriors built a settlement (today's town of Maastricht) and wealthy Romans followed, building villas and hot spring baths, planting vines, and mining the hills for marl – a clay used in building. Limburg's strategic position on the river Maas meant it was often a target of invaders.

Following the period of Spanish rule, the regions of the Netherlands developed differently. The north became a maritime trading region; the people spoke Dutch and were Protestant. In the south (Brabant and Limburg provinces) the emphasis was on manufacturing and coal mining; people spoke French and Flemish and were strongly Catholic. Limburgers, as a result, have a strong affinity to the shared past with Belgium and Germany. They appreciate outstanding French cuisine, fine wines and there's a 'joie de vivre' as well as great hospitality here.

Food specialities include an open-faced fruit tart called 'Limburger Vlaai' – delicious when prepared in the traditional fashion. The white asparagus grown here are also delicious.

Information: Call local VVVs listed throughout chapter

Venlo
The asparagus capital

Getting there: From Amsterdam, A2 south around Eindhoven, then A67 east; from
The Hague and Rotterdam, A13 then A16 south to Breda, A58 east to
Eindhoven and A67 east to Venlo.

Information: VVV, Koninginneplein 2, ☎ (077) 354 3800

Venlo's rich history began in 96 AD. It was founded by a man larger-than-life, Valuas, of
the Bructeri tribe. In folkloric events, he and his wife are still depicted as great, colourful
giants. In 1343, Venlo received its city rights from the Duke of Gelder, including the profitable right to charge a storage fee on all goods transported on the Maas before they were
traded. In the 15th century, Venlo joined the powerful Hanseatic League, and thus began a
period of prosperity. Located on the border with Germany, it has been constantly overrun
and repeatedly destroyed by tribal wars and armies over the centuries. It suffered heavy
damage in WW II and, for the most part, its ancient buildings are no more.

On the positive side, Venlo's location has made it a major trade centre, handling one-
fifth of all traffic across the German border. It is also the second most important market
garden region in the Netherlands, with over two million square meters of greenhouses.
The area supplies over 80% of the Dutch production of white asparagus. From May through
June, asparagus is King here, and a main feature in restaurants throughout the area. An
'asparagus route' runs between Roermond and Venlo. You can buy this delicacy in the markets or at farmhouses along the way, directly from the growers. Look for the sign '*Asperges
te koop*' (Asparagus for sale).

Because there are so few ancient buildings remaining in Venlo, those that exist mean a
lot to its citizens. The beautiful 16th-century Renaissance **Stadhuis** (Town Hall) on the corner of Lomstraat and Gasthuisstraat is one example. Don't miss the Council Chamber with
its highly tooled, leather-covered walls.

The 14th-century Gothic **St. Martin's Church**, Grote Kerkstraat in the centre of town, is
also interesting. Constructed between 1597-1600 and later rebuilt in neo-Renaissance style,
it was damaged by fire and again restored in 1955. It is full of important art treasures such as
a 17th-century bronze baptismal font; 17th-century paintings; and richly carved, Baroque
pulpit and choir stalls.

Don't miss the **Romerhuis** (1521) an old merchant's house on Jodenstraat, and **Huize
Schreurs** (1588), an old patrician house opposite St. Martin's.

The modern art museum **Van Bommel-Van Dam**, Deken van Oppensingel 6, ☎ (077) 351
3457, open Tues.-Sun. 11am-5pm, is well-known for its 20th-century paintings and special
Japanese print collection.

Limburgs Museum, Keulsepoort 5, ☎ (077) 352 2112, same hours as above, deals with
regional history and ancient archeology. There are displays of folk crafts, weapons, silver, coins, topographical maps, antique porcelain, glass, and tin, as well as paintings and
period rooms.

Eating out

If you want to splurge, the **Hostellerie de Hamert**, Hamert 2, in Wellerlooi, about 20 km (12 mi) north of Venlo, ☎ (077) 473 1260, is an award-winning restaurant.

Staying over

Venlo has many possibilities, including the **Wilhelmina Hotel**, Kaldenkerkerweg 1, ☎ (077) 351 6251. Check with the VVV.

Yearly events

In early June the **Tour d'Asperges** is organised. This cycling event, with daily distances of 30 or 60 km (19 or 37 mi), takes you past lovely scenery with asparagus fields, and to the best asparagus restaurants. There are various exhibitions about asparagus, from how it's grown to how it's eaten!

In the neighbourhood of Venlo

The **National Asparagus and Mushroom Museum** is north of Venlo in the town of **Horst**. Called **De Locht**, Koppertweg 5, ☎ (077) 398 7320, it's open May-Sept., 11am-5pm, Oct.-April, Tues., Thurs. & Sun. 2-5pm, it shows how mushrooms and asparagus used to be grown. It's housed in an authentic 19th-century farmstead, with a poultry house, herb and flower garden, and a bake house where bread is still made in the traditional way.

In **Arcen**, 10 km (6 mi) north of Venlo, is **Chateau Arcen Gardens**, Lingsforterweg 26, ☎ (077) 473 6020, open May-Sept., daily 10am-6pm; April, Oct.-Nov. 10am-5pm, and year-round for meals. The gardens form a permanent plant exhibition with the rosarium as its focal point, and the interesting grounds extend some 70 acres. The chateau (1750) offers a choice of restaurants.

Northern Limburg has some pleasant old villages such as **Gennep**, **Afferden** and **Bergen** at the edge of the **Leukermeer**, an active water sports centre. The **Peel** is a fine place for walking and appreciating the flat countryside west of the Maas. The river offers many diversions along its banks, including villages like **Tegelen**, known for its pottery, and **Steyl** with its Mission Museum.

Roermond
A centre of commerce

Getting there: Roermond is almost on the German border. Take A2 from the west, picking up N280 at Kelpen.

Information: VVV, Kraanpoort 1, ☎ (0900) 202 5588

Roermond, the most important commercial city in middle-Limburg, is the centre of Catholicism for the area. It obtained its city-rights as early as 1232. It was taken by William the Silent in 1572, but fell to the Spaniards within a few months. A pawn of war under Austria and France, it finally became a part of the Netherlands in 1815.

The main church, **Onze Lieve Vrouwe Munsterkerk**, Munsterplein, open April-Oct., daily 2-5pm, Nov.-March, Sat. 2-4pm, is the major attraction. It was built in 1224 as part of the convent of a Cistercian abbey. Transitional in style (Roman to Gothic), it was restored between 1864-97 by architect Cuypers. Inside is a retable, ornamentally carved in Brabant style, and the tombs of Count Gerard III and his wife Marguerite of Brabant, founders of the abbey. Nearby at the corner of Pollartstraat is a former palace, the **Prinsenhof**, dating from the period of Spanish domination.

The **Cathedral of St. Christopher** on the market square was constructed in 1410 and restored after being damaged in the last war. Notice the statue of St. Christopher, the patron saint of this city and church, on the tower.

The **Stedelijk Museum Roermond**, Andersonweg 4, ☎ (0475) 33 3496, open Tues.-Fri. 11am-5pm, Sat. & Sun., 2-5pm, honours native son Dr. P.J.H. Cuypers (1827-1921), a famous architect whose work includes the Central Station and Rijksmuseum in Amsterdam. Its permanent collection deals with the history of Roermond, and there are often temporary exhibitions.

Golfslagbad de Roerdomp, Achilleslaan 2, ☎ (0475) 34 6500, offers the distraction of a huge pool with wave action, mini-golf and games galore.

In the neighbourhood of Roermond

The **Maasplassen** lakes are directly west of Roermond. These artificial lakes provide a popular water sports centre with ideal conditions for surfers and swimmers. The **Meijnweg National Park** is southeast of town with the **Elfenmeer** campsite conveniently located at Meinweg 1, Herkenbosch, ☎ (0475) 53 1689. Several campsites border the lakes. Further south is the interesting village of **St. Odiliënberg** that we recommend you visit.

Thorn
'The White Town'
Getting there: Southwest of Roermond and west of the river Maas. On A2, take exit 41 and follow the signs south to Thorn.
Information: VVV, Wijngaard 14, ☎ (0475) 56 2761

Thorn is almost overlooked in today's hustle and bustle, but for 800 years it was an independent principality and home to the royal residence of a small kingdom. It is known as 'The White Town' due to the predominance of white painted buildings, and also as the 'Musical Town' because of the musical societies it has always supported.

Before Christianity came to these parts, a tribe of Eburons built a temple dedicated to their idol, Thor, on the site of the present Abbey Church. This may explain the origin of the name 'Thorn.'

Near the end of the 10th century, Count Ansfried, one of the richest and most powerful noblemen of his time, and his wife established a principality here and built an abbey.

They also established a double cloister, one for men and one for women, where they too could spend their last years. Their daughter was the first abbess, perhaps striking an early blow for women's rights. Women from noble and influential families came here and as abbesses and canonesses controlled the city through the management of the Abbey-church. After the French invasion in 1794, however, the Principality of Thorn ceased to exist.

The French occupation perhaps also explains why Thorn has so many white buildings. According to the story, the wealthy women who lived here fled as the French army approached, abandoning their homes to the poorer townsfolk. When the French levied a tax based on the number of windows, doors and chimneys in houses, the townsfolk, rather than paying the tax, took stones from the demolished palace to fill in most of the doors and windows. To cover up the result, they painted the houses white.

A walk around the old town will transport visitors back to the era when aristocratic ladies had everything to say about the town and its famous abbey. There are 22 VVV-suggested sites to discover as you negotiate the cobblestone streets...comfortable shoes are recommended.

▶ Stiftskerk – The Abbey Church of Thorn
Location: Follow 'Centrum' to the old part of town.
Information: VVV, ☎ (0475) 56 2761
Hours: April-Oct., daily 10am-5pm, Sat. 10am-4pm

Begin your visit at the **Abbey Church** and see the slide show (available in English) about the history of Thorn and its abbey. This complex of abbey buildings has been modified structurally throughout the years. The church is the only well-preserved building remaining. Romanesque until 1250, it was rebuilt in Gothic style at the end of the 13th century. Its late-Baroque, 15th-century additions can be seen in the priest's choir; the ladies' choir is 18th-century. The white and gilded Baroque interior accentuates the impression of space, wealth and tranquility. Visit the Gothic crypt under the sanctuary, and two 14th-15th-century apartments.

▶ Also in Thorn
The **Museum Abdijkerk** (Abbey Museum), Kerkberg 2, ☎ (0475) 56 2761, is part of the abbey complex and has the same hours. Fine church silver, paintings of abbesses and canonesses, a fine neo-Gothic reliquary and other church relics are displayed. **Het Land van Thorn Museum**, Wijngaard 14 (also the VVV office), ☎ (0475) 56 2761, open Apr.-Oct., Tues.-Sun., 10am-5pm, Mon., noon-5pm; Nov.-March, Tues.-Sun. 11am-5pm, depicts the musical heritage of Thorn to the present and describes the old principality and its abbey. It also includes the **Panorama Thorn**, a unique, moving, three-dimensional model of Thorn made by the artist Frans van den Berg.

The restaurant of hotel **La Ville Blanche**, Hoogstraat 2, ☎ (0347) 75 0423, offers excellent cuisine; you can also sit outside and watch the passersby. A delightful overnight stop in this very picturesque village.

Heerlen
Roman baths and former coal mining centre

Getting there: Coming from Maastricht, take A2 north to A79 east. From the north and west, A2 south to A76 southeast.

Information: VVV, Honigmanstraat 100, ☎ (045) 571 6200

Around 2,000 years ago the Romans built two important roads that crossed where the municipal library now stands; one from Xanten to Trier, the other from Boulogne-sur-Mer to Cologne. A settlement of merchants and craftsmen built elegant homes and called the town 'Coriovallum.' Flavius established his country seat here on what is now the centre of town. With the passing of Roman fortunes, however, it became an inconspicuous village with the 12th-century **St. Pancras Church**, as it remains today, the heart of **Heerlen**.

In the late 1800s, coal was discovered and everything changed. The sleepy town was full of mines; the sky was smoke-laden; the population doubled in ten years and by the next decade increased some 500%. However, in the 1970s the mines were no longer economically viable and the pits were closed. To survive, Heerlen became an administrative centre, and developed new industries.

▶ **Roman Thermenmuseum – Roman Baths Museum**
Location: Coriovallumstraat 9.
Information: ☎ (045) 560 5100; www.thermenmuseum.nl
Hours: Open Tues.-Fri., 10am-5pm, Sat. & Sun., noon-5pm

The **Thermenmuseum** was built over the only excavation of a complete Roman building in the Netherlands, a 2,000-year-old bathhouse. The bathhouse was the focus of social life in Roman times, and the museum explains its role and how it worked. The ruins are very interesting, as are the models of a potter's oven, a Roman villa, and thermal baths. Utensils, jewellery and earthenware discovered in the region from the Roman period to the present are on display.

▶ **Also in Heerlen**
The **Stadsgallerij Heerlen**, Bongerd 18, ☎ (045) 577 2210, open Tues.-Fri. 11am-5pm, Thurs., 11am-8pm, Sat.-Sun. 1-5pm, has a collection of modern Dutch art and special exhibits. Another stop of interest is the observatory **Explorion Science Centre**, Schaapskooiweg 95, ☎ (045) 563 0101, www.explorion.nl, open Wed.-Fri. & Sun. 1-5pm, also Fri.

evenings 7:30-10pm. Everyone will enjoy the heathland walks, and the **Sheep and Shepherd Educational Centre** at **Brunsummerheide**, Schaapskooiweg 99, ☎ (045) 563 0355, open Tues. & Thurs. noon-5pm, Wed., Sat., Sun. 10am-5pm.

In the neighbourhood of Heerlen

North of Heerlen in **Hoensbroek** is **Hoensbroek Castle**, Klinkertstraat 118, ☎ (045) 522 7272, open daily 10am-5:30pm. It's the biggest and most impressive castle between the Maas and Rhine rivers, built in five phases between the 13th and 18th centuries. On display are antique furniture, a tin and copper collection, 16th-century pottery, period rooms, armouries and more. Every Easter the castle is set up as it was when the lord, his family and staff lived here, with everyone dressed in period costume and performing the daily activities of the time.

Kerkrade is known for **Botanische Tuin Kerkrade**, St. Hubertuslaan 74, ☎ (045) 541 5615, open Mon-Fri 9am-5pm, Sun 11am-5pm; Oct.-Mar closed Sat-Sun. This 4-acre botanical garden highlights Limburg flora. **Industrion**, Museumplein 2, ☎ (045) 567 0809, www.industrion.nl, open Tues.-Sun. 11am-5pm, is an industry museum, showing the machines and objects used in coal mining, the chemical industry, the making of roof tiles, etc. It's a hands-on museum that shows how it felt to work in a 1930s metal factory, or live in the home of a labourer. An old-fashioned steam train runs from **Schin op Guel** via **Simpelveld** to Kerkrade.

The **South Limburg Steamtrain Company**, or ZLSM, Stationstraat 20, Simpelveld, ☎ (045) 544 0018, runs year-round through the hills of southern Limburg. Its station has a 1920s-style restaurant and a museum.

Rolduc Abbey, just east of Kerkrade, is well worth a visit. Founded in 1104, this impressive Romanesque building has many lovely carvings. Its cloverleaf contains the sarcophagus of a young priest, its founder. Call the Kerkrade VVV, ☎ (0900) 9798, for opening times.

Eating out and staying over

The **Hotel Brughof** and **Restaurant Kasteel Erenstein**, Oud Erensteinerweg 6, ☎ (045) 546 1333, is a deluxe stopover. This castle hotel-restaurant has a fitness centre with sauna and other amenities. The 14th-century castle is situated in a park and the restaurant is said to be one of the best in the Netherlands.

At **Landgraaf**, Northeast of Heerlen, VVV, ☎ (0900) 9798, horse lovers will find 'manèges' and trails through the woods – for bikers too.

Valkenburg
Land of caves, castles and health resorts

Getting there: Take A2 to A79, go east to the Valkenburg exit. Maastricht is about 11 km (7mi) southwest on a local road.

Information: VVV, Th. Dorrenplein 5, ☎ (0900) 9798; www.vvvzuidlimburg.nl

It's believed the Romans had a small settlement here, and that they mined the unusual clay soil for marl, a material they used for construction. But it wasn't until 1040 when the town began to grow, and the castle was completed that Emperor Henry IV granted **Valkenburg** a town charter. Ruins of the castle are still visible on a hillside overlooking the town.

Mining continued, and by the 19th century the caves created by the miners were a curiosity for tourists. Later, wealthy visitors from Germany, Belgium and France came to Valkenburg to enjoy the healthy air and take the water. It became Limburg's primary recreation area thanks to its castle, its caves, and its health-oriented facilities.

Those are still reasons to visit Valkenburg today – its caves, its castle (one of several in the vicinity) and the spring waters below its surface, which made Valkenburg the first town in the country to win the right to call itself a 'spa.'

Valkenburg is buzzing with visitors, summer and winter. If you plan to stay the night, make reservations in advance, particularly during the holiday season.

▶ **Valkenburg Castle & Fluweelengrot**

Location: Grendelplein 13 and Daalhemerweg 27

Information: ☎ (043) 609 0110; www.kasteelvalkenburg.nl

Hours: Castle: Oct.-Mar. 10am-4:30pm; Apr.-Sept. 10am-5:30pm; Cave: Nov.-Mar., tours Mon.-Fri., at 11am & 1pm, Sat. & Sun. 11am-3pm; Apr.-June & Sept.-Oct. 11am-4pm, tours every hour; July-Aug. 10:30am-4:30pm, tours every half hour

High on the hill overlooking Valkenburg are the remains of the once-proud, 12th-century castle belonging to Walram of Arlon, a noble and major landholder who retained his independence until the French period. Practically destroyed through decades of war, the ruins still give a good impression of how the **Valkenburg Castle** looked, and offer a fine vantage point for a view of the surrounding countryside. A secret passageway leading to the **Fluweelengrot** (Velvet Grotto) was discovered in the 1930s. It was put to good use during the 1940s when it sheltered hospital patients and was a wartime hiding place for the resistance.

Other castles in Valkenburg: The Provincial VVV offices are in the **Kasteel Den Halder**, Wilhelminalaan, which in the 14th century served as part of the city's defensive wall. The present structure was built around 1635. **Kasteel Oost**, Oosterweg, is now a party centre. Built in the 16th century, much of it was rebuilt in 1830. **Kasteel Genhoes**, Oud-Valkenburgerweg, goes back to the 11th century. Burned down in 1577 during the

80 Years War, it was rebuilt in the 17th and 18th centuries. Many other castles in and around Valkenburg are now hotels; see 'Staying Over.'

▶ **Gemeentegrot – Town Cave**
Location: Cauberg 4
Information: ☎ (043) 601 2271; www.gemeentegrot.nl
Hours: Generally, 11am-4pm; for details check the website.

This cave, the **Gemeentegrot**, dates back about 2,000 years. The Romans first discovered marl as a building material, and that the hills around Valkenburg were rich in it. Over the years, stone continued to be taken from the mine so that when the mining stopped, the town was left with a maze of underground passageways. There are two ways to visit the Gemeentegrot, on foot (60 minutes), or on a small train (30 minutes). In both cases a tour guide will lead the group.

Somewhat eclectic, the cave is well worth a visit. You will see subterranean passages that go off in all directions, evidence of prehistoric fossils, and layers of shells – some of which are 100 million years old! The remarkable natural phenomena include an underground lake – light green and 'glowing' – and water that drips with clockwork regularity through the roof. In addition, as you proceed through the cave you will see sculptures and wall paintings (some from the 12th century and some present-day additions). (Wear comfortable, warm clothing.)

Other caves in Valkenburg: The **Steenkolenmijn** (Coal Mine), Daalhemerweg 31, ☎ (043) 601 2491, www.steenkolenmijn.nl, see website or call for opening times and tours, is a replica of a coal mining cave. It is designed to be as realistic as possible, showing how coal was mined in Limburg before it became uneconomical. The real mines are some distance from town, but this cave was chosen for the museum partially because its marl walls were easy to cut. What was created was a model mine, so realistic that it is considered a cultural and historic monument, an example of industrial archeology. Loudspeakers project sounds one would hear under real working conditions: the thunderous roar of explosions, trains rumbling down the tracks, and excavation machines at work. Well-lighted and warm, ex-miners guide visitors on a 75-minute visit which includes a fossil museum; you can even see the largest known lower-jaw of a Mosasaurus (185 cms).

The **Roman Catacombs**, Plenkertstraat 55 (in the Rotspark), ☎ (043) 601 2554, open Apr.-Aug., daily 11am-4pm; Sept.-March, Sat.-Sun. 2pm tour, is a faithful reproduction of parts of the best-known Roman catacombs. They were laid out around 1910 under the guidance of Dutch architect P.J.H. Cuypers.

In addition there are all sorts of activities at **Rotspark**, including a theatre in the woods, and a cable car to **Wilhelminatoren**...the views are superb. **Valkenier Fun Park**, Koningswinkelstraat 53, ☎ (043) 601 2289, has attractions that include autoscooters, a roller-coaster, House of Horrors, mini-car circuit, toboggan run, playground and restaurant.

Valkenburgs Grottenaquarium (Grotto Aquarium), Trichtergrubbe 2, ☎ (043) 604 2929, open Easter-Oct., 11am-4pm, July & Aug. 10:30am-4:30pm, is a cavern with piranha, crocodiles, an electric eel and more in 35 aquariums hewn out of the cave's walls. The **Lourdes Grotto** (near the Gemeentegroot) is a copy of its famous French counterpart.

▶ **Thermae 2000 – Spa**

Location:	Cauberg 27
Information:	☎ (043) 609 2000; www.thermae2000.nl
Hours:	Daily 9am-11pm

Thermae 2000 is an extraordinary Roman-type spa. It is situated on top of the Cauberg overlooking the countryside, as well as over a 40,000-year-old underground water reservoir. Three wells have been drilled to make use of the pure mineral-rich water. One provides fresh drinking water for those wanting to 'take the cure,' while the other two supply warm thermal waters for the baths.

The sauna complex includes steam baths, eucalyptus and sauna cabins, a solarium and indoor and outdoor pools connected by water-filled corridors, so one can swim from one bathing area to the next. The 33° waters contain sodium chloride and fluorine.

You can be as active or as passive as you wish. There is a yoga-meditation centre under a glass pyramid, hydro gymnastics, and massage. Outdoor walking paths take you through the botanical garden, or along wooded hillsides.

Made almost entirely of glass, it offers splendid views of the valley below. For overnight stays the **Thermaetel**, ☎ (043) 609 2000, has a direct link with the baths at Thermae 2000. The restaurant **'t Hooght**, ☎ (043) 601 2048, has excellent views from its terrace, as well as healthy choices on its menu. Also on top of Cauberg is **Holland Casino**, Kuurpark Cauberg 28, ☎ (043) 609 9600, open daily, noon-3am.

▶ **Also in Valkenburg**

Valkenburg's charming 1853 railway station is the oldest still in use in the Netherlands. There are two old town gates, the **Berkelpoort** (east) and the **Grendelpoort** (west). **Streekmuseum Land van Valkenburg**, Grotestraat C31, ☎ (043) 601 6394, open Tues.-Fri. 10am-5pm, Sat. & Sun. 1-5pm, has rooms dedicated to religious, castle, and local militia memorabilia. The **Theme Park Sprookjesbos**, Sibbergrubbe 2A, ☎ (043) 601 2985, has fairy-tale woods; an African theme park section with elephants, lions, etc.; an American section with a Wild-West show and a saloon snack bar; as well as water rides, bumper boats and a laser show.

Markets

Market day is Mon. 9am-12:30pm, Walramplein. In mid-November and December. the Gemeentegrot and Fluweelengrot hold Christmas markets. You can see traditional candle-making in the cellar of the **Restaurant 't Jachthoes**, Muntstraat 10, ☎ (043) 601 3737, and make one on your own.

Eating out

One eats well in this town; there is a café or restaurant at every turn. **Restaurant Lindenhorst**, Broekhem 130, ☎ (043) 609 0345, is small and intimate with an excellent menu. **Kasteel Wittem** (Wittem Castle), Wittemerallee 3, ☎ (043) 450 1208, 10 km (6mi) southeast of town, has a cosy cocktail lounge, and their menus include a gastronomic seven-course meal (wine included) for the gourmand. The Wittem boasts a fine pastry chef and excellent wine cellar.

Should you want to try some traditional Limburg *vlaai*, the **Botterweck Banket**, Grotestraat Centrum 51, is a good choice. *Vlaai* is a flan, filled with a custard or fruit, and is a speciality of the Limburg area.

Staying over

There are so many choices in Valkenburg, the VVV can best recommend a suitable hotel according to availability and price. A moderately-priced, first-class hotel, is the **Parkhotel Rooding**, Neerhem 68, ☎ (043) 601 3241, with indoor swimming pool, lovely grounds, and a wooded area close by.

Of special note are the area's castle-hotels, which are generally expensive. **Kasteel Geulzicht**, Vogelzangweg 2, Berg en Terblijt, ☎ (043) 604 0432, was built around 1850 and has been a hotel since 1937. Some rooms come with a private whirlpool/sauna. The moated **Kasteel Schaloen**, Oud Valkenburgerweg 5, ☎ (043) 407 7400, is over 650 years old. It was badly damaged in the 80 Years War between Holland and Spain. **Chateau St. Gerlach**, Joseph Corneli Allee 1, ☎ (043) 608 8888, is a 5-star luxury hotel with apartment suites for longer stays, with restaurant, indoor pool and spa. There are also castle hotels in Kerkrade, Wittem and Vaals.

At **Epen**, on the Belgian border, is the 4-star **NH Zuid Limburg Hotel**, Julianastraat 23a, ☎ (043) 455 1818. The green countryside can be enjoyed from the terrace or balconied apartments (with kitchenettes). Like many hotels in Limburg, this one has special culinary weekend arrangements.

Tours

Stadsrondritten Otermans, ☎ (043) 601 4941, has half-hour bus tours of Valkenburg; departure from the Grendelplein. Cycling is very popular in the area. Valkenburg has hosted Tour de France events and the World Cycling Championship. The VVV can suggest cycling routes for budding 'champions,' and others for the rest of us. If you prefer to get off track, **Valkenburg Aktief & Sportief**, ☎ (043) 604 0675, can guide you on a bike ride through a cave! However, a minimum of ten people is required to book a trip. Gather up some locals or other tourists, maybe.

In the neighbourhood of Valkenburg

Margraten is the site of the **American Cemetery**, Rijksweg, open daily 9am-6pm, a worthwhile stop to briefly remember the 8,301 Americans buried here who died in 1944-45 during the battles in southeastern Holland. Each Memorial Day weekend, services are held to honour those who fell. Dignitaries, including the Queen's Commissioner, the US Ambassador and ranking generals, come from The Hague, Amsterdam, Germany and the United States to participate. It is touching to see the children from surrounding villages bringing flowers and standing by 'their' grave – representing their grandparents' generation, the Dutch who housed the US soldiers and got to know them briefly before they perished in the common cause. This is the only American WW II cemetery in the Netherlands.

Further east in the wooded area of **Gulpen** is **Kasteel Neuborg**, Riehagar-voetpad (footpath) , a 14th-century castle with a moat and drawbridge. Only its courtyard is open to the public. In nearby **Wijlre**, 17th-century **Kasteel Wijlre** has a charming, cobblestoned inner courtyard. Between Wijlre and Wittem is 15th-century **Kasteel Cartils**, not open to the public, but if you'd like to eat inside a watermill there's the **Neubourgermolen**, Molenweg 2A, ☎ (043) 450 3963. Built in 1712, it is the largest in the country. There is also a *pannekoek* restaurant, a typically Dutch affair that features all manner of pancakes, both sweet and savoury.

There are two recreation parks in Gulpen that your family may want to discover. **Rocca Klim**, Lansraderweg 13, ☎ (043) 450 4747, is a climbing and adventure centre where you can scale sheer walls, take a jump on a bungee cord, or ride a bike up a mountain. **Mosaqua**, Landsraderweg 11, ☎ (043) 450 7400, is a water paradise. Its 25-meter outdoor pool has a 90-meter waterslide and wildwater area; also whirlpools, solariums, steambaths, fitness area, and a children's pool. The **Gulpener Beerbrewery**, Rijksweg 16 (call the VVV for reservations, (0900) 9798) let's you watch the beer-making process.

Further east in **Wittem** is the 11th-century **Kasteel Wittem** (see previous 'Eating Out'). William the Silent lived here for a while, having captured it in the 80 Years War. Set in a small private park with swans on its moat, it also offers country walks, and an excellent hotel and restaurant.

Vaals is in the extreme southeastern tip of the Netherlands. Here you can ride an elevator (or climb 223 stairs) to the top of **Boudewijntoren**, ☎ (043) 306 1019, and afterwards impress people with the fact that you once saw three countries at one time. This is **Drielandenpunt**, the point where Belgium, Germany and the Netherlands come together. It is also where the **Vaalser Berg** soars 1059 feet (353 meters) above sea level. Not very high perhaps, but in a country with an average elevation of 37 feet (11 meters), this is the highest point in the Netherlands. The largest maze in Europe is also here. The **Labyrint**, ☎ (043) 306 5200, open Apr.-Oct., daily 10am-6pm, challenges you to reach its centre and exit through its high-hedged paths. Vaals also has glass-blowing demonstrations by **Gerardo Cardinale**, Tentstraat 2, ☎ (043) 306 2596, Tues.-Sun. 11am-4pm on the hour; no demonstrations Jan./Feb. For a small fee, visitors can blow their own glass. Ancient and modern glass is on display. Vaals also has two castle hotels: **Kasteel Vaalsbroek**, Vaalsbroek 1, ☎ (043) 308 9308; and **Kasteel Bloemendal**, Bloemendal-straat 150, ☎ (043) 365 9800.

We haven't yet mentioned the natural beauty that surrounds Valkenburg. The town is built on the river **Geul** that flows under its bridges past cafés and parks. Explore the Geul area south of Valkenburg with its hidden villages, woods, castles and small farms. Some of the small old villages are **Sibbe**, **Vilt**, **IJzer**, **Oud-Valkenburg**, **Geul**, **Hoathem**, **Bocholtz**, and **Walem**. The VVV has a variety of country accommodations for those who want to 'get away from it all.'

Maastricht
City with a lively Roman influence

Getting there: A2 from Amsterdam; from Rotterdam and The Hague, direction Eindhoven, then A2 south to Maastricht. Parking is difficult, use the Vrijthof (city centre) underground parking

Information: VVV, Kleine Staat 1, ☎ (043) 350 6262, www.vvvmaastricht.nl

Maastricht is the capital of Limburg, with all that implies – bustling streets, a lively international atmosphere, pavement cafés, good food and good shopping, yet 20 centuries of history, with art, culture, historic buildings and tradition to match. Its wealth of churches, mansions and treasure houses bear witness to its prosperous past, while the remains of the city walls and fortifications are relics of the turbulence that came with it.

Maastricht won world attention in 1991 when representatives of 12 European countries met here to sign an agreement to establish the European Union and to launch a common currency. Being in the centre of a changing Europe is nothing new for this city. Some 2,000 years ago it was an important Roman outpost called 'Mosae Trajectum,' implying that it lay at the junction of the river Maas with roads leading to other Roman settlements. Merchants, farmers and traders gathered at this point and business burgeoned. The outer walls were built in 1229, but the town grew so rapidly that they had to build a second wall in the 14th century.

Maastricht was a rich prize, and repeatedly came under siege by the Dutch, Spanish and French. In 1795, the French made it a provincial capital. After Napoleon's defeat at Waterloo, Belgium and the Netherlands were united under King William I. They battled constantly, however, and nine years later a partition was agreed upon, under which Maastricht remained a Dutch city.

Today, Maastricht is a vibrant cultural, educational and political centre full of *bon vivants*. Ceramics, paper, beer and cement are its main products. Students from the six universities in the area add to the city's vitality. Walking is the best way to get to know this city whose lovely centre is a declared 'protected area.' Maastricht is also rich in ancient churches with outstanding collections of religious art. The VVV has detailed walking tours to help you find the historic and modern sites, exploring the old city walls in the process. (See top photo, page 311.)

▶ **Basilica of St. Servatius**
Location: Keizer Karelplein 6
Information: VVV, ☎ (043) 350 6262
Hours: Daily 10am-5pm, Sun. 12:30-5pm

This Medieval cruciform basilica is on the site of a 6th-century Roman 'sanctuary,' its heart dating from ca. 1000. The crypts (11th and 12th centuries) hold the remains of St. Servatius, Maastricht's first bishop. Note especially the Emperor's Gallery and Hall (impressive columns); richly sculpted Gothic south portal (Berg Portal); 16th-century paintings and columns in the choir; and St. Servatius' tomb. The Treasury has a rich collection of relics, paintings, figurines and old Eastern fabrics. Most magnificent are the 12th-century relics of St. Servatius, the saint's bust sculpted in 1579, and some of his possessions. The Grameer, the nation's largest bell, hangs in the south tower of the west wall.

• **Near the Basilica of St. Servatius:** Situated next door is **St. Janskerk**, Henrie van Velde-keplein, open Easter to end-Oct., Mon.-Sat. 11am-4pm. Built in the 14th century as a Catholic parish church, it has been Protestant since 1633. It boasts a Louis XVI pulpit and some fine tombs, as well as a beautiful tower, 70-meters high. There's no charge to visit the church, but there is a small fee to climb the tower for a view of Maastricht.

Behind the two churches is the **Vrijthof**, a large square lined with shops and restaurant terraces for outdoor dining. At one time, executions took place here. Pilgrims also gathered here to view the relics of St. Servatius. The **Spanish Government House**, Vrijthof 18, ☎ (043) 321 1327; open Wed.-Sun. 1-5pm, is also on the square. It dates from 1545 and was the residence of the dukes of Brabant and the Spanish rulers. There are period rooms in Dutch, French, Italian and Liege-Maastricht styles; collections of art and artifacts; crystal chandeliers; statues and figurines and other 17th-century artifacts.

Town Hall, Markt 78, open Mon.-Fri. 8:30am-12:30pm & 2-5:30pm, is further north on the **Markt**, another large square. It was built around 1660 by architect Pieter Post. Two men ruled the city at the time, and each thought they should be the first to climb the stairs to city hall. The solution was to build a double staircase, allowing them to climb at the same time. Note the murals, archway decorations and rococo plastered ceilings as well as the paintings and fine Gobelin tapestries. The carillon tower (1684) has 49 bells that are played on Saturdays. The statue you see nearby with the burning flame honours Maastricht scientist S.P. Minckelers who invented gas lighting.

Between the Markt and the Vrijthof is the **Dominican Church** on Dominicanerplein, a 13th-century sandstone church. The remains of wall paintings on the arched roof, date from 1337 (north aisle) and 1619.

North of the Markt is **St. Matthias' Church**, Boschstraat 99, open daily 8am-6pm & 7-9pm. This church, which dates from the 14th-16th century, was financed primarily by the cloth weavers' guild. It has a beautiful 15th-century Pieta.

The **Dinghuis**, Kleine Staat 1, is down the street from the Markt. Built in 1470, it was the seat of the Chief Justice and is now home to the VVV. It has a beautiful stone gable and timbered wall on the Jodenstraat side of the building.

The **Museum De Historische Drukkerij** (Historical Printing Museum), Jodenstraat 22, ☎ (043) 321 6376, guided tours March-July & Sept.-Nov., Fri. & Sat. 1-5pm, is a printing shop dating from 1900 – its old printing presses still in operation.

▶ **Onze Lieve Vrouwe Basiliek – Basilica of Our Beloved Lady**
Location: O.L. Vrouweplein 20
Information: ☎ (043) 325 1851
Hours: Easter-Oct. Tues,-Sat. 11am-5pm, Sun. 1-5pm

Onze Lieve Vrouwe Basiliek is perhaps the oddest-looking church in the Netherlands. Its tall brick facade with hardly any windows, and its two turrets make it look more like a fort than a place of worship. In fact, it has been both. In a city that has been under siege 21 times in its history, Onze Lieve Vrouwe Basiliek served both a spiritual and a practical function as part of the city's defenses.

The west wing and crypts are the oldest parts of this 12th-century medieval basilica. The structure was built on Roman foundations and enlarged, altered and restored a number of times. The west wing and the choir are of special architectural significance. Notice the impressive columns, the richly sculpted capitals surrounding the choir, the cloisters and the crypts. The Treasure-House can be entered through the church on O.L. Vrouweplein. It has a rich collection of ecclesiastical art and artifacts, including richly embroidered garments.

Also of interest is the Stella Mare Chapel, with its 500-year old statue of Mary. In the 1600s the statue was credited with numerous miracles. As many as 20,000 people a year made the pilgrimage to Maastricht to pray before it.

▶ **Derlon Museum**
Location: Plankstraat 21. Lower floor the Derlon Hotel.
Information: VVV, ☎ (043) 350 6262
Hours: Open Sun. noon-4pm

Construction of the Derlon Hotel began in 1983 in the oldest part of the city, on what was a garden at the time. Luckily, the city's archeologists were on their toes when they surveyed the site. What they found, buried below six meters (20 feet) of soil and other deposits that had accumulated over the centuries, were the remains of a Roman settlement. Instead of destroying the ruins, or cancelling the building project, they decided to incorporate them into the hotel's design.

They are now a popular attraction, well displayed in the hotel basement. You will see part of a 2nd and 3rd-century square, a section of a 4th-century wall and gate, a 3rd-century well, and part of a pre-Roman cobblestone road. Additional artifacts are displayed in illuminated glass cabinets. There's an information sheet with details about the survey find and the display.

- **Near the Derlon Museum:** The **Stokstraat Kwartier** runs from just south of the VVV office, after the St. Servaas Bridge, to the area of the Derlon Hotel. It should be explored on foot to admire the restored period houses of the 17th and 18th centuries, and to 'appreciate' the many fine shops.

▶ **Bonnefanten Museum**

Location: Avenue Ceramique 250
Information: ☎ (043) 329 0190; www.bonnefantenmuseum.nl
Hours: Open Tues.-Sun. 11am-5pm

Bonnefanten Museum sits like a thick silver space missile on the east bank of the Maas across the water from the old town centre. This modern design, by Italian architect Aldo Rossi, houses some ancient finds – including Limburg archeological relics as old as 250,000 BC. But archeology is only one part of the museum. It also has a collection of sculpture, paintings, earthenware and silver from the 14th to 17th centuries, as well as temporary exhibits of contemporary art. Visitors may enjoy the large-scale model of Maastricht. The original maquette made in 1752 is at the Hotel des Invalides in Paris.

- **Near the Bonnefanten museum:** One pleasant walk is east into the Wijk area over the **St. Servaas Bridge** (1280-98). Originally a 9-arched wooden bridge, it is one of the oldest in the Netherlands. Having crossed it, turn left on Oeverwal to **St. Martins Church** (1858) on St. Maartenslaan. Designed in Gothic-style by P.J.H. Cuypers, it replaced an older church. Go inside to see 'The Black Crucifix,' a life-size image of Christ made of walnut. Further south, along part of the medieval ramparts, note the **Water Gate** along the stone wall and the **Meuse Tower** on the Maaspuntweg, both 13th century. Walking east from the water tower along Hoogbrugstraat, you will come to the Monumentale Panden, a former place of refuge of the deanery of Meerssen (1690). Across the street is **St. Gillishofje**, almshouses dating from 1759. Walking back along Rechtstraat, note the interesting facades and gable stones.

Centre Ceramique, Avenue Ceramique 50, ☎ (043) 350 5600, is a state-of-the-art library offering young and old the opportunity to use the latest communications and media technology. It has some 80 computers, English books, CD-ROMs, the city archives, and an exhibition area with maquettes of Maastricht's development to date.

▶ **Fortifications of Maastricht**

Location: The old city walls that are still intact are on the south and east edges of the old city centre. On the south, the walls run in the vicinity of Nieuwenhofstraat and St. Pieterstraat; on the east, they overlook the Maas River just south of Vrouweplein.

Information: VVV, ☎ (043) 350 6262

For 1500 years, Maastricht residents put up walls to protect their strategically-located city. The Romans built walls in the 4th century, but those remaining in Maastricht today were built in the 13th century and after. The walls are of interest to military buffs, but also to anyone who enjoys a nice walk through some interesting parts of the city. The VVV has a 'Fortifications Walk' brochure, a self-guided walk that takes you on top and alongside the walls, and past most of the sites such as the **Helpoort (Hell Gate)**, St. Bernardusstraat 1, ☎ (043) 325 7833, open Easter-Oct., daily 1:30-4:30pm. Set in the best-preserved section of the city wall that was built in 1229, it is the only gate in town still standing. There's no charge to visit, when the tower is open.

Close to the Helpoort on the south bank of the Jeker is a white building, the **Pesthuis** or Plague House. It was a former water-driven paper mill, but received its name from its proximity to a nearby barracks which housed plague victims. The **Onze Lieve Vrouwewal** is the section of wall which overlooks the river Maas. It too was part of the 13th-century wall. Near the parking entrance at Onze Lieve Vrouweplein are steps to climb the wall. At the base are five old cannons pointing toward the river, and there are fine views from the top.

• **Near the Fortifications:** The **Natural History Museum**, De Bosquetplein 6-7, ☎ (043) 350 5490, www.nhmmaastricht.nl, open Mon.-Fri. 10am-5pm, Sat.-Sun. 2-5pm, deals with the natural history and geology of the Limburg area. There's a permanent exhibit of rocks, minerals, fossils and flora, as well as changing exhibits. In addition, there's a traditional garden and vivarium. You can't miss the quartzite boulder next to the museum.

Nearby is the **Huys op den Jeker**, Bonnefantenstraat 5, a pretty little 17th-century structure that straddles the flowing waters of the Jeker. For a good view of it, walk around to Looiersgracht and stand behind the small statue of a donkey.

The **Bishop's Mill**, 17th-18th century, Stenenbrug 1, is close to the first wall fortifications...cross the little bridge to the back of the mill where the wheel can be seen. Visits by arrangement only.

St. Martin's Almshouse (1715), Grote Looierstraat 27, is also nearby and consists of 13 cottages. Notice the beautiful gable stone over the entrance. You can visit the courtyard. **Faliezusters Convent** (1647) is near the fortifications, just south of the Bishop's Mill. This convent was built in Maasland Renaissance style.

From 1575 to 1825, mining created a network of passageways which could be used in times of siege for the underground movement of troops and as hiding places. One such area is the **Casements**. Enter at Waldeck Bastion near Tongerplein; tours at 2pm. The guide explains all about this military monument with its domed vaults, shell-proof refuges, powder rooms, plunging steps and variety of galleries. The normal tour is one hour, but there is a three-hour tour in October (must reserve with the VVV). Interestingly, the 'fourth Musketeer,' d'Artagnan, was killed here in 1673. He took part in an attack on Maastricht by the army of Louis XIV.

▶ **Caves of Mount St. Peter**

Location:	There are two sections of the labyrinths open to the public: Northern Passage, departure from Chalet Bergrust, Luikerweg 71; the Zonneberg Caves, departure from Buitengoed Slavante, Slavante 1 (near Enci Cement Works, Maastricht).
Information:	VVV, ☎ (043) 350 6262
Hours:	Vary throughout the year; check with the VVV.

These caves resulted from centuries of excavation of marl, a clay used in building. There is a labyrinth of over 20,000 passages, over 200 kilometers (124 miles) long with some sections as high as 16 meters. Throughout history these caves have been a place of refuge, and signs of habitation can still be seen. In both World Wars they were used as escape routes between Holland and Belgium and as a place to hide Allied soldiers and resistance workers. Some of the emergency provisions are still there. Names, dates and hometowns scratched into the walls attest to the presence of American soldiers during WWII.

During the war, Rembrandt's *Night Watch* was one of many Dutch art treasures stored here to protect it from the bombings and hide it from invaders.

In the Northern Passage, there are ancient writings on the walls, and a baker's oven dating from the French occupation in 1794. The ceiling and walls are still black from the smoke that rose from it over 200 years ago. Nearby is a stone trough for feeding the animals also in the caves, and essential to those in hiding. The Southern Passage (**Zonneberg Caves**), contains charcoal drawings, old handwritings, a water reservoir, an oven and a chapel. Dress warmly even in summer, wear comfortable shoes, and bring a flashlight if possible.

● **Near the caves of mount St. Peter: Fort St. Peter** is located just a short walk from the northern entrance to the caves. Departure for the tour is from the café Fort St. Peter, Luikerweg 80. Check with the VVV for information. The fort was constructed in 1701-02 and was instrumental in the siege of Maastricht in the battle with the French in 1748. Shaped like a 5-pointed star, it has two major galleries at its centre and a gallery round its five sides. You will see the galleries, the shell-proof chambers and a well, and then you can climb up to see the wonderful view. The tour takes about an hour.

Lichtenberg Ruin, Lichtenbergweg 2, open May.-Oct., Sun. noon-4:30pm, is what's left of a 10th-century castle on the east side of Mount St. Peter. There are excellent views of the Maas Valley from here. Nearby is an old-fashioned Limburg farm bakehouse. You can watch them bake bread and pies in a wood-burning oven, and when you can no longer resist...try some. Open some Sun. 11am-4pm, but check with the VVV to be sure.

▶ .**Also in Maastricht**

Located on the west side of town behind Statensingel and between Pastoor Habetsstraat and Cabergerweg (entry on Cabergerweg), **Linie van Du Moulin** is a treat for military buffs. This complex of fortifications covers 37 acres. It was developed from 1773-77 by General Du Moulin, an expert on defense. There are dry trenches, bastions with bomb-proof shelters and mine galleries. The guide gives a one-hour tour, usually every Sun. at 3pm, but also on Mon., Wed. & Fri. in the summer and during the autumn school break...details from the VVV.

Markets

Maastricht markets draw crowds from far and near. The general market is held Wed. and Fri. 8am-1pm on the square around City Hall; an antique and curio market is held Sat. 10am-4pm on Stationsstraat.

Some Maastricht specialities worth discovering are the Limburgse flan (*vlaai*), gingerbread, apple dumplings, a local cheese called '*rommedou*,' mushrooms and trout, the Maastricht beer, wine, and their hard liquor '*Els*.'

Eating out

On the Vrijthof, there are sidewalk cafés galore: The **Monopole**, Vrijtof 3, ☎ (043) 356 1110 is inexpensive. The popular **Gauchos Grill Restaurant**, Vrijthof 52, ☎ (043) 325 5022, offers wonderful beef from Argentina and all-you-can-eat ribs.

Gourmet restaurants are numerous, and include **Le Bon Vivant**, Capucijn-enstraat 91, ☎ (043) 321 0816, in a vaulted cave; and **'t Pleuske**, Plaukstraat 6, ☎ (043) 321 8456.

The **Chateau Neercanne**, Cannerweg 800, ☎ (043) 325 1359, southwest of town on the Belgian border, is a must for any special occasion. It offers an elegant setting in a castle dating from 1698 and brimming with history. It sits high on the side of a hill – the only terraced castle in the Netherlands.

Staying over

Because of Maastricht's popularity, overnight stays should be reserved well in advance. You may consider staying in the Wyck section, east across the Maas. The railroad station, Congress Centre, and **NH Maastricht** hotel, Forum 110, ☎ (043) 383 8281, are all located here. **Hotel Beaumont**, Wyckerbrugstraat 2, ☎ (043) 325 4433, is in the heart of the Wyck shopping centre and has modern rooms in a period hotel with style; rates are moderate. **Crowne Plaza Maastricht**, De Ruiterij 1, ☎ (043) 350 9191, offers rooms and apartments – rates are at the top. A large, rambling establishment, its modern rooms have wonderful views of the city from across the river.

In the centre of town, there are many hotels to choose from, including the comfortable **Best Western Hotel Du Casque**, Helmstraat 14, ☎ (043) 321 4343. With its terrace overlooking the Vrijthof square, this hotel couldn't be more conveniently located, with cafés and restaurants close by. Service is impeccable, prices moderate to expensive.

Alternatively, the **Hotel Derlon**, O.L. Vrouweplein 6, ☎ (043) 321 6770, with its Roman antiquities 'museum' in the cellar, is a unique hotel overlooking a charming square, and offering all amenities, albeit expensive.

Yearly events

The special yearly activities include one of the largest **Carnavals** in the Netherlands just before Lent, the prestigious **International Antique Market** in March; **St. Servatius Fair** on the Vrijthof in May, and the **Burgundian Gastronomic Festivities** on the Vrijthof in August.

Tours

The VVV in Maastricht is very active and organises a number of well-worthwhile tours. It conducts a daily walking tour in English and German from early July to early September, 12:30pm, but tours in Dutch are throughout the year.

Boat Tours are offered by **Rederij Stiphout**, Maaspromenade 58, ☎ (043) 351 5300, www.stiphout.nl. They also offer a trip on the Maas and a visit to St. Pietersberg caves; a Candlelight Cruise with music, cocktails and buffet supper; a trip on the Maas from Maastricht to the Belgian border; Maastricht-Liege boat trip with a visit to the Ardennes; and a Brunch-trip, with buffet and accordion music.

You can row your own boat from **Kayak Tour Limburg**, Grote Dries, ☎ (089) 61 4424, www.kajaktourlimburg.nl. They have 'unsinkable' one, two or three-seat boats you can row on a 10 or 22-kilometer (6 or 14-mile) route downriver through the countryside. Call in advance to reserve.

If land or river tours don't excite you, how about a spin by air? **Air Service Limburg**, Maastricht Aachen Airport, ☎ (043) 364 6949, offers 15-minute to one-hour flights. Minimum of two persons. Another option is a hot air balloon tour. For information on one hour to one-and-a-half-hour trips, call the VVV.

Back to earth for something different, you can tour Maastricht on a *Toek Toek*, a 3-wheel vehicle – of Thai origin – that seats eight. From mid-April through Oct. the **Foundation Toek Toek Maastricht** (call the VVV for reservations) has half-hour tours leaving from the Vrijthof square between 11am-5pm.

In the neighbourhood of Maastricht

Eijsden is home to 17th-century **Eijsden Castle**. It's still occupied, but you're welcome to visit the French gardens, daily from 9am to sundown.

Northeast of Maastricht is **Meerssen**, an oasis of quiet where visitors can enjoy the unspoiled countryside, explore or seek out historic churches, and castles. Its **Basilica** in the centre of town is considered one of the best examples of Gothic architecture in the Maas region. This 13th-century church can be visited daily, generally from 10am to 5pm, except when a service is in progress.

Chapter 13 | The province of Zeeland

Zeeland was one of the richest and most powerful of the Dutch provinces. Middelburg, its capital, had its own East India Company. Veere was the main port for the Scottish wool trade, and the merchants of Zierikzee were known in every port on the Baltic. Gradually, its commercial importance declined and by the 18th century, agriculture had overtaken foreign trade significantly. With the farming community behind their great sea dikes being less exposed to the outside world, life in a way stood still here until World War II.

Historically, this area has always battled with the sea – a source of wealth, but also a harbinger of fearful destruction. Dry land originally, the North Sea has risen some 20 cms per century with the melting of the polar ice caps. Dikes were gradually built to protect the land, but the disastrous floods still came. The St. Elisabeth flood of 1421 destroyed 72 villages and drowned 10,000 people. More recent flood disasters were in 1911, 1916 and 1953.

The Delta Plan was born as a result of this last major flood. Its system of dikes, surge barriers and dams has not only made Zeeland safer, but also an area for water-related recreation. Zeeland consists of six areas, mostly former islands now linked together by bridges and dams: Schouwen-Duiveland (Zierikzee, Brouwershaven), Tholen (St. Annaland), Noord-Beveland (Colijnsplaat), Zuid-Beveland (Goes, Yerseke), Walcheren (Middelburg, Vlissingen, Veere), and Zeeuwsch-Vlaanderen (Terneuzen, Sluis).

Information: Provincial VVV Zeeland, ☎ (0118) 65 99 65; www.vvvzeeland.nl

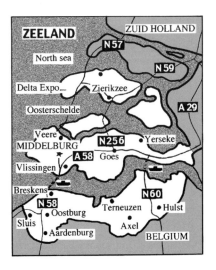

Brouwershaven
Once a busy seaport

Getting there: From the north take N57 south to the island of Schouwen-Duiveland, then follow signs to Scharendijke and on to Brouwershaven. From the east N59 to N654 north.

Information: VVV, Markt 2, ☎ (0111) 69 1940; www.vvvzeeland.nl/regios/brouwershaven

Brouwershaven received its town charter in 1477, but there is evidence that the area was inhabited even earlier. It was most prosperous from 1590, but the flood of 1682 washed away many buildings and left the fertile polders covered with salt and silt. By 1822, there were only 322 inhabitants, but things improved again gradually. From 1840-60, Brouwershaven was a busy seaport on the Grevelingen, servicing Rotterdam and Dordrecht. It had international Consular representatives, pilot services, a law court, solicitors, tax offices and some 27 hotel-cafés. However, when Rotterdam's Nieuwe Waterweg provided direct access to seagoing vessels, Brouwershaven was dealt the fatal blow.

The **Town Hall** (1599) is considered by some to be one of the most beautiful examples of the Flemish Renaissance style in the Netherlands. The inscription over the entrance reads 'The Law is for the Common Good.' Make time to see the Dutch Reformed Church, **St. Nicolas**, Korenmarkt, open mid May-mid Sept., afternoons. It is believed to have been founded as early as 1293.

In the neighbourhood of Brouwershaven

To the west toward the North Sea, just south of Brouwershaven Dam, there are lovely walks between the villages of **Renesse** and **Haamstede**, as well as 750 acres of forest and 2,000 acres of beach and dunes to explore. A former 12th-century fortified castle is located just north of Renesse, **Slot Moermond**. It has a long and interesting history, but is only open for visits in the summer. Information: VVV Renesse, Zeeanemoonweg 4A, ☎ (0111) 46 2120. www.renesseaanzee.nl

Taking N57 south over the Brouwersdam, the first stop you might make in Schouwen-Duiveland is **Scharendijke**, just east of the south exit of the dam, to see **Aquadome**, Brouwersdam 2, ☎ (0111) 67 1639, open Easter-mid July & mid Aug.-Nov. 10am-6pm; mid July-mid Aug. 10am-8pm. It's a floating aquarium with many species of fish native to the North Sea and the Oosterschelde.

South of Brouwershaven and north of Zierikzee, there are three former *terp* villages built around a central square with the local church in the centre. **Zonnemaire** is known for its illustrious citizen, Pieter Zeeman who won the Nobel Prize in 1902 for physics; **Noordgouwe**'s church dates from 1462; but **Dreischor** is the most charming, with an interesting 14th-15th-century church with a leaning tower, small moat and a town hall dating from 1637. Its agricultural museum, **Goemanszorg, Streek en Landbouwmuseum**, Molenweg 3, open mid-March-Oct., Tues.-Sat. 10am-5pm, Sun. noon-5pm; July-Aug., also open Mon. 10am-5pm, ☎ (0111) 40 2303, has a large collection of vintage farm implements as well as a typical farmer's living room and kitchen. For an overview of all 33 museums in Zeeland, see www.museainzeeland.nl.

Zierikzee
A trading town ... salt, red dye

Getting there: From the north take N57 south then N59 east; from the east, take the N59 exit off of A29 at Willemstad.

Information: VVV, Meelstraat 4, ☎ (0111) 41 2450; www.vvvzeeland.nl/regios/zierikzee

---

Zierikzee is the largest and most important town on Schouwen-Duiveland. Its colourful history spans eleven centuries. When Count Willem III granted its city rights in 1248, Zierikzee was about half its present size. In 1325 the town began to develop on both sides of the harbour – new quays were built and the whole area surrounded by a wall. Its location on the Oosterschelde and a tributary of the Gouwe enabled it to become an important port. To a large extent, it owes its development to trade between England, present-day Belgium (then Brabant and Flanders), and Holland. Zierikzee provided two products much in demand: salt and madder, a root that produces a red dye used in clothmaking.

A lovely town, you'll sense the Middle Ages atmosphere when visiting its old churches; its 16th-century town hall; its ancient prison; three picturesque town gates and a canal that encloses the old part of the city.

▶ Stadhuismuseum – Town Hall Museum
Location: Meelstraat 8. Look for the tall spire.
Information: ☎ (0111) 45 4464; www.museaschouwenduiveland.nl/stadhuis
Hours: May-Oct., Mon.-Sat. 10am-5pm. Sun. noon -5pm

The 16th-century **Town Hall** is easily identifiable by its tall delicate spire. Start your visit on the ground floor. The Mayor's office and the great hall where weddings take place can be visited if not in use. There are paintings of the town as it was in 1506. The Council Room was reconstructed in 1775 in Louis XV style, and the 'Schutterszaal' (on the next floor) is where the 17th-century Home Guard met. Notice the open roofing constructed like a reversed ship's hull. The museum deals with local history and has a collection of silver, porcelain, earthenware, costumes, paintings and drawings. Town and regional history are illustrated in a room decorated with tiles, typical of the Schouwen area.

> **Maritiem Museum – Maritime Museum**
> Location: Mol 25
> Information: ☎ (0111) 45 4464; www.museaschouwenduiveland.nl/maritiem
> Hours: April-Oct., Mon.-Sat. 10am-5pm, Sun. noon-5pm

Another ancient building in Zierikzee is its old prison, 's Gravensteen, originally built in 1358, and now part of a museum. It fell into disrepair and was replaced between 1524 and 1526. The present building housed the Count's officials, the Count's High Tribunal, and what was the prison until 1923.

There was a debtor's cell, women's cell, dormitory and infirmary. The jailer lived on the ground floor next to the room where the judges passed sentence. At the rear were the sheriff's office and the torture chambers. Among the 'residents' were prisoners awaiting trial, those serving their sentences, debtors, and prisoners of war. Many were sailors detained for smuggling, theft or violence. Inscriptions were discovered in 1969 when a layer of plaster was removed. This part of the building has not been changed. Notice the heavy oak reinforced with metal bands for security. There are large holding cells, and smaller rooms with iron cells each for two prisoners. You can look through peepholes into the dormitories and through the 'window' where food was passed to prisoners. Spend a little time reading the graffiti...notice the dates, pictures, etc.

The museum portrays Zierikzee's centuries-old struggle with the sea. There are ships' models, maps, paintings, and items relating to the history of fishing as well as archeological finds from the Scheldt. The copper statue of Neptune that graced the Town Hall spire from 1554-1976 is also here. You can hear a concert of the Town Hall carillons on Thurs. between 10:45-11:45am.

> **Also in Zierikzee**
Zierikzee has a canal that encircled the original town. Three of the town gates still stand. The **Nobelpoort**, Korte Nobelstraat, is a 14th-century water gate with a decorative 1559 facade. The **Zuidhavenpoort** and the **Noordhavenpoort** stand near each other at the end of Oude Haven. The Zuidhavenpoort is a tall, square tower with four turrets. The Noordhavenpoort has a small courtyard between the two gates.

These last two gates were built to protect the old port. This part of town is worth exploring if you are interested in early buildings with elegant facades. The front of the **White Swan**, Havenpark 1, dates from 1658. Close by is the **Museumhaven**, Oude Haven, ☎ (0111) 41 2450, open July-Aug., Tues.-Thurs. & Sat. 10am-5pm, a collection of old boats docked on the canal.

The **Burgerweeshuis Museum**, Poststraat 45, ☎ (0111) 41 2683, open July-Aug., Tues.-Sun. 11am-5pm, is in a weigh-house that dates from the 14th-17th centuries. Its collection includes a Regent's room with gold-tooled, leather-covered walls, and Louis XIV wainscoting, paintings, ceramics, etc.

Zierikzee has two interesting churches, the **Gasthuiskerk**, Havenplein 17, a 14th-century structure, and **St. Lievensmonstertoren**, Kerkhof, built in 1454. The heavy, square Gothic structure was built as a tower for a cathedral that was never finished. Designed to be over 200 meters tall, work stopped when it reached 60 meters. Nevertheless, it's a good place for a view of the area. Open April-mid Sept., Mon.-Sat. 11am-4pm, Sun. noon-4pm.

Two grain grinding mills can be visited: **De Hoop** (1874), Lange Nobelstraat 43, open on Saturdays – if you see the windmill's arms turning; and **Den Haas** (1727), Bolwerk, again open any day the mill's arms are in motion.

Markets

Regular market day is Thurs. in the town centre. From July -mid Aug. a tourist market is held every Tues. You might also buy some shellfish at the local oyster or mussel beds. Check with the VVV.

Eating out

The recommended pancake house is **'t Zeeuwsche Pannekoekenhuis**, Appelmarkt 6, ☎ (0111) 41 6179; or you can try typical Dutch dishes at **Restaurant Concordia**, Appelmarkt 29, ☎ (0111) 41 5122. Other possibilities are **De Zeelandbrug**, Weg naar de Val 10, ☎ (0111) 41 3208; and **De Zeeuwsche Herberghe**, Havenpark 2, ☎ (0111) 41 4118.

Staying over

Two moderately-priced hotels are **Mondragon**, Havenpark 21, ☎ (0111) 41 3051, and **De Drie Koningen**, Driekoningenlaan 7, ☎ (0111) 41 2323. The VVV Camping Guide will give you full details on campgrounds, accommodations, prices, etc. There are also folders on hotels, boarding houses, holiday homes and apartments. The off-season rates for 3, 5-and 8-day hotel or bungalow arrangements might also be of special interest.

Yearly events

Special folk events include the yearly market, in early June; the traditional sailing race on the Oosterschelde in early July; and tourist days, most Tuesdays from mid-July to mid-Aug.

Tours

Seasonal boat trips are offered by **Rederij Friesland**, ☎ (06) 5277 8505, June and Sept., every Tues. 2pm; July-Aug., Mon.-Thur. 10:30am and 2pm...the trip on the Oosterschelde takes you under the Zeelandbrug to Oosterscheldekering and Burghsluis. You can also sail on the Oosterschelde in a traditional sailboat in July-August, daily from 1:30-4:30pm, ☎ (0111) 41 5830.

Serooskerke, west of Zierikzee, suffered terribly when the sea dike here broke in 1953, creating enormous loss of life and property. Once the gap in the Schelphoek dike was closed, it left a deep inland creek. This area has been planted and its fine natural scenery provides birds and waterfowl with a place of refuge.

A drive east of Zierikzee along the coastline will take you to the break in the dike which caused the flood in 1953. The **Ouwerkerk Caissons**, great concrete structures, were dropped into place to breach the gap. It took from February when the break occurred, to November to complete the repairs. This quiet, secluded spot is ideal for a picnic while enjoying the views.

Bruinisse, known for its oyster culture and water-sports activities, also has two museums. The **Fishery Museum**, Oudestraat 23, open June-Aug., Mon.-Fri. 2-4:30pm, ☎ (0111) 48 1223, tells the story of the local mussel and oyster trade. The **Oudheidka-mer** (Antiquities Museum), Oudestraat 27, ☎ (0111) 48 1503, open June-Sept., Mon.-Fri. 2-4:30pm, is in an 18th-century home.

Delta Works – Oosterschelde

The worst natural disaster to strike the Netherlands in the 20th century took place on January 31, 1953. The weather forecast that morning warned of the approaching danger to the country:

8am: All areas, westerly wind, force 7.

9:30am: All areas, gale warning, west-northwest.

5pm: All areas, strong west/northwest gales.

5:15pm: Northern and western North Sea, strong westerly-northwesterly gales imminent, spreading south and east, persisting all night. Dangerously high tides at Rotterdam, Willemstad and Bergen op Zoom.

Major floods occurred every few years in the Middle Ages, but after centuries of dike-building the Dutch felt protected from the sea. Unfortunately, the dikes did not hold for this storm. Overnight, 1,855 drowned and thousands more lost their homes and possessions. The damage was overwhelming. Rescue teams and volunteers came from everywhere to help. The inundations extended to most of Duiveland, Tholen, the area north of Bergen op Zoom to the Hollands Diep, Overflakkee, the area around Hellevoetsluis, the Biesbosch, Dordrecht and even further east. The loss was so great, that immediate action was demanded to make sure a disaster of this magnitude could not happen again. This resulted in the Delta Act of 1958.

The resulting **Delta Works** project is a marvel of 20th-century engineering that took 30 years and over five billion dollars to complete. Existing dikes were repaired and improved, and new ones built along the coastline. Dams were also built inland to prevent strong currents causing further damage. Some waterways were closed off from the sea; in others storm surge barriers were created with gates that only close when the water reaches flood level. The largest part of the project was the dam at the mouth of the Oosterschelde.

Work began in 1968 to seal off the Oosterschelde, but there was opposition from environmental groups and fishermen whose livelihoods would be lost if they could not reach the North Sea to fish. After due study it was decided not to close off the estuary, but to construct a storm-surge barrier in the mouth of Oosterschelde. Had it been closed, it would have meant the end of the mussel and oyster trade, an economic loss of about 200 million guilders (the currency at that time), not to mention the social problems caused for the fishermen and their families.

All in all, this massive project has meant that the land and inhabitants are protected and the fishing industry saved; and the Delta Plan has created new recreational areas and a natural environment for birds, which feed and nest in the protected areas. It has also resulted in a new attraction for visitors called **WaterLand Neeltje Jans**.

▶ **WaterLand Neeltje Jans**
Man's battle against the sea
Location: On N57, between the islands of Schouwen and Noord Beveland. Follow signs to Neeltje Jans.
Information: ☎ (0111)-65 5655; www.deltawerken.com/Waterland-Neeltje-Jans
Hours: April-Oct., daily 10am-5:30pm; Nov.-March, Wed.-Sun. 10am-5pm

Neeltje Jans was the island used as a base by the construction crews who worked on the Delta Project. After its completion in 1986, work began to create an exhibition area on the theme of 'man's battle against the sea.' We highly recommend a visit to this fascinating and extremely educational complex, complete with a highly touted water theme park, fun for the entire family.

The Delta Expo and the Storm Surge Barrier are the main attractions. The Expo has many audiovisual and scale model exhibits to explain the history and development of the Storm Surge Barrier. One of the most popular is a large ground level model of the delta region of Zeeland. You can see how the Delta Works project operates as water levels in the model rise and fall, and the dams and barriers respond to the changing conditions. Films are in Dutch and English, and give a complete visual explanation of the immense work carried out here in Holland's constant struggle against the sea.

Details of the construction are thoroughly explained – the magnitude of the task, the solutions found and the innovations made are enormously impressive. Sixty-five prefabricated concrete piers were placed on foundation mattresses in the three channels in the mouth of the Eastern Scheldt. Sixty-two steel gates were installed – suspended between piers – that can be closed under dangerous conditions. Normally, the gates are kept raised, maintaining the difference between high and low tide at roughly three-quarters of its former range. Happily, fishermen still have access to the North Sea to continue their traditional fishing.

Another exhibition shows the advances made by the Dutch in using wind as a source of energy, and includes a 12-meter, wind-driven rotor blade, a 3,000-kilo turbine, and a computer that answers all your questions on wind energy. In Holland the force of the wind is self-evident...if you doubt it, a walk along the flood barrier should convince you. The tour concludes with a visit to a section of the barrier, giving visitors an appreciation of the enormous size of the works and the force of the water. From the roof of the Delta Expo building, you can enjoy magnificent views of the mouth of the Oosterschelde.

▶ Also at Waterland Neeltje Jans

Over the years, the area around the Oosterschelde storm surge barrier has developed into a family entertainment complex – especially suitable in summer. The barrier and the Delta Expo are open year round, but several other attractions are only open from April-Oct. These include boat trips on the Oosterschelde (every 45 minutes from 11:30am to 4:30pm), where you can see the storm surge barrier from another angle as well as some of the wildlife of the region. If you don't happen to see any interesting animals or fish on the trip, you can visit the **Waterlife** centre in the summer months. Its aquariums house some of the creatures who live in the local waters. There's also a guided nature walk every day (except Sun.) at 1pm, also at 3pm in July and Aug. For the little ones, there's a Waterplayground, and for those slightly older there's a climbing pier (supervised by an experienced climbing instructor). Another attraction open all year is the **Waterpavillion**, where an audio tour explains all about water – where it comes from and where it goes. Last but not least, visit the most fantastic water theme park in the Netherlands, **WaterLand Neeltje Jans**, where you can spend a fun day filled with amazing attractions! www.neeltjejans.nl

After visiting Delta Expo you can continue south to **North Beveland island**. On the northeast coast you will come to **Colijnsplaat**. You could also arrive here via the longest bridge in the Netherlands, the **Zeelandbrug**. There's a bona fide fish auction held Thursday and Friday afternoons on Havenplateau. Though not open to the public, if you're around in the late morning or early afternoon on auction days, you can watch the fish being unloaded.

Veere
Once the centre for the Scottish wool trade

Getting there:	Veere is only about 7 km (4 mi) north of Middelburg.
Information:	VVV, Oudestraat 28, ☎ (0118) 50 1365; www.veere.nl

Veere, a quaint old town, was once a very prosperous port for the Scottish wool trade from the late 14th to 18th centuries. The Scots acquired their special privileges to conduct trade here when the Lord of Veere married Mary, the daughter of James I of Scotland. This alliance prospered until the arrival of the French in 1795. Veere was also one of the East India

Company's headquarters. Today, trading ships can no longer enter the harbour, so the town depends on tourists and yachting enthusiasts for its livelihood.

Be sure to visit the **Town Hall**, Markt 5, dating from 1477. Built in Gothic style, the Renaissance tower was added in 1599. The facade is decorated with statues of Lords and Ladies of Veere; the Council Chamber is hung with Gobelin tapestries and paintings of note; and 47 bells are rung from its tower from July-Aug, Sat. 7-8pm; May-June & Sept.-Oct., Thurs. 3-4pm; Nov.-April, every 14 days, Thurs. 3-4pm. Inside the Town Hall, in what was formerly a courtroom, is now a local museum, **De Vierschaar**, open May-Oct. Mon-Sat. 1-5pm, ☎ (0118) 50 6064. Its interesting collection of Veere historical objects includes a famous cup belonging to Maximilian of Burgundy (1551).

The **Grote Kerk** (1348), Oudestraat, open April-Oct., daily 10am-5pm, Sun. 1-5pm, is also known as 'Onze Lieve Vrouwekerk.' History has not been kind to this old building. The interior was destroyed by fire in 1686. In 1809 the British took it over during the Walcheren expedition; and Napoleon used it as a barracks and a hospital in 1811. The stained-glass windows were destroyed and five floors, since removed, were added in the nave and transept. There is a fine view from the 42-meter tower. South of the church, the **Cistern** or Town Well was constructed in 1551 by Maximilian of Burgundy who promised the Scottish wool merchants good water, necessary to their development and trade.

As you wander the streets you will see many unusual house facades, mostly made of brick, often with step gables, and their woodwork painted in the traditional dark green and white. Look for the houses called 'The Dolphin,' 'The Phoenix,' 'The Golden Lion' and the 'Suster Anna,' with three sailing ships portrayed in full sail over the doorway, all of them around the little Town Square.

Beyond the Town Square is another green area with a series of almshouses. Take a glimpse over the walls at their colourful gardens.

Along the wharf are many step-gabled houses. One was once the Grain Stevedores' Guild and a former prison. A present-day antique shop was a little church at one time, and the smallest house – just 7-feet wide with a double door and a double window – belonged to a ship chandler. Then there are the impressive **Scottish Houses**, 'Het Lammetje' (1539) and 'De Struys' (1561), which were once warehouses and offices of the Scottish wool merchants. Now called the **Museum Schotse Huizen**, Kaai 25-27, ☎ (0118) 50 1744, open April-Oct., daily 1-5pm, it has displays of old Zeeland costumes, antique furniture, books, atlases, etc. Along the quay are the Yacht Club and the **Campveerse Tower** (15th century) that forms part of the fortifications at the harbour entrance. The **Ramparts** too, are extremely well preserved. www.schotsehuizen.nl

Shopping

Demonstrations and sale of minerals and ornaments take place at **De Aquamarijn**, Markt 37-39, ☎ (0118) 50 1980, open May-Oct., Mon.-Sat. 10am-6pm, Sun. 1:30-5pm; Nov.-April, Tues.-Sat. 11am-5pm. **De Schapekop**, Kerkstraat 3, ☎ (0118) 50 1416, has handicraft demonstrations, and there are pottery demonstrations at **Potterie S**, Simon Oomstraat 1, ☎ (0118) 50 2140.

Eating out

Suster Anna Restaurant, Markt 8, ☎ (0118) 50 1557, is a good choice near the Town Hall. **'t Waepen van Veere**, Markt 23, ☎ (0118) 50 1231, is nearby, where you can order a 'Koffietafel' (typical Dutch sandwich lunch), or regular lunch and dinner (seafood is the speciality). Another reasonably-priced restaurant along the quay, **Restaurant in den Strupkelder**, Kaai 25, ☎ (0118) 50 1392, is in an old cellar and attractively decorated in old Dutch style. For special occasions, try **Campveerse Toren**, Kaai 2, ☎ (0118) 50 1695, where William the Silent had his wedding supper! From your table in this medieval powder magazine, you can see fishing vessels gliding past. The small circular room is beautiful, with its silver and copper. Top quality service and food is offered. Expensive but worth it. Across the harbour is **d'Ouwe Werf**, Bastion 2, ☎ (0118) 50 1493, a well-recommended gourmet restaurant.

Staying over (which we heartily recommend)

While dining at the **Campveerse Toren** (see 'Eating Out') is expensive, sleeping there is not. Accommodations, ☎ (0118) 50 1291, are simple but adequate, and most have views over lake Veere. Not all rooms have private baths so do check this. The room with the most charm and loveliest views is the one furthest from the tower and the dining room. Windows on three sides of the room let you enjoy the dainty spire of the Town Hall and other illuminated buildings, the dike which leads away from the hotel (with town parking on one side) and the Veerse Meer on the other, while the third view is of the sea itself. Another recommended hotel is **'t Waepen van Veere** (see 'Eating Out'), with moderate prices that include a good Dutch breakfast.

Tours

Rederij Dijkhuizen, Vlissingen, ☎ (0118) 41 9367, offers a number of tours in the area. The boat from Veere departs from the quay behind the Campveerse Toren, Easter to mid-Sept, 11am-5pm.

In the neighbourhood of Veere

Vrouwenpolder, four miles west toward the dunes, is the place for beach, swimming and dune-exploring. **Oostkapelle**, a slightly larger town, and centre for camping and beach activities, offers a wide range of accommodations. A couple of kilometers toward the sea, you will find **Westhove Castle**. Its Orangerie houses a natural history museum, the **Zeeuws Biologisch Museum**, Duinvlietweg 6, ☎ (0118) 58 2620, open June-Aug., daily 10am-6pm; Nov.-March, Tues.-Sun. noon-5pm; Apr.-May & Sept.-Oct., Tues.-Fri. & Sun. 10am-5pm, Sat. noon-5pm. **Domburg**, south of Westhove Castle, is charming and the oldest seaside resort of Zeeland. In the 18th century, its first outdoor bathing facilities were put in place, and in 1837 the first bath pavilion was opened. A most pleasant family resort.

Middelburg
Provincial capital, Thursday market, and a miniature village

Getting there: From the north N57; from the east A58; from the south take the ferry from Perkpolder (N60) and then A58.
The Kruiningen-Perkpolder ferry operates 4:05am-11:25pm, every half hour, except Sat. and Sun., then hourly; 20 minutes each way.
See 'Vlissingen' for Vlissingen-Breskens ferry information.

Information: VVV, Nieuwe Burg 40, ☎ (0118) 65 9900; www.midddelburg.nl

Before the bridges and dams were constructed on which modern highways are built, the island of Walcheren was isolated, but not as much as some parts of Zeeland. The **Abdij** or Abbey, which dates from 1120, had a great deal of influence both on the town and the area generally. When **Middelburg** became an early convert to the Protestant faith during the uprising against the Spanish, the Abbey was dissolved and the complex of buildings used for other purposes.

The town suffered greatly under German occupation. The Allies needed to eliminate the heavy German artillery barrage coming from Vlissingen and other parts of South Beveland, which prevented badly-needed war supplies from being off-loaded in the Belgian port of Ghent. The best approach seemed to be to bomb the dikes, thus causing flooding throughout Walcheren. Furious Commando attacks followed, forcing the Germans to surrender. Middelburg in the midst of it, came under attack and suffered heavy damage.

As capital of the province of Zeeland, and its largest city with about 45,000 residents, Middelburg is an important regional centre – its busy Thursday market is living proof. Many of Middelburg's streets and buildings were successfully rebuilt after the war years, restoring some of its pre-war charm. Attractions such as a miniature village were added, making it an interesting stop for visitors.

▶ **Abdij – The Abbey**
This former abbey, founded in 1120, has several interesting features. The Norbertine religious order was housed here until 1574. Since that time it has been home to the provincial government of Zeeland, which still occupies a portion of the complex. In 1940 the **Abdij** was severely bombed, its burning tower crashing onto the buildings below, which included three churches. Now restored, the complex is one of Middelburg's treasures. For an overview see: http://middelburg.touristshop.nl/middelburg_info

The **Abdijkerken**, Ondertoren, are actually three churches in one: the **Nieuw Kerk** was built in the 16th century; the **Wandel Kerk** has a large tomb honouring Jan and Cornelis Evertsen, two brothers, both admirals killed in a battle against the English in 1666; the **Koor Kerk** contains the oldest organ in the Netherlands, built in 1481. Above the churches stands a tower nicknamed **Lange Jan** (Long John). Destroyed in 1940, the 90.5-meter (280-foot) tower was rebuilt. For those willing to make the climb (some 207 steps), it offers a panoramic view of Walcheren, the Zeeland Bridge and the Eastern Scheldt works.

The 49-bell carillon of Lange Jan plays every 15 minutes, and on Thursdays there are carillon concerts from noon to 1pm. From May to mid-September there is an additional concert on Saturday from noon to 1pm, ☎ (0118) 61 2525. www.langejanmiddelnburg.nl

The **Zeeuws Museum**, Abdij 3, ☎ (0118) 65 3000, open Mon.-Sat. 11am-5pm, Sun. noon-5pm, is located in one of the oldest quarters of the Middelburg Abbey. The collection includes traditional Zeeland costumes, Delftware, furniture, paintings and a marvellous tapestry gallery. www.zeeuwsmuseum.nl

Roosevelt Study Centre, Abdij 9, ☎ (0118) 63 1590, open April-Oct., Mon.-Fri. 10am-12:30pm & 1:30-4:30pm, is a centre of research on 20th-century American history. It has a permanent exhibit on former American presidents Theodore Roosevelt (1858-1919), his distant cousin Franklin Roosevelt (1882-1945), as well as Eleanor Roosevelt (1884-1962), a niece to Theodore and wife to Franklin. She was probably the most active and outspoken American 'First Lady.' All three had Dutch ancestors who came from this part of Holland. www.roosevelt.nl/en

Blauw or Gistpoort (Blue or Yeast Gate), the restored gatehouse of the abbey was built between 1509 and 1512, and is lined with blue stone.

▶ **Miniature Walcheren**

Location: Molenwater – just a short walk from the Abdij
Information: ☎ (0118) 61 2525; www.miniatuurwalcheren.nl
Hours: April-Oct., daily 10am-5pm; open 'til 6pm in July-Aug.

Along with serious sightseeing, it's only fair to allow the squirmy generation a chance to stretch their legs and see something of special interest to them. If you take the island of Walcheren and reduce it to 1/20th of its normal size, monuments, churches, and museums that are typically boring to the small fry suddenly become quite fascinating. Up to now, more than four million people have seen **Miniature Walcheren**, and we suggest you do too.

This scale model of the island of Walcheren shows streets, dikes, ports, 500 of the principal buildings, ships, trains, barges and a good overview of the area's water-control system. In addition, trains and buses travel along their normal routes, so there's something happening all the time. Great family site.

▶ **Also in Middelburg**

The 15th-century **Town Hall**, ☎ (0118) 67 5450, open March-Oct., Mon.-Sat. 11am-5pm, Sun. noon-5pm, is considered by some to be one of the most beautiful in Holland. Its facade dates from 1452-58. Next door is the old **Vlees Hal** (Meat Hall), which was added in 1506-20, as was the elaborate tower. In 1780 there were more additions, but in 1940 most of the building was destroyed by German bombings. There are information sheets in English and guides prepared to answer questions. You'll see the Council Chamber, Mayor's private office, Reception Hall, etc. Notice the beautifully-carved wooden chests from old Zeeland farms. Reconstruction began before the end of the war; wood not being available, steel beams were used and then decorated in Zeeland colours.

There is the old **Grain Exchange** on the Dam square; the **Koepoort** (Cow Gate), near Miniature Walcheren, was built in 1735 and is the only remaining town gate; the **Court of Justice** (1765); the **English Church** (15th century) near the Town Hall; and the picturesque **Vismarkt**, the old galleried fish market with its Doric columns and little auctioneer's house.

Markets and shopping

Middelburg is known for its Thursday market, 9am-4pm on the main Market Square – especially for old curios and the odd antique find. Colourful local costumes are worn. There is also a book market from Feb-Oct., Mon. 1-4pm. In summertime, on Thurs., a special art market is also held on the Vischmarkt. The town also has many interesting antique shops.

Eating out

Like other cities, Middelburg has a wide choice of places to eat in all price categories. Tourist menus are available at **De Huifkar**, Markt 19, ☎ (0118) 61 2998, and the **Station Restaurant**, Kanaalweg 24, ☎ (0118) 63 7601. Or you could eat at one of the food stands if you're visiting on market day (Thursday)...a shrimp or eel sandwich is a nice change of taste from a hamburger. On the expensive side, you can eat in the more elegant atmosphere of an old patrician house, **Den Gespleten Arent**, Vlasmarkt 25, ☎ (0118) 63 6122, or **Het Groot Paradys**, Damplein 13, ☎ (0118) 65 1200.

Staying over

To tempt you to stay a bit longer, the important buildings of Middelburg are illuminated during the summer months and can best be appreciated if you spend the night. Four first-rate hotels are the **Grand Hotel du Commerce**, Loskade 1, ☎ (0118) 63 60 51, **Le Beau Rivage**, Loskade 19, ☎ (0118) 63 8060; **De Nieuwe Doelen**, Loskade 3, ☎ (0118) 61 2121; and the 4-star **Arneville**, Buitenruststraat 22, ☎ (0118) 63 8456. Less expensive is **De Huifkar**, Markt 19, ☎ (0118) 61 2998.

Yearly events

You shouldn't miss the traditional horseback 'tilting for the ring' competitions. This is a unique folkloric, full-day event in July on the Abdijplein, and in August at **Molenwater**, near the main city entry gate.

Tours

Tours by horse-drawn trams, usually May-Aug. (pick-up point VVV office on Nieuwe Burg) take you to Miniature Walcheren. Canal boat tours, April-Nov., leave from the Langeviele bridge, Achter de Houttuinen 39.

In the neighbourhood of Middelburg

Westkapelle, on the coast, still bears evidence of its role in WW II. Antipersonnel fences, tank traps, cement blockhouses and gun emplacements are all here. Notice the commemorative tablet in English and Dutch marking the date, November 1, 1944. It was on this date that the British 4th Commando Brigade landed to liberate the area.

Drive along the huge dike of Westkapelle, completed in 1987. Normally, the seaside of dikes are dunes with no view. This is an exception. As part of the Delta Works, the dike was built twice as high as it had been previously. You look down on the sea – a wonderful expanse of North Sea before you.

Goes has a 15th-17th-century, late Gothic basilica, **St. Marie-Magdalenakerk**, open weekdays in summer. Goes also has a 14th-century Gothic **Town Hall** with guided tours in July and August, and the **Museum voor Zuid en Noord-Beveland**, Singelstraat 13, ☎ (0113) 22 8883, open Tues.-Fri. 10am-5pm, Sat. 1-4pm. This 15th-century convent has an interesting display of traditional Dutch costumes from North and South Beveland in its 10,000-item collection.

If you have a soft spot for steam engines, you might have to stay on to spend the afternoon traveling on an old steam train from Goes to Borsele and back. **Stoomtrein Goes-Borsele**, Stephensonsweg 9, ☎ (0113) 27 0705, open mid July-early Sept., Sun.-Fri., departs from Goes at 11am, 2pm & 4pm; April-June & mid Sept- Oct., Sun. 2pm departure; special holiday schedules, including a special Christmas train in late December. On the way back the train stops for a half hour at **Hoedekenskerk**, where you can climb the dike for a good view of the Western Scheldt river. The roundtrip usually takes two to two-and-a-half hours. www.destoomtrein.nl

The landscape is beautiful, especially when the fruit trees are in blossom in spring. It is dotted with tiny, old villages – such as **Kapelle** and **Baarsdorp** – with hardly more than a dozen houses. The VVV 'Blossom route around South Beveland' will help you explore.

Yerseke, just east of Goes, is Holland's centre for oyster and mussel culture. Mussels are fished from the Wadden Islands and brought to beds in Zeeland where they mature for two to three years before they're ready to be eaten. They are exported in great quantity to Belgium and France where they are in great demand. The mussel auction room, on Ankerweg off Julianahaven, is open on weekdays in season. For details call VVV Yerseke, ☎ (0113) 57 1864. There are many restaurants in the area specialising in oyster and mussel dishes (in season).

On the third Saturday in August, Yerseke celebrates with a Mussel Festival. Tours of the oyster beds are arranged in season (Sept.-April). Regular tours of the Oosterschelde depart from Julianahaven. The **Museum Yerseke**, Kerkplein 1, ☎ (0113) 57 1864, www.oosterscheldemuseum.nl, open Mon.-Sat. 10am-noon and 1-4pm, focuses on the vital role that the oyster and mussel play in the economy of the town.

The town of **St. Annaland** on the island of **Tholen** boasts an interesting museum, **Streekmuseum De Meestoof**, Bierensstraat 6, ☎ (0166) 65 2477, open spring through autumn, Tues.-Sat. 2-5pm. Located in the former town hall, its collection includes traditional costumes of the area, farmers' style rooms, archeological finds and a 19th-century school room. A ferry brings pedestrians and bikers from Scherpenisse to Yerseke.

Vlissingen
Summer resort, fishing and shipbuilding centre

Getting there:	Vlissingen is about 5 km (3 mi) south of Middelburg. The Vlissingen-Breskens ferry operates weekdays 4:50am-11:50pm, departing every 30 minutes from 7:20am-7:50pm; otherwise hourly at 10 minutes to the hour. Departure times are similar at weekends, but from Oct.-May, boats leave hourly at 10 minutes to the hour. Trip takes 20 minutes. From Breskens, boats leave 20 past, or 10 minutes to the hour.
Information:	VVV, Nieuwendijk 15, ☎ (0118) 41 2345; www.vvvzeeland.nl/regios/vlissingen

Like all port towns, **Vlissingen** has a long history of naval battles and military action. It was in the forefront of the fight against Spanish control. It revolted in 1572 and came under British 'care' from 1585-1616. However, the town didn't begin to develop until 1872 when the railway was built and the docks were completed. In 1940 it suffered heavily when the harbour was bombed by the Germans. Then in 1944 the dikes were breached to enable the Allies to subdue the Germans. The defenses and bunkers of that period are still visible. Vlissingen and surrounding towns were again damaged or seriously threatened in the 1953 flood.

From Vlissingen, you can take a relaxing car ferry across the Westerschelde to Breskens and drive south into Belgium. If you decide to spend the night in Vlissingen, many hotels are located on the Boulevard along the beach. From your room you may see streams of international ships passing by, heading for the Belgian port of Antwerp, which explains the tremendously varied traffic.

▶ **Het Arsenaal**

Location:	Arsenaalplein 1 – on the coast in the town centre
Information:	☎ (0118) 41 5400; www.arsenaal.com
Hours:	April-Oct., daily 10am-6pm; Nov.-Dec., Tues.-Sun. 10am-5pm; Jan.-March, Wed.-Sun. 10am-5pm

Het Arsenaal is an indoor maritime theme park that children love. It has a collection of large model ships, and a display on pirates, including their clothing, cutlasses, etc.

There's a cave, where you're greeted by a dancing chorusline of skeletons, a shipwreck simulator (not for small children), and a series of aquariums. There are small sharks in some, as well as fish found in the North Sea. Some rays swimming in a tank may allow you to rub their bellies! The Crow's Nest tops it all. An elevator takes you 65 meters (215 feet) up to an observation tower with spectacular views of Vlissingen, the waterways and ship traffic. On a clear day you can see Belgium.

- **Near Het Arsenaal:** If the children are still raring to go, next door is **Carrousel**, a family entertainment complex with a variety of games and amusements set up like a fairground, complete with merry-go-round and organ grinder.

On the quieter side, behind the Arsenaal you can take a stroll along the dike and watch pleasure boats and ocean-going ships on their way to and from the Belgian ports.

▶ **Also in Vlissingen**

Most other attractions in town are around **Bellamypark**, the tree-lined square in the town centre. **Reptielenzoo Iguana**, Bellamypark 35, ☎ (0118) 41 7219, open daily 1-5:30pm; June-Oct. also open Tues.-Wed., Fri, & Sun. 10am-5:30pm, has over 500 live reptiles on display, including crocodiles, tortoises and iguanas. www.iguana.nl

In front of the building is a stone marking the spot where a Spanish nobleman was hanged in 1572. The people of Vlissingen were among the first to rebel against Spanish rule.

The **Stedelijk Museum**, Bellamypark 19, ☎ (0118) 41 2219, open Mon.-Fri. 10am-5pm; Sat.-Sun. 1-5pm, has portraits, town silver, a room devoted to Admiral Michiel de Ruyter (1607-76), the famous native son, a painting of Vlissingen in 1664, and the remains of the 'Vliegend Hart,' a VOC (United East India Co.) merchant ship that sank just off shore.

St. Jacobskerk (1328), located on the Kleine Markt, is open to visitors. It is late Gothic with a beautifully restored tower and carillon. The church can be visited, and the tower can be climbed, July-Aug., Thurs.-Sat. 1:30-5pm. www.sintjacobskerk.nl

The new **Town Hall** (1965) is on the Boulevard next to the **Gevangentoren**, the 15th-century remains of the West Gate. Some old houses of interest are the **Beeldenhuis** (1730) at Hendrikstraat 25; the **Beursgebouw** (1635) at Plein 11; the **Lampsinhuis** (1641) at Nieuwendijk 11, and **Cornelia Quack's** (believe it or not) **hofje**, Korte Zelke. It dates from 1786, and the small gate from 1643.

A stroll around town should include a walk along the boulevard facing the river Schelde, (the street changes names from De Ruyter, to Bankert and Evertsen), with its view of tug boats, sailing ships, and ferry boats vying for position. A windmill, **Oranjemolen**, on Oranjedijk, is open Fridays 9am-4pm.

Markets

Market day is Fri. 9am-4:30pm, at Lange Zelke and Spuiplein. Flanders, across the Westerschelde, is a mecca for Dutch and Belgian shoppers.

Staying over

A favourite for its exceptional sea views and access to the beach is the **Hotel Britannia**, Boulevard Evertsen 244, ☎ (0118) 41 3255, boasting spacious rooms with wide windows; the **Piccard**, Badhuisstraat 178, ☎ (0118) 41 3551, is moderately priced.

Yearly events

Boat tours on the Westerschelde depart from Koopmanshaven in July-Aug., Tues., Thurs. and Fri, 2pm. Tour lasts two hours. Arrange through the VVV, which also has information on free pony-tram tours of the inner city and the Boulevard on Saturday afternoons in July and August.

Terneuzen
The Belgian connection

Getting there: To reach Terneuzen cross the Westerschelde by ferry from Vlissingen to Breskens, or Kruiningen to Perkpolder.

Information: VVV, Markt 11, ☎ (0115) 69 5976; www.vvvzeeland.nl/regios/zeeuwsvlaanderen/terneuzen

Terneuzen has long been an important harbour and transportation centre in Zeeland-Flanders, and it's now even more important. The Westerscheldetunnel makes it possible for motorists to reach Zeeland-Flanders without taking a car ferry or driving through Belgium.

Terneuzen is where the Westerschelde enters the Ghent-Terneuzen Canal – an active and economically important waterway for traffic to Belgium. In addition, the harbour has about 600 berths for pleasure boats, and the demand is constantly growing.

Terneuzen has an old town centre with much atmosphere. It is bordered on one side by the sparkling harbour (its wealth and its pride), and on the other by a modern housing complex. Browse around the locks, and look at ships of all nationalities, or wander through the old town. A good walk for views of both is along the Westerscheldedijk (Schelde Boulevard). If you are here at low tide, you can see large sandbanks appear – quite a sight.

At **Het Portaal van Vlaanderen** you get a close-up view of shipping, with displays and video. You see the Terneuzen canal from a viewing tower. Boat trips are possible through the harbour and to the locks to see the ocean-going ships sailing to and from Ghent. The programme starts at 1:30pm, open July-Aug, Mon-Sat; May-June, Wed & Sat; April & Sept, Wed., ☎ (0115) 69 5976.

If you want to learn more about the tunnel connecting Zeeland-Flanders to the rest of the Netherlands, visit the **Tunnelcentrum**, Willemskerkeweg 1, ☎ (0115) 64 9095, www.westerscheldetunnel.nl, open Tues.-Fri. 9am-4pm; Sat. 11am-4pm. It has a detailed model and a computerised feel of what a ride through the Westerscheldetunnel is like.

A look back at what schools were like in the olden days is possible at the **Schoolmuseum Schooltijd**, Vissteeg 4, ☎ (06) 5283 7109, open Apr.-Sept., Wed.-Sat. 2-4:45pm; Oct.-Mar., Wed. & Sat. 2-4:45pm.

Eating out

A bit expensive, but for water-view dining, try **De Kreek**, Noteneeweg 28, ☎ (0115) 62 0817. **Paviljoen Westkant**, Scheldeboulevard 1, ☎ (0115) 61 6000, also has excellent views of the waterway.

Staying over

If you need a place to rest your head, try the **Hotel Winston Churchill**, Churchillaan 700, ☎ (0115) 62 1120 (pool, air-conditioning), or **Hotel Golden Tulip L'Escaut**, Scheldekade 65, ☎ (0115) 69 4855.

Yearly events

In late May there's the **Schelde-Jazz Festival** and in July the **Port Celebration**.

Tours

If fishing is your sport, there's water everywhere: **De Braakmancreek, Otheense Creek**, or the **Westerschelde**. You can rent a boat and go on your own, or join a group. **Denick**, ☎ (0113) 38 3570, offers tours of the waterways as well as sport-fishing trips.

In the neighbourhood of Terneuzen

Zaamslag has a picturesque Town Square and former Town Hall surrounded by a park with an original bandstand. There's also the **Schelpenmuseum**, Plein 3, ☎ (0115) 43 1233, open Fri. 1-5pm & 6-9pm; Sat. 9am-noon & 1-5pm, with a collection of shells and other finds from the deep.

Axel is famous for its Saturday general goods market – the stands extend for 2 kilometers (over one mile)! Local costumes are sometimes worn. Dutch and Belgian shoppers in Flanders often cross the border, both in search of better prices on the other side (Belgians find gin, butter, cigarettes, etc., cheaper in the Netherlands).

Axel has a farm museum, **Streekmuseum Het Land Van Axel**, Noordstraat 11, ☎ (0115) 56 2885, open April-Oct., Wed.-Sat. 1:30-5pm; July-Aug., also open Tues. 1:30-5pm. The **Town Hall** tower has a 35-bell carillon. www.axel.nl/recreatie/streekmuseum

Hulst, southeast of Terneuzen on N60, has almost all its 17th-century fortifications intact. The town was first surrounded by ramparts when it became a regional trading centre in the late 12th century. The existing structures are from a 17th-century remodelling. Besides the earthen embankments, there are still parts of the old moat, nine bastions, and four town gates still in place: **Begijnepoort** (1704), **Dubbele Poort** (1771), **Gentse Poort** (1781) and **Bollewerckspoort** (1506).

St. Willibrordusbasiliek sits on 12th-century foundations, but it took over 250 years to finish building it. Originally a Catholic church, it was taken over by the Protestants in the 17th century, and shared by both groups in the 19th, a wall having been built inside to divide it into two sections. Since 1929 it was again a Catholic church, becoming a Basilica in 1935.

The **Town Hall**, Grote Markt 21, was built in 1534 – you can spot it by its tall tower. The **Streekmuseum De Vier Ambachten**, Steenstraat 28, ☎ (0114) 31 2311, open Easter to autumn holiday, daily 2-5pm, has a collection of traditional costumes from Zeeland-Flanders, as well as other items relating to local history. More information: VVV, Grote Markt 31, ☎ (0114) 38 9299, www.devierambachten.nl.

Biervliet is one of the most charming villages of Flanders. Formerly a prosperous trading town, there are remnants of the old city ramparts; a **Dutch Reformed Church** (1659) with lovely stained-glass windows, and an old grain mill, **Harmonie**, Molenstraat 9, ☎ (0115) 48 1462, open for visits by appointment. If you're here in mid-May, there's a **Pirates' Festival** (Geuzenfeesten).

Oostburg
Beaches, bowling and buying

Getting there:	Located between Breskens and Aardenburg
Information:	VVV Cadzand, ☎ (0117) 39 1298, or VVV Breskens, ☎ (0117) 38 1888; www.vvvzeeland.nl/regios/zeeuwsvlaanderen/oostburg

Oostburg is a large town in Dutch Flanders, and a major shopping centre for western Zeeland. The Wednesday market is an active and interesting place to shop. There's a cheese farm in town, **De Ysenagel**, Bakkerstraat 58, ☎ (0117) 45 2063, with a shop open Mon.-Fri. 9am-6pm, Sat. 9am-5pm. The nature reserve **Het Groote Gat** is also worth exploring. You might enjoy watching a traditional Zeeland-Flanders sport, *bollen met de krulbol*, a type of bowling with wooden cylinders, Tues. & Thurs. 7-9pm, Q. van Uffordweg 10, ☎ (0117) 45 2391.

In the neighbourhood of Oostburg

Breskens is the arrival point for the ferry from Vlissingen. Ferry schedules are discussed under 'Vlissingen.' A trout farm in the harbour at Kaai 2, ☎ (0117) 38 3158 open daily 10am-9pm, offers a tour as well as the chance to catch your own. Breskens has a Monday morning market, and a Fish Festival in mid-August.

Cadzand and **Cadzand-Bad** (Beach) is the place to relax and enjoy the North Sea beaches, the various sporting activities such as biking, bowling, tennis and squash. You can also relax in a sauna or dance at a disco. It's about 10 km (6 mi) northwest of Oostburg and about the same distance southwest of Breskens. The windmill, **Molen Nooitgedacht**, Zuidzandseweg 3, ☎ (0117) 46 1744, is open all year on Sun. from 2-6pm, also on Wed. in the summer. For information contact the VVV, Boulevard de Wielingen 44d, ☎ (0117) 39 1298.

If you want surf and sand, one of the hotels at Cadzand-Bad will be for you. There are several 4-star hotels, including **De Blanke Top**, Boulevard de Wielingen 1, ☎ (0117) 39 20 40, located on the dunes with sea views. It has a fitness centre with sauna, whirlpool and protected terrace. The **Strandhotel Jacoba's Hof**, Boulevard de Wielingen 49, ☎ (0117) 39 2110, is above the dunes with sea views, indoor pool, sauna, bowling, billiards and table tennis.

Sluis
Action-filled tourist centre

Getting there:	Located in Dutch Flanders, take the N58.
Information:	VVV, St. Annastraat 15, ☎ (0117) 46 1700; www.sluisonline.nl

In 1290 when **Sluis** received its town charter, it was already a well-known port and commercial centre. Together with the town of Damme, it was an outer harbour for ancient Bruges (Belgium). It declined over the years because of many wars fought in the area and also the silting up of the Zwin River. In the last war, 80% of the town was destroyed, but was then rebuilt by its townspeople. Wisely, these good people did not remove the old to make way for the new; rather, they blended the two and endeavoured to restore the characteristic old atmosphere as much as possible. The many visitors attest to their success.

Today, tourism is the economic mainstay of Sluis, although some industry and agriculture also play a part. Through special dispensation, dozens of attractive shops are allowed to remain open in the evenings and on Sundays – not so common in the rest of Holland. Because of this, its proximity to popular Belgian beach centres, comfortable hotels, and atmospheric cafés and restaurants, Sluis is buzzing with activity in holiday periods and at weekends.

The **Town Hall**, restored after severe damage in WW II, has the only 14th-century belfry in Holland. The wooden figure in the tower is of Flanders' oldest bell ringer, Jantje van Sluis – carved in the Middle Ages by Jacoppe van Huusse. He represents a medieval bell ringer whose warnings are reputed to have saved the town from a Spanish attack. His colourful dress makes him a sure camera target, and he indicates the time every half-hour in ingenious fashion. Special carillon concerts are given in the summer in addition to the regular chimes. The tower is open for visits July-Aug. 1-5pm.

De Brak, Nieuwstraat 26, ☎ (0117) 46 1250, open 10am-5pm, but closed Fri. in winter, is a working grain mill restored after being damaged in the war.

The ramparts, gates, and the ruin **De Steenen Beer** should not be missed. On the ramparts is a statue of 19th-century Sluis schoolmaster Johan Hendrik van Dale, famous for his compilation of the Dutch dictionary.

In the neighbourhood of Sluis

On the outskirts of Sluis is **St. Anna ter Muiden**, with a Town Square pretty enough to be officially listed for preservation. It has a picturesque village green, a unique medieval Town Hall, and a 17th-century church. The monumental tower next to it is all that remains of the original church which was destroyed during the Spanish occupation.

Aardenburg has origins dating back to the Stone Age, and was a Roman town as can be verified by a visit to the **Gemeentelijk Archeologisch Museum**, Markstraat 18, ☎ (0117) 49 2888, open late Apr.-Sept., Tues.-Sun. 1:30-5pm. It contains a collection of sarcophagi from the Roman period. Northwest of town, you can see the **Kaaipoort** (17th century), one of the gates in the old town walls. Attractive 17th-century buildings can be seen along Weststraat. The 13th-century church, **St. Baafskerk**, St. Bavostraat 5, ☎ (0117) 49 2544, can be visited May-Sept., Tues.-Fri. 1-5pm, Sat.-Sun. 2-4pm. You will see a number of stone coffins of various Counts, which were discovered in the church's restoration. Shoppers might enjoy Aardenburg's Tuesday morning market.

Chapter 14 | Beaches

Going to the beach in Holland can be a pleasant but often perplexing venture for some foreigners, as 'the system' can be different in certain ways from that in the UK or US, for example. The following tips may be helpful if you're not sure how 'the system' works.

Beach pavilions and cafés are a common sight on developed beaches in Holland. You can either sit inside and be served a snack, or rent a chair, parasol and space on the beach. A waiter will get you settled wherever you choose (in front of his establishment) and take your order. Some places offer changing rooms that can be rented for a day or half-day; others have changing rooms where you can leave your clothes, but some do not. Some have showers; many do not, but you are almost sure to find toilet facilities. You pay for what you want to use, and the cost is usually minimal. You are, however, expected to order a drink – and later, perhaps an ice cream or another drink, but you won't be bothered every few minutes. At the more sophisticated beaches, you will find cafés that offer a full meal, as well as some glass-enclosed sunbathing areas, etc.

The first visit to a Dutch beach may present the visitor with the unusual sight of sunbathers huddling behind various coloured tarpaulins. You may soon follow suit after experiencing the ever-present wind on a North Sea beach. Though you leave home convinced it's going to be a brilliant, hot, windless day, once you've put on your swim attire and reached the water's edge, you might be in for a surprise. The answer is a *windscherm*, a windscreen available at sports shops.

If you go to a less developed beach, you will probably be faced with a lack of toilet facilities. A beach café will provide the solution – there's usually one close by.

The good news is that there are fabulous beaches all along the North Sea coast, including those of the Waddenzee Islands, Flevoland, Friesland and Groningen. Those we list here are some of the better-known beaches in Zeeland, South and North Holland. Many have been given the 'blue flag,' an international award given to beaches that are clean, with water judged to be of excellent quality, and with sufficient toilet facilities, rubbish bins, and lifesaving and first aid posts on hand.

Some beaches in the Netherlands are designated as 'naturist,' a euphemism for 'nudist,' while on most beaches, topless sunbathing is fairly common today.

Domburg

Getting there: From Middelburg take N288 to Westkapelle; for Oostkapelle and
Domburg take N57 north to N287.

Information: VVV, Schuitvlotstraat, ☎ (0900) 202 0280; www.vvvzeeland.nl

Domburg is Zeeland's oldest seaside resort, and although very popular, there are plenty of other 'blue flag' beaches on the island of Walcheren to compete for the summer crowds.

Westkapelle is an old sea village, located directly behind a dike that has protected villagers from the sea since the 16th century. **Oostkapelle** is known for its summer markets, folkloric events, and a puppet theatre for the kids. You can have your photo taken in traditional costume at **Familie Louws**, Westhovenseweg 4, ☎ (0118) 58 2096. Just west of Vlissingen are two other 'blue flag' beaches, **Dishoek** and **Zoutelande** with the highest dunes on the island.

Still the primary beach and most developed resort in the area, picturesque Domburg has a number of early 20th-century homes built by the wealthy – the first to come here for its blue skies and fresh air. It was popular with Dutch artists Piet Mondriaan and Jan Toorop, as well as other prominent artists and performers. Golf and horse riding are among the many attractions.

On the drive between Domburg and Middelburg, there's an orchard area where you can try the fresh fruit and juice. For a farm lunch, stop at the old mill at Serooskerke, **Molen Taverne De Hoop** (literally 'Windmill Tavern of Hope'), Vrouwenpolderseweg 55A, ☎ (0118) 59 2842. Just past it is the dairy farm **Pitteperk**, Kokerheulweg 1, ☎ (0118) 59 6031, open Tues. & Thurs. 2-5pm, where you can see and sample the cheese and butter produced here.

Renesse

Getting there: N59 west from A29, or N57 south from Ouddorp
Information: VVV, Zeeanemoonweg 4A, ☎ (0111) 46 0360; www.vvvzeeland.nl

Along with **Burgh-Haamstede** and **Westerschouwen**, **Renesse** is part of a major seaside area, with a beach to suit almost every taste. Located on the island of Schouwen-Duiveland, Renesse and Westerschouwen are 'blue flag' beaches with very different personalities. In summer, Renesse is alive with discos, bars and restaurants, and a popular nudist beach. Westerschouwen nestles on the edge of woodlands, its beach popular with families and water sport enthusiasts. To handle the influx of summer visitors, Burgh-Haamstede has a park-and-ride facility with 24-hour security. A shuttle runs to the various beaches and facilities in the area.

Ouddorp

Getting there: Take A29 south from Rotterdam to the N59 exit. Take N59 west to N215, then southwest on N57 to Ouddorp.
Information: VVV Ouddorp, Bosweg 2, ☎ (0187) 68 1789; www.vvv-ouddorp.org

The northwestern tip of the island of Goeree-Overflakkee in Zeeland is lined with white sand, family beaches and dunes. The picturesque 'ring village' of **Ouddorp** is also worth a visit. Its 14th-century church in the marketplace is ringed by shops. The area also has numerous bike routes winding past farmhouses and fields of flowers.

East of Ouddorp is another pretty village, **Goedereede**, a North Sea port in 1312 that still has a number of buildings from that era, including a 16th-century cathedral tower that also served as a lighthouse. Further east is the village of **Stellendam**, where a fish auction is held on Friday mornings along the harbour.

Rockanje

Getting there: From A15/N15, south of Rotterdam, take exit 12 (N57) south to N496, and follow signs to Rockanje.

Information: VVV, Berberislaan 2, ☎ (0181) 40 1600; www.zuid-hollandse-eilanden.nl

Rockanje is a lovely small town in South Holland geared to families. Its dunes are ideal for exploring and its fine sand beach perfect for young children. It is wide, the water is calm, and little huts offer protection from too much sun.

Park your car at the main entrance to the beach by **Restaurant 't Golfie**, with its playground for tots, and mini-golf. There are a few beach hotels for overnight stays, as well as apartments, pensions and private homes that let rooms. About 15 minutes walk from the beach is the **Badhotel Rockanje aan Zee**, 2e Slag 1, ☎ (0181) 40 1755, which has a heated pool, and offers apartments and rooms as well as hotel accommodation.

Oostvoorne

Getting there: Southwest of Rotterdam. On A15 take exit 16 (Spijkenisse) south to N218, go west, follow signs to Oostvoorne.

Information: VVV, Hoflaan 6, ☎ (0181) 48 2749; www.zuid-hollandse-eilanden.nl

Oostvoorne originated as a settlement around a castle, and the beach here is so wide and flat that you can drive your car right onto it. There is no boardwalk, but beach cafés spring up in the summer. Ideal conditions for swimming and windsurfing can be found here.

One of Western Europe's most beautiful nature reserves lies between Oostvoorne and Rockanje – its woods and dunes rich in flora and birdlife. Cyclists can ply the free-lying paths, winding their way through the rustic landscape and visiting the picturesque villages of **Tinte**, **Zwartewaal**, **Abbenbroek** and medieval **Heenvliet**.

Rail-Toy, Hoflaan 16, ☎ (0181) 48 5085, open March-Dec. Wed.-Sat., 10:30am-4:30pm; also Tue. 10:30am-4:30pm, has wide-gauge toy trains from 1890-1940, steam engines, ships, cars, etc. – a family outing rain or shine.

For those wanting to spend a weekend or longer, there are hotels along the boulevard: The **Duinoord**, Zeeweg 23, ☎ (0181) 48 2044, and **Hotel Het Wapen van Marion**, Zeeweg 60, ☎ (0181) 48 9399, www.wapenvanmarion.nl. The VVV has a list of other accommodations.

In the neighbourhood of Oostvoorne

Brielse Meer is a lakeside recreation park that extends some 14 km (8.5 mi) from Spijkenisse to Oostvoorne along the former Brielse Maas. Natural and unspoiled, it appeals to nature lovers, campers, sailors and all lovers of water sports. As well as a large protected outdoor swimming area, there are paths for walking and biking. If you don't have a boat, you can rent one from **Botenverhuurbedrijf A. Boertje**, Brielse Veerweg 2, ☎ 06 2267 0967. They have everything from motor and sailboats, to rowboats and water bikes. (For more on Brielle, see the South Holland chapter.)

Hoek van Holland

Getting there: Slightly northwest of Rotterdam. From Rotterdam follow A20/N220 west to Hoek van Holland.

Information: VVV Infopunt, PrinsHendrikstraat 265, (0174) 31 0080; www.hoekvanholland.nl/vvv, and www.waterweg-westland.nl

From the centre of Rotterdam you can drive to the '**Hook of Holland**' in 30 minutes. There is also quick and frequent public transportation (check at Central Station), as this is the port for the daily ferry to Harwich, England, as well as a lively resort. Its wide family-type beach is relatively undeveloped, but there is much to see and do in the area. There are dunes, woods, and special VVV nature walks and bike rides, as well as museums to do with the sea; the Storm Surge Barrier; the Expo-Info Waterway Centre; and ships and sports galore. Accommodation and eateries come in all categories.

This long stretch of beach and dunes bordering the North Sea continues past the pleasant little resort of **'s Gravenzande** as far as the Afvoer Canal, which cuts through the centre of The Hague. **Scheveningen** begins on the other side of the canal, with miles of beaches and dunes stretching northward. Because the dunes are needed to protect the inland area, there is no highway parallel to the beach proper. Those wishing to explore, should leave the highway at 's Gravenzande, **Monster** or **Loosduinen**.

Scheveningen

Getting there: In The Hague, follow signs to Scheveningen.

Information: VVV Scheveningen, Gevers Deynootweg 1134, ☎ (0900) 340 3505 (€ 0,75 p. min.); www.scheveningen-info.com

Scheveningen is the best known and most developed of the North Sea beaches. It deserves its reputation, especially if you want entertainment, shopping and activity along with your enjoyment of the coast. The wide, four-kilometer-long (2.5 mi) beach has a children's play area at the foot of the pier. For sun and sea bathers, the area is well patrolled by lifeguards, with beach pavilions and restaurants galore. On the boulevard above the beach, which has glass wind protectors here and there, you can buy anything from inexpensive souvenirs to furs! You can grab a bite from a *patat* (British 'chips' or French fries) stand or have a sumptuous meal at a hotel or restaurant overlooking the water. There is something for every taste, and the seafood is fresh and tasty.

Scheveningen has been a fishing port for over 700 years. Until the 20th century, and the terrible storm of 1894 that demolished most of the fleet, fishermen had pulled their boats up onto the beach. Today, they moor them in the protected harbour alongside leisure boats at the southern end of town. As a result, this particular area is full of interesting dining-out spots.

Attractions

Besides having the most popular beach on the coast, Scheveningen has many other attractions. These include: the **Sea Museum**, the **Sea Life Centre**, the **Scheveningen Museum**, the **Sculptures By The Sea Museum**, the **Museum Ship Hr Ms Mercuur**, as well as the beautiful **Kurhaus**, and **Holland Casino** (see The Hague, Chapter 3). Following are some specific Scheveningen beach area attractions.

The **Palace Promenade** has developed into the largest, covered shopping/entertainment centre in this part of Holland. Open daily until 10pm in summer, you can find almost everything: luxury gift articles, fashion, delicatessens, café-restaurants, etc. Next door is a bowling centre at Gevers Deynootweg 990, ☎ (070) 354 3212.

From **Van der Valk's Pier**, Strandweg, ☎ (070) 306 5500, open 9am-11pm, there's a great view of the beach, either from the raised pier, or from its 50-meter watchtower. The pier's attractions include a café, restaurant and a family amusement centre. www.valk.com

If you're in the mood for a sauna, body massage, or even a sunbed on a bad day, **Kuur Thermen Vitalizee**, Strandweg 13, south of the Kurhaus, ☎ (070) 416 6500, offers the full spa treatment, www.vitalizee.nl. The more active can horse ride; call **Manage Le Cavalier**, Alkmaarsestraat 20, ☎ (070) 355 0016; rent skates at **Rollerwave**, Badhuisstraat 114, ☎ (070) 354 0059 www.rollerwave.nl, or **Go Klap**, Dr. Lelykade 44, ☎ (070) 354 8679, which also has canoes and surfboards. Rent catamarans and water-skis at **Oscars**, Gevers Deynootweg 205, ☎ (070) 352 2742; or, to do some serious sailing, call at **Minerva Maritiem**, Dr. Lelykade, ☎ (070) 351 4262, or **Het Zeilend Zeeschip**, Schokkerweg 44, ☎ (010) 448 61 86, www.eendracht.nl.

Eating out

The number of restaurants, snack bars, etc., is inexhaustible, and your greatest problem will be making a choice. If you want to eat something traditionally Dutch, walk south (the beach on your right), past the lighthouse, and turn at Vissershavenweg toward the port. At Treilerdwarsweg there's a food stand on the quay, with people blissfully eating a whole herring – their heads thrown back and mouths open, with fish overhead and fish tail between their fingers. If you can't face this nourishing delicacy (smothering it with onions as the Dutch do makes it even more *lekker*), there are numerous fish restaurants; among them, **van der Toorn**, Teilersdwarsweg 2, ☎ (070) 354 5783 (simple but good), and a variety of ethnic eateries overlooking the harbour on Dr. Lelykade.

There are a vast number of restaurants here from all over the world – including Italian, Mexican and Chinese. For Indonesian, try **Raden Mas**, Gevers Deynootplein 125, ☎ (070) 354 5432, http://radenmasschvn.orientalrestaurants.nl; for Japanese, **Sakura**, Gevers Deynootplein 155, ☎ (070) 358 4853; for American, **Applebee's**, Gevers Deynootplein, ☎ (070) 352 3002 – all near the Kurhaus. Inside the Kurhaus, you have the

choice of the elegant **Kandinsky** restaurant, Gevers Deynootplein 30, ☎ (070) 416 2636, with it's wonderful sea views, or the reasonably priced buffet served in the main lobby.

Staying over

Scheveningen is a favourite place for families wanting to mix sightseeing with sea breezes, as well as for people doing business in The Hague. Top of the line accomodation is the majestic **Steigenberger Kurhaus Hotel**, Gevers Deynootplein 30, ☎ (070) 416 2636. The less expensive **Bel Park Hotel**, Belgischeplein 38, ☎ (070) 350 5000, is only a 15-minute walk to the beach. Also there is the **Strand Hotel**, Zeekant 111, ☎ (070) 354 0193, www.strandhotel.demon.nl, with sea and dune views, and a moderate price.

In the neighbourhood of Scheveningen

Kijkduin, to the south, is The Hague's 'family beach.' It's a pleasant walk from the centre – with its sun terraces, bistros, and shops. In season, there are puppet shows for kids, and concerts for teenagers and older. A covered shopping area is open daily. North of Scheveningen is a nudist beach, followed, in contrast, by an undeveloped and therefore ideal, family-type picnic beach at **Wassenaarse Slag**.

Noordwijk aan Zee

Getting there: Located between The Hague and Haarlem, take exit 6 off of A44 to Noordwijk aan Zee.

Information: VVV, de Grent 8, ☎ (0900) 222 2333 (€ 0.50 p.m.); http://www.hollandrijnland.nl/noordwijk

This beach extends for miles up and down the coast, with hotels and guesthouses galore on the seafront and in the dunes. **Noordwijk** is conveniently located for those visiting **Keukenhof** and the bulb fields of the region. Less commercialised than Scheveningen, it is popular with foreign tourists.

There are places for horse riding near the beach and in the dunes, as well as tennis courts, a pool for indoor-outdoor swimming, mini-golf, a bowling alley, and a shopping street buzzing with activity. There are also bike paths along the coast and through the dunes inland to the lakes. (Bike rental details from the VVV.)

Close by is the beach-dune-woods area and **Noordwijkerhout**. The **Dune Reserve** between Noordwijk and Zandvoort is a protected waterfowl area open to walkers only (no bikes or dogs) – a real oasis of peace, flora and fauna.

Attractions

Oud Noordwijk Museum, Jan Kroonsplein 4, ☎ (0171) 361 7884, open June-mid Sept., Mon.-Sat. 10am-5pm, Sun. 2-5pm; May, mid Sept.-Oct., Tues.-Sat. 2-5pm, is a renovated 1880s farm where they tell the history of area fishermen. www.g-o-n.nl

Ever wonder what it feels like to be an astronaut and lose your orientation from spinning upside down?

Then head to **Noordwijk Space Expo**, Keplerlaan 3, ☎ (0171) 364 6446, open Tues.-Sun. 10am-5pm. The Multi-Axis Simulator at the Space Expo gives visitors a chance to experience that very feeling. Once your feet are planted firmly on the ground again, you can see real satellites, a space station, a moon rock, etc. There is much to see, touch, and learn here – of interest to all ages. This is also the visitors' centre for ESTEC, the European Space Agency. www.spaceexpo.nl

Jan Verwey Nature Centre, Weteringkade 27, open May-Sept., Sun. & Wed. 2-4pm, has an exhibit of area flora and fauna. **Aqualand**, at the Oranje Hotel, Koningin Wilhelmina Blvd. 20, ☎ (0171) 367 6848, offers spa and wellness treatments for indulgent pampering. www.hotelsvanoranje.com/uk

Eating out

The beach and the boulevard have many terraces for a bite or a drink, but to do it in style, the terrace of the **Grand Hotel Huis ter Duin** with its lovely view over the sea is hard to beat. Noordwijk itself has many restaurants, but for a special meal try **Het Hof van Holland** (see below).

Staying over

Away from the hustle bustle of the beach area is a hotel-restaurant with typical Dutch atmosphere: **Het Hof van Holland**, Voorstraat 79, ☎ (0171) 361 2255, on a tree-lined Square. Top of the line **Grand Hotel Huis ter Duin**, Koningin Astrid Boulevard 5, ☎ (071) 367 9220, has great views and 5-star comfort. (Contact the VVV for B&B, camping, etc.)

Tours

The VVV offers several holiday packages for visitors to Noordwijk. They include cycling packages through the dune region or the bulb fields; a golf package that includes two half-hour lessons from a golf pro; and a beauty package that includes a facial, body-scrub and sauna.

Zandvoort

Getting there:	From Haarlem, follow the signs to Zandvoort. It's about a 20-minute drive west.
Information:	VVV, Schoolplein 1, ☎ (023) 571 7947; www.vvvzk.nl, and for detailed information, www.info-zandvoort.nl

Zandvoort is Amsterdam's playground. Going along with Amsterdam's image of the avant-garde, it has a nude bathing beach, a casino, and a motor racing circuit, plus the amenities of a seaside resort. (For these attractions, see Chapter 2.)

There are 15km (9 mi) of beaches, with superb sand and water to enjoy. There are about 40 pavilions with changing facilities, food, drinks, parasols, etc. As well as the special sections for nude bathers, there are also fairly deserted stretches for those seeking peace and quiet. You can actually walk all the way to IJmuiden. To the north of Zandvoort are the beaches of **Bloemendaal aan Zee** and **IJmuiden**. If you prefer smaller and less crowded beaches and don't need attractions and amenities, these are the choices for you.

Staying over

Zandvoort has many hotels and pensions. On the high end is the **Gran Dorado**, Trompstraat 2, ☎ (023) 572 0000; or the **Golden Tulip Zandvoort**, Burg. Van Alphenstraat 63, ☎ (023) 571 3234. In the moderate range are the **Hotel Cocarde**, Hogeweg 39, ☎ (023) 571 6855, a small traditional Dutch hotel with under 20 rooms, or the **Zuiderbad**, Boulevard Paulus Loot 5, ☎ (023) 571 2613, with a café-restaurant. The **CenterParcs** bungalow park here is great for families, Parc Zandvoort, Vondellaan 60, ☎ (023) 572 0000, www.centerparcs.nl.

Eating out

Try **Cesario**, Kerkstraat 19, ☎ (023) 573 1456, for pizza and Italian food; or **'t Familie Restaurant**, Kerkstraat 27, ☎ (023) 571 2537, for rib eye, spare ribs, salmon steak, or their speciality of stewed eel! (Come on, be adventurous.) **Take Five**, Boulevaard Paulus Loot 5, ☎ (023) 571 6119, offers a sea view and delicious food, www.tfaz.nl. A family-friendly place in the dunes is **Parnassia**, on the edge of the **Kennermerduinen** national park, ☎ (023) 573 2140, www.parnassia-aan-zee.nl.

Grand Cafe Restaurant Riche, Boulevard Barnaart 67, ☎ (023) 571 2553, offers international cuisine.

Egmond aan Zee

Getting there: Just west of Alkmaar, you can reach Egmond aan Zee from the N9 via N512. Bergen aan Zee is slightly north.

Information: VVV, Voorstraat 82A, ☎ (072) 581 3100; www.vvvnoordzeekust.nl

Egmond aan Zee and **Bergen aan Zee** are two family-style beaches close to Alkmaar. The villages are in a protected national dunes and woodland area. Bergen aan Zee is a picturesque artists' centre well worth a visit. http://bergenaanzee.com/nl-nl

Schoorl is a couple of kilometers north of Bergen off north/south road N9. The Schoorl beach, only accessible by foot or bike, is therefore quieter than most beaches on this coast. Bikes can be rented. The dunes here are the widest and highest in the country. www.vvvschoorl.nl

Petten

Getting there: N9 north from Alkmaar to the Petten turnoff
Information: VVV, Zijperweg 1A, ☎ (0226) 38 1352; www.vvvpetten.nl

The beaches at **Petten** and at **St. Maartenszee** are known as peaceful seaside resorts. They have few overnight hotel facilities, as most visitors rent weekly accommodation, but their 'blue flag' beaches are a perfect place for those looking for a quiet spot to swim and enjoy the sun. The flat polder terrain is excellent for walking and cycling. Treasure hunts for children are organised at Petten and St. Maartenszee during the peak season. For family camping, see www.campingsintmaartenszee.nl

Callantsoog

Location: From Alkmaar take N9 north. Near Schagen, take N503 west to Callantsoog.
Information: VVV, Jewelweg 8, ☎ (0224) 58 1541; www.vvvcallantsoog.nl

Callantsoog is popular with both beach and nature lovers. There are miles of walking and cycling paths through the dunes and neighbouring polderlands. Some trails lead to the **Zwanenwater**, a nature reserve that is home to blue herons, spoonbills, gulls and numerous other birds.

Further north – just south of Den Helder – the **Julianadorp** beach (see Chapter 2) boasts long sunshine hours, and has an area reserved for nudists. There are a number of luxury holiday home parks, and a golf course. www.strandslagvakantie.nl

Even further north is **Huisduinen**. Like Julianadorp and Callantsoog, Huisduinen has been awarded the 'blue flag' in recognition of its high environmental quality. This old fishing village has facilities for surfing, diving, cycling, and fishing. (Read more about the attractions of this area in the 'Den Helder' section in Chapter 2.)

Just north of Callantsoog is **Grote Keeten**, another 'blue flag' beach with various hotels, bungalows and camping facilities for overnight stays.

▶ Coastal guides

For even more information on the Dutch coastal areas, visit the Coastal Guides to Europe, www.coastalguide.to/netherlands, for details and recommendations on hotels, camping, bungalows and cottages, restaurants, events, attractions, etc., in Holland.

There are over 700 campsites, and 450 bungalow parks, as well as select holiday homes in Holland. For more information see: www.eurocampings.co.uk/en/europe/netherlands/, or search by 'bungalow park' on: www2.holland.com/us.

Two chains operating popular bungalow parks throughout the country are **Landal Green Parks**, www.landal.nl, and **Center Parcs**, www.centerparcs.nl.

Chapter 15 | How it's made: crafts and industry

In our world of plastics and throwaways, it's always important to remind ourselves of some of the products still made by hand in traditional fashion, and that many have no equals in the 'ready-made' market. Every country has its own traditional products, and Holland is certainly no exception. From asparagus to wheat, beer, candles, cheese, clocks, crystal and glass, diamonds, Dutch gin, eels, furniture, mustard, peat, pewter, pottery (especially Delftware), ships, silver, textiles, wine (yes, wine) and wooden shoes, Holland is indeed a mecca for handmade and locally produced goods, some of which are indigenous to this country.

Following are a select few of the places we recommend for enjoying the local crafts and industry and, in most cases, sampling the goods.

▸ **Asparagus**
  Diffelen, Overijssel (north of Almelo). Asparagus farm with guided tour and video presentation. **Aspergeboerderij Het Nijenhuis**, Rheezerweg 127, ☎ (0523) 25 1866, www.hetnijenhuis.nl, open Mon.-Fri. 10am-6pm, Sat. 9am-5pm.

▸ **Baking and grinding wheat**
  – **Gouda**, South Holland. Baking treacle wafers (*stroopwafels*) is demonstrated at **Gebackerij van der Berg**, Lange Groenendaal 32, ☎ (0182) 52 9975, www.vd-berg.nl.
  – **Luyksgestel**, Brabant. **Bakkerijmuseum De Grenswachter**, Kapellerweg 15, ☎ (0497) 54 1314, is set up as a late 19th-century bakery and shop. www.bakkerijmuseum.nl. Baking demonstrations Wed. 1:30pm & Mon.-Sat. 1:30pm during school holidays.
  – **Schiedam**, South Holland. **De Nieuwe Palmboom**, windmill museum, Noordvest 34, ☎ (010) 426 7675, is open Tues.- Sat. 11am-5pm, Sun. 12:30-5pm.
  – **Rotterdam**, South Holland. **Distilleerketel** windmill, Voorhaven 210, Delfshaven, ☎ (010) 477 9181, open Wed. 10am-5pm, Sat. 10am-4pm.

▸ **Beer-brewing**
  – **Amersfoort**, Utrecht province. **De Drie Ringen**, Kleine Spui 18, open Thurs. 1-6pm, Fri.-Sat. 1-7pm, ☎ (033) 465 6575, offers free tours of its small brewery. www.dedrieringen.nl
  – **Amsterdam**, North Holland. **Heineken** offers a tour of its former brewery (main one now at another location), with free samples given during the visit, Stadhouderskade 78, ☎ (020) 523 9666, www.heinekeninternational.com, open Tues.-Sun. 10am-6pm.
  – **Berkel-Enschot**, Brabant. The monks at the **Trappist Monastery**, just northeast of Tilburg, have been brewing La Trappe beer since 1884, Eindhovenseweg 3,

☎ (013) 535 8147, April-Oct., Tues.-Sat. 11am-6pm, Sun. 12-6pm. Nov.-March tours only. www.latrappe.nl
- **Enschede**, Overijssel. **Grolsch** offers tours at its brewery Mon.-Fri. by appointment, adults only. Located at Brouwerslaan 1, ☎ (053) 483 3333. www.grolsch.nl
- **Gulpen**, Limburg. The **Gulpener Beer Brewery**, Rijksweg 16, ☎ (043) 450 7575, gives guided tours by appointment only.

▶ **Candle-making**
- **Gouda**, South Holland. Gouda, former headquarters of a large candle factory, is a candle-making centre as well as a cheese-producing town. **De Vergulde Kaars**, Hoge Gouwe 45a, ☎ (0182) 55 0735, makes candles in their shop. For a small fee you can pour and colour your own creation. By appointment only. www.deverguldekaars.nl
- **Hapert**, Brabant. **Kaarsenmakerij Keerf**, Dalweg 1, ☎ (0497) 38 4862, open Tues.-Sun. 11am-4pm. Watch candles being made...then make your own. Also available for children's birthday parties. Southwest of Eindhoven.
- **Scheveningen**, South Holland. **Ambachtelijke Kaarsenmakerij**, Strandweg 11, ☎ (070) 352 3486, open Mon.-Fri. 10am-5pm, weekends 11am-5pm. This workshop demonstrates all aspects of candle-making, including the age-old process of candle-dipping and casting. At the end of the programme, you can try your own hand at dipping a candle that you may take home. The modest admission fee includes the cost of your personally-made candle.
- **Zevenaar**, Gelderland. **Steenfabriek Panoven**, Panovenweg 18, April-Aug. 10am-5pm daily, rest of the year Tues.-Sun., ☎ (0316) 52 3520. www.panoven.nl. Not only do you see the candles being made here from June-Oct., but by visiting their apiary, you can see the bees that supply the wax as well. You may watch the brick-making process, too.

▶ **Cheese-making**
Cheese-making is perhaps not as readily done as you might think, considering that cheese is a major export item and a full-scale industry in the Netherlands. The small farmer usually makes cheese once a year. He keeps some for his own use and sells some privately, but much of it is sold commercially as *boerenkaas*, farmer's cheese. *Boerenkaas* is creamier than other cheeses, therefore with a higher fat content. Cheese-making is a delicate process, requiring very controlled conditions (no drafts, for instance) for the milk to set properly. For this reason, a large group of sightseers cannot usually be accommodated in a limited work space.
- **Bodegraven**, South Holland. **Cheese Museum and Centre**, Spoorstraat 15, ☎ (0172) 65 0909, open Sat. 10am-4pm.
- **Gouda**, South Holland. **De Boerinn**, Kamerik, ☎ (0348) 40 1200, www.deboerinn.nl, office open daily 9am-various hours; visit to farm by appointment only, where you can try your hand at it.

– **Katwoude**, North Holland. **Kaasmakerij Irenehoeve**, Hoogedijk 1, ☎ (0299) 65 2291, open daily 9am-6pm. Cheese and wooden shoes made here.
– **Katwoude**, North Holland. **Jacobhoeve**, Hoogedijk 8, ☎ (0299) 65 5151, open daily 9am-6pm. Sheep, goat and Gouda cheese made in the traditional way.
– **Markelo**, Overijssel. **Zuivelboerderij Effink**, Stokkumervlierweg 6, ☎ (0547) 26 0319, http://welcome.to/effink, open Sept.-April Tues. 1:30-5pm, Fri.-Sat. 9am-5pm, May-Aug. Tues. Thurs. Fri. Sat. 9am-5pm, makes cheese according to traditional methods.
– **Vreeland**, Utrecht. **De Willigen**, Nigtevechtseweg 188, ☎ (0294) 25 1668, www.dewilligen-kaas.nl, open April-Oct., Tues.-Sat. 9am-6pm; Sun. 12-6pm., closed Sun. Nov.-March.
– **Zaandam**, North Holland. **Catharinehoeve**, Zaanse Schans Zeilenmakerspad 5, ☎ (075) 621 5820, www.henriwillig.com, open March-Oct., daily 8am-6pm; Nov.-Feb., daily 8:30am-5pm, shows how Edam and Gouda cheeses are made in the traditional manner.

▶ **Clock-making**

Joure, Friesland, is home to makers of traditional Frisian clocks. You can visit **Klokkenmakerij ten Hoeve**, Midstraat 37, ☎ (0513) 41 3339, open Mon.-Fri. 8:30am-5:30pm, Sat. 10am-4pm; or **Klokkenmakerij van der Meulen**, Roazebosk 13, Scharsterbrug (just south of Joure), ☎ (0513) 41 2751, www.klokkenmakerijvandermeulen.nl, open Mon.-Sat 9am-5pm.

▶ **Crystal and glass-making**

– **Schiedam**, South Holland, Boterstraat 81, 06 110 17511, glass museum, www.glasmuseum.nl. There are regular glass-blowing demonstrations, as well as craftsmen at work creating glass products.
– **Leerdam**, South Holland. Did you know that the Dutch make crystal? They do, and very well, too. Visit **Glascentrum Leerdam**, Zuidwal, ☎ (0345) 61 4960, www.glascentrumleerdam.nl, open April-Oct., Tues.-Sat. 10am-5pm, Sun. noon-5pm, Nov.-23 Dec., Fri.-Sat. 10am-5pm, Sun. noon-5pm, to see how it's done.
– **Vaals**, Limburg. Gerardo Cardinale is one of Europe's top glass blowers. He gives demonstrations of his craft at **Glasblazerij Gerardo** at Tentstraat 2, ☎ (043) 306 2596, www.glasblazerij-gerardo.nl. Demonstrations are on the hour, Tues.-Sun., 11am-4pm. No demonstrations from Jan-Feb. You can also test your own skill at glass blowing.

▶ **Diamond-cutting**

– **Amsterdam** is known as the 'City of Diamonds' with several well-known diamond-cutting and polishing firms offering guided tours for individuals and groups. Perhaps the most customer-friendly and service-oriented is **ZaZare Diamonds**, Weteringschans 89 (just across from the Rijksmuseum), ☎ (020) 626 2798, www.zazarediamonds.com, known for its 'diamond treatment' (see ad with special offer, including diamond discount, travel coupons and champagne for readers of *Here's Holland*, on page 4). You can

353

also visit: **Amsterdam Diamond Center**, B.V., Rokin 1, ☎ (020) 624 5787; **Coster Diamonds and Museum**, Paulus Potterstraat 2-8, ☎ (020) 676 2222; **Gassan Diamonds and Museum**, Nieuwe Uilenburgerstraat 173-175,☎ (020) 622 5333; and **Van Moppes Diamonds**, Albert Cuypstraat 2-6, ☎ (020) 305 5555.

- **Rotterdam**, South Holland. **Diamond Center**, Kipstraat 7b, ☎ (010) 413 4551, open Mon.-Sat. 11am-5:30pm, closed Wed., for diamond-cutting and exhibition.
- **Volendam**, North Holland. **Biesterveld Dutch Diamond Center**, Haven 16-20, ☎ (0299) 32 1123, open daily 10am-6pm, has demonstrations of the art of diamond-cutting in its shop.

▶ **Distilleries**

Schiedam, South Holland. The **Netherlands Distillery Museum**, Lange Haven 74-76, ☎ (010) 246 9676, www.jenevermuseum.nl, has a small distillery on the ground level where visitors can watch the *jenever*-making process (*jenever* is Dutch gin). A free sample of their product is offered at the end of the tour. Open Tues.-Fri. noon-5pm, Sat.-Sun. noon-6pm.

▶ **Eel-smoking**

- **Broek Op Langedijk**, North Holland. Demonstrations given at the **Museum Broeker Veiling**, Museumweg 2, ☎ (0226) 31 3807, in April-June & Sept.-Oct., Mon.-Fri. 10am-5pm, Sat.-Sun. 11am-5pm; July-Aug., Mon.-Fri.10am-6pm, Sat.-Sun. 11am-5pm. www.broekerveiling.nl
- **Monnickendam**, North Holland. At **De Oude Visafslag**, Havenstraat 12, ☎ (0299) 65 4256, open Mon. 5am-3pm, Tues.-Fri. 5am-4pm, you can see the eel-smoking rooms in use.

▶ **Furniture & woodworking**

- **Dalfsen**, Overijssel (near Zwolle). **W. Duteweerd**, Brinkweg 3, ☎ (0529) 43 3981, makes cane and wicker products using old methods. By appointment only.
- **Hindeloopen**, Friesland. For details about visiting a factory that produces Hindeloopen furniture with its distinctive multi-coloured designs, call the VVV, ☎ (0900) 540 0001. At **Roosje Hindeloopen Holland**, Nieuwstad 44, ☎ (0514) 52 1251, Mr. E. Stallmann will demonstrate furniture being hand-painted. Cloth, used both for garments and home linens such as tablecloths, is also dyed in a unique Hindeloopen style. www.roosjehindeloopen.com
- **Staphorst**, Overijssel. Carving and woodwork by hand and machine can be watched at **Houtsnijbedrijf Timmerman**, Oranjestraat 32, ☎ (0522) 46 1369, www.atwoodcarving.nl, Mon.-Fri. 8am-noon & 1-6pm, Sat. 9am-noon, 1-4pm.

▶ **Mustard**

Doesburg, Gelderland. The **Doesburg Mustard and Vinegar Museum**, Boekholtstraat 22, ☎ (0313) 47 2230, open Mon.-Fri. 10am-5pm, Sat. 11am-4pm, makes mustard and vinegar the old-fashioned way.

▶ **Peat-digging**

Bargen Compascuum (east of Emmen), Drenthe, **National Veen Park**. It might come as a surprise but peat is still used for fuel in Europe, and this unusual occupation is explained at the Peat Park on demonstration days. Call the VVV.

▶ **Pewter-making**

Zaandam, North Holland. The **Tinkoepel Pewter Shop**, Zaanse Schans, Kalverringdijk 1, ☎ (075) 617 6204, is one place where you can watch pewter craftsmen working.

Zuidwolde, Drenthe. **Tin-Art Tingieterij**, Burgemeester Tonckensstraat 49, ☎ (0528) 37 3258, open Tues.-Sat. 10am-5pm, www.ibw.nl/tinart, makes pewter jewellery as well as other pewter items, and gives demonstrations in their shop.

▶ **Pottery-making**

There are two major manufacturers of pottery, porcelain and tiles in the Netherlands, both with a fascinating history. Makkum in Friesland, and Delft in South Holland have been rivals almost since they began.

Delft, South Holland. The **Koninklijke Porceleyne Fles**, (Royal Delftware Factory), Rotterdamseweg 196, ☎ (015) 251 2030, www.royaldelft.com, open April-Oct., Mon.-Sat. 9am-5pm, Sun. 9am- 5pm; Nov.-March, Mon.-Sat. 9am-5pm, receives visitors from all over the world, as it is the last remaining Delftware factory from the 17th century still producing entirely handmade Delftware. Famous for its blue and white designs, its artists also create pottery in black and other colours, in both classic and modern patterns.

Also in **Delft**. **De Delftse Pauw**, Delftweg 133, ☎ (015) 212 4920, www.delftsepauw. com, open April-Oct., daily 9am-4:30pm; Nov.-March, Mon.-Fri. 9am-4:30pm, Sat.-Sun. 11am-1pm. Established in 1954, this manufacturer produces pottery alongside a canal just outside the city centre – the VVV has directions. Plates can be ordered to your own design or for special occasions. Moderate prices.

Also in **Delft**. **De Candelaer**, Kerkstraat 13, ☎ (015) 213 1848, www.candelaer.nl, open Apr.-Sept., daily 9am-5:30pm; Oct.-Mar., Mon.-Sat. 9am-5pm, is a small family-operated shop. Conveniently close to the New Church, it is an easy stop for visitors. The selection of goods is smaller but also less expensive. Try here for a special order; they are very cooperative and will ship anywhere.

Makkum, Friesland. **Tichelaars Koninklijke Makkumer Aardewerk en Tegel Fabriek**, Turfmarkt 65, ☎ (0515) 23 1341, www.tichelaars.nl, open to visitors Mon.-Thurs., 11am, 1:30 & 3pm, and Fri. 11am & 1:30pm, for very interesting, conducted tours. This factory has also earned the right to add 'Royal' (*Koninklijke*) to their title, due to the quality of their work and the patronage of the House of Orange.

Giethoorn, Overijssel. Regular handmade pottery demonstrations at **Pottenbakkerij Rhoda**, Binnenpad 41, ☎ (0521) 36 2040, www.rhoda.nl, open daily March-Oct. 10am-6pm., Nov., Dec., Feb., Wed.-Sun. 10am-6pm.

Gouda, South Holland. **Adrie Moerings**, Peperstraat 76, ☎ (0182) 51 2842. Ceramics and pipe-maker. You can watch the potter at work.

Zevenaar, Gelderland. Handmade pottery using the old technique of peat-firing at **Pottery Laurens Goldewijk**, Lentemorgen 2, ☎ (0316) 52 8828, open Mon.-Tues. 1-5pm, Wed.-Fri. 2-6pm, Sat. 10am-5pm.

▶ Ship-building

- **Lelystad**, Flevoland. Replicas of 17th-century Dutch sailing ships are made at **Batavia-Werf**, Oostvaardersdijk 01-09, ☎ (0320) 26 1409, www.bataviawerf.nl, open daily 10am-5pm. Not only can you go on board the Batavia, but you can watch a replica of De Zeven Provincien, the flagship of 17th-century Dutch Admiral Michiel de Ruyter's fleet, being constructed.

- **Groningen**, Groningen province. Ships displayed in the **Noordelijk Scheepvaart-museum**, Brugstraat 24, ☎ (050) 312 2202, open Tues.-Sat. 10am-5pm, Sun. 1-5pm, are detailed model replicas made in the museum workshop. www.noordelijkscheepvaartmuseum.nl

▶ Silver-making

Schoonhoven, South Holland. Schoonhoven is known as the Dutch 'silver town,' offering a number of places where you can see how silver is worked:

The **Museum of Antique Silverware** (Edelambachtshuis), Haven 13, ☎ (0182) 38 2614, www.rikkoertjuweliers.nl, open Tues.-Fri. 10am-5:30pm, Sat. 10am-5pm, has two floors devoted to an enormous collection of old Dutch silver. You may watch the silversmith at work.

At the **Gold, Silver and Clock Museum**, Kazerneplein 4, ☎ (0182) 38 5612, you can arrange to see demonstrations by the silversmith, engraver or clockmaker.

▶ Textile-making

Tilburg, Brabant. The **Netherlands Textile Museum**, Goirkestraat 96, ☎ (013) 536 7475, www.textielmuseum.nl, open Tues.-Fri. 10am-5pm, Sat.-Sun. noon-5pm, has old textile machines in operation, and people on hand to explain the processes.

▶ Wine-making

- **Nieuwegein**, Utrecht. **Wijnkooperij Trouvaille**, Het Fort Jutphaas 3, ☎ (030) 603 1708. Wine-making demonstrations, only for groups and by appointment.

- **Vlaardingen**, South Holland. **De Wijnboerderij**, Zuidbuurt 40, ☎ (010) 460 3120. There are demonstrations of fruit wines being made in a natural way, which you can watch for a small fee.

▶ **Wooden shoemaking**

Wooden shoes (*klompen*) are made all over the Netherlands, so we will only give a few names to get you started. Other 'clog' makers can be found in **Volendam** and the **National Veen Park** (see Peat-digging) during their demonstration days.

- **Best**, Brabant (north of Eindhoven). The town of Best has more wooden shoemakers than any other in the Netherlands. The **Klompenmuseum De Platijn**, Broekdijk 14, ☎ (0499) 37 1247, www.klompenmuseumdeplatijn.nl, open July-Aug., daily noon-6pm April-Oct., Tues.-Fri., 1-5:00pm, Sat.-Sun. noon-6:00pm, is a good place to see how they were made in the old days, as well as today.

- **Keijenborg**, Gelderland (southeast of Zutphen). Makers of clogs since 1921, the Sueter family makes nearly 300 pairs a day. You can compare traditional and modern methods in their **Museum De Klompenmaker**, Uilenesterstraat 10a, ☎ (0575) 46 3030, open Mon.-Sat. 8am-5pm.

- **Lekkerkerk**, South Holland. **Van Zwienen**, Schuwacht 150, ☎ (0180) 66 1362, open Mon.-Fri. 9am-noon & 1:30-5pm, Sat. 8:30am-12:00pm, have been in business since 1815. Sawdust flies as hundreds of clogs are made daily, dried in piles in special rooms before being finished off and painted.

- **Zaandam**, North Holland. The **Zaanse Schans Klompenmakerij**, Kraaienest 4, ☎ (075) 617 7121, www.woodenshoes.nl, open March-Oct., daily 8am-6:30pm; Nov.-Feb., daily 8:30am-5pm, is a museum, a workshop where wooden shoes are made, and a shop where you can choose from the 7,000 pairs in stock. Should be enough.

Part II

Living in Holland

Chapter 16 | Living in Holland

WELCOME TO HOLLAND! To feel at home and not be threatened by an unknown system, it helps to know something of the culture, the social and general attitudes of one's hosts toward life and their place in the world, as well as discovering how the system works (see *Dealing with the Dutch* author Jacob Vossestein's exposé, 'Who are the Dutch?' on page 27). In this chapter, we will address the problem of where to go for advice and help in adjusting to life in the Netherlands.

Adjustment is not a flat concept. Knowing the language is helpful, but even verbal communication is only one aspect of 'adjustment.' For instance, many Dutchmen born in Indonesia or South Africa, who came to Holland as adults, were not happy when they first arrived because they were faced with an entirely different social and cultural atmosphere than they were used to. Also, in spite of the fact that English is spoken more often and better here than anywhere else in Continental Europe, you still may not find adjusting to life in Holland easy. We hope we can help by pointing the way toward solving the everyday problems that arise.

Reading about a culture is always helpful whether you are touring or becoming a resident in a new country. The books listed in the 'Recommended Reading' list at the end of this book can be a start. Also, before leaving home, contact the Dutch Embassy or Consulate and ask for whatever information they have for prospective residents. The Commercial Officer can answer business-related questions, and will have practical information on the cost of living in the Netherlands, etc.

The first concern of families with children is schooling. The burning questions are, what's available, where is it, and how much will it cost. Begin by contacting ACCESS, www.access-nl.org, and the Ministry of Education, (Ministerie Onderwijs, Cultuur en Wetenschappen), POB 25000, 2700 LZ Zoetermeer, ☎ (079) 323 2323, www.minocw.nl, for their booklets. You can also write to the schools listed in Chapter 19, asking for their brochures. If you are in Holland, you would naturally make an appointment to meet the principal or head, and visit the facilities.

Once here, you will probably get practical help and information through the people you meet – both Dutch and foreign. The jobholder will meet colleagues as a natural course, however, spouses and children must make their own way. For them, the best contacts are clubs and schools. Both groups are listed in this and the following chapters.

After a school is chosen and the housing situation is resolved, the next mission is to make friends and enjoy your time here to the fullest. We hope 'Part One' of this book will give you a lot of good ideas for culture and travel during your stay in Holland.

The practicalities of living, such as establishing a personal bank account, getting English-language newspapers, knowing how to get around, etc., must not be minimized. We will therefore start with the nitty-gritty of settling in, and then move on to the 'The Good Life' in Chapter 17. The chapter entitled 'The Younger Set' gives all manner of information about schools and child-oriented activities and organisations.

English-language newspapers & periodicals: Many English-language newspapers and magazines are available at city railway stations, hotels and bookstores. Major Dutch public libraries also carry a selection of newspapers and magazines published abroad.

Relocation services: There are many such organisations offering advice and help to newcomers relocating to the Netherlands. One of the best resources is **ACCESS (Administrative Committee to Coordinate English-speaking Services)**, Plein 24, 2511CS, The Hague, ☎ (070) 346 2525; and on the Herengracht 472 in Amsterdam, ☎ (020) 423 3217, www.access-nl.org. This English-speaking community service and 'help' organisation provides information and education materials and workshops promoting cultural adaptation, human development and family life. It also offers a counselling referral system. This is also an excellent place for non-employed spouses to volunteer their services, practice their skills, or learn new ones. If you have a general question about living here and don't know where to go, ACCESS can be extremely helpful. Just call and ask. (See ad on page 455.)

Outpost, www.outpostexpat.nl is a non-profit organisation providing worldwide information on the Internet to help expatriates relocate with ease.

RMS Relocation Management Services, Figeestaete, Hendrik Figeeweg 1-E, 2031 BJ Haarlem, (023) 518 3470, www.rmsrelocation.com. "Your people – Our care!" reflects RMS' commitment toward the client's needs. When relocating to the Netherlands, you may want their assistance with settling-in, immigration and tax-related issues, or property purchases, mortgage, financial and social advice. RMS also helps you find profitable Dutch Tax benefits within your specific situation. However, their foremost goal is assisting you and your family in a personal and caring manner with finding the right home in the right area, schools, medical services, registrations, childcare, sports, a bank account, child benefits, cultural programs, and so forth — in short: welcoming you to a warm new home in the Netherlands. (See ad on page 382.)

Personal Relocation, Mollenburgseweg 88, 4205 NB Gorinchem, ☎ (0183) 622 903, www.personalrelocation.nl, plays a key role by offering a complete range of support services for expatriates, returning Dutch repatriates, and the elderly, in relocating to new living accommodations. Their services are based on flexibility, individual attention and unrivaled experience. (See ad on page 455.)

Many other relocation companies for the Netherlands may be found on the website of **EuRA**, the **European Relocation Association**. www.eura-relocation.com

Money and banking

Dutch money is based on the decimal system. One hundred cents make one Euro. A euro is notated with the symbol '€'.

Salaries and recurring bills can be paid automatically through your bank, and Internet banking is increasingly used for regular bill-paying and other banking business.

ABN AMRO has an excellent expatriate service, with an all-English, on-line banking site that's very user-friendly: www.yourexpatbank.com.The ABN AMRO Expat Service is an exclusive service for expatriates who live and work in the Netherlands. The members of the Expat Account Team are familiar with the problems and needs of expats, and are able to assist them with all kinds of financial questions (see ad on page 2).

Most banks have folders in other languages explaining particular forms of payment and investments, and safe deposit boxes (*kluisjes*) are available at some.

▶ Currency Exchange

GWK (exchange offices) are at major railway stations and in larger cities. Besides changing foreign currencies, they can change travellers checks and give cash for Giro Cash cards, the Eurocard, and usual credit cards. They can also make hotel and theatre reservations. Offices are usually open Mon.-Sat. 7am-7pm, Sun. 10am-4pm. The GWK at the Amsterdam train station is open from 8am – 10pm. Most banks offer exchange facilities, so it is wise to compare rates, even though the GWK is often the best option. Check www.travelex.com to find listings of all locations throughout the Netherlands (and worldwide).

– **Amsterdam Schiphol Airport** (in the railway station), ☎ (020) 653 5121, Open 24hrs.

– Opening hours of **GWK-Travelex Lounge 1** (after passport and ticket control at Schiphol airport) both during summer and winter time 6am – 8:30pm.
Location: GWK Travelex – Arrivals (before passport and ticket control). Arrivals = *Aankomstpassage* 23, hall 3, ☎ (020) 653 5121, open: 7 days/week from 6am to 10pm.

– **GWK Travelex – Departures** (after passport and ticket control). Departures = *Vertrekpassage*, lounge 1 – pier B/C, ☎ (020) 316 2090, open 7 days/week from 6am to 8:30pm. You may use your credit or debit card to withdraw cash 24 hours a day from one of the ATMs located next to each branch.

– **GWK – Central Station**, Amsterdam, ☎ (020) 627 2731, open 7am-11pm daily.

– **Change Express**, Damrak 86, ☎ (020) 624 6681/624 6682, open 8am-11pm daily.
Leidseplein 123, ☎ (020) 622 1425, open 8am-11:30pm daily.

Credit Cards: All Dutch banks honour the *Eurocard*, which works in conjunction with Mastercard and Visa. A Eurocard can be obtained via www.eurocard.nl, at all GWK branches, and at most banks, or call the MasterCard Customer Service department ☎ (030) 283 5252.

Major credit cards are accepted in the Netherlands, though by no means everywhere. (Please be aware that of all the credit cards, American Express is the least accepted here. Be sure to bring other means just in case.) It is recommended that you take some cash with you for the first few days in Holland. Traveller's checks are a safe alternative to cash, and are handy if you do not have a credit card.

Cash-on-card services are available from selected American Express, Diners Club, MasterCard and VisaCard addresses. (These cards are also accepted by all GWK currency exchange outlets and Change Express Offices.)

(KLM airlines has an American Express card for frequent fliers whereby you can earn airmiles with each purchase using their credit card. www.klm.com)

– **American Express.** Head Office: Amsteldijk 166, 1078 AX Amsterdam; ☎ (020) 504 8504, ☎ (020) (020) 504 8666 (lost and stolen cards), Fax (+31) (020) 504 8001. Also at Damrak 66, Amsterdam, ☎ (020) 504 8777, open 9am-5pm Mon-Fri; 9am-noon Sat., closed Sun.

– **Thomas Cook** (There's no charge for cashing Thomas Cook travellers' checks.) Dam 23-25, ☎ (020) 625 0922, open 9am-8pm daily. **Branches:** Damrak 1-5, ☎ (020) 620 3236, open 8am-8pm daily. Leidseplein 31A, ☎ (020) 626 7000, open 9am-7:30pm Mon-Sat; 10am-7.30pm Sun.

– **Diners Club Head Office.** Weesperstraat 77, 1018 VN Amsterdam, ☎ (020) 557 3581 ☎ 0800 0334 toll free (lost and stolen cards), Fax: (+31) (020) 557 3425

– **Interpay Eurocard/Mastercard Nederland Head Office.** Eendrachtslaan 315, 3526 LB Utrecht, ☎ (030) 283 5111, ☎ (020) 283 5555 (lost and stolen cards), Fax: (+31) (030) 283 5518, E-mail: info@eurocard.nl

– **VSB International BV/ Visa Card Services Head Office.** Wisselwerking 32, 1112 XP Amsterdam, ☎ (020) 660 0600, ☎ (020) 660 0611 and (030) 283 5181 (lost and stolen cards), Fax: (+31) (020) 660 0688, E-mail: communicatie.visa@fortis.nl

▶ **Automatic Teller Machines (ATMs)**

If you have a foreign bank pass with a Cirrus logo, you can get money from an Automatic Teller Machine (ATM), usually open 24 hours per day. Some ATMs of the ABN AMRO bank also accept passes with the PLUS logo. Also check your pass and the ATM for EDC, EC and Maestro logos. Of course, you can also use most credit cards to obtain money from an ATM.

▶ **Personal banking**

For personal accounts, we highly recommend **ABN AMRO** bank's excellent Expat Service, all in English. www.yourexpatbank.com (See ad on page 2).

All banks allow you to sign an order form (*machtiging*) for periodic automatic payments for such items as rent, utilities, telephone bills, and the like. Also, you can still pay by 'bank *giro*' checks (provided with your bill or *factuur*) to be signed and returned by post to your bank if you would rather not pay automatically or on-line.

When opening an account, you will be given a PIN code card, with your Personal Identification Number (PIN), that you can use instead of cash payments. These are accepted in most stores, restaurants, etc. Look for the blue and white 'PIN' logo on an establishment's door or cash register (*kassa*). Shop assistants will run your card through their machine, after which you enter your PIN code number. The cost of your purchase will then be immediately deducted from your bank account. (Should you wish, you can change your given number to one easier to remember.) *Note that if you enter the wrong code three times in succession, your card will be blocked and you will have to apply and wait a week or so for a new one.* (When paying in cash, eurocents are rounded up because one eurocent and two eurocent coins were discontinued. PIN payments deduct the exact amount.)

Most Dutch financial institutions also have cash machines for use in getting cash, as well as making some other transactions. Your PIN code card and number will give you access to these.

There are several other ways of making payments other than by cash or credit card. One is the Europas, which can be used as a debit card throughout Europe and at ATM cash machines throughout the world. It should not be confused with a credit card for which you have to make a special application at the bank. The latest arrivals are the *chip-knip* and *Chipper*, smart payment cards for small amounts. *Chipknip* cards can be 'loaded' with a set amount at special bank machines, as they are issued by the banks. The Chipper is issued by the Postbank, and can be 'loaded' at the post office or by telephone, since it is also a telephone card.

The Private Bank: The Dutch are well known for their banking acumen. Some major banks with branches throughout the country are ABN AMRO, Rabobank, and ING. They handle the usual financial transactions but their system is sometimes different from other countries. As we mentioned, there are several methods of paying for purchases apart from the PIN card above:

1. A yellow *giro* payment slip (*accept girokaart*) is most often sent in place of a bill for purchases, subscriptions, monthly installments, tax payments, etc. It must be completed, signed and sent to your bank – its perforated stub kept as your receipt. The Postbank also lets you pay with postgiro slips, which can be handed into the post office or posted in envelopes they provide.

2. A bank *giro* is used for payment of an invoice (*rekening*). A supply of these printed forms is provided by your bank, along with envelopes (no stamps required). You fill in the amount to be paid, the payee's account number (bank or *postgiro*), name and town, indicate what the payment is for, under '*omschrijving*,' and then sign it. You will be given a folder to keep the daily statements of your account (*dagafschriften*) that are sent every two weeks, unless you wish to receive them more frequently. These indicate your original balance, with debits and credits, and the final balance. Every statement is numbered consecutively, starting the calendar year with '1.' (Interest is paid on current accounts in the Netherlands.) You can also, of course, conduct and check your transactions on-line, through Internet banking.

3. Bank checks or transfers can be used for payment of large sums, such as when buying a car, furniture, TV, etc. You may also PIN or use your credit card.

▶ **Major banks in the Netherlands**

– ABN AMRO Bank: http://www.abnamro.nl or http://www.abnamro.com; for Expat Service: www.yourexpat.bank.com

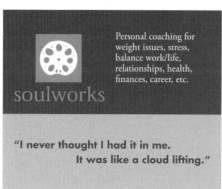
– De Nederlandsche Bank (Dutch Central Bank): http://www.dnb.nl/english
– ING Bank: http://www.inggroup.com
– Fortis Bank: http://www.fortis.com
– Postbank: http://www.postbank.nl
– Rabobank: http://www.rabobank.nl or http://www.rabobank.com
– Robeco Advies: http://www.robeco.com
– SNS Bank: http://www.sns.nl
– Staal Bankiers: http://www.staalbankiers.nl
– CenE Bank: http://www.cenebankiers.nl

The Postbank: To open a bank account through your local post office, pick up, complete, and submit an application form. Soon after you will receive acknowledgment that your form is being processed. As soon as this is done, you will receive your account number, and a request to deposit funds, followed by a folder containing *giro* forms used for paying your bills, a holder for your statements, and envelopes addressed to the city in which your account will be administered. These envelopes need no postage. If you have requested checks for paying bills (*betaalkaarten*), you will be informed when and where to collect them, your pass (*giromaatpas*) and PIN code for withdrawing cash from automatic tellers. www.postbank.nl

Note: The Post Office usually has the best rate of exchange for foreign currencies.

Medical care and health benefits

One of the first things a new resident in Holland should do is establish himself or herself, and the family, with a general practitioner doctor (*huisarts*). The whole system of medical care is very well organised in the Netherlands and it is wise to have a little background on how this works in order to avoid trouble and frustration in case of an emergency. For all physicians in locations throughout NL, see www.huisartsen.nl.

First and foremost, doctors work in regional areas of each town and will **not** take patients who live outside their area of responsibility. **You will be expected to choose a doctor in your immediate area.** This is mainly because Dutch 'GPs,' or general practitioners still make house calls in case of serious illness – and therefore want their patients to be in their vicinity – and are responsible for government-insured patients (the bulk of their practice), as well as private patients. (See 'insurance'.) As almost all segments of society are well covered by health provisions, everyone makes regular use of doctor services. This results in all doctors having very busy practices and, along with a general shortage of doctors, helps explain the need for limiting the geographic area that each doctor must cover. Therefore, you will need to find a doctor who practices in the neighbourhood in which you live.

Secondly, and perhaps the biggest bone of contention for 'expats', is the fact that you can't just *go* to an eye doctor, a pediatrician, or a heart specialist just because you can't see, are going to have a baby, or are having heart palpitations. **You must first see your own doctor, the 'huisarts', who will refer you to the appropriate specialist – if he or she thinks it's necessary.** Although some expats tend to circumvent this dictum, keep in mind that if you have not established yourself with a neighbourhood doctor and you have an emergency illness in the family, it might be difficult to get immediate attention.

For help in finding a doctor, call the Municipal Medical Service (*Gemeentelijke Geneeskundige Dienst*) of your town, ACCESS, or even your local pharmacy (*apotheek*) who is generally happy to give you a list. In the 'yellow pages' of the telephone directory, doctors are listed under 'Artsen-Huisartsen'. An excellent booklet explaining the Dutch health care system is available from ACCESS: 'The Health Care Guide to the Netherlands' (see ad on page 455, and below for contact information).

In addition to the Municipal Medical Service's overall public health duties, they give blood tests, vaccinations and other injections, and X-rays. School doctors also fall under the supervision of this organisation. The school doctor visits the school regularly, examines the children for general health, and warns parents if he/she sees anything unusual in a child's development. The school doctor also checks dental health, and arranges X-rays and other tests as needed.

▶ **Distress line**

Should a serious personal or emotional problem, or even a major crisis arise, referral to native English-speaking professional counsellors is available. The multinational community service organisation, **ACCESS,** ☎ (070) 346 2525, the Hague, and (020) 423 3217 Amsterdam, www.access-nl.org, provides such a counselling referral service, as well as general information for expatriates, and educational workshops. (See ad on page 455.) The Dutch equivalent, Stichting Algemene Christelijke Hulpdienst, has an **SOS Help Line** open 24 hours a day. If whoever answers is not fluent in English, ask to be called back as soon as possible by someone who is. (See below for more details.)

For additional counselling services, see www.counsellingeurope.com.

▶ **SOS help line**

For medical emergencies at night, weekends or holidays, call the following numbers:
– **Amsterdam:** Doctor or Dental Help: ☎ (0900) 503 242
  Emergency: SOS Line (Distress) ☎ (020) 675 7575
– **The Hague:** Doctor Help: ☎ (0900) 8600, Dental Help: ☎ (070) 311 0305 Emergency: SOS Line (Distress) ☎ (070) 345 4500

– **Rotterdam:** Doctor Help: ☎ (010) 420 1100, Dental Help: ☎ (010) 455 2155
  Emergency: SOS Line (Distress) ☎ (010) 436 2244
– **Eindhoven:** Emergency Help Line ☎ (040) 212 5566
– **Utrecht:** Emergency Help Line ☎ (030) 294 3344

Nationwide Emergency Number ☎ 112
National Emergency Child Help Line ☎ (0800) 0432

▶ **Hospitalisation**

Should you need to be admitted to hospital, your doctor or specialist will make the necessary arrangements, and you will be notified when a bed is available – except of course in emergencies. It is important that your insurance company be informed of the date you enter the hospital. As this is often done directly by the hospital administration, take your insurance particulars with you.

The type of insurance you have will largely determine the room you will occupy. Private rooms are usually only reserved for very serious or post-operative cases, so be prepared to share a room. You may ask for a telephone and TV (slight charge). You will also be informed of visiting hours, which vary from hospital to hospital. Your first visitor will be the department's internist, who will check your medical history, diet, allergies, etc. If an operation is necessary, he or she will be followed by the anesthetist. (Most doctors and nurses speak good English.)

If your child has to be admitted to the hospital, you can be sure that he/she will receive kind attention. Ask to have your child admitted to the children's section or directly to a children's hospital. (Available in Rotterdam, Amsterdam, The Hague, Utrecht and Zwolle.) Provided there are facilities available and your child's condition warrants your presence, you may be allowed to stay.

For minor accidents, remember that calling an ambulance may turn out to be very expensive, as it is not always covered by your insurance.

▶ **Pregnancy**

In Holland it is quite normal for midwives (*vroedvrouw*) to handle prenatal, delivery and postnatal care. A midwife must have three years' training before being qualified to deliver babies. Babies are delivered both at home and in hospitals. Complicated cases will be referred to an obstetrician (*vrouwenarts*), who will only deliver in a hospital with which he or she is associated. It is wise to discuss these possibilities with your doctor and decide who you want to look after your pregnancy.

Exercise classes for pregnant women are given by local Cross Associations (see next page) and are highly recommended even for non-Dutch speakers. ACCESS also has pre- and post-natal exercise classes, as well as classes on baby massage, breastfeeding, CPR for children, raising bi-lingual children, and more – all in English. ACCESS also publishes a helpful booklet, 'The Babies and Toddlers' (120 pages).

The first step in any pregnancy is to see your family doctor and to discuss the decisions you need to make. **Examples:** Do you use a midwife or a gynaecologist for pre-natal care and delivery? Should the baby be born at home (normal in the Netherlands) or in a hospital? Do you want to use some form of pain relief during childbirth (not usually done unless absolutely demanded), or have the baby by natural birth (normal in the Netherlands)? Your family doctor will also provide you with the names of midwives or gynaecologists.

If you give birth in a hospital, your stay may be brief. It's not uncommon to be released just 24 hours after delivery. If there are complications, of course, the stay will be longer. Whoever delivers the baby will want the birth to be as natural as possible; discuss the procedures well in advance. In Holland it is not a problem for husbands to be present when the baby is being born.

Three weeks after the baby's birth, the visiting nurse (*wijkverpleegster*) will come to check you both. She will also make an appointment for your first visit to the baby clinic. You may prefer to have all inoculations and vaccinations given by your doctor, but it is less expensive to use the local Cross Association (Kruisvereniging or Thuiszorg) consultation bureau or well-baby clinic – if you don't mind a possible wait. In either case, you will be given a handy booklet in which all vaccinations will be recorded.

▶ **Semi-private health organisations**

The cost of membership in a Cross or Thuiszorg home-help organisation is nominal because such organisations are subsidised by the municipal government of the city they serve. Their aim is to promote the health of the general population. They employ their own nurses and social workers, and provide home care for the sick and elderly. The following help organisations serve four major cities. To contact similar groups in other towns, you can search in every province via the national website: www.thuiszorg.nl

Cross help organisations

– **Amsterdam:** Amsterdamse Thuiszorg, ☎ (020) 886 1000;
   www.amsterdamthuiszorg.nl
– **The Hague:** Meavita, ☎ (0900) 8088; www.meavita.nl and Evitazorg,
   ☎ (070) 314 2444; www.evitazorg.nl
– **Rotterdam:** Humanitas Thuiszorg, ☎ (010) 425 010; www.humanitas-rotterdam.nl
– **Utrecht:** Agathos Thuiszorg, ☎ (010) 264 0777; www.agathos-thuiszorg.nl

▶ **Services available**

Each branch may offer a slightly different service, but they will not vary much from those listed below, and all provide medical equipment such as crutches, wheelchairs, etc., on loan. Membership for a minimum of six months is required in order to take advantage of these services, but the annual contribution is minimal.

It should be mentioned that some knowledge of the Dutch language is helpful in dealing with these organisations since their office and technical personnel are not especially trained to service foreign residents. Nevertheless, we feel that most newcomers will find it worthwhile taking a family membership.

1. **Care for Mother and Child**
   Prenatal care and exercise classes, lectures and courses to prepare the pregnant mother for the birth of her child.
   Maternity nurse (*kraamverzorgster*) to come to the house for the first 10 days following the birth of the child. You have a choice of someone who stays all day or someone who will come twice a day to help the mother and change, wash and feed the baby. If you desire this service, you may be billed with a reasonable extra charge.
   Postnatal care and general pediatric care for the baby are provided at their '*Consultatiebureaus*' or well-baby clinics.

2. **Household help in case the mother is ill** (*Gezins Verzorging*). There are two kinds of household help available: experienced help capable of running a household without direction, in case the mother should be in the hospital; and a mother's helper who will come in and work under the direction of the mother when she is confined to bed. This is limited to a period of six weeks, and is billed separately from the membership fee.

3. **Care and exercise for those recuperating, older people, etc.** A visiting, practicing nurse will come at regularly-scheduled times to bathe and exercise post-operatory patients or people confined to bed or wheelchair.

4. **Dietitian services are also available.**

▶ **Dentists**

Not all insurance covers dental care, and finding a dentist to suit your needs may not be simple. Some take only private patients, and some are so busy they accept no new patients. However, there are many good, high-standard dentists in Holland, and one should enquire locally.

▶ **The pharmacy**

Doctors' prescriptions are required for medicines. If necessary he or she will also indicate how often the pharmacist may renew this prescription. If your pharmacy is closed, a notice on the door will indicate the address of one that is open. Similarly a tape-recorded telephone message will usually give you this information if you call. Night service is listed in daily newspapers.

Havinga International Pharmacy, Prins Hendrikplein 3, The Hague, ☎ (070) 345 6100, specialises in 'international medicines.' (See ad on page 456.)

▶ **Health insurance**

Most working foreigners living in Holland are insured by the company that employs them. It is wise to be familiar with the kind of cover they give you and your family, both for sickness and life insurance. For those who are not automatically covered, since January 1, 2006, health insurance is obligatory for everyone living in the Netherlands, whether you work, stay at home or study. A good number of health insurance companies offer coverage. For more information, contact **Union of Insurance Companies (Het Verbond van Verzekeraars)** at ☎ (070) 333 8777, or contact the **Dutch Consumers' Union (Consumentenbond)**, ☎ (070) 445 4545; www.consumentenbond.nl. One website in English is www.oomverzekering.nl. Most insurance websites are in Dutch. Some insurance companies are: Zilverenkruis Achmea, Delta Lloyd, FBTO, Agis, Ohra, Centraal Beheer, and Unive. (See *verzekering* or *gezondheidsverzekering* in the 'Yellow Pages' of the phone book.

Taxes

National Tax Office: http://www.belastingdienst.nl

Ministry of Finance, Information Centre, Prinses Beatrixlaan 512, The Hague: www.minfin.nl

(*Taxation in the Netherlands*, an English guide, is published by the Ministry of Finance.)

Legal information – Immigration/permits

General: www.immigratiedienst.nl

Immigration and Naturalization Service (Immigratie en Naturalisatie Dienst, IND: www.ind.nl

Ministry of Foreign Affairs (Ministerie van Buitenlandse Zaken): www.minbuza.nl/english

Eures, European jobs: www.eu.int/eures

Work permits: www.workpermit.com/netherlands

Ministry of Justice (Ministerie van Justitie): www.justitie.nl

Dutch customs (Douane): www.douane.nl

Royal Dutch Notaries: www.notaris.nl

Legal aid Netherlands (Rechtshulp Nederland): www.rechtshulpnederland.nl

RVR (Raden voor Rechtsbijstand) legal help: www.rechtshulp.nl

The National Ombudsman: www.ombudsman.nl

Dutch Housing Association: www.eigenhuis.nl

Child Care and Protection Board: www.kinderbescherming.nl

Embassy services: www.ambassadediensten.nl, and www.embassyworld.com

Australia: www.australian-embassy.nl	Ireland: www.irishembassy.nl
Belgium: www.diplobel.org	Israel: www.israel.nl
Brazil: www.brazilianembassy.nl	Italy: www.italy.nl
Canada: www.canada.nl	Japan: www.nl.emb-japan.go.jp
China: www.chinaembassy.nl	New Zealand: www.mft.govt.nz
Denmark: www.danishembassy.nl	Norway: www.noorwegen.nl
Finland: www.finlande.nl	Pakistan: www.embassyofpakistan.com
France: www.ambafrance.nl	Russian Federation: www.netherlands.mid.ru
Germany: www.duitse-ambassade.nl	South Africa: www.zuidafrika.nl
Greece: www.greekembassy.nl	Spain: www.claboral.nl
India: www.indianembassy.nl	Sweden: www.swedenabroad.com/thehague
Indonesia: www.indonesia.nl	United Kingdom: www.britain.nl

United States of America: www.usemb.nl

Places of worship

Churches of all faiths are represented throughout the Netherlands. Those within the Randstad that hold foreign-language services are listed in the 'Quick Reference' section just before the Index. Dutch churches are listed in newspapers, in a town's particular information pamphlet, and in the VVV's weekly *What's On* magazine.

Libraries

In Holland, major city libraries lend from their extensive collections – books, CDs, DVDs, cassettes, sheet music, slides, video programmes, etc., all for a modest subscription fee. Avid readers will find English books expensive in Holland. Luckily, all large city libraries have a good selection of English as well as Dutch books. They also carry foreign-language newspapers and a selection of children's books in foreign languages. Two important private libraries in our list that follows are those of the American Womens and British Clubs in The Hague. The Volksuniversiteit Libraries are also available to the general public for a nominal membership fee.

The music departments (Muziek Afdeling) of the libraries may require your passport and proof of an address (bank statement) as security for you to join. They have extensive collections of sheet music and CDs.

▶ **Amsterdam**

Amsterdam Centrale Bibliotheek, Prinsengracht 587, ☎ (020) 523 0900, www.oba.nl, has an especially interesting collection of books on the history of Amsterdam, and a large selection of English books – including children's – and foreign newspapers. Their computers can be used for email or Internet, by appointment. Membership cost is mini-

mal. Open Mon. 1-9pm, Tues.-Thurs.10am-9pm, Fri. 10am-7pm, Sat. 10am-5pm. From
Oct.-Mar. also Sun. 1-5pm. They also have language computers you may use.

Universiteit's Bibliotheek (the University of Amsterdam Library), Singel 425, ☎ (020)
525 2301, has a reading room with 70 workstations, a copy machine, and plenty of reference books. Open Mon.-Fri. 8:30am-midnight, Sat., 9:30am-5pm, Sun.11-5pm.
http://cf.uba.uva.nl/uba2006/english

▶ **The Hague**
Openbare Bibliotheek, main public library, Spui 68, ☎ (070) 353 4455, open Mon. noon-
8pm, www.bibliotheekdenhaag.nl, Tue-Fri.10am-8 pm, Sat. 11am-5pm, Sun. noon-5pm.
This large new building in the heart of the city has a good selection of English books
and a special children's section. Minimal cost for subscription.

American Women's Club Library, Nieuwe Duinweg 25, ☎ (070) 350 6007, is one of the
largest English language libraries in Holland with around 7,500 English-language books.
Non-club members may join for an annual fee per family per year. www.awcthehague.org

British Club Library, Plein 24, ☎ (070) 346 1973, has an extensive library which is
also open to non-members for a small fee. www.bwclubthehague.demon.nl

▶ **Rotterdam**
Centrale Gemeente Bibliotheek (Central Municipal Library), Hoogstraat 110, ☎ (010)
281 6181, www.bibliotheek.rotterdam.nl, open Mon. 1-8pm, Tues.-Fri. 10am-8pm, Sat.
10am-5pm, Sun. 1-5pm, has many English-language books and videos available. Students will find extensive reference material and trade journals. Computers are freely
available except for Internet use, which has to be paid for. The 'Leeszaal' (Reading Hall)
has sections for English, French, German and Dutch novels. A Central Youth Library is
also located here and has the same hours. Bright and cheerful with green plants hanging from various levels à la gardens of Babylon. There's a coffee shop and a library theatre used for special events and occasional foreign-language programmes. Most foreign
newspapers are available and there is a gallery with changing exhibits.

Rotterdam Reading Room (Rotterdamsch Leeskabinet) is worth investigating for
scientific works, dictionaries, journals and even such light relief as mystery thrillers
and some children's books. A private enterprise with a long history, it is now located in
the Erasmus University, Burgemeester Oudlaan 50, ☎ (010) 408 1195.

Social and business organisations
There are numerous social and business organisations of interest to foreign residents. It is
not possible to list them all here, but selections are given in Chapter 19 (The Younger Set),
and in 'Quick Reference' at the end of the book.

▶ **National society organisations**
Most foreign businessmen and women, in cooperation with their embassy officials, will
promote such clubs as the Netherlands-America Institute, the Netherlands-Japan Club,

and the Netherlands-England Society. There are similar clubs for other foreign nationals represented in Holland. The purpose of these groups is to meet socially and become better acquainted in order to promote matters of interest to the visitor and host countries. Call your embassy for details, or check the list on www.expatica.com.

▶ **Women's social organisations**

These groups provide friendship and support through social activities, lectures and group outings. Some also operate community services. The American Women's Club in The Hague has a clubhouse with its own extensive library – the British Club similarly – while the International Women's Contact, perhaps the largest women's group in The Hague, holds its meetings in a conference centre. Clubs in other parts of the country are listed, along with business and social clubs for men and women in the 'Quick Reference' section. Should your area not be listed, we suggest you contact ACCESS, ☎ (070) 346 2525, The Hague, or ☎ (020) 423 3217 Amsterdam, www.access-nl.org.

▶ **Business networks**

There are also a number of business networking clubs, providing opportunities to hear speakers and exchange business cards while enjoying refreshments. (See the list in Chapter 21.)

Adult education opportunities

Educational opportunities are far-ranging, from working for a university degree to taking art classes on the Riviera!

▶ **University programmes**

Attending a Dutch university may be difficult because the demand for space by Dutch students is so great that acceptance of foreigners has to be kept to a minimum. Information about higher education for foreigners can be obtained abroad through the Netherlands Embassy or the **Dutch Ministry of Education**, ☎ (079) 323 2323; or from the **Foreign Student Service**, Oranje Nassaulaan 5, 1075 AH Amsterdam, ☎ (020) 671 5915. They publish a 'Concise Guide to Study in the Netherlands' for foreign students, and also list 'Non-university Dutch Language Courses.'

    Fulbright Center (Netherlands-American Commission for Education Exchange), Herengracht 472, 1017 BZ Amsterdam, ☎ (020) 531 5930, has information on international exchange programmes, and a documentation center, open 9am-noon. www.fulbright.nl

▶ **NUFFIC**

One of the best places to start your search is at NUFFIC, the **Netherlands Organization for International Cooperation in Higher Education**. Their website, www.nuffic.nl, lists all of the possible international studies in the Netherlands. They work in close cooperation with other universities abroad, offering the possibility to spend part of your study time on another campus. Currently over 1,000 courses are offered in English, and their database-driven search site (see English pages, grants, scholarships, cooperation, etc.) makes it incredibly easy to find just what you're looking for.

Another excellent resource for study information in the Netherlands can be found on www.studytrack.com. The Netherlands is attracting over 6,000 foreign students needing visas yearly, in addition to students from countries within the European Union. Want to study in Holland? See www.studyin.nl.

Education Resources

www.international-students.nl – resources for international students
www.minowc.nl/english – Dutch ministry of education and culture
www.vsnu.nl – association of universities in the Netherlands
www.hasb.nl – HES Amsterdam School of Business – International MBA programme
www.webster.nl – Webster University
www.leiden.edu – Leiden University
www.erasmusuniversiteit.nl – Bachelor & Masters programs, Rotterdam
www.rsm.nl – Rotterdam School of Management
www.tudelft.nl – Delft Technical University
www.uu.nl – University of Utrecht
www.rug.nl – Rijksuniversiteit Groningen
www.unimaas.nl – Maastricht University
www.roac.nl – Roosevelt Academy (part of University of Utrecht)
www.euruni.edu – European University
www.uva.nl – University of Amsterdam
www.vu.nl/english – Vrije Universiteit
www.thehagueuniversity.nl – 3-year English program, Bachelor in European studies
www.nyenrode.nl – Nyenrode Business University
www.inholland.nl – In Holland HBO University
www.mon3aan.nl – Mondriaan International Business School (MIBS) The Hague
www.volksuniversiteitamsterdam.nl – People's University
www.schoolweb.nl – Scope on the Globe, student fair

Distance Learning
www.ou.nl – Open University
www.oubs.nl – MBA programs (distance learning)
www.henley.nl -management college with 8,000 global executive students
www.uop.nl – University of Phoenix

For students
www.study-in-holland.com – specialist in visa and work permits
http://universititen-studieverenigingen.nl/pagina – student associations
www.studytrade.com – see The Netherlands

▶ **English-language universities offering degrees here**

Webster University, Boommarkt 1, 2311 EA Leiden, ☎ (071) 514 4341, www.webster.nl, is part of Webster University in St. Louis, Missouri, and offers undergraduate and graduate programmes in International Relations, International Business, Management, Marketing, and Psychology.

European University, Nassauplein 25, 2585 EC The Hague, ☎ (070) 360 4479, offers undergraduate and graduate degree programmes in Business Administration, Business Communication, and Public Relations. All classes are taught in English. www.euruni.be

Haagse Hogeschool University, Johanna Westerdijkplein 75, 2521 EN The Hague, ☎ 070) 445 8284, fax (070) 445 8194; gsc@sem.hhs.nl, www.sem.hhs.nl/gsc, offers English language MBA and International Bachelor Degrees in Business.

The University of Maryland, Horizonstraat 75 K3, 6466 SC Brunssum, ☎ (045) 523 1431, offers Associate and Bachelor degrees in business and computer studies; also BA in History and Psychology through their Open University and weekend seminars.

The British Open University, POB 91496, 2509 EB, The Hague, ☎ (070) 322 2335, or J.Ellis@open.ac.uk, has over 200 degree and fully accredited business courses. Students receive correspondence packages throughout the year, work from set books and BBC TV programmes. Credit is earned on the basis of completed written assignments and exams.

Erasmus University in Rotterdam, ☎ (010) 408 1111, www.eur.nl For enquiries, ICIR@asv.oos.eur.nl, offers a programme leading to a Masters of Business Administration ... taught in English.

Volks-Universiteit Classes. There are more than 100 public universities or *Volksuniversiteiten* in the Netherlands offering lectures and courses in a wide variety of craft subjects such as photography, drawing, painting, spinning, textile weaving, etc. They also have an extensive language department, including Dutch classes.
Main Address: www.volksuniversiteit.nl. **Amsterdam:** Herenmarkt 93,
☎ (020) 626 1626. **Amstelveen:** ☎ (020) 545 1424. **The Hague:** Nieuwe Duinweg 6 -14,
☎ (070) 358 9585. **Rotterdam:** Heemraadsingel 275-277, ☎ (010) 476 1200.
Utrecht: ☎ (030) 231 3395. **Hilversum:** ☎ (035) 621 9741.
The telephone directory will list those of other towns.

The British Language Training Centre, Nieuwezijds Voorburgwal 328E Amsterdam, ☎ (020) 622 3634, offers the internationally-recognised CELTA Certificate course to those wishing to become English-language teachers. Similarly, the **Hogeschool** in Diemen offers an International Degree in English and Education (IDEE).

▶ **Dutch language schools**

If you manage to learn the language, there is no doubt your stay here will benefit. Apart from those of the Volksuniversiteit, there are countless courses in all price categories, geared in intensity for all levels. Look in the 'Yellow Pages' under 'Talenonderwijs' (Language Education) or 'Volwassenonderwijs' (Adult Education). If you need advice, Helen Vandervelde's book, *How to Choose a Dutch Language Course*, may help you.

One of the best-known courses used often by professionals who are funded by their companies, is **Talenpracticum Regina Coeli**, Martinlaan 12, Vucht, ☎ (073) 657 0200. It is a total immersion, residential course originally offered by 'the nuns,' though nowadays there are many language instructors. www.reginacoeli.nl

If you prefer a private tutor, ACCESS should be able to recommend one in your area. The following two language institutes, however, provide courses in the major towns and cities in the Netherlands:

Elycio Talen: individual and group courses as well as remote learning in six locations throughout the country. www.learndutchnow.nl

Linguarama: professional language training, ☎ 0800 822 5596, www.linguarama.nl

Amsterdam:

Talencoach, Kloveniersburgwal 138, (☎ (020) 622 3231, (See ad on page 382.)

British Language Training Centre, Nieuwezijds Voorburgwal 328E,☎ (020) 622 3634, www.bltc.nl

The Hague:

The city of The Hague publishes a free booklet on all the language schools in the city. www.denhaag.nl

Direct Dutch, Piet Heinplein 1a, ☎ (070) 365 4677 (See ad on page 380.)

Language Learning Resources

www.directdutch.com	www.iberlingua.nl
www.berlitz.com	www.britishschool.nl
www.linguarama.nl	www.vtn-online.nl
www.lexicon.nl	www.taalthuis.com
www.easydutchplus.nl	www.feedbacktalen.nl
www.alliance-francaise.nl	www.languagesolution.net
www.babel.nl	www.pcitalen.nl
www.language-unites.org	www.talencoach.nl
www.bltc.nl	www.learndutch.com
www.icb-leiden.nl/en/opmaat.htm	

Music schools

There are many Dutch schools of dance, music, art, drama, etc., but as instruction is in Dutch, it might mean coming to grips with the language, too. As a rule, a *Conservatorium* trains those wishing to become professional, while the *Muziekscholen* (music schools) are more geared to those who simply wish to learn to play an instrument. The hobbyist should look under 'Musiekscholen' in the 'pink pages' of the telephone book, or contact ACCESS, who have a list of English-language music teachers, as well as a file of musical activities ranging from choirs to bagpipe-playing. The following music schools may help in searching out the best possibilities (registration is in April):

Amsterdam: Stichting Muziekschool Amsterdam, Bachstraat 5, ☎ (020) 578 7373, in locations throughout the city. **Sweelinck Conservatorium**, van Baerlestraat 27, ☎ (020) 571 2500.

The Hague: **Cecilia International Music School**, International School, T.M. Bouw-meesterlaan 75, ☎ (070) 328 3848 Individual lessons on most instruments by qualified staff, and in several languages. **Koninklijk Conservatorium**, Juliana van Stolberglaan 1, ☎ (070) 381 4251. **Muziekschool Wolthuis**, Burg. Hovylaan 12, ☎ (070) 391 0484. **Koorenhuis Centrum voor Kunst en Cultuur**, Prinsengracht 45, ☎ (070) 342 2722.

Rotterdam: Rotterdams Conservatorium, Pieter de Hoochweg 222,☎ (010) 476 7399. **SKVR Muziekschool**, Calandstraat 7, 3016 CA Rotterdam, ☎ (010) 436 1366, also dance and other activities. Various outlets.

▶ **Dance schools**
There are extremely helpful organisations to guide the newcomer on everything from classical ballet, line dancing and Scottish reels, to belly dancing. ACCESS will have a useful listing.

Nederlands Theater Instituut, Herengracht 684, Amsterdam, ☎ (020) 551 3300, has a list of recommended teachers and schools for all of Holland. They speak English and can give any information required about dance instruction. All schools take pupils from six years of age.

The English Dance Studio, Waverstraat 16, 1079 VL Amsterdam, ☎ (020) 644 2431, has been recommended for both classic and modern dance.

Dancers' Studio, Kerkstraat 75, Wassenaar, ☎ (070) 511 5050, international teaching staff for adults and youngsters. Ballet, modern dance, jazz etc.

Scottish Dancing, a recreational form of rather intricate folk dancing – great exercise too! Contact the **St. Andrew's Society**, or Drusilla Wishart, ☎ (071) 517 1047, Mr. van Zon ☎ (070) 320 2352, or ACCESS (see below).

▶ **Special classes, lectures and groups**
The following list covers a wide spectrum of activities, from problem-solving to learning and personal enhancement, to just plain fun. Some are a bridge to understanding the Netherlands.
– **ACCESS**, ☎ (070) 346 2525 in the Hague, and (020) 423 3217 in Amsterdam, www.access-nl.org, offers workshops on cultural adaptation, human development, family, career, pregnancy, and financial matters – all in English.
– **Alliance Francaise**, offers French language courses. It also organises activities to promote French culture, such as lectures, films and diverse cultural groups from France. In Amsterdam, ☎ (020) 627 9271; The Hague, ☎ (070) 362 1523; Rotterdam, ☎ (010) 436 0421; or the French Embassy, ☎ (070) 312 5800.
– **Amateur and Semi-Professional Drama Groups (Little Theater)**. Frustrated thespians might want to investigate the Anglo-American Theater Group in The Hague. www.aatg.nl
– **American Repertory Theater**, ☎ (020) 627 6162, www.amrep.org, and **The In Players International Drama Group in Amsterdam:** www.inplayers.org. (For a complete list see chapter 21 'Quick Reference.')

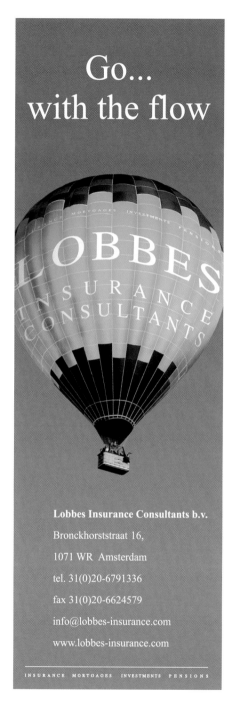

DutchNews.nl

Check out www.DutchNews.nl for your daily Dutch news round-up

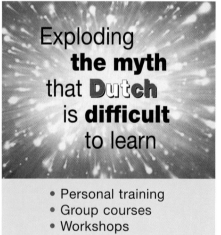

- **The British Choir**, The Hague, ☎ (070) 238 3848, www.cecilia-choir.com
- **Decoding the Netherlands**, evening lectures organised by ACCESS, in The Hague, ☎ (070) 346 2525, and ☎ (020) 423 3217 in Amsterdam, www.access-nl.org, an introduction to the Netherlands by quality speakers.
- **Decorative and Fine Arts Society of The Hague**, ☎ (070) 517 9003, professional lectures on all aspects of fine art.
- **Images International Photography Club**, The Hague, ☎ (070) 354 5964 www.imagesphotoclub.com
- **International Art Club in The Hague**, ☎ (070) 362 3347, has its own studio and holds regular workshops for amateur artists 'with some skill.' www.nadfas.org.uk
- **Museum Orientation and Educational Programmes**. Most large museums have an Education Department to encourage the public's appreciation of their collection. Most helpful, they can often arrange English-language group tours and lectures. Call the museum for information.
- **NIVON** (Netherlands Institute for Adult Education and Nature Work) offers members courses, camps and study trips. It has 17 'nature-homes' in Holland. Contact them for information at Hilversumstraat 332, Amsterdam, ☎ (020) 435 0700; also open to non-members. www.nivon.nl

Shopping

Sometimes, when spirits are low, browsing through an open-air market, traditional stores or fancy boutiques can be therapeutic ('retail therapy'). Many town markets are indicated in our chapters on each province; markets can be found in both cities and small towns, especially in summer. However, the problem may well arise of making oneself understood. Personnel in small shops, greengrocers, bakeries etc., do not always speak or understand English. In cities and in large department stores you have a better chance.

'Late Night Shopping': Most stores are open from 9am-5:30pm, but in most all towns, one evening a week is designated for shopping until 9pm. Also, certain 'Shopping Sundays' (*koopzondagen*) are also featured – often once per month – and some grocery stores have extended their hours to 8 or 9pm, with a few open until 10pm in urban areas. *Koopavond* or shop evening in Amsterdam and The Hague is on Thursdays; in Rotterdam on Fridays. Major cities have several small grocery stores that stay open at night. Check your phone directory for 'Avondverkoop' (evening sale) or 'Avondwinkel' (evening shop).

▶ **Supermarkets**

Albert Heijn, perhaps the best and biggest supermarket chain in the Netherlands, has branches all over the country. They carry most things you normally buy in a supermarket, from meats and groceries to household items, drinks, flowers, etc. They even have a home delivery service! Other popular supermarkets are **Super de Boer**, **Vomar**, **C1000**, **Deka Markt**, **Aldi**, **Dirck van den Broeck**, **Konmar** and **Lidl**.

Various chain stores may have familiar names, like **IKEA**, specialising in furniture, **Etos** and **Kruidvat** for toileteries and pharmacy, **Blokker** and **Marskramer** for kitchen equipment and household articles, **Megapool**, and **IT's** for electrical equipment, and **Gamma** and **Praxis** for DIY.

▶ **Department stores**

There are two major department stores in the Netherlands – **De Bijenkorf** and **Vroom and Dreesman** – that carry everything from a garlic press to a houseful of furniture. They each have large branches in Amsterdam, The Hague and Rotterdam, with various branches in many other cities throughout the country. For the newcomer, they facilitate shopping by offering a wide selection of goods under one roof. A 'Charge Account Service' is available, and they will exchange or refund unsatisfactory merchandise if returned within a few days of purchase together with your receipt or *bon*. Remember to keep it.

De Bijenkorf: Special departments for baby, teenager and adult clothing; china and glassware; beauty products and perfume; leather goods; toys; sports equipment; books in English, French, German and Dutch; CDs; photographic supplies; household articles; linens; furniture, and so on.

Amsterdam: Dam 1, ☎ (0900) 0919. Amstelveen: Galerij 152, ☎ (0900) 0919. The Hague: Wagenstraat 32, ☎ (0900) 0919. Rotterdam: Coolsingel 105, ☎ (0900) 0919. There are also medium-sized Bijenkorf stores in Arnhem, Breda, Eindhoven, Enschede, Den Bosch, Groningen, Maastricht, Utrecht and Venlo. (See www.bijenkorf.nl for a complete listing and opening times.)

Vroom and Dreesman: Special departments for baby, youngster and adult clothes; sports equipment; toys; foreign language books; CDs; photo supplies; baby furniture and supplies; excellent food store; etc. The **La Place** self-service restaurants are a super place to pause for refreshments while shopping. The food is always fresh and delicious – including one of the few 'salad bars' anywhere in Holland – and, as with any buffet-style restaurant, you can see what you're getting! See www.vroomendreesman.nl for a complete listing and opening times, ☎ (0900)-235 8363. Below are the three major ones.

- Amsterdam: Kalverstraat 203, ☎ (0900) 235 8363.
- The Hague: Spui 3, ☎ (0900) 235 8363.
- Rotterdam: Hoogstraat 185, ☎ (0900) 235 8363.

▶ **Speciality stores**

Some of the following chain stores can also be found in other major European cities, and are more specialised in their merchandise than the department stores mentioned above. If our list does not include the type of store you need, call ACCESS who may be able to help you.

- **C&A:** Especially good for children's clothes – from tots to teenagers. Amsterdam: Beurspassage 2, ☎ (020) 530 7150. The Hague: Grote Marktstraat 59, ☎ (070) 312 0720.

Rotterdam: Coolsingel 80, ☎ (010) 281 6666. See www.c-en-a.nl/stores for a complete listing of store locations and opening times.

- **Hennes & Maurits:** H&M, great fashions, accessories, reasonably priced. www.hm.com/nl

- **HEMA:** For inexpensive clothing, good value cold cuts and wine, as well as miscellaneous household articles. Amsterdam: Nieuwendijk 174-176, ☎ (020) 623 4176. The Hague: Grote Marktstraat 57, ☎ (070) 365 9844. Rotterdam: Beursplein 2, ☎ (010) 282 9900. See www.hema.nl for a complete listing of store locations and opening times.

- **Perry Sport:** Specialising in sports clothing; ski supplies in winter, swimwear in summer, tennis and riding clothes, etc. Some sports and camping equipment available. Amsterdam: Kalverstraat 99, ☎ (020) 624 7131, The Hague: Spuistraat 63, ☎ (070) 364 7840, Rotterdam: Lijnbaan 91, ☎ (010) 411 9011. See www.perrysport.nl for a complete listing of store locations and opening times.

▶ **Shopping for art**

Paintings, drawings, prints – various media: Art plays an important part in Dutch life. True to tradition, Holland inspires many artists, and the country is full of galleries of varying quality and prices.

Many visitors frequent auction houses here to buy old paintings; you can also attend the end-of-year exhibit of students of the Art Academies for a varied choice of modern pieces. For other less expensive options, we recommend the following: both the American Women's and British Clubs, as well as the International Art Club in The Hague, have exhibits from time to time. Call for enquires. (See clubs and organisations.) It is also possible to rent art! www.kunstuitleen.nu. For a directory of all the addresses of the *kunstuitleens*, see www.fku.nl, Federatie Kunstuitleen in NL.

For a reasonable fee you could even choose a quality drawing or painting direct from a professional artist, who will also take commissions (house portraits, a favourite scene or a subject you would like to have immortalised). A portfolio is also available with a wide range of paintings in various mediums should you prefer to select a painting without the extra cost of gallery commission. For details write The Artist, POB 34119, 3012 AC Rotterdam; email: abdolmans@gmail.com. What better memento of your stay. (See ad on page 141.)

For breathtaking still lifes and church interiors, visit Dutch artist Henk Helmantel, www.helmantel.nl, north of the city of Groningen. (See Chapter 9, and ad on page 277.)

▶ **Shopping for parties!**

Nothing can be more fun than organising an unusual and imaginative party. To get you started, look in the 'Yellow Pages' under *feestartikelen* or *verhuur feest artikelen*.

▸ Shopping for English language books

Although most bookshops have a good section of English language books, a few need to be mentioned in particular:

- **Amsterdam: American Book Center (ABC)**, Spui 12, ☎ (020) 625 5537; fax (020) 624 8042; www.abc.nl. (See ad on page 38.) **Waterstone's**, Kalverstraat 152, ☎ (020) 638 3821. **The English Book Shop**, Lauriergracht 71, ☎ (020) 626 4230. **Scheltema** – Dutch bookshop in Amsterdam, with English selections, Koningsplein 20, ☎ (020) 523 1411. **De Slegte** – Kalverstraat 48-52, is a supermarket of book surpluses and healthy discounts. www.deslegte.nl. On Fridays there is an open-air book market on the Plein in front of the ABC store, on Spui.

- **The Hague: American Book Center (ABC)**, Lange Poten 23, ☎ (070) 364 2742. www.abc.nl (See ad on page 38.)

- *XPatMedia*: Publisher XPat Media has some of the very best books about Holland on offer from their online web shop, www.hollandbooks.nl. Books are also on sale in local bookshops and at the annual expat fairs in Amsterdam and The Hague. The most popular book for almost 10 years is the annual *Holland Handbook*, a rich encyclopaedia for living and working in the Netherlands, with contributions from more than 30 professionals writing on their field of expertise. *Housing in Holland* tells you everything you need to know about renting or buying. www.housinginholland.nl, while other titles include *The Low Sky*, *The Food Shoppers Guide to Holland*, *Living with the Dutch*, *Dealing with the Dutch* and *Minding Your Manners*, to name but a few. They are also known for the stunningly beautiful photography in their books on a variety of places in the Netherlands, and the aerial views in the book *High over Holland*. For anything you want to read about the Netherlands, here are the books you need!

▸ Shopping for hobbies

Arts and crafts, painting, needlepoint and stamp collecting are among many possible hobbies, and ACCESS has a list of suppliers for such – a good place to start. Otherwise department stores may be able to assist you. Every town has a good art supply store; you will find it listed under 'Kunstenaarsbenodigheden.'

- **Stamp Collecting**: There are established stores, but also open-air (covered) stamp exchanges on regular days during the week. **Amsterdam:** Nieuwezijds Voorburgwal opposite No. 280, Sat. 1-4pm. **The Hague:** Corner of Noordeinde-Paleisstraat, Wed. & Sat. noon-4pm. **Rotterdam:** Grote Kerkplein, every Tues. & Sat. 10am-4pm. Big dealers are present but so are the small dealers bringing their albums in shopping bags. Stamps can be bought for 25 cents up!

- **Craft Shops and Painting Supplies**: Try the larger department stores...or check the 'yellow pages' under 'Kunst Schildersbenodigheden.' Art supply shops are easier to find these days...the best are usually close to Art Schools.

Pets

If you don't already have a pet, you might consider getting one when you have settled in. With this new member of the family, you will need to know about vets, grooming and where to leave your pet when you go on holiday. Should it get lost, you will need to know about 'Amivedi, a non-profit organisation that registers lost animals and assists in animal emergencies, road accidents etc.

Though many are listed under 'dierenhandel' in the 'Yellow Pages', resist the temptation to buy puppies from a shop, as they are not controlled by the Kennelclub.

Be sure, in any case, to ask for the animal's vaccination papers in the case of dogs and cats. If you just want a family pet, why not visit the local pound, 'dierenasiel,' where a variety of animals are crying out for adoption. Here you can pick out a healthy pet for a reasonable price. Cats will have been spayed and, like dogs, will have received all necessary shots. They can also help you find a solution if you can no longer keep your pet. For a complete listing throughout the country, see www.dierenasiels.com.

For a pedigree dog, contact the **Dutch Kennel Club,** ☎ (020) 664 4471, who will put you in touch with various breed clubs, reputable breeders, etc. www.kennelclub.nl

Veterinarians can be found in your telephone book under 'dierenarts.'

▶ **Grooming of dogs**

Salons will vary in quality. Look in the telephone book under 'hondenkapper,' 'hondenkapsalon' or 'hondentrimsalon.'

▶ **Holiday Kennels**

Leaving your pet when going on trips can create anxiety. Be sure, therefore, to leave it in expert hands. Consult your local kennel club or vet for reliable addresses, and be sure to book well in advance of holidays. Visit the kennel before you reserve too!

The **Animal Rescue Organisation, 'Nederlandse Vereniging tot Bescherming van Dieren'** is a very reliable private organisation that takes care of stray, unwanted and sick animals, commonly known as **'Dierenbescherming'** – so listed in the telephone directory. www.dierenbescherming.nl

Pet Emergencies: Police or Ambulance ☎ 112

You may also contact the 'dierenambulance' or animal ambulance. This organisation will pick up the animal and take it for medical care or disposal. www.dierenambulance.nl

Although the website is in Dutch, there is a good amount of helpful information – with links to organisations having to do with pets – on the veterinarian online site. For veterinarians online: www.dierenartsonline.nl

Chapter 17 | The good life: out and about

Entertainment and the Netherlands go hand-in-hand. Besides all the cultural venues, you have a wide choice of nightclubs in major cities like Amsterdam, The Hague, Breda, Rotterdam and Maastricht. Trendy *Grand Cafés*, typical *Bruin Cafés* (local pubs) and terrace restaurants (in summer) are popular places to relax and do some 'people-watching.' Jazz clubs can be found all over Holland, but are most prevalent in bigger towns and cities. The VVV will have a list.

▶ What's going on?

A non-Dutch reader need no longer have difficulty finding out what's going on. Newspapers list films and entertainment and, after a little practice, you will be surprised at how much you can actually understand even when you don't read Dutch. However, there are many other publications – both print and on-line – with regularly updated information about what's going on:

In Amsterdam:

– *Uitkrant*, a monthly VVV publication, lists movies, plays, concerts, cultural activities, museums, cabarets, special exhibits, concerts and other entertainment. Available from the VVV and Uit Buro (AUB). www.uitkrant.nl and www.amsterdamsuitburo.nl For English text: www.iamsterdam.com

– *Amsterdam Weekly*: www.amsterdamweekly.com, free cultural and events news. PDF issue online.

In The Hague:

– *Den Haag Agenda* lists activities and entertainment for the month in Dutch and English for the Hague, Scheveningen and Kijkduin, available from the VVV. www.haagsuitburo.nl

In Rotterdam:

– *R' Uit Magazine* is available from the VVV. It lists theatre, music and dance performances, and other happenings and events. Most large towns have their own version. www.rotterdamsuitburo.nl

In all three cities:

– *The Amsterdam-Hague-Rotterdam Times*, www.thehollandtimes.nl, is distributed free in Amsterdam, the Hague and Rotterdam.

▶ On-line publications and websites

– *Dutch News.nl*, www.dutchnews.nl, provides news in English everyday at 4pm, free to subscribers.

– *Expatica*, www.expatica.com, provides on-line news, information and events. Annual 'Expat Fair' in October, as well as other events, such as SpeedDating, Wine Tasting.

– *TheHagueOnLine*, www.thehagueonline.com, provides a calendar of events and news for The Hague and region.
– *Roundabout*, www.roundabout.nl, provides a summary of events around the country, every 14 days.

▶ **Movies and TV**

Because Holland is a small country and the expense of dubbing films would not be viable, foreigners are fortunate in being able to see movies and TV programmes in the original language. English-speakers can also watch BBC, NBC and CNN on the Dutch cable system.

In the case of a very popular movie at the cinema, it is wise to reserve seats ahead of time. This can be done in person a few hours before the performance, by telephone or often on-line. There is a slight charge for telephone reservations, and tickets will be held until a half hour before the show. (Personnel usually speak English.)

Movies are not listed daily in newspapers, as they are in the US and other countries, but rather in the Thursday edition. So, if you're a movie-mad family, save your Thursday entertainment section for use on the weekend.

Parents should know that the Netherlands is strict regarding what movies children are allowed to see. Unlike in the US where parents can assume responsibility by accompanying their child, in Holland if the age limit is 16 years and your child is obviously younger, he or she will not be allowed entry – even if you are with him. (For details, see 'The Younger Set,' Chapter 19.)

Television programmes are listed daily in newspapers, but as there is no Sunday edition; Saturday's paper will list programmes for the whole weekend.

▶ **Casinos**

French and American Roulette, Blackjack, Baccarat and slot machines can all be found at the casinos in Amsterdam, Breda, Eindhoven, Groningen, Zandvoort, Valkenburg, Nijmegen, Scheveningen, Rotterdam and at Schiphol Airport. (Addresses are given in the various province chapters under the appropriate town.) Casinos are generally open from 1:30pm-2am daily. Minimum age for entry is 18 years.

▶ **Amateur theatre**

There are a number of 'Little Theatre' groups in the Randstad area that provide entertainment to the foreign resident who really misses theatre productions that he or she can understand. Naturally, most plays are produced in Dutch, but these amateur theatre groups offer an international programme. (See Chapter 21 for listings.)

The performing arts

The full gambit of performing arts is available in the Netherlands: concerts, ballet, opera, musicals, circuses, ice-skating reviews, and more.

▶ **Buying tickets and season tickets**

Regular tickets and season tickets may be purchased through theatre box offices or the VVV. Box offices are usually open during the day, though some remain open up until the performance. Generally, reservations can be made up to one month in advance. For countrywide listings: www.uitburo.nl

In **Amsterdam**, contact the theatre directly, the Amsterdam Uit Buro (AUB), Leidseplein, ☎ (0900) 0191 (75 cents per minute), open daily 10am-6pm, Thurs. 9pm, or the VVV. www.aub.nl (English site)

In **the Hague**, tickets can be obtained from the VVV, from the theatre, or from Nederlands Theaterbureau, Zeekant 102, ☎ (070) 354 3411. www.haagsuitburo.nl

In **Rotterdam**, the VVV and theatres have the same reservation facilities as above. For advance discounted reservations, enquire as of May about a free booklet entitled 'Theater Seizoen,' which gives details of coming events for the year. Reservations must be made by August 31 – earlier for the best seats. The booklet can be picked up at box offices, the Doelen (see below), or sent by mail. www.rotterdamsuitburo.nl

See also: Maastricht, www.maastrichtsuitburo.nl, and Groningen, www.groningeruitburo.nl

▶ **Symphony**

The **Royal Concertgebouw Orchestra** and the **Netherlands Philharmonic of Amsterdam** need no introduction. Their recordings are famous worldwide. The Royal Concertgebouw Orchestra's home is the **Concertgebouw** in Amsterdam, where the first concert was held in 1888. www.concertgebouworkest.nl, and www.orkest.nl

The **Rotterdam Philharmonic Orchestra** has also carved out a fine reputation, giving a series of concerts throughout the year at **De Doelen**, Rotterdam's Concert Hall, with its outstanding acoustics. www.rpho.nl

The **Hague Residentie-Orkest** performs in the **Anton Philipszaal**. www.residentieorkest.nl. From time to time, certain composers are featured with a series of concerts dedicated to their works.

The **Netherlands Chamber Music Orchestra** (Nederlands Kamerorkest) performs at all the above concert halls.

▶ **Dance**

There are three major ballet companies in the Netherlands: **Het Nationale Ballet** (headquartered in the **Muziek Theater** in Amsterdam), the **Netherlands Dance Theater**, which performs in the **Lucent Danstheater** in The Hague, and the **Scapino Ballet** of Rotterdam, which specialises in ballets appealing to children. There are many smaller, modern ballet groups with a fine reputation. www.het-nationale-ballet.nl, and www.scapinoballet.nl; www.ndt.nl

▶ **Opera**

The **Netherlands Opera Foundation** numbers about 100 voices. They often have excellent visiting performers, directors and conductors – many from the United States. They perform in the **Muziektheater** in Amsterdam. For information, contact the **Netherlands Opera Foundation**, Waterlooplein 22, ☎ (020) 551 8117, and box office (020) 625 5455. www.hetmuziektheater.nl

▶ **Theatres and auditoriums**

In a country with a long history of appreciation for the performing arts, some of the theatre buildings in Holland are of significance in their own right. When older buildings were no longer able to serve the needs of the theatre-going public, innovative new, often avant-garde architecture resulted. Here are some examples:

Amsterdam

–**Concertgebouw,** Concertgebouwplein 2-6, ☎ (020) 671 8345 has 2,200 seats in the Main Hall and 492 in the Recital Hall. Built in 1888, it is known for its fine architecture and world-famous acoustics. Box office is open daily 10am-7pm; telephone reservations from 10am-5pm. www.concertgebouw.nl

–**Het Muziektheater**, Amstel 3, ☎ (06) 25 5455, is part of the controversial Stopera building, which overlooks the Amstel River and incorporates City Hall. It houses the Dutch National Ballet, the Netherlands Opera and the Foundation 'Het Muziektheater.' The box office is open Mon.-Sat. 10am-6pm, Sun. 11:30am-6pm. www.hetmuziektheater.nl

–**Muziek gebouw aan Het IJ** holds various concerts in a new venue along the Ij River near Central Station. Piet Heinkade 1, ☎ (020) 788 20 00. www.muziekgebouw.nl

–**Theater Carré**, Amstel 115-125, ☎ (020) 549 452, is on the east side of the Amstel River, between the Nieuwe Prinsengracht and the Nieuwe Achtergracht, in a famous theatre built in 1887 to stage circuses – which it still does occasionally at Christmas. Shows of all types are staged here from opera to theatre-in-the-round. Open daily 8am-9pm. www.theatercarre.nl (Parking garage opposite the Magere Brug, 'Skinny Bridge'.)

–**Stadsschouwburg**, Leidseplein 26, ☎ (020) 624 2311, has enormous chandeliers and decorative ceiling paintings from Belgium. Mainly Dutch theatre performances, but occasionally international and dance productions during Holland Festival. Ticket office open Mon.-Sat. 10am to time of performance. www.stadsschouwburgamsterdam.nl

–**Nieuwe de la Mar Theater,** Marnixstraat 404, ☎ (020) 530 5301, has a rich tradition of cabaret, earning it an international reputation. Box office open daily 11am-6pm. www.theaterbellevue.nl

–**Tuschinski Movie Theatre**, Reguliersbreestraat 26, ☎ (020) 626 2633, offers regular guided tours to see this cinema, an outstanding example of Art Deco (Jugendstil) and the Amsterdam School. Decorations include expressionist paintings, exotic wood, coloured marble, chandeliers and sculpture. The Wurlitzer Pipe Organ was brought from North Tonawanda, USA, to accompany silent movies, and is occasionally used for concerts. Guided tours in summer. www.tuschinski.nl. Spend more time there by watching a movie. Reservations: 0900-1458

– **Beurs van Berlage**, Damrak 277, ☎ (020) 530 4141, offers concerts in this skillfully converted Stock Exchange building, now home to The Netherlands Philharmonic Symphony Orchestra. They also host special exhibitions. http://en.beurs-van-berlage.nl

– **Boom Chicago Theatre, Leidseplein Theatre**, Leidseplein 12, ☎ (020) 423 0101, Amsterdam's leading improvisation/stand-up comedy show, in English. A very popular club – many Boom alumni are now comedy stars in the US. Open almost every night, with a surprisingly good dinner option. www.boomchicago.nl (See ad on page 40.)

– **Comedy Cafe**, Max Euweplein 43-45, ☎ (020) 628 3971. Improvisation/stand-up comedy with international performers. www.comedycafe.nl

– **Bimhuis**, Piet Heinkade 3, ☎ (020) 788 2188, is Holland's main jazz venue, in the same building as the Muziekgebouw, along the IJ shores (behind Central Station). www.bimhuis.nl

– **Diridas Poppentheater** (puppet theatre), Hobbemakade 68, ☎ (020) 662 1588.

– **Kindertheater Circus Elleboog**, Passeerdersgracht 32, ☎ (020) 623 5326, www.elleboog.nl

– (See www.theaterinstituut.nl for a full listing of venues, and www.gids4kids.nl for a large selection of children's activities.)

– **Felix Meritis Theater**, Keizersgracht 324, ☎ (020) 623 1311, www.felix.meritis.nl/english

– **The Vondel Park Open-Air Theatre**, ☎ (020) 673 1499, offers summertime performances with specific days for theatre, music, children's shows, and pop concerts. Wednesday lunch concerts at noon, children's shows at 3pm; theatre on Friday and Saturday nights at 9pm. All shows free of charge. www.amsterdam.info/parks/vondelpark

– **Film Museum,** Vondelpark 3, ☎ (020) 589 1400, www.filmmuseum.nl

– **English Church**, Begijnhof 48, ☎ (020) 624 9665, for a variety of concerts, www.ercadam.nl

The Hague and Scheveningen

The Hague Agenda, lists all cultural events in The Hague and is published monthly by the VVV. Also www.haagsuitburo.nl, ☎ 0900 828 29 99 (0,45 p.m.)

– **Nederlands Congres Centrum**, Churchillplein 10, ☎ (070) 306 6366, was built primarily to host international conferences, but it also holds all kinds of meetings, commercial, art and antique fairs, theatre and opera. www.congresscentre.nl

– **Dr. Anton Philipszaal**, Spuiplein 150, ☎ (070) 360 9810, www.ldt.nl, with its modern architecture, provides an elegant home for the Residentie Orkest. The building adjoins a fine hotel and good Japanese restaurant for convenient pre-theatre dining.

- **Koninklijke Schouwburg**, Korte Voorhout 3, ☎ 0900 3456789 (10cpm), www.ks.nl, first opened its doors to the public in 1804. Productions include plays, concerts, cabarets, puppet shows, and speciality acts from Holland and abroad.
- **Diligentia Theater**, Lange Voorhout 5, ☎ 0900 - 4104 104 (€ 0.15 p.m.), www.theater-diligentia.nl, has concerts, plays and other programmes that might appeal to non-Dutch-speaking audiences, as well as some special programmes in English. Coffee and lunch concerts also.
- **Fortis Circus Theater**, Circusstraat 4, ☎ (070) 416 7600, www.theater-online.nl, near the Kurhaus in Scheveningen, was once the site of a real circus. This building now houses musicals, top performing artists, shows and concerts. For tickets: ☎ 0900 300 5000.
- **Puppet Theaters**
  - **Poppentheater Guido Van Deth and the Puppetry Museum**, Nassau Dillenburgstraat 8, ☎ (070) 328 0208, has performances for children and adults. The theatre has over 1,000 puppets, including many colourful and interesting examples from France, Sicily, India, Germany, Java and Holland. It has a large library and a collection of 500 prints. Tours on request.
  - **Poppentheater Frank Kooman**, Frankenstraat 66, ☎ (070) 355 9305, www.kooman-poppentheater.nl, is operated by a happy man who needs no other hobby than his work. Frank Kooman is this lucky man who gives pleasure to young and old. In one month, he may give 44 performances to a total of 10,000 children. Mr. Kooman makes his own puppets, writes the plays, composes the music and is all the voices of his characters. Adult plays run about two hours; children's about one hour. (For a comprehensive list of puppet theatres, see Chapter 19.)

Rotterdam

- **De Doelen** (Music and Congress Centre), Schouwburgplein 50,
  ☎ (010) 217 1717, www.dedoelen.nl, box office open daily 10am-6pm, Fri.7pm; evening of performances 7-8:30pm. De Doelen, home of the Rotterdam Philharmonic Orchestra, is a modern concert hall with exceptional acoustics. Free lunch concerts are held on Wednesdays.
- **De Rotterdamse Schouwburg**, Schouwburgplein 25, ☎ (010) 411 8110, www.schouwburg.rotterdam.nl, is a controversial, starkly modern theatre of the eighties. Performances of opera, dance and theatre (mainly Dutch).
- **De Lantaren/Venster Theater**, Gouvernestraat 133, ☎ (010) 277 2277, www.lantaren-venster.nl, is a cinema that also presents theatre, dance and music in a season that runs from Sept.-June.
- **Luxor Theater**, Posthumalaan 1, ☎ (010) 484 3333 is the main locale for the annual International Film Festival, and many international artists perform here regularly. www.luxortheater.nl
- **Theater Zuidplein**, Zuidplein 60-64, ☎ (010) 20 30 203, www.theaterzuidplein. nl, often hosts performances of American and English companies in plays, opera,

musicals and concerts. The ticket office is open Mon.-Sat. 10am 6pm; sales for evening performances begin two hours before curtain.

– **Ahoy's Sport Complex**, Ahoyweg 10, ☎ (010) 293 3300, south of the river, is a huge hall that hosts such international events as the world tennis championships, ice hockey playoffs, pop concerts, circus, etc. Special shows for holiday periods such as 'Holiday on Ice' and the 'Christmas Circus.' www.ahoy.nl

Dining out

Chapter One describes some restaurant chains popular in the Netherlands. VVV offices have a complete list of recommended restaurants, often giving ethnic type, price, address, telephone number and directions.

Reasonably priced 'dish of the day' meals are available at 'Eet Cafés,' at railway station and department store restaurants, and at pancake restaurants.

Eating out with children is a special experience, as the Dutch really take them into consideration, often with special play areas and dishes. Restaurants and foods they particularly like are discussed herein, as well as the best (and most expensive) places to dine out on special occasions.

In Part One, recommended restaurants are listed under 'Eating Out'. The list of 'tried and true' restaurants in Amsterdam, The Hague and Rotterdam is too long to include in the province chapters, so they appear at the end of this chapter.

▶ **Indonesian restaurants**

Thicker than flies on honey in every town in the Netherlands, due to the many years the Dutch were settled in Indonesia, this cuisine is almost a national dish in Holland. As it is not as familiar to newcomers as other international foods, a bit of description may be helpful. Most Indonesian restaurants also serve Chinese cuisine, but purists may prefer a restaurant that specialises in one or the other. 'Rijstafel' is the Indonesian speciality and consists of many small dishes such as chicken prepared in various ways, saté (meat or chicken cooked over charcoal then served on a skewer covered with peanut sauce), rice, vegetables in different guises, and so on. For those who like their food spicy hot, there are always sauces on the side.

These restaurants usually offer a choice of two, three or six-person menus, either emphasising Indonesian or Chinese dishes, and sometimes a combination of the two. They are generally a good value.

Dutch taste treats

Patat (french fries) stands and *Automatieks* (vending machine foods) dot the landscape in summertime. Students gravitate to these eateries for a quick snack any time of the day or night. Some common snacks or fast foods are:

Patat or Friet: Probably the most universally-eaten food in the Netherlands – known in the United States as 'French-fries' and in England as 'chips.' Here you must specify if you want them with or without mayonnaise: 'met' means 'with,' and 'zonder' means 'without.' They might also be offered with ketchup or saté sauce.

Kroketten (kroket for singular): Similar to timbales, rissoles or croquettes, but with much less meat. Children – and many 'grown children' love these things, despite not knowing what's really in them.

Bitterballen: The same as kroketten but in small round balls. Offered as a cocktail snack and served hot with mustard.

Frikandel: Made of pure ground meat (usually beef and pork mixed) and shaped like a frankfurter sausage.

Worst: Sausage. Some are long, some short; most are thin, though some are fat. The kind of sausage you find in your green pea soup (erwtensoep), or the kind that kids buy at a patat stand. They look like hot dogs but taste rather different.

Gehaktbal: A meatball of ground meat (usually half beef and half pork) seasoned with nutmeg, dipped in egg and breadcrumbs and deep fried.

Slaatjes: Potato salad, mixed salad or green salad with mayonnaise.

Nasi Bal: An Indonesian meatball made with a mix of rice and hot spices, then deep fried. Too spicy for most children.

Bami Hapje: Ditto above, but noodles are used in place of the rice.

Loempia: Another Indonesian speciality that resembles a spring roll, filled with a mixture of chicken, bean sprouts, vegetables and hot spices. A meal in itself – fairly nutritious, but may be quite spicy.

Oliebollen: Like donuts without the hole, dipped in powdered sugar; traditional fare on New Year's Eve and during winter markets and fairs.

Saucijzebroodje: Flaky puff pastry with meat filling. Available from the bakery and other convenient places. (Small ones make tasty appetizers!)

Haring: Herring (raw). You may go for this right from the start, or you won't even consider trying it. Still, it is very typically Dutch and you should at least give it a try. To be properly traditional, the raw herring should be eaten whole (cleaned and minus the head). You hold it up by the tail, position your mouth beneath it and bite into the headless end. It can also be smothered in raw onion. The piece of tail you are left with may be discarded. Go on, try it! If you're like most expatriates (or even tourists), you'll eventually end up liking it. And – it's extremely healthy.

Herring stands often include a choice of chopped herring on bread or toast; and shrimp sandwiches or smoked eel sandwiches (yes, eel) – all with or without mayonnaise, and quite good. Incidentally, herring stands also sell the most marvelous, huge, crispy pickles that can be enjoyed with or without the herring, of course.

Herring is at its best and most expensive from June (when the first 'green' herrings are landed) to September. The Queen is presented with the first herring of the season, after which they are available to all.

Poffertjes: Mini-pancakes made on a special griddle, which has silver-dollar-sized depressions. You can have poffertjes absolutely dripping in butter and coated with powdered sugar – the usual way – or 'spliced' with alcohol, like rum, which makes them a bit more 'interesting.' *Poffertjes* are only available at a special *poffertjes* stand or restaurant, usually in the centre of town, at fairgrounds, etc. Children love them.

Pannekoeken: Dutch 'pancakes' are more like French crèpes and not like the traditional American pancake, nor are they eaten at breakfast here, but for lunch and dinner or in between – sweet or savoury. Dutch *pannekoeken* are about 14 inches across, and need special plates to accommodate them. You can order them with a variety of toppings – anything from apples, bacon, ham, cheese and pineapple – with *stroop* (a dark-coloured syrup similar in taste to simple maple syrup), and so forth. Here are some well-established pancake restaurants for you to try:

▶ **Pancake restaurants**

(Look for 'Pannekoekhuis'): Generally informal and often in scenic or touristy places, pancake restaurants are usually a good choice when children are in tow, and they appeal to most people who aren't dieting! For pancakes in each province see the national *pannekoek* site: www.pannekoekenhuizen.org. Our favorites in the Randstad area include:

Amsterdam:
– **Pancake Bakery**, Prinsengracht 191, ☎ (020) 625 1333. www.pancake.nl, with play area for kids
– **Het Pannekoekhuis**, Prinsengracht 358, ☎ (020) 620 8448
– **Bredero**, O.Z. Voorburgwal 244/3, ☎ (020) 427 7921
– **Boerderij Meerzicht**, Pancake House in the Amsterdam forest, Koenkade 56, ☎ (020) 679 2744.

Delft:
– **Stads-Koffyhuis**, Oude Delft 133, ☎ (015) 212 4625, www.stads-koffyhuis.nl, is an old favourite.
– **Stadspannekoekhuys**, Oude Delft 113-115, ☎ (015) 213 0193
Gouda:
– **Goudse Winkeltje**, Achter de Kerk 9a, ☎ (0182) 52 7874
Leiden:
– **Oudt Leyden,** Steenstraat 49, ☎ (071) 513 3144, www.oudtleyden.nl, with two restaurants, one the pancake house and the other a top-notch venue.
– **Leidse Hout**, Houtlaan 100, ☎ (071) 515 3476, www.deleidsehout.nl
– **De Schaapsbel**, Beestenmarkt 7, ☎ (071) 512 4650, www.schaapsbel.nl
The Hague:
– **Maliehuys Restaurant,** Maliestraat 10, ☎ (070) 346 2474
– **Malieveld Paviljoen**, Koekamplaan 6, ☎ (070) 363 9250, www.malieveld.nl, a well-known stop.
Rotterdam:
– **Pannekoekhuis Boshut de Big**, Kralingseweg 20, ☎ (010) 452 6874, in the woods.

– **Pannekoekhuis De Nachtegaal**, Princes Beatrixlaan 11, ☎ (010) 452 7361, www.pannenkoekenhuisdenachtegaal.nl

Other traditional Dutch dishes

– **Uitsmijter:** An open-faced sandwich of sorts with ham, beef or other meat, and/or cheese, topped with lightly fried eggs; a popular luncheon choice.
– **Erwtensoep:** Old-fashioned split pea soup the real traditional way, with pieces of sausage and fat bacon...a typical winter dish and a hearty meal in itself. A real Dutch speciality.
– **Capucijners:** Another winter dish, this one of beans (similar to chickpeas) cooked with onions, bacon and potatoes.

Cookies and candies

It would seem every town in every province has its own recipe for delicious Dutch cookie specialities. Even if we knew them all, we couldn't list them all. Enjoy!
– **Kruidkoek:** 'Pain d'epices' or a kind of gingerbread, a speciality of Friesland (can also be purchased throughout Holland.)
– **Suikerbrood:** Also from Friesland, this is a wonderful sugar-topped cake, usually eaten at breakfast.
– **Blauwvingers:** Literally 'blue fingers,' these cookies with almonds are shaped in the form of ladyfingers and come from Zwolle (Overijssel province).
– **Arnhemse meisjes:** Literally 'Arnhem girls.'
– **Sprits:** A small butter cookie from Utrecht.
– **Stroopwafels:** A specialty of Gouda (South Holland). Unusual cookies made in a waffle-patterned mould and filled with a delicious caramel syrup.
– **Vlaaien:** From Limburg and the south, these open-faced tarts (flans) are usually filled with seasonal fruits – apricot and cherry are favourites.
– **Korstjes:** From the Eindhoven area (Brabant province), an anise-flavoured cookie.
– **Speculaas:** Wherever they originated, they are available all over the Netherlands and come in small, crunchy varieties as well as the 4-5-foot-tall cookies made in the form of Saint Nicholas during the holiday season...a rich spicy flavour and delicious. The large ones keep for weeks.
– **Hopje, Dropje and Zuurtjes:** Most drugstores sell these candies that come in all shapes, colours and flavours. The most famous are perhaps the *Haagse hopjes* made by Raademakers in The Hague...tasty coffee-flavoured, hard candies. *Dropjes* come in varying shades from light grey to pitch black and are licorice-flavoured, some hard and some soft. *Zuurtjes* are the hard candies that come in all colours of the rainbow – including stripes – and in all flavours... the fruit ones, *fruit* (pronounced 'frowt') *zuurtjes*, being especially popular.
– **Muisjes and Hagelslag:** *Muisjes* (literally 'little mice') are anise-flavoured, while *Hagelslag* is a chocolate-flavoured, grain-like topping. These become favourites with

foreign children who quickly imitate the Dutch in sprinkling them on bread, in yogurt, etc. When a new baby is born, it is customary to offer visitors *muisjes* on a rusk – pink for a girl and blue for a boy.

▶ **Eating out with children**

Holland is one of the most densely populated countries in the world – and this means lots of children. In the inimitable style of the Dutch, they have come up with a highly civilised solution to eating out with children – the *kindermenu* (children's menu), which is available in most restaurants here, with the exception of those definitely catering to adults only. No matter which restaurant you patronise, the chances are ten to one that the children's menu will feature grilled chicken, French fries and applesauce. We don't know who researched and discovered this magic formula, but somehow it works. The portions are child-sized and priced accordingly. Some restaurants even offer a choice of two or three children's menus...the second most popular will probably feature *kroketten*.

In addition to eating out 'en famille,' the older children will probably want to 'go it alone' at the local *patat* stand. While sightseeing or in-town shopping, an easy stop with children is, of course, a McDonald's or Burger King, or the cafés in major department stores. For something really fun for your 6- to 12-year-olds, take them to **Kinder Kook Kafé** (Children's Cooking Café), O.Z. Achterburgwal 193, Amsterdam, ☎ (020) 625 3257. (Reservations necessary; Saturdays between noon and 2pm.) You can deposit your child here and return three hours later to a delicious three-course meal prepared and served by their own hands! Delightfully inexpensive and good for their Dutch. Birthday or school groups can be accommodated. www.dinnersite.nl/kinderkookkafe

▶ **Randstad restaurants**

The restaurants listed on the following pages start with some known and reliable favourites for Amsterdam, The Hague, Rotterdam and smaller towns in the immediate area. They are listed according to price categories, old-Dutch atmosphere or unusual decor. If you have other suggestions, don't hesitate to let us know. We're still eating our way through Holland.

We also include some of the best – and most expensive – places to dine, for those very special occasions. Many have a Michelin one-star rating (one or two have two stars), as well as accolades from other top Dutch and foreign gastronomic organisations.

Amsterdam restaurants

'Eet Cafés' and inexpensive suggestions:
- **Brasserie van Baerle**, van Baerlestraat 158, ☎ (020) 679 1532
- **Broodje van Kootje,** Leidseplein 20, ☎ (020) 623 2036; Spui 28, ☎ (020) 623 7451, for sandwiches
- **Dante**, Spuistraat 320, ☎ (020) 638 8839

– **De Doffer**, Runstraat 12, ☎ (020) 622 6686
– **Haesje Claes,** Spuistraat 275, ☎ (020) 624 9998, www.haesjeclaes.nl, classic Dutch dishes and fish
– **Land van Walem**, Keizersgracht 449, ☎ (020) 625 3544, www.cafewalem.nl, popular eatery along the canal, with nice terrace view – and good food.
– **Molenpad**, Prinsengracht 653, ☎ (020) 625 9680
– **'t Nieuwe Café**, Eggertstraat 8, ☎ (020) 627 2830, on the Dam square, built into the outer wall of the New Church opposite the Palace. Ideal for coffee or reasonably-priced lunches...terrific ice cream and pastries!
– **Rum Runners** (Caribbean), Prinsengracht 227, ☎ (020) 627 4079

Moderate-priced:

– **Café Americain**, Hotel American, Leidsekade 97, ☎ (020) 624 5322, where Mata Hari had her wedding reception; excellent coffee and cakes, and an Art Deco interior that has been designated an historic landmark.
– **Casa di David**, Singel 426, ☎ (020) 624 5093 www.casadidavid.com, for Italian specialities.
– **de Oesterbar**, Leidseplein 10, ☎ (020) 623 2988. Good fish and oysters. www.oesterbar.nl.
– **Hans en Grietje**, Spiegelgracht 27, ☎ (020) 624 6782
– **Indonesia**, Korte Leidsedwarsstraat 18, ☎ (020) 623 2035
– **Sama Sebo**, P.C. Hooftstraat 267, ☎ (020) 662 8146, ask for the *bordje* or chef's special, a combination of traditional Indonesian dishes.
– **Koriander**, Amstel 212, ☎ (020) 626 1199, overlooking the Amstel River.
– **Mayur**, Korte Leidsedwarsstraat 203, ☎ (020) 623 2142, www.mayur.nl, for fine Indian dishes.
– **Speciaal**, Nieuwe Leliestraat 142, ☎ (020) 624 9706, simple decor, good food.

Expensive:

– **De Prinsenkelder**, Prinsengracht 438, ☎ (020) 422 2777, www.prinsenkelder.nl
– **Kort**, Amstelveld 12, ☎ (020) 626 1199, French cuisine in the restored Amstel Raden Mas Church, Stadhouderskade 6, ☎ (020) 685 4041.
– **'t Swarte Schaep**, Korte Leidsedwarsstraat 24A, ☎ (020) 622 3021, for French cuisine.
– **De Tuinhuys**, Reguliersdwarsstraat 28, ☎ (020) 627 6603, full menu at lunch also.
– **De Vijf Vlieghen**, Spuistraat 294-302, ☎ (020) 624 8369, www.d-vijffvlieghen.com

Old Dutch/Medieval:

– **Boerderij Meerzicht**, Koenenkade 56, ☎ (020) 679 2744, www.boerderijmeerzicht.nl, an old farm restaurant in the Amsterdamse Bos (woods) with a playground, terrace and a Nature Museum. Take the Haarlemmermeer *museumtram* – get off at the Bos (Woods) stop.
– **Die Port van Cleve**, N.Z. Voorburgwal 176-180, ☎ (020) 624 0047, an old inn dating from 1887, specialising in native Dutch dishes. Thursday evenings in winter, a 'winterdish' buffet' is offered; other times, pea soup and steaks.

- **Hollands Glorie**, Kerkstraat 220-222, ☎ (020) 4204041
- **Dorrius**, Nieuwezijds Voorburgwaal 5, ☎ (020) 420 2224, www.dorius.nl, traditional Dutch.
- **Piet de Leeuw**, Noorderstraat 11, ☎ (020) 623 7181, www.pietdeleeuw.nl

The Hague restaurants

(Also Scheveningen and Wassenaar)
'Eet Cafés" and inexpensive suggestions:
- **De Boterwaag**, Grote Markt 8a, ☎ (070) 365 9686, in an historic setting.
- **Brasserie Corona**, Buitenhof 39, ☎ (070) 363 7930
- **Malieveld Paviljoen**, Koekamplaan 6, ☎ (070) 363 9250, www.malieveld.nl, one of The Hague's oldest.
- **de Posthoorn**, Lange Voorhout 39a, ☎ (070) 360 4906, www.bodegadeposthoorn. nl, opposite the US Embassy. Typical Dutch café atmosphere and pleasant terrace in summer.
- **'t Goude Hooft**, Groenmarkt 13, ☎ (070) 346 9713, a typical Dutch café-restaurant, with a large pleasant terrace (also serves pancakes).
- **de Mollige Haan**, Strandweg 137, ☎ (070) 355 2575, www.demolligehaan.nl, for inexpensive chicken.

Moderate-priced:
- **Aubergerie,** Nieuwe Schoolstraat 19, ☎ (070) 364 8070, French cuisine and fun.
- **Gauchos**, Molenstraat 26, ☎ (070) 360 3154, also Denneweg 71, ☎ (070) 365 1015, for Argentine beef.
- **Luden**, Frederikstraat 36, ☎ (070) 360 1733. www.luden.nl, very reasonable French menus.
- **Marco Polo**, Kettingstraat 9/11, ☎ (070) 365 2080, for Italian.
- **Le Mouton,** Kazernestraat 62 (enter Nieuwe Schoolstraat), ☎ (070) 310 6888, www.le-mouton.nl
- **Park Lane**, Parkstraat 37, ☎ (070) 365 3754, delicious food and pleasant service.
- **Perlier**, Nieuwe Schoolstraat 13d, ☎ (070) 365 0887, very reasonable prices.
- **Schlemmer**, Lange Houtstraat 17, ☎ (070) 360 9000, www.schlemmer.nl, original atmosphere, soothing music. Pleasant for lunch...also serves breakfasts & Sunday brunches.
- **Tampat Senang**, Laan v. Meerdervoort 6, ☎ (070) 363 6787, www.tampatsenang.nl, a favourite Indonesian venue. Intriguing decor and garden. Depending on your order, can be expensive.
- **Terraza**, Laan van Meerdervoort 209, ☎ (070) 365 2525. Good Italian fare.

Expensive:
- **Le Bistroquet**, Lange Voorhout 98, ☎ (070) 360 1170, www.bistroquet.nl, nice bright atmosphere.

- **Restaurant Julien**, Vos van Tuinstraat 2a, ☎ (070) 365 8602, www.julien.nl, a local favourite.
- **Shirasagi**, Stadhouderslaan 76R, ☎ (070) 346 4700, www.shirasagi.nl, for Japanese, downtown, near city hall.

Old Dutch Atmosphere:
- **Restaurant 'Meerrust' (More Rest)**, Dorpstraat 5, Warmond, ☎ (071) 301 0817, waterside farm restaurant with lots of local colour and reasonable prices.

Scheveningen

- **Bali**, Badhuisweg 1, ☎ (070) 358 77 78. www.bali-scheveningen.nl, for Indonesian food and original atmosphere.
- **China Delight**, Dr. Lelykade 116, ☎ (070) 355 5450
- **Golden Duck,** Dr. Lelykade 29, ☎ (070) 354 1095
- **Ducdalf**, Dr. Lelykade 5, ☎ (070) 355 7692, www.ducdalf.nl, for fish specialities... reasonable prices.

Rotterdam restaurants

'Eet Cafés' and inexpensive suggestions:
- **De Admiraliteit**, Admiraliteitstraat 17B, ☎ (010) 413 4289
- **De Ballentent**, Parkkade 1, ☎ (010) 436 0462, www.deballentent.nl
- **Big Ben**, Stadhuisplein 3, ☎ (010) 414 9992
- **Grand Café Loos**, Westplein 1, ☎ (010) 411 7723, www.loos-rotterdam.nl
- **Dudok Brasserie,** Meent 88, ☎ (010) 433 3102

Moderate-Expensive:
- **Blits Eten en Drinken,** Boompjes 701, ☎ (010) 413 6070, www.blits-rotterdam.nl, good food and a pleasant river view.
- **Chalet Suisse**, Kievitslaan 31, ☎ (010) 436 5462, situated on the edge of the park, overlooking the gardens...a lovely spot.
- **De Pijp**, Gaffelstraat 90a, ☎ (010) 436 6896. During WW II, this historic 'speakeasy' served as a meeting place for the Dutch resistance. Some of the feel of that era is still evident – dark interior, long bare tables to sit at family-style. Traditionally a students' hangout, every September 5th the restaurant is open to the new college (Erasmus University) arrivals who hear stories of the past from 'oldtimers.' Fraternities were forbidden by the Germans, so students gathered secretly here to work with the resistance movement. A century old in 1998, the Pijp's clientele is what makes it unique. Noisy... everyone talks to his or her neighbour, most of whom speak English. This is one of the few places a foreigner can mix easily with local people without a formal introduction. Note the collection of patrons' ties hanging from the ceiling. The extensive menu is displayed on a blackboard. You should reserve ahead.
- **El Gaucho**, van Vollenhovenstraat 58, ☎ (010) 414 1602, for steak and more steak.
- **Indonesia**, Rodezand 34, ☎ (010) 414 8588

- **Ocean Paradise**, Parkhaven 21 (opposite Euromast), ☎ (010) 436 1702. A red and gold Chinese barge to rival those of Hong Kong. Long menu with great variety of dishes (also Indonesian). A perfect place to take the family. Try to get a table on the far side away from the quay, where you can get a view of the Maas River traffic.
- **Portofino**, Nieuwe Binnenweg 151, ☎ (010) 436 5163. See the cook throwing pizzas 4-5 feet in the air, stretching the dough to the right size. Reserve ahead.
- **Taj Mahal**, Mariniersweg 18, ☎ (010) 412 0812, for Indian food.

Old Dutch atmosphere:

- **Old Dutch**, Rochussenstraat 20, ☎ (010) 436 0344, traditional Dutch food and interior.
- **Kasteel van Rhoon**, Dorpsdijk 63, Rhoon (south of Rotterdam), ☎ (010) 501 8886, www.hetkasteelvanrhoon.nl, in a castle dating from 1433...fine restaurant with romantic terrace dining.
- **In den Rustwat,** Honingerdijk 96, ☎ (010) 413 4110, www.indenrustwat.nl, an atmospheric old inn dating from 1597...fine cuisine and service.
- **De Zwetheul**, Rotterdamseweg 480 (between Delft and Rotterdam), ☎ (010) 470 4166, fine cuisine; pleasant waterside terrace for summer drinks.

Schiedam restaurants

- **Hosman Frères**, Korte Dam 8-10, ☎ (010) 426 4096, French atmosphere in this good restaurant that hugs the canal. Downstairs moderate; upstairs expensive.
- **Noordmolen**, Noordvest 38, ☎ (010) 426 3104. Eat in a working windmill, illuminated at night and paddles turning...simple but nice family atmosphere; moderate.

Maassluis

- **Ridderhof**, Sportlaan 2, ☎ (010) 591 2212. This 17th-century farmhouse has been converted into an extremely attractive restaurant. A reasonable meal is possible in the section of the farmhouse reserved for 'plate service,' and children can visit the animals in the nearby field.

Delft

- **Stadsherberg De Mol,** Molslaan 104, ☎ (015) 212 1343. This former orphanage from 1563 has been transposed into a 16th-century inn, trying to recapture its youth by inviting you to dine in medieval style. You will be attended by wenches in period dress, along with music, dancing, and meat roasting over an open fire. Call for specifics.
- **L'Orage**, Oude Delft 111b, ☎ (015) 212 3629
- **Klikspaan,** Korenmarkt 85, ☎ (015) 214 15 62, www.klikspaandelft.nl
- **Café de Vlaanderen**, Beestenmarkt 16, ☎ (015) 213 3311. Pleasant terrace and Sunday brunches.

– **De Kurk,** Kromstraat 20, ☎ (015) 214 1474, www.dekurk.nl. Good value; conservatory-type room for in- and outdoor dining. Open fire in winter.

▶ **Fine dining**

For a romantic anniversary or birthday dinner out on the town, the variety of restaurants and the quality of the preparation of dishes in Holland's top restaurants are hard to beat anywhere in Europe. Price, of course, is a factor to be considered...the best places are always expensive... but a number of starred restaurants offer two menus – one more moderate than the full gourmet meal. There is no harm in asking the price of their 'prix fixe' menu when calling to make reservations.

As a convenience to readers for special occasions, a list of some of the best-regarded restaurants in the Randstad area follows. Restaurants with an asterisk indicate that they have Michelin stars. These ratings vary from year to year, but the meal in such an establishment is rarely disappointing.

Amstelveen:
– **De Jonge Dikkert**, Amsterdamseweg 104a, ☎ (020) 641 1378, www.jongedikkert.nl

Amsterdam:
– **Christophe***, Leliegracht 46, ☎ (020) 625 0807
– **Dikker en Thijs**, Prinsengracht 444, ☎ (020) 620 1212, www.dtfh.nl
– **Le Garage,** Ruysdaelstraat 54-56, ☎ (020) 679 7176, www.restaurantlegarage.nl, famous chef, and show biz set.
– **De Kersentuin** (French), Dijsselhofplantsoen 7, ☎ (020) 570 5600
– **Paardenburg**, Amstelzijde 55, Oudekerk a/d Amstel, ☎ (020) 496 1210
– **En Route**, Hobbemakade 63, ☎ (020) 671 1263
– **Tout Court**, Runstraat 13, ☎ (020) 625 8637, for French cuisine.

Bergambacht:
– **Puccini,** Molenlaan 14, ☎ (0182) 35 1000

Delft:
– **De Zwetheul***, Rotterdamseweg 480, ☎ (010) 470 4166, with terrace.

The Hague:
– **Restaurant Corona**, Buitenhof 39-42, ☎ (070) 363 7930, www.corona.nl
– **Da Roberto**, Noordeinde 196, ☎ (070) 346 4977
– **Saur**, Lange Voorhout 47-53, ☎ (070) 346 2565. An old favourite with outstanding fish specialities. Elegant restaurant upstairs, while the bar-restaurant on the ground floor is more relaxed.

Oegstgeest:
– **De Beukenhof**, Terweeweg 2-4, ☎ (071) 517 3188

Rotterdam:
– **Dewi Sri**, Westerkade 20, ☎ (010) 436 0263, www.dewisri.nl, for Indonesian cuisine.
– **Parkheuvel***, Heuvellaan 21, ☎ (010) 436 0530, www.parkheuvel.nl, at the Maas river end of the park...modern and exclusive.

− **La Vilette,** Westblaak 160, ☎ (010) 414 8692, www.lavilette.nl, modern, with nouvelle cuisine.

Scheveningen:

− **Kandinsky,** Gevers Deynootplein 30, ☎ (070) 416 2636, www.kurhaus.nl, overlooks the sea from the Kurhaus Hotel.

Schiedam:

− **La Duchesse,** Maasboulevard 7, ☎ (010) 426 4625, good reputation; attractive and cosy interior.

− **PAN,** Parkweg 367-369, ☎ (010) 246 0340, International cuisine.

− **Lepels Eten en Drinken,** Korte Haven 5, ☎ (010) 246 7358, French/Mediterranean

Wassenaar:

− **Auberge de Kieviet**, Stoeplaan 29, Wassenaar, ☎ (070) 347 750 418, www.hoteldekieviet.nl, elegant country setting with fine French cuisine.

− **De keuken van Waarde,** Walsdorperlaan 43, ☎ (070) 328 1167, French, romantic, dine on terrace.

− **Theepaviljoen de Horsten,** Landgoed de Horsten, Kaaphorst 6, ☎ (070) 511 26 19, afternoon tea, (lunch) on wooded estate; closes 5 pm.

▶ **Online ratings**

To search and compare by city, type of restaurant, price and location, along with reviews from people who have been there, the following are the top dining websites for delicious dining tips for the Netherlands:

− **Iens Independent Index** − guides available in English, close to 3,000 restaurants reviewed; also a guide for kid-friendly dining and regional guides. www.iens.nl

− **Special Bite** − over 600 restaurants and tips for dining with children, www.specialbite.com

− **Lekker** − the food magazine/dining guide for the Netherlands; the editors choose the top 500 restaurants in the Netherlands. www.lekker.nl

− **The Red Guide**, Michelin − In the Benelux region, there are 770 Dutch restaurants and 700 hotels listed. www.viamichelin.nl

− **Dinnersite** − Search 9,000 restaurants by category. www.dinnersite.nl

Chapter 18 | Sports

There are those who enjoy watching and those who enjoy doing, so we have divided this chapter into these two categories. Dutch *voetbal*, or what some of us still call 'soccer,' probably heads the list as the most popular spectator sport here in Holland, while sailing tops the list of favourites in active sports. (The sports are listed alphabetically...not according to popularity.)

Spectator sports

We do not attempt to include every spectator sport. Each town has its own offerings at different times of the year, and many of these events have been noted throughout the book. For the very sports-minded, the Monday editions of the local newspapers are highly recommended. They list the sports activities of the previous week with scores, etc., and also the sports events for the coming week. Obviously written in Dutch, but not too difficult for enthusiasts to follow.

▸ **Biking and cycling**

Holland couldn't be a more ideal country to enjoy biking and cycling...its generally flat terrain is perfect for enjoying these sports. However, exciting indoor cycling events are also regularly held in **Amsterdam's Velodrome**. Information from the VVV or ☎ (020) 408 2133. www.velodrome.nl

▸ **Boating competitions**

While sailing is the most visual of the water sports, rowing meets, canoe competitions and speed boating are also popular. Canoe races – the **Zaan Regatta** – are held in Zaandam (near Amsterdam) in June. For more information, contact the local VVVs. www.nlroei.nl

Rowing meets: A rowing competition of national importance is held in September on the Bergse Voorplas, Rotterdam. Organised by the Nautilus Club, ☎ (010) 413 8791. Amsterdam holds its **'Head of the River' races** on the Amstel in April, while Groningen has an important **International Rowing Regatta** on the Eemskanaal in mid-June. For information: Royal Dutch Rowing Federation: www.knrb.nl

Sailing races: Serious sailors participate in the **North Sea Race** that takes place at Whitsun. There are actually two races – the race between the Dutch boats from the Hook of Holland to Harwich (England), and the main race from Harwich to the Hook of Holland, with English and Dutch boats in competition. For exact dates, ask the VVV. www.sail.nl

There are a number of sailing regattas throughout the country, an **International Sailing Regatta** in Veere, Zeeland during Easter; and international **deep-sea sailing**

races at Delfzijl (Groningen province) at Whitsun. In May, the **International Olympic class sailing races** are held in Medemblik (North Holland). In July it's **Deltaweek** with international sailing contests of round and flat-bottomed boats on the Oosterschelde (Zeeland province). About the same time and into August, a very colourful sailing event takes place on the Frisian Lakes, **'Skûtsjesilen.'** Traditional historic, flat-bottomed boats, formerly used for transporting goods, are truly a sight to be seen. **'Sneek Week'** is an international sailing week of races in August; don't miss the festive first day. October is a good time to visit Enkhuizen (North Holland) when the **'Enkhuizer Klipperrace,'** (*klippers* are a special class of Dutch boat), and the **International Sailing Competitions** of round and flat-bottomed boats take place. www.hollandregatta.org, and www.sailing.org, and www.wv-almere.nl/almere/klipperrace

▶ **Car and motorcycle racing**

Exciting races can be seen at Zandvoort (North Holland), as well as Assen in Drenthe. **Zandvoort's Circuit,** ☎ (023) 574 0740, is a car and motorcycle track that attracts a lot of spectators at holiday weekends like Whitsun, and in September. The season's schedules can be obtained from the VVVs of Haarlem and Zandvoort. www.circuit-zandvoort.nl

The province of Drenthe keeps its 'Drenthe Circuit' from gathering moss by scheduling a number of annual events, starting with the **National Motorcycle Championships** on Ascension Day, then the European championship road races, which are followed by the **International Grand Prix Motor Races,** known as the 'TT,' in Assen at the end of June. (There is also a 4-day cycling tour in Assen in July.) For information, contact the Assen VVV, ☎ (0900) 202 2393. www.vvvassen.nl

▶ **Horse shows**

'Jumping Amsterdam' is a yearly indoor International Horse Show held in the RAI at the end of November/beginning December – widely advertised and well attended. The awards are a special Netherlands Grand Prix, and an International Jumping Grand Prix. Tickets for these events are at a premium, so make your reservations well in advance. www.jumpingamsterdam.nl

Rotterdam is the site of another annual **International Horse Show, (CHIO),** held in August in Kralingen – a five-day event with outstanding competitors from all over the world. Members of the Royal Family usually attend, officiating at the closing award ceremonies. The more expensive seats are in a covered area (a blanket or pillow can soften the seating). www.chio.nl

Groningen is particularly known for its fine horses. At the end of December-January, national horse events take place in Veendam, and there are trotting races in Groningen's Stadspark. Check with the VVV.

Don't miss **The Hague Horse Days** in June, or the **Breda Paard** military horse show, May/June. Also, keep in mind that in even years an **International Concours Hippique** is held in **Boekeloo** (Overijssel province). www.ch-eindhoven.nl, and www.bredahippique.nl

Horseracing – flat-racing and trotting: From the middle of March to the middle of November, you can watch flat-racing and trotting at **Duindigt** (South Holland), ☎ (070) 314 8740. This race course is located at the edge of Wassenaar near The Hague. On the last Sunday in June, a special international trotting race, the **Grand Prix of the Low Countries**, is held. www.vriendenvanduindigt.nl. The two main tracks in Holland are Duindigt (6/8 mile) and Wolvega (5/8 mile), followed by Groningen (5/8), Alkmaar (4/10 mile) and a couple of county fair tracks in Emmeloord, Eenrum, Joure, and Leek that only have races a couple of days a year.

▶ Ice hockey, ice skating races, & figure skating events

A relative newcomer to the scene of spectator sports in Europe, ice hockey is growing rapidly in popularity. The **Netherlands Ice Hockey Team**, which is centred in The Hague, has Americans and Canadians on the team. Announcements of international games held in De Uithof, The Hague or in Eindhoven, will be found in the VVV programme guides, the sports section of the newspapers, or by calling the VVV. Most championship skating races are held in Eindhoven at the Kunst IJsbaan, ☎ (040) 238 1200, while major figure skating events take place in The Hague. www.ijssportcentrum.nl

Although it is more and more rare to see the classic **Eleven Towns Race** (**Elfstedentocht**) due to lack of solid ice these days (the last race was in 1997), races are held from time to time in the northern provinces, in particular at Deventer and Heerenveen. Should you happen to be there during a good freeze, make sure you don't miss the traditional races on the canals ... information from the Friesland VVV. More details: www.elfstedentocht.nl (English pages) (See photo on page 415.)

▶ Soccer (voetbal)

Dutch football or what some of us still call 'soccer,' heads the list as the most popular spectator sport in the Netherlands. Every city, village and town in Holland has its own team and often more than one. The two best-known teams are **AJAX** of Amsterdam and **FEYENOORD** of Rotterdam. When these two clash, everything else in the two cities comes to a standstill. The excitement of the supporters is so great that storeowners in both cities have been known to board up their windows as a protection against possible damage, as there can be problems with hooligans and vandalism.
www.ajax.nl, and www.feyenoord.nl

Youngsters with talent can play football by joining one of the amateur clubs. There are teams for boys under 12 years, called '*aspiranten*' (or beginners); 12-16 years called 'juniors' and from 16 years on, 'seniors.' Most Dutch boys join a private club and play on Saturday or Sunday from September to April, with a training evening during the week.

▶ Swimming

Anyone living in the Netherlands can well understand why swimming is a required subject in school. There is just so much water everywhere, in this land below sea level. Every community has access to an indoor pool, and sometimes an outdoor pool, as well as fresh water swimming in lakes or natural ponds. Check with the VVV or Sports and Recreation Department of your City Hall for the names of major pools in your area. They will also be able to tell you of any swimming competitions of special interest, or call the 'Dienst voor Sports en Recreatie,' or see the 'Yellow Pages' under '*zwembad*.' The **Royal Netherlands Swimming Bond** can also provide information on synchronized swimming and water polo, Nieuwegein, ☎ (030) 605 7575, www.knzb.nl. A chilling event is the traditional **New Year's Day Dive** in the North Sea, which takes place on the beaches of Scheveningen and Zandvoort.

▶ **Tennis**

Tennis is an extremely popular sport in Holland. The **ABN-AMRO International Tennis Tournament** in which all the top players participate is held in the AHOY hall, Rotterdam, in Feb.-March; and the **Dutch Open Championships** are held in the Amstelpark Club, Amsterdam in July.

You may have difficulty in finding a teacher available to give lessons... determination and persistence will help. Even joining a tennis club is difficult; though renting a court for a specific time period is simpler. For assistance in locating clubs, teachers, or courts, contact your local VVV or Sports and Recreation Office. The **Koninklijke Nederlandse Lawn Tennis Bond**, in Amersfoort, ☎ (033) 454 2600, www.knltb.nl, offers information on competitions, youth and wheelchair tennis, and lessons, in addition to listings for all clubs.

Active sports opportunities

The greatest problem about listing various sports available in the Netherlands is how to fit them all in. For full information about a sport that interests you and which is not mentioned below, contact the **NOC/NSF Arnhem**, ☎ (026) 483 4659, the local VVV or town hall (Gemeente) Sports and Recreation department. More information: www.sport.nl.

For the younger set, sports courses are offered during school spring and summer vacations at the British School in Voorschoten, ☎ (071) 560 2251, for particulars. See www.sio.nl for websites and listings of all the international schools in the Netherlands, some of which may also offer extracurricular sports programmes.

▶ **Badminton**

Fans should contact the **Netherlands Badminton Bond Association**, Nieuwegein, ☎ (030) 608 4150. www.eurobadminton.org/netherlands

▶ **Baseball and softball**

There are more than 200 clubs in the Netherlands, and they gladly welcome foreign members of both sexes from age six. Call the **KNBSB**, ☎ (023) 539 0244, in Zandvoort for details. www.knbsb.nl

The **American Baseball Foundation (ABF)**: This organisation was established by a group of sports-minded businessmen and educators to provide sports activities primarily for the American Community in Holland, but open to all nationalities. Some of the sports offered are baseball, basketball, bowling, flag football, soccer, softball and cycling. (See Chapter 19 for more details.) Clubhouse address: Ammonslaantje 1, Wassenaar, ☎ (070) 514 6115, weekends only. www.abfsport.nl

▶ Basketball

The **Netherlands Basketball Bond** is at Runnenburg 12, Bunnik, ☎ (030) 656 6500. Basketball probably originated from the Dutch game of *Korfbal*, which is still played and is the only sport with mixed teams. www.basketball.nl

▶ Cycling

In the Netherlands, cycling is a way of life; for most foreigners it's a delightfully new or relearned experience. Bikes can be rented at most railway stations, and from bike shops in town for a minimal fee. (Deposit and ID required.) The VVV has a list. To get out of town, you can transport your own bike by train without a problem.

Holland has an excellent network of bicycle paths through the countryside and bicycle lanes through the towns. On minor roads, the hexagonal white signs with a red bike indicate a particularly scenic route. There are many organised or semi-organised tour groups which will lead you into some of the most beautiful Dutch landscapes for a day, a week or longer.

– www.enfb.nl	the NL bicyclists union (*fietsersbond*) with many pages of links, routes and clubs
– www.holland.com	tourist bureaus nationwide; bike routes, bike rental
– www.cycletours.com	boat and bike tours in English
– www.fietsersbond.nl	everything about bikes, accessories and travel
– www.fietsen123.nl	over 5,000 cycling routes
– www.fietspad.nl	routes, links, touring
– www.ns.nl	train info, bike on train, and rentals
– http://fietsvakantie.pagina.nl	cycling vacations and bicycle info
– http://fiets.pagina.nl	for bicycles, accessories and more

> **Important**
> www.3vo.nl – traffic signs

Repairs, parts, accessories, rain ponchos, helmets, and service and more at the bicycle shop, listed under '*fietsen*' and '*fietsonderdelen*' or the old-fashioned word, '*rijwielhandel*.'

> **TIP!** www.cyclingaroundtheworld.nl has a handy bicycle translation dictionary in 12 languages.

But first, it is wise to learn some of the rules of the road.

BIKING RULES OF THE ROAD

1. **Learn the international traffic signs** (see previous page) – they often apply to cyclists as well as the motorist.
2. **Travel on the path reserved for cyclists** whenever there is one. These are well-marked with signs saying 'Fietspad' or sometimes 'Rijwielpad.' Incidentally, cycling is not allowed on the sidewalks, although very young children can get away with it.
3. **Signal when turning**, but watch carefully that you are not cutting in front of a car. If you are turning, the car has priority.
4. **Have your bike in good working order**, including headlight, back light, red rear reflector below the saddle, reflecting sidewall tires, a functioning bell, and a white or yellow rear mudguard. This is all compulsory and available from your local bike shop.

A visit to the ANWB (Royal Touring Club) is recommended for serious cyclists who want to get out into the country. The ANWB can suggest especially scenic routes, maps with bike trails marked, hostels along the way, information about clubs or groups which meet and bike together or about, and semi-organised area trips with the Netherlands Railways. www.anwb.nl – includes bicycle rentals and route maps.

The VVV can also advise on local and national bicycle routes. They have brochures with routes for cycling in their cities and surrounding areas. There are specific bike tours through the dunes and the tulip fields. You can also bike in the Hoge Veluwe (Gelderland province); free loan of bicycle. For information, contact the local VVV, or enquire at the Central Station.

Let's Go, ☎ (020) 600 1809, www.letsgo-amsterdam.com, will organise day tours from Amsterdam in small groups with a guide and a bike for the day. You can take a windmill/castle tour through the countryside, or go to Edam and Volendam with a picnic lunch (weather permitting) ... tour departs at 10am, April-mid Oct. from the Amstel Station (Amsterdam); also cycling through the tulip fields when in bloom.

Yellow Bike, Nieuwezijds Kolk 29, ☎ (020) 620 6940, can offer a similar seven-hour countryside tour, or a three-hour tour of Amsterdam. www.yellowbike.nl

▶ **Bowling**
Netherlands Bowling Federation, www.bowlingnbf.nl under 'centra' lists all of the bowling centres in the country, plus information on competitions. Or check 'Bowling' in your 'Pink' or 'Yellow Pages,' or contact the local VVV. Some well-known centres are:
– **Amsterdam:** Bowling Centrum Knijn, Schelderplein 3, ☎ (020) 664 2211
– **The Hague:** Bowling Centre Wijndaelerduin 25, ☎ (070) 368 6639
– **Breda:** Nassausingel 28, ☎ (076) 521 8452

- **Rotterdam:**   Dok 99, Straatweg 99, ☎ (010) 422 0011
- **Scheveningen:**   Dolfijn Bowling Centre, Gevers Deynootweg 990, ☎ (070)354 3212

▶ Canoeing

Kayaks and canoes are popular and a very suitable means of getting away from it all. Many provinces are restoring old canals for this purpose. In Overijssel there are 400 km (248.5 mi) and in Groningen 850 km (528 mi) of sheltered waterways. **Nederlandse Kano Bond**, Nieuwegein, ☎ (030)751 3750. www.nkb.nl

▶ Cricket

The **Koninklijke Nederlandse Cricket Bond** headquarters is in Nieuwegein, ☎ (030) 751 378. Local cricket and football associations offer boys from the age of 8 an opportunity to play cricket in the summer and football in winter. Most clubs welcome foreign members. For other clubs: **Amstelveen,** V.R.A,☎ (0020) 641 8525, **Rotterdam**, Pak Dutch,☎ (010) 465 4283, **The Hague,** H.B.S., ☎ (070) 368 1960, and K.H.C, ☎ (070) 324 8361, and Quick H., ☎ (070) 368, 0323; in **Amsterdam,** V.R.A., ☎ (020) 641 8525; A.C.C., ☎ (020) 647 5513, in **Haarlem,** Rood en Wit, ☎ (023) 528 7085, in **Utrecht**, Kampong, ☎ (030) 251 4530, in **Voorburg,** ☎ (070) 320 2905, www.voorburg-cricket-club.nl. The official site of Royal Dutch Cricket is www.kncb.nl. For listings of all clubs see: www.cricinfo.com under 'national members Netherlands.'

▶ Fencing

The **Koninklijke Nederlandse Algemene Schermbond** in Rosmalen, ☎ (073) 528 0067, can supply you with names and addresses of groups, courses and coaches, or see www.knas.nl.

▶ Fishing

You can fish in any canal that strikes your fancy, or in the lakes, rivers or sea if you have a permit. There are different types, of 'VISpas' – 'Junior,' 'Klein' and 'Zee' – for fishing club and non-club members. It comes in a credit card format with a 'List of fishing waters' booklet, and can be purchased from the local post office or VVV, from the **NVVS** (Sport fishing Fed.) in Bilthoven, ☎ (030) 605 8400, or from any fish and tackle shop. No permits are needed for sea-fishing. Deep-sea fishing or sea angling is possible from about 70 Dutch fishing ports. You can also order permits online: www.sportvisserijnederland.nl/vispas/

▶ Flying

For information, contact the **KNVVL**, in The Hague, ☎ (0900) 582 4877. If you have a plane to fly or want to take lessons, that is possible at Zestienhoven, Rotterdam's airport, where Kroonduif Air Flying School, ☎ (010) 415 7855, and Zestienhoven Flying School, ☎ (010) 437 4090, are based. You can also take flying lessons at **Ben Air**, Hilversum, ☎ (035) 577 1300. See www.aviation.nl/flightschols for complete listings countrywide. Further air-related activities include: Gliders, www.zweefportal.nl; Micro-lights, www.microlight.nl; Hang-gliding, www.zeilvliegen.nl; and hot-air ballooning, www.knwlballoonvaren.nl; and of course model airplane clubs, www.modelvliegsport.nl.

▶ **Football (Soccer)**

Football is the most important sport in the Netherlands. Children with talent can apply to join a local team from age six. Contact the **Koninklijke Nederlandse Voetbal Bond,** ☎ (0900) 8075. (Dutch spoken) or visit the official website: www.knvb.nl/english
  Private clubs in the main cities that welcome young foreign players are:
– **Amsterdam**: AFC, Sportpark Goed Genoeg, De Boelelaan 50, Buitenveldert,
  ☎ (020) 644 5575
– **Amstelveen**: Amstelveen Heemraad, Sportcomplex Startbaan, Sportlaan 37,
  ☎ (020) 645 2443
– **Haarlem**: KHFC, Stadion en Sportpark, Sportweg 8, ☎ (023) 525 2233
– **The Hague**: HBS, Sportpark Craeyenhout, Evert Wijtemaweg 3, ☎ (070) 368 1960;
  HVV, Sportpark De Diepput, van Hogenhoucklaan 37, ☎ (070) 324 8361, Quick H.,
  Sportpark Nieuw Hanenburg, De Savornin Lohmanlaan 215, ☎ (070) 368 0323.
– **Rotterdam**: VOC, (Cricket and Football), Sportpark, Hazelaarweg 7,
  ☎ (010) 422 4918
– **Utrecht**: Kampong, Laan van Maarschalkerweerd 2, (behind Utrecht F.C. Stadium),
  ☎ (030) 251 4530
There are over 2,700 football clubs in the Netherlands, some in existence since 1895. To search by the city or the name of the club, see: www.gidsnl.nl. In The Hague is a Dutch football club with a large international section. www.pgsinternational.tk

▶ **American football**

Gaining in popularity in the Netherlands since 1981, when the very first game was played on Easter Sunday. There are clubs throughout the country, with senior, junior (16-19) and minis (5 against 5) for the younger players. Contact the **American Football Bond**, Hoorn, ☎ (0229) 214 801. See (Dutch sites) www.afbn.nl, and www.afbn.org under links for listings of clubs and contact information.

▶ **Golf**

If this is your game, the **Netherlands Golf Federation** in de Meern, ☎ (030) 662 18 88, can give you a list of public and private golf clubs in your area. Golf has grown rapidly in popularity and the courses are crowded. There are about 150 private clubs and over 30 public courses. Many have had to have their naturally flat terrain radically altered to make the game more of a challenge – the more interesting courses being along the North Sea coast and in wooded areas. They can also provide information on tours within the European Golfing Federation, and youth events, www.ngf.nl. For a list of all of the golf courses in the

Netherlands, see: www.equipegolf.nl/banen, and for even more options to play both here and further afield: www.golfeurope.com/euro_clubs/netherlands-golf-courses

▶ **Hockey (field hockey)**

The **Royal NL Hockey Bond**, in Nieuwegein, ☎ (030) 751 3400, www.knhb.nl, lists 350 clubs in Holland, most of them in the larger towns. All have men's, women's and 'minis' (from age 6 years) sections. Hockey is a very popular game and Holland has a strong women's international team.

▶ **Horseback riding**

Koninklijke Nederlandse Hippische Sportfederatie in Ermelo ☎ (0577) 40 8300, www.knhs.nl, lists over 2,000 riding clubs and stables (manèges) in the Netherlands. Choosing the right one for you might depend to a great extent on finding one where the teachers do not object to speaking English. The **Hippisch Sport Bond Baarn**, ☎ (035) 548 3660, may also be of help. Call above or your local Sports and Recreation Office (Dienst voor Sport en Recreatie).

▶ **Ice skating**

Before coming to the Netherlands, perhaps you had a mental picture of a flat country with windmills, lots of water, and people in colourful costumes scooting here and there on their homemade Hans-Brinker-type skates! Well, it does happen – now very rarely, however – that the lakes and canals freeze and suddenly, from out of nowhere, the children appear in multi-coloured woollen hats, scarves and gloves, making bright contrasts to the ice.

But let's assume that this is a good icy winter. If the freeze lasts long enough, it will be possible to skate almost anywhere. Lakes are tested for safety, so before going out, be sure that the flag is up indicating that the ice is safe … a red flag means danger.

One of the traditional places to skate is Friesland, but closer to home perhaps, is **Kinderdijk**. Grab the skates, pile the family in the car, and join the many Dutch people that have been skating here for years. This site of 19 windmills is impressive any time, but even more so when snow-clad and in sharp relief against a winter sky. People come from far and wide to skate on the frozen canals around the mills and to enjoy the beauty of these majestic structures.

In the good old days, the popular 'Koek en Zopie' stands were everywhere to provide the chilly skaters with hot steaming cups of anise milk (anijsmelk) and spice cake, or hot chocolate. Today, you can 'do it yourself' by buying the anise-flavoured sugar cubes (look for Smelta and De Ruijter brand names) and dropping them into the warm milk.

Should there be a good freeze, you could participate in the five-lakes races, or do the traditional Rotterdam to Gouda run – buy a Gouda pipe, down some Bols genever (gin) to keep the circulation going, and then skate back to Rotterdam… the pipe intact. (For those who are not familiar with Gouda pipes, these are long, delicate white clay pipes often seen in paintings by the old masters.) In the north, there is the famous traditional **Eleven Cities race**, the **Elfstedentocht**, with its thousands of participants. The ice must be very thick for this race to take place, thus there has not been one since 1997. To stay the course is an achievement, but to win is extremely prestigious. (See photo on page 415.)

In addition to the canals and lakes that freeze naturally, there are tennis clubs that flood their courts and set up an 'ice palace' where, for a small entrance fee, you may join others of all ages and abilities, skating to appropriate music. These ice rinks usually stay frozen longer than the lakes or canals. Amsterdam encourages its skaters in winter by freezing the section of the Leidseplein surrounded by cafés, from where it's almost as much fun to watch as it is to participate.

Ice sculpture events with glistening exhibitions are also held in Eindhoven, www.sculpture-events.nl; in The Hague, www.inice.nl; and in Maastricht, an ice bar! www.icecarving.nl. For full exhibition agenda see: www.inaxi.com; they also arrange the international sand-carving events throughout Holland in the summer months.

Those who do not want to depend on the whims of winter can enjoy the facilities of an artificial ice rink (*ijsbaan*) throughout the Netherlands. For instance, in **Amsterdam,** go to Kunstijsbaan Jaap Eden, Radioweg 64, ☎ (020) 694 9652; and in **The Hague,** IJsbaan 'Uithof,' Jaap Edenweg 10, ☎ (070) 309 9649; and Prins Willem Alexander SilverDome, Van der Hagenstraat 20, in **Zoetermeer,** ☎ (079) 330 5000. In **Leiden**, the Ijshal Leiden, Vondellaaan 41, ☎ (071) 576 9344; and in **Haarlem**, the Kunstijsbaan Kennemerland, IJsbaanlaan 2, ☎ (023) 525 4000. Other outdoor rinks exist throughout the Netherlands. They open in October and close by April.

See www.knsb.nl/content/ijsbanen for complete listings and links to all websites, plus schedules. To check conditions for outdoor skating, www.natuurijsschaatsen.nl, or call the ANWB Wintersportlijn, ☎ (0900) 9623 (€ 0.45 p. min.).

The Dutch have been competing in skating competitions for over 125 years, organized through the **Koninklijke Nederlanse Schaatssport Bond**, Amersfoort, ☎ (033) 489 2000, www.knsb.nl. They have information on all aspects of ice sports and skating from racing to figure skating, and lists of all indoor rinks throughout the country. Children begin taking skating lessons at an early age, and the Dutch have won a considerable number of prizes in international skating competitions.

▶ **Judo, Ju Jitsu, Tai Chi, Aikido and Karate**

These Far Eastern martial arts are also popular in the Netherlands. Some towns have classes for children from eight years. For information, contact the **Judo Bond NL**, Nieuwegein, ☎ (030) 603 8114, or your local VVV or city Sport and Recreation office. The JBN's members are comprised of the members of the approximately 750 affiliated sports schools and associations in the Netherlands, which are subdivided into seven regions. Of the 54,700 members, some 40,000 are under the age of 19. www.jbn.nl, and www.judobondnederland.nl; see English pages.

For karate see: www.stichtingkaratenederland.net

▶ Rugby

There are now approximately 97 clubs spread over the Netherlands, each with two or three teams. Youngsters from the age of six may join the junior teams. For information call the **Nederlandse Rugby Bond**, Amsterdam, ☎ (020) 480 8100, www.rugby.nl, and www.rugbynederland.nl.

If you want to play with fellow international residents and English-speaking groups: ARC Clubhuis/Clubhouse, Sportlaan 25A, **Amstelveen** (near Amsterdam), ☎ (020) 643 8979, www.aacrugby.com; **Utrecht**, Sportpark Terweide, Hoge-weide 1, ☎ (030) 666 2025, www.utrechtrugby.nl, In **The Hague**, there are two clubs: www.haagscherugbyclub.com, and www.rugby-tewerve.com; and in **Haarlem**, www.rugbyclubhaarlem.nl. For ladies fond of a good game, try **Dutch Women's Rugby**: www.damesrugby.nl. There are also competitions for wheelchair rugby. www.wheelchairrugby.nl

▶ Gaelic football

The **Gaelic Athletic Association** is dedicated to promoting the games of hurling, football, handball, rounders, and camogie, as well as providing social venues for supporting activities that enrich their culture, Gaelic ideals, Irish language, music and dance. www.amsterdamgac.com, and, of course, Gaelic football in The Hague. www.geocities.com/denhaag

▶ Sailing and windsurfing

These are outstanding Dutch sports that are open to all. In addition to the fine summer sailing camps available north and south, it is possible to take lessons through private clubs. For those in your area, check with the **Koninklijke Ned. Watersport Bond**, Nieuwegein, ☎ (030) 751 3700. www.watersportverbond.nl. Often there are qualified young men interested in giving private lessons and who can be contacted through these clubs. Children are not usually taught to sail until they are 12 years old because they are not considered strong enough to handle a boat under difficult weather conditions. http://windsurf.pagina.nl, or www.kitesurfschool.nl

Boats can be rented and prices vary according to the type, and the season. **Top of Holland Yacht-charter** has extensive online links featuring the better-known companies, plus a number of DVD guides you may request online: www.topofholland.com. If you have your own yacht, there are also a number of yachting clubs. www.fotw.net/flags/nl-water.html

Windsurfing is not recommended on Dutch canals; in fact it is forbidden. Windsurfing is usually taught at conventional sailing schools. Enquire at **Sail, Ski and Surf School**, Wilhelminalaan 12, de Kaag, ☎ (0252) 54 4333, www.kaag.nl, or look through the 'Pink Pages' under 'ZeilSurf-en Vaarscholen,' or under water sports on the websites of www.hiswa.nl, and www.watersportverbond.nl.

For a listing of all yacht harbours see: http://jachthavens.allepaginas.nl

Amsterdam: The Royal Rowing and Sailing Club the Hoop, Weesperzijde 1046a, Amsterdam, ☎ (020) 665 7844, www.xs4all.nl/~karvhoop, and the Amstel club, Hobbemakade 122. www.amstelroei.nl

Rotterdam: The Royal Rowing and Sailing Club the Maas, Veerdam 1, Rotterdam, ☎ (010) 413 8514, www.de-maas.nl, or Nautilus, Plantagelaan 3, ☎ (010) 413 8791, also a good rowing club for beginners. See also: www.nlroei.nl

The Hague: The Netherlands International Yacht Club meets at **Woubrugge**, near the beautiful Braassemer lake. A family-oriented club, it aims to promote international 'entente.' Members come from many different countries but are predominantly British or from the Commonwealth. **Netherlands International Yacht Club,** ☎ (0172) 518 437, or Oude Wetering, ☎ (070) 382 1357.

If you've ever dreamed of renting a traditional Dutch sailing vessel with crew, contact **Hollands Glorie**, Haringvliet 619, ☎ (010) 415 6600. It can be rented for any length of time ... even a day, or for an evening party. Home port is **Rotterdam**, but trips can include **Zeeland** or **Friesland** harbours as well as North Sea crossings to England, Belgium or France.

The VVV has a good booklet about renting all kinds of boats – from 2-berth motor boats to huge sailing ships – and lists the many organisations arranging special tour packages.

For boat rentals of *skutsjesilen*, traditional Frisian yachts, www.skutsjesilen.nl. For general boat rentals: http://botenverhuur.pagina.nl/, under the heading '*skutjes.*'

The **First Dutch Dragon Boat Club** (Eerste Hollandse Drakenboot Club) is out on the water from March through October. The EHDC boathouse is located at Langbroekpad 3, in Amsterdam. See the website for contact details, as well as clubs in other areas. www.ehdc.nl.

▶ **Diving**

The **Randstad Harings Dive Club** is an international group of diving enthusiasts from Amsterdam, The Hague, Utrecht and Rotterdam who regularly suit up and take to the water, in a variety of locations. Dives also take place in Zeeland, in the south of Holland, where there are over 55 dive sites. This provides a combination of tidal and non-tidal, freshwater, seawater and brackish water sites for divers to explore. Members range from beginner to first-class diver, as well as National Instructors and instructor trainees. www.randstad-harings.demon.nl

▶ **Squash**

This sport has become more popular and clubs have sprung up all over Holland. Contact the **Squash Bond Nederland**, Scheglaan 12, Zoetermeer, ☎ (079)) 361 5400. www.squash.nl

▶ **Walking**

It may surprise many foreigners that walking isn't done quite as casually in the Netherlands as in other countries. In the first place, before you can walk in many scenic areas, you must have a special permit, a *wandelkaartje*. These may be obtained through local VVVs, the ANWB, or other places like kiosks or restaurants on the spot.

In this country where there is so little woodland, and little variety of landscape, 'Wandelterreinen' or 'Walking Areas' supply both, though in a somewhat regimented fashion. Duneland is often devoted to this purpose, other areas being protected as Nature Reserves. There are as many as eight different National Conservation Societies, but the 'Natuur Monumenten' publishes the most compact and comprehensive booklet (*Handboek*), available in Dutch only. For yearly membership and a handbook listing nearly all the Dutch nature reserves and walking areas (also what plants, animals or birds are likely to be found in each), write to: **Natuurmonumenten**, Noordeinde 60, 1243 ZR 's Graveland, ☎ (035) 655 9933. www.natuurmonumenten.nl and for the mapped routes www.natuurkaart.nl

Especially recommended areas for walking are the 'Wandelterreinen' and 'Natuur Reservaten' at **Oostvoorne** and **Rockanje**; the Staelduinse Bos, **'s Gravenzande** (near Hook of Holland); Meijendel in **The Hague**; Schaap en Burg in **Hilversum**; and Duin en Kruidberg in **Zandvoort**.

Listed below are some carefully-selected special walks showing the best of the countryside in various areas. Some of these allow access to areas that are otherwise restricted:

– Dune walks at Castricum and National Park Kennemerduinen, near IJmuiden.
– Wood walk, Hulshorst and Nunspeet
– Wood walk, Lunteren
– Wood walk, Mastbos, Breda
– Walk along the River Linge, Leerdam and Beesd
– Thijse (nature) walk, Wolfhese and Westerbouwing
– Fenswalk, Oisterwijk (with small nature museum and café)
– Beach walk, IJmuiden and Zandvoort

For further information contact the **Nederlandse Wandelsport Bond**, Pieterskerkhof 22, Utrecht, ☎ (030) 231 9458. www.nwb-wandelen.nl

For routes see: www.wandelzoekpagina.nl

Hiking maps (*wandelkaarten*) are also available from the ANWB (auto club) and from the local VVV in the region in which you wish to explore. http://wandel.pagina.nl provides lots of details.

Nordic walking has become very popular; in fact, the **Nordic Walking International Association** is quite active in Holland. See www.nordicwalking.com for an English explanation, and www.nordicwalking.nl for the Dutch clubs and routes, as well as listings and products. http://nordicwalking.startpagina.nl

The **Pieterpad** is the most famous of the longer hiking routes in Holland, so-called as it goes from **Pieterburen** (Groningen province) in the north to **Sint Pieterberg** (Limburg) in the southeast – a total of 485 km (301 mi). People tend to walk portions of it, usually over a few years. It is divided into 27 segments.

Details can be found on: http://pieterpad.pagina.nl

▶ Wadlopen

Very Dutch activity, whereby you can literally walk to an island! *Wadlopen* is a muddy, sport (that's an understatement) in which you walk or trudge over mudflats from the mainland of Holland to an island – when the tide is out. Only those with stamina need attempt this, but it is truly a once-in-a-lifetime experience. www.wadlopen.net (See photo on page 415).

▶ Running

The **Hash House Harriers Running Club** is a lively yet socialized version of 'Hare and Hounds,' whereby runners join the pack of 'hounds' to chase down a paper trail set out by the hare or hares – also known as 'harriers' or 'harriettes.' They constitute a kennel made up of the runners or 'hash.' A 'kennel' of harriers joins together after the hash for a little social activity known as the 'On In or Down Down.' There are currently over 1,600 hashes found in every major city in the world. It's a great way to make friends and have fun. Their 'global trash site' links clubs and 'runs' around the world at www.gthhh. com. Here in Holland, join the fun with other hashers: **Amsterdam**, www.harrier.nl; **Assen**, www.assenh3.net, **The Hague**, www.haguehash.nl. There is also an expat runners' club. www.hagueroadrunners.nl

Also, for a more serious pace, the '*hardlopers*,' or runners' site with races, marathons, city-races, and more, www.loopwereld.nl, as well as the **Koninklijke Nederlandse Atletiek Unie** (KNAU), joining some 300 running clubs. www.atletiek.nl/loopservice

▶ Inline skating

Skate nights on '*skeelers*' or rollerblades are held in a number of cities during the summer months; look under 'Nightskates NL' for events. Protective gear is mandatory! http://skeeler.startpagina.nl also has information on other in-line skating events and skate-related gear.

Chapter 19 | The younger set

A child's life in Holland is something to be envied. It isn't easy, however, to come to a new country, not know the language, enter a new school and have to make new friends. But there are so many compensations, once the newness has worn off, that it's hard not to feel at home and become part of the scene. Firstly, most Dutch children speak some English – or at least are not afraid to try, so the communication barrier need not be a serious one. Secondly, the international schools are top-of-the-line – if you choose that route over local schools. Extracurricular sports, band/orchestra, art and music activities, and special school outings are all there.

Without a doubt, sports are an important part of Dutch life. Before you know it, your expatriate children, affectionately known as 'expat kids,' may replace some of the sports they have been familiar with by participating in soccer, hockey, tennis, swimming, and ice skating – the last of which the Dutch are particularly famous when global warming doesn't interfere. Distances are small, and the whole country is peppered with great recreation parks, zoos, beaches and museums galore.

To the English-speaking expat's delight, most films and many TV programmes are in English, although this doesn't help your progress with the Dutch language! (To see what's on, www.tvgids.nl lists all of the programming, and www.eurotv.com lists the programmes in English.) The air is great here, outdoor life is highly valued (despite so many days of rain), and there's a general sense of security for youngsters to get out on their own; transportation is plentiful and of a high standard, and the pace of life is reasonably relaxed. All in all, Holland is a great place to raise children.

We'll start this chapter with baby-sitting, followed by information on education, summer camps and schools, organisations of special interest, and entertainment in all its guises.

Babysitting

Finding a responsible babysitter can be a bit of a problem no matter where you live, particularly when you do not live in a major city where there are organisations, clubs and church groups, as well as many students willing to be available. (See lists in 'Quick Reference' for your area.) Check with the following resources, and, when all else fails, you might consider approaching a local high school. Dutch students usually speak good English.

The Hague: The **American Women's Club** (AWC) has a roster of recommended sitters and will perhaps be able to refer you to one living in your area. During AWC meetings, they also have crèche facilities in their clubhouse for members, ☎ (070) 350 6007. The American School 'Bulletin' usually has a listing of students who babysit.

ACCESS has a list of sitters for The Hague area, ☎ (070) 346 2525, and Amsterdam area, ☎ 020 423 3217.

The **British Club** will put you in touch with a 'Mother and Toddler' group in your area, ☎ (070) 346 1973.

Praktische Thuis Help is an organisation specialised in assisting parents with handicapped children, ☎ (010) 282 1111. www.handicap.info

Dutch Babysitting Agencies can be found in your telephone directory under '*Oppascentralen*.'

Here are some websites to further your search:

– www.zoekppas.nl	There are 19,000 registered sitters throughout the country!
– www.kinderopvang.nl	daycare centres
– www.kinderopvang.net	network for childcare
– www.kinderopvang.net	addresses throughout the country
– www.skon.nl	National Childcare information (SKON: Stichting Kinderopvang Nederland)
– www.catalpa.nl	65 day care centres
– www.humanitas-kov.nl	70 day care centres
– http://kinderopvang.pagina.nl	all facilities nationwide

Regional

– www.hopmarjanneke.nl	for working parents
– www.kidsplus.nl	Montessori day care
– www.kindergarden.nl	childcare locations
– www.berendbotje.nl	North Holland
– www.impuls.nl	Amsterdam
– www.kriterionoppas.org	Amsterdam area
– www.kinderopvangdak.nl	The Hague
– www.koba.nl	The Hague
– www.kinderopvang-heerhugowaard.nl	Heerhugowaard
– www.kiekeboekinderopvang.nl	Lombardijen-Rotterdam
– www.kol.nl	Kinderopvang Online search
– www.rolykids.nl	Rotterdam
– www.kinderrijk.nl	Amstelveen
– www.oppasservice.com	Brabant
– www.skar.nl	Arnhem
– www.skv.nl	Vlaardingen

Education

For information on the Dutch educational system, including Montessori, Dalton, religious, public or special, and including foreign-language schools and government-subsidised schools, see **The Ministry of Education, Culture and Science**: www.minocw.nl For those with an English or international stream, see www.intschools.nl. (The latter are Dutch schools that prepare students for the British IGCE, IGCSE, and/or the International Bacca-laureate. They have the advantage of giving youngsters the opportunity to learn Dutch more easily and, therefore, to integrate better into the local community.)

For specific questions regarding Dutch schools, call the toll free number 0800-5010, or search: www.50tien.nl

NUFFIC, The Netherlands Organisation for International Cooperation in Higher Education, will provide everything you want to know about education in Holland. Their website, www.nuffic.nl, lists all possible international studies in the country. Over 1,000 courses are offered in English, and their data-base driven search site (see English pages, grants, scholarships, cooperation, etc.) makes it incredibly easy to find just what you're looking for. Cooperation with other universities abroad provides the possibility of spending a portion of study time on a foreign campus. For additional practical information on 'study in Holland,' see www.studyin.nl, and also www.studytrack.com under the Netherlands.

For a complete list of schools in your local area, you can contact your town hall (Gemeentehuis).

Non-Dutch speakers in Dutch schools

Children can attend school from age 4, but it is compulsory between ages 5 to 16. Those over 11 who do not speak Dutch well enough can be streamed into Dutch language education via an 'International Bridge Class,' which is available in several schools in the major cities. See also: http://netherlands.english-schools.org

▸ **The Hague (South Holland)**
The International School of The Hague, Theo Mann-Bouwmeesterlaan 75, 2597 GV The Hague, ☎ (070) 328 1450, www.ishthehague.nl
The Rijnlands Lyceum, Backershagenlaan 5, 2243 AB Wassenaar,
☎ (070) 519 3555, www.ishthehague.com
Haagsche School Vereniging International Stream, Nassaulaan 26, 2514 JT,
☎ (070) 363 8531, www.hsvdenhaag.nl

▸ **Eindhoven (Brabant)**
International Secondary School, Henegouwenlaan 2A, 5628 WK Eindhoven,
☎ (040) 264 5999, www.dse.nl

▸ **Groningen (Groningen)**
Sint Maartenscollege, Roksstraatweg 24, 9752 AE Groningen, ☎ (050) 534 0084, www.sintmaartenscollege.nl

▸ **Hilversum (Utrecht)**
International School Alberdingk Thijm, Emmastraat 56, 1213 AL Hilversum,
☎ (035) 672 9931, Secondary school; Violenstraat 3, 1214 CJ, ☎ (035) 621 6053, Junior school; www.klg.nl/ish

▶ **Maastricht (Limburg)**
Jeanne d'Arc College/Porto Mosana, Oude Molenweg 130, 6228 XW Maastricht,
☎ (043) 356 5856, www.jeanne-d-arc-college.nl

▶ **Oegstgeest (South Holland)**
International School The Rijnlands Lyceum, Apollolaan 1, 2341 BA Oegstgeest,
☎ (071) 519 3555, www.isrlo.nl

▶ **Rotterdam (South Holland)**
Wolfert van Borselen School International Dept., Bentincklaan 280,
3039 KK Rotterdam, ☎ (010) 467 3522, www.riss.wolfert.nl
De Blijberg, Gordelweg 216, 3039 GA Rotterdam, ☎ (010) 466 9629, www.blijberg.nl

INTERNATIONAL SCHOOLS

The international schools are best for families who are only temporarily assigned to the Netherlands and want their children to continue in their 'home' system. Write them directly, requesting their brochures that describe ages covered, type of education provided, prices, time-schedules, transfer policies, etc. In addition to the Randstad-area schools, there are several primary and secondary schools in other parts of the country, some of which offer boarding facilities. They are listed following the Randstad schools.

Pre-school: nursery schools, crèches, play groups

Local international schools have or can offer help in locating nursery schools. The women's clubs are also a good source of information about support groups for parents with small children. The ever-useful organisation, **ACCESS**, is also an excellent point of reference for lists of mother and young children's groups. They can even help you find a support group for mothers of handicapped children.

The **British Club** members organise a number of playgroups and 'Mother and Toddler' groups in and around The Hague. Ask about one in your area, ☎ (070) 346 1973. Wassenaar has two excellent international pre-school and daycare centres:

– **The Clown Club**, Johan de Wittstraat 33, 2242 LA Wassenaar, ☎ (070) 514 0981, where pre-schoolers are kept busy with structured and creative activities both outdoors and in. www.clownclub.nl (See ad on page 424.)
– **The Activity Shop**, Hallekensstraat 28 A, 2242 VD Wassenaar, ☎ (070) 514 6738. www.tasid.nl
There are also 'Early Learning Centres' in The Hague, Breda and other towns. They have a helpful staff that can advise you, and offer daycare play and education facilities for little ones. Check with ACCESS.

Kindergarten through high school

The larger schools are the American and British schools in The Hague, Rotterdam and Amsterdam, and the Japanese School near Amsterdam. If English instruction is desired, it is wise to investigate all the schools located near one's residence in order to have the broad picture and make the right choice for your child.

▶ **Amsterdam**
 – **The British School of Amsterdam**, Jan van Eijkstraat 21, 1077 LG, ☎ (020) 679 7840, www.britams.nl (See ad on page 416.)
 – **Ecole Française d'Amsterdam**, Uitenwaardenstraat 60a, 1079 CB, ☎ (020) 644 6507, elementary school
 – **International School in Amsterdam**, Sportlaan 45, 1185 TB, ☎ (020) 347 1111, www.isa.nl
 – **The Japanese School** in the Netherlands, Karel Klinkenbergstraat 137, 1061 AL, ☎ (020) 611 8136, ages 6 – 15
 – **Amsterdam International Community School**, Uiterwaardenstraat 263, 1079 CR, ☎ (020) 642 8246 primary-school; and Wodanstraat 3, 1076 CC, ☎ (020) 577 1245, secondary school, www.aics-esprit-sq.nl
 – **International School Almere**, Schelvisstraat 3, 1317 SG Almere, ☎ (036) 548 9525, www.internationalschoolalmere.nl

▶ **The Hague**
 – **The American School of The Hague**, Rijksstraatweg 200, 2242 BX Wassenaar. ☎ (070) 512 1060, www.ash.nl (See ad on page 416.)
 – **The British School in the Netherlands**, Vlaskamp 19, 2592 AA The Hague, ☎ (070) 333 8111, and Jan van Hooflaan 3, 2252 BG Voorschoten, ☎ (071) 560 2222, www.britishschool.nl
 – **German School**, Van Bleiswijkstraat 125, 1282 LB The Hague, ☎ (070) 354 9454, www.disdh.nl
 – **Lycee Francais Vincent van Gogh**, Scheveningseweg 237, 2584AA The Hague, ☎ (070) 358 7111, www.lyceevangogh.nl

▶ **Rotterdam**
 – **The American International School of Rotterdam**,Verhulstlaan 21, 3055 WJ Rotterdam, ☎ (010) 422 5351, www.aisr.nl (See ad on page 424.)
 – **The Japanese School of Rotterdam**, Verhulstlaan 19, 3055 WJ Rotterdam, ☎ (010) 422 1211, www.jsrotte.nl

English-language schools outside the Randstad

▶ **Assen (Drenthe)**
 – **British School of the Netherlands (Helen Sharman British School)** (named after British astronaut, Helen Sharman), Lottingstraat 17, 9406LX Assen,
 ☎ (059) 234 4590, www.britishschool.nl

▶ **Bergen (North Holland)**
 – **European School**, Molenweidtje 5, 1860 AB Bergen, ☎ (072) 589 0109, www.eursc.org

▶ **Ommen (Overijssel)**
 – **International School Eerde**, Kasteellaan 1, 7731 PJ, ☎ (0529) 45 1452 (boarders and non-boarders), www.eerde.nl

The **Stichting International Onderwijs** (Foundation for International Education) provides information and links for every international school throughout the country, making it easy to choose by location, compare costs, and take a virtual tour through www.sio.nl

Museum orientation and creative classes

There are a number of extracurricular classes in the arts worth mentioning.

The Museum Orientation Programmes offered by most major museums may appeal to your youngsters. For older children with a real interest in art, there are often imaginative and well-planned, hands-on programmes and guided tours related to the museum collection to spur their imagination. To find out what is available and whether it would be suitable for non-Dutch speakers, telephone the Education Department of the museum.

The Volks Universiteit (see Chapter 16 for addresses) offers classes on Wednesdays afternoons when Dutch schools are closed. This makes it difficult for those children attending international schools to take advantage, however, if your child is free on Wednesdays, classes for children six to 12 years are given in drawing, painting and many crafts. Instruction is in Dutch, but most teachers speak English.

Dance, Drama and Music Groups are also available for talented children. (A discussion about music, dance and ballet schools is given in Chapter 16.) The international schools and ACCESS would also know of qualified English-speaking teachers in your community. For local Dutch teachers or groups, contact your town hall, library or one of the organisations listed herein.

Church and Club Choirs welcome good voices, as would the **British Choir of The Hague**; call ACCESS for details. Rotterdam has an Arts Council, **Kunst Stichting**, Mauritsweg 35, ☎ (010) 414 1666, with information on all creative possibilities in the city.

University education

An American, British or Japanese child will most likely decide to attend a university in his or her own country. The first place to seek advice about universities is your child's counsellor, the school library, or ACCESS. See also: www.studytrade.com

Netherlands American Commission for Educational Exchange, (NACEE) Herengracht 472, Amsterdam, ☎ (020) 531 5930, is a group that administers the Fulbright-Hays Educational Exchange programme between the Netherlands and the United States. In addition to its basic programme of exchange opportunities for research scholars, lecturers, teachers and graduate students, the Counselling Office gives information to Dutch students wanting to study in the US. www.fulbright.nl

University Education in English. For the student who wants to remain in the Netherlands while pursuing an English language education, there are various opportunities; www.studyin.nl provides practical information, resources, and over 850 courses available in the Netherlands, while www.study-in-holland.com specialises in visa and work permits. The **Open Universiteit Nederland**, founded in 1984 makes higher education accessible to anyone with the necessary aptitudes and interests, regardless of formal qualifications. Some courses on www.ou.nl are offered in English, though for a broader choice see www.open.co.uk. The **British Open University** offers services to their English-speaking students at the study centre located on Lange Houtstraat 11 in The Hague, ☎ (070) 361 4701. (See Chapter 16.)

Webster University, Boommarkt 1, 2311 EA Leiden, ☎ (071) 514 4341, is part of Webster University, in St. Louis, Missouri. Undergraduate as well as graduate classes leading to BA, MA and MBA degrees are offered. www.webster.nl

Studying in a Dutch university

Enrolment in a Dutch university may not be easy for foreign undergraduates, as Dutch students have priority and demand for places is great. Consent of the Dutch Education Department is also required for admission. Lectures being in Dutch, a knowledge of the language is obligatory. MBA programmes, however, are often in English. Details regarding study in Holland can be obtained from Dutch embassies and consulates abroad, or from the education department of the **Ministerie Onderwijs**, Cultuur en Wetenschappen, POB 25000, 2700 LZ Zoetermeer. ☎ (079) 323 2323. Two organisations in Holland that can help you further are:

Foreign Student Service, (FSS) Oranje-Nassaulaan 5, 1075 AH Amsterdam, ☎ (020) 671 5915, provides general information regarding study in the Netherlands, including practical personal assistance in finding accommodation, insurance, etc. They also organise a number of recreational activities and publish a monthly English-language bulletin. www.foreignstudents.nl (See also www.studytrack.com under the Netherlands for more information for foreign students, grants, etc.)

Netherlands Universities Foundation for International Cooperation and Netherlands Centre for International Academic Mobility, (NUFFIC-VISUM) Kortenaerkade

11-12, 2518 AX The Hague, ☎ (070) 426 0260, 1-4pm. www.nuffic.nl This group supplies information and documentation on international higher education in Holland and the value of specific diplomas abroad. Its library has a large collection of university and college catalogues as well as periodicals on higher education, open Mon.-Fri., 9am-5pm. (Downloadable PDF booklets, resources for studying in the Netherlands, with a directory database listing all schools; numerous publications.)

Libraries

Many parents assume that because they are living in a foreign country, they must buy books for their children instead of belonging to a library. Fortunately, that is not the case here in Holland.

Public libraries

There are several good library sources with large children's sections in English, French and German in the main libraries in the Randstad area, and even in other major town centres in the Netherlands. In addition, school libraries have many good classic and current books.

To find a library in any location, check www.bibliotheek.nl An initiative from the public libraries to help newcomers to the Netherlands is www.ainp.nl where you can find helpful information in six languages.

▶ **Amsterdam**
  – The Amsterdam Central Library, Prinsengracht 587, ☎ (020) 523 0800, has 30 locations throughout the city. A new, ultra-modern library is being built on Oosterdokseiland. www.oba.nl

▶ **The Hague**
  – American Women's Club Library, Nieuwe Duinweg 25, ☎ (070) 350 6007, www.awcthehague.org
  – British Club Library, Societeit de Witte, Plein 24, ☎ (070) 346 1973. www.bwclubthehague.demon.nl
  – Openbare Bibliotheek, Spui 68, ☎ (070) 338 3838, www.bibliotheekdenhaag.nl

▶ **Rotterdam**
  – Central Public Library (Centrale Gemeente Bibliotheek), Hoogstraat 110, ☎ (010) 281 6100, www.bibliotheek.rotterdam.nl
  – Rotterdam Reading Room, Erasmus University, Burg. Oudlaan 50, ☎ (010) 408 1195. Membership necessary.

Music-lending libraries

Your local library will have a wide selection of music as well as books. You can take out CDs, and possibly sheet music. (A more in-depth description is given in Chapter 16, as well as information about how to become a member.)

Cultural, educational and work exchange programmes

There are a number of organisations that provide helpful guidance to students over sixteen. They are a mixed bag offering a wide range of opportunities to study abroad or in Holland, to take educational tours or participate in international exchange programmes. Further, they can offer assistance with legal matters, and so on.

We have broken them down into three individual categories: Cultural Exchange, Travel, and Work Programmes, though most of the organisations cover everything.

Cultural exchange

In Europe, the coordinating body for student exchange is **Erasmus Student Network**. Check www.esn.org and http://ec.europa.eu/educationprogrammes/socrates/erasmus/ students, for contact information per country.

AFS (Inter-Cultural Exchanges), Herenweg 115 C, Vinkeveen, ☎ (0297) 214 076, or write to: 313 East 43rd Street, NY 10017, USA. They can arrange exchanges of Dutch and foreign students, 16-18 years old, as well as language and further education courses for participants; branches in 72 countries. www.afs.org/AFSI

Travel – educational and recreational

NBBS Reizen, Head Office Schipholweg 101, 2316 XC Leiden, ☎ (071) 523 2020, with branches in other major cities. They organise inexpensive travel, including educational trips to and from Holland. Special facilities for group, school and faculty trips, ☎ (0900) 102 0300. www.nbbs.nl

▶ **Hostels**

Stayokay (Netherlands Youth Hostels Centers), There are 30 youth hostels in Holland. Local addresses are always available from the VVV.

For more information: www.stayokay.nl

YMCARE – Foundation YMCA Youth Care, F.C. Dondersstraat 23, 3572 JB Utrecht, ☎ (030) 271 7191, www.ymcare.nl

See also:

– http://hostelworld.com

– www.europeanhostelguide.com

– www.europeanhostels.com

– www.trav.com/countries/hostels

Work programmes

- **Camps IVN:** Institute for Nature Protection Education, organises work camps for English speakers. Plantage Midden, 1018DD Amsterdam. ☎ (020) 622 8115, http://yee.ecn.cz/holland.htm
- **SIW:** (Stichting Internationaal Werkkampen) – International Work Projects, summer camps, (18-30 years old) Willemstraat 7, 3511RJ Utrecht, ☎ (030) 231 7721. www.siw.nl/english

▶ **Au Pairs**

Au pairs in Holland are generally ensured good working conditions through the **Netherlands Au Pair Organisation** (NAPO), www.napoweb.nl, who sets the work standards. There are also agencies for nannies.

- **Nanny Association**, Heuvelpoort 310, 5038 DT Tilburg, ☎ (013) 543 78 85, www.nanny.nl
- **Au Pair Agency Mondiaal**, Van Boetzaerlaan 42, 2581 AK The Hague, ☎ (070) 365 1401, www.aupair-agency.nl
- **Au Pair & Nanny Worldwide**, Burg. Hogguerstraat 785, 1064 EB Amsterdam, ☎ (020) 411 6010, www.worldwideaupair-nanny.com
- **Activity International,** Brammelaarstraat 15, 7511 JG Enschede, ☎ (053) 483 1040, www.activityinternational.nl
- **Au Pair Interactive**, Frans Halslaan 5, 1412 HS Naarden, ☎ (035) 632 1190, www.aupairinteractive.com.
- **Happy Family Au Pairs**, Rotterdamse Rijweg 9, 3043 BE Rotterdam, ☎ (010) 478 1470, www.happyfamilyaupairs.nl
- **Travel Active Programmes**, P.O. Box 107, 5800 AC Venray, ☎ (0478) 551 900, www.travelactive.nl
- **House-o-Orange Au Pairs**, Oostduinlaan 115, 2596 JJ The Hague, ☎ (070) 324 5903, www.house-o-orange.nl
- **S-AuPair Intermediate**, Hinthamerstraat 34, 5211 MP 's-Hertogenbosch, ☎ (073) 614 9483, www.saupair.com

▶ **Legal assistance**

The best advice for legal help is to contact your own embassy in Holland and ask for referrals.

Summer camps and schools

Based on recommendations by organisations and parents, the summer camps and schools we list here serve as aids in locating a good holiday experience for children among their peers. However, we can offer no guarantees, and readers are strongly advised to thoroughly investigate the camps or schools before determining which – if any – your child will enjoy. Bear in mind that situations (and prices) vary from year to year.

Certain organisations like the **Stichting Vrije Recreatie**, ☎ (018) 335 2741, are set up specifically to help, with brochures, lists, advice, etc. www.svr.nl

Netherlands Children's Camping Association of the ANWB, Wassenaarseweg 220, The Hague, ☎ (070) 314 7147. No camp can be listed until it has been in operation for four years. Information on type of accommodations, reputation and suitability is given. www.anwb.nl/camping

Netherlands Youth Hostels (NJHC), known as **Stayokay Hostels**, Prof. Tulpsplaan 2-6, 1018 HA Amsterdam, ☎ (020) 551 3155. The NJHC sponsors youth hostels all over the Netherlands and Europe. Minimum age is 14 years. At their hostels in Sneek, Grouw and Heeg (all in Friesland), and at Reeuwijk and De Kaag (South Holland), one-week yachting courses are given every summer. They also list riding camps offered by various youth hostels, and trips by covered wagon in Drenthe. www.stayokay.nl

Both the **VVV** and **ANWB** have brochures and information about youth camps, sailing and riding camps. Make enquiries as to which camp would be most suitable for non-Dutch speakers and whether they have a 'Kindervakantie' list that covers pony, camping and sailing camps. (VVV and ANWB addresses are given in Chapter 1.)

▶ **Scout camps**

A number of regular Boy Scouts of America-operated scout camps can be found in Europe; for details write the **Transatlantic Council, BSA**, 68232 Mannheim, Germany, ☎ (00) (49) (621) 47 1476; or the **BSA District Office**, Steenweg op Leuven 13, 1940 St. Steens-Woluwe, Belgium, ☎ (00) (32) (272) 09 0156. A local contact to call in The Hague area would be Scout Master, Mr. Martin Nieuwenhuis, ☎ (0712) 55 8757. www.scout.org, and www.internationalscouting.com

▶ **Riding camps**

Riding groups can be found all over the Netherlands and there are *manèges* in most towns. Perhaps more reliable than checking for them in the 'Pink Pages,' the best source of information would be the **Federation of Netherlands Riding Schools**, Amsterdamsestraatweg 57, 3744 MA Baarn, ☎ (035) 548 3660.

▶ **Sailing schools**

For approved sailing camps and schools, contact:
– **Nederlands Watersport Bond**, Van Eeghenstraat 94, Amsterdam, ☎ (020) 664 2611. Other good contacts are the ANWB or VVV offices for the provinces of North and South Holland, Friesland, Groningen, Flevoland and Zeeland. Ask which schools or camps they might recommend for English-speaking children. Following are the better-known clubs in Amsterdam and Rotterdam.
– **Amstel Roei en Zeilvereniging**, Hobbemakade 121, Amsterdam, ☎ (020) 671 9105
– **Stichting Kralingse Zeilschool**, Plaszoom 350, Rotterdam, ☎ (010) 452 7170

–**Royal Rowing and Sailing Club de Maas**, (Koninklijke Roei en Zeilvereniging), Veerdam 1, Rotterdam, ☎ (010) 413 8514

See also: www.yachtcharter-albatros.com, and http://southernholland.angloinfo.com/countries/holland/sailing

▶ **International summer camps**

A newcomer is often at a loss as to where to start looking for tried and true summer camps. The ones we list below have been in operation for many years and have excellent reputations. Start by writing to find out what they offer and their dates – usually two-week programmes, but sometimes there are facilities for older children to stay the entire summer. Read their material carefully and ask for references.

–**American School in The Hague** organises summer and winter camps with sports and activities, ☎ (070) 512 1060 for details. www.ash.nl

–**International Summer Camp Montana** (also ski camp), La Moubra, CH-3962, Montana, Switzerland. www.campmontana.ch

–**International Summer Camp** at Pully and Vennes-Lausanne, Switzerland. Write: 7 Dynamostrasse, 5400 Baden, Switzerland. www.itc-ijc.com

–**Le Chateau des Enfants** (a programme of the American School in Switzerland). Write: Le Chateau des Enfants, the American School in Switzerland, 6926 Montagnola-Lugano, Switzerland. www.tasis.com

Fun and games

No doubt about it, there's a lot on offer for children in Holland. Check out the really outstanding amusement parks, safari parks, zoos and beaches that are discussed in Part I. Major zoos can be found in Amersfoort (U), Amsterdam (NH), Arnhem (G), Emmen (D) and Rotterdam (ZH). Beaches in the Randstad area get an entire chapter to themselves (Chapter 14).

Take note of the many 'farms' that exist in most towns, called 'Kinderboerderijen.' This is the Dutch way to introduce children to familiar animals that they would not likely find in a zoo. Usually it's possible to touch the animals in the farm area, see baby chicks and rabbits at close range, feed the goats, deer and sheep with approved fodder, and generally get to feel comfortable with such animals. (Check with the VVV for one near your home.)

Scouting is international and needs no introduction, and there are flourishing groups for boys and girls in Holland, including international groups. If your child speaks Dutch, there are a number of Dutch groups to choose from, including sea scouts. For information on English-language groups: **Scouts of America**, ☎ (0172) 58 8757, and guides ☎ (071) 561 6849; **UK Scouts**, ☎ (071) 561 9836, and guides, ☎ (010) 451 0529; ACCESS or the local schools. For Dutch groups, contact **Scouting Nederland**, Larikslaan 5, 3830 AE Leusden, ☎ (033) 496 0911. www.scouting.nl

Once settled in a group, scouts and guides must be outfitted. Scout shops all carry camping goods, English books on scouting, songbooks, cookbooks, uniforms, shoes, knives, whistles, compasses, pennants... everything to make a cub scout's heart beat faster.

Anything and everything the 'open air" child from 7 years up (including his parents) could want, is available from De ScoutShop, Scouting Nederland's online webshop and catalog. www.scoutshop.scouting.nl For locations of all 15 stores and opening times, look on the site under '*winkels.*'

– **Amsterdam**: Kruislan 230 A, ☎ (020) 693 9877; Mondays 7pm-9pm evenings, Wed. 1:30-3:30, Sat., 10am-noon. http://amstel.scouting.nl/scoutshop.html
– **The Hague**: Scouting Steunpunt Zuid-Holland, Waldeck Pyrmontkade 904, ☎ (070) 310 6454, http://denhaag.scouting.nl/static/regio/scoutshop
– **Rotterdam**: Heemraadssingel 129, ☎ (010) 477 2393, Wed. 1-5pm, Fri., 3:30-8:30pm. Sat., 10am-1pm. http://rotterdam.scouting.nl/Scoutshop
– **The American Baseball Foundation**, (ABF), Deylerweg 155, Wassenaar, ☎ (070) 511 9067 (weekends only). www.abfsport.nl, is a volunteer organisation that provides sports programmes for children of all nationalities, from age four. These programmes run throughout the year in soccer, basketball and baseball – depending on the season – and take place at the weekend. Sign-up for activities takes place in late August and early February. More than 600 families currently take part.

Entertainment and the arts

Luckily for English-speaking children, Holland is a small country where it is not economical to dub films in Dutch. Consequently, films made in foreign countries are shown with the original sound track –most often in English.

Movies are listed in the Wednesday evening or Thursday morning editions of Dutch newspapers. Note that there are special 'Kindermatinees' (children's matinees) shown on Wednesday, Sunday and holiday afternoons.

TV listings are given daily in the newspapers – after a little practice, you'll be surprised by how much you can actually understand. There is no Sunday edition, so TV programmes for both days are listed in the Saturday edition.

Some theatres run a children's movie until about 7pm, and then put on a film for an older audience. Children of all ages are permitted in any evening movie which has an 'AL' listing (see below). Be aware: children's movies are not usually in English as these are, indeed, dubbed for the not-yet-linguists.

– **AL**   OK for all ages
– **12**   Over 12 years of age
– **16**   Over 16 years of age
– **N**   Dutch language film
– **F**   French-language film
– **D**   German-language film
– **E**   English language film

'AL' means the film is in Dutch and all ages are permitted; 16 E means children must be 16 years or older and the film is in English. For information about advance purchase of tickets, see Chapter 17.

For television programmes, codes are given with pictograms:
www.kijkwijzer.nl

'Kijkwijzer' warns parents and educators of up to what age a television programme or film can be harmful to children, by giving an age recommendation: All Ages, 6 years, 12 years and 16 years. In addition, pictograms are used
to show the reason for the recommendation: violence, fear, sex, discrimination, drug and/or alcohol abuse and coarse language.

AL = Not harmful/All Ages

6 = Caution with children under 6

12 = Caution with children under 12

16 = Caution with children under 16

= Violence

= Fear

= Sex

= Discrimination

= Drugs- and alcohol abuse

= Coarse Language

The cultural scene

Before describing theatre, concerts and ballet productions of interest to children, we'd
like to explain about the Youth Cultural Passport, which gives young people (15 to 26
years old), who are residents of the Netherlands, reduced rates for them, as well as for
films, museums, journals and magazines.

Youth Cultural Passport. Sponsored by the Art for Youth Foundation, membership
is nominal and includes a subscription to the local monthly programme calendar and
reduced entrance fees. Application should be made at the main VVV or town hall. Bring
a passport photo for your membership card and proof of date of birth. (Passport or driver's licence.) www.cjp.nl

The Symphony and the Ballet welcome 'well-behaved' children to any of their performances. Children from eight years on are often taken to the symphony or to the ballet

in Holland. No one considers them a nuisance for the very reason that they are usually not. Here is a chance to introduce your child to the professional theatre without it being prohibitive cost-wise. If you have a budding young ballerina at home, take her to see the Scapino Ballet… or if you have a determined drummer banging away on your upper floor, a trip to hear the symphony orchestra of your choice might encourage a little more control. With the exception of opera and plays that are given in French, Italian, German or Dutch, there is a wide choice of evening performances appealing to children. The 'Little Theatre' productions in English are another introduction to the world of make-believe. Look in the 'Pink Pages' under Kindertheater. Teenagers, of course, will develop their own interests and artistic tastes and find many summer programmes such as jazz festivals to enjoy. Theatres that do attract the younger set are the puppet theatres … again, the language is universal; however, it never hurts to ask for an English synopsis. See www.uitmetkinderen.nl under '*poppentheatre.*'

▶ **Amsterdam**

Diridas Poppentheater, Hobbemakade 68, ☎ (020) 662 1588, Tram 16

Kindertheater Circus Elleboog, Passeerdersgracht 32, ☎ (020) 626 9370, children's theatre, www.elleboog.nl

The Vondel Park Open-Air Theater in Amsterdam is famous, attracting mostly young adults; however, on Wednesdays at 3pm, there's a children's performance, ☎ (020) 523 7790. Theatre and music is played during June, July and August. The open-air theatre takes place five days a week; entry is free. www.openluchttheater.nl

▶ **The Hague**

Poppentheater Guido Van Deth and the Puppetry Museum, Nassau Dillenburgstraat 8, ☎ (070) 328 0208, Bus 18. Conducted tours can be arranged upon request. (For details about the theatre and its history, see Chapter 17.)

Kooman's Poppentheater, Frankenstraat 66, ☎ (070) 355 9305, Buses 4, 65 and 89. (See Chapter 17 for details about Mr. Kooman and the theatre, www.kooman-poppentheater.nl)

▶ **Rotterdam**

De Lantaren Theater, Gouvernestraat 133, ☎ (010) 277 2277, has special children's performances. www.lantaren-venster.nl

▶ **Hilversum**

Hilvert's Hofje Poppentheatre, (Hilvertshof Shopping Centre), Wed. and Sat.; no charge. This group also organises pre-arranged English presentations, ☎ (021) 526 4194, another good idea for parties.

Chapter 20 | Yearly special events

There's no need to ever be bored in Holland. In fact, we'd venture to say that it's nearly impossible, what with the magnitude of annual events alone. This chapter provides a capsulised view of those events, around the country. Add to that the impromptu additions, and you have yourself a full calendar.

Our own calendar has been devised as a quick aid to planning a day out or an extended holiday, whether you're visiting or living in the Netherlands. Major events that occur annually are listed, but you may happen upon many that are 'spur of the moment' or a celebration for that year only, commemorating something like a national event. These we cannot anticipate and are not listed. If you want to fit some special event into your schedule, we recommend you check with the local VVV. The provincial abbreviations are:

ZH	South Holland	**F**	Flevoland	**D**	Drenthe
NH	North Holland	**B**	Brabant	**O**	Overijssel
U	Utrecht	**Fr**	Friesland	**L**	Limburg
G	Gelderland	**Gr**	Groningen	**Z**	Zeeland

Following the calendar are explanations of Dutch special events, as well as a list of annual foreign events organised by members of international organisations in the Netherlands.

The Calendar

JANUARY

Early Jan.	Lisse (SH)	Mid-winter flora – exhibition, CNB Halls
Early Jan.	Amsterdam (NH)	Vakantiebeurs – largest public vacation trade fair full of exciting and adventurous ideas.
Late Jan. – Feb.	Rotterdam (SH)	International Film Festival – more than 300 non-commercial films from around the world www.filmfestivalrotterdam.com
Late Jan.– Feb.	Amsterdam (NH)	Chinese New Year – celebrate with festivities in Chinatown in the Zeedijk area of Amsterdam, chasing away evil spirits, celebrating with fireworks all day long, and the Chinese Lion dance
Mid-Jan.	Amsterdam (NH)	Amsterdam Fashion Week, promoting the city as a centre of creativity. Also in July. www.amsterdamfashionweek.com

FEBRUARY

February	All over	Carnival celebrations with parades, balls and parties. Especially in Limburg (Maastricht), Brabant (Breda, 's Hertogenbosch) and in most towns in these southern provinces.
Mid Feb.	Rotterdam (SH)	ABN-AMRO World Tennis Tournament, Ahoy Hall
Mid Feb.	Rotterdam (SH)	Huishoudbeurs – the largest public trade show with all the newest household products and plenty of free samples, Ahoy Hall
Late Feb.	Bovenkarspel (NH)	West-Frisian Flora – flower show and home exhibition
Late Feb.	Amsterdam (NH)	HISWA, international water sport and boat show, RAI
Feb.-March	Assen (D)	Ice-speedweek – ice speed races, De Smelt rink

MARCH

Mid March	's Hertogenbosch (B)	Indoor Brabant – equestrian competition
Mid March	Maastricht (L)	The European Fine Art Fair (TEFAF) – paintings, furniture, contemporary art, jewellery, antiques, etc. www.tefaf.com
Late March	The Hague (SH)	International Half Marathon, Lange Voorhout
Late March-May	Lisse (SH)	Keukenhof – open air flower exhibition and pavilions – bulb fields. www.keukenhof.nl
Late March-May	Vogelenzang (SH)	Tulip show at Holland Tulip Park (Frans Roozen) – gardens, fields and greenhouses
Lent	All over	Performances of Bach's St. Matthew's Passion
Palm Sunday	Denekamp, (O)	Palmpasenoptocht – procession with palms Oostmarsum, through the town Delden, etc.

APRIL

Easter	Ootmarsum, (O)	Paasvuur – traditional lighting of huge Easter Day Markelo, bonfires Enschede etc.
Easter	Ootmarsum (O)	Vloggeln – traditional Easter procession through town, singing of religious hymns
Easter weekend	Zwolle (O)	Pasar Malam Bali – Indonesian market, with articles for sale; music of oriental countries
1 April	Brielle (SH)	1 April Feesten – folk celebration re-enacting the capture of the town by the 'sea beggars' in 1572
Mid April	Zuidlaren (D)	Zuidlaardermarkt – spring fair with horse and pony auction and market with 200 stands
Mid April	Rotterdam (SH)	Generale Bank Marathon Rotterdam
Late April	Noordwijk (SH)	Flower Parade Bollenstreek – floats go from to Haarlem (NH) Noordwijk, through Sassen-heim, Lisse, Hillegom, Bennebroek, and Heem-stede to Haarlem. Floats on display in Haarlem Saturday night and Sunday. www.bloemencorso-bollenstreek.nl
30 April	All over	Koninginnedag – celebration of the Queen's Birthday, a national holiday. Fairs (*Kermis*), organ-grinders, flags and decorations, and sell-your-own-goods flea markets around the streets throughout the country (Vondelpark in Amsterdam is a prime venue sure to excite.)
April – May	Amsterdam (NH)	World Press Photo, exhibition, Nieuwe Kerk
April – May	Tiel (G)	Blossom Tour Route – fruit trees in bloom
April – Sept.	Alkmaar (NH)	Cheese market with bearers in historic guild uniforms; craft demonstrations; Fridays 10 am-noon

MAY

Early May	Amsterdam (NH)	Art Amsterdam (KunstRAI International Art Fair) draws gallery owners and collectors from all over the world; paintings, glass, jewellery
5 May	All over	Liberation Day celebrations, concerts in many cities. www.bevrijdingsfestivals.nl

Mid May	Amsterdam (NH)	The Amsterdam Literary Festival (ALF) puts the delightful Dutch capital on the world literary map, showcasing authors and speakers, events. www.amsterdamliteraryfestival.com
Mid May	All over	National Windmill Day. Well over 600 windmills, water mills and pumping stations throughout the country are open to the public; demonstrations. www.molens.nl
Mid May	Buren (G)	Fortress Day – picturesque market in medieval walled town with a fair, traditional crafts, antiques, music and over 300 stalls.
Mid May	Arnhem (G)	Harley-Davidson Day – motorcycle enthusiasts
Mid May	's Hertogenbosch (B)	Jazz in Duketown
Mid May	Leeuwarden (FR)	Frisian Elfstedenwandeltocht – walking tour through 11 towns, 205 km (127 mi)
Mid May	Urk (F)	Visserijdagen – free samples of fish with events to celebrate Urk's fishing heritage; held every other year.
Mid May	Zeist (U)	Garden Market – on the Zeist castle grounds
Late May	Almelo (O)	Avondwandelvierdaagse – walking event on four evenings
Late May	Apeldoorn (G)	Pop and Jazz Festival
Late May	Breda (B)	Jazz Festival Breda – street parades and open air concerts
Late May or early June	Landgraaf (L)	Pinkpop – open air rock music festival
Late May	Leeuwarden (FR)	Elfstedentocht voor Auto's – auto tour through route of 11 Frisian towns
Late May	Urk (F)	Urkerdag – residents dress up in the traditional clothing of this old fishing village.
Late May	Zandvoort (NH)	International Motor Races
May-June	The Hague (SH)	Japanese Garden in bloom, Clingendael Park
May-June	Exloo (D)	Schaapscheerdersfeest – sheep-shearing festival with folk dancing, parade and bands
May-June	Scheveningen (SH)	International Sand Sculpture Festival

May-Sept.	The Hague (SH)	Antique market, Lange Voorhout, Thur. 9am-9pm
May-Sept.	Wadden Islands (FR)	Wadlopen – guided mud-flat walking on islands of Schiermonnikoog and Ameland
End May	Rotterdam (SH)	Ortel Dunya Festival – world cultures music festival in park by the Euromast. www.dunya.nl
End May-late June	Amsterdam (NH)	Holland Festival – Holland's largest performing arts festival for 60 years. Celebrates the end of the cultural season with the best of music, theatre, dance, film and opera, throughout Amsterdam. www.hollandfestival.nl

JUNE

Early June	Breda (B)	Military Breda CCI – International Military Horse Show
Early June	Delfzijl (Gr)	Whitsun Festival – waterfront party and other activities
Late May or early June	Landgraaf (L)	Pinkpop – international open-air pop festival
Early June	Scheveningen (SH)	Vlaggetjesdag – flag-festooned herring fleet opens the new fishing season
Early June	Texel (NH)	Catamaran race around the island of Texel, from De Koogmid
Early June	Eelde (D)	Sheep-shearing festival; old crafts demonstrated, also music, markets, herring-eating contests, etc.
Mid June	The Hague (SH)	Bijenmarkt – annual bee market; Equestrian Days, Lange Voorhout
Mid June	Amsterdam (NH)	Amsterdam Roots Festival – 8 days of global music and non-western culture, performances, at several locations. www.amsterdamroots.nl
Mid June	Rotterdam (SH)	Poetry International – poetry festival
Mid June	Scheveningen (SH)	Vliegerfeest – int. kite-flying festival

Mid June	Terschelling (Fr)	Oerol Festival – podium art across the island, an incredible, open-air theatrical experience. An internationally recognised, multi-disciplinary festival. www.oerol.nl
Mid June	Tilburg (B)	Slotmanifestatie Festival Mundial – festival of music from many different cultures
Mid June	Warmond (SH)	Kaagweek – rowing races on Kagerplassen
Mid June	Wijchen (G)	Castle Fair – home and garden fair on the grounds of Kasteel Wijchen
Mid / Late June	Arnhem (G)	Champion Arnhem, equestrian competition
Mid June	Amsterdam (NH)	Aqua-Musica-T IJ – A nautical music festival, which takes place on and around the water of Amsterdam's IJ at unique locations, such as the VOC ship, The Amsterdam.
Late June	Assen (D)	International Dutch Motorcycling TT Grand Prix
Late June	Bolsward (Fr)	Heamieldagen – festival of Frisian folk costumes, traditional costumes worn; events include tilting at the ring on horses
Late June	Den Helder (NH)	National Surf Marathon – 50 km (31 mi) surfing competition across the Wadden Sea to Texel
Late June	Eindhoven (B)	Fiesta del Sol – Latin music and dance in centre
Late June	The Hague (SH)	Parkpop – international pop music festival
Late June	The Hague (SH)	Pasar Malam Besar – large oriental bazaar, food, music, on the Malieveld
Late June	Laren (NH)	St. Janprocessie – ancient folkloric procession through the town to the cemetery where human sacrifices once took place.
Late June	Warffum (Fr)	Op Roakeldais – costumed international folkdance festival
Late June	Wassenaar (SH)	Grand Prix of the Lowlands – horse races, trotting

June-August	Amsterdam (NH)	Vondelpark open air theatre, stages with all kinds of free performances, workshops, and music from DJs during the summer. Wed. mainly child-oriented; Thurs. salsa and tango workshops; Fri.-Sun. theatre and music. www.openluchttheater.nl
June-August	Rotterdam (SH) Utrecht (U) Amsterdam (NH) The Hague (SH)	De Parade, a nomadic theatrical event, will visit several Amsterdam/The Hague cities. Performances take place in clusters of tents during two months of theatre, film, dance, opera, music, magic and more. www.deparade.nl

JULY

July	Amsterdam (NH)	Julidans – two-week summer festival of contemporary dance where theatrical choreographies, theatre, music and other disciplines merge. www.julidans.com
July	Westerbork (D)	Schaapscheerdersfeest – sheep-shearing festival on a Sunday
Early July	Denekamp (O)	Dorpsfeesten – sheep-shearing, handicrafts, market, pancakes
Early July	Den Helder (NH)	Nationale Vlootdagen – The Royal Dutch Navy Fleet on display
Early July	The Hague (SH)	International Rose Contest – rose exhibition and Golden Rose of The Hague award, in the Westbroekpark
Early July	Ommen (O)	Bissingh – authentic country fair with music and entertainment
Early July	Tilburg (B)	Jazz Meeting Tilburg – weekend jazz festival
Early July	Vlissingen (Z)	Weeklong street festival
Early July	Zwolle (O)	Open Orgeldag – Schnitger Organ recitals, St. Michael's Church
Mid July	Apeldoorn (G)	Vierdaagse – international four-day walking event
Mid July	Didam (G)	Archery Festival – with archery competition and demonstrations

Mid July	Exloo (D)	International Festival van Oude Ambachten – old trades and crafts festival
Mid July	Rotterdam (SH)	North Sea Jazz Festival – three days of music with over 1,000 musicians featuring top jazz musicians as well as new talent on over a dozen stages. One of the greatest jazz events in the world. www.northseajazz.nl
Mid July	Leiden (SH)	Leiden Summer Festival – ten-day festival, opening parade of boats on the canals
Mid July	Nijmegen (G)	Vierdaagse – international four-day walking event, 30, 40, or 60 km (19, 25, or 37 mi) routes
Mid July	Amsterdam (NH)	Amsterdam Fashion Week, promoting the city as a centre of creativity. Also held for one week in January.
Mid July	Spaarnwoude (NH)	Dance Valley, two-day festival held for over 13 years; dance lovers from across Europe will come to enjoy live acts and a whole spectrum of music. Campground. www.dancevalley.nl
Mid July	Tilburg (B)	Tilburgse Kermis – the biggest fair in the Benelux countries, live entertainment daily
Late July	Chaam (B)	Chaam Eight – cycling classic for pros, amateurs and beginners
Late July	Emmen (D) Meppel (D) Assen (D)	Drentse Rijwiel Vierdaagse – four-day tourist Hoogeveen,cycling event – 30, 40, 60, 100 or 150 km (19, 25, 37, 62 or 93 mi) routes
Late July	Joure (Fr)	Boerenbruiloft – traditional farmer's wedding in old Frisian costumes
Late July	Loosdrecht (U)	International Holland Week – sailing competition
Late July	Scheveningen (SH)	Heineken Music Scheveningen – old-style jazz and Dixieland music along the sea front
Late July	Various cities (NH)	Youth Friendship Days Holland – sporting competitions, baseball, basketball, tennis, swimming, bowling, soccer, tennis, etc.
Late July	Rotterdam (ZH)	Ortel Zomercarnaval – spectacular carnival with street parade, costumes, music, dance. www.zomercarnaval.nl

444

July-Aug.	Barneveld (G)	Old Veluwse Market – every Thursday in July, and the first two in August
July-Aug.	Borger (D)	Old Drenthe farm wedding
July-Aug.	Frisian Lakes (Fr)	Regatta with Skûtsjesilen on lakes in several Frisian towns ('Skûtsjes' are unique flat-bottomed boats.)
July-Aug.	Gouda (SH)	Kaas en Ambachtenmarkt – traditional cheese market, Thursday 10am-12:30 pm; also craft demonstrations and horse-drawn wagon tours of the old city centre.
July-Aug.	Hoogeveen (D)	Pulledagen – commemorates when farmers got payment for milk and went into town to splurge. ('Pulle' means 'milk churn.')
July-Aug.	Kampen (O)	Street fair, music, street theatre, and plenty of food, on Thursdays. Kamer Uit-dagen – on three Thursdays in July and three in August; open-air markets, handicrafts, demonstrations, etc.
July-Aug.	Kinderdijk (SH)	Molendagen – Windmill Days – mills operating Sat. 1:30-5:30pm, Sun. (beginning late July) 1-5pm; one mill open for visits, 10am-5pm; Also, boat trips on canal along the windmills.
July-Aug.	Meppel (D)	Donderdag Meppeldag – folk dancing, a village band in traditional dress, the chance to climb the church tower – Thursdays.
July-Aug.	Schagen (NH)	Westfriese Donderdagen – old crafts (lace-making sheep-shearing, etc.) demonstrated every Thursday; also market, children's games, traditional costumes.
July-Aug.	Spakenburg (U)	Spakenburg Days – folk festival on Wednesdays, with fishing boats, and old crafts, dancing, and costumes.
July-Aug.	Zwolle (O)	Blauwevingerdagen – Blue Finger Days include a fair in the city centre, flea market, and music; Wednesdays 10am-6pm

Early Aug.	Almelo (O)	Avond Fietsvierdaagse – four-day cycling event; 0, 45 and 65 km (19, 28 and 40 mi) routes
Early Aug.	Amsterdam (NH)	Gay Pride Parade – event on the city's canals
Early Aug.	Broek in Waterland (NH)	Broeker Festival – old Dutch market, folk games, food, crafts, etc.
Early Aug.	Den Bosch (NB)	Boulevard Theatre festival
1st Sun. in Aug.	Deventer (O)	Deventer Boekenmarkt – Europe's largest book market, 850 stalls, over six kilometers (4 miles) of books.
Early Aug.	Nijmegen (G)	International Cycling Days – four-day cycling event
Early Aug.	Rijnsburg (SH)	Bloemencorso – flower parade (Rijnsburg-Leiden-Katwijk-Noordwijk)
Early Aug.	Rotterdam	Heineken Fast-Forward Dance Parade – free event, 40 trucks packed with sound systems and (inter)nationally acclaimed DJs; ends traditionally with a spectacular 'after party.' www.ffwdheinekendanceparade.nl
Early Aug.	Sneek (Fr)	Sneek Week – international sailing competitions and fair
Early Aug.	Hoofddorp (NH)	Mysteryland – dance and music festival in the Floriadepark
Mid Aug.	Amsterdam (NH)	Prinsengracht Concert – classical music on boats, bridges and along the Prinsengracht. www.grachtenfestival.nl
Mid Aug.	Amersfoort (U)	Festival Dias Latinos – Latin-American Film festival
Mid Aug.	Barneveld (G)	International Etc. Fiesta – hot air balloons, model airplanes and parachute demonstrations
Mid Aug.	Biddinghuizen (FL)	Lowlands – youth-oriented 3-day pop music festival with camping facilities
Mid Aug.	Breskens (Z)	Fishery Days Festival, with fair
Mid Aug.	Doorn (U)	Castle tour, with horse-drawn carriages

Mid Aug.	Eindhoven (B)	Jazz & Blues Festival
Mid Aug.	Nijmegen (G)	Waalkade à la Carte – sample area restaurant culinary fare
Mid Aug.	Rotterdam (SH)	CHIO International Horse Show
Mid Aug.	Scheveningen (SH)	Vuurwerk Festival – international fireworks festival
Mid Aug.	Winsum (Fr)	Fierljeppen – Frisian championship of pole-vaulting across canals
Mid Aug.	Yerseke (Z)	Mussels Day – Zeeland festival, boat trips
Late Aug.	Amsterdam (NH)	Uit Markt – indoor and outdoor performances to open the city's new cultural season. www.uitmarkt.nl
Late Aug.	Amsterdam (NH)	Hartjesdagen (Days of the Hearts), lavish street festival dates back to the Middle Ages and is all about love songs and dance music, with a procession of men dressed as women and vice versa, in the Zeedijk.
Late Aug.	Breda (B)	Breda Balloon Fiesta – 30 hot air balloons
Late Aug.	Harlingen (Fr)	Visserijdagen – fishing days, with old costumes, boats, sailing race, air show, market, fair and concerts
Late Aug.	Heeze (B)	Brabant Days – historical theme parade and folk activities in town
Late Aug.	Leersum (U)	Central Holland Flower Parade; art market, music fair
Late Aug.	Maastricht (L)	Preuvenemint – Burgundian culinary fair, sampling of food and drink from some 40 restaurants
Late Aug.	Raalte (O)	Stoppelhaene – traditional harvest festival, market and fair
3rd Friday Aug.	Zwolle (O)	Straatfestival – street market and music, from 6pm to midnight
Last Sat. in Aug.	Giethoorn (O)	Gondelvaart – illuminated gondola trips on the canals

End Aug. -1st week Sept.	Middelburg (Z)	Zeeland Nazomer Festival – annual 'End of Summer' festival, dance music and literature. www.nazomerfestival.nl
End Aug./ early Sept.	Utrecht (U)	Holland Festival Oude Muziek – focus on 'really old music' from the Middle Ages and the Renaissance, to later periods. Market, lectures, workshops and symposium. www.oudemuziek.nl

SEPTEMBER

1st Sat.	Aalsmeer (NH)	Flower Parade – starts 9am in Aalsmeer and travels to Amsterdam, via Amstelveen. All the floats are on display on the Dam in Amsterdam after the parade.
Early Sept.	Amsterdam NH)	Seven Bridges – one day, free-of-charge jazz festival at the Reguliers canal by well-known jazz musicians and amazing new talent. www.sevenbridges.nl
Early Sept.	Amersfoort (U)	Keistadfeesten – annual cultural event
Early Sept.	Eelde (D)	Bloemencorso – flower parade and festival; market, fireworks, antique cars
Early Sept.	The Hague (SH)	Haagse Kermis – largest autumn fair in Holland held on the Malieveld
Early Sept.	IJmuiden (NH)	HISWA te Water – annual boat show at Seaport Marina
Early Sept.	Kinderdijk (SH)	Molens In Floodlight – illumination of windmills; boat trips to view the mills, evenings until 11pm.
Early Sept.	Leeuwarden (Fr)	Fries Straatfestival – Frisian street festival
Early Sept.	Maastricht (L)	Het Parcours – theatre festival, opening of the season
Early Sept.	Rotterdam (SH)	Wereldhaven Festival – fireworks, tours of ships and boat trips to celebrate the World Harbour Festival
Early Sept.	Zundert (B)	Dahlia flower parade, market and street theatre
Early Sept.	Zwolle (O)	International Guitar Festival

2nd Sat. Sept.	Tiel (G)	Fruitcorso Tiel – Harvest & Fruit Parade – floats made of fruit; marching bands
Mid. Sept.	All over	Open Monument Days – many museums and monuments are open free of charge
Mid Sept.	Amsterdam (NH)	Jordaanfestival – city folk festival in Jordaan
Mid Sept.	Eindhoven (B)	Torchlight procession, fireworks and events commemorating the end of World War II
2nd Tuesday in Sept.	The Hague (SH)	Prinsjesdag – opening of Parliament by the Queen, riding in a resplendent horse-drawn, golden coach through The Hague
Mid Sept.	Oosterbeek (G)	Airborne March – walking tour of 10 to 25 km (6 to 15.5 mi), visiting the sites of the 1944 Allied airborne landings
Mid Sept.	Valkenswaard (B)	Flower Parade – traditional parade with floats
Mid Sept.	Warmond (SH)	Schippertjesdgen – nautical festival with old boats and market
Late Sept.	Amsterdam (NH)	De Woonbeurs Amsterdam – public trade show with all the latest lifestyle, furniture and living trends and products
Late Sept.	Tilburg (B)	Tilburg Wijnstad/Culinary – wine and food festival
Late Sept.	Joure (Fr)	Jouster Merke – folk fair, agriculture show, horse auction
Late Sept.	Veldhoven (NB)	Cult en Tumult – cultural weekend, music, dance, theatre
Late Sept.	Zaanse Schans (NH)	Windmill Days – windmills open for visits
End Sept.-Early Oct.	Utrecht (U)	Netherland's Film Festival – every year, for ten days, film lovers and film professionals have the unique opportunity to acquaint themselves with the best and latest films from the Netherlands. www.filmfestival.nl/en

OCTOBER

1st weekend	Eindhoven (B)	Prehistoric Weekend at Prehistoric Open Air Museum – shows ancient crafts, music, dance and ancient culture
Early Oct.	Leiden (SH)	Leidens Ontzet – liberation of Leiden from the Spanish siege, celebrated with historic parade, music and fair
Early Oct.	Alkmaar (NH)	Alkmaars Ontzet – liberation of Alkmaar from the Spanish siege celebrated with a traditional festival
Early Oct.	Utrecht (U)	Studie Beurs – public orientation fair featuring educational opportunities for students, with representatives from schools in and beyond Holland. www.scopeontheglobe.com
Early Oct.	Nijmegen (G)	Kermis – annual fair
Mid Oct.	Amsterdam (NH)	ADE Amsterdam Dance Event – 3 nights, 30 clubs, 300 DJs; dance festival in venues across the city. www.amsterdam-dance-event.nl
Mid Oct.	Utrecht (U)	Camping and Caravan Show at the Jaarbeurs exhibition hall
3rd Tues.	Zuidlaren (D)	Biggest horse market in Western Europe. www.zuidlaardermarkt.info

NOVEMBER

Early Nov.	Assen (D)	Jaarmarkt – annual autumn market
1st Wed.	Coevorden (D)	Ganzenmarkt – traditional goose market
Early Nov.	Haarlem (NH)	Kunstlijn – weekend of open ateliers, galleries, visit artists and view their works
Early Nov.	Zeist, Den Treek (U)	St. Hubertus Slipjacht – hunting with horses
Early Nov.	All over	St. Nicholas Celebrations – the Saint's official arrival in Holland, by steamboat and horse
Mid Nov.	Amsterdam (NH)	PAN Amsterdam – annual Art and Antiques Fair at the RAI, a wealth of intriguing finds and rare delights. www.pan-amsterdam.nl

Mid Nov.	Amsterdam (NH)	Museum Night – more than 40 museums and institutions will open their doors from 7 pm until 2 am! All museums organise special events. www.n8.nl
Mid Nov.	Leiden (SH)	Thanksgiving Day service in Pieterskerk
Late Nov.	Maastricht (L)	JIM Jumping Indoor Maastricht – spectacular equestrian programme in MECC exhibition venue. www.jumpingindoormaastricht.nl
Last Thurs.	Valkenburg (L)	Christmas markets inside the local caves
Nov.- Dec.	All over	Christmas markets in numerous towns
Nov.-Dec.	Amsterdam (NH)	IFDA – one of the world's most prestigious documentary film festivals, over 200 high-quality documentaries and an extensive programme, workshops, readings and forums about filming. www.idfa.nl
Nov. thru Dec.	Rotterdam (SH)	Night of the Proms – 14 evenings of music performed by international artists in Ahoy hall. www.notp.com

DECEMBER

Early Dec.	Gouda (SH)	Gouda bij Kaarslicht – Gouda by candlelight – town hall and market candle-lit for ceremonial lighting of Christmas trees; carol singing
Early Dec.	Maastricht (L)	Winterland – covered and heated outdoor winter market in the city centre. www.winterland.nl
Mid. Dec.	Appledoorn (G)	Paleis Het Loo – Christmas at the royal palace, beautifully decorated
Mid. Dec.	Deventer (O)	Dickens Festival – a lovely Christmas market where the townspeople are dressed as Old English characters.
Mid. Dec.	Rotterdam (SH)	Kerstcircus Ahoy – Christmas Circus at Ahoy Hall
Late Dec.- Jan. 6	Denekamp,	Midwinterhoornblazen – traditional midwinter Ootmarsum, horn-blowing from Advent to Epiphany Borne (O)

Calendar list of events supplied by our resource: ReSpons Events Monitor, Amsterdam. www.respons.nl

Further information about select events

January in Holland seems to be the month for resting from the series of holiday festivities that took place in December, but extensive (some say too many) fireworks can be heard popping all over town on New Year's Eve and New Year's Day. January 6th is normally the date for taking down the Christmas trees, and Dutch kids love collecting them to then burn them in the streets. Also, mostly in the provinces of Brabant and Limburg (in small towns), you could be surprised on January 6th to find children dressed as the Three Kings ringing your doorbell and serenading you. In exchange for their singing, they receive cookies and sweets.

The **Queen's Birthday** is always celebrated on April 30th, so this is a date you can count on if you are interested in participating in some very colourful events. Most towns have a fair (*kermis*). The decorations in The Hague are especially colourful, with great orange balls (for the House of Orange) hanging from the trees along the Lange Vijverberg and Lange Voorhout. In all towns and cities of the Netherlands you will see the Dutch flag flying from private homes, office buildings, and town halls – and even churches and windmills bedecked with colourful bunting. Many shop windows are also specially decorated. Birthdays of other members of the Royal family are not national holidays, but flags do fly for each Royal birthday and the organ grinders will be out in full force. A special law allows organ grinders to play whenever there is a Royal family birthday and, happily, the members of the House of Orange are numerous enough to save the organ grinders from obscurity in the near future.

Folkloric markets and events are scheduled throughout the year, but especially in June, July and August – the tourist season. Every city and village turns itself inside out to attract visitors. A brand-new and often curious experience for visitors, these events based on folk tales give an insight into Dutch history and humour. A few of these extraordinary happenings of true Dutch origin are 'Op Roakeldais,' a dance festival in Groningen; '*kaatsen*' or 'handball' competitions in Friesland; 'Skotsploegh' performances in Frisian costumes; sheep-shearing in Loenen (Gelderland); Fierljeppen – pole-vaulting across canals in Friesland; and 'Skûtsjes' boat races, also in Friesland. ('Skûtsjes' are traditional old trading ships with large black or brown sails. The body of the vessel is flat and wide, and has large wooden lee boards on each side, for stability). Each province has its own folkloric event. Zeeland has a number of traditional games such as 'tilting for the ring' on bare horseback – a very old and unusual tradition seen in Middelburg and other villages between June and August; '*krulbollen*,' a type of bowling with wooden balls and archery competitions, all held in various towns.

Less folkloric, but nevertheless of note in summer are many special interest events such as garden shows, sports competitions, jazz festivals, art shows, boat regattas, and special walking tours throughout the country.

One truly unique experience which falls into this category is 'mud-flat' walking (*wadlopen*). This truly demanding walk is only possible at low tide, obviously, and in the company of an experienced guide. Not for the faint-hearted or unfit, it takes you from the mainland

Very international. Very Unique.

The right match between client and candidate: that's what it's all about. Unique Multilingual Services has a wide and varied range of candidates hailing from more than 30 different countries and with diverse specialities. We provide multilingual temporary and permanent staff and advise a large number of enterprises on their HR policy.

All our candidates are fluent in English and at least one other language. In spite of their different cultural backgrounds, our candidates have much in common. They are enthusiastic, motivated and capable of adapting quickly to new work environments. Unique Multilingual Services utilise an extensive and professional selection procedure. As a result, we are in an excellent position to meet your requirements.

Enjoy the benefits of our international experience, network and focus.

unique
multilingual services

070-311 78 00
www.uniquemls.com

454

International Pharmacy Havinga

Specialised in International Medicines

We are specialised in International Medicines. Do you need information about the availability of your medicines in the Netherlands? Do you need to (re)fill a prescription? Contact the international pharmacy. Free parking. Free delivery. Free advice.

Exclusive distributor of Roger & Galet, H_2O Plus, Vichy and La Roche-Posay skincare products.

Contact Details & Opening Hours

Prins Hendrikplein 3
2518 JA Den Haag
0031 70 3456100 (tel)
0031 70 3106702 (fax)

Monday – Friday 08.00 – 17.30
Saturday 10.00 -17.00
info@apotheek-havinga.nl
www.apotheek-havinga.nl

to the Waddenzee Islands of Schiermonnikoog and Ameland (see Friesland, and photo on page 243). An added advantage is that its timing coincides with the nesting season of the myriad of birds that come here between April and August. A very special experience for bird lovers.

Prinsjesdag is another 'not-to-be-missed' event that takes place in The Hague on the third Tuesday in September. The Queen rides from her palace to Parliament in her resplendent, golden coach drawn by a team of Royal horses. She is accompanied by her family – some riding with her and others following in perhaps less splendid, but still very impressive, coaches. The Queen is very popular and close to the people, so the streets of her route are lined with 'her citizens' – and many visitors too. It is wise to come early; but, as the wait is often long, it is not recommended for very young children.

Leiden's Ontzet takes place on October 3rd. This festival and historical parade commemorate the day the Dutch routed the Spaniards from Leiden by opening the dikes and flooding the area. In their haste to retreat, the Spaniards left their pots of stew (hutspot) on the fire. The story goes that the starving Dutch were much strengthened by this stew, and since then this fare (together with herring and bread, another of their historic staples), has been served on the colourful anniversary of the event. Similar celebrations take place in Groningen and Brielle.

Sinterklaas or St. Nicholas: The festive Christmas season starts early in the Netherlands. December 5th is when Sinterklaas comes to town, arriving by boat on various canals throughout the country. St. Nicholas' Calendar Day, December 6th, is observed in most Roman Catholic countries, but only in the Low Countries – and especially in the Netherlands – is the eve of his festival celebrated nationwide by young and old, without any religious overtones. Although Sinterklaas is always presented in the vestments of the bishop he once was, his status as a Saint, duly canonised by the church, has played no part in the Dutch mind for centuries. Rather, he is a kind of benevolent old gentleman, whose feast on the evening of December 5th is the merriest and most beguiling event of the Dutch year, with Christmas day itself being kept as a strictly religious festival. Unfortunately with commercial interests prevailing, this is changing.

St. Nicholas is based on historical fact. He was born in 271 A.D. and lived to December 6th, 342 or 343. His 4th-century tomb in the town of Myra, Asia Minor, has only been discovered by archaeologists in the last twenty years. That St. Nicholas' influence was especially strong in the Netherlands is primarily due to his role as patron saint of merchants and sailors, though he soon became better known as the benefactor of children. In the 14th century on December 6th, choirboys of St. Nicholas Churches were given pennies and the day free to celebrate. Somewhat later, pupils of church schools were apparently ceremoniously rewarded or punished by a teacher – a monk disguised as the venerable bishop, just as he is still presented today with his long white beard, his red mantle, mitre, and his gold crosier. Gradually, Sinterklaas became a household name. In due time, Sinterklaas came accompanied by his Moorish knave, Piet, a grinning fellow with a birch rod, whose sack of goodies, when emptied, is large enough to carry away naughty children!

While the American Santa Claus lives at the North Pole, it is well known that the Dutch Sinterklaas lives in Spain – how else would he have a Moorish servant? Sinterklaas arrives by boat, of course, so, in Rotterdam, for example, on a predetermined school holiday afternoon (usually the Wednesday afternoon before December 5th) Sinterklaas will arrive at Leuvehaven and dispense his goodies (spice cookies) on his way to his main rendezvous in front of City Hall, 'Stadhuis.' And so it is in most towns and cities throughout the Netherlands.

Now for the night of December 5th itself, when stores are jammed with people frantically trying to get those last-minute 'surprises,' and the streets are full of workers and shoppers hurrying home. Expensive gifts are definitely not necessary. It is the personal touch or 'do-it-yourself element' of the gift and its original presentation that counts. Small inexpensive articles chosen with care and meaning are all that is expected, although special presents are sometimes given.

The really difficult part of this festivity is writing the poem that must accompany each gift. Whether long or short, is entirely up to the rhyming talents of the giver, but it cannot be left out. The poem should deal with the good points or the weaknesses of the recipient in a light-hearted, amusing way.

Another special aspect to this gift-giving is in the preparation of the packages. Here the imagination should be given free rein. Pretty gift wrappings are definitely out. The gifts are to be carefully camouflaged and made to look like something else. This requires careful planning and preparation. No one is immune, and all manner of society can be seen – even in executive offices – preparing such concoctions as Jello within which the gift-giver may have hidden a little plastic-sealed package for the recipient. Gifts have also been known to be concealed in potatoes dressed to look like dolls; in a pudding made of coloured starch; in a glove filled with wet sand, etc. Sometimes, the recipient only finds a note in the pudding directing him to look in a cupboard, or some obscure place – the greater the imagination, the greater the fun. Each surprise is addressed to the person in question and signed by Sinterklaas, of course.

Sometimes both Sinterklaas and Piet arrive in traditional costume to deliver the gifts and offer a few pertinent words to assembled friends and family. He might say that young Anne has been too frivolous, perhaps, or that Jan has been playing football instead of studying...or he will comment if one of the children has done something special during the year. If they have been very bad, on the other hand, they might be 'put in Piet's bag and taken off'! If Sinterklaas and Piet cannot appear in person, it is likely that the doorbell will ring loudly at a prearranged time; mother will answer, opening the door just wide enough to allow a gloved hand to toss a lot of spice candies into the room, for which the children obviously make a dive. Then the real fun begins. One present is unwrapped at a time – the whole group watching while the embarrassed recipient reads aloud his or her poem. Young and old enjoy this entire holiday ritual.

▶ **Yearly foreign-community events**

As indicated earlier, the foreign community sponsors a number of special events during the year. There are also events organised by the Dutch Government and the various international schools.

January: Model United Nations. This annual event is promoted by the international schools in The Hague area. Held in the World Forum Congress Center, more than 1,500 students from 28 countries take part. The opening and closing sessions are the most exciting times to attend. For information, call the American School of The Hague, ☎ (070) 514 0113. www.ash.nl

March: The American Baseball Foundation sponsors an annual Sports Evening when team awards are presented. The evening is dedicated to football and baseball films, celebrity speakers and sports personalities. Contact ABF, Deylerweg 155, Wassenaar, ☎ (070) 514 6115, weekends. www.abfsport.nl

May: Memorial Day Ceremonies. Americans in particular might like to know about the special Memorial Day Ceremonies that are held at Margraten Cemetery outside of Maastricht (Limburg), the last weekend in May. As the largest American military cemetery in the Netherlands, it is a beautiful place to visit, and the moving Memorial Day Ceremonies are worth a special trip. The Queen's personal representative, the American Ambassador – leading military personnel, local mayors and prominent citizens – all attend, as well as other Americans, local Dutch, and many other nationalities. Dutch children from towns in the area participate by each bringing a bunch of flowers to put on a grave. There is usually a special fly-over salute and speeches; wreaths are laid, and the cemetery may be visited. As it's a good three-hour drive from Rotterdam, for example, it might be an opportunity to stay over in charming, neighbouring Valkenburg (see Chapter 12).

June: A picnic is sponsored by the American Baseball Foundation in Wassenaar, usually on the closest weekend to the end of the summer semester. It's an 'All American-Day' with baseball, children's games, and plenty to eat. For information, check with ABF (see March listing of Annual Events) or the American Women's Club, ☎ (070) 350 6007. www.awcthehague.org

Late October – November: Many foreign churches and clubs have annual charity bazaars at this time of the year. It's a great way to pick up special food items and gifts for Christmas. For information, check with individual churches, clubs or ACCESS. www.access-nl.org

November: Guy Fawkes Day (November 5th) Sponsored by the British Society in Amsterdam. For details, ☎ (020) 642 8629. There is usually a big bonfire with the effigy of Guy Fawkes being burnt on it, and also a fireworks display. www.britsoc.nl

American Thanksgiving Day: On the last Thursday of November, the American Community Council organises an ecumenical service commemorating the departure of the Pilgrims from Leiden to the New World. It is held in the historic Sint Pieterskerk (St. Peter's Church). For details, call the Leiden VVV, or the American Women's Club, ☎ (070) 350 6007.

Annual United Service for Peace: Held on the first Sunday of Advent, at the International Scots Church in Rotterdam, Schiedamsevest 119, ☎ (010) 412 4779, the service begins at 7:30 pm. The Dutch Reformed Church, the Eglise Wallone, the Church of England, the Finnish Church, the Russian Orthodox Church, the German Evangelische Gemeinde Church, the Roman Catholic Church, and the Norwegian Church are usually all represented. www.scotsintchurch.com

Chapter 21 | Quick reference

ANWB

- The Royal Dutch Touring Club , (AAA, AA and RAC equivalent), www.anwb.nl
- Emergency Road Service, ☎ (0800) 099 8888 for members. (In emergencies, non-members can join 'on the spot.')
- The Hague Head Office: Wassenaarseweg 220, ☎ (070) 314 7147
- Amsterdam: Museumplein 5, ☎ (020) 673 0844
- Breda: Nieuwe Ginnekenstraat 27, ☎ (076) 522 3232
- Eindhoven: Emmasingel 10, ☎ (040) 236 8080
- Groningen: Oosterstraat 48, ☎ (050) 318 4345
- Maastricht: Wycker Brugstraat 24, ☎ (043) 362 0666
- Rotterdam: Coolsingel 67, ☎ (010) 414 0000
- Utrecht: Van Vollenhovenlaan 277-279 , ☎ (030) 294 0939

Car rentals

- Alamo, Schiphol Airport, Amsterdam, ☎ (0800) 022 4456, www.goalamo.com
- Avis, Hogehilweg 7, Amsterdam, ☎ (020) 430 9611; Schiphol Airport,
  ☎ (020) 604 1301, USA & Canada reservations, ☎ (800) 331-1084, www.avis.com
- Budget, Overtoom 121 & Schiphol Airport, Amsterdam, ☎ (0800) 05 37, USA reservations
- ☎ (800) 472 3325, www.drivebudget.com
- Diks Car Rental, Gen. Vetterstraat 51-55, Amsterdam, ☎ (020) 617 8505, www.diks.net
- EuropCar, Overtoom 51, Amsterdam, ☎ (020) 883 2123, Schiphol Airport,
  ☎ (020) 316 4190, www.europcar.com
- Hertz, Overtoom 333, Amsterdam, ☎ (020) 612 2441, Schiphol Airport,
  ☎ (020) 601 5416, USA reservations, ☎ (800) 654 3001, www.hertz.com
- National, Overtoom 196, Amsterdam, ☎ (020) 616 2466, Schiphol Airport,
  ☎ (020) 316 4081, USA reservations, ☎ (800) 227 7368, www.nationalcar.com

Other:
- www.amsterdam.affordablecarrental-europe.com
- www.webcarhire.com
- www.drivetravel.com/carrent/holland

Motorhome rentals

- www.arrantea.com
- www.bwcampers.com
- www.dutchnomads.com

Casinos

There are 38 cities in the Netherlands that have a combined total of 50 gambling casinos – the only legal type:
www.hollandcasino.com and
www.worldcasinodirectory.com/netherlands

- **Amsterdam:** Max Euweplein 62, ☎ (020) 521 1111
- **Breda:** Kloosterplein 20, ☎ (076) 525 1100
- **Eindhoven:** Heuvel Galerie 134, ☎ (040) 235 7357
- **Enschede:** Boulevard 1945-105, ☎ (053) 750 2750
- **Groningen:** Gedempte Kattendiep 150 , ☎ (050) 317 2317
- **Leeuwarden:** Heliconweg 56, ☎ (058) 750 2222
- **Nijmegen:** Waalkade 68, ☎ (024) 381 6381
- **Rotterdam:** Weena 624, ☎ (010) 206 8206
- **Scheveningen–The Hague:** Kurhausweg 1, ☎ (070) 306 7777
- **Schiphol Airport:** Lounge 1 (at pier B & C), ☎ (023) 574 0574
  Only with boarding card!
- **Utrecht:** Overste den Oudenlaan 2, ☎ (030) 750 4750
- **Valkenburg:** Kuurpark Cauberg 28, ☎ (043) 609 9600
- **Venlo:** Magalhaesweg 4, ☎ (070) 750 2625
- **Zandvoort:** Badhuisplein 7, ☎ (023) 574 0574

Places of worship

The following locations offer services for foreigners in the Randstad. Dutch or other language services are indicated by an asterisk (*).

Amsterdam:

- **Independent Baptist Church of Amsterdam**, Frederik Hendrikstraat 17, 1051 HH,
  ☎ (020) 684 1251.
- **Blessed Trinity Parish,** (Roman Catholic), Zaaiersweg 180, 1097 ST, ☎ (020) 465 2711 /
  (020) 7772740, www.blessedtrinity.nl
- **Christ Church** (Anglical Episcopal), Groenburgwal 42, 1011 HW, ☎ (020) 624 8877,
  www.christchurch.nl
- **Church of Jesus Christ of Latter Day Saints**, Zaaiersweg 17, 1097 SM, ☎ (020) 6100622;
  services in Dutch with English translation.
- **Crossroads Christian Community** (Eucumenical), Piet Mondriaanstraat 140,
  1061 TT Amsterdam-West and various other locations, ☎ (020) 545 1444, www.xrds.nl
- ***Deutsche Evangelische Gemeinde**, Viottastraat 44, ☎ (020) 673 2522
- **English Reformed Church** (Presbyterian), Begijnhof 48, ☎ (020) 624 9665,
  www.begijnhofamsterdam.nl
- **First Church of Christ Scientist**, R. Wagnerstraat 32, ☎ (020) 662 7438

- **Friends Center (Quakers)** Vossiusstraat 20, 1071 AD, ☎ (020) 679 4238; services in Dutch with English translation.
- ***Liberal Catholic Church,** Deurloostraat 17, ☎ (020) 664 0854
- ***Liberal Jewish Community,** Jacob Soetendorpstraat 8, 1079 RM, ☎ (020) 642 3562
- ***Portuguese Synagogue**, Mr. Visserplein 3, ☎ (020) 624 5351
- ***Synagogue**, van Boechhorststraat 26, 1081 BT, ☎ (020) 646 0046, www.nihs.nl
- **Unitarian Universalist Fellowship**, Keizersgrachtkerk, Keizersgracht 566,
  ☎ (020) 470 4647

The Hague:
- **American Protestant Church,** Esther de Boer van Rijklaan 20, 2597 TJ,
  ☎ (070) 324 4490, www.apch.nl
- **Church of Jesus Christ of Latter Day Saints**, Leersumstraat 13, 2546 TE,
  ☎ (070) 329 3531
- **Church of St. John and St. Philip** (Anglican & Episcopal), Ary van de Spuiweg 1,
  ☎ (070) 355 5359, www.stjohn-stphilip.org
- **Church of St. James,** English church in British School in Voorschoten, Jan van Hooflaan 3, 2252 BG Voorschoten, ☎ (071) 561 1528, www.stjames.nl
- **Church of our Saviour**, English-speaking Roman Catholic Parish, Parish House, Ruychrocklaan 126, ☎ (070) 328 0816, www.parish.nl
- ***First Church of Christ Scientist**, Andries Bickerweg 1a, ☎ (070) 351 5032
- ***Liberal Jewish Congregation,** Prinsessegracht 26, 2514 AP, ☎ (070) 365 6893
- ***Orthodox Jewish Congregation**, Cornelis Houtmanstraat 11, 2593 RD,
  ☎ (070) 347 3201
- **Society of Friends (Quakers)** Stadhouderslaan 8, ☎ (071) 561 7461
- **Trinity Baptist Church**, Gruttolaan 23, 2261 ET Leidschendam, ☎ (070) 517 8024, www.trinitychurch-nl.com

Leiden:
- **Unitarian Universalist Fellowship**, International House, Rapenburg 6, ☎ (071) 514 0988 (every fourth Sunday).
- ***Pieterskerk** (Dutch Reformed), Pieterskerkhof 1a, ☎ (071) 512 43 19, www.pieterskerk.com (Only on American Thanksgiving Day is the service in English.)

Rotterdam:
- ***Christian Science Society Rotterdam**, Kraaiheide 38, ☎ (010) 421 5718
- **Church of English-speaking Catholics**, Leduinastraat 10, ☎ (010) 414 3384
- **Church of Jesus Christ of Latter Day Saints**, Oosteinde 73, ☎ (010) 414 9883
- ***Deutsche Evangelische Gemeinde,** 's Gravendijkwal 65, ☎ (010) 477 2070
- ***Eglise Wallone de Rotterdam**, Schiedamsevest 119, ☎ (010) 412 4779
- ***Greek Orthodox Church**, Westzeedijk 333, ☎ (010) 436 1798
- ***Orthodox Synagogue**, A.B.N. Davidsplein 4, ☎ (010) 466 9765
- ***Russian Orthodox Church**, Persijnstraat 16, ☎ (010) 477 1272

- **Scots International Church** (Presbyterian), Schiedamsevest 121, ☎ (010) 412 4779, www.scotsintchurch.com
- **St. Mary's Church** (Church of England), Pieter de Hoochweg 133, ☎ (010) 220 2474
- **★Suomen Merimieskirkko**, 's Gravendijkwal 64, ☎ (010) 436 6164

For a complete list of English language church services: www.wav.nl/scw/churches

Clubs and organisations

The following is a selection of clubs and useful organisations of particular interest to foreign residents. For more information on Women's Clubs in the Randstad area, see Chapter 16; for Youth Clubs and Organisations, see Chapter 17.

▶ **English-speaking clubs**
- American Women's Clubs, general, www.fawco.org
  - Amsterdam, ☎ 020 644 35 31, www.awca.nl
  - The Hague, ☎ 070 350 60 07, www.awcthehague.org
- American Netherlands Club Rotterdam, www.ancorotterdam.com
- American Chamber of Commerce, ☎ (020) 795 1840, www.amcham.nl
- Amsterdam-American Business Club, ☎ (020) 520 7534, www.aabc.nl
- The Rotterdam American Business Club, www.rabc.nl
- Australian & New Zealand Women's Club, The Hague, ☎ (070) 317 9881, www.anzwc.nl
- Australians in Holland, www.coolabah.com/oz/hollandsite
- Australians Abroad, www.australiansabroad.com
- Australian Business in Europe, www.abie.com.au
- AFNORTH International Club, ☎ (045) 527 4273, www.usagschinnen.eur.army.mil/sites/about/communityactivities.asp
- Amersfoort British Club, ☎ (033) 472 3941
- British Clubs
  - The Hague, ☎ (070) 346 1973, www.bwclubthehague.demon.nl
  - Amersfoort, ☎ (033) 472 3941
  - Utrecht, ☎ (030) 210 0371
- British Society of Amsterdam, Amsterdam, ☎ (020) 624 8629, www.britishsocietyofamsterdam.org
- CADS (Commercial Anglo Dutch Society), ☎ (0546) 823 244
- Canadian Women's Club of The Hague, ☎ (070) 326 4488, http://groups.msn.com/CanadianWomensLeagueoftheNetherlands-Membership
- The Canadian Expatriates Club of Amsterdam (CECA), www.spetz.ca/CECA.html

- **Commonwealth Club,** The Hague and Rotterdam, ☎ (010) 422 0458
- **Connect International,** Groningen, ☎ (050) 521 4541, www.connect-int.org
- **Connecting Women,** The Hague, ☎ (070) 365 2543, www.connectingwomen.nl
- **Club of Amsterdam,** www.clubofamsterdam.com
- **English Language Bond of Women,** Dordrecht, ☎ (078) 618 3681
- **English Speaking Ladies Club,** Uithoorn, ☎ (029) 756 5274, www.geocities.com/eslcsite
- **English Speaking Contact Group**, Haarlem, www.englishhaarlem.nl
- **English Speaking Community in the Netherlands**, www.elynx.nl
- **E.L.B.O.W.**, Dordrecht, ☎ (078) 618 3681, http://home.wanadoo.nl/elbow
- **Expat Lions Club**, The Hague, ☎ (070) 350 8693, info@lions.nl
  - **Lions Club Maastricht**, www.lionsmaastrichtmondial.nl
  - **Lions Club The Hague Universal**, Rijswijk, ☎ (070) 394 8370
- **Foreign Exchange** (Nijmegen/Arnhem region), www.fexchange.net
- **Hash House Harriers Amsterdam**, www.harrier.nl
- **Hash House Harriers The Hague**, www.haguehash.nl
- **Hash House International**, www.halfmind.com
- **International Contact**, The Hague, ☎ (070) 383 0858
- **International Business Club Eindhoven**, www.ibuc.nl
- **International Women's Club of The Hague**, ☎ (070) 355 8863, www.lwcthehague.nl
- **International Women's Contact**
  - Amsterdam, ☎ (0297) 56 3027, www.euronet.nl/users/iwc_amst
  - Breda, ☎ (076) 597 1357, www.iwcbreda.nl
  - Eindhoven, ☎ (040) 253 9699, www.iwce.nl
  - South Limburg, ☎ (043) 325 4353, www.iwc-sl.nl
  - The Hague, ☎ (070) 355 8863, www.iwcthehague.nl
  - Utrecht/Amersfoort, ☎ (033) 461 4356, www.iwcu.non-profit.nl
  - Maastricht, ☎ 043 321 54 69, website: www.iwc-sl.nl
- **International Cultural Exchange Group (I.C.E.)**, http://uk.groups.yahoo.com/group/ice_thehague
- **In-Touch**, Rotterdam, www.intouchnl.com
- **Irish Club of the Netherlands**, The Hague, ☎ (070) 427 7123, www.irishclub.nl
- **International Yacht Club**, The Hague, ☎ (070) 324 5134, or ACCESS
- **My Haarlem**, social network for professionals in Holland, www.myhaarlem.com
- **Paddyish Irish Club of Amsterdam,** ☎ (035) 685 0344, www.egroups.com/group/PADDYISH
- **The John Adams Institute**, Amsterdam, ☎ (020) 624 7280, www.john-adams.nl
- **The Netherlands England Society**
  - National contact ☎ (071) 561 5209, www.nederlandengeland.nl
  - Amsterdam, ☎ (075) 616 9936
  - Utrecht, ☎ (030) 699 1618
  - The Hague, ☎ (070) 324 7888,

- Netherlands-India Association, www.netherlands-india.nu
- Network-Club, ☎ (0522) 49 1100, www.network-club.com
- Noordwijk & District Ladies' Club, Noordwijk, ☎ (025) 237 6750
- North Holland International Friendship Club, www.nhifc.org
- Pickwick Women's Club, Rotterdam, ☎ (010) 452 6949, www.3kleur.nl/pickwick/index.pickwickclub.htm
- Petroleum Wives Club, The Hague, ☎ (070) 517 7629, www.pwc-thehague.com
- Rotary International, Amsterdam, ☎ (020) 549 1440, www.amsterdamrotary.org
- Rotary International, The Hague, www.rotary.nl
- Rotary Utrecht, www.ikzie.org
- Royal Air Force Association Amsterdam Branch, ☎ (020) 696 0133,
- www.britian.nl (See Defence pages – link to RAFA icon)
- Russian Community in The Netherlands, ☎ 0900 90 90 000, www.ruscom.nl
- Russian Netherlands Friendship, ☎ (030) 29 44023, www.rus-ned.nl
- The Randstad Harings Diving Club, www.randstad-harings.demon.nl
- Singapore-Netherlands Association, ☎ 010 511 4400, www.sna-nl.org
- South African Women's Club, The Hague, ☎ (070) 328 1512, www.sawcnl.com
- South Africa Club, www.southafricaclub.nl
- St. Andrew's Society of the Netherlands, Wassenaar, ☎ (070) 511 8151, www.standrews.nl
- Scottish Coalition, http://scottish-coalition.org
- Royal Scottish Dance – The Hague District, (information on other dance groups), ☎ (070) 320 2352
- Scandinavia Club, ☎ (070) 352 1193, www.clubscandinavia.com
- Swedish Women's International Network SWEA, ☎ (0343) 516 122,
- www.chapters-swea.org/holland
- Twente Expatriates Club, Enschede, ☎ (053) 484 9649
- Women's International Network, ☎ (020) 683 8862, www.womensinternational.net
- UFDA (United Filipino Dutch Association), ☎ (023) 539 6312
- L'Amitie Club, ☎ (070) 383 4433 or French Embassy.
- Japanese Club, ☎ (023) 545 2415 or Japanese Embassy.
- German Clubs, ☎ (020) 531 2900, www.goethe.org

▶ **English-speaking art clubs**
- The Decorative & Fine Arts Society (DFAS) of The Hague, Popular, high quality, monthly lecture program, ☎ (070) 517 9003
- International Art Club, Nieuwe Schoolstraat 22B, 2514 HZ The Hague, ☎ (070) 362 3347, www.nadfas.org.uk
- Images International Photo Club, The Hague, ☎ (070) 354 5964, www.imagesphotoclub.com

▶ **Theatre**
  – **Leiden English-Speaking Theatre Group (LEST),** Hooglandskerkgracht 20a, Leiden,
    ☎ (071) 513 0002, www.feats.org
  – **Anglo-American Theater Group (AATG),** P.O. Box 10239, 2501 HE The Hague,
    ☎ (070) 394 5988, www.aatg.nl
  – **American Repertory Theater (ART),** Rozengracht 117, 1016 LP Amsterdam,
    ☎ (020) 627 6162, www.amrep.org
  – **Theatre Works Amsterdam,** various locations, ☎ (020) 471 5636,
    www.theaterworksamsterdam.nl
  – **STET - Stichting The English Theatre,** ☎ 06 300 500 18,
    the-english-theatre@wanadoo.nl
  – **International Drama Group of English Speaking Associates (I.D.E.A),**
    ☎ (078) 617 0465, www.idea-panto.nl
  – **In-Players International Drama Group,** Amsterdam, ☎ (020) 770 4984,
    www.inplayers.org
  – **The Stadhouderij Theater Company,** Bloemgracht 57/1, Amsterdam, ☎ (020) 626 4088

▶ **Song**
  – **The British Choir of The Hague,** www.cecilia-choir.com
  – **Sweet Adelines International,** www.sweetadelines.nl

▶ **Communications**
  – **Words in Here.** Poetry collective showcasing contributors works. Writers' workshops
    and 'Versal' magazine. ☎ (020) 465 1860, www.wordsinhere.com
  – **Society of English-Native-Speaking Editors (SENSE),** www.sense-online.nl
  – **Toastmasters International,**
    – Amsterdam, www.toastmasters.nl
    – The Hague, www.toastmasters.nl/thehague (also info for Rotterdam)
  – **International Training in Communication (ITC),** www.itcintl.com

▶ **English-speaking comedy theatre**
  – **Boom Chicago.** Not cabaret, and not stand-up, Boom Chicago is a mix of sketches
    and pure improvisation. Innovative visuals and music from first-class VJ's, DJ's
    and musicians make for a unique evening out. Boom Chicago is situated in the
    Leidseplein Theatre in Amsterdam, on never-dull Leidseplein, at no. 12. Dinner
    available; shows almost every night. Tickets and reservations, ☎ (020) 423 0101,
    www.boomchicago.nl (See ad on page 40.)
  – **Without Ties.** Comedy trio of UK/USA humour performing weekly at the **Comedy
    Café** on the Max Euweplein 43-45, in Amsterdam, ☎ (020) 638 3971,
    www.withoutties.com

- **Theatre Diligentia.** English-speaking performances, music and comedy in the beautifully restored Theatre Diligenta in The Hague, ☎ 0900 414 4104, www.theater-diligentia

▶ **General information**
- **Outpost, Expat Info. Centre,** ☎ (070) 377 6530, www.outpostthehague.com
- **EXPATICA,** information, news and events, www.expatica.com (See ad on page 379.)
- **ACCESS,** Herengracht 472 (2nd floor), 1017 CA Amsterdam, ☎ (020) 423 3217, and Plein 24, 2511 CS The Hague, ☎ (070) 346 2525, www.access-nl.org (See ad on page 455.)

▶ **Sports**
- **The American Baseball Foundation,** (ABF), www.abfsport.nl
- **Amsterdam Gaelic Athletic Club,** www.amsterdamgac.com
- **Basketball Association BS Leiden,** ☎ (071) 528 9821
- **American Football Club Zwolle Warriors,** www.zwolle-warriors.dds.nl
- **De Kieviten Cricket Club,** www.kieviten.nl/cricket
- **Hilversum Cricket Club,** ☎ (035) 623 3930
- **Voorburg Cricket Club,** ☎ (070) 320 2905
- **Te Werve Rugby Club** (The Hague), www.tewerve-rugby.com
- **Utrecht Rugby Club,** www.tte.nl/urc
- **PGS/VOGEL Football Club,** ☎ (062) 705 1820
- **International Rugby Club of Amsterdam,** Amstelveen, www.arcrugby.com
- **Den Haag GAA Club - Gaelic Athletic Association,** www.geocities.com/DenHaagGAA
- **Eerste Hollandse Drakenboot Club - First Dutch Dragon Boat Club,** www.beckwith.demon.nl/ehdc

Nationwide Emergency Number ☎ 112

▶ **Police / Fire / Ambulance**
Central National Police Information, ☎ 0900 8844, www.politie.nl
To contact the fire department, Emergencies: 112; www.brandweer.nl

Holidays

Public Holidays: New Year's Day, Good Friday, Easter Sunday and Monday, Queen's Birthday (April 30), Ascension Day, Whit Sunday and Monday, Christmas, Boxing Day (day after Christmas). Shops closed except on Good Friday morning.

Remembrance Days are not public holidays; most shops are open: May 4 - WW II Remembrance Day; May 5 - Liberation Day.

NBTC – Netherlands Board Of Tourism and Conventions

Head Office: **Nederlands Bureau voor Toerisme**, Vlietweg 15, 2266 KA Leidschendam. Not for private queries or requests for publications. You will enjoy their website, however: www.nbtc.nl

Hotel and other reservations

NRC (**Netherlands Reservation Centre**), www.hotelres.nl, will handle your reservations by e-mail, while hotel, theatre, concert or other reservations can be made through the closest VVV office. (See list at the end of this section.)

Public transportation information

Call 0900 9292 (€ 0.75 cents per minute)

Telephone assistance

Information within NL:	☎ 1888 (€ 1.30 p.m.)
	☎ (0900) 8008 (operator assistance)
Information outside NL:	☎ (0900) 8418
Telegram:	☎ (0800) 0409
Customer Service:	☎ (0800) 0402
Operator Assistance:	☎ (0800) 0410
Repairs:	☎ (0800) 0407

VVV offices in Holland

VVV: Vereinigingen voor Vreemdelingenverkeer – Local tourist assistance offices. Most offices are open at least from Monday to Friday, 9am-5pm and on Saturdays from 10am-noon. During the holiday season, some are also open in the evening and on Sunday afternoons. They have much information on touring, and will make hotel, theatre and tour reservations. All numbers below beginning with a '0900' prefix are toll calls, charging from 50 to 100 cents a minute. Unfortunately, more and more of these numbers have become '0900.'

> ### For a complete up-to-date listing of all 408 VVV offices (and new ones!) in the country, see: www.vvv.nl

- **Alkmaar,** Waagplein 2-3, (072) 511 4284, North Holland, www.vvvalkmaar.nl
- **Almelo,** Rosa Luxemburgstraat 8, (0546) 818 765, Overijssel, www.vvvalmelo.nl
- **Almere,** Randstaad 2117, (036) 533 4600, Flevoland
- **Amersfoort,** Stationsplein 9-11, 0900 1122364, Utrecht, www.amersfoortyourway.nl

- **Amstelveen,** Stadsplein 102, (020) 6414126, North Holland, www.vvvamstelveen.nl
- **Amsterdam,** Stationsplein 10, 0900 4004040, North Holland, www.vvvamsterdam.nl
- **Apeldoorn,** Stationsstraat 72, (055) 526 0200, Gelderland, www.vvvapeldoorn.nl
- **Arnhem,** Stationsplein 45, 0900 21122344, Gelderland, www.vvvarnhem.nl
- **Assen,** Marktstraat 8, 0900 2022393, Drenthe, www.vvvassen.nl
- **Bergen aan Zee,** Plein 1, (072) 581 3100, North Holland, www.vvvbergen.com
- **Bergen op Zoom,** Grote Markt 1, (0164) 277 482, Brabant, www.bergenopzoom.nl
- **Breda,** Willemstraat 17-19, 0900 522 2444, Brabant, www.vvvbreda.nl
- **Delft,** Markt 85, (015) 212 6100, South Holland, www.zuid-holland.com
- **Den Haag,** (see 'Hague')
- **Den Helder,** Bernhardplein 18, (0223) 625 544, North Holland, www.vvvkopvannoordholland.nl
- **Deventer,** Keizerstraat 22, 0900 353 5355, Overijssel, www.vvvdeventer.nl
- **Doetinchem,** IJsselkade 30, (0314) 323 355, Gelderland, www.vvvdoetinchem.nl
- **Dordrecht,** Stationsweg 1, 0900 4636 888, South Holland, www.vvvdordrecht.nl
- **Drachten,** Museumplein 4 , (0512) 517 771, Friesland
- **Ede,** Molenstraat 80b, 0900 835893, Gelderland, www.vvvede.nl
- **Egmond a/zee,** Voorstraat 82a, (072) 581 3100, North Holland, www.vvvegmond.nl
- **Eindhoven,** Stationsplein 17, 0900 112 2363, Brabant, www.vvveindhoven.nl
- **Elburg,** Ledige Stede 31, (0525) 681 520, Gelderland
- **Emmen,** Hoofdstraat 22, 0900 2022393, Drenthe
- **Enschede,** Stationsplein 1/A, (053) 432 3200, Overijssel, www.vvvenschede.nl
- **Epe,** Pasteur Somstraat 6, (0578) 612 696, Gelderland, www.vvvenschede.nl
- **Gouda,** Markt 27, 0900 468 3288, South Holland, www.vvvgouda.nl
- **Groningen,** Grote Markt 25, 0900 202 3050, Groningen, www.groningen.nl
- **Haarlem,** Stationsplein 1, 0900 616 1600, North Holland, www.vvvzk.nl
- **Hague, The,** Hofweg 1, 0900 3403 505 , South Holland, www.denhaag.com
- **Harderwijk,** Bleek 102, (0341) 426 666, Gelderland, www.vvvharderwijk.nl
- **Heerlen,** Oranje Nassaustraat 16, 0900 9798, Limburg, www.vvvzuidlimburg.nl
- **Helmond,** Markt 33, (0492) 543 155, Brabant, www.vvvhelmond.nl
- **Hengelo,** Nieuwstraat 59, (074) 242 1120, Overijssel, www.vvvhengelo.nl
- **'s Hertogenbosch,** Markt 77, 0900 1122334, Brabant, www.regio-vvv.nl
- **Hilversum,** Kerkbrink 6, (035) 629 2810, North Holland, www.vvvhilversum.nl
- **Hoogeveen,** Hoofdstraat 13, (0528) 268 373, Drenthe, www.vvvhoogeveen.nl
- **IJmuiden,** Plein 1945 - 105, (0255) 515 611, North Holland, www.vvvzk.nl
- **Katwijk,** Voorstraat 41, 0900 222 2333, South Holland, www.vvvkatwijk.nl
- **Leeuwarden,** Sophialaan 4, 0900 202 4060, Friesland, www.vvvleeuwarden.nl
- **Leiden,** Stationsplein 2D, 0900 222 2333, South Holland, www.vvvleiden.nl
- **Lelystad,** Stationsplein 186, (0320) 243 444 , Flevoland
- **Lisse,** Grachtweg 53, 0900 222 2333, South Holland, www.vvvlisse.nl

- **Lochem/Laren & Barchum,** Tramstraat 4 (Lochem), (0573) 251 898, Gelderland, www.vvvlochem.nl
- **Maastricht,** Kleine Staat 1, (043) 325 2121, Limburg, www.vvvmaastricht.nl
- **Meppel,** Kromme Elleboog 2, (0522) 252 888, Drenthe, www.vvvmeppel.nl
- **Middelburg ,** Nieuwe Burg 40, (0118) 659 900, Zeeland, www.vvvzeeland.nl
- **Noordoostpolder,** De Deel 25a, Emmeloord, (0527) 612 000, Flevoland, www.vvvnoordoostpolder.nl
- **Noordwijk,** De Grent 8, 0900 222 2333, South Holland , www.vvvnoordwijk.nl
- **Nunspeet,** Stationsplein 1, 0900 253 0411, Gelderland, www.vvvnunspeet.nl
- **Nijmegen,** Keizer Karelplein 2, 0900 1122344, Gelderland, www.vvvnijmegen.nl
- **Oisterwijk,** Spoorlaan 82D, (013) 528 2345, Brabant, www.regio-vvv.nl
- **Oosterhout,** Bowlingplein 1, 0900 202 2550, Brabant, www.vvvoosterhout.nl
- **Oss,** Spoorlaan 24, (0412) 633 604, Brabant, www.regio-vvv.nl
- **Putten,** Kerkplein 15, (0341) 351 777, Gelderland, www.vvvputten.nl
- **Roermond,** Kraanpoort 1, 0900 2025588, Limburg, www.lekker-genieten.nl
- **Roosendaal,** Markt 71, (0165) 554 400, Brabant, www.vvvroosendaal.nl
- **Rotterdam,** Coolsingel 67, 0900 4034065, South Holland, www.vvv.rotterdam.nl
- **Scheveningen,** Gev. Deynootweg 1134, 0900 340 3505, South Holland, www.scheveningen.nl
- **Schiedam,** Rotterdamsedijk 441, 0900 119 2192, South Holland, www.waterweg-westland.nl
- **Schoonhoven,** Stadhuisstraat 1, (0182) 385 009, South Holland, www.vvvschoonhoven.nl
- **Sittard,** Rosmolenstraat 2, 0900 9798, Limburg, www.vvvzuidlimburg.nl
- **Sneek,** Marktstraat 18, (0515) 414 096, Friesland, www.vvvsneek.nl
- **Texel,** Emmalaan 66/den Burg, (0222) 312 847, North Holland, www.texel.net
- **Tiel,** Korenbeursplein 4 , (0344) 616 441, Gelderland, www.tiel.nl
- **Tilburg,** Spoorlaan 364, 0900 202 0815, Brabant , www.vvvtilburg.nl
- **Utrecht,** Domplein 9, 0900 128 8732, Utrecht, www.utrechtyourway.nl
- **Valkenburg,** Th. Dorrenplein 5, 0900 97 98, Limburg , www.vvvzuidlimburg.nl
- **Venlo,** Koninginneplein 2, (077) 354 3800, Limburg , www.lekker-genieten.nl
- **Vlaardingen,** Westhavenkade 39, 0900 119 2192, South Holland, www.waterweg-westland.nl
- **Vlissingen,** Oude Markt 3, 0900 2020280, Zeeland, www.vvvzeeland.nl
- **Weert,** Maasstraat 18, (0495) 536 800, Limburg, www.lekker-genieten.nl
- **Winterswijk,** Markt 17a, (0543) 512 302, Gelderland
- **Zaandam,** Ebbehout 31, 0900 400 4040, North Holland, www.amsterdamtourist.nl
- **Zandvoort,** Schoolplein 1, (023) 571 7947, North Holland, www.vvvzk.nl
- **Zeist,** Slotlaan 24, 0900 1091013, Utrecht, www.vvvzeist.nl
- **Zutphen,** Stationsplein 39, 0900 269 288, Gelderland, www.vvvzutphen.nl
- **Zwolle,** Grote Kerkplein 15 , 0900 112 2375, Overijssel, www.vvvzwolle.nl

Recommended reading

▶ **Introduction/background books**

- *The Holland Handbook*, Xpat Media, 2007 (annually), the complete reference book for international residents – a virtual encyclopedia of all you need to know about living and working in the Netherlands. A must-have for 'expats.' www.xpat.nl
- *Housing in Holland*, Xpat Media, 2007, everything about housing, renting, and buying in Holland, www.housinginholland.nl
- *Minding your Manners – A Guide to Dutch Business and Social Etiquette*, Magda Berman, Tirion, 2006, www.hollandbooks.nl
- *Dealing with the Dutch* – 3rd edition/14th update, by Jacob Vossestein, KIT Publishers, 2004, www.kit.nl
- *Living with the Dutch,* by Norean Sharpe, KIT Publishers, 2005, www.kit.nl
- *At Home in Holland*, by the American Women's Club of The Hague, 2005
- *Culture Shock! Netherlands*, by Hunt Janin, 1998
- *How To Be Happy In Holland*, by George Pogany, 1995
- *Live & Work in Belgium, the Netherlands & Luxembourg*, by Andre De Vries, 1998
- *Living and Working in the Netherlands*, by Pat Rush, UK, 2001
- *Simple Guide To Holland, Customs and Etiquette*, by Mark Hooker, 1997
- *The Xenophobe's Guide to the Dutch*, by Rodney Bolt, 1995
- *Country Review, Netherlands 1998/1999*, by Robert Kelly, editor, 1998
- *Daily Life In Rembrandt's Holland*, by Paul Zumthor, 1994
- *D is for Dutch - An Insider's Holland*, by Jules Faber, 1973
- *The Dutch Puzzle*, by Duke de Baena, 1966
- *The Dutch Republic In The Seventeenth Century*, J.L. Price, 1998
- *The Dutch Today*, by Frank E. Huggett, 1974
- *The Dutch Republic: Its Rise, Greatness, and Fall 1477-1806*, by Jonathan I. Israel, Oxford University Press, 1998
- *Embarrassment of Riches: An Interpretation of Dutch Culture in the Golden Age*, by S. Schama, 1987
- *The Hiding Place*, by Corrie ten Boom, 1970, 1986, 2005 (35th anniversary print)
- *History of the Low Countries*, by J.C.H. Blom, editor, 1999
- *The Hunger Winter: Occupied Holland 1944-1945*, by Henri Van Der Zee, 1998
- *The Low Sky: Understanding the Dutch*, by Han van der Horst, 1996
- *Of Dutch Ways*, by Helen Colijn, 1992
- *A Short History of the Netherlands*, by Rietbergen, Bekking Publishers, 1998
- *The Undutchables*, by Colin White and Laurie Bourke, 1996
- *Victims and Survivors: The Nazi Persecution of the Jews in the Netherlands 1940-1945*, by Bob Moore, 1998
- *My 'Dam Life*, by Sean Condon, 2003

▶ **Art books**
- *Art and Commerce in the Dutch Golden Age: A Social History of Seventeenth-Century Netherlandish Painting*, by Michael North, 1997
- *Dawn of the Golden Age: Northern Netherlandish Art 1580-1620*, by Ariane Van Suchtelen, et.al., 1994
- *De Stijl*, by Paul Overy, 1991
- *Dutch Painting 1600-1800*, by Seymour Slive, 1995
- *Land of Skies and Water*, by Felix Faure, Lemniscat, 1996
- *The Low Skies in Pictures*, published by Scriptum 1998, photography
- *Vermeer*, by Lawrence Gowing, et.al., 1997
- *A Worldly Art: The Dutch Republic 1585-1718*, by Mariet Westerman, 1996

▶ **Cookbooks**
- *Food Shoppers Guide to Holland*, Ada Henne Koene, Eburon, 2006
- *The Art of Dutch Cooking*, by C. Countess Van Limburg Stirum, 1997
- *Dutch Cooking*, by A.M. Halverhout, 1990
- *Dutch Delight*, Sylvia Pessireron, N&L Publishing, 2005
- *Edna Eby Heller Dutch Cookbook*, by Edna Eby Heller, 1960
- *Let's Go Dutch Again: A Second Treasury of Dutch Cuisine*, by Johanna Bates& Jan Walrabenstein, 1994

▶ **Children's books**
- *Netherlands*, by Pat Seward, Cultures of the World Series, 1995
- *The Cow Who Fell into the Canal*, Phyllis Krasilovsky, 1997
- *The Netherlands*, by Ronald Seth, Major World Nations Series, 1997
- *Netherlands In Pictures*, Visual Geography Series, 1992
- *Rembrandt and Seventeenth-Century Holland: The Dutch Nation and Its Painters*, Claudio Pescio, 1995, 9-12 year olds
- *Van Gogh: Art and Emotion*, by David Spence, Tessa Krailing, 1997, 9-12 year olds
- *Unlocking the Secret of Otherland – A Story and Activity Book for Children Living Abroad*, Mieke M.E. Janssen-Matthes, KIT Publishers, 2006, www.kit.nl

▶ **Guidebooks**
- *Backroads of Holland*, by Helen Colijn, 1992
- *Cycling The Netherlands, Belgium and Luxembourg*, by Katherine Widing, 1998
- *Fodor's Holland*, by Fodor's Travel, a division of Random House, Inc., NY (regular updates)
- *Michelin Tourist Guide to the Netherlands*, by Michelin (regular updates)
- *Nederland Museumland*, text in Dutch, but lists all the museums in detail. For the serious museum-goer, updated annually

▶ Maps

- *ANWB Noord, Zuid and Midden Maps* to the scale 1:200 000 ... clear, with indications to show interesting buildings, churches, convents, windmills, Megalithic tombs, castles, ruins, lighthouses, etc.
- *ANWB Stratenatlas*, handy book with street maps of all Dutch cities
- *De Complete Stratengids van Nederland*, every road in the country, in one thick book
- *The Tourist Atlas of Holland*, an Intermap bv Production, available from NBTC or VVV offices ... spiral form in English, German and Dutch editions ... recreation and leisure in 20 maps
- *Stedenboek van Nederland*, published by Falk, a collection of maps of Dutch cities in one convenient-sized book

▶ Publications (in English)

- *ACCESS Newsletter*, Plein 24, 2511 CS Den Haag, ☎ (070) 346 2525, bi-monthly. www.access-nl.org (See ad on page 455.)
- *The XPat Journal*, Van Essen Publishing, Van Boetzelaerlaan 153, 2581 AR The Hague, ☎ (070) 306 3310, www.xpat.nl, excellent, informative quarterly magazine about 'expat' life in the Netherlands. *The XPat Journal* has been keeping expats informed since 1998, covering issues related to working, housing, legal and financial, education, daily life, health care, art, culture, events, book reviews and more. The website www.xpat.nl is a great resource with links and addresses for many organisations of interest to foreigners, as well as cultural and business events and an online archive with the possibility to purchase back issues. With a circulation of 10,000 copies, *The XPat Journal* is without a doubt the best-read magazine for internationals in the know! Keep informed by ordering your own subscription from the expat-specialised publisher and premier source of information for Holland's international community. (See ad on page 455.)
- *XPat Media*, Publisher XPat Media has some of the best books about Holland on offer, available from their online web shop, www.hollandbooks.nl, as well as from local bookshops and annual expat fairs. Most popular is the annual *Holland Handbook*, a rich encyclopedia of living and working in NL, with contributions from more than 30 professionals. *Housing in Holland* tells you everything you need to know about renting or buying, www.housinginholland.nl, while other titles include *The Low Sky; The Food Shoppers Guide to Holland; Living with the Dutch; Dealing with the Dutch;* and *Minding Your Manners*. Top-notch books, several of which are known for their photography, and the aerial views in *High over Holland*. (See ad on page 38.)
- *The Amsterdam-Hague-Rotterdam Times,* www.thehollandtimes.nl – Distributed free in Amsterdam, The Hague and Rotterdam. (See ad on page 38.) *The Amsterdam Times* was launched in 2004 as the first English-language newspaper in NL, aimed at expats, tourists and business visitors. The Hague and Rotterdam Times pages were added later that same year, and now form a collective, printed weekly, and also available

online as *The Holland Times*, www.hollandtimes.nl, covering local and national Dutch news, cultural events, sports, and entertainment, with frequent in-depth interviews. 600 distribution points; subscriptions available. Published by Argopress.

– **Amsterdam Weekly**, www.amsterdamweekly.com – free, with cultural and events news. Read PDF issue online. (See ad on page 74.) Launched in 2004, *Amsterdam Weekly* is a free paper offering a critical guide to arts and entertainment. Inspired by alternative publications such as the *Chicago Reader* and New York's *Village Voice*, *Amsterdam Weekly* has been honoured with six European Newspaper Awards of Excellence in three categories. Print and online versions include an agenda of music, clubs, film, art and events. Practical but quirky classifieds. Nearly 700 distribution points in Amsterdam proper, as well as the Zuid-Oost area and Amstelveen.

▶ Websites

– **Dutch News.nl**, www.dutchnews.nl, news in English everyday at 4 o'clock. *Dutch News.nl* is a free, online, daily round-up of each day's main Dutch news, in English. Punchy and to the point. Sign up to receive it by e-mail via www.dutchnews.nl. Classifieds and 'What's On' calendar also. (See ad on page 381.)

– **Expatica**, www.expatica.com, online news, information and events. Expatica's website is the best place to start (or end) your day, with concise daily news and articles about living and working in NL, including a helpful employment portal and housing section. Each October they present 'I am not a Tourist,' the Expatica Welcome to the Netherlands Fair, in Amsterdam, offering a full day of information stands, workshops, speakers, books and more.

Their free, annual *Expatica Survival Guide* is filled with tips and information for newcomers. Regular events include speed-dating, wine tasting, and Halloween and Valentine parties. You needn't go alone, as they also offer an online dating site. (See ad on page 379.)

– **TheHagueOnLine,** www.thehagueonline.com, community news for The Hague and region. An excellent way to keep on top of everything that's going on, this daily English-language website informs the international community in and around The Hague about national and local news, upcoming social and cultural events, clubs, associations, business initiatives, goods and services, charity events and more. Also runs a Social Club, offering at least four events every month, providing many wonderful opportunities to meet other people while having fun or learning something new. The two weekly newsletters, 'Arts & Entertainment' and 'Weekly News,' give information on leisure, dining, sports and much more. In September, TheHagueOnLine co-organises (with ACCESS) the annual **Feel at Home in The Hague – The International Fair**, a one-day event introducing expats to a variety of local organisations, services, goods and activities.

TheHagueOnline is the gateway to the growing expatriate and international community, currently estimated at 50,000 in The Hague region alone.

TheHagueOnline is the gateway to the growing expatriate and international community, currently estimated at 50,000 in The Hague region alone. (See ad on page 108.)

– **Underwater Amsterdam**, www.underwateramsterdam.com, online guide to the city created by Amsterdam British resident Pip Farquharson, with events, what's on, short tips and more.

▸ Entertainment publications

Distributed in hotels, VVV offices, etc...monthly

– **In Amsterdam:** Uitkrant lists theatre, concerts and other entertainment, www.uitkrant.nl, and www.amsterdamsuitburo.nl
For English text: www.iamsterdam.com

– **In The Hague:** *Den Haag Agenda*, Dutch and English Text; monthly events in The Hague, Scheveningen and Kijkduin. www.haagsuitburo.nl

– **In Rotterdam:** *R'Uit* magazine covers Rotterdam's films, theatrical and artistic events, in Dutch. www.rotterdamsuitburo.nl

▸ ACCESS publications

– www.access-nl.org, Plein 24, 2511 CS The Hague, ☎ (070) 346 2525
– Herengracht 472 (2nd floor), 1017 CA Amsterdam, ☎ (020) 423 3217
– *ACCESS Guide to Healthcare in the Netherlands*
– *ACCESS Babies and Toddlers*, information on having a baby and raising a child in Holland
– *Working in The Netherlands*, information on finding work in the Netherlands
– *ACCESS Information Calendar*, 16-month calendar published annually
– *ACCESS Fact Sheets*, helpful information on a variety of subjects

All of these publications, as well as other books and fact sheets on living and working in the Netherlands, and the ACCESS magazine may be ordered online through the website bookshop. (See ad on page 455.)

▸ Radio

– **Expat Radio International** is broadcast from the VLOK studios in Katwijk, near The Hague, on 88.1 cable or 106.8 FM (for Katijk Valkenburg areas), live on Wednesdays from 8pm-10pm with a repeat on Friday 10am-noon. Run by volunteers. www.radiointernational.tk

– **BBC Radio**, www.bbc.co.uk/radio

– **Radio Netherlands**, www.radionetherlands.nl, English-language broadcasts

– **Radio America**, www.radioamerica.org

Index

A

Aalsmeer 60
Aardenburg (Z) 339
Abdij, Middelburg (Z) 329
ABN AMRO 2, 362, 363
ACCESS 362, 367, 368
Adriaan Windmill 65
Aduard (Gr) 261
Aerdt (G) 187
Afferden (L) 299
Afsluitdijk (Enclosing Dike) 77, 239
Agrarisch en Wagenmuseum 78
Air travel 25
Aldfaers Erf Route 240
Alida Hoeve 88
Alkmaar 71
Allard Pierson Museum 41
Allingawier (Fr) 240, 351
Almelo (O) 292
Almere (F) 203
Almshouses (hofjes)
    Friesland 235
    Groningen 257
    Limburg 314, 315
    South Holland 110, 117, 124, 134, 157
    Utrecht 162, 164, 166
    Zeeland 327
Alphen a/d Rijn (SH) 139
Ameland (Fr) 251
Amerongen (U) 173
Amersfoort (U) 170, 351
Ammerzoden (G) 201
Amstelkring Museum 32
Amstelveen 59
Amsterdam (NH) 30, 53, 351, 353
Amsterdam ArenA 52
Amsterdam Canal Cruises Nicolaas Witsenkade 57
Amsterdam Culture & Leisure Pass 56
Amsterdam Diamant Museum 51
Amsterdam-Hague-Rotterdam Times, The 38, 56, 474
Amsterdam Historical Museum 36
Amsterdam Weekly 54, 56, 74, 474
Amusement & Theme Parks 221, 306, 333
Anloo (D) 276
Anne Frank House 41
ANWB
    Royal Dutch Touring Club 14, 461
Apeldoorn (G) 182
Appel, Karel 96, 294
Appingedam (Gr) 268
Aquariums & Sea Life 46, 128, 181, 306, 320
Arcen (L) 299
Archeologisch Museum 62
Army Museum 116
Arnhem (G) 188
Arsenaal, Vlissingen (Z) 333
Art, To Purchase 385
Artis Planetarium 46
Artis Zoo 45
Asparagus Farm Tour 351
Assen (D) 274
Asten (B) 229
Audio Tourist 58
Au Pairs 431
Automobile Museum, The National, Raamdonksveer (B) 215
Avifauna, Alphen a/d Rijn (SH) 139
Axel (Z) 336

B

Baarle-Nassau (B) 218
Baarn (U) 172
Baarsdorp (Z) 332
Babysitting 421
Badminton 408
Bakenesser Kerk 65
Bakery Tours 351
Balloerkuil (D) 276
Balloo (D) 276
Ballum (Fr) 253
Banking 364
Barneveld (G) 180
Bartolotti House 42
Baseball & Softball 408, 434
Basketball 409
Batavia-Werf, Lelystad (F) 205
Beaches 340, 437, 461
    Brabant 214
    Flevoland 203
    Friesland 249, 252, 254
    Limburg 300
    North Holland 348, 349, 350
    South Holland 128, 133, 343, 347
    Zeeland 328, 337, 340, 341, 342
Beatrix, Queen 127, 253
Bed and breakfast 24, 59
Bedum (Gr) 261
Beekse Bergen Safari Park, Hilvarenbeek (B) 222
Begijnhof 36
Beilen (D) 276
Berg, Frans van den 301
Bergen (L) 299
Bergen aan Zee (NH) 75, 349
Berg en Dal (G) 198
Bergen Op Zoom (B) 212

Bergh Kasteel Huis, 's Heerenberg (G) 186
Berkel-Enschot (B) 351
Berlage, H.P. 126, 193
Best (B) 226, 357
Beurs Van Berlage 31
Beverwijk 67
Bevrijdende Vleugels Museum, Best (B) 226
Biermuseum De Boom 72
Biervliet (Z) 337
Biesbosch (B) 214
Bijbels Museum 42
Biking
  Brabant 214
  Drenthe 284
  Flevoland 203
  Friesland 249, 252, 254
  Gelderland 191, 192
  Limburg 303, 307
  North Holland 349, 350
  Overijssel 292
  South Holland 102, 118, 127, 131, 148, 343, 347
  Utrecht 169, 177
  Zeeland 341, 342
Biking, rules of the road 19, 410
  cyclists 20
Biking competitions 405
Bimhuis 54
Binnenhof, The Hague (SH) 119
Bird watching 203, 214, 250, 251, 253, 254, 291,
  347, 350
Bisdom van Vliet Museum, Haastrecht (SH) 149
Blijdorp Zoo, Rotterdam (SH) 100
Bloemendaal aan Zee (NH) 349
Blokzijl (O) 291
Blue Flag beaches 340
Boating & Sailing
  Brabant 212, 214
  Flevoland 203, 204
  Friesland 238, 245, 246
  Groningen 268
  Overijssel 291
  South Holland 148, 344
  Utrecht 169
  Zeeland 336, 342
Boating competitions 169
Boat Tours
  Brabant 214
  Flevoland 208
  Friesland 236, 252
  Gelderland 190, 198
  Groningen 261, 269
  Limburg 318
  Overijssel 290, 291
  South Holland 104, 118, 131, 137, 148, 154, 157
  Utrecht 168
  Zeeland 323, 326, 328, 335, 336

Bodengraven (SH) 352
Boerhaave Museum, Leiden (SH) 136
Boezem, Marinus 203
Bojmans-Van Beuningen Museum, Rotterdam
  (SH) 96
Bol, Ferdinand 157
Bolsward (Fr) 239
Bonaparte, Louis 168, 183
Bonifacius Church 79
Bonnefanten Museum, Maastricht (L) 314
Book shops 386
Boom Chicago 40, 54
Borger (D) 279
Bosch, Hieronymus 96, 224
Boskoop (SH) 148
Bossuhuizen 84
Botanical Garden 52
Bourbon Street Jazz and Blues Club 54
Bourtange (gr) 270
Bowling 410
Brabant 211, 319, 405, 421
Braque, Georges 192, 228
Breda (B) 215
Breda Castle, Breda (B) 216
Brederode Castle 68
Breitner, George Hendrik 294
Breskens (Z) 337
Breughel, Peter 96
Breweries 106, 164, 308, 351, 352
Brick kilns 187
Brielle (SH) 159
Broek in Waterland 89
Broek Op Langedijk (NH) 75, 354
Brouwersgracht 43
Brouwershaven (Z) 320
Brouwershofje 63
Brown cafes 106
Brueghel, Pieter the Younger 294
Bruinisse (Z) 324
Buitenmuseum 81
Buren (Fr) 253
Buren (G) 200
Burgers' Zoo, Arnhem (G) 189
Burgh-Haamstede (Z) 341
Business organisations 373
Bus tours 131, 307

C
Cadzand (Z) 337
Café Americain 55
Café Hoppe 55
Café Kort 55
Cafés 55
Campen, Jacob van 132
Camping 24
  Brabant 213, 218, 222, 225
  Drenthe 275, 280, 283

Flevoland 204
Gelderland 192
Groningen 260, 263, 264, 266, 268
Limburg 300
North Holland 350
Overijssel 291
South Holland 132
Zeeland 328, 342
Camp Zeist (U) 178
Canal Bike 57
Canal Bus 57, 59
Canal tours 57
Candle-making 147, 307, 352
Cannenburgh Castle, Vaassen (G) 184
Canoeing 411
Captain's House 86
Car & motorhome rentals 461
Carillons
   Brabant 216, 224
   Groningen 269
   South Holland 114, 145
   Utrecht 161, 171, 199
   Zeeland 330, 334, 336, 338
Carnegie, Andrew 125
Car rentals 461
Carriage tours 118, 332
Casinos 52, 55, 102, 129, 196, 217, 257, 306, 389,
   462
Castle hotels 284, 307, 308, 309
Castles
   Brabant 216, 225, 229
   Friesland 236, 239
   Gelderland 184, 186, 189, 191, 199, 200, 201
   Groningen 262, 263, 267, 270
   Limburg 303, 304, 308, 316, 318
   North Holland 92
   Overijssel 291, 292, 293, 295
   South Holland 132
   Utrecht 168, 169, 170, 172, 173, 174, 177
   Zeeland 320, 328
Catharijneconvent Museum, Utrecht (U) 164
Catharina Gasthuis Museum, Gouda (SH) 145
Caves 305, 306, 316
Central Museum, Utrecht (U) 166
Chabot, Henry 96
Chagall, Marc 227
Charles II, King of England 215
Cheese 85
Cheese-markets 71
   Gouda (SH) 146
Cheese making 148, 337, 352
Children's farms 102, 118, 127, 131, 139, 184, 268,
   275, 280, 293, 294
Churches / Places of Worship 72, 462
   Brabant 212, 213, 223, 225, 229

Drenthe 276, 280, 284
Friesland 234, 235, 237, 238, 239, 241, 242, 246,
   252, 253
Gelderland 180, 181, 185, 187, 189, 197, 199, 200
Groningen 258, 261, 262, 263, 265, 268
Limburg 298, 300, 301, 302, 303, 310, 313, 314,
   318
North Holland 91, 93
Overijssel 287, 289, 291, 293, 294, 295, 296
South Holland 97, 106, 110, 112, 114, 115, 120, 121,
   123, 127, 134, 135, 144, 150, 152, 154, 156, 159
Utrecht 162, 163, 165, 172
Zeeland 320, 323, 327, 329, 332, 334, 337, 339
Churches – hidden 122
Church services 372
Circuit Park Zandvoort 67
Claes Claesz Anslohofje 49
Clock-making 247, 353
Clubs and organisations 464
CoBrA Museum 59
Coevorden (D) 281
Colenbrander, Theodoor 125
Colijnsplaat (Z) 326
Comedy, English-speaking theatre 467
Comenius, Jan Amos 91
Concerts, church 97, 177, 188
Corot, J.B.C. 125
Corrie ten Boom Museum – The Hiding Place 65
Coster Diamonds 51
Costumes – traditional 173, 180, 208, 245, 271, 288,
   331
Courbet, Gustave 125
Craft shops 386
Cranach, Lucas 294
Credit cards 363
Cricket 411
Crystal making 353
Culemborg (G) 199
Currency/foreign exchange 20
Cuyp, Aelbert 121, 156, 157
Cuypers, P.J.H. 93, 229, 234, 300, 305, 314
Czar Peterhuisje 70

D
d' Artagnan 316
DAF Museum, Eindhoven (B) 228
Dale, Johan Hendrik van 338
Dalfsen (O) 354
Damrak 31
Dam Square 33
Dance schools 378
Dance theatre 390
Dantzig Aan De Amstel 55
De Cocksdorp 78
Deest (G) 198
De Gooyer Windmill 49

De Haar Castle, Haarzuilens (U) 169
De Hallen 62
De Jaren 55
De Karmeliet 66
De Koog 78
Delacroix, Eugene 125
Delden (O) 295
Delfshaven (SH) 104
Delft (SH) 112, 355
Delftware 113, 355
Delfzijl (Gr) 267
De Lier (SH) 118
Delta Works (Z) 324
Delvaux, Paul 96
De Melkweg 54
Den Burg 77
Denekamp (O) 293
Den Helder 76
Den Hoorn 78
Dental care 370
De Oude Bakkerij 79
Department stores 384
De Pieper 49
De Rijp 85
Derlon Museum, Maastricht (L) 313
Deventer (O) 295
De Waal 78
De Wijk (D) 284
Diamonds 4, 51, 53, 353
Didam (G) 187
Diepenheim (O) 295
Dieren (G) 191
Diffelen (O) 351
Dishoek (Z) 341
Distilleries 109, 354
Distilleries Museum, Schiedam (SH) 109
Doelen Hotel 59
Doesburg (G) 187, 355
Dokkum (Fr) 247
Dolfinarium Harderwijk (G) 181
Dolhuys, het – The Madhouse museum 66
Dolmans, Albert 141, 385
Domburg (Z) 328, 340
Domkerk, Utrecht (U) 162
Domtoren, Utrecht (U) 161
Dongen, Kees van 106
Doorn (U) 174
Dordrecht (SH) 154
Dordrecht Museum (SH) 157
Dorst (B) 218
Dou, Gerrit 120, 134
Dreischor (Z) 320
Drenthe 273
Drents Museum, Assen (D) 274
Driebergen (U) 177

Drommedaris 81
Drouwen (D) 279
Drunen (B) 221
Dubbelde Palmboom Historical Museum, Delfshaven (SH) 105
Dudok, W.M. 93
Duinrell Recreation Park, Wassenaar (SH) 132
Duizel (B) 229
Dutch East India Company 105, 205, 334
Dutch News.nl 56, 381, 474
Dutch Reformed Church 89
Dyck, Anthony van 120

E
East Gate 84
Eating out 55, 394, 398
    with children 398
Ecomare Adult Education 78
Edam 85
Edams Museum 85
Edelambachtshuis, Schoonhoven (SH) 151
Education, adult 374
Education and Resources 361, 374, 378, 422
    Dutch universities 428
    English-language schools 427
    international schools 425
    kindergarten through high school 426
    museum orientation & creative classes 427
    pre-school 425
    university education 428
Eel-smoking 88, 354
Eemland area (U) 172
Eenrum (Gr) 265
Eersel (B) 229
Eext (D) 279
Efteling, Kaatsheuvel (B) 221
Egmond aan Zee (NH) 349
Eijsden (L) 318
Eindhoven (B) 227
Eise Eisinga Planetarium, Franeker (Fr) 232
Elburg (G) 181
Electric Tram Museum 52
Elfstedentocht 237, 246
Embassies 372
Emergencies 468
Emergency numbers 367
Emmen (D) 280
Emotional problems 367
English Church 36
Enkhuizen 80
Enschede (O) 294, 352
Entertainment 54, 434
Erasmus, Desiderius 97
Ernst, Max 96
Erotisch Museum 33
Etten Leur (B) 218

Euromast, Rotterdam (SH) 96
Exchange programmes 430
Exloo (D) 279
Exmorra (Fr) 240
Expatica 56, 379, 474
Eyck, Jan van 96

F

Fencing 411
Ferry boats
  on the IJsselmeer 246
  to England 343
  to Waddenzee Islands 250, 251, 253, 254, 255
  Zeeland 329, 333
Ferwoude (Fr) 240
Figure skating events 407
Fish auctions 326, 332, 342
Fishing 118, 131, 204, 212, 238, 250, 264, 268, 291,
  336, 337, 350
Fishing villages 208, 253
Flessenscheepjesmuseum 81
Flevoland 202
Flower auctions 118
Flower market 43
Flower parades 143, 199
Flowers, places to see 126, 140, 143, 199, 204, 206,
  207, 213
Folkloric Markets 452
Food
  asparagus 298
  cranberry wine 251
  Deventer Koek 296
  dribbled cookies 239, 240
  Limburg Vlaai 307
  mussel & oysters 332
  mustard 355
  stroopwafels 144, 147, 351
Football, American 412
Foreign community events 459
Fortress Museum 91
Fraeylemaborg Castle, Slochteren (Gr) 270
Franeker (Fr) 231
Frans Hals Museum 61, 63
Frederik Hendrik 225
Friesland 230
Fries Museum, Leeuwarden (Fr) 233
Frisia Museum 85
Friso, Johan Willem 234
Furniture making 245, 354

G

Galerij Prins Willem V 122
Gardens
  Gelderland 181, 183, 187, 191, 199
  Groningen 259, 261, 267
  Limburg 299, 303
  Overijssel 295

South Holland 102, 118, 127, 137, 140, 148
  Utrecht 162, 167, 169, 170, 172, 177
Geelvinck Hinlopen Huis 43
Gelder, Arent de 157
Gelderland 179
Gemeentegrot, Valkenburg (L) 305
Gemeentemuseum, The Hague (SH) 126
General sources of information 468
Gennep (L) 299
Geological Museum 46
Gevangenpoort, The Hague (SH) 121
Gieten (D) 279
Giethoorn (O) 290, 356
Glass making 309, 353
Goedereede (Z) 341
Goes (Z) 332
Gold, Silver & Clock Museum, Schoonhoven (SH)
  151
Golden Curve 43
Golf 159, 341, 348, 412
Gouda 144
Gouda (SH) 351, 352, 356
Goyen, Jan van 96, 120, 123, 134, 136, 137, 157, 294
Grand Westin Demeure Hotel 59
Grijpskerk (Gr) 263
Gris, Juan 192
Groenlo (G) 187
Groesbeek (G) 198
Groningen (Gr) 256
Groot Ammers (SH) 153
Groothoofdspoort, Dordrecht (SH) 156
Grote Keeten (NH) 350
Grote Kerk 62, 84, 88
Grote Kerk, Dordrecht (SH) 154
Grote Kerk, The Hague (SH) 123
Grote Kerk – St. Bavo Church 62
Grotius, Hugo 112, 114, 201
Grou (Fr) 237
Gulpen (L) 308, 352

H

Haaksbergen (O) 295
Haamstede (Z) 320
Haarlem 61
Haarzuilens (U) 169
Haastrecht (SH) 148
Haesje Claes 55
Hague, The (SH) 118
HagueOnLine, The 56, 108, 130, 474
Hals, Frans 96, 120, 164
Hapert (B) 352
Harbours & ports
  Brabant 212
  Flevoland 203, 208
  Friesland 231, 241
  Groningen 256, 267

South Holland 98, 101, 110, 129, 157, 344
Zeeland 335
Harderwijk (G) 180
Haren (Gr) 261
Harlingen (Fr) 231
Harmoniummuseum Drenthe 282
Hartenstein Airborne Museum, Oosterbeek (G) 195
Hash Marijuana Hemp Museum 33
Havelte (D) 284
Havenbuurt 89
Health care organisations 369
Heerenveen (Fr) 247
Heerlen (L) 302
Heeswijk-Dinther (B) 225
Heeze (B) 229
Heiligerlee (Gr) 269
Heineken Experience 52
Heinenoord (sh) 158
Hellendoorn (O) 292
Helmantel, Henk 261, 276, 277, 385
Helmond (B) 229
Hengelo (O) 292
Hepworth, Barbara 192
Herder windmill 79
Herengracht 42
Hervormde Kerk 89
Het Gooi 92
Het Hollands Kaasmuseum 72
Heusden (B) 225
Heyn, Piet 105, 106, 115
High over Holland 386
Hikes & walks 419
  Brabant 213, 214, 224
  Flevoland 203
  Friesland 236, 250, 254
  Gelderland 186, 191, 197
  Limburg 299, 301, 309
  North Holland 350
  Overijssel 292
  South Holland 97, 102, 104, 110, 127, 137, 157,
    343
  Utrecht 168, 169, 177
  Zeeland 320, 342
Hillegom (SH) 143
Hilvarenbeek (B) 222
Hilversum (NH) 92, 93
Hindeloopen (Fr) 245, 354
Historisch Museum Zuid-Kennemerland 64
Hobbema, Meindert 120
Hobbies 386
Hockey, field 413
Hockey, ice 407
Hoekschewaard Streek Museum, Heinenoord (SH)
  158
Hoek van Holland (SH) 343
Hoensbroek (L) 303

Hof, Dordrecht (SH) 156
Hofjes Pieter-Jansz Suyckerhoff 49
Hofje van Bakenes 65
Hofje van Loo 63
Hofje van Splinter 72
Hofje Venetiae 49
Hof van Sonoy 72
Hogebeintum (Fr) 248
Hoge Veluwe National Park (G) 192
Holbein, Hans the Younger 294
Holidays, public 468
Holland Books 38
Holland Casino 52, 55, 67
Holland Experience 47
Holland Handbook, The 386, 453
Holland Handicrafts 113
Holland International 57
Holland Resources 25
Hollandsche Schouwburg 45
Hollum (Fr) 252
Holwerd (Fr) 248
Hoofdtoren 84
Hoofdwacht 63
Hoogeland Open Air Museum, Warffum (Gr) 266
Hoogeveen (D) 284, 353
Hooghalen (D) 283
Hoorn 83
Horse, cattle markets & fairs 139, 276, 280, 288
Horse racing 132, 407
Horse riding 102, 168, 250, 252, 254, 260, 288, 292,
    303, 341, 344, 347, 413
Horse shows 406
Horst (L) 299
Hortus Botanicus 45
Hortus Botanicus, Leiden (SH) 137
Hortus Bulborum 75
Hospital care 368
Hostels 25
Hotel reservations 469
House with Heads 42
Housing in Holland 386
Houtenhuis 86
Houwerzijl (Gr) 264
Huijbergen (B) 213
Huis Doorn, Doorn (U) 177
Huisduinen (NH) 350
Huis van Achten 72
Hulsel (B) 229
Hulst (Z) 336
Hunebedden 273, 276, 279, 280, 281, 284
Huygens, Christiaan 123, 132, 136
Huygens, Constantijn 123, 132

I

Ice skating 229, 247, 260, 413
Ice skating races 237, 247, 407
Iens Independent Index 55

IJmuiden (NH) 67, 349
Indiana, Robert 228
Indonesian restaurants 394
Israels, Jozef 125, 294
iT 54

J
Janskerk 66
Janum (Fr) 248
Jan v.d. Togt Museum of Modern Art 60
Jenever 109
Jewish Historical Museum 45
Jewish quarter 44
Jordaan 49, 53
Jordaens, Jacob 120, 123
Joure (Fr) 247, 353
Judo 414
Juliana, Queen 172
Julianadorp (NH) 77, 350

K
Kaatsen 232
Kaatsheuvel (B) 221
Kaiser Wilhelm II 174, 177
Kamerik (SH) 148
Kampen (O) 289
Kandinsky, Wassily 96
Kapelle (Z) 332
Karate 414
Kathe Kruse Poppenmuseum (Doll Museum) 77
Katwoude (NH) 353
Keijenborg (G) 357
Keizersgracht 42
Kerkbuurt 89
Kerkrade (L) 303
Keukenhof, Lisse (SH) 140
Kijkduin (SH) 347
Kijkhuisje Sijtje Boes 89
Kinderdijk (SH) 153
Klooster Ter Apel 271
Knegsel (B) 229
Koch, Pyke 190
Koepoort 81
Kokoschka, Oskar 228
Kolhorn 80
Kornwerderzand (Fr) 240
Kuinre (O) 291

L
Lakenhal Museum, Leiden (SH) 136
Lakes 169, 172, 261, 264, 284, 299
Lambert Van Meerten Museum, Delft (SH) 116
Land art 203, 204, 206
Landgraaf (L) 303
Landsmeer (NH) 91
Land Van Ooit, Drunen (B) 221
Langerbroeker Wetering (U) 173

Laren (NH) 93
Lauwersoog (Gr) 264
Leek (Gr) 262
Leens (Gr) 263
Leerdam (SH) 353
Leeuwarden (Fr) 232
Leeuwenhoek, Anthony van 115, 136
Legal information – immigration/permits 371
Leiden (SH) 133, 457
Leidsestraat 53
Lekkerkerk (SH) 357
Lelystad (F) 204, 356
Let's Go Amsterdam 57
Leyden, Lucas van 136
Libeskind, Daniel 203
Libraries 372, 429
Lighthouses 208, 250, 251, 252
Limburg 297
Lindbergh 58
Lindeboom 78
Linnaeus 180
Linnaeushof Recreation Park 68
Lipchitz, Jacques 192
Lisse (SH) 139
Liszt, Franz 200
Living in Holland 361
Loevestein Castle, Woudrichem (G) 201
Loon (D) 276
Loo Palace, Het, Apeldoorn (G) 183
Loosduinen (SH) 127
Los Gauchos 66
Louis, Morris 228
Luchtvaart Museum Texel 78
Lutherse Kerk 42
Lutjegast (Gr) 263
Luyksgestel (B) 351

M
Maarplassen (L) 300
Maarssen (U) 169
Maasland (SH) 118
Maastricht (L) 309
Mac Bike 57
Madame Tussauds Amsterdam 35
Madurodam, The Hague (SH) 125
Maes, Nicolas 157
Magere Brug 44
Magna Plaza 35, 53
Makkum (Fr) 241, 356
Manet, Edouard 200
Maps 20
Margraten (L) 308
Margriet, Princess 183
Marinemuseum 76
Maris, Matthijs 125
Maritiem en Jutters Museum 78

Maritiem Museum, Zierikzee (Z) 322
Markelo (O) 353
Marken 88
Marken Express 89
Marker Museum 89
Markets 53
Market Squares 114, 145, 185, 197, 223, 271, 275, 293, 296, 310, 336
Markiezenhof City Museum, Bergen Op Zoom (B) 213
Marssum (Fr) 236
Marta Pan 192
Martinitoren, Groningen (Gr) 259
Martinuskerk Oosterend 78
Marx, Karl 200
Mary Mapes Dodge 68
Mata Hari 233
Maurits, Prince 117, 212, 215, 225
Mauritshuis Museum, The Hague (SH) 120
Mauve, Anton 125, 294
Medemblik, Twisk and Kolhorn 79
Medical care 366, 368
Medical insurance 371
Medieval towns 170, 181, 184, 199, 200, 212, 223, 268, 287, 289, 295
Meerssen (L) 318
Meier, Richard 120
Mendini, Alessandro 256
Menkemaborg Castle, Uithuizen (Gr) 267
Meppel (D) 284
Mesdag, H.W. 124, 125
Mesdag Museum, (Panorama)The Hague (SH) 124, 125
Metsu, Gabriel 120, 134
Middachten Castle (G) 191
Middelburg (z) 329
Midlaren (D) 279
Millet, Jean-Francois 125
Minckelers, S.P. 310
Miniature towns 125, 330
Miniature Walcheren, Middelburg (Z) 330
Moddergat (Fr) 248
Moderne Kunst, Museum Voor, Arnhem (G) 190
Molenmuseum 70
Molenmuseum De Valk, Leiden (SH) 135
Mondriaan, Piet 126, 172, 192, 341
Monet, Claude 96, 126, 294
Monnickendam (NH) 88, 354
Moore, Henry 192
Moriaan Pipe Museum, Gouda (SH) 146
Motor racing 263, 274, 406
Mount St. Peter Caves, Maastricht (L) 316
Movies 389, 434
Mozes en Aaronkerk 47
Muiden (NH) 93

Muiderpoort 46
Mummies 237, 274
Munttoren 43
Museum Abdij Van Egmond 75
Museumboot Rederij Lovers 57
Museum Broeker Veiling 75
Museum de Cruquius 68
Museum Grietje Tump 90
Museumjaarkaart (Museum Year Card) 22, 56
Museummolen 85
Museum quarter 50
Museums
    African Culture 198
    Alcoholic Beverages 109, 190, 197, 220
    American Pilgrims 134
    Archeology & Ethnology 101, 135, 136, 185, 196, 199, 207, 264, 274, 302, 313, 314, 339
    Architecture 96, 167
    Art: Brabant 216, 217, 220, 223, 224, 227, 229
    Art: Flevoland 203
    Art: Friesland 233, 235, 242, 250
    Art: Gelderland 186, 190, 192
    Art: Limburg 298, 302, 314
    Art: North Holland 93
    Art: Overijssel 288, 294
    Art: South Holland 96, 117, 120, 121, 124, 125, 126, 128, 157
    Art: Utrecht 164, 166
    Aviation 348
    Baby carriages 269
    Bell casting 269, 276
    Bicycles 196
    Books & printing 121, 127, 185, 186, 213, 218, 220, 260, 284, 313
    Canal houses 116, 117, 155
    Carriages 262, 303
    Cars 143, 215, 228, 291
    Cheese 146
    Clocks 151, 247
    Coins & money 167
    Comenius 91
    Communications 124
    Costumes – traditional 93, 173, 208, 227, 233, 261
    Fairs & circus 291
    Farming 127, 173, 180, 188, 225, 240, 270, 279, 291, 292, 320, 336
    Fishing 111, 173, 248, 252, 324, 332, 347
    Flowers 143
    Food & baking 93, 172, 187, 197, 218, 264, 265, 292, 295, 299
    Fortifications 196, 269, 271
    Grocery 109, 162
    Indonesian culture 115
    Lace 266
    Lifeguards 252

Medical 136, 145, 166, 171
Military 129, 172, 177, 178, 190, 200, 269
Music 111, 126, 164, 229, 290
Nature 96, 129, 137, 192, 196, 214, 220, 228, 235,
   240, 248, 250, 251, 253, 258, 287, 293, 315,
   328, 348
Old houses 149, 158, 274, 285, 293, 324
Open Air Museum Arnhem (G) 188, 206, 228,
   266, 282
Peat 292
Police 184
Pottery, tiles & ceramics 96, 116, 126, 146, 193,
   231, 234, 257, 322
Prisons 121, 276
Public transportation 99
Railroad 139, 165, 295, 303
Religion 164, 198, 223, 242, 248, 261, 301
Royal Family 114, 183, 200
Schools & universities 98, 137, 259, 336
Scissor art 152
Sea shells 290, 336
Shipping 98, 99, 147, 205, 238, 258, 263, 322
Shoes & leather 220
Silver & gold 151
Sports 102, 187, 232, 246
Taxes 101
Technology & science 126
Tobacco 258
Toys 102, 191, 218, 220, 288, 296, 342
Water management 204
Windmills 110, 135
Witches 149
World War II 102, 146, 155, 189, 195, 198, 226,
   240, 283
Museumstoomtram Hoorn-Medemblik 84
Museum Van De Twintigste Eeuw (Museum of the
   20th Century) 84
Museum Van Egmond 75
Museum Van Loon 44
Music 390
Musical Clock to Street Organ Museum, Utrecht
   (U) 164
Music schools 377
Mustard-making 355

N

Naaldwijk (SH) 118
Naarden 90
Napoleon 122, 231
Nationaal Reddingmuseum Dorus Rijkers 76
National Carriage Museum, Leek (Gr) 262
Naturalis, Leiden (SH) 137
NBTC, Netherlands
   Board of Tourism and Conventions 13, 469
Nederlands Instituut for Sound and Light 92
Nederlands Stoommachinemuseum 79

Neeltje Pater 90
Neer, Eglon van der 121
NEMO – New Metropolis Science and Technology
   Centre 48
Nes (Fr) 253
Netersel (B) 229
Neunen (B) 229
New Bali 55
Newspapers & periodicals 362
Nienoord Castle, Leek (Gr) 262
Nieuwegein (U) 356
Nieuwe Kerk 34
Nieuwe Kerk, Delft (SH) 114
Nieuwe Palmboom, Flourmill 110
Nieuweschans (Gr) 269
Nieuw Land Poldermuseum Erfgoedcentrum 204
Nieuwolda (Gr) 269
Night life 54
Nijenrode (U) 168
Nijmegen (G) 195
Noorder Dierenpark, Emmen (D) 280
Noorderhoogebrug (Gr) 261
Noordgouwe (Z) 320
Noordhorn (Gr) 261
Noordwijk (SH) 139, 347
Noort, Oliver van 152
Norg (D) 276
North Brabant Museum, 's Hertogenbosch (B) 224
Northern Shipping and Tobacco Museum, Gronin-
   gen (G 258
North Holland 29
North Sea islands 77
Nudist beaches 340

O

Observatories & planetariums 166, 232, 302
Odeon 54
Odoorn (D) 279
Oirschot (B) 229
Oldemarkt (O) 291
Oldenbarnevelt, Johan van 171
Oldenzaal (O) 295
Olympisch Stadium 52
Ommen (O) 288
Onze Lieve Vrouwe Basiliek 313
Oorlogs en Verzetsmuseum, Overloon (B) 226
Oorlogs en Verzetsmuseum Rotterdam 102
Oost-Vlieland (Fr) 249
Oostburg (Z) 337
Oosterbeek (G) 193
Oosterhout (B) 218
Oosterkerk 84
Oosterpoort 84
Oostkapelle (Z) 328, 341
Oostvoorne (Z) 342
Ootmarsum (O) 293

Open Air Museum 81, 188
Opening hours 383
Openluchtmuseum, Arnhem (G) 188
Opera 391
Operation Market Garden 193, 198, 226
Ophemert (G) 200
Orvelte (D) 282
Otterlo (G) 193
Oudegracht, Utrecht (U) 163
Oude Haven, Rotterdam (SH) 98
Oude Raadhuis, Kampen (O) 289
Oudeschild 78
Oudewater (sh) 149
Oudheden Museum, Leiden (SH) 135
Overijssel 286
Overloon (B) 225

P

P.J.H. Cuypers 79
Palaces 121, 122, 127, 172, 177, 178, 183
Pancake restaurants 396
Panorama paintings 124, 301
Papeneiland 55
Paradiso 54
Park-line 58
Parks
   City & town 102, 126, 127, 167, 184, 196, 197, 235,
     260, 294, 305
   National 191, 192, 250, 285, 300
   Nature reserves 203, 205, 214, 251, 253, 254, 291,
     292, 337, 342, 350
   Recreation 131, 132, 139, 184, 195, 197, 218, 222,
     229, 268, 275, 276, 280, 292, 305, 308
Party planning 385
Peace Palace, The Hague (SH) 125
Peat-digging 355
Performing arts 390
Personal Relocation 361, 455
Pets 387
Petten (NH) 350
Pewter-casting 105, 355
Pharmacies 370
Philips, Gerard 227
Piaam (Fr) 240
Picasso, Pablo 126, 192, 228
Pieck, Anton 182, 221
Pieterburen (Gr) 265
Pieterskerk, Leiden (SH) 134
Pilgrim Museum, Leiden (SH) 134
Pilgrims, American 106, 133, 134
Pipe-making 147
Plane rides 184, 253, 318
Pole vaulting competitions 263
Pope Hadrian VI 163
Port of Rotterdam (SH) 101
Portuguese Synagogue 45

Post, Maurits 174
Post, Pieter 123, 124, 132, 146, 310
Potter, Paulus 123
Pottery, tiles, ceramics 113, 114, 231, 241, 242
Pottery making 355
Pregnancy 368
Prehistoric Open Air Museum, Eindhoven (B) 228
Princessehof Museum, Leeuwarden (Fr) 234
Prinsengracht 43
Prinsenhof, Delft (SH) 114
Prinsjesdag 457
Prison Museum 121
Prostitution Information Centre 33
Proveniershuis 86
Puppet shows 133, 221, 341, 393, 436
Purmerends Museum 86

Q

Queen's Birthday (Koninginnedag) 55
Quick Reference 461

R

Raadhuis van Edam 86
Raamsdonksveer (B) 215
Radboud Castle 79
Radio, English 476
Railway Museum, Utrecht (U) 165
Reading, recommended 472
   entertainment 476
   maps, periodicals 474
   publications, access publications 476
   websites 475
Red Light District 32
Redon, Odilon 192
Relocation services 362
Rembrandt 46, 96, 120, 121, 123, 134, 136, 137, 157,
   164, 316
Renesse (Z) 320, 341
Restaurants (see eating out per chapter) 398
Reusel (B) 229
Rheden (G) 191
Rhenen (U) 174
Rietveld, Gerrit 167
Rijksmuseum 46
Rijksmuseum – National Gallery 50
Rijksmuseum Twenthe, Enschede (O) 294
Rijper Museum In 't Houtenhuis 85
Rijswijk (SH) 131
Rixt the Witch 253
RMS 361, 382
Robinson, John 134
Rockanje (z) 342
Rode Klif (Fr) 246
Roden (D) 276
Rodin, Auguste 192
Roermond (L) 299
Rolde (D) 276

Roman Thermenmuseum, Heerlen (L) 302
Roosendaal (B) 213
Roosevelt family 330
Rossi, Aldo 314
Rotterdam (SH) 94, 351, 354
Rouveen (O) 288
Rowing meets 405
Royal Palace 34
Royal Palace on the Dam 34
Rozendaal (G) 191
Rubens, Pieter Paul 96, 120
Rugby 417
Ruisdael, Jacob van 120
Ruyter, Michiel de 334

S
's Gravenzande (SH) 343
's Heerenberg (G) 186
's Hertogenbosch (B) 223
Sailing 417
Sailing races 405
Sailing schools 432
Scarlet Cord 33
Scharendijke (Z) 320
Scheepsvaartmuseum-Netherlands Maritime
    Museum 47
Scheepvaarthuis 49
Scheepvaartmuseum 47
Schermerhorn 85
Scheveningen (SH) 128, 343, 352
Schiedam (SH) 109, 351, 354
Schielandshuis Hist. Museum, Rotterdam (SH) 100
Schiermonnikoog (Fr) 254
Schiphol Airport 52
Schiphol Visitors Centre 52
Schipluiden (SH) 118
Schokland Museum, Ens (F) 207
Schoonhoven (SH) 150, 356
Schoonoord (D) 281
Schoorl (NH) 349
Schreierstoren 49
Schuymacher, Wim 190
Scouting 432, 433
Sea Life Centre, Scheveningen (SH) 128
Seals 250, 252, 265
Sea Palace 55
Serooskerke (Z) 324
Sheep folds 191, 279, 303
Ship building 188, 205, 242, 356
Shipping 153, 200, 335
Shopping 383
Silver-making 151, 356
Simenon, Georges 268
Simon van Gijn Museum, Dordrecht (SH) 155
Singer, William H. 93
Sinterklaas 457

Sisley, Alfred 294
Skiing 133, 250
Slagharen (O) 288
Slochteren (gr) 270
Sloten (Fr) 246
Sluis (Z) 338
Sneek (Fr) 238
Soccer 407, 412
Social organisations 373
Soestdijk Palace, Baarn (U) 172
Son en Breugel (B) 229
Spakenburg (U) 173
Spas & saunas 132, 269, 306, 344, 348
Speeltoren 86, 88
Spinoza, Baruch 120, 123
Sports, for participation 408
Sports stadiums 102
Sprookjeswonderland (Fairy-tale Land) 81
Squash 418
St. Annaland (Z) 333
St. Anna ter Muiden (Z) 339
St. Jans Gasthuis 84
Stadhuismuseum, Zierikzee (Z) 321
Stamp collecting 386
Staphorst (O) 288, 354
Statenpoort 84
Stavoren (Fr) 246
Staying over 59
Steam trains 184, 295, 303, 332
Stedelijk Museum 48, 75
Steen, Jan 96, 120, 121, 123, 134, 136, 137
Steensel (B) 229
Steenwijk (O) 291
Stellendam (Z) 342
Stiftskerk, Thorn (L) 301
Storm Surge Barrier (Z) 325
Stuart, Queen Mary 183
Stuttenburgh 88
Stuyvesant, Peter 231
Summer camps 431, 433
Supermarkets 383
Swimming 407
Swimming pools 99, 127, 132, 218, 225, 252, 268,
    275, 300, 308, 348
Symphony 390
Synagogues 45, 117, 151, 463
Sypesteyn Castle, Nieuw Loosdrechtsedijk (U) 170

T
't Smaaltje 49
't Twiske 90
't Woudt (SH) 118
Tasman, Abel 263
Tassenmuseum (Bag or Purse Museum) Hendrikje
    52
Tattoo Museum 33

Taxes 371
Tegelen (L) 299
Telephone 21
Telephone assistance 469
Television 389
Teniers, David 96
Tennis 408
Tennis tournaments 408
Ter Apel (Gr) 271
Terborch, Gerard 296
Terneuzen (z) 335
Terp villages 264
Terschelling (Fr) 250
Texel 77
Textile-making 356
Textile Museum, Tilburg (B) 219
Teylers Museum 64
Theatermuseum 42
Theatre 389
Theatres – multi-media 127
Thermae 2000, Valkenburg (L) 306
Thorn (L) 300
Tichelaar's Royal Ceramics and Tile Factory 241
Tiel (G) 199
Tilburg (B) 219, 356
Tips for travellers 20
Toorop, Jan 341
Torensluis 42
Tours and travel services 58
Town halls
    Brabant 212, 213, 216, 224
    Drenthe 280
    Friesland 231, 232, 235, 238, 239, 242, 246, 248
    Gelderland 180, 181, 185, 186, 187, 197, 199, 201
    Groningen 268
    Limburg 298, 310
    Overijssel 287, 289, 291, 296
    South Holland 106, 110, 112, 114, 120, 123, 135,
        145, 150, 152
    Zeeland 320, 321, 327, 330, 332, 336, 337, 338,
        339
Transportation 58
    Train travel 16
Transportation, public 469
Tromp, Maarten 115, 159
Tropenmuseum 46
Twisk 80

U
Uithuizen (Gr) 266
Union Museum 45
University programmes 374
Urk (F) 208
Utrecht 160

V
Vaals (L) 308, 353
Vaassen (G) 184
Valkenburg (L) 304
Valkenburg (SH) 139
Valthe (D) 279
Van Abbe Museum, Eindhoven (B) 227
Van Gogh, Vincent 96
    museum 51
Veendam (Gr) 272
Veenhuizen (D) 276
Veenpark, Barger-Compascuum (D) 282
Veenwouden (Fr) 237
Veere (Z) 326
Venlo (L) 297
Venus Temple Sex Museum 31
Verhildersum Castle, Leens (Gr) 263
Vermeer, Jan 112, 115
Vermeer Centre 116
Verweyhal 62
Verzetsmuseum 46
Vesting Museum (Fortress Museum) 91
Vestingwal 81
Vishal 63
Visserijmuseum, Vlaardingen (SH) 111
Vlaardingen (SH) 111, 357
Vliehors (Fr) 250
Vlieland (Fr) 249
Vlissingen (z) 333
Voerman, Jan 182
Vogelenzang (NH) 143
Volendam (NH) 87, 354
Volendams Museum 87
Volkenkunde Museum, Leiden (SH) 136
Volkenkunde Museum, Rotterdam (SH) 101
Vollenhove (O) 291
Vondel Park 52
Voorburg (SH) 132
Voorhout (SH) 143
Voorschoten (SH) 132
Vreeland (U) 353
Vreeswijk (SH) 153
Vries (D) 276
Vriezenveen (O) 292
Vrije Universiteit (Free University) 52
Vrouwenpolder (Z) 328
Vught (B) 225
VVV – National Dutch Tourist Offices 14, 469

W
Waag 33, 72, 84, 85, 88
Waalkade Riverfront, Nijmegen (G) 196
Waalse Kerk 66
Waalwijk (B) 220
Waardenburg (G) 200
Waddenzee Islands 249
Wadlopen 248, 265, 452

Walking 419
Wall houses 171
Warffum (Gr) 265
Warns (Fr) 246
Wassenaar (SH) 132, 347
WaterLand Neeltje Jans (Z) 325
Waterlooplein Market 47
Watermills 132, 189, 229, 293, 295, 308, 315
Water Sports
   Brabant 212
   Drenthe 284
   Flevoland 204
   Friesland 237, 238, 241, 246
   Groningen 264
   Limburg 299, 300
   North Holland 350
   South Holland 102, 118, 158, 342
   Utrecht 169
   Zeeland 341
Weeshuis 88
Weigh Houses 81, 84, 86
   Friesland 233, 242
   Gelderland 187, 189, 197, 200, 201
   Overijssel 296
   South Holland 114, 146, 152
Werkendam (B) 214
Westerbork 283
Westerkerk 43
Westerschouwen (Z) 341
Westfries (West Frisian) Museum 83
Westfriese Flora 82
Westkapelle (Z) 332, 341
West Terschelling (Fr) 250
What's on in Amsterdam 54
Wheat grinding tours 351
Wierum (Fr) 248
Wijk bij Duurstede (U) 177
Wijlre (L) 308
Wildlife 192, 205, 214
Wilhelmina, Queen 122, 183, 217
Willem-Alexander, Prince 122
Willemstad (B) 212
Willem van Haren Museum, Heerenveen (Fr) 247
Willet-Holthuysen Museum 43
William I, King 92, 136, 309
William II, King 172, 219
William III, King 183, 267
William III, Prince 155, 159, 270
William IV, Prince 234
William the Silent 112, 114, 115, 122, 133, 156, 159,
   215, 216, 299, 308
William V, Prince 122
Willink, Carel 190
Windmills 153
   Brabant 213, 225

Drenthe 276
Friesland 248, 253
Groningen 261
Overijssel 288, 291
South Holland 102, 106, 110, 135, 147, 153
Utrecht 166, 167, 177
Zeeland 323, 334, 337
Windsurfing 417
Wine-making 356
Wintersel (B) 229
Witches Weighing House, Oudewater (SH) 149
Witt, Cornelis de 120, 122, 155
Witt, Johan de 120, 122, 155, 270
Wittem (L) 308
Wiuwerd (Fr) 237
Woltheus Cruises 67
Women's organisations 374
Wooden Shoe Museum, Best (B) 227
Wooden Shoes 87, 226, 357
Woodworking 354
Woonbootmuseum 43
Workum (Fr) 242
World Arts Museum 101
World of Ajax 52
World War II sites 190, 193, 225, 226, 240, 283, 308,
   316, 332
Worship, places of 462
Woudrichem (G) 201
Woudsend (Fr) 246
Wouw (B) 213

X
XPat Journal, The 56, 455, 474
XPat Media 386

Y
Yellow Bike 57
Yerseke (Z) 332
Youth Cultural Passport 435
Ysbrechtum (Fr) 239

Z
Zaamslag (Z) 336
Zaanse Schans (NH) 353, 355, 357
Zaans Historisch Museum 70
Zakkendragershuisje 105
Zaltbommel (G) 200
Zandvoort (NH) 348
Zandvoorts Museum 67
ZaZare Diamonds 4, 51, 53, 353
Zee Aquarium 75
Zeeland 319
Zeelandbrug (Z) 326
Zeeman, Pieter 320
Zee Museum, The Hague (SH) 129
Zeewolde (F) 204
Zeist (U) 178

Zeist Palace, Zeist (U) 178
Zevenaar (G) 187, 352, 356
Zierikzee (Z) 321
Zonnemaire (Z) 320
Zoos & animal parks 100, 117, 139, 153, 183, 189, 220, 222, 236, 280, 334
Zoutelande (Z) 341
Zuid-Kennemerland National Park 67
Zuiderkerk 33
Zuiderzee 88
Zuiderzee Museum 80
Zuidlaren (D) 280
Zuidwolde (D) 355
Zuivelboerderij St. Donatus 78
Zutphen (G) 184
Zuylen Castle, Maarssen (U) 169
Zwanenwater (NH) 350

Zwartsluis (O) 292
Zweeloo (D) 281
Zwolle (O) 287

WITH THANKS TO OUR ADVERTISERS

ISBN 978-90-5972-141-8

For more information, contact:
Here's Holland
P.O. Box 34119
3005 GC Rotterdam
The Netherlands
info@heresholland.com / www.heresholland.com

Managing Editor: Shirley Agudo, Pro/PR
Contributing Editor: Connie Moser, u & i know communications
Research Assistants: Lara Geijsen, Carol Conover
Cover design: Studio Geert Hermkens, Amsterdam
Graphic design: Textcetera, The Hague
Maps: Landkaartje, Rotterdam
Photography: NBTC (Netherlands Board of Tourism and Conventions), Fryslân Marketing, Microfoto,
    Sas van Veen, Bas Silderhuis, Stephen Lewis, Maarten Uilenbroek, Paco Busteros, Albert Dolmans,
    Shirley Agudo and Grant Jonathan
Portraits: Jacques Bendien, Jacques Studios, The Hague
Technical Assistance: Grant Jonathan

Production:
Eburon Academic Publishers
P.O. Box 2867
2601 CW Delft
The Netherlands
tel.: +31 (0)15-2131484 / fax: +31 (0)15-2146888
info@eburon.nl / www.eburon.nl

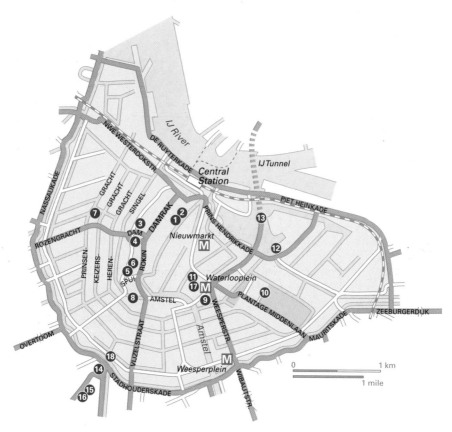

Amsterdam City Walk

Oude Kerk, 1
Amstelkring Museum, 2
Nieuwe Kerk, 3
Royal Palace, 4
Begijnhof, 5
Amsterdam Historical Museum, 6
Anne Frank House, 7
Flower Market, 8
Jewish Historical Museum, 9
Artis Zoo, 10

Rembrandt House, 11
Netherlands Maritime Museum, 12
New Metropolis Science &
            Technology Museum, 13
Rijksmuseum, 14
Van Gogh Museum, 15
Stedelijk Museum, 16
Waterlooplein Flea Market, 17
ZaZare Diamonds, 18